BANNED FILMS

BANNED FILMS

Movies, Censors and the First Amendment

Edward de Grazia and Roger K. Newman

R. R. BOWKER COMPANY
New York & London, 1982

Photographs:

The Birth of a Nation, The Spy, Ecstasy, Spain in Flames, Professor Mamlock, The Outlaw, courtesy of the Billy Rose Theatre Collection, The New York Public Library at Lincoln Center, Astor, Lenox and Tilden Foundations.

Alibi, The Birth of a Baby, Remous, The Miracle, Native Son, courtesy of the Museum of Modern Art, Film Still Archive.

Viva Maria, Copyright © 1965 Nouvelles Editions de Films. All rights reserved. Released through United Artists.

I Am Curious—Yellow, courtesy of Grove Press, Inc. Copyright © 1969 Grove Press, Inc. All rights reserved.

Last Tango in Paris, Copyright © 1972 United Artists Corporation. All rights reserved.

Published by R. R. Bowker Company
205 East Forty-second Street, New York, NY 10017
Copyright © 1982 by Edward de Grazia and Roger K. Newman
All rights reserved
Printed and bound in the United States of America
Second printing, September 1983

Library of Congress Cataloging in Publication Data

De Grazia, Edward.
    Banned Films.

    Bibliography: p.
    Includes index.
    1. Moving-pictures—Censorship—United States.
2. Moving-pictures—Censorship—United States—Digests.
I. Newman, Roger K.   II. Title.

KF4300.D43	344.73'0531	82-4314
ISBN 0-8352-1509-1	347.304531	AACR2
ISBN 0-8352-1511-3 (soft)		

To our families

Congress shall make no law . . . abridging the freedom of speech, or of the press. . . .

Amendment I, The Bill of Rights,
Constitution of the United States

. . . the censorial power is in the people over the government, and not in the government over the people.

James Madison

Contents

1960–1969

1970–1981

Illustrations

Prologue

"Would it not be good propaganda," a New York City deputy police commissioner wrote the city's license commissioner during World War I,

> when men's souls are stirred to their depths and must be reaching out for the noblest and best . . . to print each night on the screen in every motion picture house The Ten Commandments, one at a time, remaining on the screen for about two minutes, giving the people time for reflection? No embellishment or comment would be necessary, as those Commandments are "Too pure for the touch of a word."

The police official had just seen "a private exhibition" of *The Finger of Justice*, and she "most emphatically" stated her disapproval of the movie, based on what she called "my intimate knowledge of human nature."

> The scenes depicted in the bad house are an insult to the pure and clean of heart who go to the motion picture seeking innocent amusement. The young girl on the downward path sees nothing but allurement in those scenes, regardless of what comes after. The loafer of evil mind, looking at this picture, discovers an easy way whereby he can live, in following the footsteps of "Flip," the procurer. The general public receives the impression that all city officials are dishonest and depraved and, consequently, loses respect for authority. The good that the young minister does cannot compensate for the kind of filth that is shown in this picture.

For as long as movies have been made, there has been a relentless struggle to control their appearance, their morals, their ideas. This is the story of movie censorship in the United States. It is also the story of a nation struggling to come to grips with one key provision in its Constitution, the First Amendment, with its protections of speech and press. Throughout—like a "brooding omnipresence"—has been the United States Supreme Court;

nine judges, their identities and ideologies changing over the years, who have sat in darkened rooms to view films and decide for Americans the meaning of their liberty and the limits of their personal choice. From 1915, when the Court declared movies to be no part of this nation's constitutionally protected press, into the 1980s, the reasoning and decisions of these judges have helped to shape the political and moral values and the right to watch of the American people.

Freedom, like law, ideally is a "seamless web." Any give and take in one quarter has repercussions in the others. A rent in the fabric anywhere threatens a loss for all. And so, the events of movie censorship are not isolated from similar situations affecting other media, especially books and magazines. We have referred to the latter where it seemed helpful to an understanding of developments concerning movies. Long affecting these media was the work of the Roman Catholic Legion of Decency, and this is part of the story, as is the influence of the Pope and the first papal pronouncement on any popular art, the encyclical *Vigilanti Cura* (*With Vigilant Care*), on movies.

Motion pictures, more than any other art, have been primarily an American contribution. From humble beginnings, they have grown to a powerful position in the culture and, reflecting their origins, retained much of their anti-establishment coloration. Inevitably, they were difficult to control. For four decades, this nation's judicial branch remained relatively aloof from the conflict over movie censorship—allowing local, state, and federal censors and police to decide what the people could and could not see on their neighborhood and downtown movie screens. The movies were censored by police, prosecutors, Customs officials, and all sorts of city and state boards; by mayors, governors, fire, safety and health commissioners, educators and librarians as well.

The people were prevented from seeing on the movie screen what was happening around them, unless the censors considered it safe. The censorship interfered with the communication of political as well as sexual information and ideas. Movies critical of the courts or the police were frequently condemned. Newsreels that showed Hitler's Germany in an unfavorable light or Soviet workers in a favorable light were banned by the police. Even the news survey *March of Time* was censored. In the mid-1930s, an attempt was made to involve the White House in the suppression of the Czechoslovakian film *Ecstasy*, which showed a woman experiencing sexual pleasure outside of marriage. Although the movie had earned its director a prize at an international film festival in Venice, it had also shocked a Vatican representative there. On entry into the United States, it was seized by Customs police, tried, and burned.

The motion picture, no less than literature and art, is a paramount means for the circulation of ideas and for the carrying out of this nation's dialogue. Movies made in foreign countries have brought many new ideas to the United States, ideas which, because they have also been alien, have fallen under the jurisdiction of Customs police. Backed by federal attorneys and courts, these police have long tried to regulate the immigration of films—of ideas—that could bring solace and salvation, as well as subversion, to the people of this nation.

"Scarcely any political question arises in the United States," Alexis de Tocqueville wrote long ago in *Democracy in America*, "that is not resolved, sooner or later, into a judicial question." So it has been with movie censorship. Constitutional protection was not granted to a motion picture until 1952. At that point in our story, the legal issues come to the fore. Ironically, the more deeply the Supreme Court became involved in the struggle over freedom of the press and screen, the more it began to act as a censorship board, reading books and magazines, seeing movies to determine whether or not they were "obscene" or "immoral," whether they should or should not be "free." The most intense period of this activity was during the 1960s and early 1970s when this nation was embroiled in the conflict over civil rights and the war in Vietnam.

There has been much debate over the Supreme Court's role, but no one denies that chief among its vital functions is to guarantee for the people the freedoms acknowledged as belonging to them by the Bill of Rights. The high purpose of these first ten amendments, and the judges' role in securing them for all the people, was articulated most clearly by James Madison when he introduced them in the First Congress:

> If they are incorporated into the Constitution, independent tribunals of justice will consider themselves in a peculiar manner the guardians of those rights; they will be an impenetrable bulwark against every assumption of power in the Legislative or Executive; they will be naturally led to resist every encroachment upon rights expressly stipulated for in the Constitution by the declaration of rights.

The judges who have faced the issue of censorship have reacted to the materials in question as have their fellow human beings—with a bewildering variety of emotions ranging from passive resignation based on constitutional rectitude to animated revulsion. For movies have often directly and deliberately struck at the heart of accepted notions of politics, religion, and morality, and relatively few judges have been able to separate their personal feelings from the constitutional command. The attitudes and reactions of individual Supreme Court Justices can be gleaned not only from written Court opinions and contemporary comment, but also from the Justices' personal papers, as they become available following death; and we have used these where relevant.

We begin *The Story*, part one of this book, with the principal events—social, political, legal, and human—that brought the motion picture under regimes of censorship, from the early 1900s and the birth of censorship, to World War II and the post-war years, through the era of constitutional protection, and finally to the present. Here, the term *censorship* means any government or industry practice that has interfered with or changed the content of the movies as determined by its creators—from criminal prosecutions and governmental censor boards to private industry self-regulation, including war-time "voluntary cooperation" with the military.

Part two, *The Movies*, presents the individual accounts of 122 American and foreign films banned in the United States. Over the years, countless films have been censored. The "122" are representative films banned, or threatened with banning, by local, state, or federal officials, including the U.S. Customs Service; all have been the subject of officially reported court cases. These individual accounts disclose in some detail the continuous struggle that has taken place in this country's courts for almost 75 years over who shall determine what the movies will say and show.

The 122 accounts appear according to the year banned so that the movement of film censorship may be followed movie by movie, decade by decade. In following the films through the decades, what also emerges is a changing America with its shifting patterns of morals, life-styles, and social attitudes—to be glimpsed in the stories of the films and in the reasons for and the climate underlying the banning of these moving pictures. Here will be found details on the techniques of censorship and on the methods used to free movies from censorship, beginning with the suppression in 1908 of *The James Boys in Missouri* and *Night Riders* by Chicago police, and ending with the freeing in 1981 of the French film *Emmanuelle* from the town police of Covina, California.

This book presents the historical and legal record of movie censorship in the United States by officials and courts for political, religious, moral, and sexual reasons. The jurisprudence of this censorship and freedom—the theories of why and how film freedom may be legally restrained—is discussed throughout. But it gets its sharpest focus in part one, beginning with the chapter on Sacrilege and the Supreme Court, running to the end of *The Story*. Here the development of the Supreme Court's constitutional "tests" for obscenity is carefully considered, as it also is in the accounts of *The Lovers, I Am Curious—Yellow*, and *Magic Mirror*, among others in part two.

Freedom of expression may be suppressed in private ways that are immune from judicial scrutiny. For example, if the producer of a movie wants to tone down an explicit sex scene or omit a controversial political image or idea, there is little that the film's screenwriter or photographer, editor or director can do to make the movie appear as he or she wishes. The courts have no right to intervene while directors are few who gain the right of the final cut of their films.

Today, even a producer's ideas may be curtailed by the industry's rating and classification system (the Code and Rating Administration). If a producer wants to reach the largest audience, and one that includes minors, he or she must not only satisfy but anticipate the system's judgment of whether the film is suitable for youths because of sex, violence, or some other possibly harmful ingredient. These private sorts of censorship have never been recognized by the American legal system because they are impressed on the film's creators and disseminators not by "state action," but in the "private" sphere—by persons and organizations deemed legally incapable of violating anyone's constitutional rights.

The front of this book contains a list of movies banned. It confirms that censors are not deterred from their function because of cinematic or artistic merit. Witness the suppression of such films as D. W. Griffith's *The Birth of a Nation*; *Ecstasy*; *Spain in Flames* (written by John Dos Passos and Ernest Hemingway); *Professor Mamlock*; Roberto Rossellini's *The Miracle*; Elia Kazan's *Baby Doll*; Louis Malle's *The Lovers* and *Viva Maria*; Ingmar Bergman's *The Virgin Spring*; Vilgot Sjöman's *I Am Curious—Yellow*; Mike Nichols's *Carnal Knowledge*; Peter Bogdanovich's *The Last Picture Show*; and Bernardo Bertolucci's *Last Tango in Paris*. That many of these films were imported suggests the degree to which private industry self-regulation, which has almost exclusively been applied to U.S.-made films, may have been effective in preventing controversial films from ever being made by American concerns. Movies that are never made, or released, need not be censored.

Banned Films reflects the combined historical and legal backgrounds of the authors. Research included extensive examination of legal and court files and archival material, including the papers and internal memoranda of Supreme Court Justices. This is the first publication to draw on the papers of the late Justice John Marshall Harlan. Interviews were conducted with court case lawyers and with prominent figures in the motion picture industry and in the history of movie censorship.

The United States Supreme Court and Movie Censorship

The United States Supreme Court has played a crucial role in the history of movie censorship. In 1915, the Supreme Court declared that moving pictures were not constitutionally protected, were unsheltered by the First Amendment. It was not until 1952 that the Court granted that protection to a motion picture. The chief architect of freedom of expression and movie freedom has been Justice William J. Brennan, Jr. In the area of movie and book censorship, Brennan has been the "prime mover," the judicial strategist who, perhaps more than any other person, most effectively determined for the nation not only how much constitutional freedom movies and books could have, but which books might be read, which movies might be seen.

The liberal Brennan joined the Supreme Court in 1956. In *The Brethren*, Bob Woodward and Scott Armstrong depict Brennan as having acted as a sort of Vice-Chief of the Court, meeting regularly, in private, with Chief Justice Earl Warren to plan the all-important conferences at which votes were taken and decisions reached. Brennan was also influential in determining which Justices would write the Court's opinions in key cases.

Brennan did not adopt the "absolute" free speech position promoted by Justices Hugo L. Black and William O. Douglas. For him, it was too radical, and did not brook the compromises needed to produce opinions that might move the law, gradually, in the direction of greater First Amendment protection. To expand the people's freedom to communicate about sex—in books, magazines, movies, and other media—Brennan had to cope with the Justices' own attitudes in this sensitive area. Some Justices, especially Chief Justice Warren and Justice Tom C. Clark, were puritanically disposed toward sexual expression. So, too, was Warren E. Burger.

When Burger became Chief Justice during the Nixon administration, he acted to unseat Brennan from his position of power. One major objective was to restore "the right of the Nation and of the States to maintain a decent society" and to eliminate from the channels of communication the "garbage and sewage," and "environmental pollution problems" that the Warren Court's "laissez-faire" approach to the "obscenity-pornography problem" had left in its wake. In the volatile arena of the people's First Amendment rights, Burger undercut Brennan's role by assigning the writing of majority opinions in carefully selected obscenity cases to Byron R. White, Harry A. Blackmun, William H. Rehnquist, or Lewis F. Powell. But that Brennan was no longer the Court's spokesman in this field did not erase his achievements.

Perhaps not since Oliver Wendell Holmes or Louis D. Brandeis has any individual Justice contributed so much to the development of constitutional doctrine protecting expression as has Brennan. Time and again, in a wide variety of settings, Brennan wrote the opinions that made freedom of speech "the central meaning of the First Amendment," and recognized in that Amendment the "core of protection of speech without which democracy cannot function."

Once the motion picture was found entitled to First Amendment freedom, paradoxically, the members of the Court themselves began to sit as censors—as what Justice Black once decried as "about the most inappropriate Supreme Board of Censors that could be found." Inappropriate, one supposes, because the guardians of the First Amendment ought not themselves to grant or deny freedom to particular forms of expression; but this in time became one aspect of the Court's work. The first movie explicitly "cleared" in this way was Louis Malle's *The Lovers*. The first novel openly freed in this sense was Henry Miller's *Tropic of Cancer*. This was in 1964.

In cases where the Supreme Court decides to invalidate a state law or a municipal ordinance, under which a movie or book has been banned or its disseminator punished, the Court does not act as Censor. But when the Court decides to review the judgment of a state or lower federal court in upholding or denouncing the censorship imposed, then the Court can be said to be acting as Censor. In that sense, one of this book's authors himself urged the Court to behave as a Supreme Board of Censors—in efforts to free the book *Tropic of Cancer* (the Court did) and the movie *I Am Curious—Yellow* (the Court did not).

Justice Brennan defended the majority's action in freeing *The Lovers* by stating "This Court cannot avoid making an independent judgment on the facts of the case as to whether the material involved is constitutionally protected." The reason it "cannot" is because a majority of the Court has consistently shunned adopting the unqualified principle that movies and books should be entirely free of government constraint—that no judge, juror, high or low bureaucrat, no police officer or prosecutor should be able to decide that *this* movie, but not *that* movie, *this* novel, but not *that* novel, may go free.

In *The Lovers* case, six of the Court's nine Justices voted to reverse the Ohio conviction of the film's exhibitor. In the *Tropic of Cancer* case, which was decided the same day, only five of the nine voted to reverse the state of Florida's suppression of the book. It was Byron White who voted differently in those cases, presumably because he considered the book, but not the movie, "obscene." In a case involving the Swedish movie *I Am Curious— Yellow*, Thurgood Marshall voted initially to uphold its suppression by state censors; later, when the Court's composition had been altered by an appointment of President Nixon, Marshall voted to free the film from that censorship.

A majority of the Court must agree on any decision or judgment reached—for example, to free a banned movie or a book, or to uphold or invalidate a censorship statute. The written *opinion* that accompanies the Court's judgment in a particular case is usually authored by a single Justice. If the Court's judgment is unanimous and if the nine Justices also agree on a statement of the reasons for the judgment, then a single written opinion, bearing the name of the author, but joined by all other Justices, might accompany the decision and explain or rationalize it in legal terms subscribed to by the entire Court.

Every written opinion is important, not only for what it says about why the Court acted the way it did in deciding to affirm or reverse a judgment, but also for what it can be read to say about how the Court might act in a related case in the future. This, of course, is the precedential value of a case.

Frequently, all nine Justices cannot agree on the action the Court should take or the reasons for it. If a Justice disagrees with the judgment reached by a majority of the members of the Court, he or she will *dissent*. Even when a Justice agrees with the majority judgment, if he or she disagrees with part or all of the reasons given in the Court's majority opinion, he or she is free to express the departure by writing a *concurring opinion*, which articulates the difference.

Sometimes five Justices cannot agree on the reasons for a judgment reached by a majority. Here no single written opinion can record the reasons why a majority of the Court reached the decision it did (usually to affirm or reverse the judgment of the court below). Individual Justices have different reasons for deciding the way they do. In such a case, the Court's judgment or decision is accompanied not by an opinion which can properly be described as *the* opinion of *the* Court, or as a majority opinion, but rather by an opinion subscribed to by two or more Justices. This opinion states the narrowest of reasons given by any plurality of agreeing Justices supportive of the Court's decision, giving *their* reasons for the judgment reached by the Court.

This so-called *plurality opinion* can only represent the concerted viewpoint of a minority of the Justices, but often its point of view, and the reasoning, are treated by lower federal or state courts, which are called upon to decide related issues in future cases, as though it expressed *the Court's* view—that is to say, the concerted viewpoint of a majority of the Justices. While it does not do that, it contains the best guide of any other written opinion associated with the case as to how the Court might predictably act, if called upon to do so, in a future case involving related issues. Thus Justice Brennan's plurality opinion in *The Lovers* case was joined in only by Justice Arthur J. Goldberg. Nevertheless, it was widely referred to as the Court's opinion in that case and its reasoning was followed and adopted by other courts faced with similar cases. As Professor Frederick Schauer points out in his important work *The Law of Obscenity*, Brennan's declaration in that case that "the constitutional status of an allegedly obscene work must be determined on the basis of a national standard" was followed by "the overwhelming majority of lower courts which faced the problem" thereafter, including "every federal court."

Similar respect was paid by lower courts to Brennan's announcements in the same case that any book or movie "dealing with sex" that had "literary or scientific or artistic value or any other form of social importance may not be branded as obscenity and denied the constitutional protection," and that no work could constitutionally "be proscribed unless it is 'utterly' without social importance."

It was not until 1973, in an opinion written by Chief Justice Burger (in the case of *Miller* v. *California*), that a majority of the Court was organized to "overrule" such influential statements by Brennan. When that happened, Brennan took the opportunity to adopt a new, more radical position—that officials should be prevented from censoring any sexually oriented materials, including so-called obscene books and movies, and from punishing anyone from disseminating such materials—except in the contexts of distribution to juveniles or exposure to unconsenting adults. In short, under the First Amendment, adults ought to be fully free to read the books and see the movies they choose, without governmental supervision—and this, whether inside or outside of the home.

Thus, some 16 years after Brennan had said for a majority of his brethren, in the case of *Roth* v. *United States*, that "obscenity" was "outside" the protection of the First Amendment, the Court's principal metaphysician of the law of obscenity now declared (joined by his brothers Potter Stewart and Thurgood Marshall) that "obscenity"—an impossibly broad and indefinite concept—was juridically useless, except as a censor's tool to restrict and restrain freedom of expression.

Acknowledgments

We wish to thank all those who helped us in preparing this book, including Morris L. Cohen and Erika S. Chadbourn of the Harvard Law School Library and Professor Paul A. Freund of the Harvard Law School; Nancy Bressler of the Seeley G. Mudd Manuscript Library, Princeton University; Charles Silver of the Museum of Modern Art Film Study Center; Professor George H. Williams of the Harvard Divinity School and Alan Seaburg of the Andover-Harvard Theological Library, Harvard Divinity School; and archivists and staff members of the Library of Congress, Franklin D. Roosevelt Library, New York Public Library for the Performing Arts at Lincoln Center, and other repositories, who, along with others, helped us gain access to, and gave us permission to quote from, their collections. We also appreciate the cooperation of the many persons who permitted us to interview them.

Among those who contributed to the filmographic research were Christophe de Grazia, whose assistance in uncovering filmographic data and developing film synopses was particularly valuable; Elisabeth Good; and Barbara Loos. Much of the spadework for the legal research was conducted by students at the Benjamin N. Cardozo School of Law; we are indebted to Danny Cantor, Jane Carlin, Jane Darnell, Leslie Fielden, Melanie Karsh, Arthur Lewis, Terry Raskin, Peter Schwartz, and, especially, Nesa Hassanein, Marc Bogatin, Gail Markels, and Alan Yatvin. We are grateful to Stella Torgoff, whose secretarial and proofreading efforts helped bring the manuscript's numerous drafts to publishable proportions.

A special appreciation is due to our editors at R. R. Bowker Company, Book Division. Judy Garodnick, editor in chief, originally interested us in this book, and she and Nancy Volkman, senior editor, remained an unswerving source of strength throughout. They spurred us to completion, greatly improved the book, supported us, and persevered. Finally, we thank Barbara M. Preschel for preparing the index and Stephen A. Rosen for compiling the tables of cases.

The Story

"The Birth of a Nation" —and of Censorship

Movies were made before D. W. Griffith made *The Birth of a Nation*, but no other single picture has had as great an impact on the art of filmmaking or on American society. Griffith mastered what others developed—ways to build scenes and create imagery, pace sequences and bring on dramatic transitions, film fade-outs, close-ups, and long shots—and assembled it all into a powerfully constructed story. *The Birth of a Nation* vividly demonstrated the power of the new form of cultural expression. It was not only the leading American picture of the day, but also the first to deal in a grand manner with a matter of great importance: the role of blacks in American history.

The Birth of a Nation was first shown on February 8, 1915 at Clune's Auditorium in Los Angeles under the title *The Clansman*, a popular novel by Thomas Dixon, Jr., from which Griffith drew much material and his main story line. Both works took liberties with history: The Ku Klux Klan did not unite the North and the South. Griffith portrayed the values of a conquered people. He later recalled that, as a child, "I used to get under the table and listen to my father (a Confederate colonel) and his friends talk about the battles and what they'd been through and their struggles. Those things impress you deeply—and I suppose that got into *The Birth*."

The first half of the picture is a conventional tale of the Civil War. But the second half presents Griffith's romantic view of Reconstruction as inspired by Dixon's book, which ends, "Civilization has been saved, and the South redeemed from Shame." In depicting the blacks' capture of the government of South Carolina, the picture enraged many viewers. It portrayed blacks as so ignorant, uncouth, and driven by sexual lust that the Ku Klux Klan is forced to rescue young women from them and to restore order to the

3

state. In one scene a white girl plunges from a cliff to her death rather than submit to a black former family servant. Whites and blacks are separated throughout the picture, and one subtitle bluntly states that the South must be made "safe" for whites. At screenings of the movie, a symphony orchestra, generally composed of between 25 and 50 instruments, played excerpts from classical scores to fit the scenes, adding to the picture's impact on the audience.

One week after its Los Angeles opening, the movie was exhibited to the National Board of Review of Motion Pictures, a private body located in New York City whose judgments about the acceptability of films were sometimes followed by government censors in many areas of the country. A sharply divided board approved the picture, and news of its heated meeting and the movie's explosive character was printed in the press. Fearing that a "sectional conspiracy" might succeed in suppressing the film, Dixon thought to enlist the aid of his friend, President Woodrow Wilson. They had been friends since graduate school 30 years earlier; Wake Forest College had awarded Wilson an honorary law degree on Dixon's recommendation. "I've always cherished the memory of it," Wilson said when Dixon called upon him.

Dixon asked Wilson to view the film "not as the Chief Magistrate of the Republic but as a former scholar and student of history and sociology." Wilson was in mourning because of the recent death of his wife and so could not go to a theater, but suggested that if projection equipment could be brought to the White House, he would see it there and invite his Cabinet. "Of course," Dixon wrote afterwards, "I didn't dare allow the President to know the real big purpose back of my film—which was to revolutionize Northern sentiments by a presentation of history that would transform every man in my audience into a good Democrat! . . . What I told the President was that I would show him the birth of a new art—the launching of the mightiest engine for moulding public opinion in the history of the world."

"It is like writing history in lightning," was Wilson's reaction. "My only regret is that it is all so terribly true." Although Wilson later stated that he "did not approve" the film and referred to it as an "unfortunate production," Dixon had secured the *imprimatur* he wanted.

The next day, Dixon arranged to meet with Chief Justice Edward Douglass White. When he asked that White and the other Supreme Court justices view the film, White replied: "Moving picture! It's absurd, Sir. I never saw one in my life and I haven't the slightest curiosity to see one. I'm very busy. I'll have to ask you to excuse me." As he was about to leave, Dixon mentioned that the movie concerned the Ku Klux Klan. White said that he had been a Klan member and wanted to see the picture. That night the justices joined members of Congress in viewing it at the Raleigh Hotel in Washington.

Four days later, the Supreme Court handed down a unanimous decision that long hobbled the film industry. Comparing moving pictures as "mediums of thought" to "the theater, the circus, and all other shows and spectacles," the Court wrote: "It cannot be put out of view" that their exhibition is "a business pure and simple, originated and conducted for profit, like other spectacles, not to be regarded . . . as part of the press of the country or as organs of public opinion. They are mere representations of events, of ideas and sentiments published and known, vivid, useful and entertaining no doubt, but . . . capable of evil, having power for it, the greater because of their attractiveness and manner of exhibition." Perceived as just another commercial enterprise, movies were not entitled to constitutional guarantees of freedom of speech and press. It was more than 35 years from the time the Supreme Court handed down this decision, known as *Mutual Film Corporation* v. *Industrial Commission of Ohio*, that the precedent it established was discarded.

Shortly before the picture's public exhibition in New York City, Dixon learned that the theater planned to be closed that night. The distributor went to court and during the hearing its lawyer mentioned that the film had been shown at the White House. A telephone call was made and Wilson's daughter answered and affirmed that indeed it had been seen there and, she added, by the Supreme Court and Congress the following night. The court immediately withdrew the warrant for the theater closing and ordered police to protect the theater against interference.

The Birth of a Nation [3] was banned more often than any other film in motion picture history. Its right to be screened is known to have been challenged in well over 100 incidents in and out of court, as recently as 1980; in 60 instances the picture was completely banned or partially censored. From the beginning, those who sought to suppress it used a variety of tactics: initiating civil and criminal proceedings, petitioning government officials to enforce their administrative powers, seeking censorship legislation (at least eight laws were passed that aimed specifically at banning the movie), and extralegal means such as picketing, demonstrations, letter writing, pamphleteering, and sermons. The same methods were employed in future years in attempts to ban hundreds of other pictures.

In a widely distributed 1916 pamphlet entitled "The Rise and Fall of Free Speech in America," Griffith himself advocated "the freedom of the screen." He included extracts from newspaper and magazine editorials supporting *The Birth of a Nation*'s right to be exhibited and expressed the conviction that movies should have the same constitutional status as "the printed press":

> The moving picture is simply the pictorial press. The pictorial press claims the same constitutional freedom as the printed press. . . . Unjustifiable speech or publication may be punished, but cannot be forbidden in advance. Today the

censorship of moving pictures throughout the entire country is seriously hampering the growth of the art. Had intelligent opposition to censorship been employed when it first made itself manifest it could easily have been overcome. But the pigmy child of that day has grown to be, not merely a man, but a giant, and . . . he is a giant whose forces of evil are so strong that he threatens that priceless heritage of our nation—freedom of expression. . . . We have no wish to offend with indecencies or obscenities, but we do demand, as a right, the liberty to show the dark side of wrong that we may illuminate the bright side of virtue—the same liberty that is conceded to art of the written word—that art to which we owe the Bible and the works of Shakespeare.

This pamphlet did not stop the campaign, conducted largely by the National Association for the Advancement of Colored People, to ban the picture. One-third of all legal actions to ban the movie took place at the time of its release. The NAACP advised opponents of the film "to have an able lawyer, preferably a white man upon whom you can depend absolutely," examine existing local ordinances to determine if any could be applied against the film. The "play," branch offices were told, "can probably only be stopped by executive order of the Mayor whom you may be able to interest by united appeals from colored and white civic and welfare organizations, secret societies, women's clubs, etc. We urge you to be watchful and to leave no stone unturned in an effort to suppress this picture."

As front-line public officials, mayors had already become movie censors: more than a dozen banned *The Birth of a Nation*. The mayor of Newark, New Jersey banned it in 1915 on the ground that "it is not fit for decent people to look at." Three years later, the mayor of Louisville, Kentucky censored it because it was "the wisest thing." In 1931, Mayor Frank Murphy of Detroit, later an outspoken civil libertarian Supreme Court justice, threatened to revoke a theater's license if it continued to show the film after a two-day run. He objected to the picture because "of its unfair presentation of the Negro and its tendency to arouse race hatred." And the mayor of Minneapolis, after the state supreme court upheld his right to ban the movie if he wished, reversed himself and allowed it to be screened.

A revival of the film in 1924, and the release of a sound version in 1931 and again in 1938, brought more suppression. In Maryland, the film was banned for two separate periods during the 1940s and 1950s. When the Ohio censorship board disbanded in 1956, the picture returned to the state's screens after an absence of more than 40 years. In 1978, the Riverside, California City Council canceled a showing in the city on the ground that the picture was "racist," and an exhibition in Oxnard, California under Ku Klux Klan auspices caused a riot. In 1980, anti-Klan demonstrators disrupted a San Francisco showing because the picture was "pro-Nazi." It was close to two-thirds of a century since *The Birth of a Nation* had first been seen in Clune's Auditorium.[1]

Progressivism and the Fear of Films

When motion pictures first were exhibited at the turn of the century, an enthusiasm for moral uplift, social justice, and civic regeneration was sweeping the country. The main premise of this movement, called progressivism, was that reformation of the environment could be achieved by people of goodwill. Once the city, the "hope of democracy," was cleansed of its evils, the people who dwelt there would also progress. Two things appeared essential: the moral education of the country's youth and the Americanization of its immigrants. The child became the central theme of "humanitarian "progressivism," the investment in the future, the carrier of the American dream. Progressives welcomed immigrants, however cautiously, for the contributions they could surely make to the nation as long as they submitted to its ethos.

No sooner were the silent "photoplays" publicly shown than the guardians of culture began to fear the social effects of films and to denounce the irresponsibility of moviemakers. Immigrants and children were of special concern. The marvel of the movies was that:

> It is art democratic, art for the race. It is in a way a new universal language, even more elemental than music, for it is the telling of a story in a simple way that children are taught—through pictures. . . . There is no bar of language for the alien or the ignorant, but here the masses of mankind enter through the rhythm of vivid motion the light that flies before and the beauty that calls the spirit of the race. For a mere nickel, the wasted man, whose life hitherto has been toil and sleep, is kindled with wonder; he sees alien people and begins to understand how like they are to him; he sees courage and aspiration and agony and begins to understand himself. He begins to feel a brother in a race that is led by many dreams.

People who formerly had spent their spare time in poolrooms, dance halls, and, especially, saloons, now flocked to new and converted movie houses, which shortly became the *bête noir* of progressives. For immigrants and other newcomers to the cities, the moving picture house was "the substitute for the saloon." The "slums," wrote Vachel Lindsay, were "an astonishing assembly of cave-men crawling out of their shelters to exhibit for the first time in history a common interest on a tremendous scale in an art form. Below the cliff caves were bar rooms in endless lines. Yet this new thing breaks the lines as nothing ever did. Often when a moving picture house is set up, the saloon on the right hand or the left declares bankruptcy." Progressives found little comfort in this situation: movie houses and saloons appeared to them equally suspect. Some reformers maintained that "recreation is the antitoxin of delinquency, and the sooner it is administrated, . . . the milder will be the disease." "Recreation," at that time, meant activity directed at some socially useful, educational, or developmental end; leisure time was not intended to be spent socializing with peers in settings that might threaten the traditional authority of home, church, and school. Movies were not obviously healthy recreation; their potential for evil was at least as great as their disposition toward good—unless they could be controlled. To many, films loomed as a new kind of urban vice.

Public officials and civic organizations came to share the view that movies might inspire criminal activity and antisocial behavior. Mothers "could do nothing with their children, especially the boys, after they had attended moving picture shows." In Chicago, social reformer Jane Addams was not "against" movies but argued that police and citizen groups should "supervise" what could be seen in theaters. Movies, she said, could be instructive and wholesome; they "dramatized great moral lessons" and could raise the quality of life if placed under the proper guidance. The *Chicago Tribune* saw nothing good in the new entertainment form. It deplored the "nickelodeons" (which sometimes charged a dime) for lacking "a redeeming feature to warrant their existence." Since they "minister . . . to the lowest passions of childhood," it was "proper to suppress them at once." The newspaper called for "a law absolutely forbidding entrance of a boy or girl under 18" to their "wholly vicious" influence. "There is no voice raised to defend the majority of five-cent theaters," the editorial concluded, "because they cannot be defended. They are hopelessly bad."

The richness and variety of daily American life provided much subject matter for the early films. The "exploits of the policeman and burglar, cowboy and factory worker, farmer and country girl, clerk and politician, drunkard and servant girl, store keeper and mechanic" became steady grist of the early movie mill. The first moving pictures were not concerned with elevated themes, or with "fairy tales, fantasies, [or] storybook romances," because these were "far removed" from the "immediate interests" of most people. As films carrying titles such as *The Defrauding Banker* and *Adventures of an American Cowboy* played to packed theaters, Chicago's city fathers sought a social device that might prevent the exhibition of "objectionable" movies. In November 1907, the Chicago City Council passed the nation's first motion picture censorship law. It prohibited "immoral or obscene" pictures and required the police department to issue a permit before any movie was shown.

The Chicago police moved almost immediately to suppress *The James Boys in Missouri* [1] and *Night Riders* [2], two pictures that Jake Block and others "engaged in the business of operating five-and-ten-cent theaters, where moving pictures are displayed," wanted to show in their nickelodeons. When the police refused to issue any permits for these movies, Block showed them anyway, and went to court to prevent the Chicago police chief from enforcing the censorship law. His action was unsuccessful and the city's police power to regulate for the general welfare was upheld. The Supreme Court of Illinois concluded that although movies like *The James Boys* depicted "experiences connected with the history of the country . . . it does not follow that they are not immoral," since they "necessarily portray exhibitions of crime. . . . Pictures of the *Night Riders* can represent nothing but malicious mischief, arson, and murder." Had later courts followed this interpretation, much of America's frontier history would have been banished from the screen.

Chicago social reformers were still restive. Although police censors worked to remove scenes of violence, murder, and abduction from movies, and even rejected entire pictures, there was increasing pressure for the establishment of a better method of censorship. In 1914, a ten-member salaried civilian commission, composed equally of men and women, replaced the police board. It adopted a "pink permit" system whereby children could now be entirely barred from movies that received this "adults only" rating, the first in the nation. However, in 1917, a federal court found unauthorized an attempt by the Chicago police to restrict exhibition of *The Spy* [10] to adults only. Since the police had not asserted that the movie was "obscene" or "immoral," portrayed "unlawful scenes," or had a "tendency to disturb the peace," the refusal of a "general" permit, which did not exclude children, was held to be an abuse of official discretion.

Pre-exhibition "licensing" was not the only way in which movie freedom might be restrained by law. Police, prosecutors, and the courts could and did apply ordinary criminal law to punish persons who showed "immoral" or "obscene" pictures, as public or "notorious" acts of indecency. Usually, these were prosecuted as "common" law crimes, without any statutory basis. The first officially reported case of this kind of restraint involved the film *Orange Blossoms*, banned in New York in 1897, when a policeman arrested its exhibitor, John B. Doris. Police charged, and the court found this pantomime to "outrage public morals." The "outrageous" scenario, in the court's own words, consisted of

the scenic representation of a bedchamber, to which a bride and bridegroom retire late upon the night of their wedding day. The clock strikes twelve and the husband falls on his knees before his wife. She raises him up and, as she complains of a headache, he takes her to the bed, and suggests that she lie down. She requests him to leave the room so that she may undress. He refuses, declaring that they are married. She insists, however, and takes him to the door. There, he puts his hand up to indicate that he will be back in five minutes, and goes out. The woman undresses herself completely, and puts on her nightgown. She removes even her slippers, garters, and stockings. In removing her clothing, however, she skillfully limits the exposure of her person. When she is entirely ready to retire, she gets into bed, and turns down the light. At that moment (this is the end of the movie), there is a knock at the door, and she says "entrez."

At the trial, Doris's lawyer somewhat speciously argued that the movie could not be found harmful to morality because the heroine's behavior "was connected with lawful marriage." This was, in fact, the trouble with the movie. It was criminally "immoral," not obscene. "We have no doubt," the court concluded, "that the defendant's aim was not to honor, but to degrade marriage, and its sacred confidences." (The only record of the existence and contents of this picture is found in the court decision that justified its obliteration.)

The main concern that government authorities had with the early movies was their "immorality," a legal net big and durable enough to catch and condemn almost any picture. This suppression of "immoral" movies continued unchecked for more than fifty years.[2]

The National Board of Review of Motion Pictures

In 1907, as major cities throughout the country reported "nickel madness," the People's Institute of New York City launched an investigation of the commercial amusements provided to the largely immigrant working class. It was an appropriate time to do so, for in that year alone, some 1,300,000 foreigners arrived in the country. New York City's ghettos teemed with a variety of newcomers; over 3,000 people lived on one lower East Side square block alone. Seeking relief from the tedium of work, more than 1.5 million New Yorkers flocked weekly to the movies.

Thousands too went each week to programs offered by the People's Institute. A prototypical Progressive organization—"a kind of popular university," according to its director—it offered social, cultural, and educational opportunities to the working class, and was nonpartisan and above suspicion in the public eye. Movies could be beneficial if suitably regulated, claimed John Collier, who directed the institute's investigation of amusements. The "prevailing view," he announced, was that "the cinema was 'the people's theater,' and held great potential for education and for life."

This did not lay to rest the anxieties of New York City's politicians. On the day before Christmas in 1908, Mayor George B. McClellan made the spectacular move of closing every movie house in the city, over 600 in all, charging that safety hazards compelled his action. He also threatened to revoke the licenses of all exhibitors who showed movies "which tend to degrade or injure the morals of the community." Goaded into action, New York's moving picture exhibitors banded together and, two days later, obtained a court injunction that stopped the mayor's action. But the following month, the city's board of aldermen passed an ordinance that barred children under 16 from attending any movie unless accompanied by an adult. Theater owners responded by enlisting "surrogate" parents to escort children, who were believed to make up some 25 percent of the total movie audience, into their theaters.

The New York ordinance and Mayor McClellan's hostile behavior also led New York's movie exhibitors to consider the possibility of self-regulation. Certainly, this was done in order to avoid government censorship of the sort that Chicago recently had instituted and the Illinois Supreme Court had supported. Because of the fears that movie attendance by children had recently inspired, in March 1909 the New York State Association of Motion Picture Exhibitors asked the institute to create a citizen's committee to preview all movies scheduled to be shown in New York State. The People's Institute had recognized the importance of recreational programs in training children for good citizenship; and it agreed to perform this new service not only because it seemed necessary if government regulation was to be avoided, but because it was in the "public interest" to do so.

Three months later, a non-governmental organization called the National Board of Censorship of Motion Pictures was established. Representatives from the People's Institute and from other private groups in New York City, including the City Vigilance League, the Children's Aid Society, and the Neighborhood Worker's Association, joined the board. Initially, a small committee of non-salaried social reformers was assigned the job of examining the movies. But as the number of pictures made increased dramatically, the board acquired a larger group of examiners who more effectively represented "public opinion." Within a span of five years, the screening committee grew from 9 to over 100 members. By 1915, virtually the entire output of the country's movie industry was being reviewed prior to exhibition by 250 affiliated local organizations nationwide. The committee's judgment, if adverse to exhibition, could be appealed to the board's General Committee, by whose decision the cooperating producers had agreed to abide. As the board charged each producer a fee for examining the pictures, the movie industry itself bore the burden of supporting financially this first example of motion picture self-regulation.

From its inception, the board claimed to be adamantly opposed to censorship. "Selection, not censorship" was its motto. In 1915, in an effort to differentiate its work from that of government censorship agencies, and in order to dissociate itself from the connotation of the term "censorship," the board altered its name to the National Board of Review of Motion Pictures. The public, presumably, was thereby encouraged to view its role as that of movie classifier, rather than censor.

The board's operations were called "voluntary," and its power—indeed, its existence—was said to be "only through the positive and continuing wish" of the movie community. Producers, distributors, and exhibitors had no legal relationship with the board, and were under no legal compulsion to submit pictures to it. The board could neither control nor direct where any movie should or should not be shown. What it could do was decide whether pictures should be classified in a bulletin it mailed weekly to 450 "collaborators," in over 300 cities and towns nationwide, as "passed," "passed with changes as specified," or "condemned." The board had eight prohibitive standards upon which it based judgments:

1. The Board prohibits obscenity in all forms.
2. The Board prohibits vulgarity when it offends or when it verges toward indecency, unless an adequate moral purpose is served.
3. The Board prohibits the representation of crime in such a detailed way as may teach the methods of committing crime except as a warning to the whole public.
4. The Board prohibits morbid scenes of crime, where the only value of the scene is its morbidity or criminal appeal. . . .
5. The Board prohibits the unnecessary elaboration or prolongation of scenes of suffering, brutality, vulgarity, violence, or crime.
6. The Board prohibits blasphemy, by which is understood the careless or wanton or unnecessary offence against religious susceptibilities of any large number of people in the country.
7. The Board prohibits anything obviously or wantonly libelous in films, anything calculated to cause injury to persons or interests from an obviously malicious or libelous motive, and films dealing with questions of fact which relate to criminal cases pending in the courts. . . .
8. In addition to the above specifications, the Board feels in general that it is right in forbidding scenes of films which, because of elements frequently very subtle which they contain, have a deteriorating tendency on the basic moralities or necessary social standards.

On the other hand, movies that contributed to the progress and advancement of civilization, that were "inspiring," "sincerely moral," "wholesome," and "fine," were to be approved.

Although the board was not "censoring" movies, it did reduce the number of "objectionable" or "undesirable" scenes that were to be found in them. Some subjects were especially troublesome. Sex at first had been merely "hinted at" on the screen. But after 1910, according to one critic, the "sex drama," a movie using "plain, blunt language," became "a commonplace" and made "tender passion rather the worse for it in recent years." A picture that "openly used sex as its major ingredient" was finally released in 1913. *Traffic in Souls* presented "new problems" in censorship because there was no certainty as to whether such a subject as white slavery could be treated legitimately on the screen. After consulting "experts," the board's General Committee passed the movie "subject to certain changes and modifications" that amounted to the deletion of several hundred feet of film. The public, the board announced, was being offered "a high-grade picture capable of real moral teaching and dramatic entertainment, yet stripped of all questionable features, such as suggestiveness and allurement, that such a subject might carry with it."

Since it was the only "national" agency in the field, the board was fairly active. In 1913, for example, it looked at 9,000 movies and condemned 53; portions were eliminated from 401 other films. By 1916, however, with the growth of official state and local censorship boards, only some 4,200 movies were examined; the number in which changes were made rose to 530. Yet some reformers demanded stricter control over the content of movies, and, quite apparently, the board's operations were not entirely successful in forestalling the creation of government censorship boards. The board's argument that government censorship was unconstitutional and in conflict with the First Amendment's guarantee of freedom of speech and press was increasingly discounted, in part, no doubt, because it was not always apparent what difference it made whether a film was "censored" by a governmental or a non-governmental body.

In 1914, New York City's license commissioner banned *The Ordeal* [4], allegedly from fear that the movie's story about the Franco-Prussian war might offend German citizens. He cited the board's disapproval in support of his own. Thus government censors would make use of the judgments of the industry's "voluntary" censorship agency to support their own bans. The court that reviewed this action reversed the censor's decision and expressed uneasiness over government use of board opinions. Eventually, numerous cities—including Providence, Atlanta, Boston, Birmingham, Seattle, and Spokane—provided that only such movies that the board did not "pass" need be inspected.[3]

The Rise of State Censorship Boards

The example of Chicago's censorship and dissatisfaction with the National Board of Review led other cities and states to adopt prescreening censorship methods. Pennsylvania established a state board of censors in 1911, Ohio in 1913, Kansas the following year, and Maryland in 1916. (Cases involving two of these state censorship boards were *The Ordeal*, banned in Pennsylvania in 1919, and *The Easiest Way* [11], banned in Kansas in 1918.) In New York, in 1916, a governor's veto prevented the formation of a state-wide censorship system; similar bills had been introduced in the legislatures of ten other states during 1914–1915. The Pennsylvania board, which was more elaborate than city censoring structures, set the state pattern. Its members were named by the governor, were required to be residents and citizens of the state, and to be "well qualified by education and experience to act as censors." No movie could be shown in the state unless it had first received a certificate reading: "Approved by the Pennsylvania State Board of Censors." Pictures which displayed nudity, infidelity, women drinking or smoking, or prolonged passion were prohibited. A female member of the first Pennsylvania board, after viewing several weeks of filmed love drama, declared that "one yard [of film] is long enough for a kiss; young people should be torn from each other after 36 seconds." Drinking, especially by women as in *The Road to Ruin* [16], was sure to incur censors' condemnation.

Local censorship assumed various forms. Usually, the police department, empowered by a municipal ordinance and acting upon its own initiative, inspected movies; this was the case in Detroit, St. Louis, Washington, San Francisco, Louisville, and Trenton. Some cities, including Los Angeles and Birmingham, formed censorship boards within the police department or other inspection bureaus; others, such as Kansas City, created boards responsible to the mayor to carry out the censorship task.

New York City, which alone had more than 5 percent of the country's audience, was a special case. In 1911, Mayor William J. Gaynor ordered a survey of the city's entire entertainment scene and appointed a special commission to draft a law based on the findings. (In 1908, Gaynor was the judge who issued the injunction that prevented Mayor McClellan's theater-closing order from taking effect.) While the city's Board of Aldermen was considering the proposed legislation, opposition developed from among small movie house owners and stage and vaudeville interests at the same time that Tammany Hall, the city's Democratic organization, was demanding a system of prior censorship. Gaynor vetoed the bill, observing that "the criminal law is ample to prevent the exhibition of such pictures."

Gaynor proved to be an eloquent and effective defender of freedom of speech and press. When a constituent complained to him about the exhibition of prize fight pictures in theaters, he wrote:

> I do not see how it can do any good to look at them. But will you be so good as to remember that ours is a government of laws and not of men. Will you please get that well into your head. I am not able to do as I like as Mayor. I must take the law just as it is. [Mayors of] other cities [may have] ordered [that] these pictures shall not be exhibited. Indeed? Who set them up as autocrats? . . . People little know what they are doing when they try to encourage officials to resort to arbitrary power.

Gaynor's December 1912 message to the Board of Aldermen, disapproving the proposed amusement house ordinance, was an extraordinary early defense of full freedom of the screen. He had been "constrained to do this," he wrote, "because of the provisions creating a censorship." These "provided that the Board of Education shall appoint one or more censors to examine all motion pictures in advance and determine whether they may be exhibited or not." And yet, he continued, stating a principle that the United States Supreme Court did not recognize until 40 years later, "It has hitherto been the understanding in this country that no censorship may be established by law to decide in advance what may or may not be lawfully printed or published. Ours is a government of free speech and a free press. That is the cornerstone of free government. The phrase 'the press' includes all methods of expression by writing or pictures. . . ."

"The first comprehensive municipal law" in the United States for overseeing movie houses was eventually passed in August 1913. Although it did not expressly authorize the regulation of the content of pictures, and so was not a direct censorship law, the New York City license commissioner construed it to empower him to review content. Embracing a multitude of building and fire safety rules, it provided that department of licenses personnel should inspect the movie theaters regularly. Six years later, the city's Board of Aldermen rejected a plan that would have created a board of movie censors in the department of licenses and given the license commissioner explicit censorship authority.[4] Nevertheless, the license commissioner now behaved as a *de facto* movie censor as illustrated by the cases of *The Ordeal*, *The Hand That Rocks the Cradle* [7], and *The Sex Lure* [8].

Margaret Sanger and "Birth Control"

The years before World War I saw "the end of American innocence." Sex, birth control, divorce, and family problems were now discussed, although not openly. Freud had recently come to America, and realism, in psychology as well as in literature, indelibly impressed the American mind. American movies reflected some of this. There was "a loss of respect for spiritual values and an increased regard for material ones. The philosophy of self-aggrandizement, the regard for elegant clothes and polished manners, the veneration of successful businessmen and wealth, and the fashion of high-pressure salesmanship . . . now began receiving favorable attention on the screen." The advent of automobiles and airplanes brought a fast pace of life and joggled a relatively static society. Movies added "realistic" fantasies on demand and transported audiences to undreamed-of places and situations. But movies communicated ideas as well as sensations, thus heightening fears of unpredictable and unwanted change. Old-guard members of the patrician print culture were awestruck. Others, like William Dean Howells, expressed optimism: "No one can deny the wonder of this new form of the world-old mime. It is of a truly miraculous power and scope; there seems nothing it cannot do—except convince the taste and console the spirit.''

Censorship cases mirrored developing moral conflicts in the American social scene. In time, it was not enough to be able to discuss sexual problems such as contraception, venereal disease, and free love in private. Reformers wished to proselytize solutions to such problems and tried using movies to do so. As the birth control movement led by Margaret Sanger made headway, it collided with a Victorianism that sought to defend its values by insisting that the public discussion of certain subjects remain taboo. Contraceptives used to prevent pregnancy could also be used to prevent venereal diseases. A series of frank articles about venereal disease by Sanger in the *Call* in 1912 resulted in the post office's banning the magazine from the mails. Although the series was stopped, Sanger retaliated with a banner headline in the next issue: ''What Every Girl Should Know: NOTHING! By Order of the Post Office Department.''

Not long after, the New York City license commissioner again exercised his legally dubious power to censor movies by threatening to revoke the license of any theaters that showed *Fit to Win* [13], made by the American Social Hygiene Association to dramatize the public danger of venereal disease. Although the distributor promptly obtained a federal court order that restrained the commissioner from carrying out his threat, he lost it when the United States Court of Appeals decided there was ''no evidence'' that the commissioner had not ''honestly concluded'' that the picture's exhibition ''to mixed audiences will be injurious to decency and morality.''

As part of a systematic public educational campaign, Sanger made numerous personal appearances, at which she showed a movie called *Birth Control* [6]. Advertisements described it as an ''Illuminating Drama for the Ages . . . A Cheerup Photoplay for the Universe''; the National Board of Review had approved it. Largely autobiographical, the picture portrayed Mrs. Sanger as a nurse who, tempted to advise poor women on methods of birth control, refrains from doing so because of a state law that prohibited the dissemination of information on that subject. Eventually, determining to defy the law, she opens a birth control clinic. Private detectives are hired to suppress her activities, and police, tipped off about them, arrest her. The movie ends with an image of Sanger *cum* nurse in prison, and the subtitle ''No matter what happens, the work shall go on.''

Again, the New York City license commissioner took action to suppress the picture, and again his action was invalidated by a lower court, only to be revalidated on appeal. He felt that *Birth Control* was ''not a proper film to be exhibited,'' because it ''sought to teach immorality and was entirely opposed to the public welfare.'' Its ''main purpose,'' he insisted, was Mrs.

Sanger's "exploitation"; moreover, he charged, announcing a favorite grievance of censors of early social reform films, the movie "tends to bring into disrespect" law enforcement officials. (It was not until 1965, in the landmark case *Griswold* v. *Connecticut*, that the Supreme Court decided that state laws criminalizing the spread of information about birth control were unconstitutional. Seven years later, constitutional protection was extended to the distribution of contraceptives by the case of *Eisenstadt* v. *Baird* [1972].)

In addition, the commissioner charged that the movie would "have a tendency to arouse class hatred"; this was because, as trial judge Nathan Bijur "inferred" from viewing the picture, "the rich violate the law by employing contraceptive methods of which the poor are ignorant," thereby demonstrating "a certain amount of hypocrisy on the part of those who lend their active support to the enforcement of this law" while "Mrs. Sanger is activated by high and unselfish motives in condemning and even violating it." Finally, despite the seeming objectivity of the film's message, he claimed that disseminating birth control information "would cause many unmarried people to indulge in liberties from which they would otherwise refrain on account of the danger of being placed in the position of shame." The film "teaches methods of unlimited gratification of sexual desires and the avoidance of any responsibilities, as opposed to the teaching of discipline and self-control."

In an eloquent opinion that recognized movies as serving a function of free speech, Judge Bijur ordered the license commissioner not to revoke the license of any theater showing the movie. As "the public welfare may be affected" by the dominance of one or the other of "two conscientious and opposite views," it is "both appropriate and lawful that the matter be publicly considered, provided the presentation be free from gratuitous or obtrusive uncleanliness. . . ." However, the Appellate Division of the New York State Supreme Court disagreed, citing the U.S. Supreme Court's *Mutual Film Corporation* case to deny that this movie's ideas were entitled to constitutional protection. It reversed the trial judge's order on the grounds of the license commissioner's opinion that "in view of the pending war a plan to limit birth control should not be made part of amusement, entertainment, or recreation in the metropolis." The commissioner was authorized, the court decided, "and it would be his duty, to prevent any exhibition at a licensed theater that might be to the prejudice or disadvantage of the State or nation."[5]

The unfolding war in Europe soon brought reports of German aggression. As German-Americans began to organize into a potent political bloc, forming the German-American Alliance, a counterattack was launched in the arena of public opinion—an image of the German-American community "riddled with treason and conspiring under orders from Berlin." Patriotic fever was so strong that during the war one Wursterbarth, who had become a naturalized American citizen in 1882, was denaturalized on the ground that his opposition to the war demonstrated that he had taken the oath of allegiance in bad faith 35 years earlier. President Wilson, after issuing his Proclamation of Neutrality, "asked movie audiences not to cheer or to hiss either side." The case of *The Ordeal* [4] reflected this tense situation.

The defendant, once again, was New York City's militant license commissioner, George Bell. But this time, when a trial court nullified his censorship act, the nullification stood. Once the theater owner had shown the movie (the license commissioner had no prescreening licensing power), Bell told him that his license would be revoked if the exhibition were continued. Moreover, he "considered it absolutely unfit for production" in the city. One reason cited was that the National Board of Review had condemned the movie as "obviously built on the present European War and [having] portrayed such scenes as would tend to arouse partisan feeling that would lead to disturbances." Another reason was that Bell's deputy commissioner, Ephraim Kaufmann, thought that it "might occasion racial differences at this time" since, in the movie, "German soldiers are extremely cruel and show a merciless attitude dealing with combatants," which would "undoubtedly impress" a viewer with an "unfavorable impression of a nation permitting such atrocities." While insisting on real fears for "the disapproval of foreigners," Bell himself conceded there was nothing in the picture to which an American could take offense. The New York court that heard the matter reasoned that even if the movie did show a German officer "in a cruel and inhuman light," this did not form "a proper basis for preventing the exhibition." The show could go on.[6]

World War I

World War I proved the significance of the cinema in American life. Movies became a powerful propaganda vehicle, "moulding public opinion in favor of the British position." Through patriotic pictures, most producers, mainly Americans of English and Scottish descent, demonstrated their "loyalty." By the time that President Wilson, on April 2, 1917, somberly asked Congress—with nearly every member waving or wearing an American flag—to declare war against Germany, the movies already were solidly behind the war. The country's film industry had mobilized before its army.

With the country whipped to a patriotic frenzy probably unequalled before or since, Congress armed President Wilson with tools of "stern repression" that he had requested to combat domestic "disloyalty." Under the

Espionage and Trading with the Enemy Acts of 1917 and the Sedition Law of the following year, government agencies were authorized to keep a close watch over all forms of communication. A newly created Committee on Public Information, along with special bureaus within the Post Office, the Justice Department, the War Department, and the State Department, scrutinized the contents and distribution of newspapers, magazines, books, and other printed matter, as well as motion pictures, for objectionable material.

Despite Wilson's assurances to the contrary, "legitimate criticism" of war policies was no longer possible. Teddy Roosevelt demanded "one hundred percent undivided loyalty," thundering, "He who is not with us, absolutely, and without reserve of any kind, is against us, and should be treated as an alien enemy." People were criminally punished for finding fault with the Y.M.C.A. and the Red Cross. One man went to jail for impugning the integrity of the Red Cross by saying of some woman's knitting, "No soldier ever sees those socks." As conformity blended with nationalism, the government prosecuted domestic dissenters and obstructionists of the war effort almost as vigorously as it pursued the enemy on the battlefield.

Wilson was quick to appreciate the role and potential value of movies, and to flatter the producers; and he wrote the National Association of the Motion Picture Industry,

> It is in my mind not only to bring the industry into the fullest and most effective contact with the nation's needs, but to give some measure of official recognition to an increasingly important factor in the development of our national life. The film has come to rank as a very high medium for the dissemination of public intelligence, and since it speaks a universal language it lends itself importantly to the presentation of America's plans and purposes.

By the time this letter was written, in June 1917, arrangements had already been made to turn the cinema into an engine of government propaganda.

Wilson established the CPI just eight days after Congress ratified the war resolution. Under the leadership of George Creel, the CPI attempted to "sell the war to America," to convey an official line, and to provide news to the public. Its Division of Films arranged for the production, under both public and private auspices, of "documentary" films that stressed the roles of different groups in the war effort. Other movies, as Creel later wrote, "carried the gospel of Americanism to every corner of the globe." "Passing for official policy," they became "international theological weapons."

Although the CPI's film censorship activity was "voluntary," it was almost totally effective. Movies praising pacifism or denouncing war were widely banned by local censors. A Pittsburgh theater owner was arrested for distributing handbills that advertised the picture *The Battle Cry of Peace*; the authorities charged that his circulars were calculated to prevent enlistment in the armed forces. The Creel committee spearheaded a largely "patchwork" effort by which films entering or leaving the United States were liable to be censored. The CPI cautioned producers against making any picture that falsely represented American life, was derogatory to American interests, or might give "aid and comfort" to the enemy. Moviemakers were urged to avoid "mob scenes" which, although they might be innocent in and of themselves, were liable to be distorted and used against the national interest. Finally, they were advised to include, whenever possible, matter that conveyed a favorable impression of the country and its people. A failure to cooperate "voluntarily," the CPI warned, would bring direct governmental censorship of the movies. No factor of the industry wanted that. The American film medium undoubtedly felt the effects of war more strongly than did any other field of entertainment. "For all practical purposes," one study concluded, the moviemakers "quietly followed the war-party line."

A striking instance of film censorship involved *The Spirit of '76* [9]. Made by Robert Goldstein not long before the United States entered the war, it contained scenes of atrocities committed by British soldiers during the American Revolution, including one in which an American infant was whirled around on the point of a British bayonet. The movie was first shown during the summer of 1917 in Chicago, where, after much public discussion, the city's censorship board banned it. When Goldstein was denied a court injunction against this restraint, he took his picture to Los Angeles. At a private showing, local and federal governmental representatives voiced no objections to the movie, possibly because Goldstein left out certain scenes. When he restored them, in order, in his words, "to excite the audience," and later showed the picture, the local United States Attorney obtained a search warrant and seized it. Goldstein's move for its return was denied by a federal court, which said: "This is not a time for the exploitation of those things that may have the tendency or effect of sowing dissension among our people, and of creating animosity or want of confidence between us and our allies. . . . That which in ordinary times might be clearly permissible, or even commendable, in this hour of national emergency, effort, and peril, may be as clearly treasonable, and therefore properly subject to review and repression." Goldstein was later prosecuted under the Espionage Act for appealing to anti-British sentiments among German-Americans. He was convicted and sentenced to ten years of imprisonment and a $5,000 fine.[7]

The National Association of the Motion Picture Industry

Government censorship of movies in the United States has, for the most part, always been a state and local enterprise. Apart from Customs Bureau censorship of foreign movies and the intervention of the executive branch in both world wars, the federal government has been only peripherally involved. Had movies been distributed through the mails, the story surely would have been different. In that case, the inimitable special agent of the Post Office Department, Anthony Comstock, would have made his censorial presence felt. The Post Office did get itself seriously implicated in the censorship of books and magazines under the lash of Comstock's fear and anger over "smut."

Comstock resolutely "stood at what he called 'the sewer mouth' of society, alert and expert at identifying obscenity . . . and aggressive in arresting it" under a statute—the prevention of obscene mail law—which he was instrumental in getting passed. "Your Honor," he once apocryphally told a judge peering down at him from the bench, "this woman gave birth to a naked child." "Comstockery," said an angry and bemused George Bernard Shaw, "is the world's standing joke at the expense of the United States. Europe likes to hear of such things. It confirms the deep-seated conviction of the Old World that America is a provincial place, a second-rate country-town civilization after all."

The earliest attempt to bring films under the surveillance of the federal government was made in 1915. While the uproar over Griffith's *Birth of a Nation* was taking place, Georgia Congressman Dudley M. Hughes introduced legislation that would have created a Federal Motion Picture Commission as a division of the Bureau of Education in the Department of the Interior. The idea had been put forward a year earlier by William Sheafe Chase, Canon of Christ Church in Brooklyn, while testifying before the House Education Committee, of which Hughes was chairman. Noting that nearly one million children nationwide attended movies daily, Chase declared that if an "immoral" picture injured a single child, it should be a matter of concern to the federal government. Hughes's proposal was partly modeled after Pennsylvania's censorship statute. The commission, to consist of five members appointed by the president for six-year terms, would have examined, censored where appropriate, and licensed all pictures before they were allowed to enter interstate commerce. Any movie that was "obscene, indecent, immoral, or depicts a bull fight, or a prize fight, or is of such a character that its exhibition would tend to corrupt the morals of children or adults to incite crime" would be prohibited. The motion picture industry was meant to bear the cost of the commission, much as it underwrote the National Board of Review's operations, by paying for the examination of each film. After extensive hearings, the bill was defeated, as were several similar proposals introduced over the next six years.

During this period, religious organizations for the first time became active in the effort to regulate film content. There had been earlier attempts, such as one in 1910 in which the Christian Endeavor Societies of Missouri sought to ban all pictures of "improper tone" and all "spooning scenes," including scenes that showed kissing by any people except relatives or married persons; these, however, had proved ineffectual. Now the timing was more propitious. It is commonplace in American history for a conservative reaction, including a religious revival and increases in church attendance, to follow war. After World War I, Episcopalian, Presbyterian, Methodist, and Baptist groups, the New York Christian Endeavor, and the Central Conference of American Rabbis all passed resolutions critical of the movie industry and decrying the evil of, and the demoralization brought about by, motion pictures.

In an effort to avert federal censorship and, possibly, federal regulation of business practices, movie producers and directors formed the National Association of the Motion Picture Industry in July 1916. NAMPI announced a self-censorship program aimed at stopping the growing censorship movement and endorsed two changes in federal legislation affecting movies. The first took the form of a constitutional movement that called for freedom of the screen and placed films on an equal "constitutional" basis with the print media; but this made no progress at all. More successful was a 1920 revision of the federal penal code providing that movies, along with other matter including printed materials, were not to be transported by common carrier in interstate commerce if "obscene, lewd, lascivious, filthy, or of indecent character." Although this change had the superficial appearance of achieving the goal of the Hughes bill, it had no discernible effect; and by linking movies with the print media in the context of moral censorship, it actually worked to strengthen the public sense that movies, like the print media, were meant to be free of censorship.

A series of articles by motion picture commentator Benjamin Hampton in February 1921 provoked the industry into adopting a new self-censorship code in order to stem the quickening tide of criticism of movie morals. "Unless producers and exhibitors cleaned their own house and cleaned it thoroughly," Hampton wrote, "there might not be much house left." Within a month, a group of leading directors adopted for NAMPI a code known as the Thirteen Points or Standards, which placed outside the pale movies having elements or themes of the kind that censorship boards had most often disapproved. Taboo subjects included "exploiting interest in sex in an improper or suggestive manner"; white slavery; illicit love which "tends to make virtue odious and vice attractive"; nakedness; "prolonged passionate love"; crime, gambling, drunkenness, and "other unnatural practices dangerous to social morality"; instructing the "morally feeble" in crime; ridiculing or deprecating public or police officials or the military, and scenes that "tend to weaken the authority of the law"; offending any religion or religious figure; and "vulgar" scenes, "improper" gestures, and "salacious" titles. The code also provided for the expulsion from NAMPI of any member company that violated it.

The industry's strategy backfired by setting in motion a series of events that led to the demise of NAMPI and to a graver crisis yet for the movies. Reverend Wilbur S. Crafts, superintendent of the International Reform Bureau, noting the similarity among the Thirteen Points, the standards of state governmental censorship boards, and his own views, promptly ballyhooed the code as an industry-approved plan for federal censorship. The industry, put on the defensive, lost prestige and bargaining power in the state legislatures, where more censorship bills were being considered. Despite a frantic lobbying effort by NAMPI, pleading for a year's grace period to allow the industry to put its own house in order, and an opposition report in 1920 by the State Conference of Mayors, in 1921 the New York legislature passed, and Governor Nathan E. Miller signed, a bill establishing the state's first official censorship board. During this year, nearly 100 measures to regulate films were introduced in the legislatures of 37 states. The National Board of Review, created to forestall further governmental censorship, increasingly lost ground and influence as opponents accused it of being too liberal, "practically a whitewash of the whole output."

The escalating battle over movie freedom had overtones of class struggle and undercurrents of religious and racial antagonisms. When Canon Chase labeled his cohorts in the censorship movement "Patriotic Gentile Americans," he was expressing a barely disguised anti-Semitism. Reverend Crafts was more explicit when he claimed that an aim of his organization was "to rescue the motion pictures from the hands of the Devil and 500 un-Christian Jews." The film industry was especially vulnerable to such prejudices. Appealing to fellow immigrants, Jewish entrepreneurs, mostly from Eastern Europe, had gained concentrated movie power during the period from 1909 to 1913. By the time the war came, they had outmaneuvered the older companies involved in the motion picture patents trust, which had been established by Waspish elites, and now controlled most film production and were becoming the movie moguls. Before long, they supported a Protestant politician who, in turn, sought to harness the fears and angers of Irish-American Catholics concerning the effects of films.[8]

It is widely believed that the "Fatty" Arbuckle sex-murder case of 1921 cost American movies a piece of their freedom. Certainly, it was a large factor in inciting politicians to beat the drums all the louder for censorship, and in persuading the film industry of the urgency of its need for serious self-regulation. The headlines said: "ACTRESS DIES AT DRUNKEN PARTY, FAMOUS COMEDIAN CHARGED WITH MURDER." Roscoe "Fatty" Arbuckle, a gifted baggy-pants comic, second only to Charlie Chaplin at the time, was accused of killing actress Virginia Rappe. Eventually indicted for manslaughter, he was brought to trial three times. It was front page news across the nation. Two trials ended in hung juries; in the third, after deliberating for six minutes, the jury found him innocent. But Arbuckle's career was ruined: his movies were withdrawn from theaters as protests poured into the offices of Paramount Pictures, which had recently signed him to a three-year, $3 million contract.

More scandals inflamed public fear and repugnance of the movies and their makers. English director William Dean Taylor was found dead in his Hollywood home with two bullets in his back; movie people were suspected, and the murder was never solved. Next, Douglas Fairbanks and Mary Pickford, "America's Sweetheart," got married; but before long the Nevada Attorney General moved to set aside Pickford's divorce from her first husband. Although Nevada's Supreme Court eventually upheld the divorce, the adverse publicity added to the movie industry's troubles. Captains of the industry feared it was sinking. "The flow of scandal was telling at the box office." As film journalist Terry Ramsaye wrote later, "Professional enemies of the screen were capitalizing opportunity." They wished to castigate not only Hollywood for the films it made, but also its stars for their sinful personal behavior. Censors tried to stop the showing of movies whose stars had been involved in scandal or crime. In the aftermath of the Chicago Black Sox scandal of 1919, baseball had gone outside its ranks to make Federal Judge Keenesaw Mountain Landis its morality "czar." That provided an example that the movie moguls might do worse than to follow.[9]

The Rise
of Self-Regulation

In December 1921, two representatives of the motion picture industry went to Washington to see Will H. Hays, the Postmaster General of the United States. They were searching for a guardian angel. Over the previous few years, while serving as chairman of the Republican National Committee, Hays had met with movie men such as these to discuss Republicans' plans to use newsreels in the presidential election campaign of 1920. Warren Harding had won the election by a landslide, the most impressive political triumph in a century; the magnitude of that victory was generally attributed to the smoothly run party organization that Hays had created and led. Now, the industry wanted to find out if the Harding administration's chief political strategist would leave his cabinet post and join them in a major program to disarm the industry's critics and keep government out of the censorship business. They asked Hays to take the $100,000-a-year job of president of the newly formed Motion Picture Producers and Distributors Association of America. In that job, Hays became the single most important political figure in the movie industry's history.

Hays was a logical, even an ideal choice. He was from the country's heartland, an elder in the Presbyterian church, an adept administrator, and a crony of the President of the United States. Hays's morality was not subject to change. "What is immoral is always immoral," he wrote in his *Memoirs*. Throughout his movie industry career, Hays acted as though the traditional small town values of his childhood should apply to the entire United States.

The MPPDA was organized in March 1922, when its predecessor, NAMPI, dissolved after industry support for it disappeared. The new association was a fresh effort at internal reform. Its charter was vague enough to give Hays room to operate and promote the movie industry, which he did with enormous astuteness for the next 23 years. Once introduced as "the cat's whiskers of the motion picture industry," he instinctively led it through narrow places and across dangerous intersections to the advantage of the movie magnates and studio owners. Always amiable, and also shrewd, tactful, and coy, he promoted the industry by defending what he believed to be traditional American ideals. By the time he retired at the end of World War II, the "Hays Office" was a household word.

Hays's first move was to establish a "ten-point program" to foster the common interests of those engaged in moviemaking. Most important was an approaching referendum in Massachusetts meant to test, for the first time, the general public's opinion regarding censorship. Religious and secular advocates of screen regulation had effectively lobbied in the state legislature for a movie censorship bill the previous year. Hays approached the referendum as though it were another political campaign; and censorship was rejected by better than a 2½-to-1 margin of 750,000 votes cast. "The people's victory in Massachusetts," Hays later claimed, "turned the national tide." But this was wishful thinking.[1]

Proponents of screen censorship were unflagging in their efforts. In the five-year period ending in 1927, no less than 48 bills designed to impose statewide film censorship were considered by state legislatures; none of them passed. Few public officials dared to speak out against the trend toward governmental censorship. One who did was New York's Governor Alfred E. Smith. In his 1923 message to the legislature, and again in following years, he unsuccessfully urged repeal of New York's recently inaugurated movie censorship system. "Nobody will dispute that the invention of moving pictures opened the way for a new avenue of great education as well as of amusement. We have looked too lightly on guarantees of freedom of speech and of the press when we select from among our citizens three people who before the fact have the power to declare what is and what is not a violation of the statutes enacted for the protection of the morality of our people." It was a plaintive call.

Hays quickly realized that more was afoot than prospective measures of mild censorship. "It was a case of self-regulation or prohibition." The need was imperative to create a "self-governing organization" in matters of production, distribution, exhibition, and morals. Ever the politician, Hays invited "public cooperation [in] creating a demand for better pictures." The result was the formation of a Committee on Public Relations, representing over 60 civic, public welfare, fraternal, religious, professional, and educational organizations. The CPR was given a twofold job: to object to any movie of which it disapproved, and to promote patronage of every picture of which it approved, in order to encourage Hollywood "to make more of them." The committee was a political co-optation of the industry's critics that brought under the MPPDA's umbrella many of its most vociferous opponents, notably excepting such implacables as Canon Chase and Reverend Crafts. It functioned smoothly for a while, but two incidents eventually caused it to fold. In 1924, despite committee objections, Famous Players–Lasky Corporation made a film version of the book *West of the Water Tower*, which portrayed illegitimacy, a robbery, a dissolute clergyman, and petty small-town characters. The National Congress of Parents and Teachers and the General Federation of Women's Clubs promptly withdrew from the committee.

More damaging to the committee's reputation was the train of events set in motion when Hays tried to rehabilitate Fatty Arbuckle by removing the official employment ban against him. "I merely refused to stand in the man's way of earning a living in the only business he knew," Hays later wrote. "It seemed a relatively commonplace decision." But this time he grossly misread the public mood, and a cascade of denunciations poured in on him. The main criticism was that he had betrayed the public confidence placed in the MPPDA. A *New York Times* editorial suggested that Hays had been employed to "deodorize the movies." Other newspapers called for his resignation or dismissal. Forced to act immediately, the Committee on Public Relations passed a resolution asking Hays to advise the industry to "refrain from exhibiting pictures in which Mr. Arbuckle appears." Arbuckle sidestepped the issue by becoming a director of minor films.

The episode led a number of organizations to defect from the Committee on Public Relations. Some said they "did not want to be engaged in such inconsequential work." Others now viewed the committee as a "smoke screen, an obvious camouflage, an approval stamp for the salacious films and for the questionable, if not criminal, conduct of the industry and its employees." The committee was irremediably damaged.[2]

In 1925, many of the screen's local opponents banded together with proponents of national censorship to form the Federal Motion Picture Council. Their purpose was to promote the conviction that state and local censorship boards could not succeed in eliminating objectionable scenes from the movie screen and that only federal legislation would do the job. Canon Chase became the council's first general secretary as well as its most outspoken advocate. Council members lobbied actively in Washington and campaigned around the country, calling for centralized control of motion pictures.

In 1926, the House of Representatives held hearings on a bill which, like the one introduced in 1915, would have created a federal motion picture commission in the Department of the Interior. Chase pushed for this legislation, which he partly drafted, claiming that it was "the only way of effectively and promptly meeting a great new and natural evil."

> Whenever any business is so great and so intricate in its control and influence over the life and morals of the people, that business should be regulated by the United States Government or it should be regulated by some power big enough to regulate it—big enough to control it.

Only 17 persons or associations, mainly film producers or people otherwise connected with the industry, officially opposed the legislation. They asserted that voluntary censorship was improving, that self-regulation was true to the "American concept of self-government." The most influential voice belonged to President Calvin Coolidge, who declared through a spokesman that he was flatly against the bill. While governor of Massachusetts, Coolidge had vetoed a bill allowing court review of a censorship board's ruling because it did not include a provision for express trial by jury, as "provided for according to the Constitution." Congress, he now stated, should not approve a national censorship board unless the states themselves specifically approved. He pointed out that the producers' reforms were "long strides in the right direction" and that Will Hays was "a most helpful influence in this work." To the industry's relief, the bill died in committee.[3]

The juggernaut of governmental censorship was also curbed at the state level. After Hays assumed power, no new state boards were organized. Earlier, Virginia had created one in 1922, and Florida had established one the previous year. Louisiana formed one for Huey Long's political purposes in 1935, but it never exercised any power. The work of the established state boards was considerable, however, and it grew by leaps and bounds. The New York Motion Picture Commission was typical. In 1921, its censors banned or demanded deletions in 235 movies for being "indecent," "inhuman," "immoral," or "tending to incite to crime." Three years later, the number jumped to 3684. When it lacked sufficient personnel to do the job, the commission enlisted state troopers. It was not an easy task.[4]

"Self-Regulation" Guidelines

The 1920s were the Jazz Age, the Roaring Twenties, the Era of Glorious Nonsense, the Lost Generation. Liberal disillusionment was widespread: intellectuals were alienated, literary expatriates relocated in Paris, materialism was rampant. Jay Gatsby lived it up and George Babbitt believed everything that he heard and read. H. L. Mencken's savage prose brilliantly depicted the absurdities of the day. It was the time of Teapot Dome, Prohibition, bootleggers and speakeasies, flappers and "the new woman," but also of Sacco and Vanzetti, the Scopes trial, and the revival of the Ku Klux Klan.

The "talkies" arrived, and movie moguls built lavish and sumptuous palaces for their audiences; the purpose, evidently, was to see if one could outdo the next. Some assumed Grecian and Roman splendors, others imitated Chinese and Egyptian styles. Every city worth the name had at least one such secular "temple of daydreams." The most luxurious of all, S. L. Rothafel's Roxy in New York City, boasted Spanish Renaissance architecture. Its 120 ushers were reputedly ex-Marines; resplendently uniformed, they saluted patrons when they entered and eavesdropped on their comments while the films ran. "Mama," asked the boy in a *New Yorker* cartoon, standing in the lobby and gawking at the cantilevered ceiling, "does God live here?" The movies may still have been "democracy's theater," but the masses could now watch the photoplays amid surroundings in which royalty might feel at home.

Sexual permissiveness took a quantum leap during the 1920s. Many laid the blame on the movies. Theda Bara in 1915 had popularized the word *vampire*, taken from Kipling's poem, in "A Fool There Was." In 1927, Clara Bow starred in a picture called *It*, and everybody was expected to know what the "it" was. Cecil B. De Mille perfected the art of sophisticated sex appeal in his films and "practically invented the 'bathroom scene.' " "Undressing was not just the taking off of clothes," William B. De Mille observed of his brother's productions, but "a progressive revelation of entrancing beauty; a study in diminishing draperies." In competition with the canny director's eroticism were the many new "sex" and "gangster" pictures carrying messages and bearing titles that moral conservatives could not abide. These incited ever more numerous demands for "effective" government censorship.

The coming of sound in movies in 1927 spurred the industry and the art. Already ranked among the nation's ten largest industries, it grew even more powerful financially and in its public impact. By the late 1920s, the motion picture was "The Great American Art" that "symbolizes the hopes and aspirations of the unfortunate." The Depression turned the focus of America inward and helped nationalize American thought. The movie industry resorted to the old standbys, violence and sex, in new guises. Gangster films such as *Little Caesar*, *The Public Enemy*, and *Smart Money* in 1931, and *Scarface* in 1932, provided audiences with the violence; and Mae West, in movies like *She Done Him Wrong* and *I'm No Angel*, both in 1933, gave them the sex. Still, Westerns kept their place as the single most popular form of movie for all ages and all classes, perhaps because they successfully combined violence with reassuring traditional values and "moral" outcomes.

Why sex and gangster pictures were so popular with the general public when box-office receipts in general were declining is a matter for speculation. Perhaps they served as antidotes to the pervasive frustrations of the Great Depression. The "real-life" behavior of gangsters like Al Capone,

Frankie Yale, Dutch Schultz, the Diamond brothers, and the Amboy Dukes furnished popular subjects for newspapers, but American moviemakers surpassed their print competitors.

Such films became the favorite targets of women's groups which voiced concern about the influence of movies on children. A 1929 study warned that exposing youngsters to adult problems as portrayed on the movie screen could harm them. Such children, it noted, "are robbed of some of the preciousness of childhood." The League of Women Voters wanted movies to aid in civic education. The General Federation of Women's Clubs, with about three million members, "consequently endorsed" all forms of moral censorship, especially in movies. Film censorship was nearly an obsession with feminists of the period; "clubwomen ceaselessly investigated and inveighed against the movie industry." Finally, Hays assigned a former president of the General Federation of Women's Clubs to "interpret to the makers of motion pictures the feelings and wishes of womanhood in regard to the medium's development of its usefulness."

In the 1920s, books and stage plays were increasingly adapted for the screen, bringing with them the robust realism that had replaced the genteel tradition in American letters. And just as local "bluenoses" went after books with alacrity, so did motion picture reformers seek to censor their movie versions. During the period of World War I, President Woodrow Wilson personally scotched proposals to make movies from *My Four Years in Germany*, a book by former ambassador to Germany James W. Gerard; *Ambassador Morgenthau's Story*, by former ambassador to Turkey Henry Morgenthau; and Wilson's own volume, *History of the American People*. After *West of the Water Tower* was publicly released over the objection of the Hays Office, the MPPDA passed a resolution that required each member studio to submit a synopsis of all movies scheduled to be made, along with comments on any questionable aspects. But the MPPDA held no authority to reject objectionable material, or to impose penalties on members for its use.[5]

In 1926 the MPPDA established a Studio Relations Department. "I must admit," Hays later stated, "that it took some effort to persuade the producers to accept a public relations representative in Hollywood. . . ." Colonel Jason Joy, chairman of the by now defunct Committee on Public Relations, was made liaison between the studios and state and local censorship board officials around the country. He visited censors in order to clarify their standards, and passed along their views to producers. Afterwards, he described his role as a "one-man lectureship with the studio heads." Producers began showing him films before release and argued with him over his objections. Then, they gave him scripts and consulted with him about potential story problems. They gradually learned that if they followed Joy's suggestions, government censors made fewer rejections.

The experience of the Studio Relations Department was eventually codified in a series of "Don'ts and Be Carefuls," adopted at a trade practice conference in New York City in October 1927, the same month that sound was introduced. It was resolved that eleven "things"

> shall not appear in pictures produced by members of this association, irrespective of the manner in which they are treated: pointed profanity; any licentious or suggestive nudity—in fact or in silhouette; the illegal traffic in drugs; any inference of sex perversion; white slavery; miscegenation; sex hygiene and venereal diseases; scenes of actual childbirth—in fact or in silhouette; children's sex organs; ridicule of the clergy; [and] willful offense to any nation, race, or creed.

Also included was a remarkable hodgepodge of 26 other "subjects" that the producers agreed to treat with "special care" so that "vulgarity and suggestiveness may be eliminated" and "good taste may be emphasized." Among these were "the use of the flag; theft, robbery, safe-cracking and dynamiting of trains; brutality and possible gruesomeness; technique of committing murder; sympathy for criminals; sedition; the sale of women, or of a woman selling her virtue; rape or attempted rape; first-night scenes; man and woman in bed together; surgical operations; deliberate seduction of girls; the institution of marriage; the use of drugs; titles or scenes having to do with law enforcement or law-enforcing officers; excessive or lustful kissing, particularly when one character or the other is a 'heavy.' " The list is perhaps most instructive for its evidence of the kinds of subjects with which "renegade" producers were dealing during the 1920s.

The "Don'ts and Be Carefuls" resembled the British Board of Film Censors' guidelines, adopted in its initial year of operation in 1913. This board, which provided for the voluntary submission of films by manufacturers, was the first body to impose industry self-regulation in Great Britain. It was established by a professional trade group of movie exhibitors, manufacturers, and renters, the Kinematograph Manufacturers' Association. The British censors took exception to and rejected movies on grounds, among others, of "scenes calculated to act as incentive to crime"; "medical operations"; "indelicate or suggestive sexual situations"; "holding up a Minister of Religion to ridicule"; "the materialism of Christ or the Almighty"; "subjects depicting procurations, abduction and seduction"; and the "native customs in foreign lands abhorrent to British ideas."

The MPPDA's "Don'ts and Be Carefuls" were not very different from the Thirteen Points of the defunct National Association of the Motion Picture Industry; they were more exhaustive, yet hardly any more effective as a system of industry self-censorship. Since observance was optional, producers circumvented or ignored them. Implementation proved impossible without any enforcement mechanism.[6]

The Motion Picture Production Code

The nearly universal adoption of sound by 1929 prompted Hays to consider new methods of strengthening the effectiveness of his office's censorship activity. Not only did the sheer amount of language used in movies increase far beyond that employed in the subtitles of silent pictures, but the sort of language used was threatening to get out of control. New actors had been recruited, often too hurriedly for proper selection and training, from vaudeville and burlesque circuits. These, at first, improvised their lines while the movie was being filmed, creating a precarious situation that was promptly abandoned as scriptwriters adapted to the requirements of sound.

Hays was bothered by the coarse language in films. When he discovered a short subject using the word "damn" several times, he said that this "mildest of 'cuss words' " did not offend him personally but "as a matter of policy we ought to avoid expressions that rub any notable section of the public the wrong way." Two years earlier, when atheists had demanded that God be kept out of films, Hays had responded: "God is everywhere." Now, he felt that "too many objectionable things were creeping into some of the pictures." What was needed was not only a mere recital of standards but a philosophy that explained those regulations and a machinery that enforced them. A prominent lay Catholic supplied the philosophical basis.

Martin Quigley had been the publisher of the leading trade newspaper, the *Exhibitors' Herald*, for 14 years in 1929. Born in Cleveland in 1890, he attended Niagara and Catholic Universities before becoming a newspaper reporter in Detroit and Chicago, where he began his publishing career. In 1928, he acquired the *Moving Picture World* (established 1907) and combined it with the *Exhibitors' Herald* to form the *Motion Picture Herald*. He started the annual *Motion Picture Almanac* the following year and, when he moved to New York in 1931, purchased the daily *Motion Picture News*, later called *Motion Picture Daily*.

Quigley's weekly *Herald* editorials supported the making of movies suitable for mass audiences. He thought that adult pictures should be shown in designated theaters, that films did not have a responsibility to elevate their viewers, and that a theater should not be turned into a classroom. On the other hand, he felt that the producer and exhibitor had an obligation to present material that allowed a spectator to leave the theater as good a human being as when he or she entered. Films should provide enjoyment and amusement without being morally degrading. Quigley's overriding concern was for decent entertainment.

In the summer of 1929, persons within the movie industry sought Catholic support for a repeal of Chicago's censorship law. Among the backers of that law had been Quigley's priest, Father FitzGeorge Dineen, with whom he had often discussed issues of film morality. Quigley himself was "violently opposed" to governmental censorship: it was, he said, "demonstrated to be an unworkable scheme"; besides, political appointees did not know moral values. The development of sound movies would surely increase public pressure for censorship, and whereas physical scissoring of a silent film might leave it still "playable," that sort of censorship could ruin sound pictures. Quigley envisioned a plan whereby moviemakers publicly assumed responsibility to make only morally "clean" pictures. To facilitate this, he undertook to draft his version of the philosophical precepts underlying the MPPDA's "Don'ts and Be Carefuls."

To assist him, Quigley called upon the Reverend Daniel A. Lord, a professor at St. Louis University and a man of widely recognized intellectual integrity. A theologian as well as a professor of English and dramatic literature who had written one-act plays, Lord was perfectly suited to Quigley's needs. He had met Hays while serving, with a Protestant minister and a rabbi, as a "technical" advisor for Cecil B. De Mille's 1927 filming of *The King of Kings*, in which he had a minor acting role, conducting a field mass.

The result of Lord and Quigley's collaboration was the Motion Picture Production Code. Lord did the writing on the basis of a structure proposed by Quigley, who viewed it as an opportunity to read morality and decency into mass recreation. The document was divided into two parts, each reflecting its origins. The first section, the Code itself, stemmed from the MPPDA's Formula and the "Don'ts and Be Carefuls," and consisted of a preamble and a statement of general principles. The second part, "Reasons Underlying Particular Applications," was Lord's contribution. When the Hays Office presented the Code to the public in April 1930, the philosophical portion that Lord had developed was left out. This Code, Quigley's trade newspaper noted, "was formulated after intensive study by members of the industry and, according to Will H. Hays, by church leaders in the field of child education, representatives of women's clubs, educators, psychologists, dramatists, and other students of our moral, social, and family problems." In 1934, the entire Code, including the Reasons, was printed in the *Motion Picture Herald* with the following statement: "The subjoined official presentations of the content of the Code appear in two parts—first, a working abstract of the Code which has been widely accepted as the complete Code, and, second, the Code proper, which has been referred to as 'Reasons Supporting a Code.' " Information about Quigley's and Lord's roles in the Code's composition was strategically withheld because the MPPDA did not care to expose the Code's Catholic origins, even though its standards reflected American middle-class mores.

That films as entertainment and art affect the moral lives of a people and, therefore, have special obligations were the basic premises of the Code. Three general principles were enunciated:

1. No picture shall be produced which will lower the moral standards of those who see it. Hence the sympathy of the audience shall never be thrown to the side of crime, wrong-doing, evil, or sin.
2. Correct standards of life, subject only to the requirements of drama and entertainment, shall be presented.
3. Law, natural or human, shall not be ridiculed, nor shall sympathy be created for its violation.

The "Particular Applications" covered violations of the law (murder, methods of crime, illegal drug traffic, and the use of liquor); sex (adultery and illicit sex, scenes of passion, seduction, or rape, sex perversion, white slavery, miscegenation, sex hygiene, actual childbirth, and children's sex organs); vulgarity; obscenity; profanity; costume (complete nudity, undressing scenes, indecent or undue exposure, and dancing costumes); religion (ridicule, ministers of religion, and ceremonies); location; national feelings; titles; and repellent subjects (actual hangings or electrocutions, the third degree, brutality, branding, apparent cruelty, sale of women, and surgical operations). According to the Code, sin and evil were "valid dramatic material," but "sin which repels by its very nature, and sins which often attract . . . must be distinguished." If a film had any transgressions, "compensating moral values" had to be introduced.

One particularly clear example of the power of the Hays Office (and of Hollywood life) was a situation that occurred later, in 1940. Producer David O. Selznick clashed with Joseph I. Breen, the Director of the Production Code Administration, over the film *Rebecca*. In the Daphne du Maurier novel, Rebecca's husband, Max, murders her, then sends their boat, with holes drilled in it, out into the water with her body in it, to sink. Since the script lacked "compensation" for an "immoral" act, Breen revised it to a story in which Rebecca, during a confrontation with her husband, accidentally trips and kills herself while falling, and he then takes her body to the boat and proceeds in the manner of the book. Selznick almost abandoned the picture because of this "drastic change" (which Hays accepted), and even asked that du Maurier not mention it "publicly or privately," "especially as it would get us in wrong at the Hays office. . . ."

The Code was destined to represent the American movie industry's "official" morality for nearly 40 years. It entailed an industry-wide non-governmental form of censorship no less effective for being "private" and no less moralistic for being "secular." The Code imposed the judgments and tastes of the handful of individuals who came to administer it. If it was administered by those persons independently of state and municipal governmental censors as well as of the official Catholic church, it usually involved a collaboration with these institutions. It successfully constrained creative freedom of the movies until several factors began coalescing after World War II to break its grip on the industry.[7]

Enforcing—and Challenging— the Code

The Code did not affect movie contents as soon as it came into force in January 1931; enforcement machinery first had to be built. Previously, cooperating producers had sent their finished prints to New York where the Hays Office reviewed them, suggested modifications, and shipped them back to Hollywood. The Code was supposed to transform this loose, voluntary system into one that was binding. Each production manager, it provided, was to "submit in confidence a copy of each or any script to the Association of Motion Picture Producers," an entity that was legally separate from, but effectively part of, the MPPDA's West Coast office. Its special "reading department" made recommendations for revision wherever, according to Hays, "situations and dialogue are not in good taste, or where they might possibly offend a particular nation or country." After a script was passed there was a follow-up viewing of the completed picture. However, producers often flouted these provisions because there was no penalty for noncompliance. Disillusionment and disappointment with the Hays Office merged with a new disgust of the movies. At the same time, the industry was in serious economic trouble. Box office receipts dwindled precipitously as the Depression deepened. Attendance dropped from almost 100 million weekly in 1930 to 60 million in 1932. Close to one third of all theaters shut down the following year, and the fat profits of the major studios also plummeted.

Sound brought a greater variety of pictures to the screen. A 1930 sample of 500 films showed that while comedies composed 16 percent, almost all the rest dealt with crime (27 percent), sex (15 percent), and love (30 percent). By 1932, however, reformers succeeded in reducing the number of gangster movies made. Such films, *Commonweal* declared, created a "social milieu that serves as a very fair kindergarten of crime." *The Nation* attacked Hollywood for crowning the lawless "with the Romantic halo of bravery and adventure that helps to disguise their fundamental moronism." Hays told the studios that "to overemphasize the gangster's role in American life is undesirable." Throughout the 1920s, governmental censors had been more concerned with scenes of crime and brutality than with sex. When Jason Joy resigned in 1932 as the studios' liaison with the various boards to take a more lucrative position with Twentieth Century-Fox, Hays looked to a former head of the New York board as his replacement. Hays's expectation was that an ex-governmental censor was "not likely to overlook anything." He had decided, apparently, to get tough with reckless filmmakers, but his first opponent was a brilliant and unpredictable maverick, Howard Hughes.[8]

"Scarface"

In 1932, Hughes refused to revise his production plans for *Scarface* in accordance with Hays's views. Directed by Howard Hawks, and written by Ben Hecht from the novel *Shame of the Nation*, the movie would win recognition as the most violent gangster film of the day; it brought stardom to actors Paul Muni and George Raft, notoriety to Hughes, and some glamor to Al Capone. It was not Hughes's only skirmish with industry censorship; later, he helped damage the Code's credibility and influence with *The Outlaw*. This time, the Hays Office "ordered" Hughes to reduce the amount of violence and, insisting on legal retribution for Scarface's crimes, to see to it that the gangster was hanged at the end by lawmen, not merely gunned down by rival hoods. The script was returned to Hughes with the following indictment:

> Under no circumstances is this film to be made. The American public and all conscientious State Boards of Censorship find mobsters and hoodlums repugnant. Gangsterism must not be mentioned in the cinema. If you should be foolhardy enough to make *Scarface*, this office will make certain it is never released.

Hughes's response was characteristically brief and pointed. "Screw the Hays Office," he wrote Hawks. "Start the picture and make it as realistic, as exciting, as grisly as possible." Nevertheless, some cuts were made in the more violent scenes in deference to Hays's demands; but the end remained the same. The Hays Office pressed for a title change, suggesting *Shame of the Nation*. A compromise was finally struck, and *Shame of the Nation* became the film's rarely used subtitle. The muted version of *Scarface* obtained the MPPDA's Seal of Approval, needed to assure distribution by MPPDA members, and, upon its release, won critical acclaim. It is "as good as any gangster film that has been made," wrote the *National Board of Review Magazine*, ". . . more brutal, more cruel, more wholesale than any of its predecessors and, by that much, nearer to the truth." But Hays's scissoring did not satisfy all government censor boards.

Hughes's planned premiere in New York City was frustrated when the state censorship board refused to grant the movie a license. Hughes reacted with a fighting statement that pleased advocates of freedom of expression. It was widely reprinted in newspapers, thus generating even more publicity for the film:

It has become a serious threat to the freedom of honest expression in America when self-styled guardians of the public welfare, as personified by our film censor boards, lend their aid and influence to the abortive efforts of selfish and vicious interests to suppress a motion picture simply because it depicts the truth about conditions in the United States which have been front page news since the advent of Prohibition. I am convinced that the determined opposition to *Scarface* is actuated by political motives. The picture, as originally filmed eight months ago, has been enthusiastically praised by foremost authorities on crime and law enforcement [such as the California State Crime Commission] and by leading screen reviewers. It seems to be the unanimous opinion of these authorities that *Scarface* is an honest and powerful indictment of gang rule in America and, as such, will be a tremendous force in compelling our State and Federal governments to take drastic action to rid the country of gangsterism.

The *New York Herald Tribune* praised Hughes as the "only Hollywood producer who has had the courage to come out and fight this censorship menace in the open" and wished him "a smashing victory." He successfully appealed the censors' decision, restored the cuts and original ending, and released the film. But, not surprisingly, *Scarface* was banned in Al Capone's home turf, Chicago, and in several states.[9]

The Depression forced many Americans to abandon their characteristic optimism. As opportunities diminished, despair mounted, and breadlines grew longer and more numerous. It was publicly noticed that young women were engaging in prostitution. Reformers blanched when a host of "fallen women" movies dramatized such events. "In the harsh world of supply and demand, they had nothing to sell but sex," social observers said. And Hollywood learned how to glamorize such women and capitalize on their sexual immorality.

Just as Franklin D. Roosevelt offered the nation hope in his March 1933 inaugural address that the fog that had settled on America might be lifted ("The only thing we have to fear is fear itself"), Mae West's *She Done Him Wrong* opened in New York. Always the sexual aggressor, West was able to give her audiences "a powerful lift . . . out of the depression mire." Her suggestive one-liners and titillating *double-entendres* mocked middle-class morality and, worse, subverted it. The allure of sex had not previously been missing from the screen, but rarely had it been so blatantly entwined with the themes of films. Where West gave Americans the impression that she enjoyed sex, felt no guilt, suffered no retribution—and implied, "So can you!"—the gangster movie conveyed similar attitudes toward crime. The seeming preoccupation of the industry with both subjects, however, only served to heighten public pressure for more effective censorship.

In February 1932, a progressive Republican looking for reelection, Senator Smith Brookhart of Iowa, introduced a resolution to investigate the film industry. The Hays Office was targeted. Hays, he claimed, "has done nothing toward improving the moral tone of the movies." By the end of the year almost 40 religious, educational, and citizen groups passed resolutions calling for some sort of federal regulation of the industry. The Hays Office was apparently failing in its main function: to forestall the establishment of federal censorship and the proliferation of state and local boards.

At a time when Hays was being criticized from all sides, the May and June 1933 issues of the *Christian Century* and *Survey Graphic* magazines respectively publicized the results of the first comprehensive study of the social effects of moving pictures, supported by a $200,000 grant from the Payne Fund. The study had been oriented toward effects on the nation's youth, and some of the findings were that movies worked permanent and deep psychological effects on viewers. The publication of these findings "symbolized the culmination of the long struggle to make the motion picture industry more responsive to certain public attitudes." More important, the conclusions "tend to confirm some of the suspicions of reformers who for years had counseled that uncontrolled influence of the medium had created an undesirable and dangerous socializing force." Reformers now had an empirical as well as a moral argument in their battle to control the screen.

The moral argument could be posed two ways. The more strident crusaders were essentially concerned with eliminating "evil." Others, such as Mary G. Hawks, were guided by a conception of "good" and "beauty" and worked toward its fulfillment. Her presidential address to the National Council of Catholic Women in October 1933 laid the thesis for Catholic action against movie immorality. It was not merely that movies were failing to live up to their potential for good.

> [Movies] are a menace to the physical, mental and moral welfare of the nation. . . . These injurious effects are greatly enhanced by the shameless sex appeal of the advertising. Constant exposure to screen stories of successful gangsters and "slick" racketeers, of flaming passion and high-power emotionalism, may easily nullify every standard of life and conduct set up at home and will almost inevitably effect a moral decline at the very outset of life's adventure.

Accordingly, Hawks proposed "a Catholic standard of judgment *in re* movies, drama, and literature" and "determined elimination . . . of all that violates that standard." She wanted "to use the facilities of organization to educate public opinion to this standard of selection," which is "that highest expression of human life—the power of choice"; and "to carry to Catholic mothers generally by means of organization facilities in parishes, etc., information regarding the menace to health and morals of the movies." "*Demand* good pictures," she said, and "*protest* bad ones." "Patronize the former and boycott the latter if protest is unheeded."

During its first few years of operation, the Hays Office's Production Code had not attained the results desired. According to Martin Quigley, the reason was the lack of "sufficient pressure and support by public opinion to encourage or compel the industry at large to conform with the letter and spirit of its regulations." In some quarters, he admitted, the Code that he had prepared was regarded as "extreme," even "somewhat fanatical."[10] And the problem did not go away. By the fall of 1933, the situation prompted Catholic reformers to take direct action.

The Struggle
for Control
of the Screen

Motion pictures had been a concern of the Catholic church long before the 1930s. As early as 1916, the Church had banned the movie *Power of the Cross* and threatened its producer, A. M. Kennedy, with excommunication if he released it. In 1922, the International Federation of Catholic Alumnae began publishing reviews of "recommended" films while the Detroit Council of Catholic Organizations issued periodic lists of "objectionable" ones. The following year, Bishop John J. Cantwell of Los Angeles, wishing "to form some sort of organization amongst the Catholic picture people," established the Catholic Motion Picture Actors' Guild. Its goal was "the spiritual, social, and material advancement of our people." By 1927, some of the larger studios were sending scripts to the National Catholic Welfare Council for approval.

These were uncoordinated developments and did not represent a structured Catholic program with respect to the cinema. The Catholic press carried sporadic stories about Catholics prominent in the industry and how Catholic themes were treated in films, but not until the late 1920s did it overtly recognize movies as an art form and as a vehicle of social power. With the introduction of sound, the attention given the screen significantly increased. Movies were now perceived as a threat to moral values that the Church could no longer ignore.

Before the 1930s, the Church's concern was largely expressed through the Index of Forbidden Books and fostering "purity in print." Literary censorship was "decidedly on the wane" by 1929, and authors and publishers were enjoying more freedom than ever before. One reason was that books were not considered "quite so important any more" because movies were partly replacing them as popular entertainment. The Church had to shift with the times.

An indication of future Catholic action to control the screen came in 1926. Pointing to the proliferation of pictures and their deep hold on public taste, a Milwaukee priest argued that the movies' potential for good was great, but unfulfilled. "Some films indeed are very elevating, instructive, and edifying," he said. However, as these were not the rule but the "exception," parish priests and parishioners were told to undertake a threefold program of "direct action," including economic boycott, organized protest, and the influencing of government censors.[1]

The Legion of Decency

Catholics first became directly involved with the motion picture industry with the drafting of the Motion Picture Production Code. In 1932, American bishops appealed to movie producers to adhere more closely to the Code, but their call fell on deaf ears. The year before, however, at the prodding of a Philadelphia reporter named Joseph I. Breen who had directed public relations for the 1925 Eucharistic Congress, Universal Pictures rewrote the script for a movie based on Charles Norris's novel *Seed*. The original version, according to one diocesan newspaper, was "hardly more than subtle propaganda for birth control." Now, several men—including two laymen (Quigley and Breen), three Jesuits (Lord, Parsons, and Dineen) and the rector of Catholic University (Monsignor Joseph M. Corrigan)— "labored, first, to provide a solution for the problem of movie morals, and then to provide pressure to make the solution work." The solution lay in the Production Code that Quigley and Lord had written; the pressure would come from the Catholic bishops.

Bishop Cantwell, in whose archdiocese Hollywood was located, was "personally . . . averse to any attempt to legislate morality," and "consequently . . . not an advocate of Federal censorship of motion pictures." Instead, he advocated seeking reform through persuading influential people. One such person was A. H. Giannini, president of United Artists and brother and partner of A. P. Giannini, founder of the Bank of America, which often had supplied "indispensable" financing to major studios. Giannini told Hays that the high hopes held by the Vatican at the time of the Code's enactment had been dashed. He threatened not to underwrite new productions unless the industry succeeded in raising the moral tone of movies. Similar pressure had been exerted on the studios in the past by George Cardinal Mundelein of Chicago. The stock market collapse of 1929 brought some important studios under the financial control of the Chicago-based underwriting firm of Halsey, Stuart and Company. These bankers leaned on the industry to adopt the new code at the prompting of Cardinal Mundelein, who lunched regularly with them.

American bishops had been alerted to their new obligations with respect to movies by the Apostolic Delegate to the United States, Archbishop Amleto Cicognani, shortly after his appointment. His address to the National Conference of Catholic Charities in October 1933 was a call to arms:

> An example of forces of evil in our day is the moving picture, with its incalculable influence for evil. What a massacre of innocence of youth is taking place hour by hour! How shall the crimes that have their direct source in immoral motion pictures be measured? Catholics are called by God, the Pope, the bishops, and the priests to a united and vigorous campaign for the purification of the cinema, which has become a deadly menace to morals.

August authority now had been invoked, but what exactly were Catholics to do? The answer came the next month at the annual bishops' meeting. Cantwell took the lead, giving a lengthy report that confirmed the Church's worst fears about movies. In response, after "barely staving off" a petition calling for federal censorship, the prelates voted to create an Episcopal Committee on Motion Pictures to improve the moral quality of films.

The spring and summer of 1934 witnessed hectic activity by Catholic film reformers, including the formation of the Legion of Decency in April. A pledge was proposed by the bishops' committee whereby Catholics would promise to refrain from viewing all objectionable movies or attending any theater that showed such films. The pledge read:

> I wish to join the Legion of Decency, which condemns vile and unwholesome moving pictures. I unite with all who protest against them as a grave menace to youth, to home life, to country, and to religion. . . . Considering these evils, I hereby promise to remain away from all motion pictures except those which do not offend decency and Christian morality. I promise further to secure as many members as possible for the Legion of Decency. I make this protest in a spirit of self-respect, and with the conviction that the American public does not demand filthy pictures, but clean entertainment and educational features.

An estimated 10,000,000 Catholics signed this voluntary oath pledging themselves to "rid the country of its greatest menace—the salacious motion picture." At the urging of local bishops, protestors threatened offending exhibitors with public demonstrations against any who persisted in offering pictures that had been condemned in diocesan newspapers. Communicants were told that attendance at such a movie would constitute a venial sin. By February 1936, the Legion had evolved a rating system by class. Class A-I films were morally unobjectionable for general patronage; A-II, morally unobjectionable for adults and adolescents; A-III, morally unobjectionable for adults; A-IV, morally unobjectionable for adults with reservations; Class B, morally objectionable in part for all; and Class C—Condemned, "positively bad." The "Class B" category was a residual classification, although the Legion did urge its members to stay away from these films.[2]

In Philadelphia, Catholics boycotted all movie houses in response to an appeal by Dennis Cardinal Dougherty. Local box-office receipts decreased by 40 percent; and the manager of the Philadelphia area's chain of Warner theaters complained that he would have to shut down if the boycott were not discontinued. The Catholic press launched a vigorous anti-movie campaign. The "tragic thing about the producers," said one cleric, "is that they seem to have set aside the permanent code of the Ten Commandments which binds every human being." Members of other religions were invited to join the Catholic crusade, and some did. Nationally, more than 50 Protestant and Jewish groups and individual ministers and rabbis pledged their support. Al Smith became head of the Council of the Legion. The Church had a powerful weapon, and in 1934 the life of the movie industry was at stake.

The Hays Office moved quickly. When Quigley was invited to attend a meeting of the bishops' committee by its chairman, Archbishop John T. McNicholas of Cincinnati, Hays asked him to go as the MPPDA's representative and gave him, as Quigley requested, full power to act on its behalf. He and Breen, the only nonclerics at the meeting, were the archbishop's house guests. Afterwards, they reported to a relieved Hays that "the war had been called off." "If given adequate enforcement," the bishops advised the American hierarchy, the industry Code "will materially and constructively influence the character of screen entertainment." The next day, June 22, the Studio Relations Department was renamed the Production Code Administration (PCA), with Breen as its head. A new rule strengthened his grip: a $25,000 fine would be levied against any MPPDA member company that released a film without a PCA certificate and seal of approval. This sanction was in addition to the rule that no member-controlled theater circuit could book a picture lacking this stamp of approval. "At last," Hays recalled with satisfaction, "we had a police department, or at least a civilian-defense force."

Unlike some fundamentalist Protestant groups, the Church evidenced no desire to strangle the industry entirely. It wished, rather, to improve the quality of films made and shown in accordance with its moral views. For this, organized public opinion proved to be the best approach. The hierarchy was divided, however, over how far Catholics should exercise their power in the marketplace. In September, Cardinal Dougherty announced that the boycott in Philadelphia would continue, although Cardinal Mundelein argued that Catholics should suspend the campaign to evaluate the industry's response.

In the 1930s, the Church was still attempting to define for itself an identity at once Catholic and American. In the preservation of American "innocence," a world of rationality, predictability, and the genteel rendering of accepted forms of behavior, many Catholics found grounds for claiming both a completely loyal Catholicity and a fully respectable Americanism. Cardinal Dougherty brought back from Rome papal messages that supported the activities of the Legion of Decency. Cardinal Mundelein worked through secular channels in his efforts to further the campaign.[3]

Mundelein had a warm friendship with Franklin D. Roosevelt, and he now wrote to the president, "with the purpose of keeping you informed as to the action the Catholic bishops have inaugurated for the elimination of indecency from the moving pictures."

> We decided to use our own organization first in the endeavor to bring these picture people to a realization of the attitude of decent people of their own accord, before we would call on "the strong arm" of the Government. Personally I doubt that we will have much success except in cutting down the box-office receipts. The background here is lacking. These people simply do not know different. Many of them have come up from the burlesque houses and they still cling to the standard they learned there. However, we will do our best; in any event I wanted the President to know first hand just what we are doing, in case the matter comes up before him.

Roosevelt, not wishing to be drawn politically into this old controversy, answered perfunctorily in a "personal" letter, making a passing reference to the Code of Fair Competition of the National Industrial Recovery Act. (Passed in 1933, the National Industrial Recovery Act was later found unconstitutional by the Supreme Court. The movie industry code was the longest of the more than 600 codes of business practices drawn up under the act's auspices. It pledged to maintain "right moral standards" in film production and "in the best standards of advertising and publicity procedure"—all by means of "self-regulation.") But F.D.R.'s real response came, as it did so often, through his wife Eleanor. In the initial radio broadcast that she gave as First Lady, on July 9, 1934, Mrs. Roosevelt hailed the motion picture industry's announcement of "voluntary censorship" as a "distinct advance" in its "campaign for decency."

> The matter of moving pictures is very important to the whole country. I am extremely happy the film industry has appointed a censor within its own ranks. . . . This new announcement should do much to make these organizations feel that the film industry as a whole desires to cooperate and use its tremendous power for the improvement of the country.

Mrs. Roosevelt's announcement strengthened the hand of Will Hays. Nevertheless, his position at the helm of the MPPDA was not an enviable one. He continually had to walk a thin line between the "best interests" of the industry, for which he was the spokesman and which existed to make profits, and its vociferous, action-oriented critics, whom he had to placate and whose morality he shared. He also had to contend with the fact that his own conservatism made him somewhat ill at ease in his devotion to the screen.[4]

The Papal Encyclical

The Legion of Decency's success prompted the first papal pronouncement on any popular art, the *Vigilanti Cura* ("With Vigilant Care") encyclical of Pope Pius XI, in 1936.

This document was a consequence of the Pope's earlier activity. In 1934 and 1935, he had given his blessing to the Legion's campaign. The following year, after renewing an appeal for purer films, he invoked the "supreme power" of his "teaching authority" to reveal sixteen thousand words of Church doctrine, in a letter to the clergy and parishioners. The exact authorship of the encyclical is unknown. Bishop (later Cardinal) Francis Spellman later that year traveled in the United States with his close friend, Eugenio Cardinal Pacelli, Vatican Secretary of State and shortly Pope Pius XII. Certainly, they influenced its composition. But Martin Quigley probably played the major role. For years he had considered the Church to be neglecting motion pictures in order to attend to the older forms of communication, especially literature. He had advised the hierarchy about screen morals and had also drawn up public statements about them for the Church. Now the Church called on this publisher of movie newspapers to articulate its position regarding a pressing social problem. Quigley's hand can be seen in the entire document. "The encyclical came out of my father's mouth," claims Martin Quigley, Jr. "Many of the potent thoughts in it came from him."

The encyclical came at a time when the American Church, historically sensitive to its minority status, sought to extend its influence and power. The 1920s witnessed the beginnings of a Catholic cultural and social renewal; lay activity greatly increased and new organizations and publications were spawned. But the obstacles to stronger political power proved formidable; a "ghetto mentality" developed in the urban centers and was reinforced by the activities of the Ku Klux Klan. Then there was Herbert Hoover's resounding victory in the 1928 presidental election over Alfred E. Smith, the Democratic party's "happy warrior" and New York's Catholic governor. Smith's defeat, and the unexpected wave of anti-Catholicism that accompanied it, struck a tough blow to Catholic aspirations. It was, in the view of one partisan observer, "the night of sixteen million tragedies." The editor of *America* magazine, Father Wilfrid Parsons, expressed Catholic feeling when, in the election's wake, he said: "We are strangers in our own land."

The encyclical was a pronouncement on film aesthetics as well as a statement concerning a social medium of communication; it was also, in the Pope's words, a commentary on the "lamentable state of the motion picture art and industry in the portrayal of sin and vice." Pius complimented the Legion of Decency and urged the Catholics of other countries to follow that organization's lead. However, when he lauded government censorship and urged Catholics to "place a ban on bad motion pictures," he departed from the position developed by Quigley and others associated with the American Church, which eschewed government censorship in favor of self-regulation supervised by Catholics. Pius agreed that the Legion's campaign had "improved" movies "from the moral standpoint" without harming their artistic values or fulfilling any of the predictions of resulting financial doom for the industry.

It is interesting to note that the Pope described the conditions of movie viewing in psychological terms:

> The cinema speaks not to individuals but to multitudes and does so in circumstances, time, place and surroundings which are the most apt to arouse unusual enthusiasm for good as well as bad and to conduct that collective exaltation which, as experience teaches us, may assume the most morbid form.

> A motion picture is viewed by people who are seated in a dark theater and whose faculties, mental, physical and often spiritual, are relaxed. . . .

> Moreover, the acting-out of the plot is done by men and women selected for their art, for all those natural gifts, and the employment of those expedients which can become for youth particularly the instruments of seduction.

> Further, the motion picture has enlisted in its service luxurious appointments, pleasing music, the vigor of realism and every form of whim and fancy. For this very reason it attracts and fascinates particularly the young adolescent or even the child. . . .

The thrust of the Church's concern, however, was this stern warning to the movie industry:

> [W]hen one thinks of the havoc wrought in the souls of youth and childhood, of the loss of innocence so often suffered in motion picture theaters, there comes to mind the terrible condemnation pronounced by Our Lord upon the corrupters of the little ones: Whosoever shall scandalize one of these little ones who believe in Me, it were better that a millstone be hanged around his neck and he be drowned in the depths of the sea.

Pope Pius commended the American Church for its salutary work:

> [The] bishops of the United States are determined at all costs to safeguard the recreation of the people in whatever form that recreation may take. . . . Because of [Catholics'] vigilance and because of the pressure which has been brought to bear by public opinion, the motion picture has shown improvement

from the moral standpoint; crime and vice are portrayed less frequently; sin no longer is so openly approved or acclaimed; false ideas of life no longer are presented in so flagrant a manner to the impressionable minds of youth.

And to the American movie producers:

In particular, you Venerable Bretheren of the United States will be able to insist with justice that the industry in your country has recognized and accepted its responsibility before society.

Will Hays welcomed the Legion of Decency "with open arms," for it worked to support "moral standards we had ourselves adopted." Together, Hays and the Legion "created a 'mutual defense pact' that finally made the Code a working reality." The Pope repaid Hays for his devotion by granting him a private audience during a visit to Italy. Hays received "the appreciation of the Church for the improvement in the moral content of American motion pictures," and also the Pope's acknowledgment of the Presbyterian elder's power: "You sit at the valve in the conduit through which flows the principal amusement of the great majority of all the people in the world. Your impress is upon the quality of this entertainment and you are very important to us."[5]

"Ecstasy"

Books published abroad had long been subject to being blocked from entry into the United States under a law enacted in 1890 prohibiting the importation of obscene printed matter. James Joyce's *Ulysses* was prevented from reaching American readers by enforcement of this law, from the time of its original publication in Paris in 1922 to 1933, when the famous court cases overruled the Secretary of the Treasury's exclusion. The customs censorship law requires the United States Attorney for the district where the port of entry is located to ask a federal court's permission to destroy a book or a film which he believes should be excluded from the country. In the cases of both the book *Ulysses* and the movie *Ecstasy* [18], that U.S. Attorney was Martin Conboy.

Conboy had been director of the draft for New York City during World War I and had long been a political friend of President Roosevelt. He had served in 1920 as counsel to New York State's legislative committee, investigating the qualifications of Socialist Assemblymen; in court, in that role, he described the Socialist party in the United States as "an organization of perpetual traitors." President of the Catholic Club of New York from 1922 to 1927, Conboy was also director of the National Council of Catholic Men and was named a Knight Commander of St. Gregory the Great by Pope Pius XI, who received him on a visit to Rome in 1925.

In attempting to suppress the Czech-made *Ecstasy*, Conboy argued that the film was both "obscene and immoral" and therefore not to be admitted into the United States on two grounds: first, because "this film's portraying in the most minute detail a woman's facial expressions and reactions during orgasm accompanying sexual intercourse is obscene and immoral"; second, because "the episode and theme of adulterous intercourse pervades and dominates the entire film and supplies the title and climax of the film."

To counteract the precedential weight of the *Ulysses* case, in which a book that was allegedly "obscene" in part was admitted to the country in view of its "artistic merit and scientific insight," Conboy contended that a court should not apply such a standard to *Ecstasy*. "Would this court not hold obscene or immoral a motion picture of the book *Ulysses* including the parts admittedly grossly obscene?" he asked. The federal jury that decided the case agreed with Conboy: the litigated print of *Ecstasy* was forbidden entry into the United States and, before an appeal could be made, burned by a federal marshal.

The movie's famous nude scenes were also criticized by Conboy, but seem not to have bothered the jury nor to have been stressed in the judge's instructions to the jury on the question of whether the movie was "obscene and immoral." "It was the close-ups of [actress Hedy Lamarr's] facial expressions which chiefly shocked the jury," the *New York Times* reported after the trial. *Hollywood* magazine concurred: "All you see, all the camera gives you, is Eva's face. Hundreds of film-feet of Hedy's face, covering the whole range of love. You get it from her expression or you don't get it at all."

Ecstasy, directed by the innovative Gustav Machaty, is a screen classic whose cinematic values have been all but totally obscured by its sensational treatment at the hands of government and industry censors and the press. It was first shown at the 1934 Venice Film Exposition, where Machaty won an award for his "understanding and spontaneous interpretation of nature" and for "the great efficiency achieved with the simplest narrative art." The film historian Tyler Parker speaks of the movie as an "impressionistic poem rather than a modern triangle drama," which "influenced the world's experimental film movement more than is suspected." In fact, it is a sound movie with dialogue so spare and well chosen that audiences of any nation might readily comprehend it, without the few subtitles that were made to accompany its international distribution. "Far from seeming tame, the symbolic and implied sex of [the film] remains strikingly stimulating," William Emerson has written. "Film students of the seventies, inured to total nudity and sexual acrobatics in current porn movies, have been heard to gasp the traditional 'Oh, wow!' at scenes in *Ecstasy* that express sexual desire solely through lighting and symbols." By comparison, the federal judge who urged a jury to condemn the film said that its moral standards resembled those of "the forests of Africa" or of "certain European countries," which, however, he did not name.

Even Al Smith, evidently representing the Legion of Decency, wired President Roosevelt to urge banning the film so that it could not enter the country. Adolf Hitler reportedly banned it in Germany because its star, Hedy Lamarr, was Jewish. After the federal government destroyed the seized copy of *Ecstasy*, another, presumably altered print passed Customs without difficulty, but was banned by the New York censorship board for obscenity. The censors particularly objected to the scene that showed close-ups of the adulterous young wife's face as she experienced orgasm. The movie's distributor futilely argued that "the proper test is not whether certain scenes taken from their context and judged by themselves alone may be offensive, but whether the dominant effect of the picture as a whole is obscene."

Because, in the court's view, the picture "unduly emphasize[d] the carnal side of the sex relationship," the censorship board's decision was amply supported. A freshly scissored and partly rewritten version was subsequently submitted to New York's censors, but this too they found obscene and, in that, were seconded by the state courts. Elsewhere, the movie met with mixed reactions: some censors banned it altogether; others let it be shown with cuts. Most states deleted the nude scenes and those that were sexually symbolic. In one version or another, the film was shown throughout most of the country, grossing around three million dollars by 1943. The Hays Office, under Breen, repeatedly refused to give it a seal. In 1937, a seal was denied, among other reasons, because:

> It is a story of illicit love and frustrated sex, treated in detail and without sufficient compensating moral values, the portrayal of a mare in heat, and of a rearing stallion, the actual scene in the cabin where the woman's face registers the varying emotions of the sexual act—all are designed to stimulate the lower and baser element and are suggestive, lustful and obscene. [It] is designed to glorify sexual intercourse between human beings and between animals, and to arouse lustful feelings in those who see it.

The enmity of Breen toward the movie was so great that he urged that the MPPDA's seal "should never be placed upon any version of this picture, under the same name." According to Breen, the distributor expressed "a willingness to make any deletions required to bring the picture into conformity with the Code in order to secure additional public exhibitions in theaters which properly refuse to exhibit pictures which violate the standards of common decency mirrored in the Production Code." Since the film was irremediably identified with the title *Ecstasy* in the public eye, no deletions, however drastic, even if they were "to destroy the plot completely," should be permitted to entitle the movie to a seal. The MPPDA's board of directors affirmed Breen's extraordinarily hostile ruling because, among other reasons, "although the heroine had adequate grounds for divorce" (her elderly husband's apparent impotence), she had a "craving for sexual satisfaction . . . so pronounced that she dashes through a terrific storm to commit adultery with a man who has caught her fancy, as uninhibited by legal or moral considerations as her father's mare, which ran away with her clothes at the neigh and scent of a stallion." The board also expressly disapproved of the scene of adultery "recording the flow of expression over her face while thus 'biologically engaged.' " Finally, after Lamarr's Viennese industrialist husband tried in vain to "wipe out" the "haunted" film by buying and destroying every available print, the New York censorship board licensed a version of *Ecstasy* in November 1940.[6]

"When the Movies Really Counted"

Radio and movies were the communication media that dominated the redefinition of American culture in the 1930s. Radio competed more and more successfully with the newspapers. It also brought into American homes the variety shows and serial stories of Jack Benny, Fred Allen, George Burns and Gracie Allen, Edgar Bergen and Charlie McCarthy; culture heroes such as Jack Armstrong, the All-American boy, and the Lone Ranger; the tragic romances of "Our Gal Sunday" and "Life Can Be Beautiful"; and the voice of Franklin D. Roosevelt, strong, confident, relaxing, serene, and resonating with unruffled patrician assurance that was nearly hypnotic. There were, Roosevelt once told Orson Welles, only two great actors in America: the other one was Welles.

When Welles panicked the national radio audience with his documentary-like invasion of Earth by men from Mars, and Mae West burlesqued Adam and Eve on Edgar Bergen's radio show, an avalanche of criticism fell. The Legion of Decency threatened a crusade against West's suggestiveness; the program's sponsor abjectly apologized to the public; the advertising agency begged the forgiveness of NBC, which hoped the Federal Communications Commission would not attack it. Through it all, West stayed calm. Her defenders on the political left maintained that she had "never been properly appreciated as the First Artist of the Republic." West also picked up supporters within the country's ideological center. "You don't hear any shooting from the boys in the street, do you?" one network executive asked. They "like that stuff." NBC's hierarchy, however, did not, and banned all further reference to Mae West's name by the stations that it operated under license from the FCC.

Although radio was most effective in the way its voices entered homes in even the smallest, most remote towns, the movies offered people the unrivalled opportunity to see as well as hear their idols; this experience indelibly impressed an entire generation. During the 1930s, "movies really counted"; in 1937, 61 percent of the population trooped to them every week. When Clark Gable, in *It Happened One Night* (1934), undressed to show a torso but no undershirt, the men's underwear business declined 50 percent within a year. By providing a shared visual experience the movies helped to make the country more unified than ever and gave it a "common bond of knowledge." Their ability to "span geographic frontiers" and "give the old something to talk about with the young" was noticed. Movies would "crumble the barriers between people of different educations and different economic backgrounds." At their best, they could ease sectional tensions and reduce religious and racial friction. At something less than their best, they, like radio, presented stereotypes that served to heighten group misperceptions and prejudice.

Moviegoers from the Depression to World War II, especially the young among them, gained a "fantasy life in common, from which," as one child of the 1930s later put it, "we are still dragging up the images that obsess us." The movies became "nothing less than a kind of Jungian collective unconscious, a decade of coming attractions out of which some of the truths of our maturity have been formed." Hollywood "possessed the nation," Arthur Schlesinger, Jr., wrote. "It formed our images and shaped our dreams." During the 1930s, "the movies were near the operative center of the nation's consciousness. They played an indispensable role in sustaining and stimulating the national imagination." In time, however, the close cultural ties that had been forged between American audiences and American films were strained, if not severed. The "first blow" was delivered by the industry Code, which "imposed on filmmaking a set of rigid requirements and taboos which would have destroyed Shakespeare, Ibsen, and Shaw and which the lesser talents of Hollywood could not overcome. . . . [I]t began the process of cutting the films off from the realities of American experience. Then, as political action and economic improvement began to replenish the sense of national confidence in the course of the decade, the need for cinematic reassurance became less intense."[7]

"Gone With the Wind"

During the 1930s, three young but proven producers, Irving Thalberg, Darryl F. Zanuck, and David O. Selznick, turned literary classics and best-selling novels into respectable, elevated, yet exciting films, grounded not in the present but in the past. Theirs was a solid achievement: in just a few years they produced *Mutiny on the Bounty* and *The Barretts of Wimpole Street* (Thalberg); *The House of Rothschild* and *Les Miserables* (Zanuck); and *David Copperfield, Anna Karenina,* and *A Tale of Two Cities* (Selznick). "There are," Selznick noted, "only two kinds of merchandise that can be made profitably in this business—either the very cheap pictures or the expensive." The son-in-law of Louis B. Mayer, Selznick preferred making the most expensive. One of these was an adaptation of a book that was uncharacteristically, for Hollywood, "not even established as a success." Its title was *Gone With the Wind*.

Called "the epoch-making picture of our time," it still stands as a monument to Selznick and the producer's craft. "Great films," he wrote, "are made in every detail according to the vision of one man." Claiming that the "sum total of all these things" distinguished him from other producers, he compared the producer's role to that of "the conductor of an orchestra." Selznick's monument was stamped with his confidence, perfectionism, and passion, qualities that benefitted him when *Gone With the Wind* collided with Hollywood's moral arbiters, a collision that forced an amendment to the Production Code.

The most notorious line in the movie—Gable's "Frankly, my dear, I don't give a damn"—was not in the original script. Selznick injected the expletive—knowing the Code specifically forbade the use of "damn"—when "a couple of other endings" missed the desired impact. The expression was tried "with considerable trepidation" and, to his "delighted surprise," worked. The earlier script had read, "Frankly, my dear, I don't care," and this was the ending that the Production Code Administration approved. When the Hays Office objected to Gable's use of "damn," Selznick argued that "the *Oxford Dictionary* clearly indicates that this use of it is not considered even mild profanity, but simply a colloquialism." Still, PCA Director Breen refused to allow the word change. Breen wrote Hays: "David seems to think that because this picture is a screen characterization of a really great American novel, it is a sort of classic and that, as such, he should be permitted to use this line from the book. . . . We have withheld this line as profanity."

Selznick initially thought to ask a principal financial backer of the film, John Hay Whitney, to get Hays to call an emergency meeting of the MPPDA's board of directors to approve the change. It was, as he put it, "a silly point"; he "imagined" that "two or three" company heads "would tell Hays to forget it." But first, Selznick appealed directly to Hays. "A great deal of the force and drama [of the film]," he wrote, is "dependent [upon the word] damn; [its omission] spoils the picture. [As used, it is] not an oath or a curse. The worst that could be said against it is that it is a vulgarism," but, he pointed out, "such moral publications as *Women's Home Companion, Saturday Evening Post, Collier's*, and the *Atlantic Monthly* use this word freely." And then, in a shrewd endeavor to enlist on his side the industry censor's appreciation of power, Selznick observed: "If you were to permit our using this dramatic word in its rightfully dramatic place, in a line that is known and remembered by millions of readers, it would establish a helpful precedent, a precedent which would give to Joe Breen discretionary powers to allow the use of certain harmless oaths and ejaculations whenever, in his opinion, they are not prejudicial to public morals." With the picture in the process of final editing, Selznick (who had shot the final scene both with and without the offending line) asked that Hays give the matter his "immediate attention."

It was one of the rare instances in Hays's long tenure when he overruled Breen. After a four-hour meeting with the producer, Hays approved Gable's saying "damn." But he also told Selznick to pay a $5,000 fine for violating the Code, thereby saving both its and his face. One week later, the MPPDA's board of directors amended the Code to forbid "damn" and "hell"—*except* when their use "shall be essential and required for portrayal, in proper historical context, or any scene or dialogue based upon historical fact or folklore . . . or a quotation from a literary work provided that no such use shall be permitted which is intrinsically objectionable or offends good taste."

The Legion of Decency gave the picture its "B" rating—"morally objectionable in part for all"—finding fault with "the low moral character, principles, and behavior of the main figures as depicted in the film; suggestive implications; the attractive portrayal of the immoral character of a supporting role in the story."[8] But the tens of millions who have seen the movie over more than 40 years have apparently felt otherwise.

Newsreels and Documentary Films

The emergence of documentary films and feature movies of social significance during the 1930s obliged government censors to ban new types of movies. The filming of news events was among the earliest uses made of motion pictures. With their acute representation of reality and startling ability to bring the world into the neighborhood theater, newsreels [14] quickly achieved popular acceptance. Understandably, their political impact made them both valuable and feared—and easy prey for the censor's scissors. By the time of the Depression, documentary films on urgent social issues were also being made on a wide scale. Although they informed audiences by their apparent objectivity, they also inevitably advanced a certain viewpoint. The subject of these bold experiments in pictorial journalism, as well as their interpretations of social and political events, brought them under the special scrutiny of governmental and private censors.

The *March of Time* was a serial survey of the news, dramatically presented for viewers. Stylistically a blend of newsreel and documentary forms, and combining reporting and editorial functions, it allowed producers to "stage-direct" public officials and other prominent personalities "to perform more effectively than any Hollywood extras." The series regularly played to a monthly audience of 18 million people. Censors pounced on the products. In late 1938, a police board barred *Inside Nazi Germany* from Chicago movie screens, stating that it "reflects on the Hitler government with which the U.S. government is now on friendly terms." Both the German vice-consul in Washington and the head of the German-American Bund objected to the film, demanding that portions be deleted. Chicago's ban was revoked the next day, after a public outcry. Several theaters around the country that were planning to show the picture received bomb threats and canceled their showings.

After the American Nazi Party threatened to prevent "at any cost" the showing of *From the Ramparts We Watch*, also about Nazi Germany, it was banned in Pennsylvania. In Kansas, the state censorship board ordered a speech by Senator Burton K. Wheeler cut from a current *March of Time* showing, despite a provision in the censorship statute expressly exempting current events newsreels from its operations. The speech opposed President Roosevelt's bill to enlarge the Supreme Court. The reason given for the cut was: "We feel this dialogue is partisan and biased." Although the governor refused to intervene, popular protests against the censorship induced the board to rescind its decision.[9]

Release of *The Birth of a Baby* [22] in 1939 brought an outcry of a different kind. Although the film documented a universal human experience, government censors in Cincinnati, Omaha, Lynchburg, Virginia, and New York State banned it. This film was conceived not by Hollywood, but by the American Committee for Maternal Welfare. The picture immediately won wide support, including endorsements from the American Medical Association, the United States Public Health Service, the American Hospital Association, and state medical societies in nearly a dozen states. The *Ohio State Medical Journal* rhetorically asked whether New York's movie censors considered "bigshot gangsters, twentieth-century Casanovas, [and] Gold Coast harems" more desirable movie fare than this dramatization of the process of childbirth. One mother, addressing the Boston Diocesan Congress of Catholic Women, fully approved it. The picture, said Eleanor Roosevelt, "could not be harmful because it is honest." The Legion of Decency agreed with the movie's supporters concerning its quality. It had "considerable merit," they said, "from the medical, educational, social, and technical points of view" and was "moral in tone." Nor could the Legion deny the "sincere ultimate purposes" of the movie's sponsors; nevertheless, the film was classified as "unsuited for entertainment and inappropriate for general theatrical exhibition."

Public officials were divided over the movie's acceptability. Cincinnati's city manager, acting on a report by the chief of police ("The picture is positively terrible, and I can see nothing educational in it"), banned it. Likewise, the Lynchburg, Virginia city manager claimed that the picture violated city ordinances prohibiting the showing of obscene and indecent films. But courts in both states, noting that the state legislatures had preempted the field of motion picture censorship and that state censors had approved the film, overturned the municipal bans. New York courts, however, upheld the action of the state censorship board, the Board of Regents, which granted the picture a special permit for exhibition as an educational picture only, banning it from ordinary movie houses. In Omaha, the mayor reversed a decision of the city's welfare board that had permitted the film to be generally exhibited. Two of the board's five members had approved it, one had not, and two had abstained. The mayor ruled that a majority of the five would have to vote "yes" before the movie could be approved. Although he insisted that his private opinion had nothing to do with his official action, he admitted, "Personally, I don't think the film is necessary. It commercializes the most sacred thing in life." Those who banned the picture, quipped one observer, "should change their name to the Society for the Perpetuation of the Stork Legend."[10]

By the late 1930s, the combination of governmental censorship and industry self-regulation threatened to suffocate American movie creativity. Scripts had to be altered, plots changed, and content adjusted to meet the demands of the Hays Office and of state and municipal censors. "Innumerable sacred cows" had restrained producers' freedom, said Carl Laemmle of Universal, after selling his theaters; he was "glad [to be] out of the business."

The International Federation of Catholic Alumnae, which reviewed and classified pictures for the Legion of Decency, noted with satisfaction in late 1938 that not a single film made by a major Hollywood producer had been "totally condemned" since the inception of the Production Code Administration. But to some, censorship by the back door of private bigotry and prejudice was far more insidious than by the more open method of governmental regulation. Hitler's book burnings rekindled fears that governmental control might yet completely stifle the American cinema and stage. One New York independent theater owner stated the common sense of the matter: "No three-man board should tell millions of people what they should or should not see." The censors performed an "utterly useless function. [To justify their existence, they] slice out a shot of a kiss, or a boy holding a girl's hand—something that upsets the community. It's ridiculous."

The head New York censor disagreed. He claimed that censorship was "more effective" than relying on existing laws to guard against offense. Showing an offending film and prosecuting later, he said, was "just like locking the barn door after the horse is stolen." Censors and freedom fighters were at loggerheads. Before long, unanticipated events in Europe dimmed the urgency of skirmishes over movie censorship, but the federal government quietly and unobtrusively entered into a national censorship of Hollywood's films—in cooperation with the movie moguls.[11]

Domestic Controversies and Foreign Films

The 1930s were politically tumultuous. Citizens cast their votes in unprecedented numbers for candidates to the left and right. In 1932, the Socialist party candidate for President, Norman Thomas, received almost 900,000 votes; in 1936 he and the American Labor party together garnered around 500,000. Huey Long, the Louisiana "Kingfish" who carried out a populistic program of social improvement some considered akin to a dictatorship of the state, talked of running for president; he was assassinated the year before the 1936 election. Father Charles E. Coughlin, the "radio priest" of Royal Oak, Michigan, raised the spectre of American fascism. These extremists frightened the film industry at every level and brought it directly into politics.

Movie magnates worked feverishly to defeat the Democratic candidate, Upton Sinclair, in the 1934 California gubernatorial election. His utopian socialism and his "End Poverty in California" platform panicked the major studio owners. "Why," he asked a reporter, "should not the State of California rent the idle studios and let the unemployed actors make a few pictures of their own?" This remark brought film executives out of the studios and into the campaign arena; they were determined to "Stop Sinclair." It was "the first all-out public relations *Blitzkrieg* in American politics." Faked newsreels played all over the state with "interviews" of sympathetic citizens and pillars of the community solemnly declaring support for the Republican candidate, Governor Frank F. Merriam, an agreeable conservative.

Producers raised half a million dollars, in part by "asking" all studio employees, including performers and directors earning over $90 weekly, to contribute one day's salary to save California from "Russianization." Will Hays saw Communists "openly and identifiably" in Hollywood "for the first time." The *Los Angeles Times* ignored Sinclair in its news columns except to state that he attacked the Bible and was un-Christian; but it did show a "news photo"—in reality a still from the movie *Wild Boys of the Road*—of a freight car loaded with "tramps" going to California to live off EPIC.

It also lent its chief political correspondent to the MPPDA to work alongside the leader of the Stop Sinclair campaign and Republican state vice-chairman, Louis B. Mayer.

In 1935, novelist Sinclair Lewis wrote *It Can't Happen Here* after having "exciting discussions" with his wife, foreign correspondent Dorothy Thompson. MGM promptly paid $200,000 for the film rights to this satirical best-selling story of a fascist takeover of the United States, which depicted organized violence, Nazi-like secret police, and American concentration camps. After Sidney Howard wrote a screenplay, the project was submitted to the Hays Office. When MGM broke the news that it had decided to abandon the film, rumor had it that Hays himself had scuttled it, in fear of "mob uprisings," international complications, and the displeasure of the Republican party. Hays denied this. Mayer stated the decision was made because the movie "would cost too much," while Samuel Goldwyn, who was slated to be its producer, blamed casting difficulties. Howard, however, said he had seen a memorandum by Breen pointing out "dangerous material" in the script, which had to be drastically revised. The memo reportedly also revealed that the decision to forego production was jointly made by Hays, Breen, and MGM.

Although Lewis had no financial interest in the production of a film, he expressed "shock" at the apparent infringement of free speech. Two college students and a young dramatist launched a postcard campaign to pressure MGM into production, calling their group the Legion of Freedom in obvious mockery of the Legion of Decency. The Typographical Union of the American Federation of Labor adopted a resolution calling on the Hays Office to lift its putative ban. Nothing availed, however; the film was never made.[12]

The politicization of movie censorship that occurred during the 1930s was epitomized not only by the censoring of newsreels but also in court battles over Russian films and films about Russia and Spain. In 1935, the Detroit police commissioner prevented showing of the Soviet-made *The Youth of Maxim* [19] on the ground that it was "pure Soviet propaganda and is likely to instill class hatred of the existing government and social order of the United States." However, since the police censor had acted under an ordinance that authorized the banning only of "immoral or indecent" films, the Michigan Supreme Court reversed the prohibition, rejecting the city's contention that the term "immoral" could include any content "contrary to good order or public welfare."

Maxim was one of the first sound pictures to come from the Russian studios. Tracing the evolution of a factory worker from a simple peasant to an experienced revolutionary, it could well have been entitled *The Making of a Bolshevik*. This message obviously disturbed American movie censors. According to one critic, with *Maxim*, "Soviet cinema . . . ceases to be a vehicle of propaganda and becomes a medium of highly successful entertainment. . . . The music (by Shostakovitch) is guaranteed to make you want to leave your seat and join the workers in their rebellion against Czarist oppression.''

Pennsylvania censors were similarly disturbed by the Russian film *Baltic Deputy*, which portrayed incidents in the life of a Soviet scientist who becomes a Bolshevik at the time of the revolution. They claimed that it was ''immoral,'' ''rabble-rousing,'' and liable to ''incite people to destroy government.'' The censorship board, however, failed to record officially its reasons for banning the movie, as required by law. Judge Curtis J. Bok of the Philadelphia Court of Common Pleas, in reversing the ruling, called this ''inexcusable neglect.'' The censors' testimony, according to Judge Bok, meant that ''a revolution by Communists is objectionable, whereas a revolution against Communists would not be; a bitter attack against government in Russia is immoral, but one in France is not immoral because France and Russia are different countries. It is difficult to decide a law case on stuff and nonsense like this.''

Professor Mamlock [23], also made in the Soviet Union, was one of the first films to depict the Nazi persecution and murder of Jews. It was banned in four different states. Based on a play by Friedrick Wolf, a German writer who had come to the United States in flight from his homeland, the movie told the story of a Jewish physician's humiliation and struggle to survive, and of his son's enlistment in the ranks of the Communist Party, during the early stages of the Nazi persecution. When the Providence, Rhode Island ''amusement inspector'' was asked in court why he had barred the film from exhibition, he claimed it did not have the approval of the National Board of Review of Motion Pictures. Although that board had not yet even seen the film, the censorship was held lawful on appeal. Censorship board bans in Ohio and Chicago were rescinded after newspapers denounced them. In Boston, censors refused to license the picture for showing on Sundays because it ''might incite to riot.''[13]

Public concern over the Spanish Civil War offered a change from the domestic controversies that racked the decade. The left and the intellectual community found themselves in a painful predicament and followed the struggle in Spain ''with great . . . intensity.'' The conflict provided ''the last occasion in the 1930s when liberals and radicals could unite in defense of their most precious ideals,'' Richard Pells has written, and ''the defeat of the Loyalists in 1939 came as a crushing blow to the hopes of an entire generation.'' It was also a ''wound in the heart'' for many who found themselves divided among religious and political lines. Many non-Catholics supported the Loyalists, who received Russian military aid and several thousand

American volunteers. Supporters of the Franco-led and Nazi-and-Fascist-supplied insurgents tended to be Catholic. President Roosevelt wavered, equivocated, weighed domestic politics, and eventually kept the nation neutral. The deep feelings engendered by the war, however, led to a revival of anti-Catholicism and to the banning in numerous communities of movies dealing with that war.[14]

Spain in Flames [20], a pro-Loyalist and bitterly anti-Fascist film based on screenplays by Ernest Hemingway and John Dos Passos, was suppressed by Pennsylvania censors. But Judge Louis E. Levinthal, sitting on the same bench as Judge Bok, saw "no immorality in any of the dialogue and subtitles and assuredly no immorality so great as the suppression of free speech." He concluded that the picture was a "newsreel" and thereby exempt from censorship under the state statute. The Waterbury, Connecticut chief of police denied the movie a permit on the grounds that it was "controversial, anti-Catholic, and opposed by the Knights of Columbus." The Ohio board refused to license the film because although it "did not contain any harmful propaganda . . . the dialogue of the narrator made [it] very harmful"; it was also "not in keeping with the neutrality laws of the country," anti-religious, and provocative of race hatred. Another pro-Loyalist movie, *Heart of Spain*, portraying modern blood transfusion techniques used in Loyalist hospitals, was banned by the mayor of Fall River, Massachusetts, for being "communistic and not for the best interests of this community."

The American-made *Blockade* caused the greatest furor, but its suppression was not challenged in court. Written by John Howard Lawson, "the screenwriter and the Communist par excellence," it showed the "horror visited on women and children by the bombing of cities and the starvation of civilian population." The movie's makers, hoping to avoid opposition from the Hays Office and the Roosevelt administration, had not identified the warring sides; still, it was clear enough that the events took place in Spain. The picture promptly gained the enmity of the Legion of Decency and the Knights of Columbus, whose members boycotted and picketed this "Marxist propaganda," making what *The Nation* called "fantastic accusations." The groups also complained to the Hays Office, seeking to have the picture banned throughout the country. Especially objectionable to the movie's opponents was the final line: "It's not war. War is between soldiers. It's murder, murder of innocent people. There's no sense to it."

After viewing the film, the Legion announced that it felt compelled to widen the scope of its activities to include scrutiny for political themes, and to oppose the propaganda on screen of any "false, atheistic, and immoral doctrines." The largest Hollywood trade union, the International Alliance of Theatrical Stage Employees, adopted a resolution forbidding union projectionists to "be responsible for the handling of propaganda films," and labeled *Blockade* "propaganda." After the film's release, Lawson acknowledged that it had made a point that neither he nor Walter Wanger, its producer, intended: *Blockade* offered "clear evidence that the screen is *not* at present free, and that even the simplest humanitarian statement is regarded as 'alarming' and 'dangerous' to those who want to keep the motion picture in swaddling clothes."

The characterization of American movies as the "ostrich of the art" rang largely true by 1940. Many of Hollywood's films did not consider the world outside Hollywood because of the "fear of political reprisal and persecution." This "millstone" about the industry's neck, as Darryl Zanuck put it, "prevented free expression on the screen and retarded its development." When, in 1941, a Senate committee asked the industry to account for its activities, "We were pilloried with the accusation that we were allegedly making anti-Nazi films which might be offensive to Germany." The resolution that authorized the investigation was sponsored by the adamantly isolationist senators Gerald Nye and Bennett Clark. Its official purpose was to learn about "any propaganda disseminated by motion pictures and radio or any other activity of the motion picture industry to influence public sentiment in the direction of participation by the United States in the . . . European war." In a widely reported radio address, Senator Nye attacked the industry for "propagandizing in a most insidious manner, disguised as entertainment." It was only after Germany banned American films in 1939 that Hollywood began issuing anti-Nazi pictures such as *Confessions of a Nazi Spy, Mortal Storm, Manhunt*, and Chaplin's *The Great Dictator*. In all, 50 such movies were released between 1939 and December 7, 1941. It took Pearl Harbor to end the Nye investigation and the pressure on Hollywood not to make "interventionist" films, and to unify the warring sides in the battle over screen censorship for a far greater cause.[15]

World War II and the Postwar Years

When World War II settled in Europe, the Roosevelt administration was aiding the British and the armed forces cooperated with the motion picture studios in making war pictures. Hollywood was producing films that not only extolled the virtues of military life, but garnered sympathy for the British position. Internationally, in those countries where American movies were allowed entry, they served to generate goodwill and to muster support in counteracting the Axis powers; domestically, the movies greatly influenced public opinion. Because of the intense ideological struggle over the position the United States should take regarding the war in Europe, the content of movies was of keen interest to the government. The screen, according to film historian Arthur Knight, undertook a "kind of orientation course, introducing the American people to their future allies, exposing the nature of their future enemies."

Once the United States declared war, a law that originated in World War I automatically became effective, requiring every foreign film to be reviewed and granted a permit prior to entering the country. There was, however, no law empowering the national government to censor American-made films. In June 1942, President Roosevelt created the Office of War Information, directing it to act as a liaison between the federal government and the radio and movie industries. Within OWI, a Bureau of Motion Pictures was promptly established. To help the industry "raise its sights," the BMP wrote a "Manual for the Motion-Picture Industry" noting that the war was not merely a struggle for survival but a people's war between fascism and democracy, between a totalitarian state and one based on the Four Freedoms—freedom of speech and religion and freedom from want and fear.

The OWI solicited Hollywood to carry the New Deal's message of liberal democracy throughout the world.

At first, BMP's chief, Lowell Mellett, told industry leaders that "the motion picture must remain free. . . . I want no censorship." He advised producers to "use your own judgment." Soon, however, BMP sought to prevent the release of films that it considered possibly harmful to war policies or American relations with allies. It did this on the basis not of legal authority but of appeals to patriotism. The Bureau persuaded major studios to let it review their movies, following production but before release. When Twentieth Century-Fox released *Little Tokio, U.S.A.* over its objections, the Bureau attempted to introduce a system that would affect studio decisions at the production stage. In an unprecedented step, studios were asked to submit their scripts for pre-production review. Some cooperated willingly, while others complied reluctantly. By the end of 1942, films of all types, even gangster pictures and movies depicting race relations at home, reflected the impact of OWI.

The armed forces independently formed relationships with Hollywood, supplying men, equipment, and advice, and examining scripts as well as completed films. The industry rebelled when BMP's Mellett told the studios to submit to his office the "long cut," the last stage before prints were made, as well as synopses of projected movies. This was a "complete censorship over the policy and content of pictures," said one film executive. The OWI, according to Walter Wanger, then president of the Academy of Motion Picture Arts and Sciences, displayed "a growing desire to *write things into* scripts" and "a mounting urge to dominate production." For the moment, Mellett retreated and he and Elmer Davis, the head of OWI, both assured the studios that they were free to make and distribute any picture they wished that did not violate the treason laws.[1]

Portraying the Russians was delicate business and virulent anti-Communist themes did not reach the movie screen. A 1943 adaptation by Warner Brothers of former Ambassador Joseph E. Davies's memoirs, *Mission to Moscow*—made at the prompting of Roosevelt and with the assistance of the State Department—did not persuade its audience that Americans and Russians were "brothers under the skin." The Bureau of Motion Pictures suggested but did not insist upon changes in the script, concluding that the film would make "an outstanding contribution" to wartime unity.

A new censorship code, issued in December 1942 by OWI's Office of Censorship, strengthened BMP's powers. It prohibited the exportation of movies that showed economic preparations for a long war, such as rationing; scenes of lawlessness in which order was not restored nor offenders punished; and portrayals of labor or class conflict since World War I. When an official complained that the new code was not restrictive enough,

BMP's Hollywood office answered: "Fascist methods need not be used to defeat the common enemy of fascism."

Nevertheless, "from mid-1943 until the end of the war," as one study concluded, "OWI exerted an influence over an American mass medium never equalled before or since by a government agency." Its surveillance of the contents of movies was made easier by a compliant industry. Hollywood's desire to help the war effort was matched by its leaders' wish that nothing diminish profits. Gratified by the rise in movie attendance that took place during the war, the studios were now planning to enter the postwar foreign market on a grand scale. In fact, OWI would play an important role in bringing that about. With the agency's approval, American movies could and did follow American troops to the front. Admission monies collected by OWI overseas were put in trust for the studios; and by paving the way with foreign authorities for the exhibition of American films, the OWI was instrumental in expanding the industry's postwar international audience.

Government involvement in motion pictures was far more extensive in World War II than in World War I. The bureaucratic structure was more extensive, its activities more regularized, and by this time of course the industry itself had grown. Government involvement became a fact of life during the war. The OWI's aim "resembled that of the propagandist: to inspire right-thinking and acceptable forms of behavior." This wartime involvement also set a precedent for peacetime that may have encouraged censorship. For a generation thereafter, allusions to the Defense Department, the armed forces, or the Federal Bureau of Investigation in any movie were sent for approval to the appropriate security division or, in the case of the FBI, to J. Edgar Hoover.[2]

The Motion Picture Association
of America

In September 1945, within a fortnight of V-J Day, Will Hays unexpectedly resigned as president of the MPPDA. It was the end of an era. Hays had lost the support of some studio heads, significantly impairing his effectiveness. In previous years he would have zestfully fought their opposition; but now, having suffered a heart attack, which he kept secret, he was tired and felt he had taken "too much abuse" over the years. "A quarter century," he told his son, "is enough of this." Hays worked as a consultant to the MPPDA for the next five years and took part in various other business, legal, and civic endeavors until his death in 1954. In his *Memoirs,* he wrote, "I find that my fundamental convictions have changed little."

The policies of the MPPDA mattered to any administration, and in May 1944, Roosevelt learned that Hays's successor would be Eric Johnston, president of the U.S. Chamber of Commerce. Johnston's moderate political and social views were useful at this time. An organization called the Motion Picture Alliance for the Preservation of American Ideals had been formed "to fight . . . any effort of any group or individual to divert the loyalty of the screen from the free America that gave it birth" or, as one member more colorfully put it, to "turn off the faucets which dripped red water into film scripts."

During the spring and summer of 1945, Hollywood was beset with strikes, with allegedly Communist-controlled craft and set unions at the core. A booklet called *Communist Infiltration in the United States,* issued by the Chamber of Commerce, warned the public that Communists were seeking to control the entertainment and information media. Movie moguls and financiers considered that the head of the Chamber might benefit business and influence critics. Johnston was not only an articulate spokesman for the nation's business community, but he had been an official guest of the Soviet Union and an able conciliator in bringing about labor's no-strike pledge of World War II. His rags-to-riches career was in the mold of Horatio Alger.

Johnston's early years in office were dominated by the investigations of the House Un-American Activities Committee into Communist activities in Hollywood. These hearings, the Hollywood Ten (and Nineteen), the blacklist, the informers who, as Victor Navasky has noted, "named names" as a "test of virtue" and cooperated with HUAC's "degradation ceremonies"— all were part of a lamented time in the history of American liberty. Hundreds of Hollywood careers were ruined, while the intellectual content of movies was strained and distorted for over a decade.

Ronald Reagan, then president of the Screen Actors Guild, testified at the HUAC hearings. Believing that 99 percent of the movie industry was loyal, he made it clear that he disliked the Communist philosophy but did not want Americans to compromise the fundamentals of democracy out of fear. If there were proof that the Communist party was an agent of a foreign government, that would be "another matter. The best thing to do is to make democracy work. I think that democracy can do it."

In order to call attention to his new administration and to remove what some considered the stigma of the Hays Office, Johnston changed the MPPDA's name to the Motion Picture Association of America. He lived in Washington, D.C., where the Association's headquarters were located, and although he traveled weekly to its New York office for meetings, he rarely went to California. Most of his time was spent dealing with foreign trade and industry diplomacy. This resulted in greater freedom for the New York branch, where the legal division was located, and virtual autonomy for the Hollywood office and its Production Code Administration, the latter now widely referred to as the "Breen Office."[3]

"The Outlaw"

A movie made in 1941, called *The Outlaw* [26], might have proved to be just another version of the saga of Billy the Kid, but the eccentric Howard Hughes produced and directed it; most everything associated with him led to controversy. The movie launched Hollywood's "mammary madness." As Murray Schumach has written, Jane Russell's breasts "were to Hollywood what Eve's apple was to sin." Hughes was not searching for acting ability in Russell, who had been a receptionist and model in her teens when he discovered her. Joe Breen was wary at first: "I 'see by the papers,' as Mr. Dooley used to say, that you have begun shooting on your picture," he wrote, asking Hughes for a copy of the script. After reading it, he was dismayed: "Certain elements [will] render it unacceptable." Russell, he said, must "be fully covered"; she should put a bathrobe on over her nightgown. In the end, Breen objected to over 100 scenes. Then, having "had the pleasure of witnessing a projection room showing" of the completed film, Breen notified Hughes that his "picture was definitely and specifically in violation of our Production Code and because of this cannot be approved." An "inescapable suggestion of an illicit relationship between Doc and Rio and between Bill and Rio" had not escaped the censor's attention. Breen also complained to Hays:

> In my more than ten years of critical examination of motion pictures, I have never seen anything quite so unacceptable as the shots of the breasts of the character of Rio. This is the young girl whom Mr. Hughes recently picked up and who has never before, according to my information, appeared on the motion picture screen. Throughout almost half the picture the girl's breasts, which are quite large and prominent, are shockingly uncovered.

Breen feared this as the most conspicuous example of a trend to "undrape women's breasts." When Hughes appealed Breen's decision to Hays, the latter promised to grant a seal of approval for the picture's exhibition if Russell's breasts were covered and one line in the script eliminated. The changes were made and the seal issued in May 1941. Hays warned Hughes: "You understand, of course, that political [state and local] censorship boards are likely to insist upon additional eliminations."

When *The Outlaw* opened at a theater in San Francisco in February 1943, it was the advertising, not the film, that created a furor. A women's group wrote Hays: "A very disgusting portrayal of the feminine star was displayed throughout the San Francisco Bay section on large billboards." Darryl Zanuck, head of the Twentieth Century-Fox studios, said it was a "hell of a job keeping the boys in line. . . . The whole campaign on this picture is a disgrace to the industry." The movie, after breaking local box-office records, closed when Hughes became engrossed with producing a fighter-bomber plane for the air force to use in the war.

It was early 1946 before he returned to the picture. He hired Russell Bird-well, a spectacular publicity man, and the two jointly engineered a campaign for *The Outlaw* that included skywriting and a blimp flying over Los Angeles, advertising the film, as well as revealing pictures of Russell with captions that asked: "How would you like to tussle with Russell?" The Hollywood establishment was infuriated at the vulgarity of the movie and its advertising blitz. The newspaper *Variety* complained of a backlash: "[The] move toward liberalization of censorship, both inside and outside the industry, has been pretty well shelved by the current ruckus over *The Outlaw*. . . . Hughes's unorthodox selling of one picture must have an invidious effect on the rest of the picture industry." Because Hughes had not submitted the advertising to the PCA, as required by the Code rules, the PCA took the unprecedented action of revoking a seal of approval it had previously granted. When Johnston rejected Hughes's appeal, Hughes sued the MPAA for restraint of trade.

He lost. The dispute is a "narrow one," observed Federal Judge John Bright, relating "only to the alleged rejection of certain advertising matter" which Hughes admitted was just "a small portion" of the whole. His "sole object," the court felt, "is a selfish one." Indecent advertising could harm the industry as much as pictures that are not "morally acceptable." Once a seal has been granted, the public "is led to understand" that the film has been approved and "may properly assume" that its "advertising and promotional matter" are also approved. "The blame for improper, salacious, or false advertising is . . . placed as much at the door of the [MPAA] as of the producer."

Despite critics' continuing ridicule, crowds nationwide thronged to *The Outlaw*, breaking attendance records in city after city; it earned more money in Atlanta than *Gone With the Wind*. Some government censors, as Johnston had predicted, demanded deletions or banned the film outright. In Maryland, a trial judge claimed that Russell's breasts "hung over the picture like a thunderstorm spread over a landscape. They were everywhere." Church protests caused cancellations of the picture in Philadelphia, Minneapolis, and St. Paul.

In New York City the police and license commissioners, employing a 30-year-old tactic, warned theater owners that they would lose their licenses if the film were shown. They did not show it. This led United Artists to sue one of the theaters for breaking its contract to exhibit the movie; it also prompted Hughes to sue the commissioners. Although both cases were lost, the picture opened in New York City to great fanfare. When it played at Radio City Music Hall, the marquee proclaimed: "The Music Hall Gets the

Big Ones! What Are the Two Great Reasons for Jane Russell's Rise to Stardom?'' By then, few did not know the answer, and the Production Code Administration quietly restored to the movie the seal of approval.

Eventually, even the Church withdrew its objections, but not before significant cuts were made. Earlier when Hughes had heard the movie was slated to receive a C (Condemned) rating, he invited Los Angeles Archbishop Devlin to visit him. Devlin replied, ''I don't go to anybody.'' Hughes then promised to visit him. He arrived at one o'clock in the morning—as Father Francis Weber relates the story—driving a ''banged-up'' 1935 Chevrolet and ''dressed like a bum.'' ''I can't have the movie condemned,'' he told Devlin. ''What is your price?'' ''I don't have any price,'' the archbishop responded. ''What do you mean?'' asked Hughes. ''Everybody in the industry has his price.'' ''Goodbye, good night,'' were Devlin's parting words.

After the outcries faded and the movie played itself out, a Hughes aide contacted Cardinal Spellman of New York to use his ''influence'' with the Legion of Decency. Hughes had cut some of the more offensive scenes, and shortly thereafter, the Legion, although still objecting to ''immodest clothing,'' changed its rating to B.

The perfect candidate had failed in an oblique attempt to crack the Code. Hughes had almost unlimited financial resources at his disposal and, as he came from outside the movie industry establishment, he was immune to internal pressures. Defiantly, he had shown his seal-less picture at any theater that would risk the outcry and possible loss of future bookings. In later years, theaters took this risk more frequently, but generally only for critically acclaimed movies. ''The censors may not like it,'' Hughes said of *The Outlaw*, ''but the public does.'' Critics found it poor and hardly less salacious than its promotion. Russell Birdwell, using a wartime term, claimed the film ''proved conclusively that sex has not been rationed.'' Although diluted by industry and church censors, sex on the screen continued to attract Americans.[4]

A Country—and an Industry— in Transition

The postwar years might have become, in the words of a Sam Goldwyn film, ''the best years of our lives.'' Although the picture with that title won nine Academy Awards, the period did not live up to the claim. There was, above all, McCarthyism. For a while, the spirit of victory, of having defeated a totalitarian foe, was dominant. But before long uncertainty and anxiety—political, social, and economic—set in. The nation's unsurpassed military power and material well-being contrasted with fears of the atomic cloud overhead, which the government itself sanctioned. "What do you want to be when you grow up?" a reporter asked an eight-year-old boy. "Alive," the child answered.

Overseas GIs had discovered books by such American writers as Henry Miller and Frank Harris, which had been sold in the United States only underground; they now were brought home in duffel bags. A new sexually oriented literature mushroomed. "Girlie" magazines had become popular during the war, but a shortage of legal manpower and the press of other duties precluded any significant measure of censorship. The subject of sex was still not openly discussed when Alfred C. Kinsey startled the country in 1948 with his exhaustive reports on the private premarital and extramarital sex lives of American men. Kinsey's *Sexual Behavior in the Human Male* ran counter to almost all prevailing notions about the subject. Such information as previously existed had been kept under professional wraps or was to be found mainly among the pages of such novels as Erskine Caldwell's *God's Little Acre*, William Faulkner's *Sanctuary*, Lillian Smith's *Strange Fruit*, James Farrell's *Studs Lonigan*, and Edmund Wilson's *Memoirs of Hecate County*—all banned in various places in the United States.

Kinsey's book quickly became a best-seller, and its findings were generally accepted as valid (as would be those of his study of the sexual behavior of women five years later), although not altogether without reservations by the scientific and academic communities. For his breaking of taboos regarding a heretofore virtually unexplored area, Kinsey was, however, castigated. Some newspapers refused even to mention the report, while the Catholic church attempted to dissuade its members from buying or reading it. Although the Church condemned it outright and the National Council of Catholic Women called it "an insult to the American people," the editor of the Jesuit periodical *America*, Father Harold Gardiner, reassuringly observed that its findings did not justify any major change in existing sex laws. Believing that "indiscriminate knowledge improperly acquired and applied is an incentive to a lack of virtue," he proposed that the book's sale be limited to clergy, doctors, social workers, police, judges, and penal authorities. Around this time, a small underground of pornographic books and films also developed.

Movies imported from Italy and France, although still few in number, were especially influential; there was the work of the Italian neo-realists, especially the films of Roberto Rossellini and Vittorio de Sica. These presented realistic, matter-of-fact, nonpuritanical points of view on human relationships and behavior that defied the mores of the American film industry's Production Code. They provided an aesthetic impetus to such American directors as Elia Kazan, in movies like *A Streetcar Named Desire* and *Baby Doll* [38], that helped revolutionize the morality of Hollywood films and unsettled the foundations of church, industry, and government censorship.

Hollywood's economic decline following the war was unexpected: 1946 had been a banner year, with admission revenues at a level greater than ever before or ever after. Yet movie audiences steadily decreased, plummeting from 82 million to 36 million by 1950; the movies were losing middle-aged patrons. At the same time, production costs rose dramatically. In Washington, the United States Supreme Court decided that major studios had to divest themselves of the theater chains they owned; and in England, Hollywood's largest foreign market, the government imposed a 75 percent tax on film profits. While automobile sales boomed and many Americans took to the new super highways, many others stayed at home watching television and participating in the country's largest postwar industry, having and raising children. Drive-in theaters suddenly dotted the suburban landscape, multiplying geometrically from 100 at the war's end to more than 5,000 ten years later. By 1951, they represented 15 percent of the total number of theaters; even more significantly, drive-ins accounted for nearly 20 percent of receipts.

The source of Hollywood's biggest postwar problem is best revealed by statistics. In 1946 there were 7,000 television sets in the United States; in 1948, there still were fewer than 200,000. But within the next two years, as many as a quarter of a million sets were installed each month in American homes; the 1950 census reported that some five million families had television. The visual immediacy of television matched that of the movies, even though its size and artistry did not. With the added advantages of availability on impulse in the home and being free of charge, television quickly dominated American popular culture. By mid-decade, with 50 million sets in American homes, and 15,000 more added daily, TV had transformed American life. The movie industry never fully recovered. Only by revolutionizing its product did it survive.[5]

In 1948, the Supreme Court ruled in *United States* v. *Paramount Pictures* that studio control of the production, distribution, and exhibition of movies was an illegal combination and conspiracy to restrain trade under the Sherman Anti-Trust Act. This brought to an end the traditional structure of the motion picture industry. Loew's Metro-Goldwyn-Mayer, Paramount, Twentieth Century-Fox, Warner, and RKO were forced to dispose of their theaters. Along with Columbia, Universal, and United Artists, they were also forbidden to engage in certain monopolistic practices, such as block booking. The suit, which had been filed a decade earlier after five years of threats by the Roosevelt administration, had been quiescent during the war, when government and industry were embracing a common cause. The Justice who wrote the Court's revolutionary opinion was its specialist on economic affairs, and one of its principal free speech advocates, William O. Douglas.

Will Hays had for years tried to persuade Roosevelt and the Justice Department of the inappropriateness of their action. The government's case was aggressively pursued by the head of Justice's Anti-Trust Division, Assistant Attorney General Thurman Arnold. The men who drafted the Sherman Act, H. L. Mencken wrote Arnold, made only one mistake: they forgot to provide for capital punishment. But in this trial of the major studio system, Arnold asked for the extreme penalty. When the Supreme Court granted it, the face of entertainment in the United States changed. With studios stripped of their top-to-bottom control, exhibitors were free to bargain for and choose the pictures they thought film audiences wanted to see. The major studios' power over the character of the movies was indeed diminished by the new competition in exhibition, and their grip on film content through domination of the Production Code was also loosened.[6]

Racial and Religious Prejudice— and the Production Code

The late 1940s were a time of fresh responsibilities abroad and a new seriousness at home. Victory over the Nazis and Fascists overseas encouraged American liberals to overcome bigotry at home. Films exploring such subjects as anti-Semitism and the situation of blacks began to appear. *Gentleman's Agreement*, made in 1947, and *Pinky* [35] in 1949 were produced by Darryl Zanuck, who was, in his biographer's words, "a master at humanizing a situation of social concern." Both were directed by Elia Kazan. Many Jews in Hollywood, Kazan said, did not want *Gentleman's Agreement* made; they did not want anti-Semitism "stirred up." When the movie *Crossfire* was still in the planning stage, the American Jewish Committee approached producer Dore Schary with a similar fear, but Schary was not dissuaded.

The film community was only slightly more relaxed about movies dealing with racial prejudice. The industry, overcoming a mythic concern with the "Southern box office" that had long conditioned its approach to movies about racial problems, produced several pictures on the subject. *Pinky* concerned the travail of a white-skinned, but part black, nurse who returns to her native Mississippi after having been raised in the North. A theater manager in Texas was fined for showing it after a hastily formed censorship board banned it. The United States Supreme Court later overturned the ban. *Lost Boundaries*, the story of a black physician and his family who pass as whites, was barred in Memphis, Tennessee by Lloyd Binford, the chairman of the city's censorship board; for years he had prescribed what its residents could see on the screen. His edict was that the picture "couldn't play in the South. It deals with social equality between whites and Negroes in a way that we do not have in the South." An Atlanta censorship board also banned the film on the ground that it "would adversely affect the peace, morals, and good order" of the city, although the film played in Jackson, Mississippi and Birmingham, Alabama—as *Pinky* had in Atlanta—with no adverse public or box-office repercussions.

Such censorship by local governments deeply concerned MPAA head Eric Johnston. The period of trade association collaboration with state and city censors was drawing to a close. In 1949, an appellate court upheld a Memphis censorship board ban on *Curley* [29], which showed a desegregated school class, because "the South does not permit Negroes in white schools nor recognize social equality between the races, even in children." Johnston, who was a member of the Board of the National Association for the Advancement of Colored People, vowed that the MPAA "intends to meet the issue of political censorship head-on in the highest court in the land. We're after a clear-cut decision that will give the screen the full protection and freedom guaranteed by our American Bill of Rights." He compared this coming struggle to that of John Peter Zenger for a free press. The MPAA appealed the decision to the Supreme Court, which refused to hear the case.[7]

By this time, Breen was administering the Production Code with an iron hand. "There are two Codes," he would say, "one written, the other one mine"; or, even more to the point, "I don't interpret the Code. I make it." While Hays had been in charge, no one was inclined to dispute Breen. He brought the savvy of the streets, a "notoriously low boiling point," and "not the slightest seed of self-doubt regarding his mission or his rectitude" to a strong yet delicate position. "Look here," he told Elihu Winer, Universal Studio's liaison with his office, in 1946, "20,000,000 people have to see every picture Universal makes before you get five cents of your salary. We can't afford to offend *anybody*!" Breen could find something in almost every movie that vexed his sense of propriety, and if what was submitted failed to meet his standards, he rejected it.

Before the advent of television, each studio had its own expert on the Code who counseled the studio as well as argued its case and defended its scripts in the "court" of the Breen Office. After the studio received the list of changes suggested by Breen and his eight assistants, the negotiations began. "There would be trade-offs, such as one 'hell' for three 'damns,' " recalls Winer, presently of the Writers Guild of America East. "One wrote the best one could. Obviously there were no dirty words and no bedroom scenes. It was a game in which everybody knew the rules and they were subject to them, and then one side would try desperately to outwit the other.'' There was, for example, a time when Universal proposed to make a picture in which a black teenage boy had a major part. The Breen Office rewrote the script, casting him as a shoeshine boy, and rather than degrade the character to that role, Universal scrapped the idea for the film.

It was widely believed in Hollywood that if one of the major studios or a great deal of money were involved, Breen lowered his rigid standards. But few ventured to express the notion publicly, fearing he might judge their next picture more harshly. One who did make this claim openly was Mary Pickford, co-founder with Douglas Fairbanks, Charlie Chaplin, and D. W. Griffith of the independent United Artists. ''As things stand now,'' she said in 1946, ''the Big Five are both Congress and the Supreme Court. They not only make the rules, but they sit in judgment on the operation of them, so that an independent has no recourse.'' This is not to imply that the Big Five always had an easy time with the Breen Office. There are many examples of studio heads and producers complaining about Breen's objections.

When Hays retired and new types of films made their way onto American movie screens after the war, the smooth working relationship between the Legion of Decency and the MPAA began to disintegrate. Considered in some circles as an anachronism, the Legion ''modernized'' its outlook and began to look more favorably, or at least not with abject disapproval, upon certain adult pictures, which in the past might have received approval only with reservations. Other private and religious groups that were interested in the morality of films became active. The reaction of Jewish organizations to the 1947 British screen adaptation of Dickens's *Oliver Twist* was a case in point; their protests played a major role in the picture's unimpressive box-office performance. Asserting that the film violated the Code by ''characterizing a race unfairly,'' the Breen Office denied it a seal of approval. Later, one was granted after the film was considerably revised. The New York State Board of Rabbis successfully pressured New York's censors to ban the movie.[8]

Raising First Amendment Questions

The censorship activity sponsored by private and religious groups almost always went unchallenged in the courts. The Code itself functioned as a ''private prior restraint'' and amounted to an industry-organized, pre-licensing censoring system in the form of self-regulation. It entailed consultation and collaboration with religious and patriotic groups and with state and local government censorship agencies. Such arrangements, which invaded constitutional freedom of expression, differed from the classic forms of ''prior restraint'' against the publication or sale of books and magazines only by the absence of "state action," that is, governmental involvement. Obviously, the Code restricted and inhibited artistic creativity and placed a premium on ingeniousness in the circumvention of its limitations. Some films censored in this "private" way never reached the public. Thus an accepted fact of industry life kept many human and social concerns off the screen. American movie audiences could know what they missed only by seeing foreign films. These too might be denied if protests by pressure groups and boycotts took effect, as they did with the British *Oliver Twist*.

Most films banned in the 1940s for reasons other than political were banned because of sexual immorality or alleged "obscenity." *Webster's* defined *obscene* as: "ill-looking, filthy, obscene. 1. Offensive to taste; foul; loathsome, disgusting. 2. Offensive to chastity of mind or to modesty; expressing or presenting to the mind or view something that delicacy, purity, and decency forbid to expose; lewd, indecent; as, obscene language, dances, images. Characterized by or given to obscenity; as, an obscene mind or person. 3. Inauspicious; ill-omened." The English and American courts, which had been using the expression since *Regina* v. *Hicklin* in 1868, had hardly improved upon that definition, but they were beginning to be troubled by its vague and broad meaning. "There must be ascertainable standards of guilt," the Supreme Court noted in a related context. "Men of common intelligence cannot be required to guess at its meaning."[9]

In 1946, Edmund Wilson, the most distinguished American literary critic of his generation, published *Memoirs of Hecate County*, his first novel since 1929. Wilson, surely a man of more than "common intelligence," called it "probably the best damn thing I ever wrote—at least it has given me more satisfaction . . . than anything else." The longest of the novel's six related stories about residents of an upper-class New York City suburb contained a detailed and sensuous description of sexual intercourse. Two publishers afraid to take it on rejected the book before Doubleday, allegedly "not at all worried" about what Wilson admitted was its "impropriety," published it. Wilson's friends were surprised by his candor ("Do not let it fall into the hands of children," he told one). Most people, Wilson wrily observed, "sound as if they thought that I made an unsuccessful attempt to write something like *Fanny Hill*." It quickly became a best-seller, "mainly," he wrote, "because people think it's scandalous."

The book aroused the New York Society for the Suppression of Vice and, working with the police and the Catholic church, the anti-vice group raided New York bookstores that sold the work. Due to their pressures, Doubleday was charged with publishing and selling an obscene book. The trial court found Doubleday guilty on both counts, but wrote no opinion and gave no reasons. On appeal, the New York courts, also without opinion, affirmed.

The nation's highest tribunal, the United States Supreme Court, came next in 1948. This court had never before faced the issue of whether the criminal conviction of a publisher for selling an "obscene" book was in violation of freedom of the press.

The case was fully briefed. The sole issue the Court was asked to decide was whether a work of literature dealing with sex was not entitled to the same sort of constitutional protection as literature dealing with any other subject. Doubleday asserted that only if such a work created a "clear and present danger" to some substantial interest of the state might it properly be suppressed, and that no such danger could conceivably have been present in this case. This was also the doctrinal approach that the American Civil Liberties Union took towards literary censorship. During oral argument, Justice Robert H. Jackson expressed his fear that the Court "would become the High Court of Obscenity" if it decided "constitutional issues on the merits of literary works."

Curiously, this first time that the Court considered whether First Amendment freedoms protected sexual expression in literature, a full bench did not decide the issue. Justice Felix Frankfurter, a friend of Edmund Wilson for some 25 years, disqualified himself from the case, leaving an eight-member court. In its closed conference, the voting Justices of the Court divided equally, four-to-four: Justices Jackson, Harold H. Burton, and Stanley Reed and Chief Justice Fred Vinson voted to affirm the conviction, and Justices Hugo L. Black, William O. Douglas, Frank Murphy (with apparent reluctance), and Wiley Rutledge voted to reverse. The even vote meant that the censorship brought about by the Society for the Suppression of Vice, as upheld by the New York courts, stood. The first well-considered assault on the constitutionality of obscenity laws had misfired.[10]

In the next year, 1949, the question of obscenity in literature was considered in different cases by Jerome Frank and Curtis Bok, two unusually reflective and literate judges. Frank of the Federal Court of Appeals in New York concurred in affirming a trial court's order upholding the Postmaster General's exclusion from the mails of *Waggish Tales from the Czechs* and *Droll Stories*. However, he said he did so "with bewilderment," for his court's decision, he felt, "may put into peril other writings, of a higher order of excellence, which any man who happens at the moment to be Postmaster General happens to find offensive."

> [Such] immense administrative censorship authority in one fallible man makes him an almost despotic arbiter of literary products. If one day he bans a mediocre book, another day he may do the same to a work of genius. Originality is not so common that we should lightly contemplate its potential stifling. And censorship does more than to keep finished books from being sold: it keeps many from ever being written.

A few years later, in 1955, Postmaster General Arthur Summerfield tried to exclude from the mails a copy of Aristophanes' *Lysistrata*. He relinquished the book when a bookseller, represented by Washington attorney Edward de Grazia, sued in federal court, claiming the statute under which he acted was an unconstitutional abridgement of free expression. Similar concerns could, of course, be directed at censorship of movies.

Curtis Bok, the son of *Ladies' Home Journal* publisher Edward Bok, was a local Philadelphia judge and, like Frank, an author of note. After Philadelphia police raided bookstores and confiscated hundreds of copies of nine books—among them James Farrell's *Studs Lonigan* trilogy and *A World I Never Made*, William Faulkner's *Sanctuary* and *Wild Palms*, and Erskine Caldwell's *God's Little Acre*—Bok found the books not obscene, deeming them, instead, to be "obvious efforts to show life as it is." He went on to say:

> I should prefer that my own three daughters meet the facts of life and the literature of the world in my library than behind a neighbor's barn, for I can face the adversary there directly. . . . If [one] reads an obscene book when his sensuality is low, he will yawn over it or find that its suggestibility leads him off on quite different paths. If he reads the Mechanics Lien Act while his sensuality is high, things stand between him and the page that have no business there. How can anyone say that he will infallibly be affected one way or the other? . . . All that is relied upon, in a prosecution, is an indefinable fear for other people's moral standard—a fear that I regard as a democratic anomaly.

Judges and scholars examined First Amendment issues more seriously than ever. The most important theoretical contribution came from a philosopher and former Amherst College president, Alexander Meiklejohn, who asserted that any speech bearing on "self-government," helping Americans to perform their public duties as citizens, must be completely free; all media that disseminate information to this end must necessarily be unrestricted. In 1947, a distinguished Commission on the Freedom of the Press, under the chairmanship of the Chancellor of the University of Chicago, Robert M. Hutchins, was privately sponsored by *Time* and the *Encyclopaedia Britannica* "to consider the freedom, functions, and responsibilities of the major agencies of mass communication in our time." Its report, widely discussed, ended with a recommendation that motion pictures should be included, along with the print media and radio, as part of the press. This, of course, diametrically opposed the view the Supreme Court had taken in the *Mutual Film* case.

Ruth Inglis's study, entitled *Freedom of the Movies*, also sponsored by the commission, invited the industry to face up to its responsibilities. While she suggested it amend and improve its scheme of self-regulation, to which she gave qualified approval, she also supported Eric Johnston's expressed interest in initiating a court challenge to the power of government censorship boards. Finally, Zechariah Chafee, Jr., the leading First Amendment scholar of the day, pointedly observed that were an appeal to be taken to the Supreme Court from, for example, a censor board's banning of newsreels like the *March of Time* series, "we might hope for an illuminating reconsideration of the place of the film in modern society."

In a dictum contained in its opinion in the *United States* v. *Paramount Pictures* anti-trust case, the Supreme Court itself had held out some such revolutionary promise: "We have no doubt," said Justice William O. Douglas for the Court, "that moving pictures, like newspapers and radio, are included in the press whose freedom is guaranteed by the First Amendment." The Court refused to hear the *Curley* case in 1950. It was inevitable that another film test the censor's power, but what type of film and under what circumstances?[11]

Sacrilege and
the Supreme Court

In the history of film censorship, the 1950s was the decade of *The Miracle* [30]. The decision in this case was handed down by the Supreme Court in 1952. It granted constitutional protection to motion pictures for the first time and radically altered the course of freedom of the screen.

The key figure in *The Miracle* case was film distributor and entrepreneur Joseph Burstyn. He was born in Poland in 1901. After coming to the United States in 1921, he worked as a diamond polisher and then as a press agent and stage manager for the Yiddish theater in New York. During the 1930s, he became a fledgling distributor of foreign films and formed a partnership with Arthur L. Mayer, who was then the publicity director for Paramount Pictures. Over the next 15 years, Mayer and Burstyn imported foreign films and managed "art houses" in large cities along the East Coast. Mayer also ran the independent Rialto Theater in New York City. Here he "consistently showed the worst" movies, but he plowed Rialto profits into the Mayer-Burstyn effort in order to bring high-quality, but low-grossing, European films to American audiences. The spirited and well-liked Mayer showed pictures that lacked (and probably could not qualify for) the MPAA seal of approval; for this waywardness he was fondly called the "Merchant of Menace" and, for his "arty" foreign films, "Monsignor" and "Signor."

Short, hunchbacked, and single-minded, "simultaneously an aesthete and a tough negotiator," Burstyn was extremely knowledgeable about the European movie market and had, Mayer felt, "something approaching genius in acquiring, editing, and merchandising its product." He was the first independent exhibitor to string short artistic movies into a feature-length showing and bill them under one title. Mayer-Burstyn was the first distributor to deal almost exclusively in foreign films, and its success in that area encouraged others to follow. It also influenced American moviemakers, who soon grasped the artistic, ideological, and economic achievements their European counterparts had constructed upon the ruins of World War II. From the Italian school alone, Mayer and Burstyn imported *Open City* (1945), *Paisan* (1946), *Shoe-Shine* (1946), and *The Bicycle Thief* (1948)—movies that fed American audiences' hunger for themes that presumed they were adults.

The foreign imports immediately ran into trouble with state and local censors. Brought to the United States in 1939, *Remous* [24], patterned after *Ecstasy*, told the story of a bridegroom who became impotent as a result of an injury suffered on his honeymoon. The New York censorship board passed it after many cuts had distorted its meaning. In the French film *Generals without Buttons*, five-year-old boys were shown with their buttocks exposed. Various censorship boards demanded the scene be eliminated, while others allowed a brief, long-range shot of it to be included. It was in this form that the picture finally was released in this country in 1938. Mayer-Burstyn tried to get an MPAA seal of approval for Roberto Rossellini's *Open City*; this was refused until a scene of a small boy on a potty was cut out. Such references to the elimination of bodily wastes were apparently an American taboo.

In Vittorio de Sica's *The Bicycle Thief*, a working man's bicycle is stolen. He spends hours searching for the irreplaceable bicycle through the back streets of Rome with his young son. After several hours, the boy can no longer contain himself, and turning his back to the camera, he urinates against a building. This time, when the Breen Office insisted the footage be cut, Burstyn refused and released the movie without a seal. New York State censors also thought the scene was "obscene." Nevertheless, Burstyn's lawyer persuaded the Board of Regents to authorize a license for the film uncut by pointing out that the censors would appear ridiculous were it to be known that they believed the average New Yorker would be aroused or offended by the sight of a boy urinating. *The Bicycle Thief* won de Sica an Academy Award for the best foreign-language film in 1950.

The lawyer who aided Burstyn was Ephraim London; he became the leading anti-film censorship lawyer of his generation. Then in his late thirties, tall and courtly, London came from a New York family of nearly two dozen lawyers. His general practice had a literary flavor and he later edited a two-volume work on law and literature and taught a course on the subject. In the 1950s, he was the lawyer that other lawyers sought for counsel in the field of movie censorship.

"The Miracle"

The Miracle was an Italian film directed by Roberto Rossellini and written by Federico Fellini, starring Anna Magnani. It told the story of a simple peasant girl who is made drunk and seduced by a bearded vagrant (played by Fellini). Imagining that the vagrant is Saint Joseph and that the child she conceives is a miracle, she tells her belief to the villagers, who taunt her and crown her with a wash-basin "halo"; she is forced to flee into the hills. Never doubting the miracle, she concludes, "It's the grace of God," and delivers her child in a remote and forlorn church.

The parallels between the story and the biblical account of the conception and birth of Christ were obvious. After *The Miracle* was shown at the Venice Film Festival in August 1948, a column in *L'Osservatore Romano* suggested that, despite certain "serious" questions of a religious nature, there were "passages of undoubted cinematic distinction. . . . We continue to believe in Rossellini's art and we look forward to his next achievement." Although the Vatican's censorship agency found the picture "in effect an abominable profanation from religious and moral viewpoints," it did not invoke any governmental sanction and gave it a regular clearance. Freely shown throughout Italy, the movie was brought to the United States, where it passed Customs censorship without difficulty and was licensed by New York's censors in March 1949. Shortly afterwards, the Mayer-Burstyn partnership dissolved, when Burstyn bought out Mayer.

Not until December 1950 was *The Miracle* shown in New York. It appeared then only as part of a trilogy called *Ways of Love*, which also included two French pictures and was licensed as such by the New York board. The Legion of Decency promptly attacked *The Miracle* as "a sacrilegious and blasphemous mockery of Christian religious truth," while critics had little but praise for the film. New York City's commissioner of licenses then proclaimed it "officially and personally blasphemous" and ordered the Paris Theater to stop showing it at the risk of losing its operating license. Burstyn resorted to a state court, which ruled that the commissioner had no authority to censor films in this way, stating that he was "not the protector of a large proportion of our citizens or even of all of them."

The controversy then took a new turn. On January 7, 1951, a statement by New York's Francis Cardinal Spellman was read at Saint Patrick's Cathedral and at masses at other churches. He condemned this "vile and harmful picture" as "a despicable affront to every Christian." "We believe in miracles," he said. "This picture ridicules that belief." Spellman called on "all right-thinking citizens" to unite against immoral films, especially through economic boycott. Rossellini cabled Cardinal Spellman:

> In *The Miracle* men are still without pity because they still have not come back to God, but God is already present in the faith, however confused, of that poor, persecuted woman; and since God is wherever a human being suffers and is misunderstood, *The Miracle* occurs when at the birth of the child the poor, demented woman regains sanity in her maternal love.

Action against the film became more direct. Pickets from Catholic organizations paraded before the theater—as many as 1,000 on one Sunday—

while bomb threats emptied the packed theater on two successive Saturday evenings. One theater telephone line was cut and another reportedly tapped; London suspected his line also was tapped. At the order of the New York fire commissioner, a fire inspector issued a summons to the theater manager because people waiting for seats blocked the aisles. The Fire Department also opened an inspection of "bribe-giving" at the theater. Martin Quigley warned the New York Film Critics, who were expected to award *Ways of Love* a citation as best foreign picture of the year at a ceremony at Radio City Music Hall, that such a presentation would offend Cardinal Spellman and provoke a Church-sponsored boycott of the Music Hall. When the chancellor of the archdiocese confirmed this threat in a letter to Radio City managers, the critics moved the ceremony.

The chairman of the New York Board of Regents, claiming to have received hundreds of protests, appointed three regents to review the action of the Education Department's censors in granting *The Miracle* a license. The New York statute provided:

> The director of the [motion picture] division of the education department, or when authorized by the regents, the officers of a local office or bureau shall cause to be promptly examined every motion picture film submitted to them as herein required, and unless such film or a part thereof is obscene, indecent, immoral, inhuman, sacrilegious, or is of such a character that its exhibitor would tend to corrupt morals or incite to crime, shall issue a license therefore.

The committee viewed the picture and labeled it "sacrilegious"; now the regents ordered Burstyn to show cause why his license to show the movie should not be revoked on that ground. Unable, apparently, to show cause satisfactory to the regents, the movie's license was revoked on the ground that the "mockery or profaning of beliefs that are sacred to any portion of our citizenship is abhorrent to the laws of this great State." The film closed and Burstyn went to court. After New York's highest court upheld the regents' action, affirming the censor's ban, Burstyn appealed to the United States Supreme Court.[1]

Burstyn v. *Wilson*

Ephraim London thought from the beginning that *The Miracle* case might reach the Supreme Court. He had argued the case before New York's highest court, but not in the lower courts; he was, however, involved from the case's inception and the briefs reflected his counsel. The lower courts had ruled on the issues as London framed them in the briefs, thereby preserving them in that shape for consideration by the Supreme Court. This was his first argument in the Supreme Court and his contentions were direct: that any censorship of motion pictures was an unconstitutional prior restraint on free expression; that the New York statute violated constitutional guarantees of "separation" of church from state and of the "free exercise" of religion; and that the term *sacrilegious* was so vague and indefinite as to deny liberty of expression without due process of law.

The Supreme Court handled the case with dispatch. Argued in April 1952, it was decided just one month later. At oral argument, the justices, in the usual manner, asked London many questions; none appeared hostile to his position. Justice Felix Frankfurter characteristically posed as many queries as the rest of the Bench combined. For the first time a movie was privately shown the justices as a body. Some of them considered *The Miracle* "very poor entertainment"; Justice Sherman Minton remarked later that if he had paid "anything" to see "that film" it would have been "too much." Justices Hugo Black, Frankfurter, and Douglas refused to attend the showing. Frankfurter felt that it was "inappropriate" for a judge, in his judicial capacity, to do so and that he should rely solely on the written record in deciding the case. In conference the week following the argument, the Court unanimously voted to reverse the New York decision.

Chief Justice Fred Vinson assigned the opinion to Justice Tom C. Clark, one of the Court's most conservative members. Clark had been Attorney General when President Harry Truman appointed him to the Bench in 1949 and was now in his third term. His opinions usually were brief and workmanlike, dealing with the questions at hand, without unnecessary exploration of historical background or analysis of the underlying philosophical problems. *The Miracle* was treated no differently.

The overriding issue, Clark noted at the outset of his opinion, was the constitutionality of the New York statute that authorized government officials to ban films on the ground, among others, that they were "sacrilegious." It "cannot be doubted," he observed, transforming a "dictum" of the *Paramount Pictures* anti-trust case into a holding of this case, "that motion pictures are a significant medium for the communication of ideas" and, for that reason, protected by the constitutional guarantees of freedom of speech and press. This was because movies "may affect public attitudes and behavior in a variety of ways, ranging from direct espousal of a political or social doctrine to the subtle shaping of thought which characterizes all artistic expression." Moreover, "the importance of motion pictures as an organ of public opinion is not lessened by the fact that they are designed to entertain as well as to inform."

Clark refused to accept the New York courts' contention that the *Mutual Film* case required the Court to uphold the censors' point of view. "That books, newspapers, and magazines are published and sold for profit," he continued, "does not prevent them from being a form of expression whose liberty is safeguarded by the First Amendment. We fail to see why operation for profit should have any different effect in the case of motion pictures. . . . Expression by means of motion pictures is included within the free speech and free press guaranty of the First and Fourteenth Amendments. To the extent that language in the *Mutual Film* opinion is out of harmony with the views here set forth, we no longer adhere to it.''

The fact that movie expression was protected by constitutional guarantees was "not the end of the problem. It does not follow that the Constitution requires absolute freedom to exhibit every motion picture of every kind at all times and all places. . . . Nor does it follow that motion pictures are necessarily subject to the precise rules governing any other particular method of expression. Each method tends to present its own peculiar problems.'' New York's system, requiring that permission to communicate ideas be obtained in advance from state officials who judge the acceptability of the content of the words and pictures, was "a form of infringement upon freedom of expression to be especially condemned.'' The New York courts had interpreted the censorship law's authorization to ban "sacrilegious" films to mean that, in movies, "no religion . . . shall be treated with contempt, mockery, scorn, and ridicule.'' But this definition was so broad and all-inclusive as to set the censors "adrift upon a boundless sea amid a myriad of conflicting currents of religious views, with no charts but those provided by the most vocal and powerful orthodoxies.'' A state "cannot vest such unlimited restraining control over motion pictures in a censor.''

The Court nevertheless took care to say that it was not also deciding "whether a state may censor motion pictures under a clearly drawn statute designed and applied to prevent the showing of obscene films.'' That was deemed to be a "very different question from the one'' it was deciding, against censorship. Justice Clark cautiously wrote: "We hold only that under the First and Fourteenth Amendments a state may not ban a film on the basis of a censor's conclusion that it is 'sacrilegious.' ''

Justice Frankfurter wrote a typically long but discursive concurring opinion, in which he traced the changing meaning of sacrilege since ancient times. Before writing it, however, he contacted George La Piana, a Harvard professor who was an authority on church history and who sent Frankfurter a bibliography on the concept of sacrilege as it has "come down through the ages in the Church of Rome.'' La Piana affirmed Frankfurter's "assumption'' that the concept evolved through varied interpretations and applications; and he prepared for him a summary of its history and doctrine. Frankfurter then asked for further references which established his proposition, and La Piana supplied him with those, along with another brief historical review. In a highly unusual procedure, the Justice incorporated some of these sources and used parts of the professor's statements almost verbatim in his opinion.

The Court's holding was purposely narrow, but satisfying in the unanimous recognition that movies were fully entitled to constitutional protection. The freedom-denying *Mutual Film* case was overruled, discounted as a relic of the thinking of a bygone day. It had taken thirty-five years, but motion pictures at last were given constitutional protection.

The decision should have meant even more to the film industry than to Joseph Burstyn, but when a reporter questioned studio executives about the implications, they were "either so afraid that they refused" to comment, or they made "meaningless, innocuous remarks." The fears that inhibited them from speaking out in favor of freedom of the screen remained. Some may well have preferred censorship to the hazards of freedom, for it had mainly been "independent" and "foreign" moviemakers who had been handicapped by censorship in recent years. Without such handicaps, their productions could well present major studios with stiffer competition at the box office.

Burstyn clearly saw the connection between artistic freedom and financial success in the competitive movie business. He waged his lonely battle for both. "Sure, I am a businessman," he said. "But freedom is the life blood of business." The movies were in "bad shape because they allowed themselves to be stifled in their freedom of expression." His case went "far beyond one picture. It has to do with censorship of the screen. The screen has let itself speak only to immature people. If the industry wants to sleep comfortably, let it. It will wake up one day to find there is no business left"—or that it had all gone to "outsiders" like him. He had fought for each of his pictures and "insisted on presenting films as freely as a writer writes a book or a painter paints a picture." He spent two years and $75,000 to make a point that the movie establishment, for unexplained reasons, had never seriously tried to make. He received no support or encouragement from the MPAA or anyone connected with the American movie industry. *New York Times* film critic Bosley Crowther was one of the very few who supported Burstyn's fight for freedom of expression. Burstyn initiated a battle that Ephraim London carried to victory. One year later, on an airplane to Europe, Burstyn had a heart attack. By the time the plane could make an emergency landing, he was dead. His achievement would long survive him.[2]

In the Wake of "The Miracle"

The Supreme Court followed *The Miracle* case with a remarkable series of *per curiam* opinions that reversed, without written opinions, five state supreme court decisions that had upheld the banning of films by censorship boards. These unsigned decisions by the nation's highest court invalidated, on the basis of *The Miracle* case, all but one of the principal statutory censorship criteria that censors had applied for decades to prevent the showing of films. The now condemned criteria had embraced films deemed to be "immoral" or tending to "corrupt morals" (*La Ronde* [31]); "other than moral, educational, amusing or harmless" (*M* [33]); "of such character as to be prejudicial to the best interests of the people of said City" (*Pinky* [35]); "cruel, obscene, indecent, or immoral, or such as tend to debase or corrupt morals" (*The Moon Is Blue* [36]); and "harmful" or "conducive [to] immorality [or] crime" (*Native Son* [37]).

Taken together, these decisions implied that all of the terms (except "obscene") within the given phrases were struck down as overbroad criteria for movie censorship; they did not mean merely that the terms had been unconstitutionally *applied* by censors to condemn these particular movies. Statutory authority to censor "obscene" movies was understood to remain constitutionally viable because of the dictum to that effect in *The Miracle* case and because none of the laws voided under these new decisions were solely directed at "obscene" or "indecent" films. But no opinions were issued to explain the decisions.

It appeared, in fact, that the Court was somewhat uncertain how to proceed. While considering the *La Ronde* and *M* cases, for example, Justice Frankfurter wrote to Justice Black: "A unanimous decision announcing in unequivocal terms that there can be no censorship would . . . prove as nothing else could prove that censorship is out. But I put it to you, that since at least six members of the Court would deny any such absolute, is it not far better to have us *per cur* unanimously (barring at most Justice Stanley Reed) on *Burstyn* v. *Wilson*, than to have at least six members of the Court invite, however unwittingly, censorship legislation by giving rise to the inference that some censorship laws would pass muster."

The Court was already involved in one controversial struggle in connection with school desegregation cases and the prospect of engaging in another—for sex was controversial—must have been unappealing. More important, perhaps, was the Court's inclination to allow the issues to germinate and be aired at lower levels of the federal judiciary and among state courts, augmented by professional commentary and analysis, rather than to step in and resolve the issues authoritatively. The *per curiam* opinions indicated the direction of the Justices' thinking, without casting it in concrete. [3]

The impact of these judicial progeny of *Burstyn* was immediate and great. Now on the defensive, members of the six existing state movie censorship boards met. Their practices, it was conceded, had been thrown into "great confusion," and they called for new statutes to prevent the exhibition of "obscene and immoral" films and to justify their continued existence. The invitation for the meeting was extended by Hugh M. Flick, head of the New York censorship board and one of the more open-minded of the country's second generation of movie censors. He had been stymied in his proposal to substitute for the state's draconian "yes-or-no" licensing system a more flexible one that could limit the showing of some pictures to "adults only." Nevertheless, in the summer of 1954, Flick publicly stated that "the most offensive movies were made by independent producers" and consisted "largely of 'girly shows' and borderline subjects such as sex hygiene, drug addiction, and clinical subjects including operations and childbirth." Without any government control, he imagined, "these films would be able to prey on the more susceptible elements of the community." Flick raised no objection to the New York legislature's amending of the censorship statute to limit the coverage of the terms "immoral" and "tend to corrupt morals" to movies expressive of "sexual immorality." Much filmed material under this rubric would still be subject to censorship.

The industry's own censorship Code was also undergoing problems at this time. Sam Goldwyn had recommended to Eric Johnston that revisions be made, inasmuch as under the Code's present wording even the tales of Mother Goose could be barred from the screen. Walt Disney's films came closer to Mother Goose than those of any other director, and one of his films was indeed banned by government censors. *The Vanishing Prairie* (1954) had won an Academy Award for the best documentary feature picture, but it was banned by New York's censors as "indecent" because it showed a buffalo giving birth. No human being appeared in this story about wild birds and animals who, on the verge of extinction, somehow managed to survive. Furthermore, no one had opposed it; rather, representatives of national organizations, including leading religious ones, uniformly approved it for "family" showing. However, the acting chairman of the New York censorship board, serving while the chairman was on vacation, refused to pass it.

A stunned Disney, seeking to make amends, pointed out that the objectionable two-minute scene was presented "as part of the life cycle in the animal kingdom" and was not "dwelt upon unnaturally or sensationally." "Never," he apologized, would it "have appeared on the screen if I believed it might offend an audience. It would be a shame if New York children had to believe the stork brings buffalos, too." After the American Civil Liberties Union had lodged a complaint, the board of censors reversed itself, in light of what its chairman described as "a modification of an ancient precedent," and permitted the film to be exhibited intact. According to the *New Yorker*'s movie critic, Disney showed his audiences "the birth of a buffalo calf—an episode that . . . caused the state censors (who themselves must at one time have been born) a bit of uneasiness. I lived through that scene, and I suspect you will, too."

The Supreme Court's rulings indirectly undermined the intellectual and legal authority of the industry's Production Code. Stripped of much of its effective conceptual and moral basis, it now could be effectively challenged. As early as 1944, Otto Preminger had struggled with Breen Office censors and the Legion of Decency over his right to save intact a scene from *In the Meantime, Darling* that showed a husband and wife sleeping in the same bed. Concerning *Forever Amber,* he had even joined the priest who was the head of the Legion in the projection room in an effort to come to an agreement as to what could and could not be shown. It was a "painful" experience that Preminger would not soon forget.[4]

"The Moon Is Blue"

Everyone except the Breen Office considered Preminger's production of *The Moon Is Blue* [36] a rather innocuous romantic comedy. It was due to be distributed in 1953 by the newly reorganized and independent company, United Artists. As an aspect of his arrangement with the studio, Preminger had complete editing control over the picture. When the Breen Office announced it would reject the script unless six lines were changed, he simply refused. Breen found the movie objectionable because of its use of the words "virgin," "seduce," and "pregnant," and the phrase, "You are shallow, cynical, selfish, and immoral, and I like you!" Under the Code it was not possible for a person to be both immoral and likeable. The MPAA's board of governors rejected Preminger's appeal after Nicholas Schenck, president of Loews, made an impassioned speech in which he stated, "I wouldn't let my daughter see it. It's true that the girl is not seduced in the time she spends with the boy, but other girls in a similar situation might get closer to the flame. I vote no." Eric Johnston announced that "the Board has reaffirmed its firm and wholehearted support of the Code. . . . The Code has nothing to do with 'styles' or changing customs. It is a document that deals with principles of morality and good taste." These, according to Johnston, were "timeless."

Preminger, on the other hand, insisted the Code was "antiquated" and that many pictures approved by the Breen Office were more objectionable than *The Moon Is Blue.* "I am not a crusader or anything like that," he explained. "But it gives me great pleasure to fight for my rights. If you don't fight for your rights, you lose them." Later he said, "[We have] not only the right, but the duty to defend this right of free expression; because if this right deteriorates, that is the first step to dictatorship, to totalitarian government." In the face of at least one studio head's prediction that "not more than five theaters" would show the film without a Code seal, United Artists distributed the movie without one. Critics liked it, calling it "as pure as Goldilocks" and "never once in bad taste."

Some government censors, including those of New York and Pennsylvania, licensed the film without objection, but censors in Ohio and Kansas banned it. The United States Supreme Court eventually overturned the Kansas action and invalidated the state censorship law. In Jersey City, New Jersey, a theater manager showing the movie was arrested at the order of the mayor, who claimed *The Moon Is Blue* was "obscene, indecent, and immoral." When the Milwaukee Motion Picture Commission banned it, suburban drive-ins beyond the city's legal reach played the film to capacity audiences. After Maryland censors barred it, citing the Production Code's refusal of a seal, United Artists went to court. In reversing that ban, in December 1953, the Maryland court observed that "if the Production Code were law, it would be plainly unconstitutional." The film's legal battles received wide publicity, inspiring the comment: "Provocative Subject equals Protests equals Publicity equals Profits." *The Moon Is Blue* grossed more than $6 million for Preminger and United Artists, as more than 8,000 theaters showed it. The theory that economic disaster resulted for any picture distributed without the MPAA seal was laid to rest.

The Legion of Decency had fought to suppress the film even before it was released. Martin Quigley privately asked United Artists president Arthur Krim to alter the movie. The story's lighthearted treatment of "free love," he claimed, violated the Code's provision that "pictures shall not infer that low forms of sex relationship are the accepted or common thing." Preminger argued with Breen that his female lead got her man because of decency, not sex. Breen disagreed. To him, a colleague wrote, "this was an issue involving the original set of values on which the Code was founded." First principles were at stake, and Breen sought public support to protect them and the Code. At his suggestion, a Hearst newspaper columnist castigated the movie. The New York Archdiocese labeled it "an occasion of sin" that broke the moral law and the ideal of wholesome standards in the name of public entertainment. The Archbishop of Philadelphia issued a similar statement and tried, but failed, to keep the movie out of city theaters. Once the tempest over the film had subsided, an "influential party" in the Legion admitted that the organization had acted to condemn the film not because of its immoral character, "but for extrinsic considerations—namely to support the Code and prevent the seamless garment from being rent."

For Joe Breen it was a momentous defeat. His friends in the Legion, the Catholic hierarchy, and the *Motion Picture Herald* had always proved effective allies in the battle against screen immorality. This time they had fought hard, but lost. For two years, in response to pressures from within and outside the industry to liberalize the Code, Breen had periodically submitted his resignation to Eric Johnston. While at first Johnston refused to consider it, he now began looking for a replacement; on the recommendation of Quigley, he picked a New York City family court judge, Steven Jackson, as Breen's replacement. The choice was not propitious; Jackson served as acting director of the Production Code Administration for only a year and a half, and Breen did not formally resign but instead went on leave. During this interregnum, Breen disputed Jackson over censorship standards and decisions. It was soon clear that a new industry chief censor would have to be found. When Breen left, he did not depart emptyhanded. In honor of his achievements and his unstinting service to the industry, the Academy of Motion Picture Arts and Sciences awarded him a special Golden Academy Award: an Oscar for the censor.[5]

The old taboos were losing their force. Howard Hughes's new "bosom brouhaha" fizzled despite the old kind of publicity ("Jane Russell in 3-Dimensions—and what dimensions!"), largely because the movie, *The French Line*, was "more to be pitied than censored." A liberalized era began with Geoffrey Shurlock's appointment to administer the Production Code in October 1954. Short, stocky, then already 60 years old, Shurlock seemed out of place in Hollywood. A British-born Phi Beta Kappa graduate of Dartmouth whose mind raced ahead of his tongue, he was cultured and well read. He was not a reformer; eradicating evil was not his job. His "inclination" was "to yield to the force of events without making an issue." He realized that his influence on the film world was small and did not wish to increase it. Implicit was his belief that the moral climate changes and that movies—which are "to a large extent based on those novels and plays that have won the widest approval"—must necessarily follow. Widely respected, Shurlock administered the Code (within what was now sometimes called the Johnston Office, never the Shurlock Office) evenhandedly. He had been with the office from the beginning and had chafed under Breen's rigid control. Unlike him, Shurlock was compromising, a moderating force. In his custody, it was inevitable that the Code would be applied more leniently.

When Joe Breen finally left, the Church hoped that his successor would be a member of the Code staff who represented its viewpoint. Quigley spoke to Jack Vizzard. He had been a member of the staff for ten years and had come to the office through Breen's son, with whom he had attended seminary. But Quigley was "disappointed" that Vizzard had not effectively influenced Shurlock "to keep him more moderate." Quigley asked Vizzard to make a minority report when he disagreed with Shurlock. It was his "duty," Quigley told Vizzard, to oppose Shurlock. "The Code is operating at variance with the Legion of Decency. The spread is becoming wider to the point that it is becoming a matter of conscience. The voice of the Legion is the representative voice of the Hierarchy in the United States. That is an obediential voice. You are obliged to accommodate it." These were not propositions Shurlock, Vizzard, or even Johnston, who was responsible to the major studio heads, could readily accept.[6]

McCarthyism

A demand for loyalty to "higher" sovereignties was common in the United States in the early 1950s. At the close of World War II, President Harry Truman inaugurated a federal program to remove "disloyal and subversive elements" from government. "We must not, however," he said, "permit employees of the federal government to be labeled as disloyal . . . when no valid basis exists for arriving at such a conclusion." Many such employees were nevertheless counted as disloyal. Fear and suspicion of Communism were pervasive; this was a time of demagoguery and character assassination. It was called McCarthyism, but Senator Joseph McCarthy from Wisconsin was a latecomer to the movement that took his name. By the end of 1952, more than six and a half million people had been checked for their "loyalty" by a government intelligence dragnet, with some 25,000 receiving full FBI field investigations. Truman's injunctions against red-baiting and for fair legal procedures in the adjudication of loyalty were routinely disregarded.[7]

In this constrictive atmosphere, book censorship was widespread. Few good authors were exempt. Government commissions were set up at state, county, and local levels to decide what materials were proper for Americans to read. *The Nation* magazine was barred from New York City and Newark, New Jersey public schools and from state colleges in Massachusetts; the librarian of the Bartlesville, Oklahoma public library was discharged after 30 years of service for ordering it and the equally heretical *New Republic*. McCarthy took the chair of the Senate Committee on Government Operations in 1953 and made his influence felt even more in the executive branch. His committee's counsel, Roy Cohn, and the latter's assistant, G. David Schine, toured the libraries of the United States Information Agency in Europe to remove "Communist" literature from their shelves. Secretary of State John Foster Dulles then banned from departmental libraries "the works of all Communist authors" and "any publication which continually publishes Communist propaganda." Off the shelves came books by such writers as Foster Rhea Dulles (the cousin of John Foster Dulles), Arthur Schlesinger, Jr., W. H. Auden, John Dewey, Stephen Vincent Benét, and Tom Paine; some volumes were even burned.

Finally, President Dwight D. Eisenhower, in a June 1953 commencement address at Dartmouth College, said,

Don't join the book burners. Don't think you are going to conceal faults by concealing evidence that they ever existed. Don't be afraid to go to your library and read every book, as long as that document doesn't offend your own ideas of decency. That should be the only censorship. . . . We have got to fight [Communism] with something better. Not try to conceal the thinking of our own people. They are part of America and even if they think ideas that are contrary to ours they have a right to record them and a right to have them in places where they are accessible to others.

One week later, Eisenhower (in a letter drafted by his assistant Emmett John Hughes) wrote to the American Library Association of "the precious liberties of our nation: freedom of inquiry, freedom of the spoken and written word, freedom of exchange of ideas. Upon these clear principles, democracy depends for its very life. . . . Full unfettered . . . knowledge . . . is a free people's greatest strength. . . . And any who act as if freedom's defenses are to be found in suppression and suspicion and fear confess a doctrine that is alien to America." This kind of talk did not stem McCarthyism.[8]

Movies reflected the prevalent patriotism. Hollywood released 86 "Cold War films" during the 1950s; 18 alone were made in 1952. The Pentagon assisted in making half of these pictures by providing government film footage or permitting the use of military bases and equipment. Its only condition was the power to approve the script. Other movies depicted "patriots" seeking to stamp out anti-Americanism; these could be regularly frustrated by legal "technicalities." In *Big Jim McClain* (1952), John Wayne rooted out and captured Communists only to see them gain release by relying on the Fifth Amendment. Undaunted, he continued his search for enemy agents. His motives? "I don't know the whys. I shot at the man on the other side of the perimeter because he was the enemy."

Anti-intellectualism was encouraged by the movies of the 1950s. According to the historian Richard Hofstadter, it consisted of "a resentment and suspicion of the life of the mind and of those who are considered to represent it" as well as "a disposition constantly to minimize the value of that life." In *My Son John* (1952), a bureaucrat becomes a Communist when a male college professor exposes him to allegedly "radical" ideas and a female Communist seduces him. Ultimately, he recognizes his mistake, thanks to his mother's religious faith and his father's good old-fashioned Americanism. It was, Stefan Kanfer noted in *A Journal of the Plague Years*, "a crackpot primer for Americans. . . . Stimulants led to narcotics, colloquy to atheism, intellectual curiosity to Communism."

Themes of paranoia dominated many pictures—the fear of being falsely accused, the chance that anyone at all might be a spy, the threat of nuclear annihilation, the failure of authority figures. These attitudes prevailed among the right wing during the 1950s; many of its adherents felt "dispossessed" because "their" America had been taken away from them. *Invasion of the Body Snatchers* (1956) eptomized the "era of the secret identity," and *On the Beach* (1959) that of the atom bomb. The "central image" in the "paranoid style," Hofstadter wrote, is that of a "vast and sinister conspiracy, a gigantic and yet subtle machinery of influence set in motion to undermine and destroy a way of life." The "realism" of these fantasy films—one bringing to the surface the fear of a Communist invasion by posing a parallel threat from outer space, the other "realizing" the possibility of the end of the world from a series of atomic explosions—resembled the "elaborate concern with demonstration" which paranoid literature "almost invariably shows. . . . The paranoid tendency is aroused by a confrontation of opposed interests which are (or are felt to be) totally irreconcilable, and thus by nature not susceptible to the normal political processes of bargain and compromise." Like so many politicians of the time, Hollywood films of the 1950s frequently forfeited the middle ground.[9]

Amending the Production Code

The success of *The Moon Is Blue* encouraged Otto Preminger to act again in advancing freedom of the screen. After reading Nelson Algren's novel about a heroin addict, *The Man with the Golden Arm* [41], he bought the film rights and United Artists agreed to distribute it, even though it was plain that the Production Code forbade even the mention of addictive drugs. When *Golden Arm* was denied a seal, Preminger attacked the MPAA as the "private club of the major studios." Johnston intervened on the film's behalf, but the MPAA board refused to overturn the Code Administration's decision. One board member thought the film was unacceptably "sordid"; another noted the director's remark that he did not "care too much" whether it received a seal. Preminger felt the movie carried "a very strong moral lesson, or a moral balance at least," and that "if anything, [it was] a warning against the consequences of taking narcotics." To placate the Legion of Decency, Preminger deleted a 30-second scene that showed actor Frank Sinatra preparing heroin in a spoon; the Legion then gave the film a B rating, marking the first time that a movie without the MPAA seal was not condemned. Starring Sinatra and Kim Novak, and carrying no seal, the film played every major theater circuit and brought large box-office returns. It was banned by Maryland censors, but freed by the state's highest court.

The situation angered some studio heads, who felt that the entire self-regulation structure was jeopardized. Members of the MPAA had pledged not to release a movie without a seal. United Artists' violation of this agreement, with *The Moon Is Blue*, was passed over by the industry because the movie was not expected to have much popular success. When that expectation proved to be wrong, the major studios restrained themselves and did not protest publicly. But *The Man with the Golden Arm* presented another situation entirely: starring one of the entertainment world's biggest names, its box-office appeal was obvious. When other MPAA members denounced it, United Artists quit the group.

It was a move that jolted the industry—when combined with a demand, jointly made by UA and Preminger, that the Code be amended to permit films on narcotics to be made. Why should the MPAA forbid the subject to be explored by motion pictures when newspapers and magazines did so regularly and freely? And then, not outdone by the independent United Artists, the "major" Twentieth Century-Fox paid $250,000 for the screen rights to Michael Gazzo's play *A Hatful of Rain*, also dealing with drug addiction.

While a besieged Eric Johnston announced that he expected no changes to be made in the Code in the "foreseeable future," he nonetheless appointed a committee of MPAA board members to re-examine the industry's self-regulation machinery. Late in 1956, he announced that, for the first time since its inception more than 25 years before, substantial revisions were being made in the industry's Code of morality. Largely concerned with the removal of four absolute taboos—portrayals of illicit narcotics practices, abortion, prostitution, and kidnapping—the amended Code frowned upon them, but allowed their depiction within bounds. Dropped entirely from the Code was its ban on miscegenation; simultaneously, the use of racial slurs was more directly discouraged. Overall, one critic said, the Code was " 'streamlined' into a body of instructions to producers rather than laws."

Not all of the changes increased freedom of the screen. Possibly as a pacifier to the Church, the word "divine" was added to the third General Principle, which thereupon read: "Law—divine, natural, or human—shall not be ridiculed, nor shall sympathy be created for its violation." This three-pronged division of law was borrowed from Saint Thomas Aquinas's *Summa Theologica*. To counteract the blow delivered to the hierarchy's interests by the Supreme Court decision in *The Miracle* case, the Code now also included a ban on blasphemy: "Ministers of religion, or persons posing as such, shall not be portrayed as comic characters or as villains so as to cast disrespect on religion." Manifestly, however, the new prohibition could not be used to withhold approval of a film such as *The Miracle*, whose allusions were to religious beliefs rather than to the ministers of such beliefs. The reason given for the new stipulation was "because the attitude taken toward [ministers] may easily become the attitude taken toward religion in general."

Critic Bosley Crowther hoped the revisions of the Code were a step on the road to "some day . . . eliminating the Code itself." In opposition, Martin Quigley claimed the amendments actually "reaffirmed and preserved inviolate the basic moral principles and provisions of the earlier Code." In any event, the philosophy behind it surely was eroding.[10]

"Baby Doll"

The Legion of Decency's opposition to Elia Kazan's *Baby Doll* [38] was not surprising, but in its ardor it overstepped itself. Not much earlier in 1951, the Legion had tangled somewhat successfully with Kazan over his film treatment of Tennessee Williams's hit play, *A Streetcar Named Desire*. Dealing in part with a woman's being sexually molested by her brother-in-law, the movie was, as Geoffrey Shurlock later said, "obviously not family entertainment." But, after script changes were negotiated with the industry's censor, Breen, and "compensating moral values" added, the picture was scheduled to open at New York City's Radio City Music Hall, traditionally a "family" movie theater. Before Warner Brothers released the film, however, the Legion condemned it. Fearing boycotts and pickets at theaters, the producer "secretly" agreed to cut more than three minutes of footage, 12 cuts in all, without Kazan's approval. One of the cuts showed the expression on actress Kim Hunter's face while contemplating her animalistic husband, played by Marlon Brando. These excisions had been demanded at Quigley's request. Despite glowing reviews and the cuts, the Legion classified *Streetcar* as "morally objectionable in part for all."

Five years later, when Kazan made *Baby Doll*, he, and not the Warner studio, had final-cut rights. Baby Doll (Carroll Baker) is the "untouched" bride of a southern bigot who, frustrated by sexual and financial problems, burns down a competitor's cotton mill. Seeking revenge, the competitor terrorizes Baby Doll into signing a confession of her husband's guilt and then seduces her; the husband runs amok, shoots his rifle into the night, hunting futilely for his rival, and gets hauled away by the local gendarme to an asylum. Although the Legion of Decency attacked the film vigorously, the MPAA, under Shurlock, gave it its seal. In a publicly released statement the Legion condemned *Baby Doll* for offending the entire community, claiming that its subject matter was "morally repellent both in theme and treatment." It dwelt, said the Legion, "almost without variation or relief upon carnal suggestiveness in action, dialogue, and costuming. Its unmitigating emphasis on lust and cruelty are degrading and corruptive. As such it is grievously offensive to Christian and traditional standards of morality and decency." Moreover, the picture's approval evidenced "an open disregard of the Code by its administrators." Quigley seconded this accusation by charging in the *Motion Picture Daily* that the film violated all three of the Code's General Principles. Kazan responded:

> I made *Baby Doll* as I saw it. I did the best I could to get on film what I felt in the South. Not the way things should be. Not the way they will some day be. But the way they appeared to me there and then. I wasn't trying to be moral or immoral, only truthful. I did the best I could, and I like the film as it is. I have

no intention of being pressured. I cut my own films with the help of a good film editor of my own choosing. As for the judgment of the Legion of Decency, I think in our country all people equally will and should judge for themselves.

Cardinal Spellman mounted the pulpit of Saint Patrick's Cathedral for the first time in nearly eight years to tell Catholics not to see the film "under pain of sin." Although he had not himself seen it, he claimed it involved a "contemptuous defiance of natural law" and a "definite corruptive moral influence" on American society. Noting that his censure might "induce many people to view this picture and thus make it a material success," he also said, "If this be the case, it will be an indictment of those who defy God's law and contribute to corruption in America."

The movie then opened to mixed reviews. Kazan's direction and the acting were praised, but little else; even Bosley Crowther was upset by its "foreignness." *Time* called it "the dirtiest American-made motion picture that has ever been legally exhibited." Catholic clerics told parishioners to boycott for six months theaters that showed the film. There were pickets and even some bomb scares. Businessman and diplomat Joseph P. Kennedy did not show it in his chain of New England theaters, declaring: "I have been in business 45 years, and I think this is the worst thing that has ever been done to the people and to the industry. I think it should be banned everywhere." His son, Senator John F. Kennedy, would be up for reelection in two years and the father did not wish to alienate Catholic voters.

Bishop James A. Pike of New York's Cathedral of Saint John the Divine attended *Baby Doll*'s premiere with his wife and, along with a rabbi and priest, told the press of their opposition to "political censorship." The next Sunday he spoke about the film from his pulpit. Charging that Spellman's attack represented the "efforts of a minority group to impose its wishes on the city," Pike defended *Baby Doll*'s exploration of human problems and criticized Spellman's view of the role of a church with respect to motion picture freedom. "The task of the Church," he said, is to provide its members with "the right canons of interpretation and to furnish them with answers to questions asked in depth."

Baby Doll did well, but not as well as expected, probably because of the many circuit cancellations; it played at 4,000 instead of 20,000 theaters. Kazan was "outraged" by Cardinal Spellman's suggestion that he and the film were somehow "unpatriotic." The Church's opposition to the film was a high point in its long campaign to keep the public from seeing immoral films, but from now on it had to confront a new America, socially and legally.[11]

Defining "Obscenity":
Roth v. United States

By 1957, it was generally supposed that films could constitutionally be banned only on account of their obscenity or sexual immorality. Most other reasons that legislative bodies had authorized officials to use in the suppression of movies had by then been invalidated by the Supreme Court. The sexual objections could take various forms, as the Supreme Court had never set forth its views on exactly what obscenity was. In 1957, it had a chance to do so.

Samuel Roth first gained notoriety in the New York publishing world in the late 1920s for publishing "obscene" books and magazines, some of which had surreptitiously entered the country. His activities brought him to the attention of the New York Society for the Suppression of Vice and the federal postal authorities. For his transgressions, he served several jail terms. In late 1956, after being convicted of violating the postal statute for mailing "obscene" materials, the judgment against him was affirmed by the Federal Court of Appeals for the Second Circuit; a memorable concurring opinion by Judge Jerome Frank resembled a dissent in everything but name. It contained an appendix of some 20 pages in which questions were raised about the nature of obscenity and obscenity law that to this day have not been satisfactorily answered.

The Roth case was argued in the Supreme Court in April 1957. Roth's lawyers contended that the federal and postal obscenity laws violated constitutional freedom of expression and, because of the vagueness of the concept of obscenity, due process of law. The federal government opposed these contentions in part by maintaining that 90 percent of material "actually caught in the net" of the federal statute's provisions comprised "black-market" or "hard-core" pornography—books, pamphlets, photographs, and films that blatantly depicted normal and abnormal sexual activity. To prove his point, the Solicitor General offered the Court a carton of hard-core materials to examine. During oral argument, the government made this material available "if any of the Court should wish to look at it." Even though the matter mailed by Roth was not hard core, the Court "assumed" it was "obscene."

The opinion to support the Court's vote to uphold Roth's conviction was assigned to Justice William J. Brennan, Jr., a 51-year-old newcomer to the high bench. Already, in his first term on the Court, Brennan displayed a broad and humane approach to constitutional problems, an intellectually powerful mind, a capacity for hard work, and an accomplished technical proficiency. In writing the Roth opinion, Brennan took on a work that he continued for more than twenty years; he became the nation's high metaphysician of the law of obscenity. In *Roth*, he fashioned a rationale for the suppression of "obscenity" that also accorded freedom to ideas about sex and that, amended in certain respects, dominated the constitutional law of obscenity up to the present. That was a remarkable achievement in any field, especially a heavily litigated one, and it was extraordinary for a novice justice.

The "dispositive question," Brennan wrote, was "whether obscenity is utterance within the area of protected speech and press." Protected expression included *ideas*. "All ideas having even the slightest redeeming social importance—unorthodox ideas, controversial ideas, even ideas hateful to the prevailing climate of opinion"— were protected unless they were "utterly without redeeming social importance." But was sexually oriented material protected?

> Sex and obscenity are not synonymous. Obscene material is material which deals with sex in a manner appealing to prurient interest. The portrayal of sex, *e.g.*, in art, literature, and scientific works, is not itself sufficient reason to deny material the constitutional protection of freedom of speech and press. Sex, a great and mysterious motive force in human life, has indisputably been a subject of absorbing interest to mankind through the ages; it is one of the vital problems of human interest and public concern.

The nub of the problem seemed to be how to distinguish obscenity from the "portrayal of sex" in art, literature, and other works. Brennan offered the following "test" for obscenity; the question was:

> whether to the average person, applying contemporary community standards, the dominant theme of the material taken as a whole appeals to prurient interest.

If so, the material was constitutionally unprotected obscenity; if not, it was presumably expression that was constitutionally protected. "We hold," said Brennan—as though satisfied that his definition of *obscenity* could readily be applied by anyone concerned in the distribution of books, magazines, or films dealing with sex—"that obscenity is not within the area of constitutionally protected speech or press."

Three other opinions were written. One of these, by dissenting Justice William O. Douglas, joined in by Justice Hugo L. Black, took umbrage with Brennan's approach. "These convictions," Douglas wrote, make "the legality of a publication turn on the purity of thought which a book or tract instills in the mind of the reader." It inflicts punishment "for thoughts provoked, not for overt acts or antisocial conduct." The new standard fashioned by the Court "does not require any nexus between the literature which is prohibited and action which the legislature can regulate or prohibit. . . . I have the same confidence in the ability of our people to reject noxious literature as I have in their capacity to sort out the true from the false in theology, economics, politics, or any other field."[12]

The *Roth* decision was handed down by the high court at a time when national self-confidence was about to be unsettled by the Soviet Union's orbit of its satellite Sputnik. The prevailing lull was challenged as well by an unaccustomed noise—and stridency. The noise was rock and roll and the stridency was typified by Elvis Presley. They would both mesmerize Americans for years to come. Presley's records, sensuality, and sexuality enticed and brought together a generation of uncommitted youth; the reaction of the establishment was swift. One disc jockey was fired for playing his records and police ordered Presley to "clean up" his show.

Playboy, founded in 1953 on a personal investment of $600 by a young man named Hugh Hefner, epitomized an upwardly mobile life-style for males. It quickly became the fastest growing magazine in the country. Aimed at urban bachelors, each issue featured a full-color centerfold of a nubile and nude "girl next door." Within five years it was selling a million copies monthly, and Hefner's bills for defending his magazine against censors rose proportionally; but Americans increasingly insisted on and tolerated new forms of sexual expression.[13]

"Lady Chatterley's Lover"

The late 1950s were troubled times for the American film industry. Hollywood was well along the road to becoming Television City, and one quarter of the nation's theaters had closed. The age of the moguls was over: Louis B. Mayer died in 1957; Harry Cohn in 1958; Darryl Zanuck resigned as production head of Twentieth Century-Fox in 1956; Sam Goldwyn and David Selznick stopped making movies; only Jack Warner held onto his power. At the beginning of the decade the major studios released 320 films yearly; by the end, 189. By 1960 new foreign pictures outnumbered American ones by close to four to one and, overwhelmingly, the imports played without a Code seal. Innovation in the film world, and satisfaction, too, came from abroad. For many, the industry seal was an anachronism.

The "new wave" French filmmakers stressed a strong individuality, freshness, and daring that competed with Italian neo-Realism; both schools outshone their American counterparts. The creation of European motion pictures had become a matter of personal expression. The director was *auteur*—the one who gave a film its distinctive shape and style. The product bore the director's stamp, not that of the producer. With few exceptions, Hollywood, and its structured and weighty studio system, seemed hardly to grasp this development. After having been dominated by American movies,

French directors and critics rebelled, designing their own free-flowing approaches to the cinema. In the United States, new European pictures were shown at "art theaters," which had suddenly spread across the country, attracting a growing audience of increasingly sophisticated viewers and, especially, a fast-expanding new film generation from within and outside of colleges and universities. If American filmmakers such as Preminger and Kazan broke the back of the industry's Code, it was mainly foreign directors, from Italy and France, whose works provoked those acts of censorship that ultimately led to a sharp curtailment of all movie censorship.[14]

Lady Chatterley's Lover [43], a French-made (though not new wave) film version of D. H. Lawrence's notorious novel, was denied a license for exhibition in New York in 1957 by state censors who charged that the "whole theme" of the picture was "immoral": it presented adultery "as a desirable, acceptable, and proper pattern of behavior." "We rest our determination," the censorship board stated, "upon the fundamental recognition by our society that adultery is condemned by God-given law (Sixth Commandment given to Moses on Mount Sinai) and man-made law (sections 100–103 of the Penal Law)." When the courts of New York upheld the ban, the movie's distributor appealed to the Supreme Court; once again, Ephraim London was the lawyer.

In the opinion he wrote for the Court, in June 1959, Justice Potter Stewart stated: by denying a license to a film that "approvingly portrays an adulterous relationship, quite without reference to the manner of the portrayal," New York had acted to "prevent the exhibition of a motion picture because that picture advocates an idea—that adultery under certain circumstances may be proper behavior." But, Stewart continued,

> the First Amendment's basic guarantee is of freedom to advocate ideas. The State, quite simply, has thus struck at the very heart of constitutionally protected liberty. [The Constitution] protects advocacy of the opinion that adultery may sometimes be proper, no less than advocacy of socialism or the single tax.

The Court ruled that government cannot interfere with the exhibition of a film because it disapproves of an idea expressed, even a sexual idea. The Constitution safeguards even the most "immoral," offensive, and even dangerous of ideas. "Ideological obscenity"—which goes to the content, not the manner, of expression—was dead. While London was not surprised over the ruling, the head of the New York censorship board observed that "some segments of the community were very upset . . . not so much on the erotic aspects but on the advocacy of what they consider an immoral idea." Taking a lesson, the board liberalized its policies with respect to nudity and illicit love and proceeded to restore a scene from another French film, *Love*

Is My Profession, starring Brigitte Bardot. With her back to the camera, the actress was seen walking from the shower to the living room, unclothed.

The five concurring opinions filed by Justices Black, Frankfurter, Douglas, Harlan, and Clark in the *Lady Chatterley's Lover* case indicated how divided the Court was on the matter of censorship. The Court's decision startled conservatives, and columnist David Lawrence warned: "Either the Supreme Court justices or the Constitution now will have to be changed to get a different result."

In another case that arose before the end of the year (*Smith* v. *California*), five separate opinions were written; the Court held that a bookseller could not constitutionally be found liable for selling obscene books without having knowledge of their contents, lest he "tend to restrict the books he sells to those he has inspected," for this self-censorship would restrain non-obscene as well as obscene literature. In both the *Lady Chatterley's Lover* case and this case the justices were unanimously of the judgment that the lower court's decision upholding the censorship should be reversed. It seemed that now only sexual "obscenity"—an epithet going to the manner of presenting sexual images and ideas—remained as a ground to ban movies. The direction the Court might take in this elusive field was unknown. Predictably, it depended upon the specific materials brought before the Court and upon the ways that lawyers framed the issues presented by the actions of the censors.[15]

The Era of Constitutionalization

The election of John F. Kennedy to the Presidency in 1960 was instrumental in transforming the American spirit. He offered hope and vitality to a quiescent country recovering from McCarthyism. A huge literature of protest emerged. Change was also significant in the Catholic church, and Kennedy's success was instrumental in bringing Catholics into the mainstream of American life. The brief and warm-spirited reign of Pope John XXIII, with his ecumenical bent, minimized theological differences and accented common values. His appeal for *aggiornamento*, an updating and renewal of Catholicism in response to modern conditions, struck a responsive chord.

There were those who, like Father John Courtney Murray, sought to amalgamate Americanism with Catholicism. Murray's appearance on a *Time* cover in 1960 celebrated the publication of his outspoken book, *We Hold These Truths*. In it he said, "No society should expect very much in the way of moral uplift from its censorship statutes. . . . Particularly in the field of sexual morality the expectations are very small . . . smaller here than anywhere else. . . . Philip Wylie may have been right in saying that American society is technically insane in the matter of sex. If so, it cannot be coerced into sanity by the force of law." For such efforts, Murray was periodically silenced by the Vatican.

With a Catholic in the White House, an Ecumenical Council convened by Pope John in Rome, and parishioners increasingly reluctant to accept clerical orders, Martin Quigley foresaw that the Legion of Decency might be drained of its power. And so he placed his connections and talent on the other side. After a script for a movie version of Nabokov's *Lolita* had been rejected outright by the Code administrators, the film's producer hired him to guide it back through the Code machinery. He did, and a seal was issued, though the Legion had asked him to cut portions that he personally thought best to retain. Twentieth Century-Fox engaged him for a similar task with *Cleopatra*, and the Code censors accepted the version presented.

Quigley could apply leverage against the Legion, if need be; but the Legion, too, was maturing: a new, long overdue category, "A-IV: morally unobjectionable for adults, with reservations," was created in 1963 to notify Catholics of movies that treated "serious themes" maturely. Meanwhile, the Code itself was under pressure for liberalization: among other areas affected, the production of a number of pictures dealing with "sex perversion" persuaded the MPAA to ease its restraints on references to, and depictions of, homosexuality. In any event, good foreign and domestic movies could now be shown successfully without the seal: both *Room at the Top* and *Never on Sunday* returned substantial profits and were extended into second, third, and fourth runs.

State and local censorship boards still actively wielded prior restraint, sometimes in collusion with the Code's administrators. In Atlanta, a librarian had been deciding since the end of World War II what films its residents could see. She claimed that she was "flexible": the word for a female dog was "perfectly acceptable" when applied to that animal but not when applied to a man's wife while she is having "a conversation with his mistress." In one year she forbade the people of Atlanta to see both *Room at the Top* and *Never on Sunday* [50], neither of which carried the PCA seal; both actions wound up in court. Her ban on the latter, a film that gave the "whore with a heart of gold" formula a new twist, caused the distributor, Lopert Pictures, to "appeal" to the city's Library Board. When the trustees also ruled that the picture was obscene because it "presented an unacceptable idea," Lopert sought relief from censorship from the Georgia Supreme Court. That court, however, denied his request—taking no notice, on a technical procedural ground, of the United States Supreme Court's holding in the *Lady Chatterley's Lover* case, which prohibited any censorship of "sexual immorality" or "ideological obscenity." But in the case involving *Room at the Top*, the court reversed the librarian's action on the ground that "liberty of speech, or of the press" could not be invaded "for one second in any conceivable manner." Atlanta's Charter provisions and ordinance providing for the censorship of movies were also declared void.

The new constitutional thinking of the Supreme Court had an impact. Within two years, movie censorship laws in Pennsylvania, Oregon, and Georgia were likewise invalidated by state courts, as censorship laws in Ohio in the *M* case [33] and in Massachusetts in the *Miss Julie* case [34] had been before them.[1]

"Don Juan"

The Supreme Court was given, but declined, the opportunity to outlaw entirely all film licensing laws. In the *Don Juan* [48] case, decided in 1961, the high court dampened the growing excitement of advocates of full freedom for the screen. Three years earlier, Times Film Corporation, an importer and distributor of foreign pictures, brought a test case against Chicago's censorship ordinance. A screen version of Mozart's opera *Don Giovanni* was the vehicle: it did not involve sex or obscenity, so censors could scarcely argue that it appealed to "prurient interests." "Our main object," Times Film's lawyer Felix Bilgrey later wrote in an unpublished memoir, was "to focus attention on the discrepancy between the judiciary's movie censorship appeals and those affecting other media."

The Times Film lawyers, in a brief largely written by Chicago lawyer Abner Mikva, advocated a radical position in this regard: that the nature of the movie was irrelevant to the constitutional issue, and that even if the film amounted to pornography, incitement to riot, or forceful overthrow of orderly government, it might nevertheless be shown without prior submission for examination by Chicago's censors. This was, of course, a pure interpretation of the prior restraint doctrine. After paying the required licensing fee to Chicago's censorship board, Times Film refused to submit the picture. It claimed that the city's censorship statute was "null and void on constitutional grounds" and that if the city wished to prevent *Don Juan* from being shown, it should invoke the criminal process against those who showed it *after* it had been shown. The city returned the fee, saying there was "nothing . . . to decide." After federal district and appellate courts upheld the city's action, or inaction, Times Film petitioned the Supreme Court for review. The Court agreed to hear the case.

The MPAA supported Bilgrey's argument that all government prelicensing arrangements should be invalidated and submitted an *amicus curiae* (friend of the court) brief stressing that there was no justifiable ground for a distinction in treatment of motion pictures and other media of communication. When the decision came down, a majority of the Supreme Court sharply disagreed with the principle urged by Times Film and the MPAA. The section of Chicago's censorship statute requiring submission of films prior to public exhibition, Justice Clark wrote, was not, "on the grounds set forth, void on its face." The issue was the censor's "basic authority": "whether the ambit of constitutional protection includes complete and absolute freedom to exhibit, at least once, any and every kind of motion picture."

The city of Chicago had argued that if Times Film's propositions were adopted, it could not protect the people of Chicago "against the dangers of obscenity in the public exhibition of motion pictures." If *Don Juan* were obscene, Clark reasoned, "certainly petitioner's broadside attack does not warrant . . . our saying that . . . the State is stripped of all constitutional power to prevent, in the most effective fashion, the utterance of this class of speech." At the suggestion of Justice John M. Harlan, Clark "narrowed" the Court's holding to "no more than this—that we are dealing only with motion pictures and, even as to them, only in the context of the broadside attack presented on this record."

Chief Justice Earl Warren wrote a dissenting opinion denouncing all prior restraints against movies. Clark's suggestion that the movie might, for all the Court knew, be obscene did not concern him. Warren also privately expressed "outrage" at pornographers who "sold their wares to the young." But for Warren the principle was crucial: prior restraint could be equally applied against other media. The decision, he contended, "presents a real danger of eventual censorship for every form of communication, be it newspapers, journals, books, magazines, television, radio, or public speeches." Its effects gave

> official license to the censors . . . formal sanction to censorship in its purest and most far-reaching form, to a classical plan of licensing that, in our country, most closely approaches the English licensing laws of the seventeenth century which were commonly used to suppress dissent in the mother country and in the colonies. . . . The censor performs free from all of the procedural safeguards afforded litigants in a court of law. The likelihood of a fair and impartial trial disappears when the censor is both prosecutor and judge. There is a complete absence of the rules of evidence; the fact is that there is usually no evidence at all as the system at bar vividly illustrates. How different from a judicial proceeding where a full case is presented by the litigants. The inexistence of a jury to determine contemporary community standards is a vital flaw. . . . [Chicago's licensing system] officially unleashes the censor and permits him to roam at will, limited only by an ordinance which contains some standards that, although concededly not before us in this case, are patently imprecise.

But the censors had won the day. The Court's opinion generated nervousness among other media groups, which feared that the licensing the Court had sanctioned for movies might be applied to them. After the opinion was published, Chicago officials promptly announced that the city's ordinance would be revised to tighten its licensing provision. City authorities planned to crack down on allegedly pornographic magazines sold on newsstands.

Within a week after the decision, the MPAA appointed Anna Rosenberg, former Assistant Secretary of Defense, who handled its public relations, to deal with the alarm the case had generated. She was to coordinate efforts by a number of media organizations to file *amicus curiae* briefs if Times Film were to request a rehearing by the Court. Times Film sought reconsideration of the issue largely to give the television and print groups an opportunity to be heard. Its request was denied. Felix Bilgrey hoped a later Court might see the issue differently, at least if the issue were presented more diplomatically; that day would come. In the two years after *Times Film*, nearly 20 censorship boards became inactive or were disbanded. The "unfinished public business" of which John Kennedy spoke when running for President evidently did not include film censorship. But over the next several years, a handful of Supreme Court cases changed the shape of obscenity law and film censorship.[2]

The restrictions—the First Amendment weaknesses—of *Roth* had to be overcome. If obscenity were not constitutionally protected as *Roth* indicated, merely because it appealed to prurient interests (thus arousing lustful thoughts), did not this imply that the Court had ceded to government censors' jurisdiction over thought? In *Roth*, Brennan himself had said that "sex [was] a great mysterious motive force in human life [and] indisputably . . . a subject of absorbing interest to mankind through the ages; it is one of the vital problems of human interest and public concern." Did this mean, then, that the government could limit the human mind and imagination? Did this also imply that the freedom of all modes of cultural expression could be scrutinized by the police and the courts so that they might regulate its sexual content as they saw fit?

On the Court itself, Harlan especially was unhappy with Brennan's nondefinition of obscenity in *Roth*. In his concurring opinion in that case, he suggested that Brennan had begged the question of why obscene expression was not constitutionally protected in stating that this was because it was "utterly without redeeming social importance." Moreover, Harlan observed, Brennan's opinion seemed "to assume that 'obscenity' is a particular genus of 'speech and press,' which is as distinct, recognizable, and classifiable as poison ivy is among other plants." And there Harlan was right, for there was nothing in *Roth* to help a poet or a policeman, a movie exhibitor or a prosecutor, a librarian or a judge to differentiate between legitimate expression about sex and illegitimate obscenity. All Brennan had said was that "obscene material" was "material which deals with sex in a manner appealing to prurient interest . . . i.e., material having a tendency to excite lustful thoughts." Any item in a library or a bookstore, in a movie distributor's catalog or on a newsstand, might have a "tendency" to do that.

Elsewhere in his opinion, Brennan had done American First Amendment jurisprudence the service of ridding it of the *Hicklin* rule, established in England in 1868 (*Regina* v. *Hicklin*). This rule defined obscenity in terms of its putative "tendency to deprave and corrupt those whose minds are open to such immoral influences, and into whose hands a publication of this sort may fall," especially "to the minds of the young of either sex, or even to persons of more advanced years." The opinion also discarded the *Hicklin* dictum that allegedly obscene material might be judged by the supposed effect of even an "isolated passage" upon a person into whose hands it might fall. But this was inadequate achievement for the critics of Brennan's *Roth* opinion.

In 1962, the Supreme Court added to the definition of obscenity in an opinion written not by Brennan but by Harlan, which, however, only Stewart joined. This significant event occurred in connection with the Court's reversal of the Post Office's ban on three homosexual magazines sent through the mail (*Manual Enterprises* v. *Day*). On a draft of Harlan's opinion, Brennan commented:

> I have no doubt that we must some day give further thought to the *Roth* test. [But] I lean to the idea that we ought let the widespread ferment continue a bit longer in legal periodicals and courts over the soundness and meaning of the *Roth* test before we re-examine it. I am particularly persuaded to that view, of course, by the fact that the Court is hopelessly divided in this area and there appears almost no prospect of an agreement of five of us upon anything.

Harlan had proposed "patent offensiveness" as a new obscenity standard. Choosing this terminology had not been an easy task. He first used "inherently sexually obscene"; but Justice Stewart, hoping that "a more satisfactory phrase can be found," thought that "obnoxiously debasing portrayals of sex" was "much closer" to the mark. Harlan's choice of "patent offensiveness" gave Brennan "some difficulty." "I have the reaction," he told Harlan, "that this element would only serve to limit obscenity to 'hard core' pornography. . . . And I have trouble defining 'hard core,' although no trouble at all recognizing it when I see it. In sum, I wonder whether the introduction of the element of 'patent offensiveness' would really be an improvement upon the *Roth* test, or only result in still further confusing an already confused subject." But Harlan announced the judgment of the Court in this case and modified the legal definition of obscenity. It was no longer sufficient to condemn a book or movie, or to punish its disseminator, on the basis that it might evoke lustful feelings in its audience. Now the government had to show that the material was "so offensive on [its] face as to affront current contemporary standards of decency." The scope of obscenity censorship laws was tightened another notch.

Harlan described obscenity as an "elusive field." Brennan called it "an already confused subject," and admitted that the members of the Court were "hopelessly divided" on what, exactly, obscenity was. Yet booksellers such as Samuel Yudkin (*Yudkin* v. *Maryland*) and movie exhibitors such as Nico Jacobellis (*Jacobellis* v. *Ohio*) were soon threatened with jail for not knowing what obscenity was or was not. Moviemakers, publishers, and librarians were all intimidated by the uncertainty clouding the issue. Yet, during the Sixties, no justice admitted to what Brennan finally admitted in 1973, that the concept of obscenity was indefinable for legal purposes, was hopelessly and unconstitutionally vague. Only Black and Douglas contended, passionately and consistently, that no one should be punished, and that no book or movie should be suppressed, because a government organ, or the Supreme Court, imagined it knew what obscenity was.

Justices Black and Douglas had almost given up hope of converting the brethren to their point of view. When the *Times Film* case of 1961 was decided, a disappointed Douglas told a friend:

> My views on obscenity are so far out of line with the majority of the Court that it seems almost hopeless to keep pounding away for them. Once in a while I see some minor step being taken which is a small, tiny advance, and hence I succumb to the feeling that perhaps I serve the cause of the First Amendment best by lending my weight to that meagre advance. Yet in the long haul, I think . . . that these moments of acquiescence accomplish nothing.

In 1960, one of the legal academic establishment's brightest members turned to what Justice Harlan later referred to as the "intractable problem of 'obscenity.'" Concerned for the welfare of the First Amendment, Professor Harry Kalven, Jr., of the University of Chicago suggested (in a *Supreme Court Review* article) a path the Supreme Court could take to square *Roth*'s lame holding with what Brennan the following year called the "transcendent value of speech." This was one of three articles written by law professors that significantly influenced the development of the law of obscenity in its crucial years.

The other two articles were written by the dean of Minnesota Law School, William Lockhart, and his colleague, Robert McClure. The first Lockhart and McClure piece appeared three years before *Roth* was decided. It called persuasively for the constitutionalization of the obscenity field, citing the Supreme Court's equally divided vote upholding Doubleday's conviction for publishing Edmund Wilson's *Memoirs of Hecate County* as evidence that the Court sooner or later needed to face the problematic relationship between obscenity and free literary and artistic expression. The second article advanced the concept of "variable obscenity"—"a chameleonic quality of material that changes with time, place, and circumstance," and "is judged by its appeal to and effect upon the audience" to which it is "primarily directed."

Kalven's piece, entitled "The Metaphysics of the Law of Obscenity," was a brilliant analysis of the *Roth* opinion within the context of the Court's First Amendment jurisprudence. He criticized what Brennan had done or, perhaps, what he had not done: the opinion's "irritating . . . oversimplification," its question-begging aspects, the unacceptable logic that appeared "to lead to the conclusion that, in [Brennan's and the Court's] view, such books as *Lady Chatterley's Lover*, *Memoirs of Hecate County*, and *Strange Fruit*, all of which had been held 'obscene' by distinguished courts, are in the category of speech which is 'utterly without redeeming social importance.' '' That last (single quoted) phrase had been the *reason* Brennan gave in *Roth* for excluding obscenity from the constitutional protections of free speech and press. This was an exclusion that he claimed to have found "implicit" in the history of the First Amendment and "mirrored in the universal judgment that obscenity should be restrained."

Kalven knew that despite its shortcomings *Roth* was unlikely, so soon, to be overruled and replaced by another definition. In order to make the best of a bad metaphysical situation, he proposed an interpretation of *Roth* that, if adopted by the Court, would turn *Roth* into a vehicle for "a major advance in liberating literature and art from the censor." To do this Kalven turned Brennan's reasoning in *Roth* on its head: "If," Kalven said, tracking Brennan's logic, "the obscene is constitutionally subject to ban because it is worthless [i.e., utterly without redeeming social importance], it must follow that the obscene can include only that which is worthless." For Kalven, "worthless" material included "so-called hard-core pornography," which he described as "discussions of sex which are not integral parts of anything else." If the "socially worthless" criterion, alluded to in *Roth*, was hereafter to be "taken seriously" in obscenity court cases, then books, magazines, films, and other works of art would be invulnerable to government censorship. Kalven thus offered the Supreme Court a logical way out of the corner it had painted itself into—when in *Roth*, Brennan described, but did not *define*, the "obscene" as "worthless" or "utterly without redeeming social importance."[3]

"Tropic of Cancer" and a National Standard

If Harlan's criterion of "patent offensiveness" had determined whether *Tropic of Cancer*, by Henry Miller, was obscene, the work probably would have been found obscene. "Patently offensive" was one of the nicer terms attributed to this novel, but to poet Karl Shapiro it was "a poem in the best and broadest sense of the word." Edmund Wilson referred to it as the "epitaph for the whole generation of writers and artists" who migrated to Paris following World War I. And to critic Horace Gregory it was a "triumph of the comic spirit."

The *Tropic of Cancer* case is particularly significant because it represented the first effective request of the Supreme Court to mandate a uniform national standard for the protection of sexually oriented material. In addition, it was the first case in which the Supreme Court held a specific literary or artistic work "not obscene" and constitutionally protected—for the entire nation. Defying a 27-year legal ban, the book had been released in an American edition by Barney Rosset's avant-garde Grove Press. Litigation promptly developed in 21 states. Rosset's publishing, and later, film distribution activities made Grove an important force in the development of a new sexual openness and a new radical politics in American life, but the expenses incurred to defend *Tropic of Cancer* all over the country wiped out its profits and left the small publishing house on the edge of financial disaster. Grove defended booksellers even when it was without legal obligation to do so. The results were a mixed bag. When an intermediate appellate court in Florida upheld a Dade County jury's finding of the book obscene, Grove decided to appeal to the United States Supreme Court and asked lawyer Edward de Grazia to undertake the job.

At this time, Rosset had in his warehouse other books, including Miller's *Tropic of Capricorn* and William Burroughs's *Naked Lunch*, which he feared to sell because of the unpredictable legal and financial consequences. Grove finally published them when de Grazia agreed to defend them. In July 1966, *Naked Lunch* was found not obscene and constitutionally protected by the Massachusetts Supreme Court in a case handled by de Grazia (*Attorney General* v. *Naked Lunch*). De Grazia had written an *amicus* brief on behalf of the American Civil Liberties Union in defense of Samuel Yudkin's sale of *Tropic of Cancer* when the bookseller had been convicted and was appealing to the Court of Appeals of Maryland. This brief defended the novel as a work of art and, pressing Kalven's thesis, also argued that the Constitution must protect any "recognizable" work of literature or art. The brief was widely circulated and de Grazia was asked to formulate a new policy on obscenity for the ACLU to replace the "clear and present danger" test, which the *Roth* decision had rendered useless.

De Grazia's petition for *certiorari*, asking the Supreme Court to hear the Florida *Tropic of Cancer* case, emphasized four points: (1) *Tropic of Cancer* was "a work of literature, not a piece of pornography," and (citing Kalven's article) was certainly not "*worthless* obscenity"; (2) since, on the contrary, it had "literary, artistic, or other social importance," it could not be condemned; (3) the lower courts erroneously had made no judgment independent of the jury's as to whether the book was entitled to constitutional protection; and (4) the jury had been required to evaluate the book's obscenity exclusively on the basis of local standards, whereas a unified national standard should have been mandated. He had, he felt, "a hundred-to-one chance" of persuading the Court to consider the case.

At this same time, the Supreme Court had before it a case dealing with French filmmaker Louis Malle's movie *The Lovers* [49]. Nico Jacobellis, the manager of a suburban Cleveland theater, had been convicted for showing this allegedly obscene picture and had appealed. The Court first heard the argument in the spring of 1963, after which Justice Brennan drafted a short *per curiam* opinion, reversing the conviction on the ground that the movie was not obscene. But the justices were unsatisfied and wished to explore further the matter of a national standard, on which no consensus within the Court had developed. The case was reargued, and the opposing lawyers were questioned on the point although the briefs had not considered it.

Brennan's judgment for the Court in *Jacobellis* v. *Ohio* announced:

> We do not see how any "local" definition of the "community" could properly be employed in delineating the area of expression that is protected by the Constitution. . . . To sustain the suppression of a particular book or film in one locality would deter its dissemination in other localities where it might be held not obscene, since sellers and exhibitors would be reluctant to risk criminal conviction in testing the variation between the two places. . . . The constitutional status of an allegedly obscene work must be determined on the basis of a national standard. It is, after all, a national Constitution we are expounding.

Justice Stewart wrote a short concurring opinion. In *Roth*, he admitted, the Court was "trying to define what may be undefinable," and its decisions since then, he felt, seemed to have limited what could be suppressed to "hard-core pornography." But what was hard-core pornography? "I shall not," Stewart said, "today attempt further to define the kinds of materials I understand to be embraced within that shorthand definition; and perhaps I could never succeed in intelligibly doing so. But I know it when I see it, and the motion picture involved in this case is not that." His was a memorable answer that demonstrated the degree to which a judgment is inherently intuitive and subjective regarding what is and what is not obscene. Stewart came to regret his definition. When he retired in 1981, he said the phrase " 'I know it when I see it' [is] going to be engraved on my tombstone," even though "it's far from deathless."

Six obscenity cases, including the *Tropic of Cancer* appeal, had been held over until *Jacobellis* v. *Ohio* could be decided. On June 18, 1964, Brennan circulated a memorandum within the Court stating that he had read *Tropic of Cancer*, along with a book in another case, and did "not think they are obscene under the *Roth* standard. I would grant [*certiorari*] and reverse citing *Roth*." At its weekly conference the following day, the Court decided, five to four, to grant the petition for *certiorari* in the *Tropic of Cancer* case and summarily reverse the lower court judgment in a *per curiam* opinion that Brennan prepared. Justices Black, Douglas, Brennan, Stewart, and Arthur J. Goldberg voted to reverse for the same reasons given in their *Jacobellis* opinions, handed down the same day, while Chief Justice Warren and Justices Clark, Harlan, and Byron R. White would not have heard the case at all. No briefs on the "merits" were submitted nor argument held. *Tropic of Cancer* could now be sold anywhere in the United States.

The decisions in the *Tropic of Cancer* and *Jacobellis* cases established several new and significant points: (1) Courts were required (they "cannot avoid") to make an independent constitutional judgment "whether the material involved is obscene." This meant that no trial judge or jury could have the final say on a book or film's alleged obscenity. (2) The only proper "community standards" to be applied in determining whether a work was "patently offensive" was a "national standard." A local standard had "the intolerable consequence of denying some sections of the country access to material, there deemed acceptable, which in others might be considered offensive to prevailing community standards of decency." (3) A work could not be proscribed as obscene "unless it is 'utterly' without social importance." If it "has literary or scientific or artistic value or any other form of social importance," it "may not be branded as 'obscenity' and denied the constitutional protection." To make plain that "any social importance" should free a work from forfeiting constitutional protection, even if it otherwise seemed obscene, Brennan added: "Nor may the constitutional status of the material be made to turn on a 'weighing' of its social importance against its prurient appeal, for a work cannot be proscribed unless it is 'utterly' without social importance."

Brennan, as Kalven had urged, turned *Roth* on its head. The only sexually oriented expression that could now be deemed constitutionally obscene was "worthless" matter, "utterly without social importance." Once this revision of *Roth* made its way into courtrooms across the nation, defenders of free expression had a new and powerful constitutional lever to use against censors.

In his opinion in *The Lovers* case (*Jacobellis* v. *Ohio*), Justice Brennan applied those points de Grazia had raised in his *certiorari* petition on behalf of *Tropic of Cancer*. The book had reached the Court too late in the term to permit oral argument or the writing of a full-scale opinion, which, in any event, might have invited criticism. It might well have been politically injudicious to have announced a radical reconstruction of *Roth* in a case involving a widely known but sexually explicit work and a controversial publisher, when an alternative was readily available in the case of *The Lovers* and the unknown exhibitor Nico Jacobellis.[4]

By the time she appeared in the Supreme Court in 1966, *Fanny Hill* was a much litigated young woman. Her timing had improved over the years, for the Supreme Court was now moving toward excluding from constitutional protection only socially "worthless" or "hard-core" materials. However, as one justice conceded, a majority had "not yet" reached that point. The "woman of pleasure" sped the Court's arrival. Her "memoirs" did not reveal her techniques; that was left for her lawyer Charles Rembar: all were agreed that she had very slight redeeming value.

Once again, Justice Brennan delivered the judgment of the Court. He restated the *Roth* definition of obscenity as improved upon in the *Manual Enterprises* case ("patently offensive" added) and the *Jacobellis* and *Tropic of Cancer* cases ("utterly without social importance" added):

> [I]t must be established that (a) the dominant theme of the material taken as a whole appeals to a prurient interest in sex; (b) the material is patently offensive because it affronts contemporary community standards; and (c) the material is utterly without redeeming social value.

This formulation included no new factor; but it combined the previously announced ingredients into a single, three-pronged rule. "A book cannot be proscribed," Brennan emphasized, "unless it is found to be *utterly* without redeeming social value. This is so even though the book is found to possess the requisite prurient appeal and to be patently offensive. Each of the three federal constitutional criteria is to be applied independently; the social value of the book can neither be weighed against nor canceled by its prurient appeal or patent offensiveness." This point was important because its absence permitted courts to deem material obscene and undeserving of constitutional protection, notwithstanding its ("outweighed") possession of social value. Without the caveat that a work's social value was not to be "weighed" against its sexual components, the legal status of books and movies in the United States was similar to their status in England, where works of admitted "merit" may nonetheless be found obscene and banned, if they are believed also to have the tendency to corrupt the morals of those into whose hands they might fall. That is a nonconstitutionally protected status.

To Justice Clark, dissenting, the new Brennan doctrine was too much: the book was "nothing more than a series of minutely and vividly described sexual episodes." "In view of Brother Clark's passion for detail," Justice Douglas quipped to the brethren, "why don't we all chip in and buy him a copy of *My Life and Loves*, by Frank Harris, published by Grove Press?"

A Book Named "John Cleland's Memoirs of a Woman of Pleasure" v. *Attorney General* was one of three obscenity cases decided in March 1966. The Court was deeply fragmented in those cases, with 14 opinions written in all. It acted, however, to uphold criminal convictions of the publishers of printed materials in the other two: Ralph Ginzburg, for "pandering" his publications, *Eros*, *Liaison*, and *The Housewife's Handbook on Selective Promiscuity*, and Edward Mishkin, for producing and selling sadomasochistic books laying no claim to social value. These led Justice Black to conclude in dissent that "not even the most learned judge, much less a layman, is capable of knowing in advance of an ultimate decision in his particular case by this Court whether certain material comes within the area of 'obscenity' as that term is confused by the Court today." The law of obscenity plainly was a "constitutional disaster area" for some; but, in the absence of special circumstances, it was largely supposed that all except hard-core materials might now circulate freely.

The setback by the Supreme Court had made Times Film Corporation and Felix Bilgrey the more determined to defeat "city-hall censorship" of the Chicago type. Bilgrey, who also was counsel to the International Film Importers and Distributors Association, was called one day by a Baltimore exhibitor named Ronald Freedman who wanted to overturn Maryland's system of film censorship. Several times Freedman had fought with the Maryland board for the freedom to show "exploitation" films with scenes the censors had specifically told him to remove. And despite, or perhaps because of, his winning appellate court decisions overturning the board rulings, Freedman was now a man with a cause. Bilgrey considered it "the opportunity of a lifetime," suggesting a course that Freedman agreed to follow: he was to exhibit an unobjectionable picture in his Baltimore theater without the required license in order to challenge the validity of the Maryland law, and his local lawyer and Bilgrey would defend him as far as the case needed to go. Times Film recommended a movie, *Revenge at Daybreak* [58], about the Irish revolution of 1916–1917. The issue not presented in the *Don Juan* case could be squarely presented in this case: whether a criminal conviction based solely on an exhibitor's refusal to submit an unobjectionable picture in advance of its public screening (an action required by the Maryland censorship law) violated his rights of free speech and press.

When Ronald Freedman was arrested, the marquee over his theater read "Fight for Freedom of the Screen." He had called the press to publicize his action, and the battle began. The MPAA immediately grasped the importance of the case and gave the movie a Code seal of approval. But the MPAA decided not to participate as *amicus* if the case reached the Supreme Court. The Maryland courts duly convicted Freedman, and his case rose to the high Court in 1965. This time Brennan, not Clark, wrote the Court's opinion; there was no dissent. It was a landmark opinion: a censor board could no longer act to bar a film without prompt judicial supervision.

Brennan announced:

> We hold that a noncriminal process which requires the prior submission of a film to a censor avoids constitutional infirmity only if it takes place under procedural safeguards designed to obviate the dangers of a censorship system.

First, the burden of proving that the film is unprotected expression must rest on the censor. . . . Second, while the State may require advance submission of all films, in order to proceed effectively to bar all showings of unprotected films, the requirement cannot be administered in a manner which would lend an effect of finality to the censor's determination whether a film constitutes protected expression. . . . The exhibitor must be assured, by statute or authoritative judicial construction, that the censor will, within a specified brief period, either issue a license or go to court to restrain showing the film. Any restraint imposed in advance of a final judicial determination on the merits must similarly be limited to preservation of the status quo for the shortest fixed period compatible with sound judicial resolution. . . . The procedure must also assure a prompt final judicial decision, to minimize the deterrent effect of an interim and possibly erroneous denial of a license.[5]

Stanley v. *Georgia*

In 1968, Richard Nixon campaigned for the presidency on a "law and order" platform in which the stamping out of obscenity was a strong plank. In 1969, President Nixon made his first appointment to the Supreme Court, Chief Justice Warren E. Burger, who had been a conservative judge on the Court of Appeals for the District of Columbia. Before this appointment, however, the Court expanded the "ambit of intellectual effort which the First Amendment was designed to protect" in *Stanley* v. *Georgia*. Police obtained a warrant to search Stanley's home for evidence of unlawful bookmaking activities; instead, they found films that, when viewed, appeared to them to be obscene. The films were seized and introduced as evidence in his trial, not for bookmaking, but for possessing obscene materials. The "mere possession of obscene matter," Justice Thurgood Marshall announced in reversing the conviction, "cannot constitutionally be made a crime."

> [The First Amendment] right to receive information and ideas, regardless of their social worth, is fundamental to our free society. . . . Also fundamental is the right to be free, except in very limited circumstances, from unwarranted intrusions into one's privacy. . . . Whatever may be the justifications for other statutes regulating obscenity, we do not think they reach into the privacy of one's own home. If the Amendment means anything, it means that a State has no business telling a man, sitting alone in his own house, what books he may read or what films he may watch. Our whole constitutional heritage rebels at the thought of giving government the power to control men's minds.

The opinion the Court handed down in April 1969 was somewhat narrower than in preliminary drafts. Marshall had originally written, "It is now well established that the Constitution protects the rights to receive, as well as to distribute, information and ideas." Justice Harlan objected to the phrase "as well as to distribute" because "the suggestion of a correlation between the right to distribute and the right to receive might carry implications of dilution with respect to our other obscenity cases (which are concerned solely with the right to sell), which I am sure your opinion does not intend." What Harlan was diplomatically pointing out to Marshall was that the Court, in *Roth*, had maintained there was no constitutional right to distribute obscene material. Unless *Roth* were to be repudiated, the rationale for reversing Stanley's conviction for possessing obscenity had to be grounded on a distinguishable proposition—the recognition of a right (not to distribute but) to receive and possess obscenity. *Roth* had held that the distribution of obscenity was *excluded* from the protection of the First Amendment. *Stanley* held that a man's possession and enjoyment of obscenity—the right to read and observe what he pleases—at home, was *included* within the protections of the First Amendment and a constitutionally derived "right of privacy." Of the other justices, besides Harlan, who concurred in Marshall's opinion (Brennan, the author of *Roth*, was conspicuously absent), Chief Justice Warren retired at the end of the Court's term; Fortas would soon be driven to resign; and opponents of Douglas would move to have him impeached. But *Stanley* v. *Georgia* had established the very important proposition that in the privacy of the home even obscenity was a constitutionally protected expression.[6]

Protection
Amidst Turbulence

By the mid-1960s, the motion picture industry was undergoing one of its periodic upheavals. The moviegoing public was younger than ever, and by 1968 nearly half the audience was between the ages of 16 and 24. A new group of directors, actors, and actresses commanded attention. In 1963, the president of the Motion Picture Association of America, Eric Johnston, died and a search began for a Democratic replacement. Theodore C. Sorenson and Lawrence F. O'Brien, aides to the assassinated President Kennedy, were mentioned as possibilities. Adlai Stevenson, twice the Democratic candidate for president, "declined" the post (although it was never officially offered to him). When Jack Valenti, special assistant to President Lyndon B. Johnson, was offered the position, he accepted and in May 1966 became the third head of the association. The industry, in a time of declining fortunes, again had a pipeline to the White House.

Valenti immediately turned his attention to reconsideration of the Code. The Code's administrator, Geoffrey Shurlock, certified more films than ever without changes. It was at this time, in 1966, that a new film challenged the Code's profanity provisions. The film was the screen adaptation of Edward Albee's play, *Who's Afraid of Virginia Woolf?*, with Elizabeth Taylor and Richard Burton. The Code administration denied the movie a seal; but on appeal, the MPAA's board of directors approved the film after its producer, Warner Brothers, agreed to make concessions. Scenes were cut and some objectionable dialogue changed. ("Screw you!" was replaced by "Goddam you!") But, more important, at Valenti's suggestion Warner Brothers agreed to advertise the picture as "Suggested for Mature Audiences" (SMA) and inserted into all contracts with exhibitors a clause prohibiting anyone under 18 from seeing it unless accompanied by a parent. This was an unprecedented strategy in motion picture distribution. Previously, the industry had opposed the adoption of any practice that might exclude a portion of its customers, especially minors. Now, even the National Catholic Office for Motion Pictures, as the Legion of Decency had renamed itself, rated the film "morally unobjectionable."

In September 1966, the MPAA board issued a streamlined version of the Code, which allowed certain types of films to be labeled as "Suggested for Mature Audiences." It directed that the label be used "cautiously" and only when a film's subject matter was "blatant." This was a successful innovation, but not without difficulties. When the Code office rejected several nude scenes in Michelangelo Antonioni's *Blow-Up*, the film's distributor, Metro-Goldwyn-Mayer, released it without a seal through a subsidiary company that was not a signatory to the Code agreement. Despite condemnation by the National Catholic Office of Motion Pictures, the movie was an artistic and financial success. When this happened again, the MPAA changed direction, for such avoidance undermined the authority of the seal and the Code. The Code office was told to set aside the "blatant" criterion for issuance of the SMA seal and instead to "warn" parents that a movie "might not be suitable" for children. The upshot of this change was that now 60 percent of all pictures examined were placed in the SMA category. After a third of a century, the Code had perhaps outlived its usefulness and the Motion Picture Association of America had to consider exactly what might replace it.

In 1967, Congress passed a resolution creating a presidential commission, the Commission on Obscenity and Pornography, to study the "causal relationship of [sexually oriented] materials to anti-social behavior," especially in minors, and to recommend "appropriate and constitutional means to deal effectively" with obscenity and pornography. President Johnson appointed its members early the next year, with William Lockhart, the leading academic expert on obscenity law, as chairman. Realizing the sensitivity of the undertaking, Lockhart urged the members to treat all commission matters confidentially. He knew, he later said, that "we'd be pilloried no matter what we did. Right-thinking people were the only ones I cared about." "Of course," he added, "those were the ones who thought the way I did." Panels were appointed, research projects in different disciplines assigned, and the commission was scheduled to report to the President and the country in two years. Conservatives evidently hoped that the report might show some causal connection existed between "obscene" materials and crime and juvenile delinquency.[1]

"*Viva Maria*"

In March 1968, two Supreme Court cases concerning the access of minors to "obscene" books and "harmful" films helped determine the type of system of self-regulation the industry now adopted. In a case arising out of the Dallas censorship of the French film *Viva Maria* [67], the Court struck down an ordinance providing for the classification of movies as suitable or not suitable for minors. *Viva Maria*, a zany western released in 1965, starred Jeanne Moreau and Brigitte Bardot; Louis Malle was the director. Moreau and Bardot, a traveling music hall/circus team, were swept up in the revolutionary events of peasants in San Miguel. The action included a pigeon dropping hand grenades, Bardot swinging through trees, and a circus strong man who bent jailhouse bars, to allow Moreau to make love to her chained lover. Dallas censors feared the movie would "incite or encourage crime, delinquency, or sexual promiscuity" and classified it so that no one under 16 could be admitted, even with a parent. The Supreme Court, however, freed the film for general exhibition when it struck down the Dallas law because of its "vagueness" and "failure to place any limits on the censor's discretion."

The positive response of the movie industry to this decision was only slightly lessened by another decision involving censorship for minors that was delivered by the Supreme Court the same day. The case, *Ginsberg* v. *New York*, involved the criminal conviction of the owner of "Sam's Stationery and Luncheonette" in Bellemore, Long Island. He had sold "girlie" magazines to a 16-year-old. The boy had been enlisted by his mother to go to the store and buy them, so that its owner could be arrested and prosecuted. The New York law prohibited anyone from knowingly selling to a minor "any material that depicts nudity" and that is "harmful to minors." The "harmful to minors" criterion was as vague on its face and as questionable constitutionally as the "not suitable for young persons" standard voided in the *Viva Maria* case. However, the Supreme Court read the New York law as "virtually identical to [its own] most recent statement of the elements of obscenity," in the *Fanny Hill* case. The statute thus gave persons "adequate notice of what is prohibited" and was construed to outlaw the sale of printed materials that were constitutionally obscene to minors.

In effect, the Court ruling implied that minors did not have the same constitutional rights to freedom of expression as adults. As Justice Stewart put the point, in his separate concurring opinion: "[A] child—like someone in a captive audience—is not possessed of that full capacity for individual choice which is the presupposition of First Amendment guarantees. It is only upon such a premise, I should suppose, that a state may deprive children of other rights—the right to marry, for example, or the right to vote—deprivations that would be constitutionally intolerable for adults." Justice Brennan's majority opinion, however, noted that New York's "prohibition against sales to minors does not bar parents who so desire from purchasing the [forbidden] magazines for their children." The *Ginsberg* and *Viva Maria* decisions encouraged the movie industry, under Valenti's leadership, to abandon the Production Code and move toward the adoption of an age classification system.

These decisions, concerning what limitations might constitutionally be placed upon movies and magazines read by young people, came before the Court within the context of national turmoil. Three weeks earlier, President Johnson had announced he would not seek re-election. Martin Luther King, Jr., had been assassinated two weeks earlier. In the rioting that followed, the National Guard protected the Capitol building for the first time since the Civil War—its guns on the east portico pointing towards the Supreme Court building across the street. Five weeks later, Robert F. Kennedy was assassinated while campaigning for the Democratic nomination.

The country was also in the midst of a cultural polarity. Virtually all matter that was openly printed or screened received legal protection, presuming it possessed the required modicum of social value. Law enforcement officials were occupied with attempts to contain the protests of opponents of the Vietnam War. A sexual revolution was advanced by the contraceptive "pill"; and the "permissive society"—in speech, life-style, and outlook—represented a new freedom. More than ever, films reflected reality; like the generation to which they appealed, they were more direct, explicit, and daring. Meanwhile, traditionalists sought to protect time-tested values.[2]

Following the *Viva Maria* and *Ginsberg* cases in 1968, President Johnson nominated Justice Abe Fortas as Chief Justice to replace the retiring Earl Warren. One of the witnesses at the Senate hearings was James J. Clancy, an attorney for the Citizens for Decent Literature. By coincidence, he was in Washington to meet with several members of Congress in order to urge the introduction of stronger legislation against sending obscene material through the mail. "The smut industry," he charged, "takes its direction from the Supreme Court, advancing a giant step forward each time that the United States Supreme Court hands down a decision adverse to the people's interest. How much longer are the parents, the Christian people, the wholesome people, the right-thinking people going to put up with this kind of thing?"

Senator Strom Thurmond decided to show in the hearing room of the Senate several films the Court had freed. One of his aims evidently was to discredit Fortas as unduly permissive in the obscenity area. Earlier in 1968, Fortas had dissented vigorously, for example, from the criminal conviction in the *Ginsberg* case. Thurmond invited the press, as well as members of the Senate, to the viewing. A senator present said that such pictures were a "scandalization of the womanhood of the United States and of the world. If the nominee were my brother, I would not vote for him." The senators ignored the fact that Fortas was no radical on the obscenity issue. He had helped Justice Brennan construct the "pandering" theory used to uphold publisher Ralph Ginzburg's federal criminal conviction in 1966, and was a pragmatic liberal. The "absolute" approach to the First Amendment, to which Justices Black and Douglas were devoted, was to Fortas more of a philosophical abstraction, more an ideal, than a practical reality. He expressed sympathy with their views, but said they were "whoring after principle." Fortas did not become Chief Justice for other reasons, but the opposition to the judicial viewpoint he represented only intensified, and in 1969 he resigned from the high court. (Fortas returned to the Supreme Court for the first time in 13 years in March 1982, arguing a case that involved Puerto Rico's election laws. Presiding was Chief Justice Warren E. Burger, whose very seat President Johnson had wanted him to fill. Two weeks later, the 71-year-old former justice died in Washington, D.C.)[3]

The Age-Classification System

In this atmosphere Jack Valenti decided the MPAA should move quickly if it were to forestall a series of new censorship statutes, purportedly designed to protect children. By the time of the *Ginsberg* and *Viva Maria* decisions in 1968, one house of the New York legislature had already passed a film age-classification statute. Dallas began rewriting its invalidated code, and legislation was proposed in California to establish a state board of review in order to determine a picture's suitability for children and require exhibitors to advertise as such. The head of the National Association of Theater Owners, representing three-quarters of the country's movie houses, stated that the invalidated Dallas ordinance would have meant that half the current films (including box-office hits like *The Graduate* and *Bonnie and Clyde*) could not be shown to young people.

The idea of classification was not new. As far back as Will Hays's day, it had been discussed, and Chicago and New York censors had experimented with it earlier. Hays claimed classification did not have enough public support to work, even though the Legion of Decency had employed its own classification system. Under Johnston it had been considered at length and the MPAA staff suggested that he bring it before the Board of Governors, but he "never made that determination," notes Kenneth Clark, currently vice president of the association. He "didn't think the time was right." And the studio heads, fearing adverse exhibitor reaction, turned a deaf ear to the proposal. Now, however, the industry considered adopting some such system to ward off governmental intervention and financial loss. Almost all MPAA members by this time were receptive to a rating system even if differences remained regarding its form. Valenti met with studio heads, producers, distributors, and exhibitors to obtain the necessary support. Louis

Nizer, the MPAA's general counsel, thought that classification "would give public notice" that the industry was "doing everything possible to distinguish between adult entertainment," which the Supreme Court had freed for adults, and "films suitable for all ages." The final product reflected the competing interests of various groups.

Under this new system, still in effect, all films produced or distributed by MPAA members and, therefore, most movies shown in the United States, are submitted to the Code and Rating Administration, which issues a preliminary "probable" rating, including "suggestions" for changes that may improve upon the probable rating. When the finished films are viewed, CARA's objections are stated so that producers will know what changes they must make to obtain a less restrictive rating. The official ratings are:

G—suggested for general audiences, including children of all ages;

PG—parental guidance suggested, as some material may not be suitable for pre-teenagers;

R—restricted; persons under 17 are not admitted unless accompanied by parent or adult guardian;

X—persons under 17 not admitted.

These ratings, according to the MPAA, are not qualitative but only inform the public of a picture's suitability for children.

The standards applied to determine the ratings are those rewritten in connection with the Code's 1966 streamlining; they include: upholding the dignity of human life, exercising restraint in portraying juvenile crime, not demeaning religion, and prohibiting extreme violence and brutality, as well as obscene speech, gestures, or movements. Finally, sexual content and nudity are to be limited. A film rated G, PG, or R can receive the MPAA seal of approval, but an X-rated movie cannot; the rating must appear on all prints of the picture distributed in the United States and in all advertising for the film, which must be approved by the Code's director of advertising. A producer dissatisfied with the classification of a film may appeal to the Code and Rating Appeals Board, which includes the head of the MPAA, 12 of its board members, studio officials, eight members of the NATO Board, two members each from the Producers Guild of America and IFIDA distributors, for a total of 25. A two-thirds vote of the board is necessary to uphold an X rating, while a majority vote suffices to confirm other CARA decisions.

Although the new classification system has been attacked by some as an unconstitutional restraint on freedom of screen expression, the system has inhibited the enactment of new governmental censorship legislation aimed to protect children. Governmental systems protecting minors are operating, however, in Chicago, Dallas, and other cities. Complaints do arise periodically that CARA is not harsh enough in rating films and that films of major studios often receive most favorable ratings.

Apart from the above ordinances, and the federal customs law, the MPAA's classification system is currently the only prescreening restriction on freedom of the screen. Its "obligation," claimed Valenti, is "to reflect the contemporary opinion of parents"; the aim is the protection of children. Major changes made since its inception have reflected a liberalization of community standards. Sexual language and material that once earned a picture an X rating now produce an R rating, although "hard-core" material still receives an X rating. The X ratings, which were previously applied mostly in the area of sex, are now applied to violence as well. Films formerly rated PG for violence are now rated R. And finally, pictures containing strong language and language that is sexually oriented may receive R ratings. Since most box-office hits are rated either PG or R, a producer may include a few profane words to bring about such a rating. But neither designation informs parents or children why it was conferred—whether the R rating was due to the sex, violence, strong and possibly offensive language, all, or some combination. The PG rating does not indicate to parents specifically what to watch for in choosing films.

The usefulness of the rating system has been increasingly questioned by its critics. As to the X rating, film critic William Wolf observed, the "very choice of the letter (why not Y or Z?) connotes a crossing out, a negative," implying disapproval. The picture *Cruising*, about a psychopathic killer who has sexual relations with homosexuals and then mutilates them with a knife, was given an R rating. The film *Raiders of the Lost Ark*, which attracted an audience of children as well as adults, contains images of melting skulls, snakes, and dozens of violent deaths; it received a rating of PG. Though the Code and Rating Administration may be less than an ideal system and though it may restrict the artistic freedom of the filmmaker, it is not government censorship. Nevertheless, by prohibiting anyone under 17 from seeing certain films, it usurps the rights of parents to give children access to expression they may deem suitable. Minors may also be prevented from viewing what they are constitutionally entitled to see.[4]

"I Am Curious—Yellow"

On a Sunday in September 1966, Sweden's greatest film director, Ingmar Bergman, was dining with his protégé, Vilgot Sjöman, in Stockholm. They spoke of many things, including Sjöman's falling out with the production company, Svensk Filmindustri. Sjöman's spirits rose a little when he told Bergman about a new film he wanted to make with the young actress Lena Nyman. Bergman recalled the previous year when he had "lost the taste for everything. The only idea that cheered me up was being able to make a film with Bibi [Andersson] and Liv [Ullmann]." As Bergman had gone on to make that film, the haunting *Persona*, so Sjöman made his shocking *I Am Curious—Yellow*. In it, Lena Nyman broke, under Sjöman's direction, just about every sexual taboo listed in the MPAA Production Code, and box-office records as well.

An earlier Sjöman film called *491* had been stopped by U.S. Customs; after a federal court ruled that it was obscene, an appellate court reversed and ruled that the film could enter the country. Written by the Swedish author Lars Gorling from his novel of the same name, the script called for a teenage actress to appear nude. Sjöman had been disgruntled at having to defer to what he called Hollywood "clichés." He could not direct or portray her nude. The results also dissatisfied him because the actress had to wear gauze coverings in the "nude" scenes and the male lead flesh-colored tights. It was then he resolved that one day he would make a film in which actors would be nude when they were supposed to be nude. If they were supposed to be making love, wherever it was—on a mattress or on a floor—he would film them making love. And he did.

Once Sjöman began breaking sexual taboos in the film *I Am Curious—Yellow*, he did not stop until he had filmed Lena and her young lover in the nude in what were the most controversial series of sexual scenes in the history of movies. As Judge Paul R. Hays said for the Federal Second Circuit Court of Appeals, which viewed the film after its seizure by U.S. Customs:

> There are a number of scenes which show the young girl and her lover nude. Several scenes depict sexual intercourse under varying circumstances, some of them quite unusual. There are scenes of oral genital activity. It seems to be conceded that the sexual content of the film is presented with greater explicitness than has been seen in any other film produced for general viewing.

Nevertheless, overriding the jury, the court found the movie constitutionally protected and not obscene. Chief Judge J. Edward Lumbard dissented. "Except for the sexual scenes," he complained, the film "was a continuous and unrelieved boredom." Those scenes had interest mainly "from the uncertainty of the method of mutual sexual gratification in which hero and heroine will next indulge." Furthermore, "while the sex was heterosexual, the participants engage in acts of fellatio and cunnilingus. Needless to say, these acts have no conceivable relevance to any social value, except that of box-office appeal."

Although the sexual scenes accounted for approximately ten minutes of the film's two hours, Chief Judge Lumbard was disturbed by the "enormous visual impact of a motion picture as distinguished from other media. . . . The combination of sight and sound, in the darkness of a movie theater, results in a uniquely forceful impact on the audience." Therefore, he claimed, "Sexual scenes in a motion picture may transcend the bounds of constitutional protection long before a frank description of the same scenes in a book or magazine." That, however, was an argument that the contemporary Supreme Court had rejected.

It was an old argument. In 1915, the Supreme Court had ruled that movies were not entitled to constitutional protection because, in part, they were "mere representations of events, of ideas and sentiments published and known, vivid, useful, and entertaining no doubt, but as we have said, capable of evil, having power for it, the greater because of their attractiveness and manner of exhibition." But the modern Court, in 1952, nullified that hoary proposition. In *The Miracle* case, the Supreme Court said that "any greater capacity for evil" that movies might be presumed to have did not warrant "disqualifying them from First Amendment protection."

The importer and distributor of *I Am Curious—Yellow* was Grove Press, owned by Barney Rosset, which had also published *Tropic of Cancer*. At the time, the FBI, the CIA, and the Army were keeping Rosset and his firm under surveillance; for example, intelligence files were maintained. According to the Rockefeller Commission report of 1975, Grove was the only American publisher whose activities were monitored. In 1965, its political magazine, *Evergreen Review*, carried Ché Guevara on the cover as a sort of "Man of the Year." Shortly thereafter, its building in New York's Greenwich Village was bombed, presumably by anti-Castro Cuban exiles. A group of young women then raided Grove's offices, protesting against its "sado-masochistic literature and pornographic films that dehumanize and degrade women." Rosset believes the FBI and CIA backed these and other actions. Given what is now known about American intelligence "black-bag" operations, penetrations into sensitive communications institutions and relations with the Cuban exile community, his suspicions are not to be dismissed out of hand.

Rosset asked Edward de Grazia, who handled the Supreme Court case that freed *Tropic of Cancer*, and New York publishing lawyer Richard Gallen to try to free *I Am Curious—Yellow* from Customs. Despite the testimony of 12 expert witnesses that the film was an important, not a worthless, motion picture, having substantial artistic and ideological values, a federal jury concluded it was obscene. Among the witnesses at the trial were film critic John Simon, then of *The New Leader*, currently of *New York* magazine; Stanley Kauffmann of *The New Republic*; Paul Zimmerman of *Newsweek*; novelist Norman Mailer; Professor Charles Winick of the City College of New York; the Reverend Dr. Howard Moody of the Judson Memorial Church in New York; and the film's director, Vilgot Sjöman.

Sjöman testified that his film was an attempt to "make a portrait of Sweden right now." The movie was "built around Lena" as a focus for that theme—"a girl who asks for the same freedom as men always have done, and who is sort of unconscious of what is going on inside her." She is a "portrait of a new kind of female, young female, coming in the front light of our country." On cross examination concerning the sexual scenes, the director said he had tried to "break away from the ordinary way of presenting very arranged love scenes, and to approach reality and reconstruct reality, and to give the audience the feeling that this is more likely to be the real behavior than what is shown in many other films. But I must add one thing: that part of the intention was also to satirize, as there is also a lot of parody. . . ." The government's lawyer was also "curious" and questioned Sjöman closely about one scene: "Did Lena actually kiss [her lover's] penis?" The director responded: "Do you mean if her lips actually touched his penis?" When the lawyer said "yes," Sjöman continued: "I can't answer that because I wasn't that close, and I can't tell from the image either. I have a feeling it was possible for her just to have her lips a couple of millimeters above the penis. If she actually touched it or not, I didn't ask her and I didn't ask him either."

It was plain to de Grazia and Gallen that the film was entitled to constitutional protection. The government's lawyers had argued that the images communicated by movies were far more vivid and dangerous than those presented by the printed word. The answer given by the film's lawyers was that movie audiences can as readily shut their eyes to objectionable images as book readers can close the cover of books upon confronting objectionable passages. Even if one thought that the picture had breached contemporary community standards with respect to the description of sexual acts, there was no question, according to the lawyers and expert witnesses, that its dominant theme was not an appeal to prurient interests in sex and no doubt that, as Judge Hays said, the film "had unquestionable social importance." Its values were far more evident than those of the book *Fanny Hill*, for example, which the Supreme Court had cleared of a Massachusetts charge of being obscene. After the appellate court ruled that the Customs Service and the federal jury could not keep *I Am Curious—Yellow* out of the country on the claim that it was obscene, the Department of Justice debated whether to appeal the case to the Supreme Court.

Will Wilson, the Assistant Attorney General for the Criminal Division, wanted to ask the high court to reverse the court of appeals' action freeing *I Am Curious—Yellow*, but Solicitor General Erwin Griswold, former dean of the Harvard Law School, did not consider such an appeal propitious and declined to ask the Supreme Court to review. There is little doubt that the Court, at the time, would have upheld the film's right to constitutional protection.

Rosset's experience with the *Tropic of Cancer* case had shown that the costs and risks of nationwide litigation could financially destabilize Grove. He put the problem to de Grazia, who suggested a litigation strategy to be used if, despite the Second Circuit decision, attempts were made to censor *I Am Curious—Yellow* in other parts of the country. The strategy was adopted, and the plan worked. De Grazia located lawyers to defend the film wherever trouble arose, under an arrangement whereby the fee Grove paid to the lawyers came from the box-office proceeds where the picture was banned. This motivated the lawyers engaged by Grove to keep the film playing while litigation took place; for their fee was contingent upon the movie being free.

As dozens of cities and states attempted to censor *I Am Curious—Yellow*, local civil liberties lawyers were found to defend it, frequently upon the recommendation of the then legal director of the American Civil Liberties Union, Melvin Wulf. And far more often than not, they succeeded in the effort to keep it showing. It was not until 1970 that Vilgot Sjöman's film came before the Supreme Court on appeals from decisions in Maryland and Massachusetts. By then, Grove had grossed more than eight million dollars from the film and had its legal fees for defending the movie's freedom well in hand.[5]

During the 1960s, the fields covered by legislation expanded, especially in such areas as civil rights, the environment, safety, and consumer protection, and more subjects were committed to the courts. Public awareness of the law had greatly increased and the Supreme Court felt the pressures. Whereas in the 1961 term it had 2,500 cases on its docket, by 1970 there were nearly 4,200. By this time, the Court had several hundred obscenity petitions on its annual docket, which reflected the growing availability and public acceptance of sexually oriented materials. It did not, however, solve the problem for the Court inasmuch as police, prosecutors, and trial courts generated litigation. So the justices watched more movies that censors had banned.

The Supreme Court set up the screening room in the basement. These nine middle-aged and elderly men, one, Justice Harlan, virtually blind, viewed pictures that, but for their job, they would almost certainly never have seen. Their law clerks often went along; on at least one occasion, Chief Justice Warren did not view the film but charged his clerks "collectively—not trusting them individually in this matter—with viewing it and then reporting to me. . . ." He felt "obligated to abide by their decision." Justice Harlan, who arranged the showings, sometimes joked about them in the memoranda he sent notifying his brethren of the dates and times. No tickets are required, he noted. Douglas, in turn, once asked him if there were "any charge."

It is interesting to compare the screening conditions that exist when a film has been seized by U.S. Customs. Before any judge or court sees the film, lawyers and expert witnesses must be permitted to view it in order to prepare their case. After viewing *I Am Curious—Yellow* as a prospective witness for that film's distributor, Grove Press, Joseph Gelmis described those conditions:

> Films grabbed by the government are shown in a screening room at the U.S. Customs Building at 201 Varick St., Manhattan. Poorly ventilated and nearly always superheated by capacity audiences of heavy breathers, the room has cinder-block walls, stale air, and the look of a bomb shelter. Considering the government's attitude about the kind of films shown here, it's a bomb shelter meant to protect the outside world from what's going on inside. . . . Sex, this place suggests, is a greater threat to civilization than war.
>
> There are two movie projectors, to allow for uninterrupted change of reels. The projectors are in the room with the audience, rather than being enclosed behind soundproof glass as in a custom-built studio screening room. Each projector's whir creates a homey atmosphere, which is a form of psychological conditioning. Instead of feeling that you are watching a feature film at a theater or a studio screening room, you are reminded of the conspiratorial atmosphere that surrounds the showing of dirty movies in somebody's suburban basement.
>
> The seats are hard chairs. One sits uncomfortably on wood for nearly two hours. There are no cushions. The room is so small that the chairs are sandwiched closer together than the tourist seats in a nonscheduled airliner. They are arranged three abreast on either side of the narrow aisle. They can't be moved out of alignment without interfering with the vision of the person behind, or, alternatively, without blocking the projected image on the screen. The projectors are placed at head level in the rear of the room and the tallest members of the audience become stars of the movie, in silhouette, whenever they sit upright at their normal heights.
>
> In the case of subtitled foreign films, this presents a problem. It is almost impossible to read the subtitles. So the tendency is to stop trying to read them at all and to neglect whatever intellectual pretensions the film has and just concentrate on the nudity and sex.

After viewing the films, the Supreme Court often freed material on the basis of a 1967 case, *Redrup* v. *New York*, which led to a practice called "Redruping." In a brief *per curiam* opinion, the Supreme Court had reversed the judgments of three lower courts, which upheld censoring of a dozen books and magazines, including *Gent*, *Swank*, and *Modern Man*. Upon examination of the materials, the Court decided that none "was of a character described as obscene in the constitutional sense. . . . [T]he distribution of the publication in each of these cases is protected by the First and Fourteenth Amendments from governmental suppression, whether criminal or civil, *in personam* or *in rem.*"

The significance of the case lay in the fact that although no more than three of the justices could agree on *why* such materials were constitutionally protected and not obscene, at least five agreed they were so protected. Thus began "Redruping," whereby the Court examined particular materials condemned as obscene by inferior courts; if it did not find the material obscene the convictions would be summarily reversed, citing *Redrup*. This practice signalled the suspension of the use of the three-pronged definition of obscenity that had been developed by Justice Brennan in the *Roth*, *Jacobellis*, and *Memoirs* v. *Massachusetts* series of cases and included the "utterly without social importance" test generated by Professor Kalven, until a new version would later be adopted by the Court.[6]

One of the first films the justices saw in 1970 was *I Am Curious—Yellow*. A three-judge federal court had issued a temporary injunction against the prosecution by the state of Massachusetts of the exhibitor of the film; the state asked the Supreme Court to dissolve that injunction. About the same time, the Maryland motion picture censorship board, the sole remaining state board, denied a license for the movie's exhibition, an action which the Maryland Supreme Court upheld. On behalf of Grove Press, Edward de Grazia asked the Supreme Court to reverse Maryland's censors, but now the Bench lacked the liberal Fortas and had the conservative Burger, with one vacancy awaiting appointment by President Nixon. Shortly before the justices voted to hear this case, Justice Harlan drafted a short prospective dissent based on an "understanding" that a single-line *per curiam* opinion, reversing the Maryland ban on the basis of the *Redrup* case, would be circulated.

Harlan's reasoning was not based on the movie's alleged obscenity or lack thereof, but was in accordance with his view of the Court's limited role in reviewing *state*, rather than federal, actions of censorship. "Even in the light of the much greater flexibility that I have always thought should be accorded to the States in this field," he wrote, "suppression of this particular film presents a borderline question. However, laying aside my own personal estimate of the film, I cannot say that Maryland has exceeded the constitutional speed limit in banning public showing of the film within its borders."

At the time Harlan circulated his draft dissent, a majority of the eight-member bench presumably had decided that *I Am Curious—Yellow* was "protected by the First and Fourteenth Amendments from governmental suppression," just as were the publications involved in *Redrup*. Judging from the past and future, the lineup of the votes probably was as follows: for freeing the movie—Black, Brennan, Douglas, Stewart, and Marshall; for banning it—Harlan, White, and Burger. One week later, however, the

Court must have been evenly divided. For now Justice Marshall evidently switched his vote and joined a draft dissenting opinion that Justice White had circulated.

In his prospective opinion, White objected to the Court's readiness to issue a summary order granting constitutional protection to a film depicting sexual intercourse. He could not conceive of such a movie having any social value, and objected to the Court placing it beyond the reach of local community standards. The Court's decision appeared to demean the high purposes of the First Amendment by spreading its mantle of protection over *I Am Curious—Yellow*. It would be a different matter if the Court's members were legislators considering the advisability of enacting obscenity laws. But they were not, and for his part he believed that Maryland had not trespassed on constitutionally protected ground when it banned from public theaters a film portraying sexual intercourse. This opinion reflected White's private definition of obscenity—any display of erect penises, sexual intercourse, or oral or anal sodomy.

The Court set down for argument the two *I Am Curious—Yellow* cases in late April, but the clerk of the Court now advised Grove Press's lawyers that the Maryland case might be put before the Court during its following term, by which time the Fortas vacancy should have been filled. Since his resignation, the Court had only eight members, who were sharply divided on the question of whether the movie was constitutionally protected or obscene. At the same time the Court had scheduled argument on a group of appeals, called the *Younger* cases, which presented the question of whether federal courts could properly stay or enjoin pending state court criminal proceedings, except under special circumstances. Since the Massachusetts case, *Byrne* v. *Karalexis*, also raised this issue, it was heard in April, along with the *Younger* cases, but the Maryland case was left in abeyance.

Now Justice Douglas disqualified himself from participation in the *I Am Curious—Yellow* cases. Grove Press's magazine *Evergreen Review* had published an excerpt from his recent book, *Points of Rebellion*, with its publisher's permission but without Douglas's knowledge; he had received a small payment on this use of serial rights. On April 15, after a long staff investigation that was made with the assistance of the Nixon administration, Congressman Gerald R. Ford threatened to lead an "impeach Douglas" movement on grounds, among others, of conflict of interest. Speaking to members of the House of Representatives, Ford showed a copy of *Evergreen Review*: photographs of nude women were displayed a few pages away from the words of Justice Douglas. Ford's remarks came one week after the Senate had rejected G. Harrold Carswell for the Court seat left vacant by Fortas's resignation.

The Court did hear both *I Am Curious—Yellow* cases (the Massachusetts case for the second time) the following term, by which time Harry A. Blackmun had joined the Court, but Justice Douglas still did not take part. In both cases it issued *per curiam* opinions: the injunction the federal court had issued against prosecution in *Byrne* v. *Karalexis* was vacated (thrown out) and the case remanded in light of *Younger* v. *Harris*; in the judgment of the Massachusetts case Justice Stewart concurred, while Justices Brennan, White, and Marshall dissented. Had Justice Douglas taken part the first time it was considered, the Court would surely have been evenly split and the lower court opinion, upholding the injunction, would have been affirmed, thus freeing the film for showing in Massachusetts. In the Maryland case, Douglas's vote would most assuredly have meant *national* freedom for the movie since, without him, an equally divided Court (Marshall evidently having returned to the film's side) affirmed the Maryland court's upholding of the censors' ban. Justice Douglas's disqualification, though it may have been politically coerced, made the difference in both cases.[7]

The President's Commission on Obscenity and Pornography

The President's Commission on Obscenity and Pornography had been functioning smoothly since its first meeting during the summer of 1968. Researchers under contract were working on projects across the country and even abroad. The commissioners were diverse professionally and politically, ranging from judges and social scientists to public officials and the clergy. The first meeting was held at the Kinsey Institute in Indiana, where the commissioners saw old "blue" movies, as well as contemporary "sexploitation" films.

In June 1969, President Nixon appointed Charles H. Keating, Jr., an attorney from Cincinnati, to replace a member who had resigned to take an ambassadorial position. Keating's record as founder and driving force behind the Citizens for Decent Literature had led hometown newspaper reporters to call him "Mr. Clean." His appointment introduced an element of discord that disturbed the commission's operations for the rest of its days. Keating was concerned that Commission Chairman Lockhart and General Counsel Paul Bender both were members of the American Civil Liberties Union, even though Bender had successfully presented the government's case against publisher Ralph Ginzburg in the Supreme Court. Keating also believed that holding public meetings only publicized erotic materials, and so he boycotted all commission sessions until the final report was in preparation.

Lockhart classified himself, prior to his work with the commission, as being "on the moderate to conservative side among constitutional lawyers who have written on the obscenity-pornography problem." He had "assumed there was some substantial effect on behavior by exposure" to allegedly pornographic materials, but "he didn't know for sure." Now the commission's extended empirical studies in areas where "amazingly little was known" changed his mind, and thus influenced the other members.

The commission recommended that: (1) laws should not forbid adults from obtaining, reading, or viewing sexual material of their choice, and that existing laws prohibiting the sale, exhibition, or distribution of obscene materials should be repealed; (2) states wishing to forbid the sale to minors of objectively described, carefully defined pictorial sexual material, unless parental consent were obtained, could do so, and also forbid the public display of such material where young people might see it; and (3) laws also could proscribe the thrusting of offensive sexual material on those who did not wish to see it, for example, by prohibiting its mailing to those people. But there was "no warrant," the report stated, "for continued government interference with the full freedom of adults because extensive empirical investigation, by both the commission and others, provides no evidence that exposure to or use of explicit sexual materials plays a significant role in the causation of social or individual harms, such as crime, delinquency, sexual or nonsexual deviancy, or severe emotional disturbances." As radical as they seemed to some, the commission's conclusions were not out of line with public opinion. A major national survey authorized by the commission had shown that 60 percent of all adults believed that there should be no control over material available to persons over 21, while 93 percent felt sales to children should be controlled.

The commission "deliberately did not seek to water down" its recommendations "in order to try to arrive at a consensus." In order to clarify the issues, noted Lockhart, "it was better to let our divisions stand." He had little choice. Some members of the majority had quibbles with the report, but agreed with it almost completely. Two members would have gone further, however, and recommended the repeal of all existing statutes concerned with obscenity and pornography, even as to children. There was "no substantial evidence," sociologist Otto Larsen and criminologist Marvin Wolfgang wrote, "that exposure to juveniles is necessarily harmful. There may even be beneficial effects if for no other reason than the encouragement of open discussion about sex between parents and children relatively early in young lives."

Commission members Father Morton Hill and Reverend Winfrey Link, from Hermitage, Tennessee, wrote a strong dissent, which Chief Justice Burger later cited to support his decision upholding the validity of laws prohibiting the circulation of sexual materials to adults. "The commission's majority report," they began, "is a Magna Carta for the pornographer, [which] ignores [the] basic question . . . whether and to what extent society may establish and maintain certain moral standards." Obscenity law, they maintained, "in no way legislates individual morality, but provides protection for public morality." Morever, they asserted, Lockhart and Bender had steered the commission to positions "most compatible" with the ACLU's viewpoint.

Keating's disdain for the commission increased. At the final meeting, he referred to himself as the "Nixon representative" and warned of the political opposition that the report would incite. Because he did not treat commission documents as confidential, he did not receive the final draft and other materials. Claiming he had White House support, he sought a federal court order barring publication of the report; a temporary restraining order was issued. But he and Lockhart compromised, and Keating received the data he requested. He then wrote a forceful dissent criticizing almost everything that related to the "runaway commission." He concluded with a quotation which he attributed to Alexis de Tocqueville in the late 1830s: "America is great because she is good—and if America ceases to be good, America will cease to be great."

The commission's report was controversial even before its release. When a preliminary version was leaked to a House subcommittee, one congressman expressed horror that nearly two dozen college men had been exposed to "stag" films and other erotic materials for extended periods. The Nixon administration heralded the fact that the Johnson administration had appointed the commission. Attorney General John Mitchell asserted that the Department of Justice would continue to curb pornography, for society owed it to its citizens "to encourage the best and discourage the worst." The White House moved to disassociate itself completely from the commission.

The main attack was led by Vice President Spiro Agnew. Leading Republican senators criticized the findings, which the postmaster general noted were not legally binding. The commission's report became a weapon in a campaign against "radical liberals" and a "permissive society." The Senate voted overwhelmingly to denounce the report and to reject its findings. Before reading them, President Nixon rejected the "morally bankrupt" conclusions, saying that the commission had "performed a disservice" to the nation and that "American morality is not to be trifled with."[8]

Decentralization
of Censorship
of the Screen

The backlash President Nixon cultivated found its intellectual counterpart in neo-conservatism. Adherents of neo-conservatism were largely former liberals who had been disillusioned by the turbulence of the Sixties, and their issues, vocabulary, and roles were reminiscent of progressivism. They were concerned with stability, morality (and moralism), tone, manners, tradition, culture, order, authority, virtue. Those concerns appeared in the writings of Walter Berns, Irving Kristol, and Alexander M. Bickel. The "case for censorship," Berns stated, "arises initially out of a consideration of . . . what is good for the polity. . . . When obscenity is employed as it is today [1971], merely to capture an audience, or to shock without elevating, or in the effort to set loose idiosyncratic 'selfs' doing their own things, or to bring down the constitutional order, it is not justified, for it lacks the ground on which to claim exemption from law. The modern advocates of obscenity . . . have obliterated the distinction between art and trash. . . . The objection, '*I* like it,' is sufficiently rebutted by, 'We don't.' "

Kristol, who was later joined by such groups as Women Against Pornography—which proved to be even more vehement than he in lending their voices to the condemnation of pornography—based his argument for the censorship of pornography on the ground that a democracy has a right to be concerned about its "republican morality." Obscenity is a "peculiar vision of humanity: what it is really about is ethics and metaphysics. What is at stake is civilization and humanity, nothing less. The idea that everything is permitted . . . rests on the premise of nihilism and has nihilistic implications. . . . The relationship of pornography and/or obscenity to democracy, and especially to the quality of public life on which democratic government ultimately rests," concerned him. "If you care for the quality of life in our American democracy, then you have to be for censorship."

Alexander Bickel was the leading advocate of neo-conservatism in the legal sphere. His philosophy was "a combination of unequal parts of Edmund Burke and 'Fiddler on the Roof,' " in the words of his Yale Law School colleague Robert Bork. He stressed law as evolutionary and argued that its rules must be morally acceptable to society at the time. The federal government, Bickel said, "should stay out of the business of censorship altogether, because its idiocies, when they occur, affect the whole country. . . . But the Supreme Court, while exercising procedural oversight, ought to let state and local governments run the risks [of enforcing obscenity laws] if they wish." This echoed Justice Harlan's position, which he held to the end. A few months after Bickel penned these words, Justices Black and Harlan both retired, one week apart, because of deteriorating health. This gave President Nixon an opportunity to appoint two more members to the Court.

Another conservative advocate of censorship was Judge Robert Bork, currently a member of the Court of Appeals for the District of Columbia and one of the leading candidates for the next opening on the Supreme Court. Bork took the position that constitutional protection should be accorded only to speech that is explicitly political. There is no basis for judicial intervention to protect any other form of expression, be it scientific, literary, or that variety of expression we call obscene or pornographic. "Moreover, [even] within that category of speech we ordinarily call political, there should be no constitutional obstruction to laws making criminal any speech that advocates forcible overthrow of the government or the violation of any law." Bork therefore *excludes* from constitutional protection not only obscenity or pornography (as the *Roth* and *Miller* v. *California* decisions do), but all nonpolitical scientific and literary works, and motion pictures as well as speech advocating violations of law. Most of the expression the Supreme Court has brought within the ambit of constitutional guarantees since World War I would be deprived of that protection if Bork's view prevailed.

Redefining "Obscenity"

At the time Black and Harlan retired, the high court's docket was still growing and included many obscenity cases, and Chief Justice Burger appointed a study group to make recommendations for changes to reduce the burden on the justices. Alexander Bickel was appointed as one of its members, and he and Burger could now discuss the obscenity issue.[1]

The Supreme Court heard arguments on more than half a dozen obscenity cases in January 1973. Attention focused on two cases, *Miller* v. *California* and the *Magic Mirror* case [102] (*Paris Adult Theatre I* v. *Slaton*), which gave the Court an opportunity to deal with some of the unresolved questions on obscenity. In the first case, Marvin Miller was convicted of mailing unsolicited advertisements containing sexually explicit materials in violation of a California statute. He had obtained his lists of prospective customers from a company in Los Angeles that grouped mail-order patrons by the sorts of merchandise, ranging from car parts to household supplies, that they had previously ordered. In the other appeal, the Atlanta district attorney went to court to prevent two "adult" theaters from showing allegedly obscene films; the trial court had dismissed the district attorney's petition, but the Georgia Supreme Court reversed.

The outcomes, at least initially, were by no means certain. Lewis F. Powell, Jr., a corporate lawyer from Virginia, and William H. Rehnquist, an assistant attorney general, had replaced Justices Black and Harlan on the Supreme Court. Justices Douglas, Brennan, Stewart, and Marshall favored granting constitutional protection to the materials, while Chief Justice Burger and Justice Rehnquist did not. For a time, Justices White, Powell, and Blackmun were uncommitted. After Burger revised his draft opinion to meet their objections, they joined him.

This must have been a moment that Chief Justice Burger had waited for. In several earlier dissents, he had expressed great concern over the use of scurrilous language, which he felt was leading the country back "to the law of the jungle"; individuals must, he maintained, express themselves in "acceptable, civil terms." Decisions permitting caustic and vehement speech were "small but symptomatic steps. If continued, this permissiveness will tend further to erode public confidence in the law—that subtle but indispensable ingredient of ordered liberty."

In *Miller* v. *California* Burger reviewed the "somewhat tortured course" of the court's obscenity decision, and then laid to rest what Boston Superior Court Chief Justice G. Joseph Tauro, in 1969, referred to as the "Brennan doctrine," and set up instead new "basic guidelines" for the "trier of the fact":

(a) Whether "the average person, applying contemporary community standards" would find that the work, taken as a whole, appeals to the prurient interest.

(b) Whether the work depicts or describes, in a patently offensive way, sexual conduct specifically defined by the applicable state law.

(c) Whether the work, taken as a whole, lacks serious literary, artistic, political, or scientific value.

The Chief Justice gave "a few plain examples of what a state statute could define for regulation":

(a) Patently offensive representations of descriptions of ultimate sexual acts, normal or perverted, actual or simulated.

(b) Patently offensive representations of descriptions of masturbation, excretory functions, and lewd exhibition of the genitals.

For the first time since *Roth*, Burger noted, a majority of the Court was agreed on "concrete guidelines to isolate 'hard-core' pornography" from constitutionally protected expression. It could now "abandon the casual practice" of *Redrup* and "attempt to provide positive guidance to federal and state courts alike." This would not be "an easy road, free from difficulty. But no amount of 'fatigue' should lead us to adopt a convenient 'institutional' rationale—an absolutist, 'anything goes' view of the First Amendment—because it would lighten our burdens." Determining what appeals to the "prurient interest" and what is "patently offensive" are "essentially questions of fact, and our nation is simply too big and too diverse to expect that such standards could be articulated in a single formulation. . . . To require a state to structure obscenity proceedings around evidence of a *national* 'community standard' would be an exercise in futility," as these are "hypothetical" and "unascertainable."

Chief Justice Tauro's views antedated those of Burger's by four years. In an unreported 1969 opinion involving *I Am Curious—Yellow*, he had criticized Brennan's opinions in *Jacobellis* and *Memoirs* v. *Massachusetts*, which created the "social value" or "utterly without social importance" tests, as "opinions of individual judges" which he did not feel compelled to follow, because they lacked "majority support and agreement." The "most vexing and most subtle criterion of [Brennan's] constitutional definition is the requirement that obscenity be utterly without redeeming social value. . . . Few, if any, works will be found where some expert testimony cannot be elicited in support of the presence of some bare minimum of social value which would, according to the Brennan doctrine, preempt the court from coming to a different conclusion." Tauro also declared that the permissiveness of the Brennan doctrine had brought about a situation in literature and entertainment akin to the pollution of our waterways and atmosphere which some experts now assess as irreversible. "Should our literature, theaters, and television channels be similarly polluted with smut and trash, the damage would be far more pervasive than the contamination of Lake Erie or Boston Harbor."

Burger also noted that it is "neither realistic nor constitutionally sound to read the First Amendment as requiring that the people of Maine or Mississippi accept public depiction of conduct found tolerable in Las Vegas or New York City." (Note the comparison of states to cities.) "People in different states vary in their tastes and attitudes, and this diversity is not to be strangled by the absolutism of imposed uniformity." Thus did the Supreme Court's new majority seek to delegate to "local communities" the power to disapprove of movies and other materials that offended their standards in descriptions or depictions of sex.

The Chief Justice found "no evidence, empirical or historical, that the stern nineteenth-century American censorship of public distribution and display of material relating to sex in any way limited or affected expression of serious literary, artistic, political, or scientific ideas. On the contrary, it is beyond any question that the era following Thomas Jefferson to Theodore Roosevelt was an 'extraordinarily vigorous period,' not just in economics and politics, but in *belles lettres* and in 'the outlying fields of social and political philosophies.' "

Thus ignored were the voluminously documented activities of Anthony Comstock, his New York Society for the Suppression of Vice, the many similar groups it spawned, and the experiences of D. M. Bennett, Ezra Haywood, the sisters Victoria Claflin Woodhull and Tennessee Claflin, and other late nineteenth-century reformers who spent time in jail for propagating their ideas, not to mention the mountain of serious material banned, censored, destroyed, or which was never allowed to reach the public because of some person's or some group's qualms.

Burger conceded, though, that the recent "sexual revolution" may have been useful in airing issues. But it did not follow that no regulation of patently offensive hard-core materials was needed or permissible; "civilized people do not allow unregulated access to heroin because it is a derivative of medicinal morphine."

Burger continued his reasoning in this vein in the *Magic Mirror* case (entitled *Paris Adult Theatre I* v. *Slaton*) by attacking the main conclusions of the Lockhart Commission on Obscenity and Pornography and presenting the neo-conservative view. "We categorically disapprove the theory . . . that obscene, pornographic films acquire constitutional immunity from state regulation simply because they are exhibited for consenting adults only." "Legitimate state interests," he held, "are at stake in stemming the tide of commercialized obscenity against exposure to juveniles and to passers-by." Relying directly now on the writings of Bickel, Kristol, and Berns, he insisted that among the rights and interests involved are "the interest of the public in the quality of life and the total community environment, the tone of commerce in the great city centers, and, possibly, the public safety itself." In addition, there "remains one problem of large proportions aptly described by Professor Bickel," and the Chief Justice quoted:

> It concerns the tone of the society, the mode, or to use terms that have perhaps greater currency, the style and quality of life now and in the future. A man may be entitled to read an obscene book in his room [as, indeed, the Supreme Court had decided in *Stanley* v. *Georgia*], or expose himself indecently there. . . . We should protect his privacy. But if he demands a right to obtain the books and pictures he wants in the market, and to foregather in public places—discreet, if you will, but accessible to all—with others who share his tastes, then to grant him his right is to affect the world about the rest of us,

and to impinge on other privacies. Even supposing that each of us can, if he wishes, effectively avert the eye and stop the ear (which, in truth, we cannot), what is commonly read and seen and heard and done intrudes upon us all, want it or not.

Burger also rejected the Lockhart Commission's conclusion that because there was no proof linking antisocial behavior and the distribution of obscene material, obscenity laws could not do good, although by censoring they did much harm.

> From the beginning of civilized societies, legislators and judges have acted on various unprovable assumptions. . . . Understandably, those who entertain an absolutist view of the First Amendment find it uncomfortable to explain why rights of association, speech, and press should be severely restrained in the marketplace of goods and money, but not in the marketplace of pornography.

The Chief Justice found no right of privacy of the *Stanley* v. *Georgia* type to watch "obscene" films in places of *public* accommodation, which, according to him, included movie theaters. Furthermore:

> conduct or depictions of conduct that the state police power can prohibit on a public street do not become automatically protected by the Constitution merely because the conduct is moved to a bar or a "live" theater stage, any more than a "live" performance of a man and woman locked in a sexual embrace at high noon in Times Square is protected by the Constitution because they simultaneously engage in a valid political dialogue. . . . Preventing unlimited display or distribution of obscene material, which by definition [or rather by the definition the Court gave it long after the fact] lacks any serious literary, artistic, political, or scientific value as communication, is distinct from a control of reason and the intellect. . . . For us to say that our Constitution incorporates the proposition that conduct involving consenting adults only is always beyond state regulation is a step we are unable to take.

Not "unable," critics might have observed, but "unwilling."

Justices Douglas and Brennan wrote dissents in both the *Miller* and the *Paris Adult Theatre* cases. Douglas's opinion was characteristic: "[The First Amendment] was not fashioned as a vehicle for dispensing tranquilizers to the people. Its prime function was to keep debate open to 'offensive' as well as to 'staid' people." He applauded, in *Paris Adult Theatre*, "the effort of my Brother Brennan to forsake the low road which the Court has followed in this field." Brennan's opinion, which Justices Stewart and Marshall joined, was a landmark expression of dissent. In it, he departed from the premises of *Roth*, which he himself authored; it was a significant admission of a past misstep, a rebuttal of the Court majority on its own ground, and a statement which on different levels portended greater freedom for all media, information, and entertainment. "I am convinced,"

Brennan noted, "that the approach initiated 16 years ago in *Roth*, and culminating in the Court's decision today, cannot bring stability to this area of the law without jeopardizing fundamental First Amendment values, and I have concluded that the time has come to make a significant departure from that approach." He admitted, too, that although he had not joined the Court's opinion in *Stanley* v. *Georgia*, he was "now inclined to agree that the Constitution protects the right to receive information and ideas . . . *regardless of their social worth*" [italics supplied], which was to say, even so-called obscenity. This meant that Brennan had now also departed not only from *Roth*, but from the measures to free sexual expression in literature, art, and film which he had adopted in the *Fanny Hill* and *The Lovers* cases by his doctrine that the mantle of constitutional protection covered all that was not "utterly without social importance."

Brennan based his dissent exclusively on the void-for-vagueness doctrine.

> No one definition [of "obscenity"], no matter how precisely or narrowly drawn, can possibly suffice for all situations, or carve out fully suppressible expression from all media without also creating a substantial risk of encroachment upon the guarantees of the due process and the First Amendment. [A vague statute] fails to provide adequate notice to persons who are engaged in the type of conduct that the statute could be thought to proscribe.

"Chilling" protected speech is also a "grave" problem: "stricter standards of permissible statutory vagueness," the Court had indicated in the past, "may be applied to a statute having a potentially inhibiting effect on speech; a man may the less be required to act at his peril here, because the free dissemination of ideas may be the loser." Another concern, he observed, is the "institutional stress that inevitably results where the line separating protected from unprotected speech is excessively vague." There is "no probability of regularity in obscenity decisions by state and lower federal courts . . . and one cannot say with certainty that material is obscene until at least five members of this Court, applying inevitably obscure standards, have pronounced it so." One test to determine explicit sexual conduct, he noted, "apparently requires an effort to distinguish between . . . 'erect penises' and 'semi-erect penises,' and between 'ongoing sexual activity' and 'imminent sexual activity.' "

Having stated the problems that persuaded him that "a significant change of direction is urgently required," Brennan considered the alternatives available. Drawing a new line as to what material should be protected was not feasible, nor could he accept the Court's decision or leave the matter to juries, or even accept "the view, urged so forcefully since 1957 by our Brothers Black and Douglas, that the First Amendment bars the suppression of any sexually oriented expression." He sought to strike a "better balance between the guarantee of free expression and the states' legitimate interests." Were Brennan writing for the majority, he would have held that "at least in the absence of distribution to juveniles or obtrusive exposure to unconsenting adults, the First and Fourteenth Amendments prohibit the state and federal governments from attempting wholly to suppress sexually oriented materials on the basis of their allegedly 'obscene' contents."[2]

The *Miller* and *Paris Adult Theatre* decisions caused a "fig leaf crisis" and "confusion to the core" in the motion picture industry. The fear was that, under the new balkanization of the First Amendment, prosecutors around the country would "grandstand" and juries could "take a crack" at any movie that offended their standards of decency. Studios cancelled pictures spiced with sex. As in earlier times, directors filmed two versions of questionable scenes or lines of dialogue. However, the hard-core market which the new Burger doctrine was supposed to snuff out—and whose products had been involved in the *Miller* and *Paris Adult Theatre* cases— continued to flourish. The costs of production were very low and audiences grew. Movies not entirely devoid of cinematic value, such as *Deep Throat* [107], *The Devil in Miss Jones* [117], and *Behind the Green Door* [109], played to full middle-class houses; and in New York and Washington, D.C., pornography dealers reported that some customers were stockpiling "morally questionable" books and films because of anticipated hard times. Many applauded the Court's rulings. The group known as Morality in Media hailed the decisions as "a manifestation of the beauty of America's inner soul." Alexander Bickel supported them because "we were approaching a position allowing virtually anything, with exceptions that the Court couldn't explain or justify." Such a position, he felt, "has no warrant in the First Amendment, in prior history or practice—judicial or legislative—or in the history of other civilized societies from the dawn of recorded time."

At first, Jack Valenti supposed that the decisions would have "no effect" on the "responsible" part of the industry. He would be "concerned if local communities denied exhibition to well-intended films, seriously made by recognized artistic filmmakers." But the MPAA was worried and proposed a "model" obscenity law aimed at isolating hard-core pornography. Its representatives also met, as after the *Times Film* case 12 years before, with a number of publishing organizations. As a result, the American Library Association and the Association of American Publishers filed petitions for rehearing with the Supreme Court; these were denied. More than anything else, however, an action taken by the Georgia Supreme Court deflated any initial optimism of the MPAA.

"Carnal Knowledge"

The week after the *Miller* and *Paris Adult Theatre* cases were handed down, the Georgia court upheld a jury conviction of Billy Jenkins, a theater operator from Albany, Georgia, for showing *Carnal Knowledge* [105]. The Georgia jury had decided that it was obscene, and the Georgia courts agreed. "I spoke too soon," Valenti admitted. "The great fear that exists in the responsible motion picture industry is concern that this legal hysteria will become a contagion and sweep across the country." He wanted to protect "responsible" films.

Carnal Knowledge was indeed a responsible film. Produced by Joseph E. Levine, directed by Mike Nichols, and starring Jack Nicholson and Ann-Margret, it was generally acclaimed as one of the ten best motion pictures of 1971. The MPAA supported Jenkins's appeal to the Supreme Court, which agreed to hear it, and Louis Nizer argued the case. In contrast to the strategies adopted by some lawyers who argued for freedom of films, Nizer was concerned more with freeing this particular film than with carving out a broader space for liberty of movie expression. More than half a dozen screen and publishing groups submitted *amicus curiae* briefs to the Court, and some of these he thought were "purists" who wanted to see *Miller* v. *California* "destroyed."

They sought to point up *Miller*'s failure in the *Carnal Knowledge* case and to predict the inevitability of other repressions. To Nizer this was the "wrong strategy." "On principle as well as persuasive wisdom," he agreed with the *Miller* decision that hard-core pornography "should be ruled out. Our position," he felt, "ought to be that *Carnal Knowledge* was not hard core." *Miller* "needed a follow-up, not a chastisement."

In his argument before the high court, Nizer attempted to show that film merit, like "literary value," cannot be tested as one tests "offensiveness," by community standards. "A literary work," he reminded the justices, "survives even the illiteracy of its readers"; and thus *Carnal Knowledge* deserved to rest comfortably under the shelter of the First Amendment. The Supreme Court agreed. As it had done before in the *Tropic of Cancer* case, and as the Second Circuit Court of Appeals had done in the *I Am Curious—Yellow* case [71], it now made an independent constitutional fact determination and overturned a jury's verdict, only this time a criminal jury's verdict. Justice Rehnquist wrote for the same five-member majority that had upheld censorship in the *Miller* case: "It would be a serious misreading of *Miller* to conclude that juries have unbridled discretion in determining what is 'patently offensive.' " The other four justices also voted to reverse the conviction, on other grounds, and both *Carnal Knowledge* and Billy Jenkins were free again.[3]

"Deep Throat"

Harry Reems (whose given name was Herbert Streicher) was a minor actor who had played bit roles for the National Shakespeare Company and in

Off-Off-Broadway productions in the late 1960s. When one of his colleagues told him that the blue movie industry was making "white coaters," he changed costumes and began specializing in portraying crazy doctors. Some of the films in which he acted earned millions, and he became a mainstay of what most probably agreed were hard-core pornographic movies. In January 1972, he went to Miami with Gerard Damiano, a Queens, New York hairdresser and aspiring director, to help make a film.

Supposedly, Reems was working behind the camera when Damiano was having difficulty selecting a male lead. Reems volunteered, shot two sex scenes, which were later edited to look like many more, and was paid $100 for his day's work. To receive his fee, he signed a standard day-player's contract, waiving all artistic (that is, editing), marketing, and distribution rights to the movie, which he saw only when it was released.

His co-star in the movie was Linda Lovelace. Feeling "no tingle" in her sex life, the young woman played by Ms. Lovelace consulted Dr. Young (Reems), who discovered that nature had misplaced her clitoris in her throat. Only through fellatio could she achieve sexual satisfaction, he advised her, and she lost no time in taking advantage of her newly gained knowledge. Audiences by the millions viewed her techniques as *Deep Throat*, opening in late 1972, and sometimes at fashionable theaters, eventually grossed more than $25 million.

In some cities, police moved quickly against the picture. In New York City, before the *Miller* case had been decided, a Manhattan criminal court judge, sitting without a jury, found it obscene. He called it a "feast of carrion and squalor," a "nadir of decadence," and a "Sodom and Gomorrah gone wild before the fire." Just over the borough line, a Bronx county jury, applying its "community standards" as redefined in *Miller*, found the film not obscene. Prosecutors around the country brought more actions against this film than against any previous film except *The Birth of a Nation*. Box-office receipts soared, and many juries found *Deep Throat* not obscene. When the New York distributor later released a version of the movie with some scenes cut out, the local district attorney took no new action. "We've got more serious cases than we can handle already," he said. "When we have got more homicides, more rapes, and more assaults, prosecuting prostitution or pornography has to be low in priority."

Not only pornographic films but massage parlors and other commercialized sex establishments appeared across the country in greater numbers than ever. Commerce in erotica, variously defined, was booming. *Miller* v. *California* had hardly been decided when the Department of Justice announced a crackdown on interstate shipment of allegedly obscene materials, regardless of what individual states permitted. Under the federal transportation and conspiracy statutes, the department decided to prosecute all persons involved with the creation or selling of *Deep Throat*. The government, making use of the statute that allows it to bring a criminal action in any jurisdiction through which the film had passed, decided to prosecute in Memphis, Tennessee.

The "conspirators" would be prosecuted by Assistant United States Attorney Larry Parrish. In his early thirties, devout and evangelical, Parrish claimed he was not prosecuting because of his personal feelings but because a federal law was being "flagrantly and openly violated." However, he also told the Adult Film Association, "If you want to know why I am a prosecutor, you can read Romans 13." That chapter of the New Testament is a warning to evildoers that God has appointed ministers on earth to carry out his wrath against them. Pornography, Parrish once said, has a "much more pervasive effect" on people than hard drugs. Meanwhile, the expenses in this court case cost taxpayers some four million dollars starting in 1972.

One night in July 1974, while Reems was sleeping in his apartment in New York City, he was awakened by the FBI. He had been indicted as part of a nationwide conspiracy to transport across state lines "an obscene, lewd, lascivious, and filthy motion picture." Reems was the first performer or artist to be prosecuted on the federal level for his work. Georgina Spelvin, the lead in *The Devil in Miss Jones*, was indicted at the same time, but her case never came to trial. The prosecutions of comedian Lenny Bruce had all been local. Henry Miller had been indicted in Brooklyn, New York, under a state law, for writing *Tropic of Cancer*, but the case was never pursued.

Indicted along with Reems were 11 other persons and five corporations. In addition, there were 98 unindicted co-conspirators, including the advertising agency that had prepared the newspaper ads for the film and the scriptwriter (both from New York); a lighting technician from Miami; a distributor from Boston; a Chicago publicist; projectionists at some of the theaters where the film had been shown around the country; and the ticket taker at one of the theaters in Vermont. By working that single day on the movie, the indictment claimed, Reems was guilty of "vicarious responsibility." As Parrish said in his opening statement to the jury:

> Once a person joins a conspiracy, he is liable for everything that happens in that conspiracy until it is ended. [He is responsible for the acts of all persons involved. The only way out is to withdraw, but even that is not enough.] You must cease doing anything to further the conspiracy but, more than that, you have to take up affirmative actions to defeat and destroy the conspiracy.

The defendants claimed that the First Amendment protected them, but Federal District Judge Harry W. Wellford did not accept that defense. During a pre-trial hearing, he told Reems's lawyer that "if you do argue that your client's conduct is protected by the First Amendment, I am going to charge the jury that what he did is not protected expression and that this trial is not a First Amendment case"—which is just how the judge did charge the jury. He also pointed out that "if it weren't for Mr. Reems, we wouldn't have movies like *Deep Throat*.'' Before deliberating, the jury viewed the picture; it shocked them. "They wouldn't look us in the eye," Reems's lawyer said afterwards. "They saw things on the screen that they had never even thought about." Stripped of their First Amendment defense, and in the heart of the Bible Belt, the defendants were convicted in April 1976.

Reems planned to appeal and wanted a new lawyer. He asked Roy Grutman and Ephraim London to represent him; Grutman had successfully defended *Penthouse* magazine in its many obscenity trials. Both turned him down. London saw the film. "It went too far," he later said. "I couldn't defend it." Reems then approached Alan Dershowitz, a professor of law at Harvard, who had argued the Massachusetts *I Am Curious—Yellow* case. Dershowitz developed the argument that when Reems acted in the picture he had no way of knowing what the final product would look like, especially since he did not participate in its final editing or production. Nor, claimed Dershowitz, did he have any way of withdrawing from the alleged conspiracy. Moreover, all of Reems's acts had taken place prior to the Supreme Court's tightening of the definition of obscenity in the *Miller* case; yet the jury had been instructed as though the *Miller* test were applicable to Reems's conduct.

While entertainment celebrities contributed money for the expected appeal, and while Reems's sentencing was being withheld, his lawyers moved for a new trial. Their application was granted largely because, as Judge Wellford wrote, "all his activities clearly took place prior to *Miller*." Dershowitz was not Reems's lawyer of record, but he was the central draftsman of the legal issues and arguments. When the government declined to put Reems to trial again, with the pre-*Miller* test, the only actor ever to be federally prosecuted for his role in a movie was free.[4]

The waves of censorship that were forecast as a result of *Miller*'s redefinition of obscenity failed to materialize. Despite the conventional wisdom that the case would make it easier for prosecutors to deal with the noticeably larger amount of hard-core materials available, fewer obscenity prosecutions were brought nationally, and the conviction rate remained constant with that obtained under the *Roth-Memoirs* standard. Law enforcement officials accorded a lowered priority to obscenity and, despite the greater censorship powers granted by the Court to local communities, these appeared to grow only increasingly more tolerant. This was the conclusion of an extensive empirical inquiry, undertaken by New York University Law School, concerning *Miller*'s effects on the prosecution and distribution of obscenity.

Other means to control obscenity, besides criminal prosecution, were employed. After the Supreme Court's decision in *Young* v. *American Mini-*

Theatres in 1976, zoning restrictions became more popular. (The *Emmanuelle* case [122] also involved a governmental attempt to censor by use of zoning restriction.) The Court upheld a Detroit scheme that prohibited "adult entertainment" establishments from locating within 500 feet of any residential area or within 1,000 feet of any "regulated use"; but only a plurality of the justices agreed that the contents of the challenged entertainment could serve as a valid basis for regulation. For the pornography problem, zoning is an alternative approach to piecemeal criminal prosecution. It recognizes the interests both of dealers and of that part of the public that does not use or is offended by such matter, and it is often the most politically acceptable solution. For such reason Boston, for example, set up its "Combat Zone," in which X-rated films were freely shown. Some communities have used "red light abatement" laws and other "nuisance" statutes, most of which date from the turn of the century, to censor motion pictures. They are a catchall, vague and general enough to control bothersome activities, but the Supreme Court found them unconstitutional when applied to close a theater that had shown *Deep Throat*. As a tool to curb obscenity, they have been applied throughout the country, most frequently in the South.

In recent years, prosecutors have begun to invest their limited resources selectively, moving against only the most extreme films or books or those that gain enough notoriety that a reasonable chance of successful prosecution exists. Lost cases sometimes have resulted in prosecutorial policy changes. After the district attorney in Houston, Texas tried and failed twice to keep *Deep Throat* from exhibition in the city, he announced that future obscenity prosecutions would only be directed against materials depicting bestiality, excretory functions, or sex acts involving minors.

The film penetrated public consciousness to the extent that the authors of a major book about the Watergate crisis and the demise of the Nixon administration (*All the President's Men*, by Carl Bernstein and Bob Woodward) labeled a leading informant "Deep Throat." Watergate also had the effect, however temporarily, of heightening the country's *public* morality. But the changes that had taken place during the 1960s were by now more deeply ingrained. In 1976, a public opinion survey in California and Ohio asked: "Is it your opinion that in recent years the standards of your community have changed so that depictions of nudity and sex in movies and publications available only to adults are now more acceptable or less?" More than 60 percent of those who answered replied that such depictions were now more acceptable. Other polls, although not without ambiguities, elicited different results, but did not contradict that conclusion. One year later, the FBI directed its agents to concentrate only on obvious hard-core pornography and to refrain from pursuing sources of merely "highly questionable" obscenity. Jury acquittals of the disseminators of the type of materials that previously had been found obscene became commonplace. A Philadelphia jury, after prolonged deliberation, announced such a verdict to an empty courtroom, sensing, as the judge later said, that "nobody cared about obscenity." To most people obscenity was not as important as it once had been.

The state of bewilderment that marked obscenity law remained largely unchanged. The *Miller* guidelines required law enforcement officials to make inevitably subjective judgments of any given material's obscenity. As a "practical matter," said one prosecutor, this made enforcement a "hit or miss proposition." The relevant "community" continued to be left undefined, or rather left up to individual judges to define, and the trier of fact still had to apply obscure but allegedly objective standards of "prurient interest," "patent offensiveness," and "serious value" to materials judged often more by personal predilections. *Miller* v. *California* in action, the New York University study concluded, had "only a minimal effect on the conduct of prosecutors and pornographers." Some subjects, by their very nature, defy analysis. The *Miller* tale was one of continuing confusion.[5]

Some critics have viewed the advent of the 1980s as a time of hedonism, typified by the title of a best-selling book, *Looking Out for* #1. Historian Christopher Lasch considered it a period of "narcissistic preoccupation with the self." Might a retreat to more strictly personal concerns be a reason why, by the late 1970s, the traffic in pornography was yielding annual profits greater than the earnings of the film and record industries combined? The sex business, according to one estimate, grossed some five billion dollars yearly. New intensive drives to eliminate it sprang up in certain areas, with, however, limited success.

The increasing alienation felt by many individuals led to the growth of movements and organizations that served social, non-theological functions of established religions, as well as to a resurgence of the religious right. Nearly two decades of secular public life aroused fundamentalists. This, together with great concern over such issues as abortion, homosexual rights, and school busing gave birth in 1979 to the Moral Majority, a broadly based "moral action" group led by the Reverend Jerry Falwell.

As Richard Hofstadter wrote in *Anti-Intellectualism in American Life*, this is the kind of view that "looks upon the world as an arena for conflict between absolute good and absolute evil, and accordingly it scorns compromises and can tolerate no ambiguities. It cannot find serious importance in what it believes to be trifling degrees of difference. . . ." It "begins with a definition of that which is absolutely right, and looks upon politics as an arena in which that right must be realized." "We have a religious mandate," declared the head of the Moral Majority's California branch.

"We must return to the broad principles of Biblical law to restore order to our society."

"Secular humanism"—the "wisdom of man, as opposed to Godliness," which is "the wisdom of God as revealed in the Bible"—is its special enemy. In the elections of 1980, the Moral Majority actively sought to defeat liberal candidates, and it was successful. In his campaign for the presidency, Ronald Reagan told evangelical leaders that he was "shocked" to hear that the First Amendment was being "used as a reason to keep traditional moral values away from policy-making." It had been adopted, he claimed, "not to protect the people and their laws from religious values, but to protect those values from government tyranny." Moreover, "religious America is awakening. . . ." Within months of Reagan's campaign victory, attempts to remove "immoral" and controversial books from public libraries increased fivefold. A coalition of conservative groups began to monitor television programs to reduce the amount of "violence, vulgarity, sex, and profanity"; they also threatened boycotts of the products of companies that did not withdraw sponsorship of such programs.

Curiously, motion pictures were exempt from these pressures. Reverend Falwell remarked, "I'm more concerned about the television screen than the movie screen because we don't have to go to that." Perhaps the MPAA's new rating system was considered sufficient control. Yet, some prosecutors in the South did move to ban films on religious grounds. The corporate owner of a theater in Hattiesburg, Mississippi had been convicted in 1975 for showing *The Exorcist* [110], a picture about a demoniacally possessed girl and the exorcism that freed her. The conviction was under a state statute vaguely prohibiting the exhibition of "obscene, indecent, and immoral" pictures. The law was one of the few remaining that authorized the criminal punishment of persons disseminating materials for reasons other than obscenity. On appeal, the old law, unchanged since its enactment in 1920, was declared unconstitutionally "overbroad" in violation of the First Amendment.

The British group Monty Python's film, *Life of Bryan*, was a spoof about the life of a contemporary of Jesus, who, mistaken for the Messiah, is crucified by the Romans. Some Protestant, Catholic, and Jewish spokespersons condemned it as blasphemous. The movie was picketed and engagements of it were canceled in several cities, mainly in the South. At the request of local church groups that claimed it distorted the life of Jesus, a judge in Valdosta, Georgia granted an injunction against its showing. The next day, however, he lifted the order without comment. *Life of Bryan* and *The Exorcist* appear to have been the only movies banned on grounds other than obscenity in over 20 years.[6]

Rapid changes in the moral climate continued to be reflected in the collapse of venerable institutions. The National Catholic Office of Motion Pictures closed in October 1980. Financial considerations were given as the reason, but the office's purposes may no longer have seemed relevant. The Church's social actions, during recent years, have focused on the issue of abortion and its doctrine regarding birth control and divorce; movies have become less important. Nevertheless, the office's original parent body, the United States Catholic Conference, continued to rate films by way of its Department of Communication and circulated these ratings to parishes. But now there were fewer priests and nuns, and there had been defections among them. A new generation, influenced by Pope John and the Vatican Ecumenical Council, was most influential. Said one member of the Catholic Conference staff, "when three nuns are killed in El Salvador, you can't still be too interested in a movie."

The Catholic church continues to classify films, but as of January 1, 1982, it liberalized its system. Most significantly, it has given up the prerogative of qualifying a film by a "Class C" for "Condemned" rating. That classification, as well as the classification "Class B, morally objectionable in part for all," has been replaced with a single category called "O, morally offensive." Recently, statements of the Holy See have stressed the relevance of competent reviews and criticism of film materials "that assess their worth, morality, and religious value." The new listings will also contain "recommended" pictures of unusual merit, which are meant "to help Catholics in the crucial task of forming their conscience in an area that is especially difficult, particularly with regard to 'problem' films." Like other contemporary institutions, the Church has moved away from the position of censor to that of advisor.

The Maryland censorship board disbanded after 65 years of service; in June 1981, the state legislature refused to renew its charter. This board, which successfully prevented Maryland residents from viewing *I Am Curious—Yellow*, had been the only functioning state censorship agency over the past 15 years. Its demise, the retiring chairwoman warned, was "just another step toward our becoming lovers of pleasure rather than lovers of our fellow man. America is degraded." Having long lobbied to halt the board's operations, the MPAA was pleased. "This removes a staining blot on the Constitution," said Jack Valenti. "It makes Maryland, the fabled Free State, a free state at last, along with the other 49." Government, at all levels, finally was not licensing movies before they could be shown—except for minors.

In some locales, private groups moved to fill a void left by government boards. Demonstrators claimed that *Fort Apache, the Bronx*, a fictionalized account of police working in a run-down South Bronx (New York) precinct, had stereotyped blacks and Puerto Ricans as "savages, criminals, and degenerates." Their action, protected by the First Amendment, caused two

New York City theaters to cancel the picture's opening. Though none of its members had seen the film, a New York City Council committee assailed it and urged a public boycott. The movie, the resolution concluded, "will only retard" efforts by citizens of the area to rebuild their community, "fails to reflect their inherent goodness," and "will foster a negative self-image among area youth." But the full council reversed the committee's measure and eventually voided it, despite charges of racism and charges that it supported "sickness in the name of free speech." As one member noted, condemning movies or books "is not a function for which we were elected."[7]

"Caligula"

Caligula [121] had made headlines long before it was released in early 1980. It was co-produced by Robert Guccione, the publisher of *Penthouse* magazine, and it had more than the usual share of production difficulties. Gore Vidal, from whose original screenplay the film was adapted, sued to have his name removed from the credits, and the director quit because of what he called "irreconcilable creative differences" with Guccione. On the assumption that the movie would receive an X rating, Guccione did not submit it to the MPAA. Instead, he assigned it his own "MA" (Mature Audience) rating, instructing theaters showing it not to admit any person under 18.

Caligula retells the bizarre story of the young Roman emperor whose reign began benignly in A.D. 37 and ended in cruelty and violence four years later. It was a lavishly financed film ($17 million), and portions of it featured internationally distinguished actors, including Peter O'Toole, Malcolm McDowell, and Sir John Gielgud. The movie explicitly depicted sexual activities, including, but not limited to, sadism, torture, bestiality, necrophilia, gore, and extreme violence. With few exceptions, reviewers panned it. Guccione explained the situation: "Comparing an X-rated film to *Caligula* is like comparing the shootout at the O.K. Corral to the Second World War."

The movie came to the attention of Morality in Media, which alerts prosecutors throughout the country to the existence of allegedly obscene books, films, plays, and radio programs and assists in their suppression. Morality in Media aims to eradicate obscenity by encouraging legal and community efforts to combat it. One of its members, for example, complained to the Federal Communications Commission that the morals of his 13-year-old son were impaired by New York radio station WBAI's broadcast of comedian George Carlin's "seven dirty words" monologue. This situation induced the Supreme Court in 1978 to recognize, over the objections of book publishers, librarians, and broadcasters, a power in the FCC to censor broadcast program content at least during hours when children might be listening.

When the first print of *Caligula* arrived in the United States in April 1979, Customs officials at Kennedy Airport in New York examined it and advised the local United States Attorney that the film was obscene under the *Miller* v. *California* guidelines. Members of the Department of Justice's Criminal Division, along with Deputy Attorney General Benjamin R. Civiletti, viewed the movie. The department, exercising its administrative "discretion," declined to ask the courts to suppress the picture, thus permitting its entry into the country.

One hour after *Caligula* opened in New York City on February 1, 1980, the theater manager was handed a warrant of arrest, unusual in being based "upon an admiralty and maritime claim." The "claimants" were Father Hill, head of Morality in Media, and Hinson McAuliffe, the solicitor general of Fulton County, Georgia, who had long been active in the anti-pornography movement. Both were represented by Larry Parrish, who prosecuted the *Deep Throat* case in Tennessee. The complaint, in the form of a class action suit, claimed to represent more than 3,300 Roman Catholic clergymen in New York, Chicago, and Los Angeles, having the responsibility "to protect and maintain public morality consistent with the work and family ethic" of three million parishioners, and over 2,200 prosecutors located throughout the United States. The claimants charged that Justice Department officials had "failed to perform their non-discretionary duty" when they declined to move to prevent the film from entry into the United States.

Judge Vincent L. Broderick rejected Parrish's attempt to assert a private right of action and dismissed the complaint. Broderick concluded that neither the United States Attorney nor the Attorney General had any "mandatory duty" under the Customs Act "to proceed judicially against the film." In June, the Court of Appeals for the Second Circuit affirmed the lower court's judgment, noting that one of the purposes of the Customs Act—"to screen imported materials for obscenity at the border under rigorous procedural safeguards—would be frustrated by the private right of action." Morality in Media then took new action. Within two weeks, citing complaints from citizens and religious groups that *Caligula* was obscene, police in Boston seized the film from a theater where it was being shown outside the X-rated Combat Zone. The phrase "banned in Boston" rang out again.

The trial before Chief Judge Harry Elam of the Boston Municipal Court lasted nearly two weeks, with portions locally televised. Viewers saw and heard an array of witnesses testify on behalf of both sides. Judge Elam, without the aid of a jury, and applying the *Miller* v. *California* standards, decided that the film appealed to the prurient interest, depicted and described sexual conduct in a patently offensive way, and lacked serious literary, artistic, and scientific value. He went on to observe, however, that political science professor Andrew Hacker "articulated rather effectively" that a "serious political theme ran throughout the film":

> namely that absolute power corrupts absolutely. He was able to show the frightening effect of power in the hands of a single person, how power was used to emasculate, debase, and exploit sexually. And he was able to relate convincingly all of this to its historical context, as reported by ancient Roman historians. He projected the sobering thought that it was important to be aware of this and other such degrading periods in the history of our world, lest they are allowed to repeat themselves.

When the prosecution neglected to rebut this testimony, thereby failing to prove "beyond a reasonable doubt" that *Caligula* lacked "serious political value," the court held the film not obscene and thus constitutionally protected.

Atlanta prosecutor McAuliffe had made it "abundantly clear," even though he had not seen the movie, that he would institute criminal proceedings against *Penthouse* magazine and any Atlanta theater owner if *Caligula* were shown in Fulton County. By the fall of 1980, the film had been shown in over 100 cities in 20 northern and western states. In an effort to tap the southern market, *Penthouse* asked a federal court in Atlanta to declare that the film was not obscene and sought an order preventing McAuliffe from interfering with its exhibition. The prosecutor did not object. "I think filing it before anyone is arrested is the best way to do it. If the obscenity of a film is strongly suspect before it is shown, that observation ought to be made before it is brought into the area. Let the judge decide if it is obscene. I'm all for that." This strategy meant that the film would not be shown in Atlanta until after a trial took place.

The judge did decide: the film was not obscene on account of the artistic and political values "convincingly" depicted at the trial by, among others, Robert Sklar, a professor at New York University and author of *Movie-Made America*. The three-pronged "Brennan doctrine," though scorned in the *Miller* case by Chief Justice Burger, was still at work, protecting the freedom of any film or book able to lay claim to some form of social importance. After *Caligula* was found not obscene in Atlanta, Guccione submitted a version to the MPAA, with the more blatant sexual and violent scenes deleted. It received an X rating and was distributed throughout the South and elsewhere. To date, *Caligula* is the largest grossing independently produced X-rated film ever made in the United States.[8]

There is no telling what the Supreme Court would do if the issue whether a person may be punished for exhibiting *Caligula* were squarely presented to it. In the past, the Court has shown itself unable, unequivocally, to answer that sort of question with regard to the book *Memoirs of Hecate County* and the film *I Am Curious—Yellow*, although it did give a clear answer in the case of the movie *Carnal Knowledge*. Given the state of the law today, the matter would resolve itself into the more concrete issue: Would at least four members of the Court consider the question worth deciding, and, if so, would at least five Justices, after viewing the film, be prepared to take the position that the film is entitled to constitutional protection? The continuing inability even of constitutional lawyers to give any certain answer to this question is fair measure of the extent to which movies in this country are still not really free—despite the command of the First Amendment.

Notes

References to extended passages appear within a single note. Titles of works cited more than once in a chapter are abbreviated following the first complete reference in that chapter. In addition to references for books and journal articles, various archival and manuscript collections are also cited. Materials at the Library and Museum of the Performing Arts of the New York Public Library (NYPL), the Motion Picture Association of America (MPAA), and the Museum of Modern Art Library (MOMA), all located in New York City, are referred to by the name of the file and the institution's acronym (for example, *Gone With the Wind* file, MOMA).

The papers of other institutions and individuals are identified by the title of the manuscript collection (for example, Roosevelt Papers). Collections cited, and their locations, are: Hugo L. Black Papers; Harold H. Burton Papers; Huntington Cairns Papers; Felix Frankfurter Papers; and William O. Douglas Papers (all in Manuscript Division, Library of Congress, Washington, D.C.); Edmond Cahn Papers (in private possession, New York, N.Y.); Felix Frankfurter Papers (Harvard Law School Library, Harvard University, Cambridge, Mass.); John Marshall Harlan Papers (Seeley G. Mudd Manuscript Library, Princeton University, Princeton, N.J.); George La Piana Papers (Andover-Harvard Theological Library, Harvard Divinity School, Harvard University, Cambridge, Mass.); New York City Archives (New York City Municipal Archives, Department of Records and Information Services, New York, N.Y.); People's Institute Papers (Cooper Union for the Advancement of Science and Art, New York, N.Y.); and Franklin D. Roosevelt Papers (Franklin D. Roosevelt Library, Hyde Park, N.Y.).

"The Birth of a Nation"
—and of Censorship

1. Lewis Jacobs, *The Rise of the American Film* (New York: Harcourt, 1939), 171–188; Raymond A. Cook, *Thomas Dixon* (New York: Twayne, 1974), 109–122; Cook, "The Man Behind '*The Birth of a Nation*,' " *North Carolina Historical Review*, v. 39 (1962), 519; Thomas Dixon, Jr., *The Clansman* (New York: Grosset & Dunlap, 1905), 374; Seymour Stern, "*The Birth of a Nation*," *Cinemages* (Special Issue No. 1) (1955), 6–8; Arthur S. Link, *Wilson: The New Freedom* (Princeton: Princeton Univ. Pr., 1956), 252–254; *The Papers of Woodrow Wilson*, Link, ed., v. 32 (1980), 142, 267; *Focus on "The Birth of a Nation*," Fred Silva, ed. (Englewood Cliffs, N.J.: Prentice-Hall, 1971), 3; Thomas Cripps, *Slow Fade to Black: The Negro in American Film, 1900–1942* (New York: Oxford, 1977), 41–69; Cripps, "The Reaction of the Negro to the Motion Picture *Birth of a Nation*," *The Historian*, v. 26 (1963), 344; Russell Merritt, "Dixon, Griffith, and the Southern Legend," *Cinema Journal*, v. 12 (Fall 1972), 26; Nickieann Fleener-Marzec, "D. W. Griffith's *The Birth of a Nation*: Controversy, Suppression, and the First Amendment as It Applies to Filmic Expression, 1915–1973" (Ph.D. dissertation, Univ. of Wisconsin, 1977) (an exhaustive study); Daniel J. Leab, *From Sambo to Superspade: The Black Experience in Motion Pictures* (Boston: Houghton Mifflin, 1975), 23–40; Mutual Film Corporation v. Industrial Commission of Ohio, 236 U.S. 230 (1915); *Variety*, May 9, 1956, Nov. 5, 1958, May 15, 1978; *New York Times*, Aug. 3, 1978, Sept. 16, 1980; *San Francisco Examiner*, June 12, 1980; *Birth of a Nation* file, MOMA.

2. Robert H. Wiebe, *The Search for Order, 1877–1920* (New York: Hill & Wang, 1967), 169; Garth Jowett, *Film: The Democratic Art* (Boston: Little, 1976), 42; Vachel Lindsay, *The Art of the Moving Picture* (New York: Liveright, 1922), ch. 15 ("The Substitute for the Saloon"); Kathleen D. McCarthy, "Nickel Vice and Virtue: Movie Censorship in Chicago, 1907–1915," *Journal of Popular Film*, v. 5 (1976), 38; Russell Merritt, "Nickelodeon Theaters 1905–1914: Building an Audience for the Movies," in Tino Balio, ed., *The American Film Industry* (Madison: Univ. of Wisconsin Pr., 1976), 61; Terry Ramsaye, *A Million and One Nights* (New York: Simon & Schuster, 1926), 473; James R. McGovern, "The American Woman's Pre-World War I Freedom in Manners and Morals," *Journal of American History*, v. 55 (1968), 319; Jacobs, *Rise of American Film*, 67; *The James Boys in Missouri* case: Block v. City of Chicago, 87 N.E. 1011, 1016 (1909); Robert Sklar, *Movie-Made America: A Cultural History of American Movies* (New York: Random, 1975), 128; People v. Doris, 14 N.Y.S. 571 (1897).

3. Sklar, *Movie-Made America*, 19; Frederic C. Howe, *The Confessions of a Reformer* (New York: Scribner, 1925), 240; John Collier, *From Every Zenith: A Memoir—and Some Essays* (Denver: Sage, 1963), 71; Robert Fisher, *The People's Institute of New York City: Culture, Progressive Democracy, and the People* (Ph.D. dissertation, New York Univ., 1974); Kenneth R. Philp, *John Collier's Crusade for Indian Reform, 1920–1954* (Tucson, Ariz.: Univ. of Arizona Pr., 1974), 10–13; Jowett, *Film, 63, 111–113; Ramsaye, A Million and One*

Nights, 476–485, 612–619; John Collier, "Censorship and the National Board," *Survey*, v. 35 (Oct. 2, 1915), 10, 14; Howe, "What to Do with the Motion Picture Show: Shall It Be Censored?" *Outlook*, June 20, 1914, 414; *Standards of Judgment of the National Board of Censorship of Motion Pictures* (New York: Board, 1914), 3; Wilton A. Barrett, "The Work of the National Board of Review," *Annals of the American Academy of Political and Social Science*, v. 128 (1926), 185; McGovern, "American Woman's Pre-World War I Freedom," 332; Henry F. May, *The End of American Innocence—A Study of the First Years of Our Own Time, 1912–1917* (New York: Knopf, 1959), 343–344; Lary May, *Screening Out the Past: The Birth of Mass Culture and the Motion Picture Industry* (New York: Oxford, 1980), 49–50 (this book must be used warily; see Sklar's review in *Cinéaste*, v. 11, No. 2 [1981], 44); Orrin G. Cocks, "Applying Standards to Motion Picture Films," *Survey*, v. 32 (June 27, 1914), 337; "The Legal Aspect of Motion Picture Censorship," 44 *Harvard Law Review* 113 (1930); and the following in People's Institute Papers: "Special Report on Cheap Amusements," in *People's Institute, Eleventh Annual Report* (October 1908), 21–22; *People's Institute, Sixteenth Annual Report* (1913), 5; "Report of the Assistant Director of the People's Institute to the Chairman of the Board of Trustees of the People's Institute," covering the activities of the Institute from Oct. 1, 1914 to June 1, 1915, 17; *Report of the National Board of Censorship*, April 1915; *People's Institute, Seventeenth Annual Report* (1914), 6–7; National Board of Review of Motion Pictures, "Report Regarding Pictures Reviewed, Jan. 1, 1916–Jan. 1, 1917," 19–20.

4. *Public Papers of Governor Charles Seymour Whitman, 1916* (Albany, 1919), 111–116; Report of the Assistant Director of the National Board of Review, Nov. 1, 1914–June 1, 1915, Report of the National Board of Review, March 1915, People's Institute Papers; Ford H. MacGregor, "Official Censorship Legislation," *Annals of the American Academy of Political and Social Science*, v. 128 (1926), 166–168, 170–173; Mark Sullivan, *Our Times: The War Begins* (New York: Scribner, 1932), IV, 22; Ivan Brychta, "The Ohio Film Censorship Law," 13 *Ohio State Law Journal* 350 (1952); Jowett, *Film*, 114–119, 136; *Some of Mayor Gaynor's Letters and Speeches* (New York: Greaves, 1931), 25, 130–133, 213; Louis H. Pink, *Gaynor, the Tammany Mayor Who Swallowed the Tiger— Lawyer, Judge, Philosopher* (New York: International, 1931), 177; May, *Screening Out the Past*, 52–53; *New York Times*, Dec. 28, 1919.

5. Henry May, *End of American Innocence*, 334–337; Jacobs, *Rise of American Film*, 275; Myron Lounsbury, " 'Flashes of Lightning': The Moving Picture in the Progressive Era," *Journal of Popular Culture*, v. 3 (1970), 769; Margaret Sanger, *Margaret Sanger: An Autobiography* (New York: Norton, 1938), 77; *Fit to Win* case: Silverman v. Gilchrist, 260 F. 564, 566 (2d Cir. 1919); George H. Bell, affidavit, May 12, 1917, Paul H. Blakely to Bell, May 9, 1917, in Message Photoplay Co. v. Bell file, New York City Archives; *Birth Control* case: Message Photoplay Co. v. Bell, 100 Misc. 267, 167 N.Y.S. 129 (1917), reversed 166 N.Y.S. 338, 179 App. Div. 13 (1917); David M. Kennedy, *Birth Control in America: The Career of Margaret Sanger* (New Haven: Yale Univ. Pr., 1970), 83–87. On Bijur, see *American Jewish Year Book* 1904–1905 (Philadelphia,

1904), VI, 65; ibid. 1931–1932 (Philadelphia, 1931), XXXIII, 373; *The Universal Jewish Encyclopedia* (New York, 1948), II, 351.

6. United States v. Wursterbarth, 249 F. 908 (1919); John Higham, *Strangers in the Land: Patterns of American Nativism 1860–1925* (New York: Atheneum, 1963), 197; William E. Leuchtenburg, *The Perils of Prosperity 1914–1932* (Chicago: Univ. of Chicago Pr., 1958), 14; Peter A. Soderbergh, " 'Aux Armes': The Rise of the Hollywood War Film, 1916–1930," *South Atlantic Quarterly*, v. 65 (1966), 512; Ephraim Kaufmann, affidavit, Nov. 10, 1914, William P. Capes, affidavit, Nov. 9, 1914, George Bell to Hammerstein Opera Company, Nov. 2, 1914, memorandum, April 24, 1915, Life Photo Film Corporation v. Bell file, New York City Archives; *The Ordeal* case: Life Photo Film Corporation v. Bell, 90 Misc. 469 (1915).

7. Jowett, *Film*, 66; James R. Mock and Cedric Larson, *Words that Won the War: The Story of the Committee on Public Information, 1917–1919* (Princeton: Princeton Univ. Pr., 1939), 132, 147–148; Higham, *Strangers in the Land*, 204; Timothy J. Lyons, "Hollywood and World War I, 1914–1918," *Journal of Popular Film*, v. 1 (1972), 15; Woodrow Wilson, "Message to Congress, April 2, 1917," in Richard N. Current, John A. Garraty, and Julius Weinberg, eds., *Words that Made American History—Since the Civil War* (3rd ed.) (Boston: Little, 1972), II, 344; David M. Kennedy, *Over Here: The First World War and American Society* (New York: Oxford, 1980), 25; William Henry Harbaugh, *The Life and Times of Theodore Roosevelt* (New York: Macmillan, 1963), 475; Leuchtenburg, *Perils of Prosperity*, 44; Zechariah Chafee, *Free Speech in the United States* (Cambridge, Mass.: Harvard Univ. Pr., 1941), 51; Ray Stannard Baker, *Woodrow Wilson: Life and Letters* (Garden City, N.Y.: Doubleday, 1939), VIII, 135; Michael T. Isenberg, "The Mirror of Democracy: Reflections on the War Films of World War I, 1917–1919," *Journal of Popular Culture*, v. 9 (1976), 879; Stephen Vaughn, *Democracy, Nationalism, and the Committee on Public Information* (Chapel Hill, N.C.: Univ. of North Carolina Pr., 1980), 33, 203–213; Mock, *Censorship 1917* (Princeton: Princeton Univ. Pr., 1917), 173–181, 188; Horace C. Peterson and Gilbert C. Fite, *Opponents of War, 1917–1918* (Madison: Univ. of Wisconsin Pr., 1957), 93; United States v. Motion Picture Film *The Spirit of '76,* 252 F. 946 (S.D. Calif. 1917), affirmed Goldstein v. United States, 258 F. 908 (9th Cir. 1919).

8. Anthony Comstock, *Traps for the Young*, Robert H. Bremner, ed. (Cambridge, Mass.: Harvard Univ. Pr., 1967) (originally published 1883), vii; Heywood Broun and Margaret Leech, *Anthony Comstock—Roundsman of the Lord* (New York: Boni, 1927), opposite 254; Morris L. Ernst and Alexander Lindey, *The Censor Marches On* (Garden City, N.Y.: Doubleday, 1940), 60; MacGregor, "Official Censorship Legislation," 164–165; Jowett, *Film*, 115–116, 157–159, 465; House of Representatives Bill 14805, Sixty-third Congress, second session, 1914; Arthur E. McClure, "Censor of the Movies: Early Attempts to Regulate the Content of Motion Pictures in America, 1907–1936," in McClure, ed., *The Movies: An American Idiom—A Social History* (Rutherford, N.J.: Fairleigh Dickinson Univ. Pr., 1971), 136, 141–142; Sullivan, *Our Times: The*

War Begins, 562; Ruth A. Inglis, *Freedom of the Movies* (Chicago: Univ. of Chicago Pr., 1947), 69–70; Amy Woods, "Boston and the 'Movie' Censorship," *Survey*, April 17, 1920; "Censorship," ibid., May 21, 1921; W. D. McGuire, Jr., "Freedom of the Screen vs. Censorship," ibid., May 1, 1920; Fisher, "Film Censorship and Progressive Reform: The National Board of Censorship of Motion Pictures, 1909–1922," *Journal of Popular Film*, v. 4 (1975), 149–152; Sklar, *Movie-Made America*, 124; Murray Schumach, *The Face on the Cutting Room Floor* (New York: Morrow, 1964), 17; *New York Times*, July 16, 1940.

9. Sklar, *Movie-Made America*, 78; Inglis, *Freedom of the Movies*, 67; Ramsaye, *A Million and One Nights*, 815, 816.

The Rise of Self-Regulation

1. Will H. Hays, *Memoirs* (Garden City, N.Y.: Doubleday, 1955), 1, 2, 323–333, 441; Terry Ramsaye, *A Million and One Nights* (New York: Simon & Schuster, 1926), 809–817; "The Hays Office," *Fortune* (December 1938) in Tino Balio, ed., *American Film Industry* (Madison: Univ. of Wisconsin Pr., 1976), 300, 303–304; Garth Jowett, *Film: The Democratic Art* (Boston: Little, 1976), 167–169.

2. Morris L. Ernst and Alexander Lindey, *The Censor Marches On* (New York: Doubleday, 1940), 80; Alfred E. Smith, *Up to Now: An Autobiography* (New York: Viking, 1929), 266; *Public Papers of Governor Alfred E. Smith* 1923, 60–61; ibid. 1924, 66; ibid. 1926, 64–65; ibid. 1927, 63; Henry F. Pringle, *Alfred E. Smith: A Critical Study* (New York: Macy-Macius, 1927), 339–341; David R. Colburn, "Governor Alfred E. Smith and the Red Scare, 1919–1920," *Political Science Quarterly*, v. 88 (1973), 433, 435–436; Hays, *Memoirs*, 331, 335, 352, 353, 360–361; Ruth A. Inglis, *Freedom of the Movies* (Chicago: Univ. of Chicago Pr., 1947), 101–111; Raymond Moley, *Twenty-seven Masters of Politics* (New York: Funk & Wagnalls, 1949), 184; Jowett, *Film*, 175, 236; Howard T. Lewis, *The Motion Picture Industry* (New York: Van Nostrand, 1933), 372–373, 375.

3. "The Eyes of the Movie," in Lewis Jacobs, ed., *The Compound Cinema: The Film Writings of Harry Alan Potamkin (1900–1933)* (New York: Teacher's College, 1977), 266; *New York Times*, Aug. 10, 1925; Jowett, *Film*, 170; Lewis, *Motion Picture Industry*, 377–378; James N. Rosenberg, "Censorship in the United States," an address before the Association of the Bar of the City of New York on March 15, 1928.

4. Jowett, *Film*, 169; *New York Times*, March 26, 1929; "Film Censorship: An Administrative Analysis," 39 *Columbia Law Review* 1383, 1385 (1939); "Censorship of Motion Pictures," 49 *Yale Law Journal* 87, 93 (1939); Rosenberg, "Censorship in the United States."

5. Lloyd Lewis, "The Deluxe Picture Palace," *The New Republic* (March 27, 1929); Kenneth McGowan, *Behind the Screen* (New York: Dell, 1965), 257; Pare Lorentz, *Lorentz on Film—Movies 1927 to 1941* (New York: Hopkinson & Blake, 1975), 47; Ben M. Hall, *The Best Remaining Seats: The Story of the*

Golden Age of the Movie Palace (New York: Bramhall, 1961), 123; Russell Merritt, "Nickelodeon Theaters 1905–1914: Building an Audience for the Movies," in Tino Balio, ed., *The American Film Industry* (Madison: Univ. of Wisconsin Pr., 1976), 61; Robert Sklar, *Movie-Made America: A Cultural History of American Movies* (New York: Random, 1975), 149; Charlotte Herzog, "The Movie Palace and the Theatrical Sources of Its Architectural Style," *Cinema Journal*, v. 20, No. 2 (Spring 1981), 15; Douglas Gomery, "The Picture Palace: Economic Sense or Hollywood Nonsense?" *Quarterly Review of Film Studies*, v. 3 (1978), 23; Arthur Knight, *The Liveliest Art* (New York: New American Lib., 1979), 116; Jowett, "Bullets, Beer, and the Hays Office: *Public Enemy*," in John E. O'Connor and Martin A. Jackson, eds., *American History/ American Film—Interpreting the Hollywood Image* (New York: Ungar, 1979), 68; Jowett, *Film*, 178–180, 205, 219, 236–237; William L. O'Neill, *Everyone Was Brave* (Chicago: Quadrangle, 1969), 261; *New York Times*, Jan. 29, 1927; Inglis, *Freedom of the Movies*, 112–113.

6. Hays, *Memoirs*, 353; Inglis, *Freedom of the Movies*, 113–116; Jowett, *Film*, 237, 466–467; Rachel Low, *The History of the British Film 1906–1914* (New York: Bowker, 1973), 84–91.

7. *Public Relations of the Motion Picture Industry—A Report by the Federal Council of the Churches of Christ in America* (New York, 1932), 128, 129; Hays, *Memoirs*, 395, 436, 439, 440; Roger Newman, interview with Martin Quigley, Jr., May 14, 1981; Martin Quigley, *Decency in Motion Pictures* (New York: Macmillan, 1937), 22; William M. Halsey, *The Survival of American Innocence: Catholicism in an Era of Disillusionment, 1920–1940* (Notre Dame, Ind.: Univ. of Notre Dame Pr., 1980), 67; Inglis, *Freedom of the Movies*, 127–128; *Memo from David O. Selznick*, Rudy Behlmer, ed. (New York: Viking, 1972), 285, 297.

8. Lewis, *The Motion Picture Industry*, 384; Hays, *Memoirs*, 446; Jowett, *Film*, 475, 483; Malcolm M. Willey and Stuart A. Rice, "The Agencies of Communication," in President's Research Committee on Social Trends, *Recent Social Trends in the United States* (New York: McGraw-Hill, 1933), I, 208; Sklar, *Movie-Made America*, 162; Andrew Bergman, *We're in the Money: Depression America and Its Films* (New York: Harper, 1972), xxi, 3–4, 62–65; Edgar Dale, *The Content of Motion Pictures* (New York: Macmillan, 1935), 17; "Entertainment: Public Pressures and the Law," 71 *Harvard Law Review* 326, 333 (1957).

9. Noah Dietrich and Bob Thomas, *Howard—The Amazing Mr. Hughes* (Greenwich, Conn.: Fawcett, 1972), 128; John Keats, *Howard Hughes* (New York: Random, 1966), 52, 54; Stanley Kauffmann, ed., *American Film Criticism— From the Beginnings to Citizen Kane* (New York: Liveright, 1972), 260–261; *New York Times*, March 13, 1932; Jerome Lawrence, *Actor: The Life and Times of Paul Muni* (New York: Putnam, 1974), 160, 163, 165; Ben Hecht, *A Child of the Century* (New York: Simon & Schuster, 1954), 486–487; *Variety*, Oct. 11, 1932, Aug. 22, 1933.

10. Bergman, 49–50; Arthur M. Schlesinger, Jr., *The Crisis of the Old Order, 1919–1933* (Boston: Houghton Mifflin, 1957), 7; Frederic M. Wirt, *State Film*

Censorship, With Particular Reference to Ohio (Ph.D. dissertation, Ohio State Univ., 1956), 293; Jowett, *Film*, 207, 228; Mary G. Hawks, "Motion Pictures—A Problem for the Nation," an address delivered at the thirteenth annual convention of the National Council of Catholic Women, Oct. 7–11, 1933; Quigley, *Decency in Motion Pictures*, 74.

The Struggle for Control of the Screen

1. "The Eyes of the Movie," in Lewis Jacobs, ed., *The Compound Cinema: The Film Writings of Harry Alan Potamkin (1900–1933)* (New York: Teacher's College, 1977), 267; *New York Times*, Feb. 16, 1917; Francis J. Weber, "John J. Cantwell and the Legion of Decency," *American Ecclesiastical Review*, v. 151 (1964), 237, 245; Leo J. Lehmann, "The Catholic Church in Politics—II: Censorship by the Church," *The New Republic*, Nov. 23, 1938; Thomas J. Stritch, "Communications and the Church," in Philip Gleason, ed., *Contemporary Catholicism in the United States* (Notre Dame, Ind.: Univ. of Notre Dame Pr., 1969), 341; Paul S. Boyer, *Purity in Print: The Vice-Society Movement and Book Censorship in America* (New York: Scribner, 1968), 166, 207; Edward F. Garesche, S.J., "The Parish Priest and Moving-Pictures," *Ecclesiastical Review*, v. 76 (1927), 465–479.

2. Weber, "Cantwell and the Legion of Decency," 238–240; Paul W. Facey, S.J., *The Legion of Decency* (New York: Arno, 1974), 46; Will Hays, *Memoirs* (Garden City, N.Y.: Doubleday, 1955), 449; William M. Halsey, *The Survival of American Innocence: Catholicism in an Era of Disillusionment, 1920–1940* (Notre Dame, Ind.: Univ. of Notre Dame Pr., 1980), 119; *New York Times*, Oct. 2, 1933, June 22, 1934; George Cardinal Mundelein to Franklin D. Roosevelt, June 8, 1934, Roosevelt Papers; Ruth Inglis, *Freedom of the Movies* (Chicago: Univ. of Chicago Pr., 1947), 124; Richard Corliss, "The Legion of Decency," *Film Comment*, v. 4 (Summer 1968), 27, 29; Richard Griffith and Arthur L. Mayer, *The Movies* (New York: Simon & Schuster, 1957), 296.

3. Facey, *Legion of Decency*, 151; Inglis, *Freedom of the Movies*, 124; Arthur F. McClure, "Censor the Movies: Early Attempts to Regulate the Content of Motion Pictures in America, 1907–1936," in McClure, ed., *The Movies—An American Idiom* (Rutherford, N.J.: Fairleigh Dickinson Univ. Pr., 1971), 145–146; Weber, "Cantwell and the Legion of Decency," 241, 243; Cantwell, "Priests and the Motion Picture Industry," *Ecclesiastical Review*, v. 90 (1934), 136; Paul H. Furfey, "Children and the Cinema: The Pastor's Problem," ibid., 254; John F. Noll (Bishop of Fort Wayne, Indiana), "Can Catholics Really Reform the Movies?" ibid., 366; John T. McNicholas (Archbishop of Cincinnati and Chairman of the Episcopal Committee on Motion Pictures), "The Episcopal Committee and the Problem of Evil in Motion Pictures," ibid., v. 91 (1934), 113; Owen A. McGrath, "Catholic Action's Big Opportunity," ibid., 286–287; *New York Times*, July 8, 9, Sept. 22, 23, 1934; Oscar Handlin, *Al Smith and His America* (Boston: Little, 1958), 179–182; Hays, *Memoirs*, 452–454; Corliss, "Legion of Decency," 29.

4. George Cardinal Mundelein to Franklin D. Roosevelt, June 8, 1934, Roosevelt to Mundelein, June 30, 1934, Roosevelt Papers; *New York Times*, July 10, 1934; Joseph P. Lash, *Eleanor and Franklin: The Story of Their Relationship Based on Eleanor Roosevelt's Private Papers* (New York: Norton, 1971), 377, 386–387, 391, 418–420; James MacGregor Burns, *Roosevelt: The Lion and the Fox* (New York: Harcourt, 1956), 237, 475; John Gunther, *Roosevelt in Retrospect: A Profile in History* (New York: Harper, 1950), 80; Edward R. Kantowicz, "Cardinal Mundelein of Chicago and the Shaping of Twentieth-Century American Catholicism," *Journal of American History*, v. 68 (1981), 52.

5. *New York Times*, July 1, 9, Aug. 11, 12, Oct. 17, Dec. 28, 1934, April 22, 26, July 3, 4, 1936; Humani Generis, encyclical of Pope Pius XII, Aug. 12, 1950, in *1966 National Catholic Almanac* (Paterson, N.J.: St. Anthony's Guild, 1966), 187; John Cogley, *Catholic America* (New York: Dial, 1973), 168–193, 232; Roger Newman interview with Martin Quigley, Jr., May 14, 1981; Hays, *Memoirs*, 450, 521; Daniel Callahan, *The Mind of the Catholic Layman* (New York: Scribner, 1963), 83–86; Halsey, *The Survival of American Innocence*, 70, 74; David J. O'Brien, *The Renewal of American Catholicism* (New York: Oxford, 1972), 64; John Tracy Ellis, *American Catholicism* (Chicago: Univ. of Chicago Pr., 1969), 150–151.

6. United States v. One Book Called "Ulysses," 5 F. Supp. 182 (S.D.N.Y. 1933), affirmed 72 F. 2d 705 (2d Cir. 1934); Morris L. Ernst and Alexander Lindey, *The Censor Marches On* (Garden City, N.Y.: Doubleday, 1940), 83–84; Otto Preminger, *Preminger—An Autobiography* (Garden City, N.Y.: Doubleday, 1977), 39–40; Hedy Lamarr, *Ecstasy and Me—My Life as a Woman* (Greenwich, Conn.: Fawcett, 1967), 14–16, 21, 36; *Ecstasy* case: Eureka Productions v. Byrne, 300 N.Y.S. 218, 252 App. Div. 355 (1937), affirmed 300 N.Y.S. 986, 276 N.Y. 668 (1937); *Ecstasy* file, MOMA, NYPL.

7. Warren I. Susman, "The Thirties," in Stanley Coben and Lorman Ratner, eds., *The Development of an American Culture* (Englewood Cliffs, N.J.: Prentice-Hall, 1970), 183–189; Max Lerner, *America as a Civilization* (New York: Simon & Schuster, 1957), 60–61, 73; David Halberstam, *The Powers That Be* (New York: Knopf, 1979), 12; Frederick Lewis Allen, *Since Yesterday: The Nineteen Thirties in America* (New York: Bantam, 1965), 262; Daniel Aaron and Robert Bendiner, eds., *The Strenuous Decade: A Social and Intellectual Record of the Nineteen-Thirties* (Garden City, N.Y.: Anchor, 1970), 383–391; Susman, ed., *Culture and Commitment, 1929–1945* (New York: Braziller, 1973), 107–114; *New York Times*, Jan. 15, 1938; Arthur Schlesinger, Jr., "When the Movies Really Counted," *Show* (April 1963), 77; Jowett, *Film*, 266, 267, 273.

8. Robert Sklar, *Movie-Made America: A Cultural History of American Movies* (New York: Random, 1975), 189–191; *Memo from David O. Selznick*, Rudy Behlmer, ed. (New York: Viking, 1972), xiii, xv, 81–82, 91, 100, 141, 220–221, 226–231, 261, 284–285, 288–289, 488–489; Stanley Kauffmann, ed., *American Film Criticism—From the Beginnings to Citizen Kane* (New York: Liveright, 1972), 372; Murray Schumach, *The Face on the Cutting Room Floor* (New York: Morrow, 1964), 216; *New York Times*, April 21, 1940; Norman Zierold,

The Moguls (New York: Coward, 1969), 63; Bob Thomas, *Selznick* (Garden City, N.Y.: Doubleday, 1970), 168; Inglis, *Freedom of the Movies*, 207–208; William Pratt and Herbert Bridges, *Scarlett Fever: The Ultimate Pictorial Treasury of "Gone With the Wind"* (New York: Macmillan, 1977), 233.

9. Thomas W. Bohn and Lawrence W. Lichty, "The March of Time: News as Drama," *Journal of Popular Film*, v. 2 (1973), 380, 382; "Film Censorship: An Administrative Analysis," 39 *Columbia Law Review* 1383, 1386 (1939); Hays, *Memoirs*, 489; *Daily Worker*, Jan. 21, 1938; *Indianapolis News*, Feb. 14, 1938; "Censorship of Motion Pictures," 49 *Yale Law Journal* 87, 95 (1939); Censorship file, MOMA.

10. *New York World Telegram*, March 10, April 26, 1938; Ernst and Lindey, *The Censor Marches On*, 98–100; *Birth of a Baby* cases: American Committee on Maternal Welfare v. Cincinnati, 26 Ohio L. Abs. 533 (C.P. 1938); American Committee on Maternal Welfare v. Mangan, 14 N.Y.S. 2d 39, 257 App. Div. 570 (1939), affirmed 283 N.Y. 551 (1940); City of Lynchburg v. Dominion Theaters, 7 S.E. 2d 157 (1940); *New York Post*, March 11, 1938; *Variety*, June 29, 1938; Legion of Decency file, MOMA, MPAA.

11. *Lincoln* (Nebraska) *Journal*, Aug. 10, 1938; *New York Telegraph*, Sept. 3, 1938; *Lewiston* (Maine) Journal, March 10, 1939; *New York Evening Journal*, March 1, 1939.

12. Larry Ceplair and Stephen Englund, *The Inquisition in Hollywood: Politics in the Film Community, 1930–1960* (Garden City, N.Y.: Doubleday, 1980), 89–93, 304; Schlesinger, *The Politics of Upheaval* (Boston: Houghton Mifflin, 1960), 111–121; Jowett, *Film*, 294–297; Halberstam, *The Powers That Be*, 117; Hays, *Memoirs*, 479; William E. Leuchtenburg, *Franklin D. Roosevelt and the New Deal, 1932–1940* (New York: Harper, 1963), 114–115; Andrew Bergman, *We're in the Money: Depression America and Its Films* (New York: Harper, 1972), 115–118; Mark Schorer, *Sinclair Lewis: An American Life* (New York: McGraw-Hill, 1961), 614–616; Marion K. Sanders, *Dorothy Thompson: A Legend in Her Time* (New York: Avon, 1974), 208.

13. *The Youth of Maxim* case: Schuman v. Pickert, 269 N.W. 152 (1936); Ernst and Lindey, *The Censor Marches On*, 110–112; *Philadelphia Evening Bulletin*, Jan. 7, 1938; *Philadelphia Ledger*, Jan. 5, 1938; *Baltimore Evening Sun*, July 13, 1938; *Baltic Deputy* case: In re Appeal of Ankino Corp., Pa. C.P. No. 6, No. 1694 (1938); *Professor Mamlock* case: Thayer Amusement Corporation v. Moulton, 7 A. 2d 682 (1939); *Providence* (R.I.) *Bulletin*, July 17, 1939; *Providence Journal*, July 18, 1939; *Oregonian*, April 1, 1939; "Film Censorship," 1383; *Professor Mamlock* file, MOMA, MPAA, NYPL.

14. Richard H. Pells, *Radical Visions and American Dreams: Culture and Social Thought in the Depression Years* (New York: Harper, 1973), 309–310; Matthew Josephson, *Infidel in the Temple* (New York: Knopf, 1967), 407–409, 411–414, 434–436; Allen Guttmann, *The Wound in the Heart* (New York: Free Press, 1962); R. Alan Lawson, *The Failure of Independent Liberalism (1930–1941)* (New York: Putnam, 1971), 221; Charles C. Alexander, *Nationalism in American Thought, 1930–1945* (Chicago: Rand McNally, 1969), 32, 155; Burns,

Roosevelt: The Lion and the Fox (New York: Harcourt, 1956), 355–357; Robert Dallek, *Franklin D. Roosevelt and American Foreign Policy, 1932–1945* (New York: Oxford, 1979), 127–128, 135–136, 140–143, 159–161, 177–180.

15. *Spain in Flames* case: In re "Spain in Flames" 36 D.&C. 285 (1937); *Philadelphia Legal Intelligencer*, Nov. 26, 1937; 86 *University of Pennsylvania Law Review* 305 (1938); "Censorship of Motion Pictures," 98–100; Hays, *Memoirs*, 489; Ceplair and Englund, *Inquisition in Hollywood*, 65, 307–310; "Film Censorship," 1389, 1404; *New York Telegraph*, Aug. 22, 1938; Corliss, "Legion of Decency," 33; Russell Whelan, "The Legion of Decency," *American Mercury* (June 1945); Ceplair, "The Politics of Compromise in Hollywood: A Case Study," *Cinéaste*, v. 8, No. 4 (1978), 2–7; various files, MOMA, NYPL.

World War II and the Postwar Years

1. Arthur Knight, *The Liveliest Art* (New York: New American Lib., 1979), 267; Garth Jowett, *Film: The Democratic Art* (Boston: Little, 1976), 299–302, 308; Clayton R. Koppes and Gregory D. Black, "What to Show the World: The Office of War Information and Hollywood, 1942–1945," *Journal of American History*, v. 64 (1977), 87–105; John Morton Blum, *V Was For Victory: Politics and American Culture During World War II* (New York: Harcourt, 1976), 24, 25.

2. Melvin Small, "Buffoons and Brave Hearts: Hollywood Portrays the Russians, 1939–1944," *California Historical Quarterly*, v. 52 (1973), 326; David Culbert, "Our Awkward Ally: *Mission to Moscow*," in John E. O'Connor and Martin A. Jackson, eds., *American History/American Film* (New York: Ungar, 1979), 256; Culbert, ed., *Mission to Moscow* (Madison: Univ. of Wisconsin Pr., 1980), 256; Knight, *The Liveliest Art*, 300; Victor S. Navasky, *Naming Names* (New York: Viking, 1980), 104, 167; Koppes and Black, "What to Show the World," 103–104; Jowett, *Film*, 311, 475; Blum, *V Was For Victory*, 95–96; Richard Polenberg, *War and Society: The United States 1941–1945* (Philadelphia: Lippincott, 1972), 51–52; MPAA files.

3. *New York Times*, March 8, 1954, Aug. 25, 1963; Roger Newman interview with Kenneth Clark, April 6, 1982; Newman telephone interviews with Will Hays, Jr., Nov. 5, 1981, Harriet Johnston Fix, Nov. 23, 1981; Will Hays, *Memoirs* (Garden City, N.Y.: Doubleday, 1955), 569; Franklin D. Roosevelt memorandum for Stephen Early, May 13, 1944, Roosevelt Papers; Larry Ceplair and Stephen Englund, *The Inquisition in Hollywood: Politics in the Film Community, 1930–1960* (Garden City, N.Y.: Doubleday, 1980), 209–221; Robert Sklar, *Movie-Made America: A Cultural History of American Movies* (New York: Random, 1975), 256–258; John Cogley, *Report on Blacklisting: I—Movies* (Fund for the Republic, 1956), 60–67; Navasky, *Naming Names*; Ceplair and Englund, *Inquisition in Hollywood*; David Caute, *The Great Fear* (New York: Simon & Schuster, 1978), 487–520; Charles Higham, *Hollywood at Sunset* (New York: Saturday Review Pr., 1972), 64–65; Howard Suber, *The 1947 Hearings of*

the House Committee on Un-American Activities in Communism in the Hollywood Motion Picture Industry (MA thesis, Univ. of California, Los Angeles, 1966), 96.

4. Murray Schumach, *The Face on the Cutting Room Floor* (New York: Morrow, 1964), 52–62; Richard Corliss, "The Legion of Decency," *Film Comment*, v. 4 (Summer 1968), 38–41; John Keats, *Howard Hughes* (New York: Random, 1966), 137–138, 151–154, 157–158, 161–164, 170–173, 194–195; Joseph C. Goulden, *The Best Years 1945–1950* (New York: Atheneum, 1976), 197–198; Donald L. Barlett and James B. Steele, *Empire: The Life, Legend, and Madness of Howard Hughes* (New York: Norton, 1979), 107, 110, 136; Doug Fetherling, *The Five Lives of Ben Hecht* (Toronto: Lester & Orpen, 1977), 95; Noah Dietrich and Bob Thomas, *Howard—The Amazing Mr. Hughes* (Greenwich, Conn.: Fawcett, 1972), 152–160; *The Outlaw* file, MOMA; Hughes Tool Co. v. Motion Picture Assn. of America, 66 F. Supp. 1006 (S.D.N.Y. 1946); Roger Newman telephone interview with Father Francis Weber, Oct. 14, 1981; United Artists v. Amity Amusement Corp., 66 N.Y.S. 2d 299 (1946), affirmed 66 N.Y.S. 2d 621 (1946); Hughes Tool Co. v. Fielding, 73 N.Y.S. 2d 98 (1947), affirmed 75 N.Y.S. 2d 287 (1947).

5. Goulden, *The Best Years*, 5, 188–195, 203–204, 428; Martin A. Jackson, "The Uncertain Peace: *The Best Years of Our Lives*," in O'Connor and Jackson, eds., *American History/American Film*, 147; Gay Talese, *Thy Neighbor's Wife* (New York: Dell, 1981), 64, 83, 92, 120; Max Lerner, *America as a Civilization* (New York: Simon & Schuster, 1957), 679–687; Paul Blanshard, *American Freedom and Catholic Power* (Boston: Beacon, 1949), 135; Jowett, *Film*, 344, 352, 473; Douglas T. Miller and Marion Novak, *The Fifties: The Way We Really Were* (Garden City, N.Y.: Doubleday, 1977), 314; Higham, *Hollywood at Sunset*, 18–19; Theodore H. White, *In Search of History: A Personal Adventure* (New York: Harper, 1978), 381; David Halberstam, *The Powers That Be* (New York: Knopf, 1979), 132; John Brooks, *The Great Leap: The Past Twenty-Five Years in America* (New York: Harper, 1966), 162.

6. United States v. Paramount Pictures, 334 U.S. 131 (1948); Michael Conant, *Antitrust in the Motion Picture Industry: Economic and Legal Analysis* (Berkeley, Calif.: Univ. of California Pr., 1960); Gene M. Gressley, ed., *Voltaire and the Cowboy: The Letters of Thurman Arnold* (Boulder, Colo.: Colorado Associated Univ. Pr., 1977), 44; Ellis W. Hawley, *The New Deal and the Problem of Monopoly* (Princeton: Princeton Univ. Pr., 1966), 365–368; Higham, *Hollywood at Sunset*, 22–32.

7. Mel Gussow, *Don't Say Yes Until I Finish Talking: A Biography of Darryl F. Zanuck* (New York: Pocket, 1972), xiv, xv, 138; Schumach, *The Face on the Cutting Room Floor*, 104; Thomas R. Cripps, "The Myth of the Southern Box Office: A Factor in Racial Stereotyping in American Movies, 1920–1940," in James C. Curtis and Lewis L. Gould, eds., *The Black Experience in America* (Austin: Univ. of Texas Pr., 1970), 118; *Pinky* case: Gelling v. State, 247 S.W. 2d 95, reversed 343 U.S. 960 (1952); Jowett, *Film*, 371; Theodore R. Kupferman and Philip J. O'Brien, Jr., "Motion Picture Censorship—The Memphis Blues," 36 *Cornell Law Quarterly* 273, 276–278, 286 (1951); *Lost Boundaries* case: RD-

DR Corp. v. Smith, 89 F. Supp. 596 (N.D. Ga. 1950), affirmed 183 F. 2d 562 (5th Cir. 1950), certiorari denied 340 U.S. 853 (1951); "Entertainment: Public Pressures and the Law," 71 *Harvard Law Review* 326, 338 (1957); *Curley* case: United Artists Corp. v. Board of Censors, 225 S.W. 2d 550 (1949), certiorari denied 339 U.S. 853 (1950).

8. Roger Newman telephone interview with Joseph Breen, Jr., Nov. 28, 1981; Ronald Story, "Joseph Ignatius Breen," in John A. Garraty, ed., *Dictionary of American Biography* (Supplement Seven, 1961–1965) (New York: Scribner, 1981), 71; Jack Vizzard, *See No Evil: Life Inside a Hollywood Censor* (New York: Simon & Schuster, 1970), 75, 103; Elihu Winer, "See Nothing But Evil: Recollections of a Hollywood Censor," *International Writers Guild Journal*, July 1970, 24; J. P. McAvoy, "The Back of Me Hand to You," *Saturday Evening Post*, Dec. 24, 1938; Roger Newman interview with Elihu Winer, Nov. 9, 1981; Conant, *Antitrust in Motion Picture Industry*, 42; Schumach, *The Face on the Cutting Room Floor*, 88–89; Jowett, *Film*, 403; John Mason Brown, *Dramatis Personae: A Retrospective Show* (New York: Viking, 1963), 323–324; "Motion Pictures and the First Amendment," 60 *Yale Law Journal* 696, 716 (1951).

9. Morris L. Ernst and Alexander Lindey, *The Censor Marches On* (Garden City, N.Y.: Doubleday, 1940), 79; State of Ohio v. Lerner, 81 N.E. 2d 282, 286 (1948); Winters v. New York, 333 U.S. 507, 515 (1948).

10. Edmund Wilson, *Letters on Literature and Politics, 1912–1972*, Elena Wilson, ed. (New York: Farrar, Straus, 1977), 433–441, 495, 544, 559; William B. Lockhart and Robert C. McClure, "Literature, the Law of Obscenity, and the Constitution," 38 *Minnesota Law Review* 295, 295–301 (1954); Doubleday and Co. v. N.Y., 335 U.S. 848 (1948); docket books, Douglas Papers, Burton Papers.

11. Roth v. Goldman, 172 F. 2d 788, 796 (1949); Edward de Grazia, "Obscenity and the Mail," 20 *Law and Contemporary Problems*, v. 2, 609 (1955); Commonwealth v. Gordon, 66 D.&C. 101 (1949); Alexander Meiklejohn, *Free Speech and Its Relation to Self-Government* (New York: Harper, 1948); Inglis, *Freedom of Movies*, iv, 178–180, 193–194; United States v. Paramount Pictures, 334 U.S. 161, 166 (1948).

Sacrilege and the Supreme Court

1. *New York Herald Tribune*, Nov. 30, 1951; Arthur L. Mayer, *Merely Colossal* (New York: Simon & Schuster, 1953), 216–225, 228, 229; Ezra Goodman, *The Fifty-Year Decline and Fall of Hollywood* (New York: Simon & Schuster, 1961), 423–424; Mary Batten, "An Interview with Ephraim London," *Film Comment*, v. 1, No. 4 (Summer 1964), 2–19; Richard Corliss, "The Legion of Decency," *Film Comment*, v. 4, No. 4 (Summer 1968), 41–44; Alan F. Westin, *The Miracle Case: The Supreme Court and the Movies* (University, Ala.: Univ. of Alabama Pr., 1961); Bosley Crowther, "The Strange Case of *The Miracle*," *Atlantic*, April 1951, 35–39; *Remous* case: Mayer v. Byrne, 10 N.Y.S. 2d 794 (1939).

2. Docket book, Frankfurter to Brethren, April 29, 1952, Douglas Papers; Frankfurter to Brethren, April 25, 1952, Wendell P. Brown and Charles A. Brind, Jr. to Hugo L. Black, May 1, 1952, Black Papers; Frankfurter to George La Piana, no date (about Nov. 5), Nov. 26, 1951, La Piana Papers; La Piana to Frankfurter, Nov. 18, Dec. 10, 1951, Frankfurter to La Piana, Dec. 14, 1951, Frankfurter Papers, Harvard; John P. Frank, *Marble Palace: The Supreme Court in American Life* (New York: Knopf, 1958), 103; Frank, "The United States Supreme Court: 1951–52," 20 *University of Chicago Law Review* 1, 20 (1952); *New York Times*, Dec. 13, 1953; Roger Newman telephone interviews with Stanley Thayer and C. Richard Walker, Dec. 9, 1981, Abram Chayes, April 2, 1982, Marshall Small, April 5, 1982; Newman interview with Ephraim London, Feb. 21, 1980; Burstyn v. McCaffrey, 198 Misc. 884 (1951); Burstyn v. Wilson, 104 N.Y.S. 2d 740 (1951), affirmed 101 N.E. 2d 665 (1951), reversed 343 U.S. 495 (1952).

3. *Pinky* case: Gelling v. Texas, 343 U.S. 960 (1952); *Native Son* case: Classic Pictures v. Dept. of Education, 346 U.S. 587 (1954); *M* case: Superior Films v. Dept. of Education, 346 U.S. 587 (1954); *La Ronde* case: Commercial Pictures v. Board of Regents, 346 U.S. 587 (1954); *The Moon Is Blue* case: Holmby Productions v. Vaughn, 350 U.S. 870 (1955); Felix Frankfurter to Hugo L. Black, Jan. 12, 1954, Frankfurter Papers; Alexander M. Bickel, *The Morality of Consent* (New Haven, Conn.: Yale Univ. Pr., 1975), 25–28.

4. *New York Herald Tribune*, Jan. 10, 22, 1954; Hugh M. Flick, "Control and Regulation of Motion Pictures," address presented as part of the 1954 Summer Institute Series of the Univ. of Michigan Law School on Communications Media Legal and Policy Problems, June 16–18, 1954; *Public Papers of Governor Thomas E. Dewey* (Albany, N.Y., 1955), 300; Leonard Maltin, *The Disney Films* (New York: Crown, 1973), 118; *New York Post*, Aug. 13, 1954; *New York Times*, Aug. 13, 1954; *Buffalo Courier-Express*, Aug. 19, 1954; *Exhibitor* (New York), Aug. 18, 1954; Times Film Corp. v. Chicago, 365 U.S. 43, 69 (1961); Otto Preminger, *Preminger—An Autobiography* (Garden City, N.Y.: Doubleday, 1977), 103–105.

5. Preminger, *Preminger*, 103–110; Andrew Dowdy, *"Movies Are Better than Ever": Wide-Screen Memories of the Fifties* (New York: Morrow, 1973), 80–81, 85–87; Willi Frischauer, *Behind the Scenes of Otto Preminger* (New York: Morrow, 1974), 124–128; Gerald Pratley, *The Cinema of Otto Preminger* (New York: Barnes, 1971), 5; Roger Newman interviews with Kenneth Clark, April 6, 1982, Arthur Krim, April 9, 1982; Garth Jowett, *Film: The Democratic Art* (Boston: Little, 1976), 414–415; Jack Vizzard, *See No Evil: Life Inside a Hollywood Censor* (New York: Simon & Schuster, 1970), 137–144, 151–157; *New York Herald Tribune*, Jan. 10, 1954; *New York Times*, Jan. 24, 1957; Corliss, "The Legion of Decency," 48; "Entertainment: Public Pressures and the Law," 71 *Harvard Law Review* 326, 346 (1957); Ira H. Carmen, *Movies, Censorship, and the Law* (Ann Arbor: Univ. of Michigan Pr., 1966), 154.

6. Donald L. Barlett and James B. Steele, *Empire: The Life, Legend, and Madness of Howard Hughes* (New York: Norton, 1979), 195–198; John Keats, *Howard*

Hughes (New York: Random, 1966), 268–269; *New York Times*, May 25, 1954; Jack Vizzard, *See No Evil*, 158, 159, 165, 172–178, 190–196, 300, 359; *America*, April 4, 1942; Schumach, *The Face on the Cutting Room Floor*, 41–48; Roger Newman telephone interviews with Albert Van Schmus, Nov. 11, 1981, and Joseph Breen, Jr., Nov. 28, 1981.

7. Executive Order 9835, in Federal Register (v. 12), 1935; Arthur Schlesinger, Jr., in John M. Blum and others, *The National Experience* (New York: Harcourt, 1973), 727; Barton Bernstein, "America in War and Peace: The Test of Liberalism," in Bernstein, ed., *Toward a New Past: The Dissenting Essays in American History* (New York: Random, 1968), 308–309; David Caute, *The Great Fear* (New York: Simon & Schuster, 1978); Thomas I. Emerson, *The System of Freedom of Expression* (New York: Random, 1970), 205–225; Douglas T. Miller and Marion Novak, *The Fifties: The Way We Really Were* (Garden City, N.Y.: Doubleday, 1977), 21–42, 249–254.

8. Horace W. Fleming, Jr., "The Oklahoma Literature Commission: A Case Study in Administrative Regulation of Obscenity," 29 *Oklahoma Law Review* 882 (1976); Bantam Books v. Melko, 96 A. 2d 47 (1953); Walter Gellhorn, *Individual Freedom and Governmental Restraints* (Baton Rouge: Louisiana State Univ. Pr., 1956), 49–104; William B. Lockhart and Robert C. McClure, "Literature, the Law of Obscenity, and the Constitution," 38 *Minnesota Law Review* 295, 302–320 (1954); Paul Blanshard, *American Freedom and Catholic Power* (Boston: Beacon, 1958), 6, 109, 367; Herbert S. Parmet, *Eisenhower and the American Crusades* (New York: Macmillan, 1972), 259–264; Schlesinger, in Blum, *National Experience*, 741; Eric F. Goldman, *The Crucial Decade—And After* (New York: Knopf, 1956), 252–255; Anne Lyon Haight (updated and enlarged by Chandler B. Grannis), *Banned Books—387* B.C. *to 1978* A.D. (New York: Bowker, 1978), 126; Emmett John Hughes, *The Ordeal of Power* (New York: Atheneum, 1963), 94.

9. Russell E. Shain, "Cold War Films, 1948–1962: An Annotated Bibliography," *Journal of Popular Film*, v. 3 (1974), 365; Shain, "Hollywood's Cold War," ibid., 334; Gary K. Wolfe, "*Dr. Strangelove, Red Alert*, and Patterns of Paranoia in the 1950s," ibid., v. 5 (1976), 57; Arthur Knight, *The Liveliest Art* (New York: New American Lib., 1979), 303; Richard Hofstadter, *Anti-Intellectualism in American Life* (New York: Knopf, 1963), 7; Hofstadter, *The Paranoid Style in American Politics and Other Essays* (New York: Knopf, 1965), 23, 29, 35, 39; Stuart Samuels, "The Age of Conspiracy and Conformity: *Invasion of the Body Snatchers*," in John E. O'Connor and Martin A. Jackson, eds., *American History/American Film: Interpreting the Hollywood Image* (New York: Ungar, 1979), 203; Lawrence Suid, "The Pentagon and Hollywood: *Dr. Strangelove, or How I Learned to Stop Worrying and Love the Bomb*," in ibid., 219.

10. Preminger, *Preminger*, 110–113; Dowdy, "*Movies Are Better than Ever*," 88–90; Schumach, *The Face on the Cutting Room Floor*, 69; Pratley, *Cinema of Preminger*, 100, 112; Robert W. Haney, *Comstockery in America* (Boston: Beacon, 1960), 127–129; *New York Times*, Dec. 12, 1956; various files, MOMA.

11. Malcolm Boyd, *Christ and Celebrity Gods: The Church in Mass Culture* (Green-

wich, Conn.: Seabury, 1958), 106–114; Corliss, "The Legion of Decency," 44–47; Schumach, *The Face on the Cutting Room Floor*, 71–78, 95–96; Jowett, *Film*, 417–418; Vizzard, *See No Evil*, 205–215, 261; David E. Koskoff, *Joseph P. Kennedy: A Life and Times* (Englewood Cliffs, N.J.: Prentice-Hall, 1974), 333; Victor S. Navasky, *Naming Names* (New York: Viking, 1980), 199–222; Preminger, *Preminger*, 115, 119; Morris L. Ernst and Alan U. Schwartz, *Censorship: The Search for the Obscene* (New York: Macmillan, 1964), 234–235; Emmett McLoughlin, *American Culture and Catholic Schools* (New York: Lyle Stuart, 1960), 145–147.

12. Harold C. Gardiner, "Moral Principles Toward a Definition of the Obscene," 20 *Law and Contemporary Problems* 560, 567 (1955); Lockhart and McClure, "Censorship of Obscenity: The Developing Constitutional Standards," 45 *Minnesota Law Review* 5, 26 (1961); Leon Friedman, ed., *Obscenity: The Complete Oral Arguments Before the Supreme Court in the Major Obscenity Cases* (New York: Chelsea, 1970), 18; Roth v. United States, 354 U.S. 476 (1957). On Douglas, see Roger K. Newman, book review of Vern Countryman, ed., *The Douglas Opinions* (New York: Random, 1977), 6 *Hastings Constitutional Law Quarterly* 387, 396–400 (1978).

13. Goldman, *The Crucial Decade*, 308; Miller and Novak, *The Fifties*, 16–18, 301–307; Gay Talese, *Thy Neighbor's Wife* (New York: Dell, 1981), 57–58, 88–89, 107.

14. Bob Thomas, *King Cohn: The Life and Times of Harry Cohn* (New York: Bantam, 1968), 257; *New York Times*, Oct. 6, 1959; Knight, *The Liveliest Art*, 200–202, 306–319.

15. Haight/Grannis, *Banned Books*, 68–70; Abe Krash, book review of C. H. Rolph, ed., *The Trial of Lady Chatterley* (Baltimore: Penguin, 1961), 71 *Yale Law Journal* 1351 (1962); Charles Rembar, *The End of Obscenity: The Trials of Lady Chatterley, Tropic of Cancer, and Fanny Hill* (New York: Random, 1968), 59–160; Friedman, *Obscenity*, 71; *Lady Chatterley's Lover* case: Kingsley International Pictures Corporation v. Regents, 165 N.Y.S. 2d 681 (1957), affirmed 151 N.E. 2d 197 (1958), reversed 360 U.S. 684 (1959); Smith v. California, 361 U.S. 147 (1959); Lockhart and McClure, "Censorship of Obscenity," 39–43, 99–103; *New York Post*, May 17, 1959.

The Era of Constitutionalization

1. Arthur M. Schlesinger, Jr., *A Thousand Days: John F. Kennedy in the White House* (Boston: Houghton Mifflin, 1965), 726–727; John Cogley, *Catholic America* (New York: Dial, 1973), 115–122, 265–266; David J. O'Brien, *The Renewal of American Catholicism* (New York: Oxford Univ. Pr., 1972), 66–70; John Courtney Murray, *We Hold These Truths: Catholic Reflections on the American Proposition* (Garden City, N.Y.: Image, 1960), 9–10, 165, 169–171; Robert D. Cross, *The Emergence of Liberal Catholicism* (Cambridge, Mass.: Harvard Univ. Pr., 1958), 206–225; Jack Vizzard, *See No Evil: Life Inside a Hollywood Censor* (New York: Simon & Schuster, 1970), 265–271, 292–298; Garth Jowett, *Film: The Democratic Art* (Boston: Little, 1976), 419; *Newsweek*,

Feb. 13, 1961; Atlanta v. Lopert Pictures Corporation, 122 S.E. 2d 916 (1961), 125 S.E. 2d 207 (1962) (Georgia); Twentieth Century-Fox Films Corporation v. Boehm, 75 Dauph. 341 (1960) (No. 2387 in Equity) (Pennsylvania); Portland v. Welch, 367 P. 2d 403 (1961) (Oregon); Atlanta v. Twentieth Century-Fox, 133 S.E. 2d 12 (1961) (Georgia); RKO Pictures v. Department of Education, 122 N.E. 2d 769 (1954) (Ohio); Brattle Films v. Commissioner of Public Safety, 127 N.E. 2d 891 (1955) (Massachusetts).

2. Felix Bilgrey, unpublished memoir, in possession of Roger Newman; Newman interview with Bilgrey, Aug. 2, 1979; Times Film Corporation v. Chicago, 365 U.S. 43 (1961), 365 U.S. 856 (1961) (rehearing denied); John M. Harlan to Tom Clark, Nov. 3, 1960, Harlan Papers; Jack Harrison Pollack, *Earl Warren: The Judge Who Changed America* (Englewood Cliffs, N.J.: Prentice-Hall, 1979), 355; "Chief Justice Earl Warren: A Tribute," 2 *Hastings Constitutional Law Quarterly* 1, 17 (1975); *Newsweek*, June 11, 1964; Richard S. Randall, *Censorship of the Movies: The Social and Political Control of a Mass Medium* (Madison: Univ. of Wisconsin Pr., 1968), 40; Theodore H. White, *In Search of History: A Personal Adventure* (New York: Harper, 1978), 496.

3. Regina v. Hicklin [1868] L.R. 3 Q.B. 360; Manuel Enterprises v. Day, 370 U.S. 478 (1962); William J. Brennan, Jr., to John M. Harlan, June 9, 1962, Potter Stewart to Harlan, June 5, 1962, Harlan to Brennan, June 11, 1962, Harlan Papers; William O. Douglas to Edmond Cahn, Jan. 21, 1960, Cahn Papers; Yudkin v. Maryland, 182 A. 2d 798 (1962); Harry Kalven, Jr., "The Metaphysics of the Law of Obscenity," 1960 *Supreme Court Review*, Philip B. Kurland, ed. (Chicago: Univ. of Chicago Pr., 1960), 1; Interstate Circuit v. Dallas, 390 U.S. 676, 704 (1968).

4. Felice Flannery Lewis, *Literature, Obscenity, and the Law* (Carbondale, Ill.: Southern Illinois Univ. Pr., 1976), 208–209; *Henry Miller: Years of Trial and Triumph, 1962–1964*, Elmer Gertz and Felice F. Lewis, eds. (Carbondale, Ill.: Southern Illinois Univ. Pr., 1978), 315; American Civil Liberties Union and Maryland Civil Liberties Union *amici curiae* brief, in Yudkin v. Maryland, 182 A. 2d 798 (1962); Brennan draft opinion, April 15, 1963, Memorandum for the Conference, June 18, 1964, Harlan Papers; Jacobellis v. Ohio, 378 U.S. 184 (1964); Grove Press v. Gerstein, 378 U.S. 577 (1964); *New York Times*, June 20, 1981.

5. Huntington Cairns to Milton R. Konvitz, Jan. 25, 1966, Cairns Papers; A Book Named "John Cleland's Memoirs of a Woman of Pleasure" v. Attorney General, 383 U.S. 413 (1966); William O. Douglas, Memorandum for the Conference, March 15, 1966, Harlan Papers; Ginzburg v. United States, 383 U.S. 463 (1966); Mishkin v. New York, 383 U.S. 502 (1966); Charles Rembar, *The End of Obscenity: The Trials of Lady Chatterley, Tropic of Cancer and Fanny Hill* (New York: Random, 1968), 406–490; C. Peter Magrath, "The Obscenity Cases: Grapes of Roth," 1966 *Supreme Court Review* 7, 56–69; Bilgrey, unpublished memoir; Roger Newman interview with Bilgrey; Freedman v. Maryland, 380 U.S. 51 (1965).

6. Stanley v. Georgia, 394 U.S. 557 (1969); Thurgood Marshall draft opinion, March 12, 1969, John M. Harlan to Marshall, Mar. 13, 1969, Harlan Papers.

Protection Amidst Turbulence

1. John Bartlow Martin, *Adlai Stevenson and the World* (Garden City, N.Y.: Doubleday, 1977), 838; Roger Newman interview with Arthur Krim, April 9, 1982; *Washington Post*, July 9, 1981; Douglas Ayer, Roy E. Bates, and Peter J. Herman, "Self-Censorship in the Movie Industry: An Historical Perspective on Law and Social Change," 1970 *Wisconsin Law Review* 791, 800; Jack Vizzard, *See No Evil: Life Inside a Hollywood Censor* (New York: Simon & Schuster, 1970), 318–342; Richard S. Randall, *Censorship of the Movies: The Social and Political Control of a Mass Medium* (Madison: Univ. of Wisconsin Pr., 1968), 201–204. Roger Newman telephone interview with William Lockhart, Jan. 4, 1982; *New York Times*, April 25, Aug. 8, Sept. 21, 22, Oct. 5, 1967, Jan. 3, 1968.

2. Ginsberg v. New York, 390 U.S. 629 (1968); Interstate Circuit, Inc. v. City of Dallas, 390 U.S. 676 (1968); Theodore H. White, *The Making of the President 1968* (New York: Atheneum, 1969), 62–63, 226–232; "America's Two Cultures: An Interview with Theodore H. White," in *Our Troubled Press: Ten Years of the Columbia Law Review*, Alfred Balk and James Boylan, eds. (Boston: Little, 1971), 11–23; William L. O'Neill, *Coming Apart: An Informal History of America in the 1960s* (New York: Quadrangle, 1971), 212–222; Arthur M. Schlesinger, Jr., *The Crisis of Confidence: Ideas, Power, and Violence in America* (Boston: Houghton Mifflin, 1969), 194–237; Geoffrey Hodgson, *America in Our Time* (New York: Doubleday, 1976), 306–352.

3. Robert Shogan, *A Question of Judgment: The Fortas Case and the Struggle for the Supreme Court* (Indianapolis: Bobbs-Merrill, 1972), 128–129, 172–173; Gay Talese, *Thy Neighbor's Wife* (New York: Dell, 1981), 423–424; *New York Times*, July 23, 24, Sept. 6, 14, 1968.

4. Roger Newman telephone interview with Mary Looram, Dec. 3, 1981; Newman interviews with Kenneth Clark, April 6, 1982, Arthur Krim, April 9, 1982; Ayers, Bates, and Herman, "Self-Censorship in the Movie Industry," 820–836; Note, "Private Censorship of Movies," 22 *Stanford Law Review* 618, 622–625 (1970); Garth Jowett, *Film: The Democratic Art* (Boston: Little, 1976), 441–443; *New York Times*, May 24, June 16, 1981; William Wolf, "X-ing Out the Ratings," *New York* Magazine, Sept. 15, 1980; Carl T. Rowan and David M. Mazie, "Do Movie Ratings Work?," *Reader's Digest*, July 1981.

5. Milton Viorst, *Heroes and Hustlers* (New York: Simon & Schuster, 1971), 307; *Washington Star*, Aug. 12, 1979; Grove Press Files (Grove Press obtained information in a suit brought under the Freedom of Information Act); Records and Briefs, United States v. A Motion Picture Film Entitled *I Am Curious—Yellow*, 404 F. 2d 196 (1968); files of Edward de Grazia; Alan M. Dershowitz, *The Best Defense* (New York: Random, 1982), 155–174; Mutual Film Corporation v. Industrial Commission of Ohio, 236 U.S. 230 (1915).

6. Earl Warren to Felix Frankfurter, Nov. 7, 1957, Frankfurter Papers; Paris Adult Theatre I v. Slaton, 413 U.S. 49, 71 (1973); Ginsberg v. New York, 390 U.S. 629, 655 (1968); U.S. v. 12 200-Ft. Reels of Film, 413 U.S. 123, 137 (1973); Smith v. California, 361 U.S. 147, 168 (1959); Harlan, Memorandum to the Conference,

April 29, 1971, Douglas, comment on Harlan, Memorandum to the Conference, Dec. 10, 1969, Harlan Papers; Joseph Gelmis, "On Movies," *Newsday*, Feb. 11, 1968; Redrup v. New York, 386 U.S. 767 (1967).

7. Harlan, Memorandum to the Conference, Feb. 24, 1970, draft opinions, Feb. 24, 27, 1970, White draft opinion, March 6, 1970, Harlan Papers; files of Edward de Grazia; Younger v. Harris, 401 U.S. 37 (1971); Grove Press v. Maryland State Board of Censors, 401 U.S. 480 (1971); Byrne v. Karalexis, 401 U.S. 216 (1971); Bob Woodward and Scott Armstrong, *The Brethren* (New York: Simon & Schuster, 1979), 192–193; James F. Simon, *Independent Journey: The Life of William O. Douglas* (New York: Harper, 1980), 391–411; John P. MacKenzie, *The Appearance of Justice* (New York: Scribner, 1973), 44–46; William O. Douglas, *The Court Years 1939–1975: The Autobiography of William O. Douglas* (New York: Random, 1980), 355–377; *New York Times*, April 28, 1970; *Washington Post*, Dec. 9, 1970; Associate Justice William O. Douglas, Final Report by the Special Subcommittee on H. Res. 920 of the Committee on the Judiciary, House of Representatives, 91 Cong., 2d Session (Sept. 17, 1970), 42–43, 397–399, 402–403.

8. Hearings before the Subcommittee on Administrative Practice and Procedure of the Senate Judiciary Committee, 92 Cong., 1st Session, on Implementation of Recommendations of Presidential and National Commissions, May 25, 1971, 30, 32–33, 38–41, 55–56, 69, 78–82, 87–89, 92, 98; *The Report of the Commission on Obscenity and Pornography* (New York: Bantam, 1970), 57, 159, 187–189, 456, 583–584, 595, 617, 623; Roger Newman telephone interview with William B. Lockhart, Jan. 4, 1982; Newman interview with Paul Bender, Jan. 21, 1982; Talese, *Thy Neighbor's Wife*, 424–433; *New York Times*, Aug. 6, 12, 23, 26, Sept. 6, 9, 10, 15, Oct. 1, 2, 14, 25, 1970.

Decentralization of Censorship of the Screen

1. Peter Steinfels, *The Neoconservatives: The Men Who Are Changing America's Politics* (New York: Simon & Schuster, 1979), 32–41, 104–106, 171, 172; Richard Hofstadter, *The Age of Reform: From Bryan to F.D.R.* (New York: Knopf, 1955), 210–212; Walter Berns, "Pornography v. Democracy: A Case for Censorship," *The Public Interest*, No. 22 (Winter 1971), 3–24; Irving Kristol, *On the Democratic Idea in America* (New York: Harper, 1972), 31–47; Alexander M. Bickel, "Concurring and Dissenting Opinions," *The Public Interest*, No. 22 (Winter 1971), 25–26; Bickel, *The Morality of Consent* (New Haven, Conn.: Yale Univ. Pr., 1975), 29–30, 73–76, 104–109; Bickel, "Pornography, Censorship, and Common Sense," *Reader's Digest*, February 1974; Robert H. Bork, "The Legacy of Alexander M. Bickel," *Yale Law Report*, v. 26, No. 1 (Fall 1979), 11; Bork, "Neutral Principles and Some First Amendment Problems," 47 *Indiana Law Journal* 1 (1971); *Federal Judicial Center Report of the Study Group on the Case Load of the Supreme Court* (Washington, D.C., 1972).

2. Papish v. University of Missouri Curators, 410 U.S. 667, 672 (1972) (Burger

dissenting); Rosenfeld v. New Jersey, 408 U.S. 901, 902–903 (1972) (Burger dissenting); Miller v. California, 413 U.S. 15 (1973); Paris Adult Theatre I v. Slaton, 413 U.S. 49 (1973); Bob Woodward and Scott Armstrong, *The Brethren* (New York: Simon & Schuster, 1979), 254–263; *Box Office*, Nov. 24, 1969.

3. *New York Times*, June 24, 25, July 1, 20, 28, Aug. 5, Sept. 26, Oct. 10, Dec. 9, 1973; *New York Post*, July 14, 1973; *Washington Post*, July 29, 1973; Miller v. California, 414 U.S. 881 (1973) (rehearing denied); Kenneth Turan, "Unscrewing the Inscrutable," *Progressive*, December 1973; Louis Nizer, *Reflections without Mirrors* (New York: Berkley, 1979), 410–427; Jenkins v. Georgia, 418 U.S. 153 (1974).

4. *New York Times*, Sept. 28, Dec. 31, 1972, March 11, Dec. 9, 1973, May 19, 1974, Nov. 2, 1975, June 29, 1976; *New York Post*, July 14, 1973; *Los Angeles Herald-Examiner*, Oct. 19, 1973; *Atlanta Constitution*, Nov. 22, 1973; *Variety*, July 17, 1974; Nat Hentoff, "How to Make the First Amendment Obscene," *Village Voice* (New York), June 28, 1976; ibid., "But What If the Supreme Court Won't Listen?," July 5, 1976; Anthony Marro, "Prurient Interest in Memphis," *New Republic*, April 24, 1976; Ted Morgan, "United States Versus the Princes of Porn," *New York Times Magazine*, March 6, 1977; *Playboy*, February 1977; William Wolf, *Landmark Films: The Cinema and Our Century* (New York: Paddington, 1979), 360–367; Alan M. Dershowitz, *The Best Defense* (New York: Random, 1982), 163–168; Roger Newman interviews with Ephraim London, Feb. 21, 1980, Roy Grutman, Dec. 10, 1980, telephone interviews with Jay Harris, Feb. 3, 1982, Bruce Kramer, Feb. 8, 1982, Alan Dershowitz, Feb. 10, 1982; U.S. v. Peraino, 21 *Criminal Law Reporter* 2125 (W.D. Tenn. Apr. 11, 1977).

5. "Project: An Empirical Inquiry Into the Effects of Miller v. California on the Control of Obscenity," 52 *New York University Law Review* 810 (1977); "Colloquium—Violent Pornography: Degradation of Women Versus Right of Free Speech," 8 *New York University Review of Law and Social Change* 187, 285, 296 (1978–1979); Roger Newman interview with Norman Redlich, Dec. 3, 1980; William L. Prosser, *The Law of Torts*, 4th ed. (St. Paul, Minn.: West, 1971), 571–612; Erznoznik v. City of Jacksonville, 422 U.S. 205 (1975); Carl Bernstein and Bob Woodward, *All the President's Men* (New York: Simon & Schuster, 1975).

6. Robert J. Ringer, *Looking Out for #1* (New York: Fawcett, 1978); Christopher Lasch, *The Culture of Narcissism: American Life in an Age of Diminishing Expectations* (New York: Norton, 1978), xiv, xvi, 4–10, 65–66; "New Religious Movements in America" (Rockefeller Foundation Working Paper, September 1979), 27; Richard Hofstadter, *Anti-Intellectualism in American Life* (New York: Knopf, 1963), 135; "Penthouse Interview: Reverend Jerry Falwell," *Penthouse*, March 1981; *U.S. News and World Report*, June 8, 1981; Ben Stein, "The War to Clean Up TV," *Saturday Review*, February 1981; *New York Times*, Dec. 12, 1977, Aug. 23, Sept. 3, Oct. 24, 31, Dec. 11, 1980, Jan. 25, Feb. 3, 11, 12, June 22, July 5, 1981; *Washington Post*, Aug. 23, 1980; Lewis Lapham, *Washington Post Book World*, June 23, 1981; ABC Interstate Theaters,

Inc. v. State, 325 So. 2d 123 (1976); *Box Office*, Nov. 12, 1979; *Variety*, Aug. 29, 1979.

7. *Time*, Oct. 6, 1980; *New York Times*, Jan. 6, March 31, 1972, Feb. 6, 7, 15, 19, 27, June 29, Dec. 12, 1981; *New York Daily News*, Aug. 24, 1980, Feb. 27, 1981; Nat Hentoff, *Village Voice* (New York), April 28, 1980, Feb. 25, 1981; *People*, May 18, 1981; Roger Newman interview with Michael Gallagher, Sept. 11, 1981.

8. *Variety*, Nov. 14, 1979; *Washington Post*, March 31, 1980; Michael Scott, "The Highbrow Railings of Gore Vidal," *Rolling Stone*, May 15, 1980; *New York Post*, Feb. 6, 1980; *Newsday*, Feb. 10, 1980; *New York Times*, Jan. 25, Feb. 2, 10, 1980; *New York Daily News*, July 26, 1980; *Chicago Sun-Times*, Sept. 19, 1980; *Atlanta Journal*, Dec. 31, 1980; *Seattle Journal-American*, June 13, 1980; Federal Communications Commission v. Pacifica Foundation, 438 U.S. 726 (1978); *Christianity Today*, Oct. 24, 1980; Roger Newman interview with Leslie Jay, Jan. 12, 1982; File, Morality in Media v. One Motion Picture Entitled *Caligula*, No. 80-0640 (Southern District of New York), No. 80-6037 (Court of Appeals for the Second Circuit), Federal Court House, New York City; confidential source; Massachusetts v. Saxon Theater, 6 *Media Law Reporter 1979* (1980); Penthouse v. McAuliffe, 7 *Media Law Reporter 1978* (1981).

The
Movies

A Note
to the Reader

Motion pictures have been the target of censors in the United States ever since they were first made. *The Movies* presents individual accounts of the most important censorship cases, involving 122 American and foreign films banned from 1908 to 1981 for political, religious, moral, and sexual reasons. These pictures have been banned, or threatened with banning, in this country by local, state, and federal officials, including the U.S. Customs Service, and have been the subject of officially reported court cases. These accounts include cases in which the film, the act of censorship, or the legal proceedings are significant or representative. Bannings may be caused by city officials acting under city laws, state officials under state laws, or by the Customs Service and other federal officials. Many of the films have been banned in several cities and states and have been involved in numerous court cases. Actions that prevent movies from being shown are either civil or criminal. The ultimate threat always is the imprisoning or fining of a person who shows a film.

The 122 movies appear according to the year banned so that the historic movement of censorship may be followed through the decades. Each account has a number, and references to the accounts or films are found throughout the book. Accounts begin with the place and year of banning. Filmographic data provides: country(ies) of origin; year of release in the United States; distributor; running time; type (16mm or 35mm); sound or silent; color or black and white; subtitles/dubbing; producer; director; screenwriter; cinematographer; music; cast (major members); rating (referring to that, as it applies, assigned by the Motion Picture Association of America or self-imposed by the producer); festivals; awards; reviews of the film; and articles about it.

The plots of censored movies reveal individually the nation's changing life-styles and social concerns. The *censorship activity* refers to the circumstances and events that brought about the banning; the *legal importance* is a summary of the outcome of the case and a depiction of its significance in the law of movie censorship. References to sources and court cases appear in the notes at the end of the account. The reader may wish to refer to the list of abbreviations provided in the Appendix.

1908–1919

[1]
The James Boys in Missouri

Banned in Chicago, Illinois, 1908.

U.S., 1908. Dist/Prod: Essanay Film Mfg. Co. 1,000 ft. Silent. B&W.

This film was concerned with "the American historical experience" and "portray[ing] experiences of crime."[1] Another film involved in the same case was *Night Riders* [2].

Censorship Activity

Although the Chicago chief of police refused to grant a permit for the display of this movie and another called *Night Riders* in the city, Jake Block and some 200 other proprietors of "five-and-ten-cent theaters" in Chicago exhibited it. Under a Chicago ordinance passed in November 1907, it was unlawful to show "in a public place . . . any picture or series of pictures of the classes commonly shown in mutoscopes, kinetoscopes, cinematographs, and such pictures or series of pictures as are commonly . . . exhibited in so-called penny arcades, and in all other automatic or moving picture devices, without first having secured a permit thereof from the chief of police [who] must either grant or deny the permit within three days after such inspection." Block went to court, claiming that the law deprived him of "rights under the Constitution" and was void because it "discriminates against the exhibitors of moving pictures, delegates discretionary and judicial powers to the chief of police, takes the property of complainants without due process of law, and is unreasonable and oppressive." He also

177

told the court that the movies in his theater had been "taken from plays and dramas" that he asserted were "moral and in no way obscene." Judge Farlin Q. Ball dismissed Block's complaint, and the Supreme Court of Illinois affirmed.[2]

Legal Importance

This is the first known reported case of a movie banned through official denial of a permit required by law. In upholding the constitutional validity of the Chicago ordinance, which authorized the censorship of "immoral" or "obscene" pictures, Chief Justice James H. Cartwright said it was the purpose of the law "to secure decency and morality in the moving picture business, and that purpose falls within the police power. It is designed as a precautionary measure to prevent exhibitions criminal in their nature and forbidden by the laws." The court's opinion also expressed concern about the audiences of such movies, observing that the ordinance applied to "five-and-ten-cent theaters," which, "on account of the low price of admission, are frequented and patronized by a large number of children, as well as by those of limited means who do not attend the productions of plays and dramas given in the regular theaters. The audiences include those classes whose age, education, and situation in life specially entitle them to protection against the evil influence of obscene and immoral representations."

The court declined to accept Block's argument that movie exhibitors were being discriminated against by the ordinance. By singling out moving picture exhibitors, in its requirement of police permits, Block claimed, the Chicago ordinance *authorized* proprietors of "stereopticon or other stationary pictures . . . to exhibit immoral or obscene pictures, while the complainants are prohibited from doing so." This, the court contended, was a "false notion" inasmuch as the ordinance did not "sanction the exhibition of obscene or immoral pictures in stereopticon or other stationary pictures, which the statute of the state has made criminal."

Block also claimed discrimination in that "some of the same scenes displayed by moving pictures are shown in theaters where the scenes are enacted upon the stage, and there is no requirement that the show shall be given before the chief of police and a permit obtained." This argument was rejected by the court on the ground that the places where "pictures by stereopticon" or "other similar methods" were exhibited "may be inspected to ascertain whether there is any violation of law, while in the case of moving pictures, rented and passed from one exhibitor to another about the city and constantly changing it would require the constant attendance of a great force of policemen at the various exhibitions in the 200 places mentioned in the bill." The court also pointed to the "radical difference between the burden imposed" by the exhibition of films and "a requirement that a large number of actors shall go through a dramatic performance" before the chief of police. "The one is but a trifling inconvenience, while the other would verge upon the ridiculous and entail great and unnecessary expense." Since the ordinance embraced "all persons simultaneously situated and contains no discrimination as between them," it was not legally discriminatory.

Apparently, the ordinance did not require, and the police chief did not offer, applicants the opportunity to be heard before permits were denied. For, the court said, the fact that the ordinance "delegates legislative and judicial powers to the chief of police by giving him the power to determine whether a picture or a series of pictures is immoral or obscene, and not giving to the applicant for a permit a day in court for the determination of the question whether the picture or series of pictures is immoral or obscene," did not invalidate the statute. This was because "government could not be carried on if nothing could be left to the judgment and discretion of administrative officers." While it was "doubtless true" that there are differences as to what is immoral or obscene, "the average person of healthy and wholesome mind knows well enough what [the terms] 'immoral' and 'obscene' mean and can intelligently apply the test to any picture presented to him."

The court "presumed" that the chief of police, or the mayor (in case of an appeal to that office), "will perform his duty with reasonable intelligence and in accordance with the generally accepted meaning of the words." If either official abused his powers, an applicant might still apply to a court for correction of the abuse; but, said the court, no such abuse was alleged here. While it was true that pictures "representing the career of the *James Boys* illustrate experiences connected with the history of the country," it did not follow that they were "not immoral." "Pictures which attempt to exhibit that career necessarily portray exhibitions of crime, and pictures of the *Night Riders* can represent nothing but malicious mischief, arson, and murder." Thus, the court reasoned, both films were "immoral," and their exhibition "would necessarily be attended with evil effects upon youthful spectators." Moreover, "if the other pictures for which permits were refused were of similar character, the chief of police is to be commended for the refusal."

All of Block's constitutional arguments would probably prevail today. In three cases decided in the 1950s—*La Ronde* [31], *M* [33], and *The Moon Is Blue* [36], the U.S. Supreme Court ruled that the exhibition of a movie may not be prevented because it is immoral, inasmuch as this term, like some others (not including "obscene"), is too vague and uncertain a standard for censorship, giving the censor excessive discretion and the exhibitor inadequate information concerning what may and may not be shown. The permit denial procedures authorized by the Chicago ordinance would also violate

First Amendment due process requirements, as laid down in the case of *Revenge at Daybreak* [58] of 1965, notably for the failure to give would-be exhibitors any hearing whatsoever before requested permits were denied.

Finally, assuming the movie in question was a serious attempt to portray the "American historical experience," it could not have been banned as obscene, even if its dominant appeal had been to the audience's "prurient interests," under the rules laid down in the 1973 *Magic Mirror* case [102]. The Chicago police chief and the Illinois Supreme Court seem to have taken the fact that crimes were portrayed in the movie as tantamount to advocacy of such crimes, and "immoral" for that reason. Today, even the advocacy of criminal behavior, not amounting to deliberate incitement, is considered expression protected by the constitutional guarantees of free speech and press. In the *Lady Chatterley's Lover* case [43], the U.S. Supreme Court held that a movie understood by censors as advocating adultery (a crime under some state laws) was entitled to constitutional protection.

1. Block v. City of Chicago, 87 N.E. 1011, 239 Ill. 251 (1909).
2. Ibid.

[2]
Night Riders

Banned in Chicago, Illinois, 1908.
U.S., 1908. Dist/Prod: Kalem Co. 815 ft.

This film was involved in the same case as *The James Boys in Missouri* [1] and, like that picture, was concerned with "the American historical experience" and "portray[ing] experiences of crime." It depicted "malicious mischief, arson, and murder," in connection with the "tobacco war."[1]

Censorship Activity/Legal Importance
See *The James Boys in Missouri* [1].

1. Block v. City of Chicago, 87 N.E. 1011, 239 Ill. 251 (1909).

[3]
The Birth of a Nation

Banned in Minneapolis, Minnesota; Chicago, Illinois; Pittsburgh, Pennsylvania; Boston, Massachusetts; Denver, Colorado; St. Louis, Missouri; and Ohio, 1915.

U.S., 1914. Dist: Epoch Productions. 12,000 ft. 35mm. Silent. B&W. Prod/Dir: D. W. Griffith. SW: D. W. Griffith, Frank E. Woods. Cin: G. W. ("Billy") Bitzer. Cast: Henry Walthall, Mae Marsh, Violet Wilkey, Miriam Cooper, Bessie Love, Spotwade Aitken, André Beranger, Josephine Crowell, Jennie Lee, William De Vaull, Maxfield Stanley, Ralph Lewis, Elmer Cliffton, Lillian Gish, Mary Alden, Tom Wilson, Robert Harron, George Siegmann, Walter Long, Sam De Grasse, Joseph Henaberry, Alberta Lee, Wallace Reid, Howard Gaye, William Freeman, Donald Crisp, Raoul Walsh, Eugene Palette, Olga Grey, Charles Stevens, Eric von Stroheim. Reviews: *Variety*, March 12, 1915, Mark Vance; *Moving Picture World*, March 13, 1915. Articles: Lewis Jacobs, "D. W. Griffith: *The Birth of a Nation* and *Intolerance*," in *The Rise of the American Film* (New York: Harcourt, 1939), ch. XI; Seymour Stern, Part I, "The Birth of an Art, 1908–1915," *An Index to the Creative Work of David Wark Griffith* (London, 1944); Lillian Gish, "The Making of *The Birth of a Nation*," *The Movies, Mr. Griffith & Me* (Englewood Cliffs, N.J.: Prentice-Hall, 1959); Harry M. Geguld, ed., *Focus on D. W. Griffith* (Englewood Cliffs, N.J.: Prentice-Hall, 1971); Fred Silva, ed., *Focus on "The Birth of a Nation"* (Englewood Cliffs, N.J.: Prentice-Hall, 1971); Nickieann Fleener-Marzec, *D. W. Griffith's The Birth of a Nation's Controversy, Suppression, and The First Amendment as It Applies to Filmic Expression, 1915–1973* (Ph.D. dissertation, 1977, Univ. of Wisconsin).

This film was adapted in part from the novel and play *The Clansman* and in part from *The Leopard Spots*, both by Thomas Dixon, a North Carolina preacher whose uncle was the Grand Titan of the Ku Klux Klan. In 1860, Austin Stoneman, a powerful member of the U.S. House of Representatives, learns from his daughter Elsie that his sons plan to visit the Cameron family of Piedmont, South Carolina. There, amidst the plantation's black and white contentment, one son, Phil Stoneman, falls in love with Margaret Cameron, while another son, Ben Cameron, idolizes Elsie Stoneman. However, answering President Lincoln's call for volunteers, the Stoneman boys next meet the Cameron boys on the battlefield. The two families' youngest sons die in one another's arms. Ben Cameron is wounded, the Camerons lose everything, Atlanta is bombarded, and Petersburg falls. Nursed by Elsie, Ben faces a death warrant, but Elsie and Mrs. Cameron intercede with Lincoln to save him; Ben soon rejoins his family as they begin to rebuild the Cameron home. After Lincoln's assassination, to implement his own program of black equality, Austin Stoneman sends his mulatto protégé Silas Lynch to Piedmont to organize Southern blacks. Later, Phil, Elsie, and Austin Stoneman arrive and Phil tries in vain to rekindle Margaret's love for him. The blacks soon elect a largely black legislature with Lynch as lieutenant-governor. In fear of black supremacy, Ben Cameron conceives the Ku Klux Klan, and Elsie, in loyalty to her father, rejects Ben. Flora Stoneman leaps from a bluff to her death rather than submit to Gus, a former family servant who is now a black renegade militiaman. The Klan executes Gus. During Austin Stoneman's absence, Lynch sends his militiamen into the Piedmont streets and arrests Dr. Cameron for aiding the Klan. As Elsie intercedes with Lynch for Cameron, his friends free him and flee with him to a cabin, where they are surrounded by the black militia. Elsie, having rejected Lynch's proposal that she become his queen of the Black Empire, is locked in a room to await a forced marriage to him. The Klansmen, however, overcome the blacks and free Dr. Cameron and Elsie, and the Black Empire collapses under the Klan's rule. Elsie has now recognized Ben's true merit, and the two Cameron-Stoneman marriages take place.

Censorship Activity

Minneapolis Mayor W. G. Nye told the theater exhibitor that if this movie were shown, he would revoke the theater's license. The exhibitor went to court to enjoin this censorship, but the District Court of Hennepin County refused the request and the Supreme Court of Minnesota affirmed the decision.[1] In an effort to determine the "fitness" of this movie the mayor had requested "unprejudiced people of diverse callings" to view it and to report to him. "Some of the opinions solicited were favorable to the play; many were not. . . ." The mayor claimed that the production "tended to bring reproach upon the negro race . . . would invite race hatred and race riots [and] tend to disturb the public peace." There was "some evidence" that the film's showing in Minneapolis had "result[ed] in disparaging remarks regarding negroes and in subjecting them to indignities in public places." The movie, he believed, pictured historically "untrue" scenes, which "prejudiced the public mind" as to their "real nature." These "tended to inculcate in the public mind a distrust of public officials and law" and "justified lawless citizens in their attempts to organize themselves into bands to avenge real or fanciful wrongs with the avowed purpose to override public authority and take into their own hands the punishment of officers in such manner as they shall decide, irrespective of courts, public officers, and the government itself." The film contained scenes "vicious in themselves, tending to stimulate the vicious passions of mankind and to give a false report of the real conditions" during Reconstruction.

The film was also banned in Ohio by order of the governor, on the recommendation of the state board of censors; in Denver, Colorado by the city council; in Boston, where its showing reputedly caused race riots; in St. Paul, Chicago, Pittsburgh, St. Louis, and many other cities. These actions were eventually overturned by court rulings permitting the film to be shown. Over the next generation, the National Association for the Advancement of Colored People (NAACP) tried, with mixed results, to prevent its showing in various parts of the country.

Legal Importance

The main issue in the Minneapolis case was whether the court could enjoin the mayor from exercising a power that the law "expressly gives him." No issue of constitutional freedom of speech or press was raised. The Minneapolis city charter provided that any license issued by authority of the city council could be revoked by the mayor or city council at any time. "The law applicable to this case," Judge Oscar Hallam wrote, "is simple and well settled in this state." The mayor's power to revoke licenses "is not an absolute power to revoke. It cannot be used capriciously, or arbitrarily, or oppressively, but only in the exercise of an honest and reasonable discretion." On the other hand, "the discretion to be exercised is the discretion of the mayor. The power to revoke licenses is delegated to him, and not to the courts. . . . We cannot substitute the discretion of the court for that of the mayor, to whom the Legislature has specially confided its exercise. If it were otherwise, the city would be governed by the courts, and not by the city officers in whom the law vests the governmental power." The court will in such cases merely inquire "whether a fair legal discretion was exercised." It is "useless," the court noted, "to spend time arguing the question whether reasonable people might differ as to the advisability of permitting the exhibition of this play. The showing is conclusive that they differ on this point." The court had "no reason to doubt that the mayor, in proposing to revoke the plaintiff's license if he persists in presenting this play, is acting in the honest belief that such course is in the interest of public welfare and the peace and good order of the city."

1. Bainbridge v. City of Minneapolis, 154 N.W. 964 (1915); affirmed 242 U.S. 353 (1916).

[4]
The Ordeal

Banned in New York, New York, 1915.

U.S., 1914. Prod: Life Photo Film Corp. 5 reels. Sound. B&W. SW: Edward M. Roskan. Cast: Anna Laughlin.

This photoplay about the Franco-Prussian war is based upon a poem written long before World War I. It portrays the dream of a young man who goes to war, leaving his sweetheart, mother, father, and sister at home. When taken prisoner, he will not tell the hiding place of fellow soldiers, and an officer wearing a German uniform condemns the sweetheart, mother, and sister to be shot. The dream ends and the young man awakens; the whole family has come to life again, a happy group.

Censorship Activity

After this movie had been shown "once or twice" at Hammerstein's Lexington Avenue Opera House, the New York City license commissioner warned the theater's owner that his operating license would be revoked if he exhibited it again. The commissioner also told the picture's distributor that he would not permit it to be shown in any theater in the city inasmuch as a nongovernmental group of public-spirited citizens called the National Board of Review of Motion Pictures, as well as the city's deputy commissioner of licenses, thought that "it might occasion racial differences at this particular time" (World War I). When the theater's owner threatened to cancel his contract with the distributor, the distributor brought suit for an injunction to restrain the commissioner from revoking the theater's license, so that the contract might be carried out. After both the commissioner and the deputy commissioner admitted in court that "there was nothing in the picture to which an American could take offense," the state supreme court granted the injunction. [1]

Legal Importance

The commissioner's opposition to the film and his threats to revoke the theater's license were based "solely" on the fact that his deputy and the National Board of Review "feared the disapproval of foreigners." Since the board was "self-constituted" to forestall government censorship in New York and "not organized or recognized by any provision of law," and since the photoplay itself "to a sensible and ordinary mind could in no way create racial strife," it could not be censored "even if some supersensitive Teuton might consider it . . . an unfair characterization and a misrepresentation of the German army, but, as a matter of fact, this is not so." Even assuming that the photoplay did actually "show an officer of the German army in a cruel and inhuman light during the Franco-Prussian war, this . . . would not form a proper basis for preventing the exhibition in view of the testimony of the defendant commissioner and his deputy that there was nothing in [it] that could offend Americans." Since the commissioner had testified that to him the film was "unobjectionable," but that he had prevented its exhibition "based upon the judgment of an unofficial body and his deputy . . . and not upon his own," the court concluded that he should be restrained from revoking the theater's license.

1. Life Photo Film Corporation v. Bell, 90 Misc. 469 (1915) (N.Y.).

[5]
Willard-Johnson Boxing Match

Banned from entry into the United States, 1915.

Cuba, 1915. Copyright Holder: L. Lawrence Weber.

"Moving picture film of the prizefight or pugilistic encounter between Willard and Johnson."[1]

Censorship Activity

Lawrence Weber brought this movie of the Willard-Johnson boxing match for distribution from Cuba to Newark, N.J., where the collector of customs refused to admit it. Weber sought a court order that would enjoin the collector from persisting in his refusal of entry. A federal district court's denial of his request was affirmed on appeal.[2] The United States Supreme Court also affirmed.[3]

Legal Importance

The movie was refused entry into the United States under a federal law passed in 1912, which made it unlawful to send through the mails or by any express company or common carrier for interstate transportation, or to bring into the United States from abroad, any film of "any prize fight or encounter of pugilists" for "purposes of public exhibition." The movie's owner claimed the law was unconstitutional, not because it abridged freedom of speech or press, but because Congress was "in reality attempting to exercise the police power that belongs solely to the States." The court rejected this argument, asserting that the films were "articles of commerce whose exclusion from entry by Congress was no different in legal character than sponges gathered at a certain season of the year . . . imitations of coins . . . diseased cattle . . . lottery tickets" and other articles whose similar exclusion by Congress had been upheld by the courts.

The law in question had evidently been hastily enacted after the Jeffries-Johnson boxing match to prevent any reenactment in the country of that fight in which Johnson, who was black, had defeated the white heavyweight champion, James J. Jeffries. The fear of race riots in some sections of the country was given as justification for this early censorship law. The law, which was not repealed until 1940, affected newsreels and short subjects; it reputedly was "not infrequently violated."[4] It criminalized the importation and interstate transportation of fight films but not their actual exhibition, a matter which would, constitutionally, have fallen within the jurisdiction of the several states and engaged the police power of local government bodies. Today, presumably, such federal and state laws would be held unconstitutional restraints on freedom of expression in the United States, inasmuch

as movies have now been held to be a protected form of expression. (See
The Miracle case [30].) On the other hand, as recently as 1973, Chief Justice
Warren E. Burger pointed out that state laws forbidding "brutalizing" con-
tests and spectacles, such as bearbaiting, cockfighting, "bare-fist" prize
fights, and duels have not been challenged as unconstitutional.[5] And Professor Irving Kristol has defended the legal banning of such events because
they "debased and brutalized the citizenry who flocked to witness such
spectacles."[6]

1. Weber v. Freed, 224 F. 355 (1915.
2. Weber v. Freed, 224 F. 355 (1915).
3. Weber v. Freed, 239 U.S. 325 (1915).
4. Ruth A. Inglis, *Freedom of the Movies* (Chicago: Univ. of Chicago Pr., 1947), p. 69.
5. Paris Adult Theatre I v. Slaton, 413 U.S. 49 (1973).
6. Irving Kristol, *On the Democratic Idea in America* (New York: Harper, 1972), p. 33.

[6]
Birth Control

Banned in New York, New York, 1917.

U.S., 1917. Dist/Prod: Message Photo-Play Co. Silent. B&W.

Portraying various episodes in the life of Margaret Sanger, this film shows
how in the course of her duties as a nurse Sanger became interested in the
subject of birth control and eventually opened a clinic in defiance of criminal laws prohibiting the dissemination of information regarding conception
and birth control. "Some of the pictures and subheadings depict Mrs.
Sanger . . . attending an undernourished woman who is exhausted from
having too many children and is surrounded by squalor . . . in bed, in labor
pains, and about to give birth to a child, while there are several of her small
children half-starved, emaciated, and ill-clad about her. . . . [T]he birth of
her child shows the doctor warning the woman not to have another child,
and shows her pleading with him to instruct her with respect to birth control. . . . [H]e refuses the advice on the ground that the law forbids
it. . . . [The film] shows her then pleading with Mrs. Sanger for like information, and depicts the same woman resorting to malpractice to avoid the
birth of a child, from which she dies. . . . [T]hese were the circumstances
which led Mrs. Sanger to inaugurate her propaganda for birth control. The
picture further depicts her distributing pamphlets apparently containing
prescriptions to prevent conception, and her arrest and trial and

conviction; . . . the final picture shows her behind bars serving her sentence, with the subtitle 'No matter what happens, the work shall go on.' "[1] Methods of contraception were not stated or shown in any way, but the film clearly represented that such means were known to Mrs. Sanger.

Censorship Activity

The day before this film was scheduled to open at the Park Theater in New York, City License Commissioner Bell notified the theater's licensee that the movie was "immoral, indecent, and directly contrary to public welfare," that it should not "be made a part of amusement, entertainment, or recreation in the metropolis," and that if it were shown, "action will be taken against the licensee." As a result of this threat, the Park Theater refused to permit the movie's showing there, and other theaters advised the film's distributor that they would not allow its exhibition. At the distributor's request, a New York court enjoined the license commissioner from interfering with the film's exhibition on the ground that it violated the distributor's freedom of speech,[2] but this judgment was reversed on appeal.[3]

Legal Importance

The license commissioner contended that the film should be suppressed from exhibition because it "tends to ridicule the public authorities" and the state's law "forbidding the dissemination of contraceptive knowledge"; furthermore, because it teaches people "to prevent conception," being "propaganda to limit the production of children." In addition, the film "raises a class issue" by "setting before the public the squalor, poverty, and ignorance of the poor, owing to their lack of information with respect to the prevention of conception, and the luxury and small families of the rich due to their ability to acquire from physicians knowledge and means of preventing conception. . . . [It] also depicts the wealthy as contributing funds for the prosecution of those who attempt to enlighten the poor and lowly with respect to birth control and for the avowed purpose of maintaining the poor as the servant and laboring classes." The commissioner also objected to the film's clear advertisement "that conception may be controlled and that Mrs. Sanger knows how it may be prevented and how childbirth may be controlled." The distributor, on the other hand, claimed that the film's purpose was to "create public sentiment in favor of the repeal of the statute" prohibiting the spread of birth control information, maintaining that it had "a constitutional right to agitate" for such repeal. In a scholarly opinion that relied upon the views articulated in Lord Bryce's *The American Commonwealth*, de Tocqueville's *Democracy in America*, and Holy Writ, Judge Nathan Bijur ruled that the movie deals "with a great problem of life" and that the license commissioner's action violated "the constitutional right of free speech." The appellate court rejected this proposition, saying, "We are not concerned with the freedom of speech guaranteed by the Constitution,'' but only with the revoking of a theater license, ''which is not a property but merely a temporary permit to conduct a business that would be unlawful without it.'' A movie distributor ''has no constitutional or other right, on the theory of freedom of speech or of the public press or otherwise, to give public exhibition of the film,'' since the state's legislature is competent to license public motion picture exhibitions and ''also to censor such productions in order that they may be regulated and controlled in the interest of morality, decency, and public safety and welfare.''

The court's authority for this denial of constitutional freedom to the film was based, not surprisingly, on the U.S. Supreme Court's 1915 decision in the *Mutual Film Corporation* case, which held motion pictures to be a ''business pure and simple'' and no part of the nation's constitutionally protected press.[4] As the latter case was not overruled until 1952, in *The Miracle* case [30], the court's decision conformed to prevailing judicial opinion. Given the constitutional protection today afforded a motion pictures, a film that advocates the repeal or breach of criminal laws is considered expression of the type that is safeguarded by the constitutional guarantees of freedom of speech and press; see the case of *Lady Chatterley's Lover* [43]. Moreover, in 1965, the United States Supreme Court expressly ruled that a state law that criminalizes the dissemination of information regarding contraception unconstitutionally invades the rights of privacy of married persons.[5] In 1972, the constitutional protection was broadened to include the distribution of contraceptive devices, as well as information, to unmarried individuals and married couples.[6] As previously noted, the New York City license commissioner's practice of censoring films of which he disapproved by revoking or threatening to revoke the licenses of movie theaters was of dubious legality, being implied from the Code of Ordinances of the City of New York, which said no more than: ''The inspectors of the department of licenses . . . shall report to the commissioner any offense against morality, decency or public welfare. . . .'' It was not until 1921 that legislative action was taken expressly to give a government office the power to censor motion pictures shown in New York; see the *Fit to Win* case [13].

1. Opinion of Laughlin, J., in Message Photo-Play Co. v. Bell, 166 N.Y.S. 338 (1917).
2. Message Photo-Play Co. v. Bell, 167 N.Y.S. 129 (1917).
3. Message Photo-Play Co. v. Bell, 166 N.Y.S. 338 (1917).
4. Mutual Film Corporation v. Industrial Commission of Ohio, 236 U.S. 230 (1915).
5. Griswold v. Connecticut, 381 U.S. 479 (1965).
6. Eisenstadt v. Baird, 405 U.S. 438 (1972).

[7]
The Hand That Rocks the Cradle

Banned in New York, New York, 1917.

U.S., 1917. Dist: Universal Film Co. 6 reels. 35mm. Silent. B&W. Prod:
Universal Film Co. Dir/SW/Cin: Lois Weber, Phillips Smalley. Cast: Lois
Weber, Phillips Smalley, Priscilla Dean, Edgewood Nowell, Evelyn Selbie,
Harry de More. Reviews: *Morning Telegraph*, May 12, 1917; *New York
Dramatic Mirror*, May 26, 1917.

The story of this film resembles the situation of Margaret Sanger. A
doctor's wife is upset by the misery of lower classes forced by ignorance to
bring unhealthy, undesired children into homes that are already impover-
ished by too large a family. She begins to spread birth control literature.
When arrested, her husband promises the chief of police that if his wife is
released, he will see to it that she gives up her "hobby." But it is not a hobby to his wife and she continues her work. Later, she addresses a meeting of
women, is arrested, and this time sentenced to serve a prison term. There is
no apparent solution for her situation, unless education of the public will
bring about more progressive laws.

Censorship Activity

The New York City commissioner of licenses was empowered by ordinance
to issue, renew, and revoke theater operating licenses. He threatened to
cancel the license of any theater in which this film was shown. "A number
of . . . persons of high standing [and] representatives of civic societies"
had viewed the film and reported to the commissioner that "the play is *con-
tra bonos mores* (against good morals)." The state supreme court (a trial
court) denied the distributor's motion for a preliminary injunction to
restrain the commissioner from interfering with the movie's showing.[1] On
appeal, the appellate division, on the authority of the *Birth Control* case [6],
affirmed the lower court's order.[2]

Legal Importance

This case held that the city license commissioner could not be prevented
from carrying out his license revocation threat if he acted "in good faith,"
rather than arbitrarily. The distributor had not challenged the constitutionality of the commissioner's power of censorship, but sought to justify
showing the film on the basis that it was "merely an argument in favor of
the repeal of the existing law, which forbids the imparting of information
on the subject of birth control." He also urged that "under a republican
form of government it is entirely proper to educate the people by arguments
for and against the wisdom of a given piece of legislation." In response to
counsel's assertion that the state licensing statute involved ought to be

repealed because of inconsistency with the state's constitutional protection of the liberty of speech and press, the court maintained that the license commissioner had "not attempted to interfere with any such constitutional right of the citizen. We are dealing with a place of amusement . . . whose right to exhibit plays is not an absolute one, but in the nature of a privilege granted by the state. A change in the law may be effected only by the lawful methods provided by law." The commissioner was said to be authorized to deny a license to a theater that showed films "against morality, decency or public welfare."

In this film, the court noted, "a confessed violator of the law is represented as a martyr and held up to the admiration and applause of promiscuous authorities because of her violation of the law, upon the specious and pernicious plea that the law which she violated has no place upon the statute books. If the ignorant and uninformed are to be educated by being told that the laws which they do not like may be defied, and that lawbreakers deserve to be glorified as such, there would be a sorry future in store for human liberty." The court admitted that plays had been produced and exhibited in which great criminals were the principal figures. Examples included "the lives of such notorious historical and fictional bandits as Robin Hood, Captain Kidd, and men of the type of Dick Turpin." But such productions, the court reasoned, were not presented for "the purpose of accomplishing the repeal of the laws forbidding murder, robbery, or piracy," implying that had such been their purpose, those plays too could be forbidden. The court felt it could not properly "overthrow the discretion honestly exercised by the commissioner in the discharge of his duties," unless it were shown that his actions were "influenced by corrupt or dishonest considerations, the burden of proving which rests upon the moving party."

The court followed the principle established in 1915 by the U.S. Supreme Court in the subsequently overruled case of *Mutual Film Corp.* v. *Industrial Commission*,[3] to the effect that the exhibition of moving pictures was a "business pure and simple," which, "like other spectacles," was not to be regarded as "part of the press of the country or as organs of public opinion," and so not to be deemed protected by constitutional guarantees of freedom of speech and of the press. This reasoning, and its underlying principle, were not repudiated by the Supreme Court until 1952, in *The Miracle* case [30]. The arguments fruitlessly advanced by the distributor of the film censored in this case, in 1917, would have won the day, after 1952. The ruling of the New York court was that advocacy of repeal or defiance of the laws against contraception, and the glorification of lawbreakers, rendered the film a proper subject of censorship. This is contrary to more recent holdings by the U.S. Supreme Court in such cases as *Lady Chatterley's Lover* [43] and *Brandenburg* v. *Ohio*.[4]

1. Universal Film Manufacturing Co. v. Bell, 167 N.Y.S. 124, 100 Misc. Rep. 281 (1917).
2. Universal Film Manufacturing Co. v. Bell, 166 N.Y.S. 344 (1917).
3. Mutual Film Corp. v. Industrial Commission of Ohio, 236 U.S. 230 (1915).
4. Brandenburg v. Ohio, 395 U.S. 444 (1969).

[8]
The Sex Lure

Banned in New York, New York, 1917.

U.S., 1916. Copyright holder: Ivan Film Productions, Inc. 6 reels. Silent. B&W. Prod: Ivan Film Productions, Inc. Dir/Scenario: Ivan Abramson. SW: Don Dunda. Cast: James Morrison, Louisa Vale, Marie Reichardt, Donald Hall, T. B. Carnahan, Jr., W. W. Black, Frankie Mann, George Henry.

After installing herself in the family that befriends her, a girl helps kidnap the only son and lures the father into infidelity. Nevertheless, in the end, family affection triumphs over the sex lure.

Censorship Activity

The New York City license commissioner threatened to revoke the licenses of theaters exhibiting this film "on account of the title and the method of advertising," which he considered "an offense against morality, decency, and public welfare," and "purely for the purpose of holding out to the public that the photoplay is of an indecent character, thus creating an immoral curiosity as to the nature of the same." He did not object to the contents of the movie itself, since the deputy commissioner had reported to him that it might be shown "without harmful results." The distributor of the film went to court for an injunction to prevent the commissioner from interfering with its exhibition, but Judge Clarence J. Shearn of the state supreme court (special term) denied the motion.[1]

Legal Importance

This case reveals the extent to which a local government official might go in interfering with a movie exhibitor's activity, even if the movie itself was unobjectionable. The court denied the exhibitor relief from the city license commissioner's legally unauthorized suppression because of the hoary legal doctrine that a person who comes to a court of equity with "unclean hands" (here the "pandering" advertising and title) will not be given his remedy. Although the court admitted that the license commissioner plainly had been given by law no power to revoke a theater's license "simply upon the ground that the name of the play and the methods of advertising on billboards and elsewhere are objectionable," nevertheless the motion for an injunction would be denied.

License department inspectors, according to the city ordinance, were given power to "investigate the character" of films and "report to the commissioner any offense against morality, decency or public welfare committed in said exhibitions," but this was the only "subject-matter of the commissioner's jurisdiction." "The method of advertising a play may be disgusting, offensively sensational, and even dishonest, either on billboards or in the newspapers or elsewhere; but this," the court observed, "has nothing to do with the character of the exhibition itself, and is obviously not an offense committed in the exhibition." The commissioner "has no more legal right to revoke the license of a theater on these grounds than he would have because the moral character of the author of a play or of the actors employed to produce it was bad."

However, "another feature" in the case led the court to deny the relief requested by the exhibitor. "That the name and the method of advertising invite the public to a prurient and disgusting performance is only too obvious. The performance itself, however, is said to be a clean one." So the distributor "is inviting the public to the theater upon false pretenses, and seeking to capitalize whatever degenerate interest there may be created by the use of this name and the posters that go with it. Furthermore, the name and the posters taken together are indecent, nasty, and offensive. Such practices result, too, in bringing odium unjustly upon the many respectable members of the important motion picture industry."

Today, most distinctions between "equitable" and "legal" remedies having been abolished, a court would not likely deny the relief requested, in the given circumstances; the license commissioner plainly exceeded his legal authority and prevented the exhibitor's exercise of his constitutional rights of free speech. Under modern Supreme Court doctrine, "commercial speech," including advertisements, is accorded about the same constitutional protections as other kinds of speech. [See, for example, the case of *Virginia State Board of Pharmacy* v. *Virginia Consumer Council.*[2]] On the other hand, a doctrine suggestive of the one denying judicial relief because of "unclean hands" was asserted by the U.S. Supreme Court in 1966, when it upheld the criminal conviction of a publisher of printed materials having some claim to social value, and thus protected by the guarantee of free speech, because the advertising and promotional methods used by the publisher "pandered" to the prurient interest of the reader.[3]

1. Ivan Film Productions v. Bell, 167 N.Y.S. 123 (1917).
2. 425 U.S. 748 (1976).
3. Ginzburg v. United States, 390 U.S. 692 (1966).

[9]
The Spirit of '76

Banned in Los Angeles, California, 1917.

U.S., 1917. (Reissued, 1921.) Dist: All-American Film Co. 12 reels (12,000 ft.). Silent. Prod: Robert Goldstein. Dir: George Siegmann. SW: Virginia Tylor Hudson. Cast: Adda Gleason, Howard Gave, Jack Cosgrove, George Cheeseborough, Noah Berry. Reviews: *Exhibitor's Trade Review*, June 19, 1917; *Motography*, June 23, 1917. Articles: *Photoplay*, August 1918; *Moving Picture World*, August 6, 1921.

The theme of this movie is the American War of Independence. Catherine Montour, half-Indian, conspires with King George III against the English colonies to become Queen of America. When she is about to marry Lionel Esmond, with whom she plots her goal, she learns he is her brother. She falls out of favor with George III, and the America Revolution occurs, dashing her hopes for the American monarchy. Among the historical events depicted in the film are Patrick Henry's speech, Paul Revere's ride, the signing of the Declaration of Independence, and Washington's encampment at Valley Forge. An inflammatory scene portrayed the Wyoming Valley Massacre, in which a British soldier impales a baby on his bayonet and whirls it around his head. Also pictured were British soldiers shooting and bayoneting helpless American women and children and dragging them off by the hair. The producer, a tailor by profession, had supplied many of the costumes for *The Birth of a Nation* and was one of its financial backers.

Censorship Activity

Two days after this film opened at Clune's Auditorium in Los Angeles, federal agents seized it and charged its producer, Robert Goldstein, with violating the Espionage Act. Goldstein's suit for return of the seized film was denied by a federal district judge, who ruled it should be held "in the possession of the [federal] marshal until such time as, under changed conditions, it may properly be presented."[1] Goldstein was convicted for "knowingly, willfully, and unlawfully attempting to cause insubordination, disloyalty, mutiny, and reprisal of duty in the military and naval forces of the United States during war," and sentenced to imprisonment. On appeal, his conviction was affirmed.[2]

Legal Importance

The appellate court ruled that the crime of "an attempt to create disloyalty" could be committed "by showing a picture to the public, as well as by uttering a speech or publishing a writing." Even though the picture might be "a truthful representation of an historical fact," its character and the circumstances surrounding its exhibition "may well tend to show" that it was "calculated to foment disloyalty or insubordination among the naval or military forces." In time of peace, a movie such as this "might arouse but ordinary interest." But the United States was at war with Germany, enforcing draft laws, and raising a large army and navy to fight an enemy common to the British, whose very soldiers were pilloried in the movie. And so, it is only reasonable to conclude that its exhibition was "calculated to arouse antagonisms and to raise hatred in the minds of some . . . and to encourage disloyalty and refusal of duty or insubordination among the military and naval forces." Goldstein's lawyers appear not to have challenged his indictment as a violation of his constitutional freedom of speech and press, presumably in view of the U.S. Supreme Court's decision in 1915[3] that movies were not part of the constitutionally protected press. During this same period, the federal courts found other citizens, prosecuted for violating espionage laws and the laws against encouraging resistance to the draft by means of pamphlets and journals, at least entitled to raise the free speech issue in defending their punishment for speaking out against the war, the draft, and the nation's allies—despite their failure to invalidate their prosecutions and the suppressions of speech and press involved.[4] Today, Goldstein's movie would be held to come within the ambit of constitutional protection of expression; as such, it probably could not be suppressed, nor could its producer be punished, if there were no proof that it was intended and likely to incite its audience to crime or violence[5] or that it presented a direct threat to the execution of some essential incident of a war or military conscription effort.[6]

1. United States v. Motion Picture Film *The Spirit of '76*, 252 F. 946 (1917).
2. Goldstein v. United States, 258 F. 908 (1919).
3. Mutual Film Corp. v. Industrial Commission of Ohio, 236 U.S. 230 (1915).
4. See Schenck v. United States, 249 U.S. 47 (1919); Fohwerk v. United States, 249 U.S. 204 (1919); Abrams v. United States, 250 U.S. 616 (1919); Schaefer v. United States, 251 U.S. 466 (1920); Pierce v. United States, 252 U.S. 239 (1920).
5. See Brandenburg v. Ohio, 395 U.S. 444 (1969).
6. See New York Times Co. v. United States, 403 U.S. 713 (1971).

[10]
The Spy

Banned in Chicago, Illinois, 1917.

U.S., 1917. Dist: Fox Film Corporation. 6 reels. Silent. B&W. Prod: William Fox. Dir: Richard Stanton. SW: George Bronson Howard. Cast: Dustin Farnum, Winifred Kingston, William Burgess, Charles Clary, Howard Gays, William E. Lowry.

The hero of this anti-German film is an American spy who, along with his German girlfriend, is shot after refusing to reveal the hiding place of a book that contains the names of all German spies working in the United States. The scene in which the hero is put on a rack and tortured, with close-ups of his acute agony, evidently was remarkably realistic.

Censorship Activity
The Chicago police chief refused to license this film for exhibition to general audiences, stating that the distributor might have a permit to show it exclusively to adults. At the distributor's request, a federal district court enjoined the police chief from refusing the general permit.[1] This action was affirmed by a federal circuit court of appeals.[2]

Legal Importance
The Chicago ordinance, requiring a police permit as a prerequisite to the showing of a movie, authorized the denial of a permit for any "immoral or obscene" movie or one that "portrays any riotous, disorderly, or other unlawful scenes or has a tendency to disturb the public peace." But the police chief had refused to issue a general permit to exhibit this movie because of "the horrifying nature of the tortures which are portrayed as inflicted upon the hero of the play, and his ultimate shooting by a firing squad," which he considered "objectionable" for "children under the age of 21 years." According to the court, such a consideration was not authorized by the law in question, and the refusal of a permit on this ground constituted "an abuse of discretion," which properly could be corrected by the appellate court. The appellate court agreed that it was not for an ordinance's "administrator" (here, Chicago's chief of police), but, instead, for the "lawmaking body" itself, to decide whether moving pictures may be "too horrifying for children."

1. Fox Film Corporation v. Chicago, 247, F. 231 (1917).
2. City of Chicago v. Fox Film Corporation, 251 F. 883 (1918).

[11]
The Easiest Way

Banned in Kansas, 1918.

U.S., 1917. Dist: Mid-West Photo Play Corp. 8 reels. B&W. Silent. Prod: Clara Kimball Young Film Corp.—Selznick Pictures. Dir: Albert Capellani. Scenario: Frederic Chapin & Albert Capellani. Cin: Hal Young, Jacques

Monteran. Cast: Clara Kimball Young, Rockliffe Fellowes, Louis Bates, Cleo Desmond, Frank Kingdon, George Stevens.

Adapted from a play of the same name by Eugene Walter, the movie is about a fallen woman for whom "the easiest way" led from a luxurious existence and the gay night life of a city to an attempt to drown herself and final expiration and forgiveness in the arms of her true love. An MGM production starring Constance Bennett and Adolphe Menjou, directed by Jack Conway, was released in 1931.

Censorship Activity

The Kansas censorship board denied a license for the exhibition of this film on the ground that it was immoral. The distributor went to court, arguing that the film was not immoral. On review, the Wyandotte County District Court reversed the censorship board, but the Supreme Court of Kansas reversed the district court.[1]

Legal Importance

Determining whether the picture was "moral and fit for exhibition [was] an exercise of administrative power . . . specially conferred upon the board" by statute, Chief Justice William A. Johnston wrote. A court "is not warranted in substituting its judgment for that of the board." The board may have acted "mistakenly," as the distributor claimed, but there is no claim that it acted dishonestly, arbitrarily, or capriciously. Fraud or dishonesty would warrant judicial reexamination of the board's action, but not mere mistake. "Fraud and dishonesty cannot be imputed to public officials unless plainly alleged and proven. We must presume that the board acted in good faith, and that the decision that the picture is immoral was an honest exercise of the best judgment of its members." Had there been allegation and proof that the censors acted "arbitrarily or capriciously," this too would have been ground for judicial reversal of the board's decision. Justice Henry F. Mason concurred especially to "dissent from the [court's] statement that the Legislature has no power to impose" on a court the task of determining a film's fitness for exhibition. The legislature may do so, if it "thinks that course advisable. Courts are frequently called upon to decide whether particular publications are obscene . . . and I see no reason why they might not be required to decide similar questions with regard to films."

   This case is an example of the application of the doctrine that ordinarily a court should not substitute its judgment for that of an administrative (executive branch) agency in exercising the latter's lawful function. This doctrine has long been abandoned in the censorship field, in the recognition that administrative censorship encroaches on First Amendment rights of speech and press. It has been replaced by the opposite rule that it is the duty of the courts "independently" to adjudicate the question of whether a movie or other "expressive matter" is entitled to be free from governmental restraint. Thus, in the *Revenge at Daybreak* case [58], the Supreme Court held that only a *judicial* determination of whether a movie is obscene "ensures the necessary sensitivity to freedom of expression" and "suffices to impose a valid final restraint." Furthermore, "because the censor's business is to censor, there inheres the danger that he may well be less responsive than a court—part of an independent branch of government—to the constitutionally protected interests in freedom of expression." The courts have also been willing—indeed they are duty-bound in this respect—to substitute their independent judgments for those of criminal and civil juries, with respect to the issue of whether a movie is obscene or is entitled to constitutional protection (as, for example, in the cases of *The Lovers* [49], *I Am Curious—Yellow* [71], and *Carnal Knowledge* [105]). Today, the federal customs censorship law requires the customs bureau (an administrative organ) promptly to petition a federal district court and secure an adversary judicial trial and determination as to whether a movie or other matter, claimed by the administrative officials to be obscene, *is* legally obscene.[2]

Kansas was one of the first states to establish a statewide licensing system for moving pictures. The law creating a board of censors was passed in 1914; its procedures were found unconstitutional in 1966,[3] and the state legislature failed to reenact any similar law.

1. Mid-West Photo Play Corp. v. Miller, 169 P. 1154 (1919).
2. United States v. Thirty-Seven Photographs, 402 U.S. 363 (1971).
3. State ex rel. Londerholm v. Columbia Pictures, 417 P. 2d 255 (1966).

[12]
The Brand

Banned in Pennsylvania, 1919.

U.S., 1919. Dist: Goldwyn Distributing Corporation. 7 reels. Silent. B&W. Dir: Reginald Barker. Cast: Kay Laurell, Russell Simpson, Robert McKim, Robert Kunkel, Mary Jane Irving. Review: *New York Times*, March 17, 1919.

This "photoplay" was based on a Rex Beach story of Alaska and contained "many moving pictures of inherent force and beauty," "snow covered landscapes, miners' cabins, dance halls, and the men and women of the place and period." Several snowstorm scenes were said to be "especially realistic."[1] It told the story of a dancing girl amid the chaos of a mining camp. Having left her husband to live with her former lover, she has a child of doubtful parentage. The lover is branded by the husband on the brow with a knife.

Censorship Activity

The state board of censors refused to approve this movie for exhibition evidently because it showed persons "living together without marriage, and in adultery," and contained incidents "designed to inflame the mind to improper adventures," which tended to "debase or corrupt morals." The distributor appealed to a common pleas court in Philadelphia, claiming that the picture was "moral and proper" and that the censors' disapproval was "an arbitrary and oppressive abuse of discretion." That court viewed the film and reversed the censors' decision, but the Supreme Court of Pennsylvania reversed and nullified the lower court's decision.[2]

Legal Importance

The Pennsylvania movie censorship law was the first statewide licensing law. Enacted in 1911, it provided for an appeal to the court of common pleas from a censor board decision, but did not clearly indicate what reasons would justify a court to overturn the censors' disapproval of a film. Here, the lower court itself viewed the film and, apparently, made an independent judgment that it would not, as the censors believed, "tend to debase or corrupt morals." The Pennsylvania Supreme Court found this an improper judicial action because the applicable statute vested full discretion in the censors and authorized a common pleas court to reverse the censors' action only if the distributor (on whom rested the burden of proof) could show that the censors' decision rested on some ground not authorized by the statute. The censors' decision ordinarily was to be presumed correct by the reviewing court. This movie, according to the supreme court, depicted an "adulterous relationship, long continued, between a libertine and an immoral married woman, the legal wife of another, with no moral to be derived therefrom other than that the man who debauched the wife of another runs the risk . . . of having his brow scarred with a knife." This obviously violated the moral standard which "pays high deference and respect to the sanctity and purity of the home and family relation between husband and wife, upon which the home rests." Thus the censor board's refusal of a license was correct and should not have been disturbed by the lower court.

The Pennsylvania Supreme Court's decision would today be in direct conflict with such United States Supreme Court rulings as those announced in the *Lady Chatterley's Lover* case [43]—to the effect that constitutional guarantees of freedom of expression prohibit a state from refusing to license a film that portrays adultery in a favorable light—and in the *Revenge at Daybreak* case [58], which held that the burden of proof is on the censor to go to court and demonstrate that a movie it has refused to license may constitutionally be denied such a license.

1. *New York Times*, March 17, 1919.
2. In re Goldwyn Distributing Corp., 108 A. 816 (1919).

[13]
Fit to Win

Banned in New York, New York, 1919.

U.S., 1919. 6 reels. SW: Edward H. Griffith. Copyright: American Social Hygiene Association, Inc.

"The subject of the [film] is the great danger to the public of the spread of venereal diseases, results of which are displayed in the pictures."[1]

Censorship Activity

The New York City license commissioner threatened to revoke the license of a Brooklyn theater where this film was being exhibited, if its showing were not discontinued. He also notified all other theaters in the city that their operating licenses would be revoked if they exhibited the film. The owner of the film brought suit in federal court to prevent the commissioner from taking such action. The Southern District of New York granted an injunction to the owner, but the Second Circuit Court of Appeals reversed.[2]

Legal Importance

The legal action here, like that in the *Birth Control* case [6], called into question the unrestricted power of the city commissioner of licenses to revoke the right of a theater to exhibit motion pictures. The Greater New York Charter was construed by Circuit Judge Henry G. Ward to give the commissioner this broad power, imposing "no limitation" whatever upon him. The pertinent provision said only: "The commissioner of licenses shall have cognizance and control of the granting, issuing, transferring, renewing, revoking, suspending and canceling . . . of licenses in relation to theaters and concerts. . . ." This enormous discretion was not limited to moving picture theaters and, according to the court, was qualified only by the legal principle that "the license commissioner, like all officials, must exercise his discretion fairly, honestly, upon correct information, and with a view to the moral and physical welfare of the public." Since the commissioner evidently had "honestly concluded that the exhibition of the film to mixed audiences will be injurious to decency and morality," there was no ground to reverse his action. As "intelligent persons, deeply interested in the welfare of the community, especially of youth, entertain diametrically opposite opinions as to the effect of public discussions of sex questions," courts should not interfere with the "fair and honest judgment of the official primarily charged with the duty of deciding" such questions.

The case is an early example of the judicial branch ceding absolute censorship powers over motion picture expression to a governmental agency; such a delegation of motion picture power would undoubtedly be held unconstitutional today. In 1921, a state agency was created and was specially empowered to prevent the showing of objectionable movies anywhere in New York State. For examples of that censorship board's actions, see the cases involving *The Birth of a Baby* [22], *Amok* [27], *The Connection* [51], and *La Ronde* [31]. This did not prevent the New York City license commissioner from continuing to censor films by threatening theater owners with revocation of their operating licenses until 1951, when the courts decided he had no such censorship power, in a case involving *The Miracle* [30].

1. Silverman v. Gilchrist, 260 F. 564 (1919).
2. Ibid.

[3] *The Birth of a Nation*

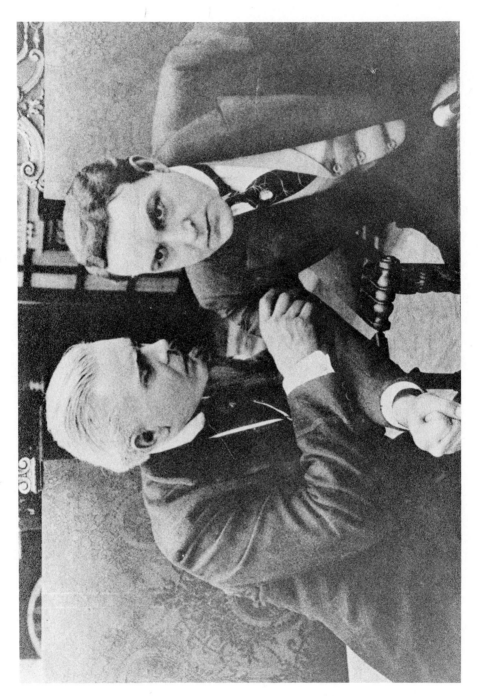

[10] *The Spy*

[16] *Alibi*

[18]   *Ecstasy*

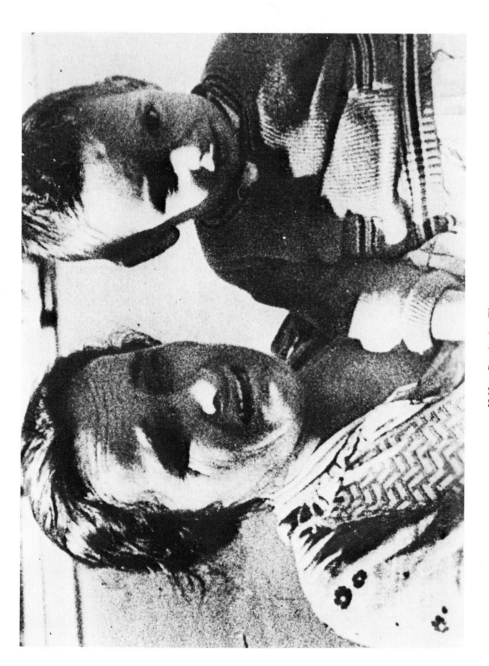

[20] *Spain in Flames*

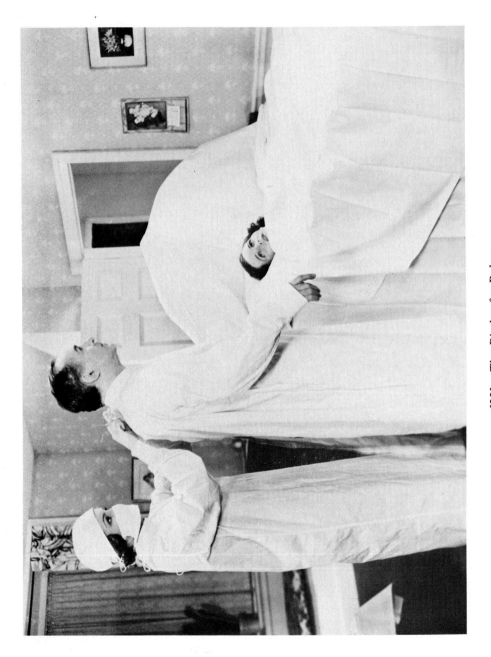

[22]   *The Birth of a Baby*

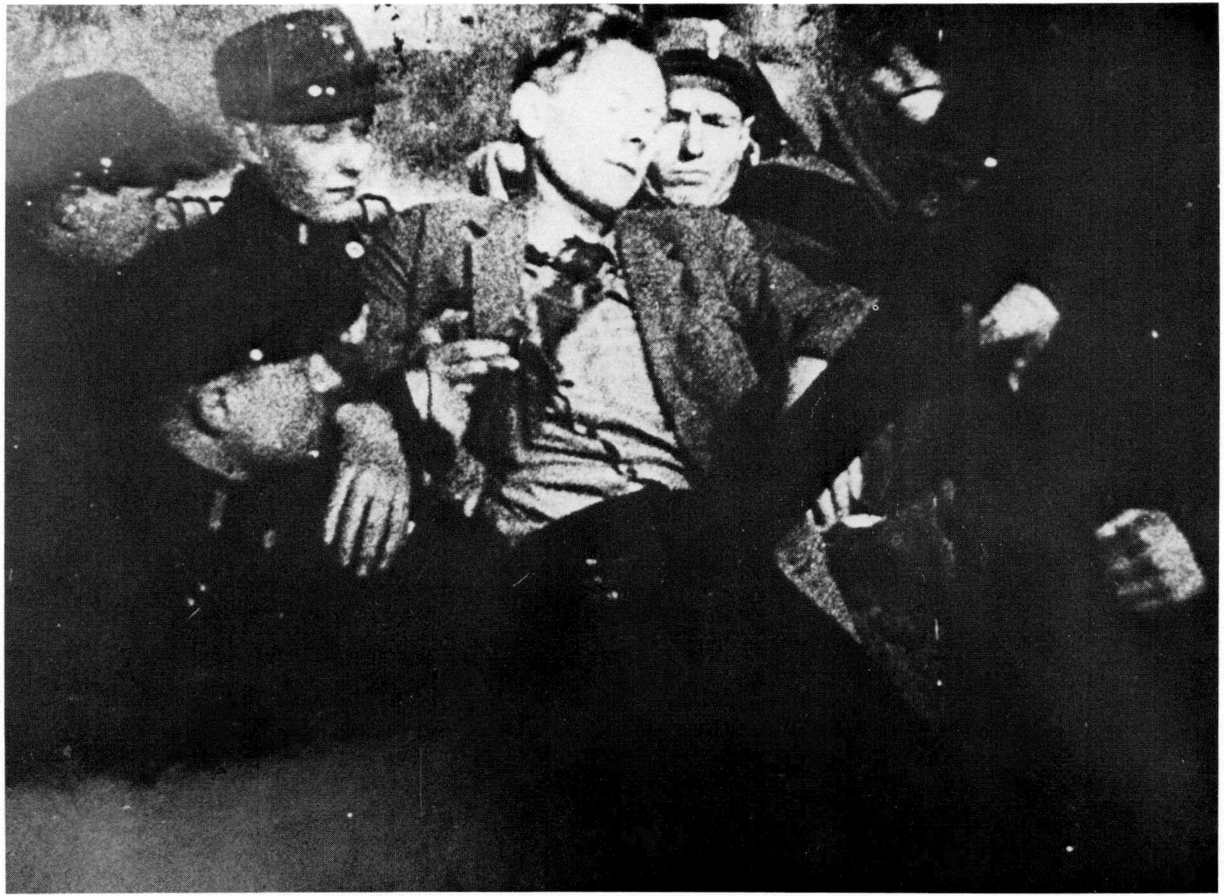

[23] *Professor Mamlock*

[24]   *Remous*

[26] *The Outlaw*

[26] *The Outlaw* (advertisement)

[30] *The Miracle*

[37]   *Native Son*

[38] *Baby Doll*

[67]   *Viva Maria*

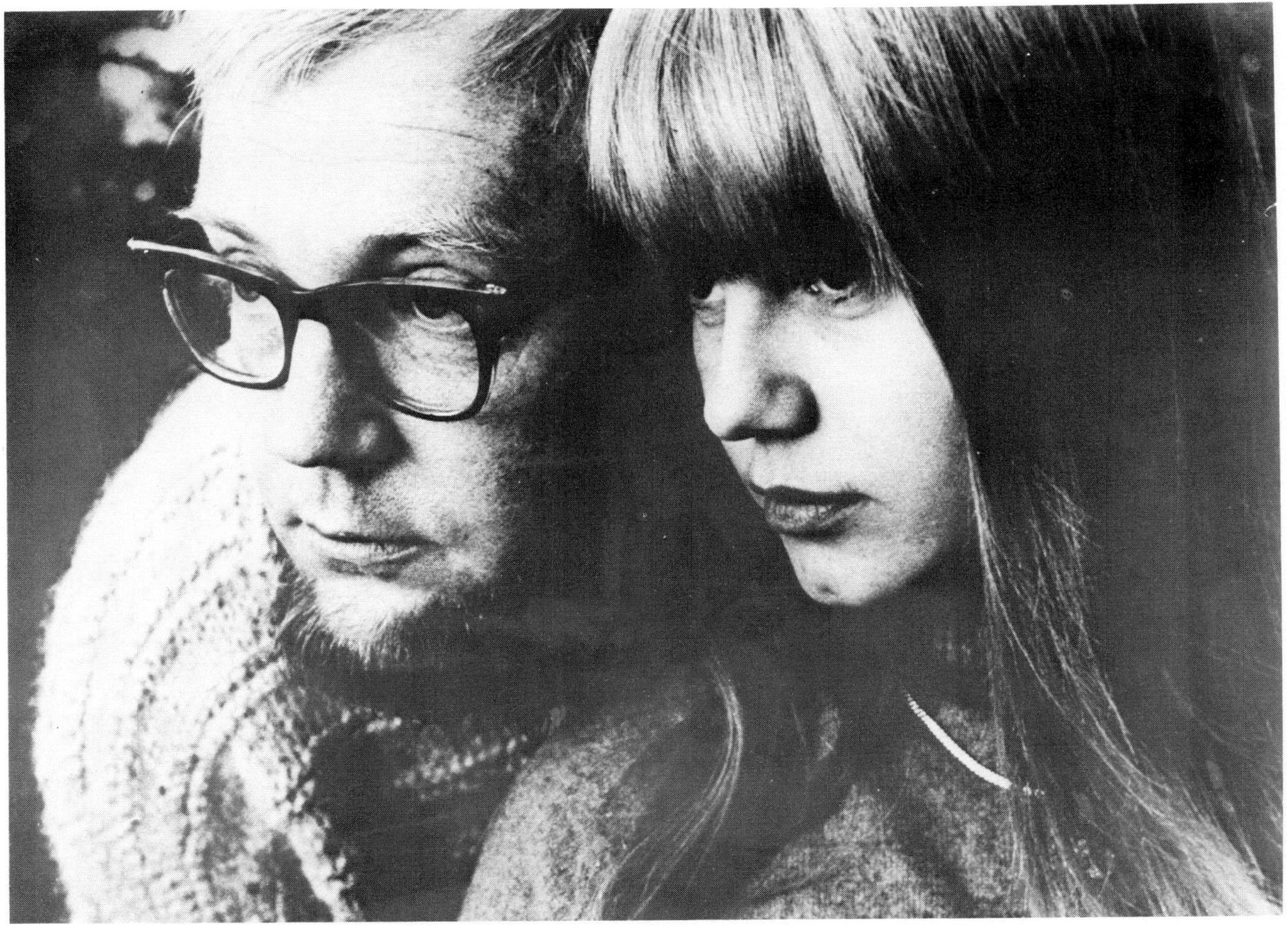

[71] *I Am Curious—Yellow*

1920–1939

[14]
Newsreels

Banned in New York, 1922; banned in Ohio, 1952.

Newsreels were produced by several movie "manufacturing" companies beginning in 1914. By 1939, five newsreel companies were releasing 104 films a year: Movietone News, MGM News of the Day (formerly Hearst Metrotone News), RKO Pathé News, Paramount News, and Universal News.[1] Pathé released "twice each week, on stated days, a motion picture 'current events' film under the designation 'Pathé News.' " According to the producer's testimony in 1922, "Such films contain no portrayal of imaginary scenes or occurrences, staged or created for the purpose of making pictures, and are not reproductions or re-enactments of the events depicted. On the contrary, the said films consist of photographs of actual transpiring events and happenings. The pictures are taken on the ground exactly as they exist or occur, with motion picture cameras."[2] The newsreel involved in the Ohio censorship case of 1952 consisted of "(1) Convention High Lights; (2) New Army Dirigible; (3) Headlines in the News: Slum Clearance—Virginia, United States Fleet—British Harbor; (4) Sports Copy—Olympics—Kayaks—England." Such newsreels "consisted of less than 1,000 linear feet of film."[3]

Censorship Activity/Legal Importance
In 1921, the New York legislature passed a law that required the "publishers" of motion picture newsreels to submit such "current event" films to the state motion picture commission to be censored prior to exhibi-

tion. Pathé sought a judicial declaration that the law violated the constitutional guarantee of freedom of the press and deprived it of property without due process of law, arguing that a newsreel was "in principle the same as an ordinary newspaper," that "no logical or reasonable distinction can be made between the two media of expression," and that "it is the news that is [constitutionally] privileged, not the method of its publication." The New York court that considered the matter decided that although a motion picture was "a medium of thought," it was "clearly distinguishable" from a newspaper, periodical, or book, being "a spectacle or show, rather than a medium of opinion." One of its differences consisted in its attraction, compared to books or newspapers, to "children and the illiterate"; "its value as an educator for good is only equalled by its danger as an instructor in evil." "The picture creates its own atmosphere so vividly, so attractively, that even the child and the illiterate adult may see and learn." Citing the 1915 holding by the U.S. Supreme Court that motion pictures are not to be considered a part of the country's press,[4] and so were liable to be censored, the New York Supreme Court (Appellate Division) refused the requested declaration, denied that "the biweekly motion picture newsreel . . . is a part of the press of the country," and held it could be regulated by the law in question.[5] This ruling was affirmed by the Court of Appeals of New York.[6]

Other state and municipal censorship boards also censored newsreels. In 1934, the New York censorship law was amended to exempt "current event" films from its requirements; the laws of Pennsylvania and Kansas also exempted them. Such exemptions were exceptions to the general rule. During the period from October 1, 1937 to September 30, 1938, Massachusetts, for example, required 13 deletions from newsreels and the March of Time series. Fake or simulated newsreels were occasionally used for political propaganda purposes; on one well-known occasion, they were used to defeat Upton Sinclair's candidacy for governor of California in 1934. During the coal strikes of 1920, newsreels considered pro-labor were banned in Ohio and Pennsylvania. Kansas censors cut from a March of Time film a speech by Senator Burton K. Wheeler of Montana that opposed President Franklin D. Roosevelt's 1937 bill for "packing" the Supreme Court. A documentary film on the civil war in Spain, *Spain in Flames* [20], was censored in Pennsylvania and Ohio.[7]

However, by 1952, when the U.S. Supreme Court recognized in *The Miracle* case [30] that movies were protected by constitutional guarantees of freedom of expression, the courts conceded that newsreels could not validly be subjected to governmental censorship. In an Ohio case, an exhibitor who refused to submit a Warner-Pathé News newsreel to the censors was found not guilty of violating the censorship law on the ground that the law itself violated constitutional freedom of the press. The court relied on *The Miracle* case to support its major premise that motion pictures were not "a business, pure and simple, not to be regarded as part of the press of the country," but were rather "an organ of public opinion [whose importance was] not lessened by the fact that they are designed to entertain as well as to inform." As such, films were deemed "included within the free speech and free press guaranty. . . ." The court also relied on the landmark case of *Grosjean* v. *American Press*[8] to find the three-dollar license fee unconstitutional. This case had found that a tax based on the gross receipts of newspapers that published advertising abridged freedom of the press. The court observed that "[a] newsreel may appear moral to one person and immoral to another," that "[w]hat to one person is educational to another may be propaganda," that "what is one man's amusement teaches another's doctrine," and that "[w]hat may appear harmless to one person may appear harmful to another, depending upon the individual's background, education, experience and environment." And the court denounced the criteria of the censorship board for licensing motion pictures as coming down to "what the particular reviewing board happens to think about the particular picture." The court found this unacceptable by standards of freedom of the press. "To subject a newsreel to [such] censorship is of itself a greater evil than the possibility of evil against which the statute was designed to protect."[9]

1. "Censorship of Motion Pictures," 49 *Yale Law Journal* 87 (1939).
2. Presentation by Pathé Exchange, Inc. in Pathé Exchange, Inc. v. Cobb, 195 N.Y.S. 661 (1922).
3. State v. Smith, 108 N.E. 2d 582 (1952).
4. Mutual Film Corp. v. Industrial Commission of Ohio, 236 U.S. 230 (1915).
5. Pathé Exchange v. Cobb, 195 N.Y.S. 661 (1922).
6. Pathé Exchange v. Cobb, 142 N.E. 274 (1923).
7. "Censorship of Motion Pictures," 49 *Yale Law Journal* 87, 90–95 (1939).
8. Grosjean v. American Press, 297 U.S. 233 (1935).
9. State v. Smith, 108 N.E. 2d 582 (1952).

[15]
The Naked Truth (T.N.T.)

Banned in New Jersey, 1926; banned in New York, 1928.

U.S., 1924 (copyright date). Dist: Public Welfare Pictures. 7 reels. 35mm. Silent. B&W. Prod: Public Welfare Pictures, Samuel Cummins. SW: George

D. Walters. Cast: Jack Mulhall, Helene Chadwick, Leo Pierson, Charles Spere, Irene Davis, Emmett King.

Clean-living young lawyer Bob, who has had good sex education, marries. Another youth becomes infected with venereal disease because his father allowed him to "have a fling." He refuses legitimate treatment, but accepts treatment from a quack doctor. His pending marriage is stopped by a legitimate doctor. A third young man does have venereal disease, consults a quack doctor, and marries. The disease eventually affects his brain and he kills his wife. Lawyer Bob gets him off by pleading insanity. The film "shows a male and a female in the nude, and, among other things, the progress of different venereal diseases and the effects thereof."[1]

Censorship Activity

Before the distributor of this film could exhibit it in Newark, New Jersey, "a private view was had," attended by the chief of the city's board of health, two members of the city's police department (known as the board of censors and appointed by William J. Brennan,[2] head of Newark's department of public safety), and also "by a number of ladies" invited by the board of censors and by Mr. Brennan. The censors objected to the movie "unless presented in a Y.M.C.A., in a school building, or a church, without charge." Commissioner Brennan then notified the distributor that "the presentation of the film was prohibited, that he would prevent the production by force, would revoke the theater license, and arrest all persons connected with the exhibition." He did not accept the distributor's offer to view the motion picture again, stating that he "confided the censorship of films" to the board of censors and that he would "stand behind their judgment." The distributor asked the court for an injunction preventing the commissioner and the city from interfering with the movie's showing, alleging "great monetary loss if . . . not allowed to produce it"; the city did not file an answering affidavit. The Court of Chancery granted the injunction.[3]

A ban of this film in New York as "obscene and indecent" was upheld two years later by the courts.[4] Here, after the New York censors refused to issue a license for its exhibition, despite several examinations, the state supreme court (Appellate Division) held—without viewing the movie—that judicial review of a censor's denial of a license was not required by law, in the absence of allegations that the denial was in bad faith, arbitrary, capricious, or without reasonable ground.

Legal Importance

The issue in the Newark case was whether "the Legislature . . . in the exercise of its police power, control[led] theaters and moving picture shows and decide[d] what are and what are not proper exhibitions." Vice Chancellor Church wrote that the Home Rule Act, which gives municipalities the power "to make [and] enforce . . . ordinances . . . as they may deem necessary and proper for the good government, order, protection of persons and property, and for the preservation of the public health, safety, and prosperity for the municipality and its inhabitants . . . [was not] specific enough to include the right to censor plays given in a theater duly licensed by the municipality." If the state legislature had granted the city the right to censor "plays," doing so here "might or might not be legal. But, certainly," the court continued, "by no stretch of the imagination can it be held that the director of public safety of a municipality can delegate to a policeman or a policewoman or a voluntary committee of women or to all combined the authority to say whether a certain play should or should not be produced." Stating that "I wish it to be distinctly understood that I am expressing no opinion as to the morality or immorality of this production," as "I have not seen it," the court relied on two unreported cases in granting the injunction. These involved *The Birth of a Nation* [3], in both of which the facts were said to be "almost identical" to those in this case.

1. Public Welfare Pictures Corporation v. Lord, 230 N.Y.S. 137 (1928).
2. William J. Brennan, the Newark Director of Public Safety, was the father of U.S. Supreme Court Justice William J. Brennan, Jr., the single most influential figure in modern obscenity law. "It is difficult to assess exactly how important [the senior Brennan's position] was in influencing the younger Brennan," a commentator has written, "but it was probably the most important single factor in shaping Brennan, Jr.'s life." David S. Jobrack, "Mr. Justice Brennan . . . the Man and the Judge," 2 *New Jersey St. B.J.* 241 (1959).
3. Public Welfare Pictures Corporation v. Brennan, 134 A. 868 (1926).
4. Public Welfare Pictures Corporation v. Lord, 230 N.Y.S. 137 (1928).

[16]
Alibi

Banned in Chicago, Illinois, 1929.

U.S., 1929. Dist: United Artists. 8,167 ft. 35mm. Sound. B&W. Prod/Dir/SW: Roland West. Cin: Ray June. Scenario: William Cameron Menzies. Cast: Chester Morris, Eleanor Griffith, Harry Stubbs, Mae Busch, James Mason. Reviews: *New York Times*, April 9, 1929, Morduant Hall; *Life*, May 3, 1929; *The Film Mercury*, March 8, 1929, Anabel Lane.

This film is based on the play *Nightstick* by John Griffith Wray, J. C. Nugent, and Elaine S. Carrington. Joan, the daughter of a police sergeant, has developed a reactive sympathy for criminals. She meets Chick, recently released from prison, who convinces her of his innocence and the cruel methods of the police. Despite her father's opposition, she dates Chick and secretly marries him. To celebrate their wedding, they go to the movies; during the intermission, Chick sneaks away and commits a robbery in the course of which he accidentally kills a policeman. The police suspect Chick of the murder, but Joan is his alibi. Chick accidentally divulges his crime to an undercover agent who Joan learns is a personal friend of her father's. She reveals his identity to Chick, who thereupon kills him. The police arrive. When they discover Chick, who is hiding in a closet, an officer who has secretly been in love with Joan fires blanks at him. Deeply shocked, Chick jumps from a window to his death. Realizing her mistake, Joan reexamines her attitude towards the police.

Censorship Activity

The Chicago superintendent of police denied the distributor of this film a permit to exhibit it in the city. The city censorship statute included the following as grounds for the denial of a permit: "if the picture is immoral or obscene, or portrays depravity, criminality, or lack of virtue of a class of citizens of any race, color, creed, or religion, and exposes them to contempt, derision, or obloquy, or tends to produce a breach of the peace or riots, or purports to represent any hanging, lynching, or burning of a human being. . . ." On this basis the superintendent refused to issue the permit, and wrote the distributor: "This picture portrays immorality, criminality, and depravity. It features the attempted robbery of a warehouse by a gang of criminals; the murder of the policeman who caught the thieves in the act; shocking and unlawful third-degree methods on the part of the police to force a confession from one of the gangsters; the murder of a man after it was discovered that he was a detective in disguise; the clever plan used by the gang to establish an alibi to cover up the robbery and the murder. The police methods used are brutal and revolting, and would tend, in the opinion of the censor board, to create contempt and hatred for the entire police force."

Judge Harry M. Fisher of the Circuit Court of Cook County granted the distributor a preliminary injunction against the superintendent's denial of a permit, but prohibited him from exhibiting the film until the court ruled on the city's motion to dissolve the order. Deciding the case solely on the basis of his viewing the film, Judge Fisher "refused to allow [the city] to examine witnesses and introduce in evidence the manuscript of the exact spoken words used by the characters in the picture. . . . The introduction of the spoken words without viewing the picture . . . cannot be regarded as evidence because it is only a part of the story told, and that so inaptly told that it can have no probative value." After viewing the film, Judge Fisher stated, "There are no parts of this picture that are immoral. . . . There is nothing in that picture—not a single scene—that could be said to come within the provisions of the ordinance before me." He then entered a permanent injunction, as the distributor had requested, preventing the city from interfering with the film's exhibition and from continuing to refuse to issue a permit for its showing. The Supreme Court of Illinois, however, reversed the lower court's decree.[1]

Legal Importance

The Illinois Supreme Court maintained that the power of a city to establish a censorship board, and to require a permit for the exhibition of a film, "cannot be doubted." "Moving picture shows, by reason of the low price of admission, are frequently patronized by large numbers of children, as well as by those who by reason of limited means or local conditions cannot attend the productions given in regular theaters. The audiences include those classes whose age, education, and situation in life especially entitle them to protection against the evil influence of obscene and immoral representations. The welfare of society demands that every effort of municipal authorities to afford such protection shall be sustained unless it is clear that some constitutional right is interfered with. Respect for law is the basis of our civilization, and any production which tends to cause disrespect for law and the officials charged with its enforcement would tend to immorality, and the exhibition of such picture would necessarily be attended with evil effects upon youthful spectators." However, that section of the censorship statute authorizing the confiscation of film apparatus, when a movie is shown in violation of the statute, was found unconstitutional as it denied due process of law: The ordinance "does not provide a forum for such confiscation, nor does it provide for notice to the owner or other persons involved in the property sought to be confiscated."

The court described its situation as "a novel one," because it did not have the film to view; "neither is the competent evidence of the manuscript of the talking part of the picture in evidence." "In a talking picture," the court said, "the words used by the actors are just as important as the scenes portrayed upon the screen. A picture apparently harmless in itself may have a very deleterious effect upon the minds of the spectators when its true meaning is brought out by the words of the actors."

The court assumed that the film's distributor, rather than its censors, had the burden of introducing the evidence necessary to resolve the issues. Since the distributor had failed to prove "by competent evidence" that the city "unreasonably and arbitrarily" refused to grant a permit for the film's showing, it could not complain. The court continued: "Suffice it to say that the picture deals with murderers on one side and the police on the other. It portrays the murder of a policeman in the discharge of his duty and the murder of a 'stool pigeon' who had won the confidence of the criminals. It contains threats of unlawful killings, made both by the criminals and by the police. It represents an exhibition of an attempt by police officers to extort evidence from prisoners by the use of what is known as the 'sweating process,' which practice has been most severely condemned by this court. . . .'' The murderer "did not expiate his crime as the result of a trial in a court of justice, but after his apprehension [when] he was threatened with instant death by officers, who aimed revolvers at him and fired several shots. While only blank cartridges were fired by the police with intent to frighten and intimidate the criminal, its effect was such as to cause him to leap to his death from an open window of the room in which he was being threatened and intimidated.'' The exhibition of the film, the court concluded, "could not fail to have a tendency to cheapen the value of human life in the minds of youthful spectators,'' and "would have a tendency toward immorality and to cause an increasing disrespect for the law and its officers.'' Therefore, the censors "were fully justified in refusing a permit for its exhibition.''

According to contemporary constitutional law doctrine, the court was decidedly in error in holding that the distributor had the burden of proving that his film was entitled to be shown, free of censorship. As the Supreme Court held in the *Revenge at Daybreak* case [58], the censor has the burden of initiating an immediate court proceeding and of proving that the film it wishes to refuse to license is not entitled to be shown.

The case is also interesting for its holding that the portrayal of immorality and of "disrespect for the law and its officers'' are valid grounds for censorship. There is no question today that such grounds present constitutionally defective bases for interfering with the circulation of films. See the cases of *Lady Chatterley's Lover* [43], *The Miracle* [30], *Native Son* [37], and *M* [33].

1. United Artists Corporation v. Thompson, 171 N.E. 742, 339 Ill. 595 (1930).

[17]
The Road to Ruin

Banned in Birmingham, Alabama, 1929.

U.S., 1928. Dist: True Life Photoplays. 6 reels (5,187 ft.). 35mm. Silent. B&W. Prod: Clifton Broughton Productions. Dir: Norton S. Parker. SW: Willis Kent. Cin: Henry Cronjager. Cast: Helen Foster, Grant Withers, Florence Turner, Charles Miller, Virginia Roye, Tom Carr. Review: *New York Times*, Feb. 21, 1928, Bosley Crowther.

Young Sally Canfield, without the benefit of guidance from parents, becomes involved with cigarettes, liquor, and affairs with older men. Picked up by police when they raid a strip poker game, she is not arrested, but is sent home. Some weeks later she learns she is pregnant. An unprincipled young man arranges for an illegal abortion if she will, in return, agree to sexual relations with another older man. The older man turns out to be her father, and Sally apparently dies of shock.

Censorship Activity

The exhibitor of this film in Birmingham, Alabama, went to federal court for an injunction to prevent the city from interfering with his showing it, alleging that he would sustain a loss of more than $3,000. The city code required the city's inspector of amusements to approve all films shown in the city. It forbade the exhibition of films illustrating "the human female in a nude state or condition, or draped or clothed with transparent or partially transparent garments, draperies, or clothing which shows or represents any indecent, obscene, lewd . . . or suggestive act [or] scene." It also prohibited "any film depicting drunkenness of any female, unless the scene is reduced to a flash . . . or any scene . . . describing the plying of the trade of procurer . . . or any seduction scene . . . depicting . . . immoral, unlawful relations of any person or persons of either sex." In addition, the code outlawed any "obscene . . . or suggestive" text accompanying the film. The exhibitor claimed that this ordinance was "so vague and uncertain" in its bearing on his film as to be "without applicability and force." The Northern District of Alabama federal court denied the injunction.[1]

Legal Importance

In holding the city censorship ordinance constitutional despite the vagueness of its language and its extraordinary reach, the court upheld a law of the type that would later be condemned in such cases as *The Miracle* [30] and *Viva Maria* [67]. The law was all-encompassing to Judge Henry D. Clayton. "It is difficult," he stated, "to imagine how a word description of a forbidden picture show could be more carefully or accurately drawn, in language more comprehensive and more definite in every particular. . . . The words seem to be exhaustive of the descriptive power of the English language." He also upheld the ordinance under the state police power: "Undoubtedly the governing authority was convinced that the business of exhibiting motion picture films might be attended with such public evil as to at once warrant and demand regulation. Here the measures adopted have reasonable relation to that end, and it is not open to the judiciary to interfere."

1. Brooks v. City of Birmingham, 32 F. 2d 274 (N.D. Ala. 1929).

[18]
Ecstasy (Extase)

Banned from entry into United States, 1935; banned in New York, 1937.

Czechoslovakia, 1933. U.S., 1940. Dist: Eureka Productions, Jewel Productions, Pix Distributing Corp. 75 min. 35mm. Sound. B&W. Prod: Elekta Films. Dir: Gustav Machaty. SW: Samuel Cummins. Dialogue: Jacques A. Koerpel. Cast: Hedy Lamarr, Jaromin Rogoz, Leopold Kramer, Aribert Mog. Music: Denes Agay, Emery H. Heim. Awards: City of Venice cup for best direction, 1934 International Cinema Congress, Venice. Reviews: *New York Daily Mirror*, Dec. 12, 1940, Dorothy Masters; *New York Times*, Dec. 25, 1940, Bosley Crowther; *New York Herald Tribune*, Dec. 27, 1940; *New York Post*, Dec. 27, 1940.

The original version of *Ecstasy* tells the story of a young woman, married to an impotent man much older than herself. She meets a young engineer from a construction camp when her horse runs away with her clothes while she is swimming nude. She subsequently runs through a fierce storm to his cabin where she gives herself to him. The film captures the ecstatic expression on the young wife's face during love-making. When her husband learns of her adultery, he commits suicide. The film ends with the woman waiting for a train, having left the engineer. A second version of *Ecstasy* contained a new diary insert, written by Samuel Cummins, in which the young woman recounts the death of her husband and her subsequent marriage to the engineer. The sexual scenes that occur between her and the engineer thus become those of husband and wife.

Censorship Activity[1]

The copy of this film initially brought to the United States was seized by the U.S. Customs Bureau and referred to a federal district court and jury, which found it immoral and obscene. Shortly thereafter, in June 1935, this print of the movie was burned by a federal marshal while an appeal from the district court's decision was pending. The appeal was then dismissed on the ground that the court had lost jurisdiction by the burning of the film.[2] A revised version of the film was subsequently imported, passing through customs without objection. In 1937, the distributor of this version was denied a license for exhibition by the New York censorship board. On review, the state supreme court's Appellate Division affirmed the censorship board's denial of a license.[3] Not until 1940 was a version of the movie licensed for exhibition in New York.

Legal Importance

A scene in this movie showed closeups of the young wife's face as she experienced orgasm. The New York censors evidently strongly objected to this scene. The state supreme court held that they were authorized to refuse to license a film for exhibition even if only part of it was objectionable. The statute required the board to issue a license for a film "unless such film *or a part thereof* [italics supplied] is obscene, indecent, [or] immoral." The distributor, taking his cue from the *Ulysses* case,[4] had argued that "the proper test is not whether certain scenes taken from their context and judged by themselves alone may be offensive, but . . . whether the dominant effect of the picture as a whole is obscene." The court, however, rejected this argument. It was enough that the picture "unduly emphasizes the carnal side of the sex relationship," and that the censorship board's decision "is amply supported by the facts."

Today, a book or film may be considered obscene only if the "*dominant theme of the material taken as a whole* [italics supplied] appeals to prurient interest"; it is improper to judge a work by "the effect of isolated" parts.[5]

The distributor earlier had brought suit in the United States District Court for the Southern District of New York for an injunction to prevent New York officials from interfering with the film's exhibition, alleging that the refusal of the state authorities to grant a permit "encroach[ed] upon federal power over foreign commerce in violation of the Constitution (Article 1, §8)." The argument was that "since the federal [customs] authorities admitted the film, determining it not to be immoral within . . . the Tariff Act of 1930, its exhibition in a state may not later be prohibited by the state authorities." The Second Circuit Court of Appeals rejected this argument, stating that "censorship by statutory regulation in the state of New York constitutes no burden upon foreign commerce. . . . In regulating the local exhibition of films, the state exercises its police power after the article has lost its character as an import and consequently does not invalidly interfere or conflict with the exercise of federal power."[6]

1. A synopsis of the unusual censorship litigation history of this film may be found in "Note: Film Censorship: An Administrative Analysis," 39 *Columbia Law Review* 1383 (1939).
2. United States v. Two Tin Boxes, 79 F. 2d 1017 (1935).
3. Eureka Productions v. Byrne, 300 N.Y.S. 218 (1937).
4. United States v. *Ulysses*, 72 F. 2d 105 (1934).
5. Roth v. United States, 354 U.S. 476 (1957).
6. Eureka Productions v. Lehman, 17 F. Supp. 259 (1936), affirmed 302 U.S. 634 (1937).

[19]
The Youth of Maxim

Banned in Detroit, Michigan, 1935.

U.S.S.R., 1935. U.S., 1935. Dist: Amkino. 85 min. 35mm. Sound. B&W. Russian, with English subtitles. Prod: Lenfilm. Dir: Gregory Kozintzev, Leonid Trauberg. Music: D. Shostakovitch. Cast: Boris Cirtov, Stephan Kayukov, V. Kibardina, M. Tarkhanov. Awards: First prize for the Leningrad Studios at the Moscow Film Festival on the 15th anniversary of Soviet cinema. Reviews: *New York Daily News*, April 19, 1935, Wanda Hale; *New York Herald Tribune*, April 20, 1935, Howard Barnes; *New York Times*, April 20, 1935, André Sennwald; *Nation*, May 1, 1935. Articles: *Time*, May 29, 1935; *Theater Arts*, June 1935; *Vanity Fair*, June 1935; *Motion Picture Herald*, Oct. 26, 1935.

This film, the first in a projected trilogy, takes place in Czarist Russia in the years 1905-1907. It is the story of the political education of Maxim, formerly an ignorant peasant, now a young factory worker in the city. Maxim's best friends are victimized or killed under capitalist working conditions and by the police. Maxim is imprisoned, then released. With much bitterness and revolutionary zeal, he joins the underground socialist movement. "A stirring, vivid and beautifully integrated document of the Russian Social-Democratic movement in 1907, it ranks high in the splendid procession of Soviet photo-plays."[1]

Censorship Activity[2]

The Detroit police commissioner granted a permit to the exhibitor of this film, but revoked it before it could be shown. A city ordinance authorized the commissioner to "inspect" films to determine whether they were "indecent or immoral" and, if so, to notify the exhibitor that they "cannot be used." The exhibitor brought suit in the Wayne County Circuit Court for a writ of *mandamus* to compel the commissioner to issue the permit. At the court hearing, "leading citizens" disagreed as to whether the film was "subversive of the accepted principles of our form of government and inflammatory in nature [and on] its probable effects upon the 'young and immature.' "

The police commissioner was not called as a witness but submitted a statement to the court "that protests were lodged with [him] by representatives of various religious, . . . veterans . . . and civic organizations protesting against the [film's] showing and averring that [its exhibition] would be likely to incite class hatred and riots." He then amended his comments to state that the movie was "immoral for the reason that [it] is pure Soviet propaganda and is likely to instill class hatred and hatred of the existing government and social order of the United States." After viewing the film, the trial court refused to grant the writ of *mandamus*, basing its decision upon an "absence of proof of flagrant abuse of discretion" on the commissioner's part. On appeal, the Supreme Court of Michigan reversed the trial court and ordered that the writ be granted.[3]

Legal Importance
The higher court rested its decision on the view that a motion picture exhibitor had "a constitutional property right to show a film which is not indecent or immoral," and that the commissioner of police lacked power to suppress films that he considered "immoral." The court declined to overrule the banning merely on the ground that the commissioner had abused his official discretion in censoring this film. Justice George E. Bushnell thus became one of the first American jurists to recognize that motion pictures were a constitutionally protected medium for the communication of ideas, anticipating a position that the U.S. Supreme Court would not adopt for another 16 years. Accepting the police commissioner's contentions, Justice Bushnell observed, "would invest him with dangerous and plainly unconstitutional power." It would enable him to "hold as 'immoral' and suppress any picture involving social problems, politics, religion, or any human activity according to his own view, and there would be no redress if his acts were supported by the opinions of witnesses. Zealots could, and would, furnish the required proof. The most conscientious and high-minded persons, as well as intense partisans, find no difficulty in supporting their contentions as moral issues, as the witnesses in this case have done. Here, they say that the picture is immoral because it has a tendency to support communism or sovietism. . . . No feeling against foreign political policies or forms of government," the court concluded, "should be permitted to establish the principle that a police officer may be invested with discretion to determine his own powers of suppression or change the plain terms of his authority." "Deep love for our own form of government is inclined to accentuate our aversion for that of others, but it should not warp our judgement or dull our vision. The petitioner has a constitutional property right to show a film which is not indecent or immoral."

1. *New York Herald Tribune*, April 20, 1935, Howard Barnes.
2. The film was also banned by the Pennsylvania board of censors.
3. Schuman v. Pickert, 269 N.W. 152, 277 Mich. 255 (1936).

[20]
Spain in Flames

Banned in Ohio, 1937.

Spain, 1937. U.S., 1937. Dist: Amkino, Film Historians, Inc. 65 min. 35mm.
Sound. B&W. Prod: Agencies of the Spanish and Russian governments. Dir:
Joris Ivens. SW: John Dos Passos (Part I); Ernest Hemingway (Part II).
Reviews: *New York Post*, Jan. 29, 1937, Irene Thiver; *New York Herald
Tribune*, Jan. 30, 1937, Howard Barnes; *New York Times*, Jan. 30, 1937,
Frank Nugent.

Spain in Flames is a full-length documentary feature, in two parts, of the
Spanish Civil War, compiled from Spanish and Soviet newsreels. The first
part, entitled "Spain, the Fight for Freedom," was filmed by Spanish
cinematographers and has an accompanying English narration written by
John Dos Passos. It deals with the historical development of the civil war:
"We learn about the people of Spain; that the farmers are among the
poorest paid in Europe; that 50 percent of them are illiterate; that they have
long been tools of a feudal system."[1] There are scenes dealing with the overthrow of Alfonso XIII, the La Rue government of 1931, and the general
strike of 1934. The second part, "No Pasaran, They Shall Not Pass," was
filmed by Soviet cinematographers and has an accompanying English narration written by Ernest Hemingway. It deals with the civil war. The film contains footage of scenes that depict the fighting between Franco's troops and
the citizens of Spain. There are also scenes of the wounded and dying, the
bombing of the Alcazar, and the burning of Madrid.

Censorship Activity

The director of Ohio's Department of Education, Division of Film Censorship, banned the exhibition of this film "upon the grounds that it was harmful in stirring up race hatred and that it was antireligious." The North
American Committee to Aid Spanish Democracy, asserting an interest in
the film's exhibition, asked the Ohio Supreme Court to "set aside and
vacate" the censor's order, which had been issued without any hearing or
trial. The court dismissed the Committee's petition without considering the
merits of the complaint.[2]

Legal Importance

The court's decision turned on a technical procedural ground. The court
ruled that because the committee filed its petition for judicial review on
April 7, 1937, rather than between April 10 and the following ten day
period, the petition to vacate the censor's order would be dismissed. The action of the Ohio censors to suppress this film, without any hearing or
judicial consideration of the proof of the validity of the suppression, would

be clearly unconstitutional under the principles announced by the U.S. Supreme Court in the *Revenge at Daybreak* case [58] and others.

1. *New York Post*, Jan. 29, 1937, Irene Thiver.
2. North American Committee to Aid Spanish Democracy v. Bowsher, 9 N.E. 2d 617 (1937).

[21]
Tomorrow's Children

Banned in New York, 1937.

U.S., 1934. Dist: Foy Productions. 70 min. 35mm. Sound. B&W. Prod: Bryan Foy. Dir/Cin: Crane Wilbur. SW: Wallace Thurman, Crane Wilbur. Cast: Don Douglas, John Preston, Diane Sunclair, Lewis Gambart, Crane Wilbur. Reviews: *Motion Picture Herald*, May 19, 1934; *Billboard*, June 2, 1934.

This film deals with sterilization. Both Mr. and Mrs. Mason are drunkards whose children include a son in jail, a physically disabled child, two who are retarded, and a normal adopted daughter. The Welfare Bureau convinces the Masons to get the whole family sterilized. Among those opposed to the sterilization are a Catholic priest, who tries to persuade the mother not to undergo the procedure, and a young physician who seeks to save the daughter, whom he loves and wants to marry. When the mother admits that the normal child is not her biological daughter, the priest and physician seek a court order to prevent the daughter's sterilization. The operation is stopped while the girl is on the surgeon's table. The daughter marries her fiancé. There is a court scene that implies that decisions about sterilization are made summarily, corruptly, and without due process. It shows the judge yielding to a politically important senator's request that a frenzied sex pervert, who has been scheduled for sterilization, be discharged. The same judge is unmoved by the cries for justice from the adopted daughter and her fiancé.

Censorship Activity

Between May 5, 1934 and August 20, 1937, the New York censorship board refused several times to issue a license for the exhibition of this film on the grounds that it was "immoral" and would "tend to corrupt morals" and "incite to crime." A state court denied the distributor's application for an order reversing the determination of the board and ordered the case transferred to the Appellate Division.[1] The Appellate Division confirmed the lower court's determination,[2] and the New York Court of Appeals affirmed the censorship, without opinion.[3]

Legal Importance

The case provided an interesting example of a film censorship based on political and ideological content, which included a daring criticism of courtroom processes. Such censorship was justified, on the one hand, by the court majority but excoriated, on the other hand, by dissenting judges who were convinced (20 years before their time) that the censorship violated constitutional freedom of expression. For the Appellate Division majority, the issue was whether the censors refused the license capriciously or arbitrarily. The law required that a film be licensed unless it or a part of it "is obscene, indecent, immoral, inhuman, sacrilegious, or is of such a character that its exhibition would tend to corrupt morals or incite to crime." The court observed: it is "academic under our law that if there is evidence to constitute a reasonable basis for the determination of the commissioner, if his determination is not arbitrary nor capricious, if the verdict of a jury reaching the same conclusion would not be set aside as against the weight of evidence, the court is not at liberty to disturb his finding."

A film was considered to be neither a book, a newspaper, nor literature, but a spectacle or show rather than a medium of opinion; and moreover, "there are some things which are happening in actual life today which should not have pictorial representation in such places of amusement as are regulated by this legislation, places where the audiences are not confined to men alone or women alone and where children are particularly attracted." This movie, said the court, was "a studied creation inherently tending to distort the minds of the unwary and of children, to teach the corruption of courts, and to portray devices for circumventing the Penal Law," which prohibited the distribution of information regarding contraception. It "publicizes and elucidates sterilization as a means to prevent the conception of children, that it is a form of birth control, contraception without penalty, and that it is 'an immoral means to a desirable end.' It declares its own immorality. It tends to inculcate the fact that venal judges in court dispense injustice, and that young girls may be mutilated, unlawfully but under the forms of law, when accident does not prevent. It demonstrates the manner how and the ease with which the law may be violated. The content of the picture is devoted to an illegal practice, which is, as a matter of common knowledge, immoral and reprehensible according to the standards of a very large part of the citizenry of the state."

"Many things," the court continued, "may be necessary in surgery which are not proper subjects for the movies. The teaching and demonstration of many facts may be necessary to the classroom of the law school, the medical school and clinic, the research laboratory, the doctor's office, and even the theological school, which are not proper subject matter for the screen." In the majority's view a public presentation of the film was "a clear violation'' of the penal law's prohibitions upon the dissemination of "any written advertisement, circular, or notice, of any kind, of a recipe to prevent conception.'' Since the state statute charged the censorship board with "the duty of protecting [children's] morals in keeping with the moral standards of the people of this state,'' the commissioner's action in rejecting this picture and in refusing a license was "neither capricious nor arbitrary,'' but "a proper exercise of the office with which he is clothed.''

A vigorous dissent was written by Justice James P. Hill, joined by Justice Christopher J. Heffernan. In their opinion, the film was "a forceful and dramatic argument against the enactment of statutes which, under certain circumstances, permit enforced operations to prevent procreation.'' Thus it dealt with a "disputatious subject of public concern.'' "The meaning of 'immoral' was uncertain. As used in this kind of statute, the term has to do with the standards of right and wrong, specifically as to the sexual relation.'' The film contains nothing lewd or lustful; no part of the human body was exposed to view, "with the possible exception of a few square inches of the abdomen visible in the preparation for an operation.'' Thus it would "require a prurient imagination to find anything of the unchaste or indecent'' in the film. Furthermore, the film's theme "no more suggests sterilization as a means of birth control than a film showing the amputation of a leg would suggest that as a means to prevent persons from walking into danger.''

Then the dissenters undertook a spirited argument as to why a film of this kind cannot be censored in a free and democratic society. The argument that sterilization should not be given publicity "presents the issue of whether our people may govern themselves or be governed; whether arguments for and against proposed and impending legislation may be presented directly in the public prints, on the stage and by films, or whether a Commission or Commissioner is to determine the limit and character of the information to be given to the public. Ministers of propaganda are favored in certain jurisdictions, but agencies of that kind have never been approved here. . . . Merited and unmerited criticism is permitted against all who hold public office. It is deemed necessary and wise under our concept of freedom of speech and of the press. The judiciary, no more than the executive and legislative, are sacrosanct. The foundation and fame of our judicial system is not so unstable as to be injured by this police court scene which is neither immoral, tending to injure morals, or to incite to crime.''

1. Foy Productions v. Graves, 299 N.Y.S. 671 (1937).
2. Foy Productions v. Graves, 3 N.Y.S. 2d 573 (1938).
3. Foy Productions v. Graves, 15 N.E. 2d 435 (1938).

[22]
The Birth of a Baby

Banned in New York, 1939; banned in Lynchburg, Virginia, 1940; also banned in Cincinnati, Ohio, and Omaha, Nebraska.

U.S., 1938. Dist: The American Committee on Maternal Welfare, Inc. 72 min. 35mm. Sound. B&W. Prod: Jack Skirboll. Dir: A. E. Christie. SW: Burke Symon, Arthur Jarrett. Cin: George Webber. Cast: Eleanor King, Richard Gordon, Ruth Matteson, Josephine Dunn, William Post, Jr. Reviews: *Variety*, March 8, 1938; *Newsweek*, March 21, 1938; *Life*, April 11, 1938; *New York Times*, Dec. 8, 1938.

The Birth of a Baby depicts a couple's life through various stages leading to the birth of their first child. The importance of consulting a reputable doctor early and often is emphasized. The story culminates in the filming of an actual delivery of a baby girl. Its message communicates the importance of good health care and of communication between patient and doctor.

Censorship Activity

The New York State censorship board refused to grant a license for the exhibition of this film on the grounds that it was "indecent," "immoral," and "would tend to corrupt morals." The Board of Regents sustained the censors' action. While offering to issue a special permit as an "educational" film, the board refused to license it for exhibition in "places of amusement." The state supreme court ordered the matter transferred to the Appellate Division, which confirmed the board's determination.[1] The New York Court of Appeals affirmed the order without opinion.[2]

Legal Importance

"Undoubtedly," wrote Appellate Division Justice Gilbert V. Schenck, "this picture may have its scientific value. It is not inherently indecent in the ordinary accepted sense of the word, but it becomes indecent when presented in places of amusement. For clinical purposes the picture may be shown under a special permit authorizing the showing of educational pictures of this character under certain restrictions. But a picture depicting the actual birth of a child becomes indecent when presented to patrons of places of public entertainment." Its exhibition "in a place of public amusement for the entertainment of an audience composed of adults and children would serve no useful purpose, although it may appeal to the morbid and curious. Aside from all other considerations," Justice Schenck noted, "this court should not substitute its judgment for the judgment of [the regents]. . . . It is a matter of opinion whether this picture is decent or indecent, and where there is room for an honest opinion, this court should not interfere[, and] may not substitute its judgment for that of the body clothed with authority to make a determination."

Justices James P. Hill and Christopher J. Heffernan dissented. The film, they wrote, "will give vital and needed information to pregnant women, many of whom fail to seek early and necessary advice. The authors and actors treated the theme in a clean, dignified, and reverent manner. To limit the exhibition to educational and clinical groups will defeat the worthy purpose of the sponsors of the film."

The film was the basis for a controversial sequence of pictures showing the birth of a baby that appeared in the centerfold of the April 11, 1938 issue of *Life* magazine. The publisher, Ralph Larsen, had written a letter to subscribers explaining that they could pull out the photographs if they did not want their children to see them, but many people received the magazine before the letter. Larsen was arrested outside of Yankee Stadium in the Bronx, New York, and charged with selling an obscene magazine. Justice Nathan D. Perlman of the Court of Special Sessions acquitted him, concluding that "the picture story, because of the manner in which it was presented, does not fall within the forbidden class. The picture story was directly based on a film produced under the auspices of a responsible medical group. There is no nudity or unnecessary disclosure. The subject has been treated with delicacy."[3]

Censorship Activity

The Virginia state censorship board, created by statute in 1922, initially refused to issue a permit for statewide exhibition of this film. Upon appeal by a theater operator, a Circuit Court of Richmond directed the board to license the film for statewide distribution. This was done, but the city manager of Lynchburg, with approval of the city council, notified a Lynchburg theater operator that the film could not be shown in the city because it violated city ordinances that prohibited the exhibition of "obscene and indecent films." The operator asked the Corporation Court of Lynchburg for an injunction to prevent the city from interfering with the film's showing. Judge Aubrey E. Strode held that the theater operator had a right to exhibit the film in Lynchburg, and the Virginia Supreme Court of Appeals affirmed.[4]

Legal Importance

In general, municipalities have only such powers as have been conferred upon them by the state; when a state exercises its power over a field or subject matter, a municipality is preempted from exercising any conflicting power. Here, the city of Lynchburg did not have the power to prohibit the exhibition of a particular film once it had been licensed for exhibition by the state censorship board. The statute providing for the regulation and examination of motion pictures was proof that the state intended to monopolize this area and not share this power with municipalities. Court of Appeals Judge Herbert B. Gregory wrote: "The State by its statute having occupied the entire field of moving picture censorship, municipalities are thereby excluded therefrom as to matters comprehended by the statute." The statute that created the motion picture censorship board was considered to embody a statewide policy. "If municipalities may censor films and determine the right of the owners to exhibit them," Judge Gregory concluded, "then the unified control plan as outlined in the State statutes would be ineffectual and inoperative to carry out the expressed intention of the legislature." (A related problem was involved in the *Virgin Spring* case [52].) The question of the film's alleged obscenity was not adjudicated.

1. American Committee on Maternal Welfare v. Mangan, 14 N.Y.S. 2d 39, 257 App. Div. 570 (1939).
2. American Committee on Maternal Welfare v. Mangan, 283 N.Y. 551 (1940).
3. People v. Larsen, 5 N.Y.S. 2d 55 (1938). See Morris L. Ernst, *The Best Is Yet* (New York: Harper, 1945), 139–140; Morris L. Ernst and Alexander Lindey, *The Censor Marches On* (Garden City, N.Y.: Doubleday, 1940), 98–100; *New York Times*, April 20, 1979, p. B4.
4. City of Lynchburg v. Dominion Theaters, 7 S.E. 2d 157 (1940).

[23]
Professor Mamlock

Banned in Providence, Rhode Island, 1939.[1]

U.S.S.R., 1938; U.S., 1938, 1941.[2] Dist: Amkino Corporation. 2,867 meters. 35mm. Sound. B&W. English subtitles. Prod: Lenfilm (U.S.S.R.). Dir: H. Rappaport, A. Minkin. SW: F. Wolf, H. Rappaport, A. Minkin. Cin: F. Filator. Music: Y. Kutchurov, M. Timofeyev. Cast: S. Mezhinsky, O. Zhakov, N. Shaternikova, V. Mercuriev. Reviews: *New York Times*, Nov. 8, 13, 1938, Frank Nugent; *New York Daily News*, Nov. 9, 1938, Dorothy Masters; *Variety*, Nov. 9, 1938; *New York Herald Tribune*, Nov. 20, 1938, Howard Barnes. Articles: *Brooklyn Daily Eagle*, Nov. 20, 1938; *Daily Worker*, Jan. 5, 20, 1939; July 12, 1941; *Providence Journal*, July 18, 1939; *London Times*, Aug. 25, 1939; *New York Times*, Aug. 30, 1939; *Motion Picture Herald*, July 12, 1941.

This film was adapted from a play of the same name by Frederick Wolf, produced in New York by a Works Progress Administration (WPA) theater group. After Hitler's rise to power, Professor Mamlock, a Jewish doctor working in a German clinic, and his family endure hardship and persecution. Despite his father's disapproval, Mamlock's son, Rolf, works underground with the Communist movement. Meanwhile, the doctor, having no particular political convictions, is deposed from his hospital post and humiliated, then pressed back into service to operate on a high Nazi official, only to be disbarred again from further practice. In a brutal climactic crowd scene, Mamlock is killed by Nazi machine guns while delivering a speech of defiance and a prayer for his beloved country, Germany. The film ends at a secret Communist Party meeting where Rolf and other anti-Nazis pledge solidarity and offer a hopeful vision for the future in spite of the hideousness of Nazism, which they must continue to resist.

Censorship Activity

After privately viewing this film, the "amusement inspector" of the Providence, Rhode Island Bureau of Police and Fire and his deputy reported that they disapproved of its public exhibition in the city "on the grounds that it was communistic propaganda; that it would not be for the public welfare but rather inimical thereto on account of its tendency to incite race hatred and class strife or to intensify them, especially in view of the present condition of the public mind with respect to the underlying theme of the picture and also because of the nature of the scenes of brutality and bloodshed there presented." The inspector also reported that despite a city statute providing that no license shall be issued for any picture not approved by the National Board of Review of Motion Pictures, the distributor planned to show the film. The bureau confirmed the inspector's action after viewing the movie. The distributor's counsel then asked the bureau to reverse its decision or to suggest changes in the picture that would make it satisfactory; the bureau denied the requests. Acting upon the bureau's intimation that no formal application had been filed, counsel filed two applications and asked that a hearing be granted. The amusement inspector and the bureau formally denied both applications and the request for a hearing. The distributor then petitioned the state supreme court, claiming that the bureau's denial of the application without granting a hearing was an error of law, and that the bureau lacked competent evidence on which to base its decision. The court rejected the distributor's contentions and annulled a writ of *certiorari* that it had improvidently granted.[3]

Legal Importance

The Supreme Court of Rhode Island considered that exhibition of motion pictures was "subject to regulation and even prohibition under the police power of the state." Moreover, according to the Rhode Island statute, any license granted to show a film might "be revoked at the pleasure of the local licensing authority." The court did not find a case in which it had decided the legality of a denial, a fact which "in itself is of no little significance." This seemed to the court to be "an indication that no one ever before thought an applicant for a license had a right to complain to th[e] court if his application was denied." There is a "well-understood belief in this state [that a license] to show motion pictures publicly for a price is necessarily a mere privilege and not in any sense a right of property." Therefore, the applicant for a license "has no right to a hearing before his application is denied." "It may be," the court noted, "that there would be less danger of arbitrary action if a hearing were made a prerequisite; but that is a matter for legislative consideration, and not for us." The court did not itself view the film, as the distributor had requested, because "under no circumstances does this court undertake on *certiorari* to review the findings of fact by an inferior tribunal, or to weigh the evidence which it had before it and on which the tribunal rested its decision." For the court to view the picture "would be to put ourselves in the place of the bureau in determining whether [it] ought to be shown. . . . [T]he petitioner would have us do . . . the very thing we cannot do, and that is weigh the evidence." "Clearly," the court concluded, in sending the case back to the bureau of police and fire, "all [the constitutional questions that the distributor had argued] only in a general way . . . are without merit."

Virtually everything the court said and did in this case was erroneous by today's law. Today, the exhibitor's "constitutional questions" would be meritorious.[4] The court would be obligated to view the film for itself and, if necessary, overturn the administrative finding.[5] The showing of motion pictures is based not on a "mere privilege" but on a constitutionally protected right,[6] and the applicant would have a constitutional right to a judicial hearing before his application to show a film could be denied.[7]

1. The film also was banned by the Chicago board of censors (*New York Post*, Nov. 17, 1938); by the Ohio State Division of Censorship (*New York Herald Tribune*, Jan. 26, 1939; *Variety*, Jan. 31, 1939); in Massachusetts, on Sundays (*Variety*, March 8, 1939); in England (*New York Herald Tribune*, April 20, 1939); and in Chungking, China (*New York Times*, Aug. 18, 1939).
2. Originally released in November, 1938, but withdrawn when the Russo-German alliance was signed; it was re-released in 1941 (*Motion Picture Herald*, July 12, 1941).
3. Thayer Amusement Corporation v. Moulton, 7 A. 2d 682 (1939).
4. *The Miracle* case [30].
5. The *Carnal Knowledge* case [105].
6. *The Miracle* case [30].
7. The *Revenge at Daybreak* case [58].

[24]
Remous (Whirlpool)

Banned in New York, 1939.

France, 1935. U.S., 1939. Dist: Alliance Cinématographique Européenne.
8,000 ft. 35mm. Sound. B&W. English subtitles. Prod/Dir: Edmond Greville.
SW: Peggy Thompson. Cast: Jeanne Boitel, Jean Galland, Maurice Maillott,
Dianna Sari. Reviews: *Morning Telegraph*, Jan. 7, 1935; *New York World
Telegram*, Feb. 9, 1935; *Variety*, April 3, 1935.

In the same vein as *Lady Chatterley's Lover*, this film portrays the plight of
a passionate woman whose husband has been paralyzed from the waist
down as a result of an auto accident that occurred during their honeymoon.
The wife eventually decides to have an affair with a young man while still
remaining spiritually faithful to her crippled husband. "Sequence after
sequence shows her struggle with her senses, in shots that recall those of the
Czech picture *Ecstasy*."[1] The wife's infidelity finally results in the suicide of
the husband.

Censorship Activity
The New York State censorship board found this picture indecent and immoral and that it would tend to corrupt morals. On review, the state
supreme court's Appellate Division held that the board's finding was not arbitrary and affirmed the determination.[2]

Legal Importance
After viewing the film, the court noted that the plot is "practically the
same" as that of *Ecstasy*, a film for which a license had also been denied;
that denial had been upheld on appeal by this same court. According to the
court, the picture purported to display the wife's nervous, emotional, and
mental state as a result of the husband's impotence, and her consequent un-
balanced moral character and indiscretions. Writing for the court's majority, Justice Bliss said that "such is not fit subject matter for screen display."

1. *Variety*, April 3, 1935.
2. Mayer v. Byrne, 10 N.Y.S. 2d 794 (1939).

1940–1959

[25]
Victory in the West (Sieg im Westen)

Attempted banning in New York, 1941.

Germany, 1941. U.S., 1941. Dist: Ufa Films, Inc. 130 min. 35mm. Sound. B&W. No English subtitles. Prod: Noldan Productions. Cin: Cameramen of the German High Command and German newsreels. Music: Herbert Windt, Hannes Sieber. Reviews: *New York Daily News*, May 8, 1941, Dorothy Masters; *New York Times*, May 11, 1941; *New York Sun*, May 16, 1941.

This German documentary film is composed in large part of newsreels that depict the German invasion of the Netherlands, Belgium, and France. It explains the mysterious seizure of Fort Eben Emael that made possible the Nazi sweep across Belgium and France. "From the start, it dogmatically asserts the necessity of the Germans to protect themselves against their enemies, and then it proceeds to show in vivid detail how the Nazi armies marched through the Low Countries and France, bombarded forts, spanned rivers, captured cities, and won the campaign in the West."[1] There are no shots of dead bodies and only a very few of wounded German soldiers. "As German troops entered France, the music openly gloated, presented an English voice singing 'We'll Hang Out the Washing on the Siegfried Line,' then mockingly played that song in slow time."[2]

Censorship Activity

A civil action was filed by one Richard R. Rollins to compel the state motion picture censorship agency, the New York State Department of Education, to subject this film to the licensing law and to deny it a license on the ground that its exhibition would tend to "incite public disorder." The Supreme Court, Special Term, Sullivan County, dismissed the action on the ground that it had no jurisdiction over the matter, such questions being left by the state law to the judgment of the Department of Education.[3] The censorship statute excluded films portraying "current events" from the requirement for a license; the department, after viewing the film, had determined that it portrayed current events and therefore needed no license.

Legal Importance

The case is noteworthy as an illustration of the way in which news or current events are sometimes exempt from governmental censorship, presumably because of their high "free speech" value. This was a Nazi propaganda film consisting in large part of official German newsreels, containing "a number of portrayals of the present war from German and other sources . . . arranged and presented from a German viewpoint." The fact that the film also presented "the historical background" of the "current events" did not mean the film was required to be licensed. As to the allegation that exhibition of the film might "incite public disorder," the court pointed out that if this were the case, "there are public officers charged with the duty of preserving the public peace," i.e., the ordinary police who, presumably, were competent to deal with such a problem, using the criminal law. The case also presents one of the few examples in which a private person, not a governmental agency, went to court in an attempt to prevent a movie from being publicly shown.

1. *New York Times*, May 11, 1941.
2. *New York Sun*, May 16, 1941.
3. Rollins v. Graves, 30 N.Y.S. 2d 510 (1941), affirmed 32 N.Y.S. 2d 11.

[26]
The Outlaw

Banned in New York, New York, 1946.

U.S., 1941, 1947. Dist: Cardinel Films, United Artists. 103 min. 35mm. Sound. Color. Prod: Howard Hughes. Dir: Howard Hawks. SW: Jules Furthman. Cin: Greg Toland. Cast: Jane Russell, Jack Buetel, Thomas Mitchell, Walter Huston, Mimi Aguglia. Reviews: *New York Herald Tribune*, Sept. 12, 1947; *New York Times*, Sept. 12, 1947, Bosley Crowther; *New Yorker*, Sept. 20, 1947. Articles: *Photoplay*, Sept. 1946, Fred. R. Simmia.

The Outlaw is about the life of Billy the Kid. It opens with a quarrel between Billy the Kid and Doc Holliday over a horse named Red, and goes on to portray the young outlaw's career. Included are the Kid's strange friendship for Sheriff Pat Garrett and his affair with a part-Indian woman named Rio. "Of course, a great attraction of the film was supposed to be some torrid love scenes, but there have been enough cuts to leave them hanging pretty much in midair."[1] The film ends with Rio and Billy the Kid seeking a new, moral life together.

Censorship Activity[2]

After New York State censors had granted a license for this film and public announcements were made of its showing at three theaters in New York City, the city's police commissioner and commissioner of licenses (having viewed the film at a "private" official showing) announced that it was obscene. They threatened to prosecute criminally and revoke the operating license of any movie exhibitor who showed the film in New York City. The film's producer applied to court for an order restraining the threatened criminal prosecutions, and to obtain a judicial declaration that since the film had been approved by the state censors for showing in New York State, any criminal proceedings based on its alleged obscenity were improper. The state court that heard the matter denied the producer's application,[3] and both the Appellate Division court[4] and the New York Court of Appeals[5] affirmed.

Legal Importance

The producer argued that the state censorship law set up an "exclusive and uniform" system of censorship for the state, but the city officials pointed out that the law establishing the censorship board's authority also provided that the law "shall not be construed to relieve any state or local peace officer in the state from the duty otherwise imposed of detecting and prosecuting violations of the laws of the State of New York." The state's penal law prohibition against anyone showing an obscene film, and the duty of law enforcement officials to enforce that law, were held not to have been nullified by the enactment of the state censorship law. The court found nothing inconsistent in the existence of the two laws "side by side." While the case was one of "first impression," the court decided that, just as the censorship law gave to film distributors a right to appeal from adverse determinations concerning the obscenity of films, so the penal law gave to law enforcement officials an avenue for appeal from censorship board decisions with which they did not agree, by bringing prosecutions against exhibitors of a film that, although licensed for showing, they nonetheless considered obscene.

1. *New York Times*, Sept. 12, 1947, Bosley Crowther.
2. Prior to the commencement of legal action by the film's producer, its distributor had applied to court for an order requiring theaters that had contracted to show the film to do so in spite of the city officials' threats to

prosecute them and revoke their operating licenses. The court denied the request, in part because it was "unthinkable that a court should order defendants to do an act which almost certainly will subject them to be convicted of a crime." United Artists v. Amity Amusement Corp., 66 N.Y.S. 2d 299 (1946), affirmed 66 N.Y.S. 2d 621 (1946).

3. Hughes Tool Co. v. Fielding, 73 N.Y.S. 2d 98 (1947).
4. Hughes Tool Co. v. Fielding, 75 N.Y.S. 2d 287 (1947).
5. Hughes Tool Co. v. Fielding, 80 N.E. 2d 540 (1948).

[27]
Amok

Banned in New York, 1947.

France, 1946. U.S., 1947. Dist: Distinguished Films. 68 min. Sound. B&W. English subtitles. Prod: Carlyle Productions. Dir: Fedor Ozep. Cast: Marcelle Chantel, Jean Yonnel, Vladimir Inkijinoff. Review: *Variety*, Oct. 23, 1946.

This film was adapted from a short story by Stefan Zweig. A lady of wealth and social position, living on a French colonial island, attempts to persuade a doctor who banished himself to the jungle to work among the natives, to give her an illegal abortion. Her husband is about to return from a year abroad and she does not want him to know of her infidelity. The doctor indignantly refuses, but then intimates that he might be persuaded to perform the operation in return for sexual favors. This is unacceptable to the wife, who resorts to a native crone, an "herb doctor," with tragic results. The doctor promises the wife on her deathbed to keep her secret, and duly tells the returned husband that she has succumbed to a heart attack. Disbelieving the story, however, the husband announces he will take the body to Europe for postmortem examination. As the casket is being lifted to the deck of the ship, the doctor cuts the rope and plunges into the sea with the casket.

Censorship Activity

The New York censorship board denied the distributor of this film a license to show it on the grounds that it was "indecent, immoral, tends to corrupt morals [and] tends to incite crime." The board recommended modifications in the dialogue between the doctor and the wife as well as in the scene "which shows the woman in extremis after the supposed abortion. . . ." The State Supreme Court, Appellate Division, confirmed the board's determination.[1]

Legal Importance

The court was not impressed by the distributor's argument that the theme in his film was "no more sordid or gross than [that of] many which have been approved," but considered that censors were entitled to use their discretion. "A standard in matters of this kind is flexible," wrote Justice James P. Hill. Since even with the suggested cuts, the same theme would remain, it was "understandable that some reviewing bodies would think this film offended," and there "doubtless is some evidence to sustain the [board's] finding." Accordingly, the ban on the film was confirmed. The possibility that the censors' behavior violated freedom of expression was not suggested.

1. Distinguished Films v. Stoddard, 68 N.Y.S. 2d 737 (1947).

[28]
Mom and Dad

Attempted banning in New Jersey, 1948; banned in New York, 1956; banned in Chicago, Illinois, 1958.

U.S., 1948. Dist: Hygienic Productions. Sound. B&W. 87 min. 35mm. Prod: Kroger Babb, Jack Jossey. Dir: William Beaudine. SW: Mildred Horn. Cin: Barney Saracky. Cast: Hardie Albright, Lois Autin, George Eldridge, June Carlson, Jimmy Clark, Bob Lowell. Reviews: *New York Herald Tribune*, Jan. 31, 1957; *New York Times*, Jan. 31, 1957, Bosley Crowther; *New York Post*, Feb. 1, 1957.

Mom and Dad is the story of a small-town high school girl who has not been told the facts of life by her squeamish mother and gets into "trouble." When the mother learns of her daughter's pregnancy, she blames herself for her puritanical attitudes and takes her daughter east to await the birth of the child. At this point in the film's original version (circa 1948), an intermission occurred during which Elliot Forbes, a "famous hygiene commentator," gave a small lecture on hygiene and sold copies of a pamphlet entitled "Secrets of Sensible Sex." The film then resumed with scenes of the actual birth, followed by a few segments of school hygiene sessions concerning the ravages of venereal disease. The film originally was shown separately to male and female audiences. In the 1957 version, "a number of the original scenes were eliminated and a number of new scenes inserted."[1]

Censorship Activity

In 1948, when the earlier version of this film was about to be released in Newark, New Jersey, the city director of public safety threatened to revoke the theater's operating license on the ground that he considered the film suitable only for noncommercial showings under educational auspices. A superior court judge held that it was not within the director's power to revoke a theater's license for showing a film under commercial auspices, the presentation of which would not be objectionable, according to the director, if shown under noncommercial circumstances.[2]

Prior to its re-release in 1957, the New York State censorship board refused to license the film on the ground that one short sequence in it, "a biological demonstration" of a human birth, under controlled conditions, was indecent. On appeal, the state supreme court's Appellate Division annulled the board's determination and ordered the film licensed.[3]

Legal Importance

The appellate court in the 1956 New York case held that the film, which it had viewed, was not indecent in the sense required "to justify prior restraint." "If the terms 'obscene' or 'indecent' could serve at all as constitutionally valid standards for prior restraint," the court wrote, "the words must be given a narrow and restricted interpretation." So interpreted, the terms were deemed "clearly not applicable" to this film. The court questioned whether the Supreme Court's decisions in *The Miracle* case [30] and in others that followed[4] left open "any area" for the states to exercise prior restraints against the showing of motion pictures. If there were "such an area," the court observed, the state would "have the 'heavy burden' of demonstrating that its statute is operative only in 'an exceptional case.' " Treating this film as "indecent" and thus refusing it a license did not meet that burden.

The later version of the film was also restrained from exhibition in Chicago, where the chief of police refused to issue a permit for its exhibition without giving reasons. This refusal was upheld by a federal district court because the judge found the film "obscene and immoral *if exhibited for entertainment.*" This decision was, however, reversed by the U.S. Court of Appeals because, after viewing the film, it "was satisfied there was absent any sound basis for outlawing the film and the absence of any reasons by the censors for their classification is a foreboding guise for arbitrary censorship running afoul of the First and Fourteenth Amendments. . . . This censorship results in a curb on free expression."[5]

1. Capitol Enterprises v. City of Chicago, 260 F. 2d 670, 671 (1958).
2. Hygienic Productions, Inc. v. Keenan, 62 A. 2d 150 (1948).
3. Capitol Enterprises v. Regents, 149 N.Y.S. 2d 920 (1956).
4. For example, Superior Films v. Department of Education and Commercial Pictures Corp. v. Regents, 346 U.S. 587 (1954).
5. Capitol Enterprises v. City of Chicago, 260 F. 2d 670 (1958).

[29]
Curley

Banned in Memphis, Tennessee, 1949.

U.S., 1947. Dist: United Artists, Hal Roach Studios. 5,040 ft. 35mm. Sound. Color. Prod: Hal Roach, Robert F. McGowan. Dir: Bernard Carr. SW: Dorothy Reid, Mary McCarthy. Cin: John W. Boyle. Cast: Larry Olden, Frances Raffery, Eilene Janssen, Dale Belding, Gerald Perreau. Review: *Motion Picture Herald*, Oct. 11, 1947.

The young students of Midvale School are apprehensive about the teacher who will replace their beloved Miss Evans, who has left town to get married. Curley, the likeable class ringleader, mistakes the new teacher's ogre of an aunt for the new teacher herself, and plans hair-raising pranks to get rid of her. The real new teacher, the young and pretty Mildred, gives Curley a ride to school; he unwittingly tells her of the pranks. Armed with this inside information, Mildred causes all the pranks to backfire. The children suspect Curley of squealing and ostracize him. At a school picnic staged by Mildred, she finally wins over her rebellious students with the athletic prowess she displays during the picnic games. When Curley rescues Mildred from a battle with the school bully, he is readmitted to the happy fold. Curley and his playmates resemble the members of *Our Gang*, a film also produced by Hal Roach.

Censorship Activity

The chairman of the Memphis, Tennessee, censorship board, after viewing the film, wrote its distributor, United Artists: "I am sorry to have to inform you that [the board] is unable to approve [for exhibition in the city] your picture with the little negroes as the South does not permit negroes in white schools nor recognize social equality between the races even in children." The film's distributor and producer, Hal Roach Studios, Inc., brought suit in the circuit court, claiming that the censorship statute denied the rights of freedom of speech and due process guaranteed under the First and Fourteenth Amendments, and that the board's denial of a license "solely on the ground that members of the colored race appear" in the film was "capricious and arbitrary" action that violated "equal protection of the laws." Refusing even to view the film, Circuit Court Judge Floyd M. Henderson dismissed the petition on the grounds that the censorship statutes were applicable only to local exhibitors, that the distributor did not show pictures in the city and had not contracted to do so, and that the board's letter, being "advisory only," did not present a "justifiable controversy." On appeal, the Supreme Court of Tennessee affirmed the lower court's judgment.[1]

Legal Importance

The court's holding that this film's distributor and producer had no legal standing to sue is an example of a court's avoiding the censorship issue and upholding an act of governmental censorship on a ground that fails to confront the questionable legality of the censor's authority. The state supreme court agreed that there was no authority in the law "to use race or color as the sole legal basis for censorship of talking-motion pictures," but maintained that the statutes and ordinances in question were deemed applicable only to "someone who has the right to speak and is denied the privilege of speaking. . . . [W]e do not understand that corporations resident in a foreign state may invoke the authority and jurisdiction of the courts of this State to strike down local laws and ordinances to aid them in carrying on their business in some other state." Apparently, no Memphis theater had contracted with the film's distributor to show the picture, and so, the court reasoned, no one's right to show the film had been violated.

1. United Artists Corporation v. Board of Censors of City of Memphis, 225 S.W. 2d 550 (1949).

[30]
The Miracle

Banned in New York, 1951.

Italy, 1948. U.S., 1950. Dist: Joseph Burstyn, Inc. 41 min. 35mm. Sound. B&W. English subtitles. Dir: Roberto Rossellini. SW: Roberto Rossellini, Tullio Pinelli. Music: Renzo Rossellini. Cin: Aldo Tonti. Cast: Anna Magnani, Federico Fellini. Reviews: *New York Herald Tribune*, Dec. 10, 1950; *New Yorker*, Dec. 16, 1950; *Variety*, Dec. 20, 1950.

This film, based on an original story by Federico Fellini, tells the tale of a simple peasant woman who, plied with wine and in a transport of religious emotion, permits a bearded stranger, whom she takes to be St. Joseph, to seduce her. She becomes pregnant and supposes she has conceived immaculately, miraculously. Her fellow villagers scorn and ridicule her, clamping a wash basin on her head for a halo. She waits alone for the birth of her child, which she delivers in an empty church.[1]

Censorship Activity

The Miracle was licensed in New York State by the motion picture division of the New York education department for showing without English subtitles on March 2, 1949. However, it was not exhibited until after a second license was issued on November 30, 1950 for the trilogy *The Ways of Love*, which combined *The Miracle* with two French films, *A Day in the Country* and *Jofroi*, and had English subtitles. After opening on December 12, 1950 at the Paris Theater in Manhattan, the film was promptly attacked by the Legion of Decency, a national Catholic organization, as a "sacrilegious and blasphemous mockery of Christian religious truth." New York City's commissioner of licenses ordered the film withdrawn under threat of suspending the license to operate the Paris Theater. One week later, the film was playing again after the New York Supreme Court had ruled that the city license commissioner was without any power of movie censorship.[2]

Next, Francis Cardinal Spellman condemned the picture and, within a few days, the New York State Board of Regents, which had authority over the New York education department, ordered the film's exhibitor to show cause why his license to show the film should not be rescinded on the ground that it was "sacrilegious." After a hearing on the matter, the regents determined that it was "sacrilegious" and for that reason ordered the commissioner of education to revoke the distributor's license to exhibit it in New York. Both the Appellate Division of the New York courts[3] and the New York Court of Appeals[4] upheld the regents' decision. On appeal to the U.S. Supreme Court, however, the decision to ban the movie was overturned.[5]

Legal Importance

The U.S. Supreme Court's decision in this case was of great moment, for it recognized for the first time that movies were "a significant medium for the communication of ideas," and were, therefore, protected by the constitutional guarantees of freedom of expression. Speaking for the court, Justice Tom C. Clark said that films "affect public attitudes and behavior in a variety of ways, ranging from direct espousal of a political or social doctrine to the subtle shaping of thought which characterizes all artistic expression. The importance of motion pictures as an organ of public opinion is not lessened by the fact that they are designed to entertain as well as to inform." Specifically, the Supreme Court held that the New York law that authorized the refusal of a license to any "sacrilegious" film was an unconstitutional "prior restraint" because it vested in a censor practically "unlimited restraining control over motion pictures."

New York courts had defined the term *sacrilegious* very broadly to mean that "no religion, as that word is understood by the ordinary reasonable person, shall be treated with contempt, mockery, scorn, and ridicule." This, the Supreme Court said, set the censor "adrift upon a boundless sea amid a myriad of conflicting currents of religious views, with no charts but those provided by the most vocal and powerful orthodoxies." In declaring the New York law and the banning of *The Miracle* unconstitutional, the Court overruled its own 1915 decision,[6] which had ruled that moving pictures were not a "part of the press of the country [nor] organs of opinion."

1. Originally distributed as part of a trilogy called *The Ways of Love* (*Amore/Amour*), which also included Jean Renoir's *A Day in the Country* and Marcel Pagnol's *Jofroi*. The complete trilogy was banned in New York, although only *The Miracle* was objectionable to censors.
2. Burstyn v. McCaffrey, 101 N.Y.S. 2d 892 (1951).
3. Burstyn v. Wilson, 104 N.Y.S. 2d 740 (1951).
4. Burstyn v. Wilson, 101 N.E. 2d 665 (1951).
5. Burstyn v. Wilson, 343 U.S. 495 (1952).
6. Mutual Film Corporation v. Industrial Commission of Ohio, 236 U.S. 230 (1915).

[31]
La Ronde

Banned in New York, 1951.

France, 1950. U.S., 1951. Dist: Goldwyn Inc. 90 min. 35mm. Sound. B&W. English subtitles. Prod: Sacha Gordine. Dir: Max Ophuls. SW: Jacques Natanson. Cin: Christian Matras. Cast: Anton Walbrook, Simone Signoret, Danielle Darieux, Odette Joyeus. Awards: First Prize in Venice Festival, 1950. British Academy Award, 1954. Reviews: *Today's Cinema*, London, April 24, 1951; *Newsweek* 38:100, Oct. 22, 1951; *Time* 58:114, Oct. 22, 1951; *Saturday Review* 34:27, Nov. 10, 1951.

La Ronde, or *The Round Dance*, was adapted from the play *Riegen* by Arthur Schnitzler. This ironic comedy, set in Vienna in the early 1900s, portrays the various amorous encounters of different couples who are all interconnected in some way. The roundabout is started when a soldier has a casual love affair with a prostitute and then falls in love with a parlor maid. The latter is more interested in her employer, who in turn is in love with a married woman. These affairs and infidelities are intricately interwoven and commented upon by the film's narrator. In the view of Judge Desmond of the Court of Appeals of New York, the film "depicts a series of illicit adventures, nothing more . . . its only discoverable theme is this: that everyone is sexually promiscuous, and that life is just a 'round' of sexual promiscuity." *Time* magazine, on the other hand, said: "*La Ronde* is all of a piece, as any round should be, setting up a mocking harmony of desire and disillusion, vanity, pleasure, and deceit. It is never prurient, smirking, or pornographic . . . it spoofs sex rather than exploits it."[1]

Censorship Activity

The New York state censorship board denied a license for the exhibition of this film on the ground that it was "immoral" and "would tend to corrupt morals." On review, the state supreme court's Appellate Division confirmed the determination.[2] The New York Court of Appeals, construing the term "immoral" in the statute to refer to "sexual immorality," affirmed the lower court.[3] The United States Supreme Court reversed.[4]

Legal Importance

In freeing this film, the U.S. Supreme Court simply cited its decision in *The Miracle* case [30], which held that motion pictures were entitled to constitutional protection from state censorship and could not be banned because censors considered them to be sacrilegious. Since the New York censors had banned the film because it was "immoral" or "sexually immoral," the U.S. Supreme Court's decision freeing the film is understood to be a holding that a state may not constitutionally censor films on the ground of such immorality. Justice William O. Douglas wrote a significant concurring opinion, in which he departed from reliance upon the ambiguous "clear and present danger" test as a means of guaranteeing freedom of expression and adopted an "absolute" standard for determining violations of the First and Fourteenth Amendment provisions protecting freedom of speech and press. According to Douglas, those provisions "say that Congress and the States shall make 'no law' which abridges freedom of speech or of the press. In order to sanction a system of censorship I would have to say that 'no law' does not mean what it says, that 'no law' is qualified to mean 'some' laws. I cannot take that step." "In this Nation," he concluded, "every writer, actor, or producer, no matter what the medium of expression he may use, should be freed from the censor." His position would grant motion pictures "absolute" freedom to communicate images and ideas.

1. *Time*, Oct. 22, 1951.
2. Commercial Pictures Corporation v. Regents, 114 N.Y.S. 2d 561, 280 App. Div. 260 (1952).
3. Commercial Pictures Corporation v. Regents, 113 N.Y. 2d 502, 305 N.Y. 336 (1953).
4. Commercial Pictures Corporation v. Regents, 346 U.S. 587 (1954).

[32]
Latuko

Banned in Newark, New Jersey, 1952.

U.S., 1952.[1] Dist: Producers Representatives, Inc. 56 min. 16mm. Sound. Color. Prod: Edgar Monsanto Queeny (under the auspices of The American Museum of Natural History). SW: Charles L. Tedford. Cin: Edgar M. Queeny, Fort B. Guerin. Narrator: Paul E. Prentiss. Reviews: *Variety*, Jan. 16, 1952; *Saturday Review of Literature*, Nov. 21, 1952.

This documentary film portrays the life, customs, and ceremonies of the Latuko tribe. It was filmed during a 1950 expedition into the province of

Equatoria in the Anglo-Egyptian Sudan by Edgar M. Queeny, board chairman of Monsanto Chemical Company. Much of the documentary concerns the readying of a Latuko youth for manhood, which includes the gouging out of two lower molars and the drawing and drinking of cow's blood.

Censorship Activity

The Newark, New Jersey, director of public safety confiscated this film, which had been produced for the American Museum of Natural History and was intended by it to be exhibited at a theater in the city. The museum and the theater owner brought suit for an injunction to prevent the public safety director from interfering with the film's showing and for the movie's return. The Superior Court Chancery Division granted the injunction and ordered that the film be returned.[2]

Legal Importance

After viewing the film in the courtroom, Judge Walter J. Freund "wholeheartedly agree[d]" with the museum's contention that "there is nothing suggestive, obscene, indecent, malicious or immoral in the showing of the Latuko aborigines in their normal living state." "While it is true," the court said, "that the men have been photographed naked and the women naked above the waist, the exposure of their bodies is not indecent; it is simply their normal way of living." It was the judge's opinion that "only a narrow or unhealthy mind could find any depravity in the film," and that the director had no authority to interfere with the presentation of "an absorbing and instructive documentation." The film apparently was not released until three years after its banning. The decision did not turn on any issue relating to the constitutional freedom of movies.

1. The film had an eight-week run in St. Louis in 1951.
2. American Museum of Natural History v. Keenan, 89 A. 2d 98 (1952).

[33]
M

Banned in Ohio, 1952.

U.S., 1951. Dist: Columbia Pictures Corp. 88 min. Sound. B&W. Prod: Seymour Nebenzal. Dir: Joseph Losey. SW: Norman Reilly Raine, Leo Katcher. Cin: Ernest Laszlo. Cast: David Wayne, Howard da Silva, Raymond Burr, Martin Gabel, Steve Brodie, Glenn Anders. Reviews: *Films in Review,* v. 11 No. 4 (April 1951), Thomas Foose; *New York Times*, June 11, 1951, Bosley Crowther.

This film is a remake of the 1932 German film by Fritz Lang and Thea von Harbon. It is the case history of a psychopathic killer who murders little

girls and then steals their shoes. In the face of an overwhelming public outcry, the police begin to round up the entire underworld, which, in order to
protect its own interests, also hunts for the killer. The dual chase for the
killer comes to a climax when the psychopath is finally trapped and must
plead his case before both the underworld and the police.

Censorship Activity

The Ohio censorship board denied a license for the exhibition of this film
because it believed its effect "on unstable persons of any age level could
lead to a serious increase in immorality and crime"; moreover, the censors
claimed that the film's "presentation of the actions and emotions of a child
killer" emphasized "complete perversion" and served no "valid educational purpose." Such a treatment "creates sympathy rather than a constructive plan for dealing with perversion." On appeal, the state supreme
court distinguished *The Miracle* case [30] and upheld the board's authority
to ban this film as one which was not of a "moral, educational, or amusing
or harmless character"—the law's criterion for licensing films. The court
admitted that these criteria "could doubtless have been made more
definite," but considered them "sufficiently" so.[1] However, the United
States Supreme Court reversed the Ohio court,[2] citing *The Miracle* case as
controlling.

Legal Importance

Like the U.S. Supreme Court's decision, without opinion, in the *La Ronde*
case [31], the high court's decision here was without opinion and signified
that states were forbidden by the constitutional protections of free speech
and press from censoring motion pictures on the basis of such vague and indefinite criteria as not having a "moral, educational, or amusing or
harmless character." As the Court said in *The Miracle* case, a state "cannot
vest such unlimited restraining control over motion pictures in a censor."

1. Superior Films v. Department of Education, 112 N.E. 2d 311, 159 Ohio St.
   315 (1953).
2. Superior Films v. Department of Education of State of Ohio, 346 U.S. 587
   (1954).

[34]
Miss Julie

Banned in Cambridge, Massachusetts, 1952.

Sweden, 1952. U.S., 1952. Dist: Trans-Global Pictures, Inc. 90 min. 35mm.
Sound. B&W. English subtitles. Prod: Sandrew Productions. Dir/SW: Alf

Sjoberg. Cin: Goran Strindberg. Cast: Anita Bjork, Ulf Palme, Marta Dorff, Anders Henrikson, Lissi Alandh, Inga Gill. Reviews: *Sight and Sound*, v. 21 No. 3 (Jan. 1952), Derick Geigs; *New York Times*, April 8, 1952, Bosley Crowther; *Saturday Review*, April 26, 1952; *Newsweek*, April 28, 1952; *Films in Review*, v. III No. 5 (May 1952), Halfdan Gregersen; *Commonweal*, May 2, 1952; *New Yorker*, Aug. 11, 1952.

Miss Julie, a screen adaptation of August Strindberg's stage play of the same title, is set in a Swedish country house in the late 1800s. Miss Julie is the only heir to the estate and lives a lonely, secluded life with her aging father and ambitious mother. The countess, Julie's mother, is an ardent feminist who "kept her daughter from dolls and other inclinations natural to a little girl and trained her to assume the role of a man."[1] While her parents are away, the 20-year-old Julie joins in the midsummer's eve party of the servants. She flirts with her father's valet, Jean. They have a long conversation and exchange life stories. "In fear of being caught together after their nightlong conversation, they flee to the valet's room and there he seduces her. To Jean the fall of his idol is as much a disappointment as a triumph, and Julie realizes that she has outlawed herself for the sake of a squalid creature who cares nothing for her."[2] Julie choses suicide as the only way out of her social disgrace. According to critic Bosley Crowther, the best things about this film are its "strong, imagistic qualities and a passionate performance of the principal role by Anita Bjork."[3]

Censorship Activity
The exhibitor of this film in Cambridge, Massachusetts, applied three times to the state commissioner of public safety and to the Cambridge city manager for permission to show the film in his theater in Cambridge on Sundays. This permission was required by state law. After both applications were denied, the exhibitor brought suit against the commissioner and the city manager in the Superior Court of Middlesex County to establish his constitutional right to show the film on Sundays. That court upheld the commissioner's objection and dismissed the suit. On appeal, the Supreme Judicial Court of Massachusetts unanimously reversed the lower court.[4]

Legal Importance
A statute proscribing the exhibition on Sundays of a film not "in keeping with the character" of the Lord's day is void on its face because it is "a prior restraint on the freedom of speech and press guaranteed by the First and Fourteenth Amendments." The statute provided that the only acceptable Sunday "public entertainment" was "a concert of sacred music, or a free open air concert . . . unless such public entertainment shall be in keeping with the character of the day and not inconsistent with its due observance and be duly licensed. . . ." The court considered its judgment that

this law was unconstitutional to be required by a series of U.S. Supreme Court decisions, beginning with *The Miracle* case [30], invalidating state laws that not only proscribed the exhibition of sacrilegious films, but also authorizing refusals to license prejudicial[5] and immoral[6] films. Similarly held to be invalid was a state law that authorized the licensing only of "moral, educational, or amusing and harmless" films.[7] Justice Raymond S. Wilkins gave the following instructive analogies: "It was unthinkable that there is a power, absent as to secular days, to require the submission to advance scrutiny by governmental authority of newspapers to be published on Sunday, of sermons to be preached on Sunday, or public addresses to be made on Sunday."

1. *Films in Review* (May 1952), p. 242.
2. *Sight and Sound* (Jan. 1952), p. 123.
3. *New York Times*, April 8, 1952.
4. Brattle Films v. Commissioner of Public Safety, 127 N.E. 2d 891 (1955).
5. Gelling v. Texas, 343 U.S. 960 (1952) (see the case of *Pinky* [35]).
6. Commercial Pictures Corporation v. Regents, 346 U.S. 587 (1954) (see the case of *La Ronde* [31]).
7. Superior Films, Inc. v. Department of Education, 346 U.S. 587 (1954) (see *M* [33] and *Native Son* [37]).

[35]
Pinky

Banned in Marshall, Texas, 1952.

U.S., 1949. Dist: Twentieth Century-Fox. 102 min. 35mm. Sound. B&W. Prod: Darryl F. Zanuck. Dir: Elia Kazan. SW: Philip Dunne, Dudley Nichols. Cin: Joe MacDonald. Cast: Jeanne Crain, Ethel Barrymore, Ethel Waters, William Lundigan, Basil Ruysdael, Nina Mae McKinney, Dan Riss. Reviews: *New York Times*, Sept. 30, 1949, Bosley Crowther; *Variety*, Oct. 5, 1949; *Time*, Oct. 10, 1949.

This film is based on the novel of the same title by Cid Ricketts Summer. Pinky is a light-skinned young black nurse who visits her grandmother's home in the South after 12 years away in Boston. Her grandmother tells Pinky that she must nurse the owner of the plantation, Miss Em, because years ago Miss Em had nursed the grandmother. Although Pinky would rather leave and marry her fiancé, a white Boston doctor, she complies with her grandmother's wishes and stays. While in the South, she is labeled a black and suffers from racist slurs and threats. Before dying, Miss Em changes her will so that she can leave the plantation to Pinky. Pinky comes to realize that she must not seek to escape her color by fleeing to Boston and marrying, but instead stay and open a nursing home for the blacks who live on the estate.

Censorship Activity

The censors of Marshall, Texas, refused to grant this film's exhibitor a license to show it, pursuant to a local ordinance authorizing them to deny a license to any movie that was "of such character as to be prejudicial to the best interests of the people of said City." The exhibitor showed the film anyway, and was convicted of violating the ordinance after a jury trial in the county court of Harrison County. Upon appeal to the Court of Criminal Appeals of Texas, his conviction was affirmed.[1] The United States Supreme Court reversed the Court of Criminal Appeals,[2] citing *The Miracle* case [30] and *Winters* v. *New York*.[3]

Legal Importance

The Texas decision was handed down five months before the U.S. Supreme Court's decision in *The Miracle* case [30], which acknowledged for the first time that motion pictures were entitled to constitutional protection from suppression. That decision overruled a 1915 decision by the Supreme Court holding that films were merely "amusement" and thus not subject to guarantees of freedom of speech. The Texas courts here had refused to accept the exhibitor's argument that "the motion picture industry had emerged from the business of amusement and become propagators of ideas entitling it to freedom of speech." It declined to acknowledge the signs that the U.S. Supreme Court's own view of film censorship had changed, saying, "We cherish the history of a federal government which has been based on a constitution as solid as the rocks and whose constancy is not shifted by the changing winds." In reversing the Texas court, the U.S. Supreme Court also cited *Winters* v. *New York*, a case that criminalized the behavior of any person who disseminated any printed matter "principally made up of criminal news, police reports, of accounts of criminal deeds, or pictures or stories of bloodshed, lust or crime . . . ," finding it void on vagueness and due process grounds. Its defectiveness lay in its propensity to "include acts fairly within the protection of a free press." The Texas law's ban on prejudicial films was equally defective because "too uncertain and indefinite," thus the statute itself, and not merely its condemnation of *Pinky*, was unconstitutional. Justice Douglas concurred, writing that the "evil of prior restraint . . . is present here in flagrant form. If a board of censors can tell the American people what it is in their best interests to see or to read or to hear, then thought is regimented, authority substituted for liberty, and the great purpose of the First Amendment to keep uncontrolled the freedom of expression defeated."

1. Gelling v. State, 247 S.W. 2d 95, 156 Tex. Cr. R. 516 (1952).
2. Gelling v. Texas, 343 U.S. 960 (1952).
3. Winters v. New York, 333 U.S. 507 (1948).

[36]
The Moon Is Blue

Banned in Kansas, 1953; also banned in Maryland, Ohio, Jersey City, New Jersey, Milwaukee, Wisconsin.

U.S., 1953. Dist: United Artists. 99 min. 35mm. Sound. B&W. Prod/Dir: Otto Preminger. SW: F. Hugh Herbert. Cin: Ernest Laszlo. Cast: William Holden, David Niven, Maggie McNamara, Tom Tully, Dawn Addams, Fortunio Bonanova. Reviews: *New York Times*, July 9, 1953, Bosley Crowther; *New York Herald Tribune*, July 9, 1953, Otis L. Guernsey, Jr.; *New Yorker*, July 18, 1953.

This film is adapted from F. Hugh Herberts' play of the same title. The film version begins with a chance meeting between boy (William Holden) and girl (Maggie McNamara) in the Empire State Building. He invites her to his apartment for dinner, but she does not know that the boy is engaged to another girl who lives with her family on the floor above. The boy's father-in-law-to-be learns of this dinner date and "comes down to do the outraged parent act but . . . stays on and makes his own pass at the girl in the most unfatherly fashion and with the easy confidence of a veteran in polite amour."[1] The young woman is startlingly frank and curious concerning sexual matters, despite her obvious innocence.

Censorship Activity
The Kansas censorship board prohibited the exhibition of this film in the state on the following grounds: "Sex theme throughout, too frank bedroom dialogue: many sexy words; both dialgue and action have sex as their theme." The distributor brought suit in Wyandotte County District Court. The court found the statute creating the board "repugnant" to the First and Fourteenth amendments because "motion pictures are protected by the First and Fourteenth Amendments to the Constitution of the United States." Moreover, the censors had given the words of the statute that authorized them to ban films, which were "cruel, obscene, indecent, or immoral, or such as tend to debase or corrupt morals," a meaning "so broad and vague as to be unconstitutional." However, the Supreme Court of Kansas reversed the lower court and upheld the constitutionality of the board's authority to pass on the fitness of the films submitted to it for licensing.[2] The United States Supreme Court reversed the Supreme Court of Kansas.[3]

Legal Importance

The U.S. Supreme Court's *per curiam* opinion reversed the Kansas supreme court's decision on the basis of *The Miracle* case [30], the *M* case [33], and the *La Ronde* case [31]. It held that the terminology "cruel, obscene, indecent, or immoral, or such as tend to debase or corrupt morals" is too vague and indefinite to support a motion picture licensing statute. The Court also held that a state may not consistently with constitutional guarantees ban a film on the basis of a censor's conclusion that it had a character that came within the scope of those words.

1. *New York Herald Tribune*, July 9, 1953, Otis L. Guernsey, Jr.
2. Holmby Productions v. Vaughn, 282 P. 2d 412, 177 Kan. 728 (1955).
3. Holmby Productions v. Vaughn, 350 U.S. 870 (1955).

[37]
Native Son

Banned in Ohio, 1953.

U.S., 1951. Dist: Classic Pictures, Inc., Walter Gould. 91 min. 35mm. Sound. B&W. Prod: James Prader. Dir: Pierre Chenal. SW: Pierre Chenal, Richard Wright. Dialogue: Richard Wright. Cin: A. V. Meray. Cast: Richard Wright, Jean Wallace, Nicholas Joy, Gloria Madison, Charles Cane, Jean Michael, George Rigaud, George Green, Willie Pearl Curtiss, Don Dean, Ruth Roberts, Ned Campbell, Charles Simmonds, Leslie Staughn, Lidia Alvs, George Nathanson, George Roos, Lewis Mackenzie, Cecile Lezard. Reviews: *New York Times*, June 18, 1951, A. H. Weiler and June 24, 1951, Bosley Crowther; *Motion Picture Herald*, June 23, 1951; *Commonweal*, June 29, 1951; *Library Journal*, July 1951; *New Republic*, July 2, 1951; *Saturday Review*, July 7, 1951; *Newsweek*, July 9, 1951.

This film was adapted from the novel by Richard Wright, who plays the protagonist in this film. A young black from Chicago's South Side slums, Bigger Thomas, is working as a chauffeur for a rich white family. One night he brings the drunken daughter back to her room, only to kill her accidentally out of fear that he may be discovered there by her blind mother. Trapped by racism and the ghetto he must live in, Bigger Thomas hopelessly struggles against a society that will not let him escape his fate.[1]

Censorship Activity[2]

The distributor of this film petitioned a court for an order compelling the Ohio motion picture censorship board to issue a license for its exhibition in the state. The board had refused on three previous occasions to license the film, although cuts and deletions had been made to eliminate objectionable elements. The board said the film "contributes to racial misunderstanding, presenting situations undesirable to the mutual interests of both races . . . undermining confidence that justice can be carried out [and presenting] racial frictions at a time when all groups should be united against everything that is subversive." The trial court denied the distributor's petition; on appeal, this denial was affirmed by the Supreme Court of Ohio.[3] The U.S. Supreme Court, however, reversed the Ohio courts.[4]

Legal Importance

The Supreme Court of Ohio took the position that although movies were entitled to constitutional freedom of expression and, in view of the recently decided *The Miracle* case [30], could not be denied a license for exhibition on the ground of being sacrilegious, censors still had discretion to refuse licenses to films they believed to contribute to immorality or crime. Similarly, the Ohio court did not believe the U.S. Supreme Court decision in the case of *Pinky* [35]—which had invalidated a Marshall, Texas motion picture ordinance that permitted censors to refuse licenses to movies believed to be "prejudicial to the best interests of the people"—necessarily meant that Ohio's censorship law was unconstitutional. The Ohio court erroneously opined that, despite the latest expressions of the United States Supreme Court on the subject of motion picture freedom, "there remains a limited field in which decency and morals may be protected from the impact of an offending motion picture film by prior restraint under proper criteria." The U.S. Supreme Court's subsequent reversal of the Supreme Court of Ohio's decision in this case meant that Ohio's motion picture censorship law was unconstitutionally vague and indefinite, and contrary to requirements of First Amendment due process, insofar as it authorized the censorship of films believed to be harmful or conducive to immorality or crime, the grounds upon which *Native Son* had been denied a license.

1. The film "was shot in Argentina and Chicago," according to *Motion Picture Herald*, June 23, 1951.
2. The case involving this film was considered together with the case of *M* [33].
3. Superior Films v. Department of Education, Classic Pictures v. Department of Education, 112 N.E. 2d 311 (1953).
4. Superior Films, Inc. v. Department of Education of Ohio, 346 U.S. 587 (1954).

[38]
Baby Doll

Banned in Aurora, Illinois, 1956.

U.S., 1956. Dist: Warner Bros. Pictures. 114 min. 35mm. Sound. B&W.
Prod/Dir: Elia Kazan (Newtown Productions). SW: Tennessee Williams. Cin:
Boris Kaufman. Music: Kenyon Hopkins. Cast: Karl Malden, Carroll Baker,
Eli Wallach, Mildred Dunnock. Reviews: *Saturday Review*, Dec. 1956; *New
York Herald Tribune*, Dec. 19, 1956, William K. Zinsser; *New York Times*,
Dec. 19, 1956, Bosley Crowther; *Time*, Dec. 24, 1956; *New Yorker*, Dec. 29,
1956; *Holiday*, Feb. 1957, Harry Kurnitz. Articles: *Look*, Dec. 25, 1956; *Life*,
Jan. 7, 1957; *New York Times*, May 25, 1957.

At the suggestion of Elia Kazan, the screenplay was derived by Tennessee
Williams from two of Williams's one-act plays, *27 Wagons Full of Cotton*
and *An Unsatisfying Supper*. Baby Doll is a pretty, vacuous Southern
"white trash" girl who at 19 still sleeps in a crib and sucks her thumb. She
has been married for two years to ineffectual, bigoted Archie Lee. The
couple have not yet consummated their marriage because Archie promised
Baby Doll's dying father that he would not touch his daughter until she said
she was "ready." He is frustrated by this strain and obliged to peek at his
squirmy half-dressed child-bride through a hole in her bedroom wall.
Archie is further humiliated and incensed by a flashy Sicilian business rival
who has recently managed to force Archie's decrepit cotton gin out of
business. In desperation and frustration, Archie burns down his rival's cotton gin one night. The rest of the story describes the Sicilian's revenge as he
blatantly pursues and seduces a distraught but sensually aroused Baby Doll,
and terrorizes her into revealing Archie's crime. Castigated by Francis Cardinal Spellman from the pulpit of St. Patrick's Cathedral as a "contemptuous defiance of the natural law," *Baby Doll* was praised and vilified by
critics and clergymen and widely boycotted by Catholic filmgoers. The film
received the Motion Picture Association of America's seal of approval but a
C (for Condemned) rating from the Legion of Decency.

Censorship Activity

Citizens at a mass meeting at the Aurora, Illinois, City Hall protested the
exhibition of this film and requested city officials to stop its showing. The
Circuit Court of Kane County granted the city's request for a temporary injunction preventing its exhibition in Aurora. The city claimed that one of
the scenes in this movie was "scandalous, indecent, immoral, lewd, and
obscene, [displayed a] young wife . . . lying on the floor or ground and her
lover places his foot on her stomach, moving it about in circular motions

and wife displays an arousal of her sexual passion." The Mayor stated in his court affidavit that this picture "is an open and flagrant violation of public morals and decency. . . . The miserable portrayal of infidelity of an under-aged wife is most dangerous and revolting. It is harmful to . . . teenage boys and girls who might slip into the show . . . and glorifies seduction and a breakdown of a family home and married life." In newspaper clippings filed with the court, Cardinal Spellman exhorted Roman Catholics not to view the film "under pain of sin," while the Rev. James Pike advised persons seeking sex to see *The Ten Commandments* instead of *Baby Doll*. On appeal, the Appellate Court of Illinois affirmed the lower court's decision.[1]

Legal Importance

According to the court, Aurora had demonstrated that the film was obscene and was correct in maintaining that an injunction to prevent its exhibition did not violate anyone's constitutional rights to freedom of expression or against prior restraint. Said the appellate court: "We are unable to detect any artistic or other merit for the normal, average person in a public demonstration of an arousal of sexual passion by means of a foot, or to conceive how this sort of expression comes within the traditional concepts of freedom of speech or of the press." Since the city had "made out a prima facie showing" that the movie was obscene, a court of equity had the power to enjoin criminal or immoral acts from being committed, although the offenders otherwise were subject to criminal prosecution—in order "to protect citizens from public wrongs and to protect the public health and welfare." Despite the court's contrary reasoning and holding, the exhibition of *Baby Doll* was entitled to constitutional protection because the film was not obscene in the constitutional sense, as the U.S. Supreme Court later made clear in *The Lovers* case [49]. This would not be made clear, however, to state and lower federal courts until the U.S. Supreme Court decision in *The Lovers* case, six years later.

1. City of Aurora v. Warner Bros. Pictures Distributing Corporation, 147 N.E. 2d 694 (1958).

- [39]
The Game of Love (Le Blé en Herbe)

Banned in Chicago, Illinois, 1956.[1]

France, 1954. U.S., 1954. Dist: Caumont (Paris); William Shelton Films, Times Film Corp. (U.S.). 108 min. 35mm. Sound. B&W. English subtitles. Prod: Franco-London Film. Dir: Claude Autant-Lara. SW: Jean Aurenche, Pierre Bost, Claude Autant-Lara. Cin: Robert LeFévre. Cast: Nicole Berger,

Pierre Michel Beck, Edwidge Feuillère, Charles Deschamps, Renée Devillers. Awards: 1954 Grand Prix du Cinéma Français. Reviews: *Variety*, March 24, 1954, Mosk.; *Hollywood Reporter*, Aug. 25, 1955, Bob Webber; *New York Post*, Dec. 15, 1954, Archer Winston. Articles: *New York World-Telegram & Sun*, Dec. 11, 1954; *Variety*, Feb. 2, March 23, 1955; *Motion Picture Herald*, Nov. 16, 1957; *Variety*, Nov. 20, 1957.

This film was adapted from *Le Blé en Herbe*, a novel written in 1933 by Colette. Raised together, practically as brother and sister because of the close ties of their families, Phillippe, a boy of 16, and Vinca, an even younger girl, spend the summer together with their families in Brittany. They endure and explore their first troubled pangs of sex and love. Phillippe encounters and becomes infatuated with a beautiful, lonely older woman, living in a nearby mansion, learns from her the ways of love, and is sent back to Vinca. "[A] tender and touching tale of the awakening of adolescence, with its infatuations, to a maturer, understanding love. . . ."[2]

Censorship Activity

The Chicago police commissioner refused to issue a permit for the exhibition of this film on the ground that it was "not acceptable to standards of decency, with immorality featured and dialogue unfit." The mayor denied an appeal on the same ground. At the request of the distributor, the United States District Court for the Northern District of Illinois appointed a master (fact finder). He ruled that the film's "calculated purpose [was] not substantially to arouse the sexual desires," that the state's interest "in preventing the probability of the arousal of sexual desires in normal persons is not a sufficiently overriding consideration to justify an ordinance authorizing prior restraint on freedom of expression," and that the Chicago censorship statute was unconstitutional because of vagueness and a lack of standards. The District Court, on review, however, decided that "the local censorship authorities were warranted in finding it obscene. . . ." The "dominant tone" of the film is "sexuality," and its "major part . . . dwells on [Phillippe's] illicit relationship with an adventurous adult woman, and later with Vinca. The film appears to casually write off this unconventional behavior as a mere interlude in the maturing process of the young hero. The Court is unable to detect any purpose other than an emphasis upon its sexuality." The court also decided that "the State's police power in the area of health and morals, which has always had constitutional protection, [would] be seriously invaded and reduced by the film industry." The court concluded that the movie was obscene, that the Chicago authorities properly exercised the police power, and that the censorship statute was constitutional.[3] On appeal, the United States Court of Appeals for the Seventh Circuit affirmed the lower court decree.[4] The United States Supreme Court, however, reversed the judgment of the Court of Appeals.[5]

Legal Importance

The Seventh Circuit Court held that the public exhibition of an obscene moving picture could be banned by proceedings under a properly drawn statute or ordinance, and that the rights of free expression enjoyed by the exhibitor of such a picture under the First and Fourteenth Amendments were not thereby violated. The ordinance was considered not vague; the words "obscene" and "immoral" were said to be "precise" and to "constitute a proper test." After viewing the film, the court found that "from beginning to end, the thread of the story is supercharged with a current of lewdness generated by a series of illicit sexual intimacies and acts. . . . We do not hesitate to say that the calculated purpose of the producer of this film, and its dominant effect, are substantially to arouse sexual desires. We are of the opinion that the probability of this effect is so great as to outweigh whatever artistic or other merits the film may possess. We think these determinations are supported by the effect which this film would have upon the normal, average person."

Without issuing any written opinion explaining its decision, the U.S. Supreme Court reversed the ban, citing the case of *Alberts* v. *California*,[6] the companion state case to the landmark federal case *Roth* v. *United States*,[7] in which the Supreme Court squarely held that "obscenity is not within the area of constitutionally protected speech or press," but also said that "all ideas having even the slightest redeeming social importance—unorthodox ideas, controversial ideas, even ideas hateful to the prevailing climate of opinion—have the full protection of the [constitutional] guarantees. . . ." The absence of any other explanation of the grounds or reasoning behind the decision caused lawyers to speculate on its meaning. (See *Variety*, Nov. 20, 1957.) What is clear, in retrospect, is that the Supreme Court was prepared to exercise its own independent judgment concerning the obscenity of a film, to overrule lower findings of obscenity and to grant constitutional freedom to a particular film. It was not prepared, however, to rule all motion picture pre-release censorship schemes unconstitutional prior restraints. (See the *Don Juan* case [48].) The case is important because it marked the first time that the Supreme Court itself decided that a particular artistic work, here a film, was not obscene but was entitled to constitutional protection from suppression. The Court did so again in *The Lovers* case [49] some seven years later, when it also did the same for a novel (for the first time), in freeing Henry Miller's *Tropic of Cancer* from Florida censorship.[8]

1. The film was also banned by the Maryland board of censors in 1955, but that ban was overturned by a Baltimore city court in an unreported decision. (See *Variety*, March 3, 1955.)
2. *Hollywood Reporter*, Aug. 25, 1955.

3. Times Film Corporation v. City of Chicago, 139 F. Supp. 837 (1956).
4. Times Film Corporation v. City of Chicago, 244 F. 2d 432 (7th Cir. 1957).
5. Times Film Corporation v. City of Chicago, 355 U.S. 35 (1957).
6. Alberts v. California, 354 U.S. 476 (1957).
7. Roth v. United States, 354 U.S. 476 (1957).
8. Grove Press v. Gerstein, 378 U.S. 577 (1964).

[40]
The Garden of Eden

Banned in New York, 1956.

U.S., 1957. Dist: Excelsior Pictures. 70 min. 35mm. Sound. Color. Prod: Walter Bibo. Dir: Max Nosseck. SW: Nat Tanchuck. Cin: Boris Kaufman. Music: Robert McBride. Cast: Mickey Knox, Jamie O'Hara, Karen Sue Trent, R. G. Armstrong. Reviews: *Variety*, Sept. 1, 1954; *Film Daily*, Dec. 18, 1957; *New York Post*, Dec. 18, 1957; *New York Times*, Dec. 18, 1957. Articles: *Variety*, Oct. 5, Nov. 16, 1955, Jan. 25, 1956; *Film Daily*, Feb. 29, 1956, *Variety*, Feb. 11, 1959; *Motion Picture Daily*, Nov. 5, 1959.

A young widow leaves the home of her father-in-law, a gruff business tycoon. When her car stalls she is rescued by inhabitants of a nearby nudist camp. Her horror subsides as she beholds the wholesome way of life of the nudists. When her father-in-law arrives, he undergoes the same transformation, and all are happier for their discovery.

Censorship Activity[1]

The New York censorship board refused to issue a license for the exhibition of this film because it was "indecent," unless scenes depicting activities of members of a nudist group in a secluded private camp were deleted. On review, the state supreme court transferred the case to the Appellate Division, which, on the basis of the *Mom and Dad* case [28], annulled the board's determination and ordered that the film be licensed.[2] The New York Court of Appeals affirmed the lower court's order.[3]

Legal Importance

This picture "cannot lawfully be banned since it is not obscene in the sense in which the law has used that term for centuries," wrote Judge Charles S. Desmond after the court viewed the film. "Nothing sexually impure is shown or suggested . . . and so there is no legal basis for censorship." Judge Desmond read the U.S. Supreme Court's opinion in *The Miracle* case [30] as "a holding that obscenity is under the First and Fourteenth Amendments the only lawful ground for denying a license. The state may take action to keep children away from movies but, unless the picture be really obscene in the traditional, historic sense of that term, license to exhibit it to adults may not be withheld." It is settled, the court observed, "that 'indecent,' standing alone and read literally, is much too broad and vague a term to make a valid censorship standard." The state's penal law, which made it a crime for any person to "willfully expose . . . his private parts in the presence of two or more persons of the opposite sex whose private parts are similarly exposed," could not be read so as to prohibit the licensing of any film showing a group of nude people of both sexes. "To say that representation of criminal activity is criminal is to abolish the drama and the novel in one stroke. . . . The showing of crimes in book, play or cinema is evil," the court concluded, "only when it is done in a dirty way or when it glorifies the criminal act. So to characterize *The Garden of Eden* is impossible."

1. This film was also involved in the following cases: Commonwealth v. Moniz, 143 N.E. 2d 196 (1957), 155 N.E. 2d 762 (1959) (Supreme Judicial Court of Massachusetts overturned lower court ban); Dickinson Operating Co. v. City of Kansas City, 317 S.W. 2d 638 (1958) (Kansas City, Missouri Court of Appeals held that it did not have jurisdiction to enforce ordinance forbidding exhibition of obscene, lewd, and indecent films); Excelsior Pictures Corp. v. City of Chicago, 182 F. Supp. 400 (1960) (the Federal District Court for the Northern District of Illinois reversed Chicago censorship board refusal to grant license for film's showing, which, at the court's suggestion, was limited to adults only).
2. Excelsior Pictures Corp. v. Regents of the University of the State of New York, 156 N.Y.S. 2d 800, 2 A.D. 2d 941 (1956).
3. Excelsior Pictures Corp. v. Regents of the University of the State of New York, 144 N.E. 2d 31, 165 N.Y.S. 2d 42, 3 N.Y. 2d 37 (1957).

[41]
The Man with the Golden Arm

Banned in Maryland, 1956.

U.S., 1955. Dist: United Artists. 119 min. 35mm. B&W. Sound. Prod/Dir: Otto Preminger. SW: Walter Newman, Lewis Meltzer. Cin: Sam Leavitt. Cast: Frank Sinatra, Eleanor Parker, Kim Novak, Arnold Stang, Darren McGavin. Reviews: *New York Times*, Dec. 16, 1955, Bosley Crowther; *New York Herald Tribune*, Dec. 1955, William K. Zinsser; *New Yorker*, Dec. 24, 1955; *Life*, Dec. 19, 1955; *Catholic World*, Feb. 1956.

This film was adapted from Nelson Algren's novel of the same title. It describes the plight of Frankie Machine, a professional card dealer in the slums of Chicago. Frankie, a man with a golden arm who can instinctively control a card game, returns to Chicago after drying out in a federal narcotics hospital. His attempt at a fresh start is foiled by a gambler who makes him deal cards again and by a dope peddler who coaxes him back onto narcotics. He finally succeeds in kicking his habit when his would-be girl friend locks him in her room to dry out. He then discovers that he is wanted for a murder he did not commit, and that his crippled wife has been maintaining her invalidism to keep him from leaving her. After his wife accidentally reveals to him her power to walk, she flees from Frankie and commits suicide. Frankie is exonerated from all criminal charges and begins a new life with the girl who helped him kick his habit.

Censorship Activity

The Maryland State Board of Censors required the elimination of a scene from this film as a condition for its exhibition in the state, on the ground that it "advocates or teaches the use of, or the methods of use of, narcotics or habit-forming drugs." The censors relied on the fact that the film had not received the seal of approval of the Motion Picture Association of America, whose Production Code disapproved of films that "portray addiction to narcotics." The film's distributor resigned from the MPAA because of that disapproval, and appealed to the courts to reverse the censors' ruling. The Baltimore City Court affirmed the censorship but the Court of Appeals of Maryland reversed, holding that although the statute authorized the censorship of a film that "advocated" the use of narcotics, it did not authorize the censorship of a film that only "discussed" such use. The appellate court viewed the objectionable scene as a "discussion," not an "advocacy," of narcotics use or addiction. It showed Frankie "rolling up his sleeve, and tying a necktie around the upper arm, while a dope 'pusher' prepares the drug for injection. While the particular kind of narcotic is not named, the picture shows the powdered narcotic, the liquid solution, the spoon, and the hypodermic needle. The 'pusher' takes the filled needle and advances toward Frankie. The actual injection is not shown, but the viewer sees the needle being removed from the arm. Just before the needle is pulled out, Frankie indicates by a facial twitch that he felt a slight pain from the injection. Complete relaxation follows."[1]

Legal Importance

The case has importance because of the pivotal distinction drawn by the court between constitutionally protected discussion and constitutionally unprotected advocacy of such ideas as the use of narcotics. The film was viewed as "discussing," not "advocating," such use. In ruling that the uncut film did not violate the provisions of the state motion picture censorship statute, the Court of Appeals avoided the need to decide whether the statute unconstitutionally abridged freedom of speech and press—as the distributor claimed—in authorizing the censorship of a film that "teaches" about drug addiction. The court considered its action analogous to that of the U.S. Supreme Court in the landmark case of *Dennis* v. *United States*,[2] where the high court interpreted the Smith Act to prohibit "advocacy [and] not discussion [of] the desirability or propriety of overthrowing any government of the United States by force or violence," despite the fact that the Act used the terminology "advocate or teach." A statute that purports to ban the teaching or discussion of any idea or practice, however controversial, probably violates constitutional freedom of expression. In this case, the Court of Appeals considered the evidence "strong and convincing" that the film did not advocate the use of narcotics, but was likely, instead, to have "a beneficial effect as a deterrent from the use of narcotics." The court gave weight to the favorable opinions about the film expressed by knowledgeable experts, government officials, and educators. As the health education coordinator in New York City said: "The picture presented an accurate portrayal of the many problems facing the drug addict and the responsibility of society." It had been shown without deletions in every state other than Maryland and, in Holland, had received a scientific and cultural award that resulted in the remission of admission taxes to patrons who viewed it. A similar result was reached by the Supreme Court of the United States in the *Lady Chatterley's Lover* case [43].

1. United Artists Corporation v. Maryland Board of Censors, 124 A. 2d 292 (1956).
2. 341 U.S. 494 (1951).

[42]
Wild Weed (Devil's Weed; She Should'a Said No!)

Banned in Pennsylvania, 1956.

U.S., 1949. Dist: Eureka Productions, Franklin Productions, Inc., Hallmark Productions.[1] 90 min. 35mm. Sound. B&W. Prod: Richard Kay. Dir: Sherman Scott. SW: Richard H. Landau. Cin: Jack Greenhalgh. Cast: Lila Leeds, Alan Baxter, Lyle Talbot. Reviews: *Variety*, Aug. 24, 1949, Wear; *Los Angeles-Examiner*, Sept. 2, 1949, Shirle Duggan; *Newsweek*, Sept. 5, 1949; *New York Times*, Jan. 31, 1957. Articles: *Los Angeles Times*, Sept. 2, 1949.

This film was adapted from a story by Arthur Hoerl. Working as a chorus girl to put her brother through college, a young woman is led by an attractive man at a party to take her first puff of marijuana. She gets involved with a dope dealer and becomes a marijuana "addict." Finally, however, she cooperates with narcotics agents to break up the drug ring. In the words of the Pennsylvania State Board of Censors: "The evils of drug traffic and addiction shown as the theme . . . in detailed dialogue and action show the use of the 'weed' leading to use of 'heroin, cocaine, opium,' excites curiosity toward escape from reality to teenagers, frustrated men and women and weak characters, and actually leads to lives of sin, corruption, horror and murder and is indecent and immoral and . . . tends to debase and corrupt morals." A federal narcotics agent testified that to give "widespread publicity and to disseminate information such as is contained in [this] moving picture" would be "dangerous" to the Commonwealth of Pennsylvania.

Censorship Activity

The Pennsylvania censorship board twice refused to issue a license for this film under the titles *Wild Weed* and *Devil's Weed* on grounds that it was "indecent and immoral and . . . tended to debase and corrupt morals." When the distributor changed the title to *She Should'a Said No!* and re-applied for a license, the board refused to issue one, giving "22 reasons why it regarded the film unfit for projection in Pennsylvania." The distributor finally appealed the censors' decision to the Court of Common Pleas of Philadelphia. On the basis of *The Miracle* case [30], the Court of Common Pleas reversed the board's order, declaring the Pennsylvania Motion Picture Censorship Act unconstitutional. The Supreme Court of Pennsylvania affirmed.[2]

Legal Importance

The case is important in signalling the end of the motion picture licensing system of Pennsylvania. The Pennsylvania censorship statute required the censorship board to disapprove of any film that was "sacrilegious, obscene, indecent, or immoral, or such as tend, in the judgment of the board, to debase or corrupt morals." This law was viewed by the Pennsylvania Supreme Court as "subject to the same fatal objections" as were the state laws that the U.S. Supreme Court had recently invalidated in the cases of *The Miracle, Pinky* [35], *M* [33], *La Ronde* [31], and *The Moon Is Blue* [36]. In ruling that the state Motion Picture Censorship Act was unconstitutional, Chief Justice Horace Stern thought it unnecessary to consider whether the statute's constitutionality "might be affected by amendments that would make its terminology more definite and specific [assuming that greater definiteness is possible in the case of such abstract terms], or whether, however amended and 'clearly drawn,' any statute censoring motion pictures must be held to be unconstitutional on the theory that motion pictures are as much entitled to the protection of the constitutional guarantee of free speech as is now enjoyed by newspapers, magazines, books, theatrical exhibitions, radio and television scripts." The court observed, however, that "even if all precensorship of motion picture films were to be held invalid this would not in and of itself affect the right to suppress objectionable films, *if exhibited* [italics supplied], or to punish their exhibitor."

In a concurring opinion, Justice John L. Bell, Jr., admitted he would have preferred to sustain the validity of the censorship statute "which has protected the interests of the highly moral and deeply religious people of Pennsylvania for over 40 years." However, he was constrained to vote with the court majority in view of the recent rulings by the U.S. Supreme Court, beginning with *The Miracle* case [30], the thrust of which were "to invalidate motion picture censorship by state tribunals."

Justice Michael A. Musmanno dissented, in terms that Chief Justice Warren E. Burger would later echo in the *Magic Mirror* case [102], writing that the "Majority Opinion is an interesting legal travelogue but it does not decide the issue in this case." The "stark question" that the case presented for him was "very simple": "Was the [censorship board], under the law, justified in declining to inflict on the people of this State [this] monstrosity of a motion picture. . . ?" His elaborate and strongly worded answer was "No."

Judge Musmanno was not satisfied that the subsequent suppression of a film like *Wild Weed,* or the subsequent punishment of its exhibitor, would satisfy the need for "mental purity" of the "good citizen" of Pennsylvania. "How," he inquired, "will the punishment of the exhibitor heal the lacerating wounds made in the delicate sensations of children and sensitive adults who witness a picture of lewdness, depravity, and immorality?" Motion picture theaters may "accommodate as many as 4000 patrons for one show." Even "[i]f a picture should last but one day, many thousands would nevertheless have seen it by the time it is withdrawn from circulation. That is why reason dictates that control over immoral films must be found in prevention and not in subsequent punishment." The good citizen must be "grateful," the judge opined, "that the government which protects him from contact with physical contagion will also have save him from association with moral trash and garbage." "The streets of a city cannot be used for immoral purposes. Why should the avenues of the mind and the soul be polluted with the parading of indecencies and obscenities which can and do sometimes appear in films?"

1. Presented by Hallmark Productions in 1957 (*New York Times*, January 31, 1957, R.W.N., 21:1).
2. Hallmark Productions v. Pennsylvania Board of Censors, 121 A. 2d 584 (1956).

[43]
Lady Chatterley's Lover (L'Amant de Lady Chatterley)

Banned in New York, 1957.

France, 1957. U.S., 1959. Dist: Kingsley International. 102 min. 35mm. Sound. B&W. Prod: Gilbert Cohn-Seat. Dir/SW: Marc Allegret. Cast: Danielle Darrieux, Erno Crisa, Leo Glenn, Berthe Tissen, Janine Crispin. Reviews: *New York Herald Tribune*, July 11, 1959, Paul V. Beckley; *New York Times*, July 11, 1959, Bosley Crowther; *Films and Filming*, v. 2 No. 12 (Sept. 1959); *Films in Review*, v. X No. 7, Aug.–Sept. 1959; *Filmfacts*, v. 11, 1959.

The film *Lady Chatterley's Lover* was adapted from the play of the same title by Gaston Bonheur and Philippe de Rothschild, which in turn was based on the famous and much-censored novel by D. H. Lawrence. It is the story of a young English woman who marries an impotent, crippled, upper class nobleman. With his tacit approval she has a few affairs in hopes of producing an heir. When Lady Chatterley falls in love with their game-keeper, who sexually awakens her, her husband is outraged by the mockery this makes of his social standing. He refuses to give her a divorce, which in turn forces her to leave him and live with the gamekeeper.

Censorship Activity

The New York censorship board found three isolated scenes in this film "immoral within the intent of our law,"[1] and refused to issue a license for its exhibition. On administrative appeal, the state board of regents upheld the finding on the ground that the film's "whole theme . . . is the presentation of adultery as a desirable, acceptable and proper pattern of behavior." When the Appellate Division of the state supreme court considered the case, it annulled the action of the regents and directed that a license be issued.[2] The New York Court of Appeals reversed the Appellate Division and upheld the regents' refusal to license the film for exhibition.[3] However, the U.S. Supreme Court unanimously reversed the Court of Appeals.[4]

Legal Importance

This is a landmark case, significant for its holding that a state law that authorized the censorship of immoral *ideas* through films violates the constitutional guarantee of free expression. Speaking for the Supreme Court, Justice Potter Stewart said: "What New York has done . . . is to prevent the exhibition of a motion picture because that picture advocates an idea— that adultery under certain circumstances may be proper behavior. Yet the First Amendment's basic guarantee is of freedom to advocate ideas. The State, quite simply, has thus struck at the very heart of constitutionally protected liberty. . . . [The constitutional] guarantee is not confined to the expression of ideas that are conventional or shared by a minority. It protects advocacy of the opinion that adultery may sometimes be proper, no less than advocacy of socialism or the single tax. And in the realm of ideas it protects expression which is eloquent no less than that which is unconvincing." The wealth of concurring opinions in this case reflects the diversity of views held by the individual justices concerning the censorship of films. Justice Hugo L. Black, who refused to view the picture, argued that the Supreme Court "is about the most inappropriate Supreme Board of Censors that could be found." "So far as I know," he wrote, "judges possess no special expertise providing exceptional competency to set standards and to supervise the private morals of the Nation."

Justice Felix Frankfurter disagreed, asserting there was a need for the Court to examine allegedly obscene films brought before it in order to determine the constitutionality of their suppression on an "instance-by-instance, case-by-case" basis. Citing D. H. Lawrence's own dictum, "But even I would censor genuine pornography, rigorously," Frankfurter claimed that "freedom of expression was no more an absolute than any other freedom." Justice William O. Douglas reaffirmed the position he first advocated in *Superior Films* v. *Department of Education*, the *M* case [33]: all "censorship of movies is unconstitutional, since it is a form of 'previous restraint' that is . . . at war with the First Amendment."

Justice John M. Harlan, while not agreeing that all film censorship was unconstitutional, or that this New York law was constitutionally defective, found himself unable to "regard this film as depicting anything more than a somewhat unusual, and rather pathetic, 'love triangle,' lacking in anything that could properly be termed obscene or corruptive of the public morals by inciting the commission of adultery." He concluded that for this reason, "in banning this film New York has exceeded constitutional limits." Justice Tom Clark agreed with his brethren in this case that the New York law's standard for censorship was too vague or "obscure," but that a law that authorized the censorship of films that "portray *acts* of sexual immorality, perversion, or lewdness," or were "pornographic," would meet "the requirements of due process."

1. The deletions ordered by the New York censors are described in Richard Randall, *Censorship of the Movies* (Madison, Wisc: Univ. of Wisconsin Pr., 1968), 62.
2. Kingsley International Pictures Corporation v. Regents of the University of the State of New York, 165 N.Y.S. 2d 681 (1957).
3. Kingsley International Pictures Corporation v. Regents of the University of the State of New York, 151 N.E. 2d 197 (1958).
4. Kingsley International Pictures v. Regents of the University of the State of New York, 360 U.S. 684 (1959).

[44]
Naked Amazon

Banned in Maryland, 1957.

Brazil, 1954. U.S., 1957. Dist: Times Film Corp. 71 min. 16mm. Sound. B&W. Prod/Dir/Cin: Zygmunt Sulistrowski. SW: Herb Meadow. Cast: Zygmunt Sulistrowski, Monique Jaubert, Caroles Roland, José Ozorio Baptista, Jeffrey Mitchell, Ary Balustein. Reviews: *Daily Mirror*, July 7, 1955, Frank Quinn; *Variety*, May 16, 1956.

This film is a semi-documentary travelogue of an expedition to the various parts of Brazil, in particular to the Matto Brosso country where the Camayura Indians live in an isolated upper Amazon River region. The expedition is led by Zygmunt Sulistrowski with a team of five men and two women. Included are shots of the jungle and snakes and jaguars, as well as nude tribespeople engaged in hunting and ritual dances. The mores and customs of the Camayura Indians are commented upon by Sulistrowski.

Censorship Activity

The Maryland censorship board ordered deletion of all scenes showing bodies of Camayura Indians naked below the waist, on the ground that their inclusion made this film obscene. On review, the Baltimore city court, noting that "intimate parts of the body cannot be seen," reversed the censor board's ruling. This decision, freeing the film without deletions, was affirmed by the Maryland Court of Appeals.[1]

Legal Importance

The appellate court did not resolve questions presented by the film's producer as to whether the statute was unconstitutional on its face and as applied. It decided in favor of the producer on the ground that the lower court was correct in finding the film "not to be obscene or pornographic." A unanimous bench rejected the board's argument that since the statute referred to "a motion picture film or view," single scenes of nudity could be considered alone, rather than in relation to the entire picture, and, if a scene's "possible obscenity outweighed any of its merits, considering that scene alone," the film could be condemned.

The censor board's chairman claimed that "the public would find the film shocking and tending to arouse sexual desires, certainly in irresponsible numbers of people." The court compared this contention to the legal doctrine espoused in discredited cases in which allegedly obscene books had been judged by the effect they might have, not on the ordinary adult person, but on "the young and immature, the ignorant and those who are sensually inclined." This was incorrect. "The correct test applies the community standard of decency . . . ," which "must be, in a sense a rough average." The court thought that only to a "prurient imagination" could this film suggest "unchaste or lustful ideas."

The censorship board misinterpreted and misapplied the statute: there was no basis, even on its theory of the law, for a finding that the film's calculated purpose and dominant effect was substantially to arouse sexual desires. Rather, the film showed "primitive unprepossessing aborigines going about their daily lives in their native surroundings unclothed, as is their custom, with no intimation of sexual activity or awareness." The film evidently had been edited, as a prerequisite to acceptance by the film industry's Production Code and to a license from the New York censorship board; this editing apparently deleted the showing of "intimate parts of the body."

1. Maryland State Board of Motion Picture Censors v. Times Film Corporation, 129 A. 2d 833 (1957).

[45]
And God Created Woman

Banned in Philadelphia, Pennsylvania, 1958.

France, 1957. U.S., 1957. Dist: Kingsley International. 92 min. 35mm. Sound. Color. English subtitles. Prod: Raoul Levy. Dir: Roger Vadim. SW: Roger Vadim, Raoul Levy. Cin: Armand Thirard. Cast: Brigitte Bardot, Curt Jurgens, Christian Marquand, Jean-Louis Trintignant. Reviews: *Films and Filming*, v. 3 No. 8 (May 1957); *New York Times*, Oct. 22, 1957, Bosley Crowther; *Films in Review*, v. IX No. 1, January 1958.

Brigitte Bardot plays a young coquette who is staying with a family in St. Tropez, France. Because she misses the family's pitch for her to marry the oldest son, the family threatens to evict her. To keep her in St. Tropez, the second son marries her. She truly cares for the oldest son and so sets a boat on fire, causing the oldest son (now her brother-in-law) to rescue her, which allows them to end up on the beach in each other's arms. This causes much family dissension and a deep depression on the part of her husband, for both she and the oldest son are unrepentant. A wealthy yachtsman who has been waiting for her disillusionment of the marriage moves in on the young wife. She gets drunk and starts dancing to hot jazz, whereupon her husband beats her into submission.

Censorship Activity

After viewing a private showing of this film three weeks prior to its scheduled public showing, a Philadelphia assistant district attorney told the distributor's lawyer that exhibiting it would violate a state law making criminal the showing of any film "of a lascivious, sacrilegious, obscene, indecent, or immoral nature," and that those responsible for its showing would be arrested and the film seized. The owners of two Philadelphia theaters at which the film was scheduled to be shown notified the district attorney that they would not exhibit the film and would breach their contract with the distributor.

The distributor then brought suit in the Philadelphia Court of Common Pleas for an injunction to prevent the district attorney from interfering with the movie's exhibition, claiming that the statute was too vague to meet the requirements of constitutional due process, that the motion picture was not obscene, and that unless the requested injunction was granted the distributor would suffer "irreparable injury." The district attorney agreed to the court's suggestion that the film be shown while the court considered the distributor's request for an injunction, but the following week, when the court refused to issue the preliminary injunction, the district attorney seized the films being shown at the two theaters and arrested the theater managers. On appeal, the Supreme Court of Pennsylvania reversed the lower court.[1]

Legal Importance

A court of equity will take jurisdiction to prevent a prosecutor from interfering with the exhibition of a film only when its distributor will suffer "irreparable harm to [his] property rights." Ordinarily, a court will not otherwise restrain the prosecution of a criminal case because the accused has an adequate opportunity to plead the invalidity of the law at the time of the prosecution. "Equity has jurisdiction because the plaintiff [here] has no adequate and complete remedy at law." The criminal prosecution was directed against the theater owners, not the film's distributor. The distributor could not protect his property rights against the district attorney in a criminal proceeding to which he was not, and could not become, a party. The pending prosecution of the theater owners thus threatened "an irreparable injury to the plaintiff corporation which distributes and leases the film." Consequently, the lower court erred in dismissing the distributor's request that the prosecution be enjoined.

In a dissenting opinion, Justice Michael A. Musmanno stated, "I am afraid that [the court's decision] has thrown a large monkey wrench into the prosecution machinery." The District Attorney "is required to enforce the obscenity statutes. . . . That is what [he] . . . attempted to do in this case and it is incredible that he should be restrained through the processes of law from doing what the law requires him to do."

At the equity court hearing, the distributor gave evidence that the film had been passed by United States Customs, licensed for exhibition in the states of New York, Virginia, and Maryland, and shown in cities located in

California, Illinois, Texas, Missouri, Ohio, Kentucky, Washington, Oregon, New York, Maryland, and Pennsylvania, as well as in Washington, D.C.

1. Kingsley International Pictures Corporation v. Blanc, 153 A. 2d 243 (1959).

[46]
The Anatomy of a Murder

Banned in Chicago, Illinois, 1959.

U.S., 1959. Dist: Columbia Pictures Corp. 161 min. 35mm. Sound. B&W. Prod/Dir: Otto Preminger. SW: Wendell Mayes. Cin: Sam Leavitt. Cast: James Stewart, Brooks West, George C. Scott, Lee Remick, Ben Gazzara. Reviews: *New York Times*, July 3, 1959, Bosley Crowther; *New Yorker*, July 11, 1959; *Saturday Review*, July 11, 1959; *Newsweek*, July 13, 1959; *Time*, July 13, 1959.

This film is based on the novel of the same title by Robert Traver. It tells the story of a local murder trial of an army lieutenant who murdered the owner of the town tavern after his wife claimed that he had raped her. Suspicion grows concerning the reliability of the wife's story. Though the lieutenant is found guilty, he is spared capital punishment due to the brilliant defense presented by his lawyer.

Censorship Activity
The Chicago censorship board refused to grant the distributor of this film a permit for its exhibition in the city, evidently because of a rape scene and the use of the words "rape" and "contraceptive"; the mayor approved the denial. The distributor brought suit in the U.S. District Court for the Northern District of Illinois for an order directing the city to issue the permit and to refrain from preventing the movie's showing. Judge Julius H. Miner granted the order.[1]

Legal Importance
Judge Miner applied the rule "generally followed in the Federal and State Courts" that "a book or play is to be judged as a whole in terms of its effect on the average, normal reader or viewer." In fact, this rule was required by the U.S. Supreme Court to be applied to allegedly obscene material in the landmark case of *Roth* v. *United States*.[2] That would not protect "obscene" material in a book or film "unless its diction or episodes are so slight or infrequent as not to convey an obscene savor to the entire book or play."

Applying these guidelines after having viewed the film, the court held that "the film cannot be placed in the category of the obscene or immoral, because its dominant effect does not tend to excite sexual passion or undermine public morals." The mention of "rape" or "contraceptive" in the film was thought not likely to "so much arouse the salacity of the normal and average viewer as to outweigh its artistic and expert presentation." And the rape of the murderer's wife "has the effect of arousing pity and revulsion rather than desire or sexual impure thoughts." Considering that the U.S. Supreme Court had recently reversed a New York ban on the exhibition of *Lady Chatterley's Lover* [43], Judge Miner regarded *Anatomy of a Murder* as not depicting "anything that could reasonably be termed obscene or corruptive of the public morals"; accordingly, he reasoned, "the censorship exceeded constitutional bounds."

1. Columbia Pictures v. City of Chicago, 184 F. Supp. 817 (1959).
2. Roth v. United States, 354 U.S. 476 (1957).

[47]
Desire Under the Elms

Banned for persons under 21 in Chicago, Illinois, 1959.

U.S., 1958. Dist: Paramount Pictures Corp. 114 min. 35mm. Sound. B&W. Prod: Don Hartman. Dir: Delbert Mann. SW: Irwin Shaw. Cin: Daniel L. Fapp. Cast: Sophia Loren, Anthony Perkins, Burl Ives. Reviews: *New York Times*, March 13, 1958, Bosley Crowther; *Saturday Review*, March 15, 1958; *Time*, March 17, 1958; *Newsweek*, March 22, 1958; *New Yorker*, March 22, 1958.

This film is based on an adaptation by Irwin Shaw of the play of the same title by Eugene O'Neill. Old Ephraim Cabot owns a large farm in New England and uses his three sons to maintain it, without offering them the hope of inheritance. Cabot weds a young woman and brings her to live on the farm. The youngest son pursues her, she becomes pregnant and gives birth to a boy, which the father thinks is his. Out of loyalty, the woman kills the child so as not to rob the young son of his birthright.

Censorship Activity

After the Chicago censorship board granted the distributor of this film a permit to exhibit it only to persons over 21, the distributor brought suit for an injunction to prevent the city from interfering with its general exhibition. The Municipal Code of Chicago provided that a film shall be granted a permit unless, among other qualities, it is immoral or obscene. However, if the picture "tends toward creating a harmful impression on the minds of children, where such tendency as to the minds of adults would not exist," a limited permit may be granted, allowing the exhibition of the film "to persons over twenty-one years." The U.S. District Court for the Northern District of Illinois issued the injunction requested by the distributor.[1]

Legal Importance

A censorship statute must be framed precisely enough for censors to have "a rational guide to their decisions." In this respect, the section of the Chicago statute that authorized limiting the audience if it might be "harmful" for children, was "defective." "Like any other censorship statute," wrote Chief Judge Sullivan, for the court, "this one must be approached with a caution dictated by the fact that it is a patent invasion of the right to freedom of speech guaranteed by the First Amendment."

The word "tend," in the ordinance, implied that a movie might be suppressible, for children, even if it merely "approached" the "harmful." And how could anyone know what a film's tendency was, with respect to its effects on a child, if the term "child" applied to every person below the age of 21? Could a 20-year-old married serviceman be prevented from seeing a film that might not be suitable for a girl of twelve? In this respect, the ordinance was deemed "hopelessly indefinite," and to violate the principle established by the U.S. Supreme Court in the case of *Butler* v. *Michigan*,[2] where a Michigan law that would "reduce the adult population of Michigan to reading only what was fit for children" was struck down as constitutionally invalid. The statute, the court concluded, is "an insufficient guide to either the censors or those who produce motion pictures." The provision authorizing the issuance of a limited license for a film that "approaches producing a harmful notion in the mind of anyone from one to 21 years of age," was "invalid . . . unconstitutional, and void."

Interestingly, the logic of Judge Sullivan's argument against the validity of this Chicago ordinance—because it would reduce the level of movies that could be seen by 20-year-olds to that which was safe for 12-year-olds—seems not to have been recognized by the Supreme Court itself when, some ten years later, in the case of *Ginsberg* v. *New York*,[3] it *upheld* the validity of a New York law restricting the level of reading material that could lawfully be sold to minors.

1. Paramount Film Distributing Corporation v. City of Chicago, 172 F. Supp. 69 (1959).
2. Butler v. Michigan, 352 U.S. 380 (1957).
3. Ginsberg v. New York, 390 U.S. 692 (1968).

[48]
Don Juan

Banned in Chicago, Illinois, 1959.

Austria, 1956. U.S., 1956. Dist: Times Film. 90 min. 35mm. Sound. Color. English subtitles. Prod: Akkond Film of Vienna. Dir/SW: H. W. Kolm-Veltee. Cin: Willy Sohm, Hannes Fuchs. Cast: Cesare Donova, Joseph Meinard, Evelyn Cormand, Hans von Borsody, Lotte Tobisch, Marianne Schooenauer. Reviews: *New York Times*, March 6, 1956, Bosley Crowther; *New Yorker*, March 17, 1956; *Catholic World*, April 1956.

This film is an adaptation of Mozart's opera *Don Giovanni*, by H. W. Kolm-Veltee, Alfred Uhl, and Ernest Henthaler. It relates the story of the nobleman, Don Juan, who compulsively conquers and morally humiliates women and their menfolk.

Censorship Activity

The distributor of this film applied to the Chicago police commissioner for a permit to exhibit it, without submitting any print of the film for examination by the censors. The commissioner notified the distributor that he would not issue a permit because, according to a Chicago ordinance, one could be granted only after the movie had been submitted for examination. The distributor refused to do this and, after unsuccessfully appealing to the mayor, went to court for an order to compel the issuance of a permit to show the film in Chicago. He claimed that the censorship ordinance—in requiring a film's submission to censors in advance of exhibition—amounted to a prior restraint on freedom of expression prohibited by the First and Fourteenth Amendments. Chief Judge William J. Campbell of the U.S. District Court for the Northern District of Illinois dismissed the complaint on the grounds that no "justiciable controversy" existed.[1] The Court of Appeals for the Seventh Circuit affirmed that judgment,[2] and was, in turn, affirmed in its action by the U.S. Supreme Court.[3]

Legal Importance

The case is important because a majority of the Supreme Court refused to acknowledge the broad and basic principle that films, like other media of expression, were protected constitutionally from prior governmental censorship. The section of Chicago's censorship statute requiring the submission of films, and the receipt of a permit, prior to their public exhibition was not void, declared Justice Tom C. Clark. The issue presented for decision was, in effect, "whether the ambit of constitutional protection includes complete and absolute freedom to exhibit, at least once, any and every kind of motion picture." The distributor's challenge was directed against the "censor's basic authority" and not against the particular statutory standards employed by the Chicago censor nor against the procedural requirements for the licensing of the film. "Yet, it has never been held that liberty of speech is absolute. Nor has it been suggested that all previous restraints on speech are invalid." The Court construed the distributor to be requesting it to hold that the public exhibition of motion pictures must be allowed "under any circumstances," with the state's "sole remedy" against an objectionable film being shown lying in "the invocation of criminal process . . . and then only after a transgression." But, Justice Clark maintained, there is no "absolute privilege against prior restraint under the First Amendment." For example, as Chief Justice Charles Evans Hughes stated in *Near* v. *Minnesota*,[4] "the primary requirements of decency . . . may be enforced against obscene publications." Chicago "emphasizes here its duty to protect its people against the dangers of obscenity in the public exhibition of motion pictures."

The film distributor's answer to this was that regardless of the alleged capacity for, or extent of, such an evil, previous restraint over movies could not be justified just as it could not be justified over newspapers or books, which, historically, have never been subject to licensing in advance of publication. In *The Miracle* case [30], Clark argued, the Court "recognized that motion pictures were not necessarily subject to the precise rules governing any other particular method of expression" and that "each method tends to present its own peculiar problems." A majority of the Court was simply unwilling to state that the State is "stripped of all constitutional power to prevent, in the most effective fashion [i.e., by prior licensing], the utterance of this class of speech." "At this time," the Court concluded, "we say no more than this—that we are dealing only with motion pictures and, even as to them, only in the context of the broadside attack presented on this record."

Chief Justice Earl Warren wrote an extensive and vigorous dissenting opinion that was joined by Justices Hugo L. Black, William O. Douglas, and William J. Brennan, Jr. For him, the case clearly presented the question of "our approval of unlimited censorship of motion pictures before exhibition through a system of administrative licensing." Moreover, the decision presented a "real danger of eventual censorship for every form of communication, be it newspapers, journals, books, magazines, television, radio, or public speeches."

The Chief Justice was aware of no constitutional principle that permitted the Court to hold that the communication of ideas through one medium may be censored while other media are immune from any such censorship. He did not "dispute that this Court has stated that the protection afforded First Amendment liberties from previous restraint is not absolutely unlimited. But, licensing or censorship was not, at any point, considered within the 'exceptional cases' discussed in the opinion in *Near*.'' The Court's decision, he continued, ''gives official license to the censor, approving a grant of power to city officials to prevent the showing of any moving picture these officials deem unworthy of a license. It thus gives formal sanction to censorship in its purest and most far-reaching form, to a classical plan of licensing that, in our country, most closely approaches the English licensing laws of the seventeenth century which were commonly used to suppress dissent in the mother country and in the colonies. The Court treats motion pictures, food for the mind, held to be within the shield of the First Amendment, little differently than it would treat edibles. . . . The Court, in no way, explains why moving pictures should be treated differently than any form of expression, why moving pictures should be denied the protection against censorship.''

1. Times Film Corporation v. City of Chicago, 180 F. Supp. 843 (1959).
2. Times Film Corporation v. City of Chicago, 272 F. 2d 90 (1959).
3. Times Film Corporation v. City of Chicago, 365 U.S. 43 (1961).
4. Near v. Minnesota, 283 U.S. 697 (1931).

[49]
The Lovers (Les Amants)

Banned in Cleveland, Ohio; Dayton, Ohio; Cuyahoga County, Ohio; Chicago, Illinois; Boston, Massachusetts; Providence, Rhode Island; Portland, Oregon; Memphis, Tennessee; and the states of New York, Virginia, and Maryland, 1959.

France, 1958. U.S., 1959. Dist: Zenith International. 90 min. 16mm. Sound. B&W. English subtitles. Prod/Dir/SW: Louis Malle. Cin: Henri Decaf. Cast: Jeanne Moreau, Alain Ainy, Jean-Marc Bory, José-Luis de Villanga, Judith Magre, Gaston Modot. Awards: Second prize, 1959 Venice Film Festival. Reviews: *Variety*, Sept. 17, 1958, Mosk.; *Saturday Review*, Aug. 8, 1959, Paul V. Beckley; *New York Herald Tribune*, Oct. 27, 1959; *New Yorker*, Nov. 7, 1959, John McCarter; *New York Times*, Dec. 27, 1959, A. H. Weiler.

This film was adapted from the nineteenth-century novel *Point de Lendemain* by Dominque Vivant. Jeanne Tournier, a 30-year-old woman living in the French province of Lyon, is trapped in an unhappy marriage. Neglected by her busy husband, who is a publisher, she is encouraged by her friend Maggy to have an affair in Paris. But the lover, a man-about-town named Raoul, offers Jeanne no real escape from her loneliness. When her husband becomes suspicious, he invites Maggy and Raoul for a weekend visit.

Jeanne's car breaks down on the way from Paris, and she accepts a ride from a young archaeologist, Bernard, who expresses contempt for the society in which she moves. Jeanne's husband invites Bernard to spend the night and after an unpleasant dinner, all but Bernard retire. Jeanne cannot sleep and goes for a moonlight walk on the grounds. She meets Bernard and they become lovers. The next morning Jeanne is unable to return to her former life and unwilling to relinquish her newly found happiness. She rejects her family, her home, and her friends, and leaves with Bernard to face an uncertain future.

Censorship Activity

The manager of a Cleveland Heights, Ohio theater who showed this motion picture was convicted in the Cuyahoga County Court of Common Pleas (Criminal Division) for exhibiting an obscene film. His conviction was upheld by the County Court of Appeals[1] and affirmed by the Supreme Court of Ohio.[2] In 1964, however, the United States Supreme Court, in *Jacobellis* v. *Ohio*, ruled that the film was constitutionally protected expression and not obscene, and reversed the theater manager's conviction.[3]

The film was also banned in Cuyahoga County, Ohio *before* the *Jacobellis* case began. A 1959 Court of Common Pleas (Criminal Division) conviction was affirmed on appeal by the Supreme Court of Ohio for the reason that "no debatable constitutional issue was involved."[4] In Dayton, Ohio, also before the start of the *Jacobellis* case, the Supreme Court of Ohio reversed a jury conviction on the ground that the statute making it a crime for a person to have possession of an obscene film, without any showing of his knowledge of the film's character, was thereby unconstitutional.[5] In Chicago, a refusal of the city's censorship board to permit the showing of this film was reversed by a federal circuit court of appeals.[6] The film is reported to have been censored but shown in New York, where before permitting the film to be exhibited, the state censorship board ordered deletions of about half a minute; in Memphis, Tennessee, where the theater manager personally expunged parts; in Boston, Massachusetts and Providence, Rhode Island, where local censorship boards allowed only a *sanitized, slightly shorter version to be shown*. In Portland, Oregon, the police ordered showings stopped. In Virginia and Maryland, theater owners reportedly refused to comply with their state censorship boards' requests for deletions in the film and canceled its showing.

Legal Importance

Justice William J. Brennan, Jr. wrote the Supreme Court's opinion, establishing the fundamental principle that "material dealing with sex in a manner that advocates ideas, or that has literary or scientific or artistic value or any other form of social importance, may not be branded as obscenity" and banned. "A work cannot be proscribed unless it is 'utterly' without social importance." Justice Potter Stewart, concurring, thought that the Court's decisions had reached the point where only "hard-core pornography" could be suppressed. Struggling with the problems of identifying what could constitutionally be banned, he said memorably: "I shall not today attempt further to define the kinds of materials I understand to be embraced within that shorthand definition; perhaps I could never succeed in intelligibly doing so. But I know it when I see it, and the motion picture involved in this case is not that."

1. State v. Jacobellis, 175 N.E. 2d 123, 115 Ohio App. 226 (1961).
2. State v. Jacobellis, 179 N.E. 2d 777, 173 Ohio St. 22 (1962).
3. 378 U.S. 184 (1964).
4. State v. Gevaras, 165 N.E. 2d 652, 170 Ohio St. 404 (1962).
5. State v. Warth, 179 N.E. 2d 772, 173 Ohio St. 15 (1962).
6. Zenith International Film Corp. v. Chicago, 291 F. 2d 785 (1961).

1960–1969

[50]
Never on Sunday

Banned in Atlanta, Georgia, 1961.

Greece, 1960. U.S., 1960. Dist: Lopert Films. 91 min. 35mm. Sound. Color. Prod/Dir/SW: Jules Dassin. Cin: Jaques Natteau. Cast: Melina Mercouri, Jules Dassin, Georges Foundas, Titos Vandis. Reviews: *New York Herald Tribune*, Oct. 19, 1960, Paul V. Beckley; *New York Post*, Oct. 19, 1960, Archer Winsten; *New York Times*, Oct. 19, 1960, Bosley Crowther.

This film tells the story of a dry, scholarly American named Homer who meets Ilya on a tour of Greece. Ilya is a happy-go-lucky prostitute who "on weekends is the bubbling sweetheart of all the sailors and shipyard workers in Piraeus, but on Sundays she's a true and virtuous patron of the ancient Greek tragedies."[1] Unlike her friend Homer, she is full of life and fun and is convinced that all the Greek tragedies that they see together end happily. The American feels that her beauty and gaiety personify Greece but that her profession denigrates her ancestral spirituality. He persuades her to quit and begins to teach her classical music, art appreciation, and philosophy. Now Homer is approached by Noface, a pimp for whom Ilya has refused to work. Noface proposes to subsidize Ilya's education in order to keep her off the streets, thus leaving more business for his girls. Believing that Noface's motives are pure, Homer accepts the offer, but when Ilya discovers this arrangement she furiously throws all of his educational "gifts" out of the window and returns to her former life. Homer sulks and, when her friends poke fun at him, threatens to start a fight. This is the first time he has ever dropped his academic armor. He realizes then that he has been trying to escape from the modern world, and from that point on begins to explore the real present-day Greece and share its zest for living.

Censorship Activity

A librarian who served as the Atlanta, Georgia motion picture censor denied the distributor of this film a permit to exhibit it within the city unless certain cuts were made. On administrative appeal, the city's board of censors, the Atlanta Public Library Board of Trustees, ruled that, with or without deletions, the film would not be licensed for exhibition. The film, said the board, "would be harmful to the average child" who might view it, and it presented "an unacceptable idea." The distributor then brought suit for an injunction to prevent the city from interfering with the movie's showing. The Superior Court, Fulton County, granted the injunction. It held that the Atlanta censorship law—which allowed the board to reject a motion picture if it affected "the peace, health, morals, and good order of the City"—was unconstitutional because it "violated the free speech provisions" of the Constitutions of Georgia and the United States, and it held that the film was not obscene. On appeal by the city, the Supreme Court of Georgia reversed the lower court's judgment.[2]

Legal Importance

The Georgia Supreme Court's unanimous decision turned on a technical procedural ground. It did not reach the merits of the case, the issue of obscenity, nor the issue of whether the Atlanta ordinance, as applied, was an unconstitutional abridgment of free speech, as the lower court had held it was. To have the Censorship Board's decision reviewed, Justice Joseph D. Quillian said, the distributor should have applied to the Superior Court by writ of certiorari. He would not allow a petition for an injunction to be substituted as a mode of application, and on this basis reversed the lower court's ruling.

1. *New York Times*, Oct. 19, 1960.
2. City of Atlanta v. Lopert Pictures Corporation, 122 S.E. 2d 916 (1961).

[51]
The Connection

Banned in New York, 1962.

U.S., 1962. Dist: The Connection Co.-Allen-Hodgon Productions. 103 min. 35mm. Sound. B&W. Dir: Shirley Clarke. SW: Jack Gelber. Cin: Arthur J. Ornitz. Music: Freddie Redd. Cast: William Redfield, Warren Finnerty, Gary

Goodrow, Jerome Raphel, James Anderson, Carl Lee, Barbara Winchester, Roscoe Lee Browne, Henry Proach. Cast-Musicians: Freddie Redd (piano), Jackie McLean (alto sax), Michael Mattos (bass), Larry Ritchie (drums). Reviews: *Film Daily*, Oct. 4, 1962; *New York Herald Tribune*, Oct. 4, 1962. Article: *Show*, August 1962, Arthur Schlesinger, Jr.

This film was written for the screen by Jack Gelber, who also wrote the play *The Connection*. It concerns eight drug addicts waiting for their connection in a New York apartment belonging to Leach. Jim Dunn, a budding film-maker, has agreed to pay for the fix if the addicts will allow him to film the connection scene. After the men get their shots, they talk Dunn into trying heroin in order to understand the subject "first hand." He becomes ill and while sleeping, Leach takes an overdose that puts him into a coma. Dunn recovers, with the aid of the connection, and writes off his film as a failure.

Censorship Activity

The New York State Board of Regents denied a license for exhibition of this film on the ground of obscenity solely because of the repeated use of the word "shit" as slang for heroin. On review, the Appellate Division of the state supreme court annulled the regents' determination.[1] This action was upheld by the state's highest tribunal, the New York Court of Appeals.[2] However, when the distributor exhibited the film at a New York theater without a license, following the state supreme court decision and while the Court of Appeals proceeding was pending, the regents obtained a court injunction against the further exhibition of the film pending a decision by New York's highest court.

Legal Importance

This case is important because the court examined the use made in the film of the objectionable word, rather than the word itself. "In most instances," the court observed, "the word is not used in its usual connotation but as a definite expression of the language of the narcotic." While the use of the word might be classified as "vulgar," it was not obscene. A related issue was decided by the U.S. Supreme Court in the 1978 case of *Federal Communications Commission* v. *Pacifica Foundation*.[3] Here, the high court decided that the repeated utterance of seven "Dirty Words" (shit, piss, fuck, cunt, cocksucker, motherfucker, and tits), in a satiric monologue by comedian George Carlin, was not constitutionally protected in the context of a radio program broadcast at a time when children were likely to be listening (2 P.M.). The procedure that prevented the film's exhibition, pending the regents' appeal from a judicial decision finding the movie not obscene, probably conflicts with the constitutional standards later enunciated by the Supreme Court in the *Revenge at Daybreak* case [58].

1. Connection Company v. Regents of the University of the State of New York, 230 N.Y.S. 2d 103 (1962).
2. Regents v. Connection Company, 234 N.Y.S. 2d 722 (1962).
3. Federal Communications Commission v. Pacifica Foundation, 438 U.S. 726 (1978).

[52]
The Virgin Spring (Jungfrukallan: Well of the Virgin)

Banned in Fort Worth, Texas, 1962.

Sweden, 1960. U.S., 1960. Dist: Janus Films. 88 min. 35mm. Sound. B&W. English subtitles. Dir: Ingmar Bergman. Scenario: Ulla Isaksson. Cin: Sven Nykvist. Music: Erik Nordgren. Cast: Max Von Sydow, Birgitta Pettersson, Gunnel Lindblom. Award: Academy Award, Best Foreign Film of 1960. Reviews: *New York Herald Tribune*, Nov. 13, 1960, Judith Crist; *New Yorker*, Nov. 19, 1960, Brendan Gill; *New York Times*, Nov. 20, 1960, Bosley Crowther; *Village Voice*, Jan. 19, 1961, Jonas Mekas.

This film was based on a thirteenth-century Swedish legend and folksong, "The Daughter of Tore o Vange" (Tores dotter i Vange). It is the story of two sisters, one a fair-haired virgin named Karin, the other, Ingeri, dark, brooding, and jealous of her sister. While on their way to bring candles to the church, Ingeri gets Karin lost in the forest. Karin comes upon three goatherds who rape and then murder her. Seeking shelter at a farmhouse, the goatherds try to sell Karin's robe to the farmer, who turns out to be the girls' father. In a fury he murders the goatherds and then goes to seek his daughter. Upon finding her nude body, he vows that he will build a church there, whereupon a spring comes gushing forth from the spot beneath her head.

Censorship Activity

The Fort Worth, Texas censorship board refused to permit the distributor of this film to exhibit it unless a 90-second "rape scene" was removed—under an ordinance that prohibited the exhibition of any film that was "indecent or injurious to the morals of the citizens of Fort Worth, or which would tend to promote or encourage indecency, immorality, or racial or sectional prejudice, or juvenile delinquency." An administrative board of review upheld the censors' denial of permission. Claiming that city officials "appl[ied] capricious and private standards of taste and judgment," in deciding whether to grant a license for the movie's showing, the distributor brought suit in the Tarrant County District Court for a temporary injunction to prevent Fort Worth officials from interfering with its exhibition.

After viewing the film at a theater in Dallas, Judge Harris Brewster refused to grant the requested injunction. On appeal, the Court of Civil Appeals of Texas affirmed the lower court's judgment, noting, "We cannot say that the trial court erred in failing to [hold the picture not obscene] when evidence available to, and which doubtless was considered by, that court is not available to us."[1] The court construed the ordinance's language to prohibit the exhibition of obscene films. The Supreme Court of Texas denied the distributor's application for a writ of error and found no reversible error in the lower court's handling of the case.[2] The film had been passed by United States Customs.

Legal Importance

The case has little importance because the Texas courts did not consider (probably because the film's distributor failed to present) such overriding issues as whether the Texas ordinance was an unconstitutionally vague and indefinite system of prior restraint lacking required procedural safeguards, under the principles established by the U.S. Supreme Court in such decisions as *The Miracle* case [30] and the *Revenge at Daybreak* case [58]; and whether the film did not have redeeming artistic or other social importance which would prevent it being suppressed as obscene, under the principles announced in such cases as *The Lovers* [49]. The Texas courts also failed to view the film itself (perhaps because it was not made part of the official record on appeal), and consider *de novo*, as an issue of mixed constitutional law and fact (as indicated in such decisions as the *Carnal Knowledge* case [105]), the question of whether the film could be held obscene, applying the principles laid down in the definitional cases of *Roth* v. *United States*,[3] *Manual Enterprises* v. *Day*,[4] and *The Lovers* case. The distributor did not contest the proposition, announced in *Roth*, that "obscenity is not a constitutionally protected form of speech or press," but rested its argument that the film was entitled to be licensed on the proposition that the censors' behavior was "capricious and private."

Some interest attaches to the anomalous legal situation in which the film's distributor was placed by overlapping state and city laws. A Texas criminal law generally proscribed the showing of obscene films except any film that had been "legally imported" into the country and had been "passed by a customs office of the United States Government at any port of entry." The Fort Worth ordinance made no such exception in the films it forbade for exhibition. Although the film's distributor argued that this inconsistency should have been resolved by giving effect to the state law alone, the court held that there was no inconsistency, and that Fort Worth, "a home rule city," held "plenary" powers to censor objectionable films. A contrary ruling would have accorded more closely with prevailing judicial opinions; see the *Birth of a Baby* case [22].

1. Janus Films, Inc. v. City of Fort Worth, 354 S.W. 2d 597 (1962).
2. Janus Films, Inc. v. City of Fort Worth, 358 S.W. 2d 589 (1962).
3. Roth v. United States, 354 U.S. 476 (1957).
4. Manual Enterprises v. Day, 370 U.S. 478 (1962).

[53]
Women of the World

Banned in Memphis, Tennessee, 1963.

Italy, 1963. U.S., 1963. Dist: Embassy Pictures. 107 min. 35mm. Sound. Color. Prod: Cineriz. Dir: Gualtiero Jacopetti, Paolo Cavara, Franco Prosperi. SW: Gualtiero Jacopetti. Cin: Antonio Climati, Benito Frattari. Narrator: Peter Ustinov. Reviews: *New York Times*, July 3, 1963, A. H. Weiler; *Time*, July 12, 1963; *Saturday Review*, Aug. 10, 1963; *New Yorker*, Aug. 24, 1963.

This feature-length documentary of the manners, mores, and amorous habits of women around the world is narrated by Peter Ustinov, who describes it as "a voyeur's dream come true." Various shots include actresses attracting attention at the Cannes Film Festival by wearing bikinis; Israeli women in combat training and bathing nude; professional mourners on Sardinia; and promiscuity in a Swedish dormitory.

Censorship Activity

The Memphis, Tennessee censorship board, acting under city charter provisions that made it unlawful to exhibit films that were "immoral, lewd, obscene or lascivious" or which were "inimical to the public safety, health, morals or welfare," told the distributor of the movie that it could not be shown in the city unless four scenes were deleted. Alleging that elimination "of these sequences would impair the continuity and diminish the [picture's] artistic and commercial value," the distributor brought suit in federal district court, claiming that the censorship statute violated its right of free speech under the First Amendment and its property rights under the Fourteenth Amendment's due process clause, and that the board's action was unconstitutional because the picture "contains nothing which can constitutionally be proscribed." The court denied the city's motion to dismiss[1] and granted the distributor the relief it requested.[2]

Legal Importance

An argument by the city, which had been upheld in the *Curley* case [29], that the distributor had no legal "standing to sue" because it was an out-of-state corporation not qualified to "do business" in Tennessee, was rejected by this court. The distributor was held "not barred from seeking relief in this court even if it is not doing business here." There was a "justiciable or actual controversy" because the board's action prevented the exhibition of the film. The court refused to invoke the doctrine of "abstention," under which a federal court defers any resolution of a federal constitutional question until the state courts have considered all state issues that might avoid the federal constitutional matter, because "[t]here is at least a limited exception to the doctrine . . . where, as here, a challenge is made to local law on the ground that it '. . . impinges on fundamental civil liberties protected by the Fourteenth Amendment.' " After the court had overruled the city's motion to dismiss the case, it granted the distributor's motion to the effect that the film was "not subject to censorship," that the city should be prevented from interfering with its exhibition and that the Memphis censorship ordinance was unconstitutional. The court found the Memphis censorship ordinance to be "a system of prior restraint."

Although the U.S. Supreme Court in *Roth* v. *United States* and *Alberts* v. *California*³ had upheld the constitutionality of state and federal statutes that made it a crime to distribute or advertise material that was "obscene or indecent," the "system of precensorship" provided for in the Memphis ordinance was unconstitutional because it did "not contain the necessary procedural safeguards [the Supreme Court] spelled out" in the *Revenge at Daybreak* case [58]. The city claimed that the constitutional requirements spelled out in that case were not applicable here because the distributor "voluntarily" submitted the film to the board for examination. "The answer to this argument," the court responded, "is that plaintiff *did* apply for a determination by the Censor Board and the Censor Board, under its ordinance authority, *did* examine the movie and *did* order that it not be shown in its entirety." The ordinance "on its face violates the Fourteenth Amendment."

1. Embassy Pictures Corporation v. Hudson, 226 F. Supp. 421 (1964).
2. Embassy Pictures Corporation v. Hudson, 242 F. Supp. 975 (1965).
3. Roth v. United States, 354 U.S. 476 (1957).

[54]
Bachelor Tom Peeping

Banned in Los Angeles County, California, 1964.

U.S., 1962. Dist: Paul Mart Productions. 61 min. 35mm. Sound. Color. Prod: Corsican Productions. Dir: Joe Castagnoli, William Dewar, Jerry Jackson. Music: Alex Sanford. Cast: Brad Dorian, Pat Casse, Sandra Lind.

This film concerns the imaginary adventures of reporter Tom Peeping, who persistently tries to enter a secluded "sun club" for women in order to mingle with and photograph naked women. In the end, Tom awakens to find himself in a sanitarium, strait-jacketed and delirious.

Censorship Activity

The producer of this film wanted to distribute it to exhibitors who wished to show it in Los Angeles County, California; but the county sheriff, his deputy, and the district attorney considered it obscene and threatened to prosecute any exhibitors. The exhibitors did not show the movie and the film's producer brought suit in federal court under the 1964 Civil Rights Act, seeking a declaration that the picture was not obscene and an order preventing county officers from interfering with its exhibition. A district court in California dismissed the complaint on the ground that it did not state a claim upon which relief could be granted. However, the Court of Appeals for the Ninth Circuit reversed the lower court.[1]

Legal Importance

The appellate court reasoned that if officials, acting under color of state law, deliberately aim to suppress "objectionable" materials and succeed in their aim, such "informal censorship" may sufficiently "inhibit" the circulation of the materials to warrant the granting of an injunction, even though the means used are mere "threats of prosecution." Authority for this holding was found in the landmark Supreme Court case of *Bantam Books* v. *Sullivan*.[2] In the present case, it was not the film's producer but its potential exhibitors who were threatened with prosecution by the state—in a proceeding in which the producer would not be able to participate. Since, in such a situation, the producer would have no opportunity to secure a hearing or any resolution of the constitutional issues affecting him in a state court, his recourse to federal court for vindication of his rights was proper and not to be precluded.

1. Corsican Productions v. Pitchess, 338 F. 2d 441 (1964).
2. Bantam Books, Inc. v. Sullivan, 372 U.S. 58 (1963).

[55]
491

Banned from entry into the United States, 1964.

Sweden, 1964. U.S., 1966. Dist: Janus Films, Peppercorn-Wormser, Inc., Svensk Filmindustri. 110 min. 35mm. Sound. B&W. English subtitles. Prod:

Svensk Filmindustri. Dir: Vilgot Sjöman. SW: Lars Gorling. Cin: Gunnar Fischer. Cast: Lars Lind, Leif Nymark, Stig Tornblom, Lena Nyman. Reviews: *Variety*, Jan. 22, 1964, Wing.; *New York Times*, Dec. 21, 1967, Howard Thompson; *Box Office*, Jan. 8, 1968. Articles: *Variety*, Jan. 15, 1964, Frederic Fleisher; *New York Times*, Oct. 21, 1966, Edward Ranzel; *Box Office*, Dec. 5, 1966.

This film was adapted by Lars Gorling from his novel of the same name. It involves an experiment in which six young delinquents are allowed to live in the home of an idealistic social worker. They must report their daily activities to an inspector, who has homosexual relations with two of the boys. Continually abusing the social worker's kindness, the boys bring home a teenage girl whom they prostitute when they need money. After they force her into perverse sexual acts, the youngest of the boys kills himself and the experiment comes to its tragic end.

Censorship Activity

When the distributor sought to import this film, it was seized by the U.S. Customs Service as obscene under the Tariff Act of 1930. Pursuant to that statute, the film was referred to the U.S. Attorney, who began an action in federal district court to have the film judicially declared obscene and forfeited. The court, after trial, found the film obscene.[1] On review, the U.S. Court of Appeals for the Second Circuit reversed, and freed the film for importation into the United States.[2]

Legal Importance

The distributor claimed the film was constitutionally protected and not obscene, largely on the basis of its claim that the film had social importance, which, under the principle laid down in U.S. Supreme Court cases such as *Memoirs* v. *Massachusetts*[3] and *The Lovers* case [49], would cloak the film with constitutional protection. The trial court had found the film obscene despite the numerous expert witnesses who testified to its social importance, including film critics, writers, ministers, and the executive director of Mobilization For Youth. A majority of the Court of Appeals, however, thought the film was "attempting to deal with social problems which in 1966 are not only on our doorstep but very much over the threshold," and, accordingly, declared it "constitutionally protected and not obscene."

1. United States v. Film Entitled *491*, 247 F. Supp. 373 (1965).
2. United States v. Film Entitled *491*, 367 F. 2d 889 (1966).
3. Memoirs v. Massachusetts, 383 U.S. 413 (1966).

[56]
Have Figure Will Travel

Banned in Maryland, 1964.

Canada. U.S., 1963. Dist: Fanfare Films. 74 min. 35mm. Sound. Color. Prod: Philip Watson. Dir: Alan Overton. SW/Cin: Stanley Lipinski. Cast: Susan Baxter, Carol MacKenzie, Marge Anderson.

With her friend Susan, Carol visits a nudist camp, unbeknownst to her strict, widowed father. After he is called away on a trip, the girls decide to take his yacht to visit other nudist camps along the Atlantic coast. With them goes another friend, Marge, who is innocent of the pleasures of nudism. The girls end their trip in Florida where officials initiate them into the camp activities.

Censorship Activity

As a condition for the issuance of a license to show this film, the Maryland censorship board ordered the distributor to delete certain "obscene" scenes showing girls cruising on a boat, unclothed above the waist. The censors did not object to other scenes in nudist camps in which there were both unclothed men and women. The board took the position that the nudity in the camps was not obscene, whereas the nudity on the boat was, because in the latter locale "it was not a normal way of life, normal people would not so comport themselves and there was no reason for its portrayal except to arouse sexual desires in the viewers." On appeal, the Baltimore City Court affirmed the board's order, but the Court of Appeals of Maryland reversed.[1]

Legal Importance

The Maryland high court rejected the distributor's claim that Maryland's film censorship system violated freedom of expression under the Maryland and United States constitutions, citing its decision in the *Revenge at Daybreak* case [58], later to be reversed by the U.S. Supreme Court. However, on the question of the obscenity *vel non* of the film, the court unanimously considered the censors' judgment to be "unwarranted." "[N]o sexual activity was shown and . . . while on the boat the girls were seen unclothed only by each other." Relying in part on the *Naked Amazon* case [44], the court noted that the "established law [is] that nudity is not necessarily obscene or lewd," and that "there is nothing to indicate that it was in the case before us." Alluding to pictures in magazines of "unclothed females in poses which might generally be thought to be offensive, . . . they, even though obviously intended to arouse sex appeal, are not strictly obscene." Therefore, the court held, the board's order to eliminate the boat scenes was improper.

1. Fanfare Films, Inc. v. Motion Picture Censor Board, 197 A. 2d 839 (1964).

[57]
Lorna

Banned in Maryland, 1964.

U.S., 1964. Dist: Eve Productions. 77 min. 35mm. Sound. B&W. Prod/Dir/ Cin: Russ Meyer. SW: James Griffith. Cast: Lorna Maitland, Mark Bradley, James Rucker, Hal Hopper, Doc Scott, James Griffith. Review: *Variety*, Aug. 18, 1965.

Voluptuous Lorna, bored with her marriage to James, a salt mine worker, often takes nude swims in a stream near their shack. One day she is discovered by an escaped criminal, who rapes her. Lorna resists at first, but later takes the man back to the shack. There the two are discovered by James, who has just returned from a fight with his coworkers concerning his sexual ability with his wife. Another fight breaks out, and Lorna and the criminal are killed. A prophet, appearing at the beginning and end of the play, reiterates that one must pay for one's sins. This was Russ Meyer's "first serious effort after six nudie pix. . . . a weak script nearly over-powered with sexploitation angles. . . ."[1]

Censorship Activity
The Maryland censorship board refused to license this film for exhibition in 1964. After viewing the picture, the Circuit Court of Baltimore affirmed the board's finding. The Maryland Court of Appeals reversed the lower court's order in October 1965.[2]

Legal Importance
The appellate court ruled that a film censorship board had the constitutional burden of proving that a film was obscene before denying it a license. This requirement was recognized by the U.S. Supreme Court in the *Revenge at Daybreak* case [58], decided March 1, 1965. Here, the board did no more than offer the film; it produced no other evidence whatever. "Enlightening testimony" was needed to determine whether a film met constitutional standards, except in the "rare [case of] the exceptional motion picture which not only speaks for itself but screams for all to hear that it is obscene." The court found this film to be "tiresome, boring, cheap, often vulgar, and

sometimes revolting,'' but did ''not feel qualified to say by virtue of a viewing of the picture only [that] the dominant theme of *Lorna* was an appeal to prurient interest, or that the picture exceeded customary limits of candor in its representations of sex or the sexual mores of the community pictured or that it was utterly without redeeming social importance or literary or artistic value.''

1. *Variety*, Aug. 18, 1965.
2. Dunn v. Maryland State Board of Censors, 213 A. 2d 751 (1965).

[58]
Revenge at Daybreak (Desperate Decision)

Banned in Maryland, 1964.

France. U.S., 1954, under the title of *Desperate Decision*. U.S., 1964, re-released under the title *Revenge at Daybreak*. Dist: Times Film Corp. 35mm. Sound. Dubbed in English. Prod: Hoche Production. Dir: Yves Allegret. SW: Jacques Siquard. Cin: Roger Hubert. Cast: Danielle Delorme, Henry Vidal, Nicholas Vogel, Maurice Rouet. Reviews: *New York Herald Tribune*, Nov. 9, 1954, Otis L. Guernsey, Jr.; *New York Times*, Nov. 9, 1954, Bosley Crowther.

The film was adapted from a novel by Catherine Beauchamp. It is set in Dublin at the time of the Anglo-Irish struggle, in 1916, when the Republicans were resisting the Free State movement with guerilla warfare. It is a melodrama of the vengeance taken by a young convent girl for the death of her brother, whom a Republican gang leader brutally executed for informing on their activities. In her search for his murderer, the young girl meets and falls in love with the gang leader, not knowing of his responsibility for her brother's gruesome death. Once she learns of this, she becomes crazed and takes revenge by murdering him.

Censorship Activity
The Maryland censorship statute required that a film must be submitted to, and ''approved and licensed'' by, the state censorship board before it lawfully could be exhibited anywhere in the state. A Baltimore theater exhibitor, in order to test the constitutionality of the statute, ''invited arrest'' by showing this movie without first having submitted it to the board. He was duly arrested and convicted in the Criminal Court of Baltimore. On appeal, the Court of Appeals of Maryland affirmed the lower court's judgment.[1] In doing so, the Court of Appeals noted that ''neither the [exhibitor] nor the State even suggests'' that the movie ''would violate any of the standards set out in the statute, and the State conceded that it would have been

approved had it been submitted for licensing." The court, however, affirmed that the statutory requirement for the licensing by the censorship board of a film before exhibition is "not void on its face and is valid and enforceable." The U.S. Supreme Court, however, reversed.[2]

Legal Importance

This decision, and Justice William J. Brennan, Jr.'s opinion for the Supreme Court, was a landmark in the history of freedom of expression for movies. It established the constitutional framework and the procedural guidelines that constrain censorship boards and law enforcement officers in their movie censorship activities. In the earlier *Don Juan* case [48], the Supreme Court had refused to declare *per se* unconstitutional all governmental systems providing for licensing of films prior to their public exhibition. In the present case, the Court stipulated minimal constitutional standards for every such system. It stated that any "noncriminal process which requires the prior submission of a film to a censor avoids constitutional infirmity only if it takes place under procedural safeguards designed to obviate the dangers of a censorship system." These safeguards were held to include statutory provisions ensuring that: (1) the burden of proving that a film was unprotected expression rested on the censor; (2) while the state might require advance submission of all films, in order to proceed effectively to bar all showings of unprotected films, the requirement could not be administered in a manner which would lend an effect "of finality" to the censor's determination that a film was not constitutionally protected expression. "The teaching of our cases," Justice Brennan wrote, is that, "because only a judicial determination in an adversary proceeding ensures the necessary sensitivity to freedom of expression, only a procedure requiring a judicial determination suffices to impose a valid final restraint." Therefore, the censor must, within a specified brief period, either issue a license or go to court to restrain showing the film; (3) "Any restraint imposed in advance of a final judicial determination on the merits must similarly be limited. . . . Therefore, the procedure must also assure a prompt final judicial decision, to minimize the deterrent effect of an interim and possibly erroneous denial of a license."

Applying these constitutionally required standards to Maryland's censorship scheme led to the judgment that the system was invalid. First, once the censor disapproved the film, the exhibitor had to assume the burden of instituting judicial proceedings and of persuading the courts that the film was protected expression. Second, once the board has acted against a film, exhibition was prohibited pending judicial review, however protracted. Third, the Maryland statute provided "no assurance of prompt judicial determination." Thus, the requirement of prior submission of films to the censorship board was an unconstitutional "prior restraint" on expression. Justice

William O. Douglas, in a concurring opinion joined by Justice Hugo L. Black, repeated his view that *all* such movie censorship systems are unconstitutional. "Movies are entitled to the same degree and kind of protection under the First Amendment as other forms of expression."

1. State v. Freedman, 197 A. 2d 232, 233 Md. 498 (1964).
2. Freedman v. Maryland, 380 U.S. 51 (1965).

[59]
A Stranger Knocks

Banned in New York, 1964; banned in Maryland, 1965.

Denmark, 1963. U.S., 1963. Dist: Trans Lux Film Corp. 81 min. 35mm. Sound. Color. Prod/Dir: Johan Jacobsen. SW: Finn Methling. Cin: Ake Borglund, Johan Jacobsen. Music: Erik Fiehn. English subtitles. Cast: Birgitte Federspiel, Preben Lerdorff. MPAA: A. Reviews: *Daily News*, April 1, 1965, Kathleen Carroll; *New York Herald Tribune*, April 1, 1965, Judith Crist; *New York Times*, April 1, 1965, Bosley Crowther.

On a stormy evening, a woman admits a stranger to her isolated cottage near the sea, unaware that he is a wartime Nazi collaborator fleeing from Danish justice. Due to her lonely life-style, she welcomes his company and responds avidly to his lovemaking. In the course of their sexual intimacies, she discovers that he is the man who tortured and killed her husband during World War II. She struggles to resolve the dilemma presented by her attraction to this ruthless stranger and her desire for retribution.

Censorship Activity
The film was denied licenses for its exhibition in the states of New York and Maryland. In New York, the state board of regents refused to license it on the ground that it was obscene; the New York Supreme Court, Appellate Division, reversed the board's ruling; the New York Court of Appeals reversed the Appellate Division, thereby reinstating the ban.[1] However, the U.S. Supreme Court granted *certiorari* and reversed New York's highest judicial bench, freeing the film for exhibition in the state.[2] In Maryland, the state board of censors disapproved the film for licensing on the ground it was obscene, and this decision was confirmed by the Circuit Court of Baltimore City. On appeal from this decision, the Court of Appeals of Maryland reversed, freeing the film for exhibition in Maryland.[3]

Legal Importance
New York's determination to ban the film was based on the distinction between "thematic obscenity," of the sort held constitutionally protected in

the *Lady Chatterley's Lover* case [43], and "obscenity in filmed behavior." The argument was that just as New York might constitutionally prohibit sexual intercourse in public, so a filmed presentation of sexual intercourse, whether real or simulated, was just as subject to state prohibition. Conceding that the "advocacy" of sexual behavior, or ideas, in a film was constitutionally protected, the Court of Appeals drew what it called "the classic line between advocating something presently against the law and actually doing it," and held that the sexual scenes in this film were "actually doing it." Once it had concluded the film was *conduct* rather than speech, and so unprotected by the constitutional guarantees of free expression, the court found it unnecessary even to apply the "test" for obscenity laid down in the landmark case of *Roth* v. *United States*. That test required that the "dominant theme of the work as a whole" appeal to "prurient interest" in sex. According to the court, "If that requirement were applicable to cases of this nature, the law would be hopeless to cope with the grossest imaginable pornography if it were included in the film as an incidental feature, collateral to the main plot."

The film contained only two scenes considered obscene by the board of regents. As depicted by the court: "The first scene presents a man and a woman on a beach embracing and caressing one another, and ends in a view of the head and shoulders of the woman with facial expressions indicative of orgasmic reaction. The second scene presents the woman astride the man on a bed. Their bodily movements are unmistakably those of the sexual act and the woman's face again registers emotions concededly indicative of orgasm." In his concurring opinion, Chief Judge Charles Desmond said that a determination to let this film be licensed would be "the first court determination in recorded history holding to be nonobscene and constitutionally protected the portrayal on stage or a screen of the very sexual act itself."

The U.S. Supreme Court's reversal of the New York ban on this film was without a written opinion; it simply cited its decision in the *Revenge at Daybreak* case [58], holding that Maryland's film censorship law was procedurally defective and "an invalid prior restraint." As a result of the Supreme Court's action, the New York Court of Appeals declared New York's film censorship law invalid.[4] Although Maryland enacted a new film censorship system designed to meet the Supreme Court's constitutional standards, the New York legislature has not resurrected any film censorship system for its state.

The Maryland censorship took place under the old Maryland law, before the *Revenge at Daybreak* case invalidated that law. The Maryland Court of Appeals reasoned differently than the New York courts when it reversed the state censors' banning of the film. After noting that the board of censors had offered no evidence in the lower court of *any* expert or other opinion indicating that the film was obscene as defined by the U.S. Supreme Court, it held the film was not obscene but rather is "a serious work of art, dealing with a subject of social importance, and does not appeal to prurient interests." Applying the teaching of Justice Brennan in *The Lovers* case [49], the court ruled that the film "may not constitutionally be denied a license for exhibition." It was in the *Revenge at Daybreak* case that the Supreme Court ruled that censor boards had a constitutionally required burden to prove that films they proposed to suppress were of a type that constituted unprotected expression, e.g., were obscene.

1. Trans-Lux Distributing Corp. v. Board of Regents, 248 N.Y.S. 2d 857 (1964).
2. Trans-Lux Distributing Corp. v. Board of Regents, 380 U.S. 259 (1965).
3. Trans-Lux Distributing Corp. v. Maryland State Board of Censors, 213 A. 2d 235 (1965).
4. Trans-Lux Distributing Corp. v. Regents, 209 N.E. 2d 558 (1965).

[60]
The Twilight Girls

Banned in New York, 1964.

France.[1] U.S., 1961. Dist: Audubon Films, Beverly Pictures. 80 min. 35mm. Sound. B&W. Prod: Safia-Sirius-Contact Organization. Dir: André Hunebelle, Radley Metzger (U.S. version). SW: Jacques Lancien, Jean Lambertie. Cin: Ed Jean Feyte. Music: Jean Marion. Cast: Gaby Morlay, Henri Guisol, Paul Guers, Marie-Hélène Arnaud, Christine Carère; (U.S. version) Georgina Spelvin.

Enrolled in boarding school, Catherine Royer falls in love with a young composer named Dean, thus incurring the jealousy of her friend Monica. After Monica nearly destroys the love affair, Catherine becomes seriously ill. Monica's guilt is too much for her and she patches up the lovers' relationship. Then the headmistress of the school talks to Monica about understanding the depth of emotions that a girl may experience as she grows into womanhood.

Censorship Activity

The New York board of regents refused to issue a license for the exhibition of this film unless certain scenes involving nudity and lesbianism, which it alleged were obscene, were eliminated. On review, the state supreme court, Appellate Division, annulled the board's determination and directed that a license be granted.² The objectionable parts of the movie did not, in the court's opinion, "constitute an appeal to the prurient interest in violation of the statute." The New York Court of Appeals affirmed the lower court's order.³

Legal Importance

The Court of Appeals' memorandum opinion simply cited the *Garden of Eden* case [40], *The Lovers* case [49], and the case of *Manual Enterprises* v. *Day*,⁴ in which the U.S. Supreme Court permitted the mailing of magazines which "consist largely of nude, or near-nude, male models," and which "cannot be deemed so offensive on their face as to affront current community standards of decency" or, as the Court labeled it, to be "patently offensive."

1. This film was originally released in France in 1957, as *Les Collégiennes*, with a running time of 88 minutes. The director of the U.S. version, Radley Metzger, cut sequences from the original version and added scenes involving sex and nudity, which he himself filmed and which featured the actress Georgina Spelvin (*American Film Institute Catalog of Motion Pictures: Feature Films 1961-1970*, edited by Richard Krafsur. New York: Bowker, 1976).
2. Metzger v. Couper, 252 N.Y.S. 2d 427 (1964).
3. Metzger v. Couper, 205 N.E. 2d 694 (1965).
4. Manual Enterprises v. Day, 378 U.S. 184 (1962).

[61]
The Bedford Incident

Attempted banning in Kansas, 1965.

U.S., 1965. Dist: Columbia Pictures. 102 min. 35mm. Sound. B&W. Prod: James B. Harris, Richard Widmark; Beford Production, Ltd. Dir: James B. Harris. SW: James Poe. Cin: Gilbert Taylor. Cast: Richard Widmark, Sidney Poitier, James MacArthur, Martin Balsam. Reviews: *Variety*, Oct. 13, 1965, Murf.; *Box Office*, Oct. 18, 1965; *Time*, Oct. 29, 1965; *Cue*, Nov. 4, 1965. Articles: *New York World Telegram*, Oct. 30, 1965, Leonard Harris; *Hollywood Reporter*, Aug. 8, 1967.

Adapted from the novel by Mark Rascovich, this is the story of a tenacious American destroyer captain in the North Atlantic during the Cold War. Feared but never questioned by his crew, the captain stalks a Russian submarine until his men are at the breaking point. Under the strain, a young ensign unwittingly fires a nuclear missile at the sub. The film ends with the certain knowledge that, before being hit, the Russian sub fired its own missiles at the American ship.

Censorship Activity/Legal Importance

For a legal analysis of the case in which this film was involved, see *Bunny Lake Is Missing* [62].

[62]
Bunny Lake Is Missing

Attempted banning in Kansas, 1965.

U.K., 1965. U.S., 1965. Dist: Columbia Pictures. 107 min. 35mm. Sound. Color. Prod/Dir: Otto Preminger. SW: John Mortimer, Penelope Mortimer. Cin: Denys Coop. Cast: Carol Lynley, Keir Dullea, Laurence Olivier, Noel Coward. Reviews: *New York Times*, Oct. 4, 1965; *Variety*, Oct. 6, 1965; *Box Office*, Oct. 18, 1965; *Newsweek*, Oct. 18, 1965. Article: *Film Daily*, July 1, 1965, Halsey Reines.

This film was adapted from the novel by Evelyn Piper. A young American unwed mother travels to London to join her brother. After only a cursory survey, she enrolls her young daughter in a British day school. But when she returns for the child that night, no one recalls having seen her. The police are called in, but all leads prove futile. Finally, the young woman stumbles upon the fact that her own brother has drugged the child and is about to strangle her. The young woman saves the child by playing children's games with her brother until the police arrive.

Censorship Activity

Seven months after the U.S. Supreme Court invalidated Maryland's motion picture licensing law in the *Revenge at Daybreak* case [58], Columbia Pictures, the distributor of this film, informed the Kansas censorship board that it would no longer submit to the board movies intended for exhibition in the state. On the assumption that the standards announced in that case rendered the Kansas censorship statute unconstitutional, the distributor showed this film and another, *The Bedford Incident* [61], at various theaters throughout Kansas without first submitting it to the board and receiving its certificate of approval. The state attorney general brought suit in Shawnee District Court to prevent the distributor from "selling, leasing, exhibiting or using" films such as these without first obtaining the board of censors' permission. Judge Marion Beatty instead held that the system of censorship, created by the Kansas statute, was an unconstitutional abridgment of freedom of expression, and enjoined the board of censors from enforcing any of the statute's provisions. On appeal, the Supreme Court of Kansas affirmed, holding the state motion picture censorship law to be unconstitutional. [1]

Legal Importance

The state censorship act procedures ran afoul the guidelines laid down in the *Revenge at Daybreak* case in the following respects: the exhibitor was assigned the burden of proving that the film was protected, whereas constitutional standards required the censor to bear the burden of proving the film was unprotected expression; exhibition of the film was prevented pending judicial review, however protracted, of the censors' decision; and a prompt final judicial decision was not assured. The Kansas law simply did not provide "adequate procedural safeguards against undue inhibition of protected expression." The legal requirement of submitting films to the board before being shown was therefore an "invalid previous restraint" that violated the First and Fourteenth Amendments to the United States Constitution. In a futile effort to bring its procedures within constitutional requirements, the board had adopted regulations based on the *Revenge at Daybreak* case. In that way, the court recognized, the board had "attempted to cure constitutional defects" in the act. But "the lawmaking power of this state," Judge Fatzer pointed out, "is vested in the legislature and the board cannot breathe life into a statute by rules and regulations. If the legislature desires to adopt the policy of complying with procedural safeguards declared in [the *Revenge at Daybreak* case,] it should incorporate those requirements in a bill."

1. State *ex rel.* Londerholm v. Columbia Pictures Corporation, 417 P. 2d 255 (1966).

[63]
The Dirty Girls

Banned in Maryland, 1965.

U.S., 1965. Dist: Audubon Films. 82 min. 35mm. Sound. B&W. Prod/Dir: Radley Metzger. SW: Peter Fernandez. Cin: Roger Duculot. Cast: Reine Rohan, Denise Roland, Madeleine Constant, Marlene Sherter, Peter Parten.

This film concerns a variety of sexual escapades engaged in by two prostitutes, Monique, a wealthy call girl from Munich, and Garance, who walks the streets of Paris. The sexual encounters include a shy young student, a sadist, a masochist, an American businessman, a movie star, and a lesbian.

Censorship Activity

Solely on the basis of a viewing of this film, a Baltimore circuit court judge upheld the Maryland censorship board's disapproval of it for exhibition. On appeal, the Maryland Court of Appeals reversed, holding that the trial judge's viewing the film did not, in itself, qualify him to determine that the motion picture was obscene under the state statute.[1]

Legal Importance

The state censorship board "did no more to meet the burden of proof of obscenity which the statute imposed on it than to offer the picture to the city court." The highest court of Maryland held that the board should have, but did not, show by appropriate probative testimony that the film met the U.S. Supreme Court's definition of obscenity, i.e., (a) that the average person, applying community standards, would find the dominant theme of the picture, taken as a whole, appeals to the prurient interest; (b) that the picture goes substantially beyond customary limits of candor in description or representation of sex or other matters; and (c) that it is "subject to proscription because it is utterly without redeeming social importance considered in light of the fact that '. . . sex and obscenity are not synonymous.' " It was in the *Revenge at Daybreak* case [58] that the U.S. Supreme Court determined that a state motion picture censorship board must bear the burden of proving that a film that it proposed not to license was "unprotected expression."

The film had been passed by censors in New York and Detroit, and had been exhibited routinely in some 50 cities, including Boston, New York, Richmond, Winston-Salem, Miami, Cleveland, Detroit, Little Rock, Nashville, Los Angeles, San Francisco, Portland, and Seattle.

1. Leighton v. Maryland State Board of Censors, 218 A. 2d 179 (1966).

[64]
The Unsatisfied (Juventud a la Intemperie)

Banned in New York, 1965.

Spain, 1961. U.S., 1964. Dist: Cambist Films. 89 min. 35mm. Sound. B&W. Prod: I.F.I. España, Ignacio F. Iquino; Lee Hessel (U.S. version). Dir: Ignacio F. Iquino. SW: Federico de Urrutia. Cin: Ricardo Albinana. Music: Enrique Escobar. Cast: Rita Cadillac, Colette Descombes, Maria del Sol, Angela Tamayo, Fernando Leon, Julian Mateos.

Bernardo, with the help of liquor and drugs, is successful at conducting crooked card games. He is tricked into arranging for the death of Suzanne, who is paid to bring wealthy men to his castle for gambling. Suzanne's lover is arrested for the murder, but he escapes and tracks down a member of Bernardo's gang, who confesses and informs on Bernardo.

Censorship Activity

After reviewing this film, New York State censors refused to issue a license unless allegedly obscene portions were eliminated. When the distributor brought suit to compel the issuance of a license, the censors counterclaimed, seeking a judicial declaration that the movie was obscene and not entitled to be licensed, and that its rules and the state film censorship statute were constitutional. On appeal, the state supreme court, Special Term (trial court), denied the relief requested by the film's distributor, but declared both the censors' official procedures and the obscenity censorship statute unconstitutional.[1]

Legal Importance

The court based its judgment and opinion on the U.S. Supreme Court's decision in the *Revenge at Daybreak* case [58], in which it was held that (1) the censor must bear the burden of instituting judicial proceedings to suppress a film; (2) any restraint on the exhibition of a film prior to a final judicial determination on the merits must be "limited to the preservation of the status quo for the shortest fixed period" possible; and (3) the procedure "must assure a prompt final judicial decision." Inasmuch as the state's licensing scheme lacked "these safeguards," the court concluded that "no valid licensing system of motion pictures now exists in New York." Since the statute and the procedural rules promulgated under it were unconstitutional, the court further decided it had "no jurisdiction" to entertain an action to declare the film obscene.

On the other hand, the court also refused to accept the distributor's argument that a license was required to be issued to show the film because, as the Supreme Court had decided in the *Don Juan* case [48], a state requirement of film licensing is not *per se* unconstitutional. The court reasoned that to require the censors to issue a license would not only make the granting of a license a *pro forma* "ministerial" duty, on the part of the censors, but would oblige the court "to impel approval" of a motion picture deemed obscene by the board of regents. The film's distributor was deliberately left free "to enter the marketplace," as with "other forms of expression, subject to the appropriate penal statutes and independent determinations on the question of the obscenity of their motion pictures." This, the court pointed out, was the same legal situation as the one that faced the distributor in the *A Stranger Knocks* case [59], where the refusal of New York censors to license that movie was invalidated by the U.S. Supreme Court because the New York censorship law failed to conform to the constitutional standards laid down in the *Revenge at Daybreak* case. Following that Supreme Court decision, the New York Court of Appeals declared "null and void" the New York censorship law, invalidated in the present case by an inferior court. The Court of Appeals' action was taken one month after the decision in the present case.

1. Cambist Films v. Board of Regents, 260 N.Y.S. 2d 804 (1965).

[65]
Un Chant d'Amour

Banned in Berkeley, California, 1966.

France, 1950. U.S., 1964. Dist: Film-Maker's Cooperative. 26 min. 35mm. Silent. B&W. Prod/Dir/SW: Jean Genet. Cin: Jacques Natteau. Reviews: *Village Voice*, Dec. 10, 1964, Jonas Mekas; *Variety*, April 21, 1971.

Set in a Paris prison and having no sound track, *Un Chant d'Amour* is the celebrated French author Jean Genet's only film. Reflecting his experience in prison, the film centers on an affair between two men living in separate cells. Various shots of these and other homosexual inmates "contain some frontal nudity and some depiction of homosexual activity. . . ."[1] A California court, having viewed the film twice, found that it "explicitly and vividly revealed acts of masturbation, oral copulation, the infamous crime against nature [sodomy], voyeurism, nudity, sadism, masochism and sex. . . ." A California appellate court, three justices dissenting, concluded it "is nothing more than hard-core pornography and should be banned." This court's opinion contains an unusually elaborate description of the film.

Censorship Activity
After Saul Landau sought to exhibit this film in Berkeley, California, the director of the special investigations bureau of the city's police department told him that the next time it was shown, "it would be confiscated and all persons responsible arrested." The exhibitor brought suit to show the film without police interference. After viewing the movie twice, Judge George W. Phillips, Jr., of the Alameda County Superior Court concluded it was obscene. On appeal, the District Court of Appeal of California (three justices dissenting) affirmed the lower court's judgment.[2] A bare majority of the U.S. Supreme Court, without stating its reasons, affirmed the judgment condemning the film, with Justices Black, Douglas, Stewart, and Fortas noting that they would have reversed.

Legal Importance

The "only question" that the District Court of Appeal considered to be before it was whether the film was obscene. After viewing it, Justice Taylor, writing for the court majority, said it "goes far beyond customary limits of candor in offensively depicting certain unorthodox sexual practices and relationships. . . . Because of the nature of the medium, we think a motion picture of sexual scenes may transcend the bounds of the constitutional guarantee [of free expression] long before a frank description of the same scenes in the written word. We cannot here disregard the potent visual impact of the movie in [various sexual acts] without any clear reference or relation to a dominant theme." Portending to apply the criteria for identifying obscenity established by the U.S. Supreme Court in *Roth* v. *United States, Mishkin* v. *New York*, and *Jacobellis* v. *Ohio*, the court concluded that the "predominant appeal of the film taken as a whole is to the prurient interest," and is obscene.

The court declined to find "any matter of social importance (including artistic merit)" in the picture, which might constitutionally redeem it and guarantee freedom for its expression. The fact that Jean Genet, "a French writer of renown," wrote, directed, and produced the film did not settle the question for the court. The court maintained that even "great artists can create the type of 'hard core' pornography proscribed by our statute," and quoted one of the exhibitor's own expert witnesses as saying the film was "a transitional work in Genet's development from a novelist into a dramatist" and was not "easily recognizable" as one of his works. The lack of an accompanying text or dialogue contributed to the film's "ambiguity and the absence of a dominant theme." Finding no discernible plot, "particular story line," or "character development" in the film, the court characterized it as a "failure." The "erotic scenes recur with increasing intensity and without direction toward any well-defined, wholesome idea, through scene after scene. The various sexual acts are graphically pictured or emphatically suggested with nothing omitted except those sexual consummations which are plainly suggested but meaningfully omitted and thus by the very fact of omission emphasized. If the film was intended as an artistic portrayal, it clearly failed in its endeavor."[3]

The California appellate court claimed it had reached its conclusion that the film was obscene (actually "hard-core pornography") partly on the basis of the constitutional principle announced by the Supreme Court in *The Lovers* case [49]—that a work "cannot be proscribed unless it is 'utterly' without social importance." It is difficult to understand how a film created by the writer Jean Genet, concerned with the enforced homosexuality of prison life, could be found obscene in the sense of being "utterly without social importance." The case is interesting also for the recorded fact that Supreme Court Justice William Brennan voted to uphold the film's suppression, despite his authorship of the quoted principle from *The Lovers* case. In no other obscenity case can he be found voting on the side opposed to the views of his brethren, Justices Black, Douglas, Stewart, and Fortas.

1. *Variety*, April 2, 1971.
2. Landau v. Fording, 245 Cal. App. 2d 820 (1966).
3. Landau v. Fording, 388 U.S. 456 (1967).

[66]
This Picture Is Censored (Censored)

Banned in Maryland, 1966.

U.S., 1966. Dist: Cinema Syndicate, Inc. 61 min. 35mm. Sound. B&W. Prod: Barry Mahon Productions. Dir: Barry Mahon. Cin: Rick Carrier.

Various film clips, which had to be cut out of sex films in order to pass censorship restrictions, are presented by Sid Berry, lecturer and critic. The clips show women dressing and undressing, cavorting in a nudist camp, acting as artists' and photographers' models, and being seduced, assaulted, tortured, and dismembered.

Censorship Activity

When the distributor of this film applied to the Maryland board of censors for a license to show it, the board denied the license on the ground the film was obscene and petitioned the Circuit Court of Baltimore for an order upholding the board's determination. The judge who took the case requested the full panel of petit jurors (25 in number) assigned to his court to view the film in the censorship board's offices and give evidence of whether it was obscene, saying their opinions would "be given great weight." The distributor's objections to this unprecedented method of securing "expert" evidence were overruled, and the court found the film obscene. On review, the Court of Appeals of Maryland reversed the trial court's decision and remanded the matter for a new trial.[1] At the film's second trial, the circuit court again found the film obscene. On appeal, this ruling was reversed and the film was held to be constitutionally protected.[2]

Legal Importance

The irregular procedure used by the trial court, without notice or opportunity for participation by counsel in the procedure, was reversible error. The jurors' "evidence" was inadmissible; it was not the province of the trial judge to procure and present evidence needed by the board to prove that the film in question was obscene. In passing, the appellate court observed that while the film, which it viewed, contained "a most generous display of the female epidermis, both fore and aft, the whole thing is about as titillating and exciting as a ton of coal."

On remand, the trial court took testimony from an assortment of persons, most of whom were deemed by the court of appeals, on review, not qualified experts on the subject matter of their testimony—whether the film was or was not obscene. Those witnesses included a probation officer supervisor, an officer of the American Legion, a rabbi, an ordained congregational minister, and a consultant to the Baltimore juvenile courts. Witnesses considered qualifiable as experts were a journalist, a moving picture critic, a drama and movie critic, and the head of a college English department.

The appellate court decided that in cases of this type it had the duty itself to scrutinize closely the trial court's rulings with respect to so-called expert witnesses, and, as declared by Justice Brennan in the landmark case of *The Lovers* [49],[3] to make "an independent judgment on the facts of the case as to whether the material involved is constitutionally protected." As the second circuit federal court of appeals said in *United States* v. *Klaw*,[4] "the various agencies, officers, judges and juries that initially find material 'obscene' do not have the last word on the matter. Rather, the Supreme Court has left no doubt that any abnegation of judicial supervision in the 'obscenity' field would be inconsistent with its duty to uphold constitutional guarantees." Thus a trial judge's rulings of "obscenity" must be assessed on appeal not merely in terms of "whether he has, or has not, abused his discretion, or that he is in error as to the law," but in light of their "objective correctness." In short, the question of whether a book or film is obscene, or constitutionally protected, can be considered *de novo* by each higher court. The correctness of this holding by the Maryland Court of Appeals received confirmation some years later, when in the *Carnal Knowledge* case [105] the U.S. Supreme Court substituted its judgment for that reached by a Georgia criminal jury that the movie *Carnal Knowledge* was obscene.

The Maryland high court reversed the trial court and decided that *This Picture Is Censored* was not obscene but was, instead, constitutionally protected, on the ground that the film's anticensorship message could not be held to be "utterly without social importance." For the Supreme Court, in the above-mentioned *The Lovers* case and in the case of *Memoirs* v. *Massachusetts*,[5] had insisted that a book or film had to be "unqualifiedly worthless," without even a "modicum of social value," before it could be deemed obscene from a constitutional standpoint. When the testimony of the "experts" produced by the censor board at trial was reviewed in the light of these legal principles, the appellate court decided it "supported, not the finding of the trial judge, but a finding that the film is not *utterly without redeeming social value,*" as claimed by its exhibitor. A final note of importance: the appellate court found that the fact that the film's producer (who testified at the trial) had used "copies" or "reenactments" of the excised portions of the censored films (instead of the actual film cuts themselves), did not destroy the film's "redeeming social value." The producer testified that such "recreation of scenes in documentary films is 'fairly standard practice' and the use of actual scenes would have greatly increased the costs of production, because of the copyright problems involved."

1. Hewitt v. Maryland State Board of Censors, 216 A. 2d 557 (1966).
2. Hewitt v. Maryland State Board of Censors, 221 A. 2d 894 (1966).
3. Jacobellis v. Ohio, 378 U.S. 184 (1964).
4. United States v. Klaw, 350 F. 2d 155 (1965).
5. Memoirs v. Massachusetts, 383 U.S. 413 (1966).

[67]
Viva Maria

Banned for minors in Dallas, Texas, 1966.

France, 1965. Italy, 1965. U.S., 1965. Dist: United Artists. 119 min. 35mm. Sound. Color. English subtitles. Prod: Nouvelles Editions de Films—Les Productions Artistes Associés, S.A. (Paris); Vides Cinematografica (Rome); Louis Malle, Oscar Dancigers. Dir: Louis Malle. SW: Louis Malle, Jean-Claude Carrière. Cin: Henri Decae. Cast: George Hamilton, Jeanne Moreau, Brigitte Bardot, Paulette Dubost, Gregor Von Rezzori, Poldo Bendandi, Claudio Brook, Carlos Lopez Moctezuma. Awards: Grand Prix du Cinéma Français. Reviews: *New York Daily News*, Dec. 20, 1965, Wanda Hale; *Hollywood Reporter*, Dec. 20, 1965, James Powers; *New York Times*, Dec. 20, 1965, Bosley Crowther; *Independent*, Dec. 25, 1965; *Motion Picture Herald*, Jan. 5, 1966, Sy Oshinsky; *Life*, Jan. 28, 1966, Richard Schickel.

As British soldiers cross a bridge to close in on her wounded Irish anarchist father, Maria Fitzgerald O'Malley blows the bridge apart, with tears in her eyes. Fleeing, she stows away with a troupe of traveling players, is taken up by an older, worldly dancer also named Maria, inadvertently invents the striptease, and becomes the toast of the small, poor country of San Miguel, learning the ways of liquor and love. Having seen the few powerful men of San Miguel exploit the country's people, Maria O'Malley furiously shoots one looter of a marauding band, and the troupe is captured by evil Don Rodriguez. While imprisoned at the don's hacienda, the two Marias are attracted to Flores, the young, handsome leader of the country's revolt, who is bound with his arms tied to a wooden yoke across his shoulders. That night, having fallen for Flores, the more experienced, yet more romantic, Maria makes love to the chained leader while he is unable to move. The next morning, taken to Rodriguez for his pleasure before disposing of them, the two women destroy his magnificent salon, Maria O'Malley cutting loose with a captured machine gun. They escape the hacienda with the prisoners led by Flores. However, as Flores, shot in the fight, soon dies, the older Maria vows to lead the revolt in his place. The two raid and destroy the hacienda, leaving Rodriguez crawling through the brush in his underwear. With success after success, the older Maria leads the growing revolution and the two Marias are hailed as the country's saviors—until they are captured by San Miguel's billiard-playing president. Facing the firing squad, the two Marias are rescued by their revolutionary followers, who have just captured the country's capital, and, with a great celebration, are sent on their way to France. There, dancing with the troupe for the wealthy elite of Orleans, the two Marias take up again their explosive, revolutionary ways.

Censorship Activity

Pursuant to a Dallas ordinance, a Motion Picture Classification Board classified this film as "not suitable for young persons," and a county court enjoined the film's exhibition without the exhibitors complying with the requirements prohibiting any person under 16 from attending the film without an accompanying parent or guardian. The classification was upheld as constitutional by the Texas Court of Appeals,[1] but voided because of vagueness by the U.S. Supreme Court.[2]

Legal Importance

The Supreme Court held that legislation regulating the access of minors to movie expression, like that regulating the access of adults, must be clearly drawn and reasonably precise "so that those who are governed by the law and those who administer it will understand its meaning and application." While a state may refuse to juveniles access to expressive materials that could not constitutionally be denied to adults, the regulation as to juveniles must be "narrowly drawn, reasonable and definite." The law in question spoke of the "portrayal . . . of sexual promiscuity as acceptable" being "obscene to minors," and required any film presenting such a portrayal to be classified as "unsuitable for minors." Such "vague standards, unless narrowed by interpretation, encourage erratic administration whether the censor be administrative or judicial . . . individual impressions become the yardstick of action and result in regulation in accordance with the beliefs of the individual censor rather than regulation by law."

1. Interstate Circuit v. Dallas, 402 S.W. 2d 770 (1966).
2. Interstate Circuit v. Dallas, 391 U.S. 53 (1968).

[68]
A Woman's Urge

Banned in Michigan, 1966.

Origin unknown. U.S., 1965. Dist: Crest Film Distributors, Sam Lake Enterprises. 83 min. 35mm. Sound. B&W. Prod: Ed Hall, A. C. Qamar. Dir: Ed Hall. Cast: Maude Ferguson, Ed Hall, Lauree Ringham, Jack Cranston.

A suicidal young woman sees a psychiatrist and flashes back on her sexually obsessed life, beginning with her drunken stepfather and moving on to a string of her conquests. These include the owner of a nightclub where she works first as a waitress, then as a featured dancer, and a photographer for whom she models and whom she seduces, vainly aspiring to a stable relationship. A weekend with a lesbian makes her more frantic and frustrated. Will the psychiatrist be able to cure her nymphomania? "The film deals with a seemingly oversexed woman."[1]

Censorship Activity

Grand Rapids, Michigan policemen and other officials went with "professors from Calvin and Acquinas Colleges" to see this movie, and reported their impressions to a prosecuting attorney. Later, members of the police vice squad bought tickets and saw the movie in its entirety, after which they proceeded to arrest the theater's projectionist as he rewound the film. Incidentally to this arrest and without a warrant, the police seized the film, which was in due course introduced in evidence at the criminal trial of the theater's manager (Bloss) despite his objection that the seizure violated the constitutional prohibition against "unreasonable searches and seizures" (Fourth Amendment). Convicted for showing an obscene motion picture, the exhibitor unsuccessfully appealed to the Court of Appeals of Michigan, which affirmed his conviction.[2] However, a petititon for writ of *certiorari* to the U.S. Supreme Court proved successful, and the conviction was reversed.[3]

Legal Importance

The Michigan Court of Appeals probably erred in ruling that the film was not seized unconstitutionally because it is settled that a *judicial* officer should determine, through an adversary hearing held *before* any seizure, the likelihood that a film, suspected by police (or others) of being obscene, is obscene. This is a special rule applicable to searches and seizures not of ordinary "contraband" such as guns, stolen goods, gambling equipment, and drugs, but of "expressive" materials, presumptively protected by the First Amendment, including books and films. However, this argument was not ruled upon by the United States Supreme Court.

The main issue was whether the film was properly deemed obscene and not protected in its circulation by the constitutional guarantees of free expression, applying the test for obscenity laid down by the Supreme Court in such cases as *Roth* v. *United States*,[4] *Memoirs* v. *Massachusetts*,[5] and *The Lovers* case [49]. In its application of that three-pronged test, the Michigan court "took into consideration not just the content of the film but also the . . . visual impact of seeing [the occurrences] acted out in a darkened room with sound accompaniment," relying on the *Un Chant d'Amour* case [65] for support for this "tightening" of the test of what is obscene. Evidently, the Michigan court misconstrued the meaning of the Supreme Court's *Un Chant d'Amour* decision, for the latter court, in a *per curiam* opinion, reversed the exhibitor's conviction for showing the movie, giving no reason for its action other than a citation to the decisions it had handed down in the cases known as *Redrup* v. *New York*.[6] Those cases had been interpreted to mean that only material that was hard-core pornography or directed at "juveniles" or "unconsenting adults" could be found unprotected by the free press guaranties and obscene.

1. Michigan v. Bloss, 171 N.W. 2d 455 (1969).
2. Michigan v. Bloss, 171 N.W. 2d 455 (1969).
3. Michigan v. Bloss, 402 U.S. 938 (1971).
4. Roth v. United States, 354 U.S. 476 (1957).
5. Memoirs v. Massachusetts, 383 U.S. 413 (1966).
6. Redrup v. New York, 386 U.S. 767 (1967).

[69]
Body of a Female

Banned in Chicago, Illinois, 1967.

U.S., 1965. U.S. Dist: Joseph Brenner Associates. 71 min. 35mm. Sound. B&W. Prod: Amlay Pictures, J. Ellsworth, Julian Marsh. Dir: J. Ellsworth, Julian Marsh. SW: Francis Ellie. Cin: Douglas Fenway, John Firth. Cast: Anna Riva, Lem Amero, Robert West.

Bruno, a drifter, is hired by wealthy, depraved Spencer to deliver a young stripper named Cindy to Spencer's New England mansion. Once there, Cindy willingly remains, with the promise of money, to perform her strip act in private for Spencer. During the act, he can barely stop himself from his intense desire to whip her. When Spencer later leaves to go into town, Bruno returns, hoping to see Cindy once more. The housekeeper tells Bruno what she observed, including her employer's obsession. Bruno finds Cindy swimming naked, but she runs into the house before he can warn her of the danger. Spencer returns, sees Cindy naked, ties her up, and whips her, but

Bruno rushes in and rescues her. The two escape to a deserted beach where Spencer finds them. In the confrontation that follows, Bruno drowns Spencer.

Censorship Activity

The Chicago censorship board refused to grant a license for the exhibition of this film and another entitled *Rent-a-Girl* [73]. On review, the Circuit Court of Cook County permanently enjoined the distributor from showing it in public places in the city. The Supreme Court of Illinois affirmed the lower court order,[1] saying: "[O]ur examination of these films shows that they deal not merely with sex, but with sexual deviations which can only appeal to those with a shameful and morbid interest in nudity and sex. . . . [T]he producers have apparently spared no effort to see that the spectator searching for the erotic is not disappointed." It "clearly go[es] beyond the customary limits of candor in this country." The U.S. Supreme Court, however, reversed the Illinois Supreme Court.[2]

Legal Importance

The Chicago motion picture censorship ordinance was held unconstitutional on its face and as applied to these films by the U.S. Supreme Court. In its opinion the Court stated that the ordinance violated the standards announced in the *Revenge at Daybreak* case [58] in two respects. First, the 50 to 57 days provided by the ordinance to complete the administrative process before the initiation of the judicial proceeding did not satisfy the constitutional requirement that the procedure assure that the censor will, within a specified brief period, either issue a license or go to court to restrain showing the film. Second, the absence of any provision for a prompt judicial decision by the trial court violated the requirement that the censorship procedure also assure a prompt final judicial decision, to minimize the deterrent effect of an interim and possibly erroneous denial of a license.

1. Cusack v. Teitel Film Corp., 230 N.E. 2d 241 (1967).
2. Teitel Film Corp. v. Cusack, 390 U.S. 139 (1968).

[70]
I, a Woman

Banned in Indiana and Kentucky, 1967.

Sweden, 1965. Denmark, 1965. U.S., 1966. Dist: Nordisk Film (Denmark), Audubon Films (U.S.). 90 min. 35mm. Sound. B&W. Dubbed in English. Prod: Novaris, Nordisk Film (Denmark), AB Europa Film (Sweden). Dir/Cin: Mac Ahlberg. SW: Peer Guldbrandsen. Cast: Essy Persson, Jorgens

Reenberg, Preben Mahrt, Bengt Brunskog, Frankie Steele. Reviews: *Variety*, Sept. 29, 1965, Kell.; *New York Times*, Oct. 12, 1966, Howard Thompson; *Box Office*, Dec. 12, 1966. Articles: *New York Times*, Aug. 10, Oct. 10, 1967; *Motion Picture Daily*, Oct. 2, 1969; *New York Daily News*, March 24, 1970.

This film was adapted from a best-selling novel by Siv Holm. A sensual young nurse, about to leave her impotent boyfriend and very religious parents, is awaiting the arrival of the chance acquaintance with whom she has made a date; she fantasizes about her past sexual encounters. She recalls her former sweetheart, a wealthy patient who seduced her during her nurse's training, a sailor, and a surgeon, the last two having hoped to marry her. She realizes that she enjoys sex too much to devote herself to any one man. In the end, she laughs at her new visitor, who proves to be her male sexual counterpart. *Variety* said: "The stable of Swedish and Danish actors . . . just stumble along, in and out of beds and dialogue. Only Essy Persson, who makes her bow in pictures with this one, seems happily unaware of the surrounding banality. She plays her role with vigor and talent, radiating sex and displaying an often-exposed body." Vincent Canby said the film, "a rather sober-sided Scandinavian tale of nympho-mania, with a good deal of nudity, has become one of the surprise hits of the current season." Purchased for "under $25,000," the film was expected to earn "more than $1 million" (*New York Times*, Oct. 10, 1967). Two sequels to this film, entitled *I, a Woman—II* and *I, a Woman—III*, were produced and released in Denmark and Sweden in 1968 and 1970, and released in the United States in 1969 and 1970.

Censorship Activity

Copies of this film were seized on October 25, 1967 in both Marion County and Indianapolis, Indiana, by police officers, after being shown at drive-in theaters located there. The seizures and the arrests of four persons concerned in the film's exhibition were carried out without judicial warrants. When criminal prosecutions were begun, the municipal court of Marion County ordered that the county sheriff or the Indianapolis police retain the films. The distributor's lawyer was allowed to possess a copy of the movie "for viewing by proposed or intended witnesses," but it was "required to be returned immediately upon demand." On the same day that the municipal court issued its order, a federal district court granted the distributor a temporary injunction and ordered the county prosecutor and the sheriff to refrain from interfering with the movie's exhibition and to return the film to its distributor, retaining one copy only for their use in connection with the pending criminal trials. On appeal, the federal court of appeals for the Seventh Circuit affirmed the federal district court's judgment.[1]

The U.S. Customs Bureau had not interfered with the film entering the country. It had been licensed for exhibition by the Maryland censorship board and shown in that state. A Chicago motion picture censorship board had approved the movie with four deletions, which also had been made in the film shown in Indianapolis and Marion County, Indiana. In cases that arose in Boston, Massachusetts, Hartford, Connecticut, Providence, Rhode Island, and Memphis, Tennessee, the picture had been found not obscene. The criminal conviction of an exhibitor in Kentucky for showing this movie was overturned, without the issuance of any written opinion, by the U.S. Supreme Court on March 23, 1970.[2]

Legal Importance

The police ban on this film in Indiana was overturned not on the ground that the film was not obscene—this issue not being reached—but on the ground that constitutional procedural requirements were not met by the action in seizing the film and preventing its exhibition. A 1964 U.S. Supreme Court decision[3] established that a prior adversary judicial hearing, focusing on the issue of obscenity, is required before law enforcement officers can seize allegedly obscene material. Applying the principle of that case, the court here ruled that "allegedly obscene publications or movies are not to be treated the same way as narcotics, gambling paraphernalia, and other contraband," and that the seizure of copies of this film, without a hearing, was unconstitutional.

1. Metzger v. Pearcy, 393 F. 2d 202 (1968).
2. Cain v. Kentucky, 397 U.S. 1081 (1970).
3. A Quantity of Copies of Books v. Kansas, 378 U.S. 205 (1964).

[71]
I Am Curious—Yellow

Banned from entry into the United States; banned in Alabama, Arizona, California, Colorado, Georgia, Kansas, Maryland, Massachusetts, Michigan, New Jersey, New Mexico, Ohio, Pennsylvania, Virginia, and Washington, 1968–1971.

Sweden, 1967. U.S., 1968. Dist: Grove Press. 120 min. 35mm. Sound. B&W. English subtitles. Prod: Sandrew, Evergreen, Goran Lindgren. Dir/SW: Vilgot Sjöman. Cin: Peter Wester. Cast: Lena Nyman, Borje Ahlstedt, Peter Lindgren. MPAA: X. Reviews: *Variety*, Nov. 1, 1967, Fred.; *Box Office*, March 10, 1969; *New York Times*, March 11, 1969, Vincent Canby; *Washington Post*, March 11, 1969, Leroy Aarons; *Cue*, March 15, 1969; *New Republic*, March 15, 1969, Stanley Kauffmann. Articles: *New York Times*, Jan. 19, 1967; *Holiday*, Dec. 1968, Richard Atcheson; *Newsweek*, Dec. 9,

1968; *New York Times*, May 21, 24, Nov. 27, 1968, Edward Ranzal; *New York Times*, Feb. 9, 1969, John Simon; *London Financial Times*, March 7, 1969, James Price; *Time*, March 14, May 30, 1969; *Saturday Review*, March 15, May 10, 1969, Hollis Alpert; *New York*, March 17, 23, Nov. 13, 26, 1969, Judith Crist; *Life*, March 21, 1969; *Newsweek*, March 24, 1969, Joseph Morgenstern; *New Leader*, March 31, 1969, John Simon; *Variety*, April 9, 1969, Morry Roth; *Christian Science Monitor*, April 16, 1969; *Film Daily*, April 16, 1969, Jay Lewis; *Cosmopolitan*, May 1969, Liz Smith; *Playboy*, May 1969, Bruce Williamson; *Saturday Review*, May 10, 1969, Hollis Alpert; *Commonweal*, May 23, 1969; *Time*, May 30, 1969; *Harper's Bazaar*, June 1969, Gerri Trotta; *National Review*, July 29, 1969, Richard Corliss; *Box Office*, Oct. 13, 1969; *New York Times*, Nov. 13, 1969; *Box Office*, Nov. 24, 1969; *New York Times*, Nov. 26, 1969; *New York Times*, March 9, 1971; *Variety*, March 10, 22, 1971; *Variety*, March 22, 1972.

Lena, an aspiring young actress making a movie for director Vilgot Sjöman while being his lover, is intensely and provocatively inquisitive, demanding and implementing new solutions to the social, political, and sexual problems that trouble her and Swedish society in the 1960s. She demonstrates against the Vietnam War outside the American embassy and interviews Stockholm citizens, union members, and returning tourists, insisting upon answers to questions that tend to accuse the persons asked. She imagines a national policy of nonviolence, "talks" to civil rights leader Martin Luther King, Jr., and desperately fantasizes about her unhappy relations with a married automobile salesman who is untroubled by politics. They play, fight, and make love, often in odd and amusing public circumstances. According to one "captive onlooker," the film's "only interest to the viewer arises from the uncertainty of the method of mutual sexual gratification in which the hero and heroine will next indulge."[1]

Censorship Activity

When the distributor of Grove Press sought to bring this Swedish film into the United States, the U.S. Customs Service seized it as obscene and went into federal district court for a judicial determination of the issue. The government requested a jury trial and the jury found the film obscene. On review, the U.S. Court of Appeals for the Second Circuit reversed, holding the movie was not obscene "under standards established by the Supreme Court" and that "the showing of the picture cannot be inhibited."[2]

Following entry into the United States, the movie became a target of censors in scores of cities and states and was found obscene in some locales and not obscene in others.[3] Finally, the Supreme Court divided 4 to 4 on the issue, in the case arising in Maryland, leaving in doubt the question of whether the film was or was not constitutionally protected.[4]

Legal Importance

This case was widely considered to have broken the grip of governmental interference with the depiction of sexual lovemaking on the screen. The director testified at the Customs trial that he deliberately broke "Hollywood" sexual taboos and clichés in making the film; and, as federal circuit Judge Henry Friendly said, in upholding the film's claim to First Amendment freedom: "It seems to be conceded that the sexual content of the film is presented with greater explicitness than has been seen in any other film produced for general viewing." There were a "number of scenes which show the young girl and her lover nude," and some of these were scenes of frontal nudity. "Several scenes depict sexual intercourse under varying circumstances. . . . There are scenes of oral-genital activity."

The court evaluated the movie's entitlement to constitutional protection under the "three-fold test" put forward by Supreme Court Justice William Brennan in the case of *The Lovers* [49] and in a case involving the book *Fanny Hill* by John Cleland.[5] "Three elements must coalesce: it must be established that (a) the dominant theme of the material taken as a whole appeals to the prurient interest in sex; (b) the material is patently offensive because it affronts contemporary community standards relating to the description or representation of sexual matters; and (c) the material is utterly without redeeming social value." Applying this test to the movie (which it viewed), the court found that "although sexual conduct is undeniably an important aspect of the picture and may be thought of as constituting one of its principal themes, it cannot be said that 'the dominant theme of the material taken as a whole appeals to a prurient interest in sex.' "

The court went on to find that "it is even more clear that *I Am Curious—Yellow* is not utterly without redeeming social value." It "does present ideas and does strive to present these ideas artistically. It falls within the ambit of intellectual effort that the First Amendment was designed to protect." The court found it unnecessary "to pass upon" the issue of whether the picture is "patently offensive because it affronts community standards relating to the description or representation of sexual matters," because the picture "is not obscene under the other two of the Supreme Court tests." Inasmuch as the government decided not to appeal this decision to the U.S. Supreme Court, the movie was freed to enter and be shown throughout the country.

When distribution and exhibition of the movie within the United States began, a large number of new legal actions, claiming the film was obscene, were brought to challenge its entitlement to freedom, notwithstanding the constitutional protection the Second Circuit Court of Appeals had granted it. Several earlier Supreme Court decisions had indicated that a "national standard'' ought to apply to the question of a movie's, or a book's, freedom, and therefore to whether a movie, or a book, could be deemed obscene. It followed that a movie found not obscene but constitutionally protected in one city or state should not be found obscene and unprotected in another, although the converse could not be true.[6] On the other hand, since a majority of the Supreme Court had never explicitly committed themselves to this position, state and local government officials in various parts of the country felt free to act as though the contrary was true, and applied their own notions of what constituted ''social value.'' As a result, *I Am Curious—Yellow* was found not obscene and constitutionally protected by some state courts, and unprotected and obscene by others.[7]

When a state court case was finally accepted for decision on the merits by the U.S. Supreme Court, the membership of the bench had substantially changed from that of the time of the Second Circuit's decision. When Justice Douglas refused to participate in the case,[8] the high court divided equally, 4 to 4, on the question whether the film was constitutionally protected or obscene.[9] This resulted in an automatic affirmance of the state decision appealed from—here, a decision by the Maryland Supreme Court that the movie was obscene. That case had arisen when the Maryland board of censors (the last of the state boards to survive) had found the movie obscene, and, that action being appealed by the distributor, the censorship was sustained by the Maryland Supreme Court.[10]

By the time the movie reached the U.S. Supreme Court, it had been shown in more than 125 communities in states from New York to New Mexico, either without legal challenge or with court approval after litigation, whereas courts in other communities including Boston, Baltimore, Kansas City, Phoenix, and Spokane had banned the movie as obscene. At that time, litigation concerning the film was also going on in San Jose, Denver, Atlanta, Detroit, Albuquerque, Cleveland, and Philadelphia; in Norfolk and Virginia Beach, Virginia; and in Livingston, Linden, and Woodbridge, New Jersey.[11] *Time* magazine reported that according to a Phoenix superior court judge, the movie ''had no plot, no economic message, and no religious dogma. Its only message is immoral copulation, public fornication, and illicit habits.''[12] According to *Washington Post* critic Leroy F. Aarons, the central theme was ''an exploration of the ways in which the impulse to violence inherent in human nature does battle with the tender, benign, constructive side of our beings.''[13]

The Jefferson County, Alabama case holds some interest because in that case the Supreme Court of Alabama declined to disturb a trial court's finding that the movie was obscene because a copy of the film, which had been introduced in evidence at the trial, had not been included in the transcript on appeal, and so the court could not see it. The prevailing legal rule is that because the constitutionality of a governmental act is placed in question by every attempt to suppress a movie, it is the duty of each court to examine and decide the issue of obscenity (when properly raised) *de novo*; to do this, it is essential for each court to view the film. In the Alabama case, an employee of the theater where the movie was being shown, having been arrested by the county sheriff, sought to enjoin a prosecution and further arrest on the ground the film was not obscene but was, instead, constitutionally protected because of its "high artistic value" and because its content was not predominantly sexual and did not appeal to prurient interests in viewers nor offend the standards of morality in the community.[14]

Three New Jersey cases were tried in a consolidated proceeding at which the court found the movie constitutionally protected and not obscene because although, in its judgment, the movie's dominant theme appealed to prurient interest and the film was patently offensive because it affronted contemporary community standards, the government had failed to prove that it was "utterly without redeeming social value." In the trial judge's view, the collective testimony of "social value" by the exhibitor's witnesses was "clearly more persuasive" than the testimony of the government's witnesses, including among them that of Father Morton Hill, a member (dissenting) of the President's Commission on Obscenity and Pornography and president of the moral action organization Morality in Media. The court observed that an "articulate witness for the defense" was John Simon, who had taught English, humanities, and comparative literature at several universities, was film critic for the *New Leader*, and drama critic for the liberal Catholic weekly magazine, *Commonweal*.[15]

Although the Maryland Supreme Court, in finding the movie to be not constitutionally protected, but obscene, had confessed that there was some "occasion for pause" on the issue of the movie's social value, it concluded that the film's concerns with social and political problems "were patently strained and contrived," and, thus, could not serve to redeem it from the charges of being "obscene."[16]

The Supreme Court of Arizona also found the movie obscene, by applying the threefold test for obscenity articulated by Supreme Court Justice William Brennan in the *Memoirs* case; but in the process it refused to follow Justice Brennan's caveat that the social value of a work should not be "weighed against" any attraction it may have for prurient interest. The Arizona court held, in effect, contrary to Brennan's admonition, that notwithstanding the film's social value, it could be found obscene because it also appealed to prurient interest and was patently offensive.[17] This mode of applying the test for obscenity appears to be erroneous even for the stricter threefold rule for finding obscenity laid down in the opinion of Chief Justice Warren Burger in the 1973 landmark case of *Miller* v. *California*—a test with which Justice Brennan strongly disagreed.[18]

The Georgia Supreme Court, "after viewing the film," stated without hesitation that it was obscene and that "if the film does not go substantially beyond the customary limits of candor in representing sexual matters, then there are no limits of candor in this country."[19] The court, obviously, had no expectation that movies like *Deep Throat* [107] and *Behind the Green Door* [109] would soon occupy state and federal courts with the argument that they were not obscene.

The Boston case was significant because the exhibitor there persuaded a federal district court that, assuming the film was "obscene," his showing of it to an adults-only audience, which had been put on notice of the film's sexual content, should be constitutionally protected.[20] This argument, in combination with the proposition that the concept of "obscenity" is unconstitutionally vague and uncertain, eventually formed the basis of Justice Brennan's doctrinal dissent from the Burger majority's approach to obscenity, in the *Magic Mirror* case [102]. The argument was based on a unanimous decision of the Supreme Court in *Stanley* v. *Georgia* that an adult had the constitutional right, in the privacy of his home, to possess and read admittedly "obscene" books and view admittedly "obscene" films.[21] In the Boston case, federal district Judge Bailey Aldrich reasoned that if a "rich Stanley" could view the movie in the privacy of his home, a "poor Stanley" should have the right to view it in a public movie theater. This argument, however, was soon to be rejected by the Burger majority of the Supreme Court in the *Magic Mirror* case [102].

1. United States v. "I Am Curious—Yellow," 404 F. 2d 196 (1968) (Chief Judge Lumbard dissenting).
2. United States v. "I Am Curious—Yellow," 404 F. 2d 196 (1968).
3. ("Obscene" in Ohio) Grove Press v. Flask, 326 F. Supp. 574 (1970); ("Obscene" in Alabama) Grove Press v. Bailey, 318 F. Supp. 244 (1970); (Not "obscene" in New Jersey) Lordi v. UA Theatres, 259 A. 2d 734 (1969); ("Obscene" in Missouri) Hoffman v. Dickinson, 468 S.W. 2d 27 (1971).
4. Grove Press v. Maryland State Board of Censors, 401 U.S. 480 (1971).
5. Memoirs of a Woman of Pleasure v. Attorney General, 865 Ct. 975 (1966).
6. Jacobellis v. Ohio, 378 U.S. 184 (1964). Justice Brennan said: "[T]he constitutional status of an allegedly obscene work must be determined on the basis of a national standard. It is, after all, a national constitution we are expounding."
7. See note 3.
8. Justice Douglas disqualified himself from the *I Am Curious—Yellow* cases that were pending before the Court at the time when a move to impeach him was underway in the Congress. Though he gave no reason for his recusancy, it was widely noted that the film was distributed by Grove Press, which had not long before paid $200 for the right to reprint in its

magazine, *Evergreen Review*, excerpts from Douglas's recently published book, *Points of Rebellion*. See *Time*, May 11, 1970.

9. An affirmance resulting from an equally divided (here 4 to 4) Supreme Court is "conclusive and binding upon the parties [to the case] as respects the controversy [in the case]." However, "the lack of an agreement by a majority of the Court on the principle of law involved prevents it from being an authoritative determination for other cases." [United States v. Pink, 315 U.S. 203 (1942).] This means, among other things, that the same division (4 to 4) of the Supreme Court, on any state (or federal) decision coming to it that had *upheld* the entitlement to constitutional protection of the film, or its exhibitor, would have resulted in an upholding of the freedom of the movie.

10. Wagonheim v. Maryland, 258 A. 2d 240 (1969).
11. Private files of Edward de Grazia.
12. *Time*, May 11, 1970.
13. *The Washington Post*, March 11, 1969.
14. Cooper v. Sheriff of Jefferson County, 257 So. 2d 332 (1972).
15. Lordi v. UA New Jersey Theatres, 259 A. 2d 734 (1969).
16. Wagonheim v. Maryland, 258 A. 2d 240 (1969), affirmed by an equally divided court, 401 U.S. 480 (1971).
17. NGC Theatre Corp. v. Mummert, 489 P. 2d 823 (1971).
18. Miller v. California, 413 U.S. 15 (1973).
19. Evans Theatre Corp. v. Slaton, 180 S.E. 2d 712 (1971).
20. Karalexis v. Byrne, 306 F. Supp. 1363 (1969). Professor Alan Dershowitz was the lawyer who presented this argument.
21. Stanley v. Georgia, 394 U.S. 557 (1969).

[72]
Mondo Freudo (The World of Freud)

Banned in Tennessee, 1967.

U.S., 1966. Dist: Olympic International Films. 80 min. 35mm. Sound. Color. Prod: Olympic International Films, R. W. Cresse. Dir: R. L. Frost. Cin: Kasem Salhmadine, Seasu Hakasomi, David Kayne (pseudonym for R. W. Cresse, R. L. Frost). Cast: Judy Adler.

In this film record of sexual practices around the world, clips include: a beauty contest in Las Vegas; marriage rites for young girls in primitive societies; child cocaine addicts in Ecuador; a man who believes he is Rudolph Valentino reincarnated; inside an oriental opium den and an Arabian beauty parlor; and "parlor games" played by English adults.

Censorship Activity

Pursuant to statute, the District Attorney brought suit to prevent exhibition of *Mondo Freudo* and an advertising trailer called *Olga's Girls* on the ground that they were obscene. After trial, the criminal court found the films to be obscene. On review, the Supreme Court of Tennessee affirmed the finding of obscenity and the suppression of the film's further exhibition.[1]

Legal Importance

The court applied the principle announced in *The Lovers* case [49] holding that a film can be excluded from constitutional protection only if it is "utterly without redeeming social importance." Despite testimony by a psychiatrist, a psychologist, and a movie reviewer concerning the film's social importance in informing people of "existing conditions concerning sex," the Supreme Court of Tennessee, having viewed the film, found it "devoid of any literary, scientific, or artistic value and utterly without social importance." The court said "the effect of the film is just to add to the sexual filth already in the world." The case is another example of the way in which even the "liberal" test for obscenity, formulated by Justice Brennan in *The Lovers* case, can be applied to ban a film that apparently has redeeming value for some people.

1. Robert Arthur Management v. State, 414 S.W. 2d 638 (1967).

[73]
Rent-a-Girl (Rented)

Banned in Chicago, Illinois, 1967.

U.S., 1965. Dist: Cambist Films, Lambs Films. 77 min. 35mm. Sound. B&W. Prod/Dir/SW: William L. Rose. Cin: Maximilian Strasser. Cast: Barbara Wood, Frank Spencer, Inge Christopher, David Ransom, Teresa Morgano, Elizabeth Walker, Gary Takata, Darlene Bennett, Paul Dare, June Roberts, Margareta Lindblom, Gigi Darlene.

The "model agency" run by Evelyn Marshall and her brother Adam in reality provides women for sex-seeking clients. Unsuspecting Karen Anderson is hired and attends a client's party where she is to be the star attraction of the orgy he plans. After she is branded and whipped, hysterical Karen and the other women who are present put up a fight. The police arrive to end the party as well as the agency's business.

Censorship Activity/Legal Importance

For a legal analysis of the case in which this film was banned, see *Body of a Female* [69].

[74]
Alimony Lovers

Banned in Maryland, 1968.

U.S., 1969. Dist: Clover Films. 74 min. 35mm. Sound. Color. Prod: William
Dancer. Dir: Harold Perkins. Music: Nova. Cast: Will Gary, Lisa Cameron,
Joy Kahl, Chris Mathis, Kathy Williams, Cathy Fox, Sebastian Gregory.

In the luxury apartment complex where he lives, Roger Rose discovers that
sexual activities are the main amusement among the divorcées living on
alimony checks. Newly divorced himself and bitter about it, Rose decides
on a way to pay his rent; he persuades the women to perform their acts
before paying audiences. When the police move in, Rose turns on to the
female lawyer who has taken his case.

Censorship Activity

The Maryland censorship board disapproved this film and another, *The
Wicked Die Slow* [80], as obscene, and the circuit court of Baltimore City
affirmed. The distributor then argued in the Maryland Court of Appeals
that it was entitled to show the films without board approvals because the
statutory licensing procedure had not been strictly followed. The court of
appeals rejected this argument and affirmed the lower court's decision.[1]

Legal Importance

The case has interest because it was the first motion picture censorship case
presented to the Maryland Court of Appeals after the state legislature
amended the censorship statute to comply with the procedural guidelines
laid down by the U.S. Supreme Court for the constitutional licensing of motion pictures (in the *Revenge at Daybreak* case [58]). The new law gave the
board five days to approve or disapprove a film for licensing following its
submission to it, three additional days after any disapproval to petition the
court for an order affirming the disapproval, another five days for the court
to commence a hearing on the film, and two days from the hearing for the
court to reach a decision on whether the film should be licensed or not.

Because the parties stipulated that the court need not view the suspect
films, the court did not, and said: "Our relief at this is great, and joy fills
our hearts." The court declined to accept the exhibitor's somewhat
technical argument that because the circuit court had not tried the matter
within the statutorily specified five days, the films could be shown without
approval. "[T]here is no need to decide . . . ," wrote Chief Justice Hall
Hammond, whether the board's failure to act within five days initially or to
go to court within three days after that, or the court's failure to hear and
decide the case within seven days, "would entitle an exhibitor to show a film
without approval or in the face of late approval." Since the circuit court

heard and decided the case within seven days, "the result is the same as if it had heard it in full on the fifth day and then decided it on the seventh . . . the exhibitor had his final answer within the statutory period of 15 days. . . ." He had enjoyed his "full constitutional protection." The court simply was "not prepared to say that . . . the statutory scheme of film censorship has been made impotent . . . merely because the Board's petition was not heard on the fifth day and decided on the seventh, but was [both] heard and decided on the seventh day."

The exhibitor argued that the legislature intended there to be two days after the close of the hearing, prior to the court's decision, and that in failing to abide by this schedule the judge "had so much less time for consideration that his decision is subject to suspicion. . . ." "This argument," said the court, "leaves us cold." The lower court had written "a reasoned and analytical opinion," and the exhibitor had not claimed that "the wrong result" was reached nor challenged the judge's holding that the films were obscene.

1. Hewitt v. Maryland State Board of Censors, 258 A. 2d 217 (1969).

[75]
Carmen, Baby

Banned in Richland, Washington, 1968.

Yugoslavia/West Germany, 1967. U.S., 1967. Dist: Audubon Films, Amsterdam Film Corp. 90 min. 35mm. Sound. Color. Dubbed in English. Prod/Dir: Radley Metzger. SW: Jesse Vogel. Cin: Hans Jura. Music: Daniel Hart. Cast: Uta Levka, Carl Mahner, Barbara Valentine, Walter Wiltz, Christians Rucker, Michael Munzer, Doris Arden. Reviews: *Variety*, Oct. 11, 1967, Rabe; *New York Times*, Oct. 17, 1967, Vincent Canby.

This film was very loosely adapted from Bizet's opera *Carmen* and concerns a cafe waitress/prostitute who, in order to escape a criminal charge, seduces a policeman, who covers for her. After a short stint in jail, the policeman and Carmen become lovers. But one day the policeman finds Carmen with his superior, and kills him. The lovers run off to a villa where they earn money by blackmailing sex-seeking tourists. Carmen meets the head of the parole board, has sex with him, and in return wins the release of her husband, who is in prison. Then Carmen leaves her lover for a rock-and-roll star. Enraged, the policeman kills Carmen's husband, follows her to the nightclub where her new lover is singing, quarrels with Carmen outside in the square, and then kills her with his knife.

Censorship Activity

On August 28, 1968, a Richland, Washington, police officer stood outside the fence of the Park Y drive-in theater and watched a part of this film. The following night, the Richland city attorney joined him in viewing the movie. The picture was visible from nearby homes, to persons standing outside the fence, and to passing motorists. After the officer described some of the more "objectionable" scenes of the film to a Richland justice of the peace, noting that he had observed pre-teenage children watching it, the manager was arrested and two reels of the movie seized. He was convicted in the Richland District Court of violating the state obscenity statute and of "caus[ing] to be exhibited an obscene, indecent and immoral show." On appeal, at a trial *de novo* in the Benton County Superior Court, he was again found guilty. The Supreme Court of Washington affirmed the trial court's judgment,[1] but the U.S. Supreme Court reversed.[2]

Legal Importance

The U.S. Supreme Court held "that a state may not criminally punish the exhibition at a drive-in theater of a motion picture where the statute, used to support the conviction, has not given fair notice that the location of the exhibition was a vital element of the offense." "To avoid the constitutional vice of vagueness," the Court announced, by way of a *per curiam* opinion, "it is necessary, at a minimum, that a statute give fair notice that certain conduct is proscribed." The statute involved in this case "made no mention that the 'context' or location of the exhibition was an element of the offense somehow modifying the word 'obscene.' " Under the lower court's interpretation of the statute, the petitioner would have been able to exhibit the film—which the court described as "a loose adaptation" of Bizet's opera, *Carmen*, "containing sexually frank scenes but no instances of sexual consummation"—to adults, in an indoor theater, with impunity. So construed, the statute was impermissibly vague because the exhibitor had no fair notice that criminal liability was dependent "upon the place where the film was shown," and no notice that otherwise permissible speech "would nevertheless not be tolerated in certain places."

Chief Justice Warren Burger, joined by Justice William Rehnquist, concurred in the decision to reverse the theater manager's conviction, "solely on the ground that petitioner's conviction under Washington's general obscenity statute cannot, under the circumstances of this case, be sustained consistent with the fundamental notice requirements of the due process clause." However, public displays of explicit materials of the sort contained in this film "are not significantly different from any noxious public nuisance traditionally within the power of the States to regulate and prohibit, and, in my view, involve no significant countervailing First Amendment considerations." The record thus showed "an offensive nuisance that could properly be prohibited," the Chief Justice concluded, "but the state statute and charge did not give the notice constitutionally required."

1. State v. Rabe, 484 P. 2d 917, 79 Wash. 2d 254 (1971).
2. Rabe v. Washington, 405 U.S. 313 (1971).

[76]
The Female

Banned in Middlesboro, Kentucky, 1968.

Argentina, 1962. U.S., 1968. Dist: Cambist Films. 85–92 min. 35mm. Sound. B&W. Prod: Araucania Films, Antonio P. Motti. Dir: Leo Towers (pseudonym for Leopoldo Torre Nilsson). SW: Beatriz Guido, Leopoldo Torre Nilsson. Cin: Ricardo Younis. Cast: Isabel Sarli, Francisco Rabal, Jardel Filho. Festivals: Cannes Film, 1961–62. Reviews: *Variety*, May 30, 1962, Mosk.; *Variety*, March 20, 1968.

This film is based on two stories appearing in *Setenta veces siete* by Dalmiro A. Sáenz. Now a prostitute in a rundown bordello, Laura does not respond to customers' advances, which angers the madam. Finally, she does take a customer and during the time spent with him, she thinks about her past. She recalls that she left her parents' home in the pampas to accompany a shepherd to his mountain hut. There she discovers a horse thief who has been shot and tries to help him, but the shepherd wants to kill the criminal. Instead, Laura persuades the shepherd to let the man live so that he can help the shepherd to dig a well. With the well nearly dug, the shepherd discovers the money belt of the fugitive and tells Laura that they should steal it and run off to buy a farm. But Laura is attracted to the horse thief, and when he suggests that the two of them should run off together, leaving the shepherd behind, she cannot make up her mind. So she leaves both men in the well to die and flees to the city and the life she now lives.

Censorship Activity

This film was seized, pursuant to a magistrate's search warrant, by town police at a theater in Middlesboro, Kentucky where it was being shown. The warrant was based on a detective's affidavit that the film "showed men and women nude and engaging in acts and conduct which indicated they were having sexual intercourse" and thus was obscene within the meaning of the state criminal obscenity law. Although the magistrate issuing the warrant had not viewed the film, before or after its seizure, he claimed there was sufficient evidence to justify holding it "in custody" and referring the case to the grand jury scheduled to meet some five months later. The distributor sued to prevent his prosecution and any interference with the movie's exhibition and for compensatory and punitive damages from the magistrate and prosecuting attorneys. A three-judge federal district court ordered that the film be returned to the distributor because the affidavit on which the magistrate based his warrant to seize it contained "only slightly more than conclusory allegations."[1]

Legal Importance

The procedure used by the police to seize the film failed to comply with the standards laid down by the U.S. Supreme Court in the landmark cases of *A Quantity of Books* v. *Kansas*[2] and *Marcus* v. *Search Warrants*[3] for drawing "the line between protected and unprotected speech." Those standards meant that "the dissemination of a particular work which is alleged to be obscene, should be completely undisturbed until an independent determination of obscenity has been made by a judicial officer, at an adversary hearing." The constitution required a procedure "designed to focus searchingly on the question of obscenity before speech can be regulated or suppressed." However, the court denied that the Kentucky obscenity statute was unconstitutional on its face, and, having itself viewed the film, judged it obscene. "The dominant theme, presented through repeated scenes of sexual gratification, in one form or another, is blatantly designed to appeal to a prurient interest. . . . The Biblical passage presented at the beginning of the film does not *ipso facto* clothe it with constitutional protection nor camouflage its dominant theme. The entire film is devoid of literary or artistic merit. The offensive themes are done with grossness, not subtlety, and have little relation to the simple plot."

1. Cambist Films v. Tribell, 293 F. Supp. 407 (1968).
2. A Quantity of Books v. Kansas, 378 U.S. 205 (1964).
3. Marcus v. Search Warrants, 367 U.S. 717 (1961).

[77]
The Fox

Banned in Jackson, Mississippi, 1968.

U.S., 1968. Dist: Claridge Pictures. 109 min. 35mm. Sound. Color. Prod: Raymond Stross. Dir: Mark Rydell. SW: Lewis J. Carlino, Howard Koch. Cin: Bill Fraker. Cast: Sandy Dennis, Anne Heywood, Keir Dullea. MPAA: MAO. Reviews: *New York Post*, Feb. 14, 1968, Frances Herridge; *Time*, Feb. 16, 1968; *New York Times*, Feb. 25, 1968, Renata Adler; *Washington Post*, March 1, 1968, Richard L. Coe.

The Fox is a loose adaptation of D. H. Lawrence's novel of the same title. It tells the story of two college friends, Jill and March, who live together after college on Jill's farm in Canada. As the only two residents of this isolated farm, the young women develop a symbiotic relationship. Jill takes care of the cooking and cleaning, while March assumes the role of protector and provider. However, March cannot bring herself to shoot the fox that is harassing their henhouse. Into this delicate balance comes Paul, a sailor on shore leave, and the grandson of the farm's late owner. Jill, imagining Paul would be the perfect man for her, asks him to stay. He does, but promptly falls in love with March whom he wants to marry. March hesitates to accept Paul's proposal because of Jill's dependency and jealousy. "The attractions are physical. We glimpse the naked March in moments of self-eroticism. We are shown her physical appreciation of Paul. We see the two girls making love in their double bed."[1] The film reaches its climax when Jill refuses to move from the path of a tree that March and Paul are cutting down.

Censorship Activity

Following a public showing of this movie at a Jackson, Mississippi theater, two city police officers and the city attorney, who had viewed it "as paid guests," arrested the theater operators for violating a state law which made punishable the exhibition of an obscene "moving picture show" and, without warrant, seized the film. The operators initially were convicted upon pleas of "no contest" in magistrate's court before a police justice of the peace. Upon receiving a jury trial in the county court of Hinds County, where the case was tried anew, they were acquitted. A mistrial was granted in the case of the theater corporation, also charged with violating the state criminal law. The operators and the theater thereafter brought suit in the U.S. District Court for the Southern District of Mississippi, seeking a permanent injunction preventing the state from prosecuting them under the statute and for the return of the seized film. A three-judge district court denied the relief requested, holding the film was obscene.[2]

Legal Importance

The decision is significant for the errors it contains. Under principles announced by the U.S. Supreme Court in a series of opinions beginning in 1965 with the *Revenge at Daybreak* case [58], and later including the *Blue Movie* [82] and *Cindy and Donna* [97] cases, it is unconstitutional for police to seize a film in the absence, at a minimum, of a previous determination by a "neutral magistrate," or judicial officer, that the film is probably obscene. No such determination having been made in this case, the film's seizure by the police officers who arrested the theater operators was an act of censorship that violated freedom of expression; the court should have ordered the film's return. In addition, the Mississippi criminal law, under which the film's exhibitors were prosecuted, was constitutionally defective inasmuch as it was judicially construed to permit a movie (or book) to be found obscene if any portions contained "portrayals of conduct [that] would be obscene if performed in public or on the public streets"—contrary to the rules laid down in such landmark cases as *Roth* v. *United States*,[3] the *Lovers* case [49], and *Miller* v. *California*.[4]

Also noteworthy is the extent to which the Mississippi federal court's judgment, dissented to by circuit Judge Rives concerning the obscenity of the film, was subjectively arrived at. Judge William Harold Cox's opinion is replete with such representations as that *The Fox* was "sordid and bizarre," as a whole, with scenes "extremely repulsive and offensive [that] contaminate the show as an entirety," where "sex is employed . . . solely as a box office pitch to the morbidly curious," containing "lurid and carnal scenes . . . which so exceeded all bounds of propriety, and common decency" as to be "a classic case of hard-core pornography wherein sex is pandered solely for profit."

1. *Washington Post*, March 1, 1968, Richard L. Coe.
2. McGrew v. City of Jackson, 307 F. Supp. 754 (1969).
3. 354 U.S. 476 (1957).
4. 413 U.S. 15 (1973).

[78]
Therese and Isabelle (Therese und Isabell)

Banned in Allegheny County, Pennsylvania, 1968.

U.S./West Germany, 1968. Dist: Audubon Films. 118 min. 35mm. Sound. B&W. Prod: Amsterdam Film Corp.—Berolina Films. A Radley H. Metzger Production. Dir: Radley H. Metzger. SW: Jesse Vogel. Cin: Hans Jura. Music: Georges Auric. Cast: Essy Persson, Anna Gael, Barbara Laage, Anne Vernon, Maurice Teynac, Remy Longa, Simone Paris, Suzanne Marchellier, Nathalie Nort, Darcy Pullian, Martine Leclerc, Bernadette Stern. Reviews: *New York Times*, May 15, 1968, Renata Adler; *Saturday Review*, May 25, 1968; *Newsweek*, May 27, 1968; *Esquire*, November 1968.

This film was adapted from the novel of the same name by Violette Leduc. It tells the story of a boarding-school romance between Therese and Isabelle, two unhappy adolescent girls who consummate their love one night on the school grounds, only to be separated the following morning when Isabelle's mother unaccountably removes her daughter from the school. The story unfolds as a flashback haunting memory of Therese, now a woman in her thirties, when she pays a visit with her fiancé to her old school. "The dominant theme of the [film] is that of loneliness, the loneliness of a young girl, not wanted by her mother, who turns to another young girl for affection. As a result of this lack of maternal affection . . . the girl becomes entwined in a homosexual relationship."[1]

Censorship Activity

The district attorney in Allegheny, Pennsylvania obtained a temporary injunction against the showing of this movie because it was obscene; it was nullified on appeal. Following a full trial of the movie's alleged obscenity, he secured a permanent injunction prohibiting it from being shown. On appeal, the Supreme Court of Pennsylvania reversed and vacated the decree preventing the movie's exhibition.[2]

Legal Importance

Although there was no statutory authority for the issuance of an injunction to prevent a movie being shown, the Pennsylvania high court ruled such an "equitable" proceeding was available to the district attorney to eliminate what he considered to be a public harm. However, the question of whether the movie was obscene or was constitutionally protected was not a matter to be decided by the district attorney, but by the state supreme court itself, exercising its "independent constitutional judgment on the facts of the case," following the admonition to this effect made by U.S. Supreme Court Justice William Brennan in *The Lovers* case [49]. Applying the threefold test for obscenity laid down in that case and in the case of *Memoirs* v. *Massachusetts*,[3] the Pennsylvania Supreme Court found the movie was not obscene but was constitutionally protected expression. In doing so, the court refused to accept an argument made by the district attorney that, because of the more vivid impact that movies have, the test of its obscenity should be different from that applicable to books. One reason, according to the court, was that "a nude figure seen on a screen for a short time may very well have less impact than a nude figure in a magazine, which can be leered at leisurely."

1. Duggan v. Guild Theatre, 258 A. 2d 858 (1969).
2. Duggan v. Guild Theatre, 258 A. 2d 858 (1969).
3. Memoirs v. Massachusetts, 383 U.S. 413 (1966).

[79]
Titicut Follies

Banned in Massachusetts, 1968.

U.S., 1967. Dist: Titicut Follies Film Distributing Co., Grove Press. 87 min. 16mm. Sound. B&W. Prod: Frederick Wiseman, Bridgewater Film Co. Dir:

Frederick Wiseman. Cin: John Marshall. Festivals: New York Film (1967). Reviews: *New York Times*, Oct. 4, 1967, Vincent Canby; *Variety*, Oct. 4, 1967, Byro; *Cue*, Oct. 21, 1967. Articles: *New York Times*, Sept. 29, 1967; *Motion Picture Daily*, Oct. 17, 1967; *Newsweek*, Oct. 23, 1967, Joseph Morgenstern; *Variety*, Oct. 25, Nov. 8, 1967; *Life*, Dec. 1, 1967, Richard Schickel; *New York Times*, Jan. 5, 1968; *Variety*, Jan. 10, 1968; *New York Times*, Dec. 1, 1968, June 25, 1969, June 16, 1970.

This film is a documentary on the conditions in a state prison for the criminally insane at Bridgewater, Massachusetts, with scenes of a musical show put on by and for the inmates and the staff before and after the filming of several incidents of the inmates' lives in the prison. "The film shows detailed close-ups of such episodes as the forced nose-feeding of an inmate on a hunger strike and his later death and burial; the explosive reaction of an inmate to repeated taunting by correction officers about his failure to keep his cell clean; the degrading process of subjecting inmates to stripping off their clothes publicly for a 'skin search' conducted by correction officers for the purpose of discovering contraband; the questioning by a staff psychiatrist of a young paranoid husband and father committed for sex attacks on children; and the unhappy protests of a young, articulate schizophrenic to the effect that after one and a half years as an inmate he is being driven insane by the surroundings and by the poor treatment or lack of treatment by the staff."[1]

Censorship Activity

Exhibition of the film to the general public on a commercial basis was enjoined, on behalf of the filmed inmates, by a Suffolk County superior court judge, because inmates were pictured naked or exhibiting painful aspects of mental disease, amounting to a collective indecent intrusion into the most private aspects of their lives. On appeal, the injunction was modified so as to permit restricted showings to legislators, judges, lawyers, doctors, psychiatrists, students in those or related fields, and organizations dealing with the social problems of custodial care and mental infirmity.[2] The U.S. Supreme Court declined to review the case, with Justices Harlan, Brennan, and Douglas voting to take review and set the case down for full consideration.[3]

Legal Importance

As Justice Harlan observed in his dissent from the Supreme Court's denial of the film producer's petition for review, *Titicut Follies* "is at once a scathing indictment of the inhumane conditions that prevailed at the time of the film and an undeniable infringement of the privacy of the inmates filmed, who are shown nude and engaged in acts that would unquestionably embarrass an individual of normal sensitivity." The case presented a stark conflict between the constitutional "commitment to the principle that debate on public issues should be uninhibited, robust, and wide-open . . . and the individual's interest in privacy and dignity. . . ." The public has a "right to know" about conditions in public institutions. The issue created by a collision of that right with the individual's right to privacy was resolved by limiting the film's exhibition to persons professionally concerned with conditions at such institutions.

In a related New York case,[4] an action for defamation and invasion of privacy was brought by officials of the Bridgewater institution, seeking to enjoin exhibition of the film. Here, a federal district court ruled that the film "was expression included within the free speech and free press [guaranties] of the First and Fourteenth Amendments"; and, as such, could not be suppressed unless it "amounted to a false report made with knowledge of its falsity or in reckless disregard of the truth," or was obscene. Since the film was neither sort of "unprotected" communication, the requested injunction was denied.

1. Cullen v. Grove Press, Inc., 276 F. Supp. 727 (1967).
2. Commonwealth v. Wiseman, 249 N.E. 2d 610 (1969).
3. Wiseman v. Massachusetts, 398 U.S. 960 (1970).
4. Cullen v. Grove Press, Inc., 276 F. Supp. 727 (1967).

[80]
The Wicked Die Slow

Banned in Maryland, 1968.

U.S., 1968. Dist: Cannon Releasing Corp. 75 min. 35mm. Sound. Color. Prod: Cannon Productions, Donald C. Dennis. Dir: William K. Hennigar. SW: Gary Allen, Jeff Kanen. Cin: Amin Chaudhri. Cast: Gary Allen, Steve Rivard, Jeff Kanen, Susannah Campbell.

Bent on avenging the rape of his girl friend by Indians, The Kid, an infamous gunfighter, with Armadillo, his Mexican companion, roam the post-Civil War West. In their travels, they kill the members of a gang who raped a woman and beat a man and his daughter. With the defeat of the gang leader, The Kid has proven that "the wicked die slow."

Censorship Activity/Legal Importance
For a legal analysis of the case involving this film, see *Alimony Lovers* [74].

[81]
Angelique in Black Leather (Angelique)

Banned in Richmond, Virginia, 1969.

U.S., 1968. Dist: Imperial Pictures. 65 min. 35mm. Sound. Color. Prod/Dir: Angelique Bouchet. Cast: Angelique Bouchet, Maria Lennard, Solange Canard.

After Suzanne goes off for a date, her lesbian lover Angelique follows her but soon loses her in the crowd. Angelique then meets and spends the afternoon with Domenique, with whom she falls in love. Angelique deliberately allows Suzanne to find her with her new love and torments Suzanne by arousing feelings of both jealousy and desire.

Censorship Activity

After purchasing tickets of admission, viewing this film, and obtaining a search warrant from a city magistrate, the Richmond, Virginia police seized it at a theater at which it was being shown and charged the theater with possessing and exhibiting an obscene motion picture. The prosecutor claimed the law did not mandate that an adversary hearing be held before a judge on the question of obscenity prior to any seizure of the movie, and that he did not intend to afford one in future similar situations "unless and until" he was "satisfied" that he was legally required to do so. Judge Robert R. Mehrige, Jr., of the federal district court for the Eastern District of Virginia granted an injunction, requested by the exhibitor, directing the city to return the film, and enjoined the police "from seizing allegedly obscene motion pictures without affording a prior adversary hearing to the possessors and exhibitors of same."[1] On appeal, the Court of Appeals for the Fourth Circuit affirmed the lower court judgment, but required the theater to make the film "reasonably available" to the prosecutor for evidentiary purposes.[2]

Legal Importance

The Constitution has been interpreted by the U.S. Supreme Court to require an adversary hearing to focus searchingly on the question of whether a book or film is obscene before it can be seized by police. "We find support" in the *I, a Woman* case [70], "a situation identical to ours in every significant way," Judge John D. Butzner, Sr., wrote. "The police lacked a search warrant there, but that provides no basis for distinguishing the case because the court focused on the lack of the hearing." The purpose of the hearing, as the U.S. Supreme Court noted in *A Quantity of Books* v. *Kansas*,[3] is to safeguard against governmental suppression of non-obscene expression which is protected from suppression by the First Amendment. The court here held that the theater was not entitled to an injunction restraining the police from seizing films in the future, because the lower court admitted that the prosecutor had acted "in good faith," but "in all other respects" affirmed the judgment.

1. Tyrone, Inc. v. Wilkinson, 294 F. Supp. 1330 (1969).
2. Tyrone, Inc. v. Wilkinson, 410 F. 2d 639 (1969).
3. A Quantity of Books v. Kansas, 378 U.S. 205 (1964).

[82]
Blue Movie/Fuck

Banned in New York, 1969.

U.S., 1969. Dist: Andy Warhol Films, Inc. 105 min.[1] 16mm. Sound. Color. Prod: Andy Warhol, Factory Films, Paul Morrissey. Dir/Cin: Andy Warhol. Cast: Viva Waldon, Louis Waldon. Reviews: *Variety*, June 25, 1969, Kent; *New York Post*, July 25, 1969, Archer Winsten; *Cue*, Aug. 2, 1969; *New York Times*, Aug. 2, 1969, Vincent Canby. Articles: *Variety*, June 18, 1969; *Daily Variety*, Aug. 4, 1969; *Variety*, Aug. 6, 1969; *New York Times*, Sept. 17, 18, 1969, Morris Kaplan; *Box Office*, Sept. 29, 1969; *New York Daily News*, Dec. 2, 1971.

This movie depicts an afternoon in a Manhattan apartment where Viva and Louis discuss current social issues while lying in bed. Louis makes sexual advances and Viva giggles; they indulge in sexual foreplay and then intercourse. They talk about the Vietnam War, watch television, get dressed, eat, discuss Louis's unhappy marriage, and finally take a shower, more and more aware of the presence of a camera. After more sex play in and out of the shower, Viva stares at the camera and asks, "Is it on?"

Censorship Activity

After seeing part of this film, New York City police officers relayed their observations to a New York County assistant district attorney who requested a criminal court judge to view it. The judge did so and, concluding there was probable cause for prosecution, signed a search warrant for its seizure and three "John Doe" warrants for the arrests of the theater manager, the projectionist, and the ticket-taker—because "it was and is my opinion that that film is obscene. . . ." Police officers immediately executed the warrants and seized a copy of the film "to preserve it as evidence." On motion of the prosecutor, the cases against the ticket-taker and projectionist were dismissed. At the theater manager's criminal trial, Judges William K. Ringel, Bernard Moldow, and Morton R. Tolleris viewed the movie and found the defendant theater manager guilty of "promot[ing] . . . obscene material."

Next, the state supreme court, Appellate Term, viewed the film and affirmed the manager's conviction. Finally, the New York Court of Appeals viewed the picture and in 1971 affirmed the lower decisions.[2] This court ruled that the film was obscene and that there had been no constitutional need for the court to hold an adversary hearing prior to issuing the warrants for arrest of the manager and seizure of the film, because "when a Magistrate sees a film, it is not much help to him, or indeed to the parties, in deciding probable cause to have counsel on one side tell him what he has just seen and on the other what he has not." The U.S. Supreme Court vacated the state court's judgment and remanded the case for reconsideration of the finding that the film was "obscene" in light of the standards it announced in *Miller* v. *California*[3] and the *Magic Mirror* case [102].[4]

Legal Importance

There were two issues in this case: (1) was *Blue Movie* obscene under prevailing Supreme Court standards, and (2) whether, and if so, under what conditions, the Constitution required an adversary hearing on the question of obscenity prior to a judge's issuance of warrants for the seizure of a film and the arrest of its exhibitor.

New York's highest state court in 1971 held that such an adversary hearing was not required and that "the judicial determination which occurred prior to seizure in this case was constitutionally sufficient." This court also held the movie to be obscene as "simple pornography unrelieved by any merit," applying the standards announced in such cases as *The Lovers* [49].

On the issue of unconstitutionality of the film's seizure, Chief Justice Burger, writing for the Supreme Court in 1973, said that the Court "has never held, or even implied, that there is an absolute First or Fourteenth Amendment right to a prior adversary hearing applicable to all cases where allegedly obscene material is seized. In particular, there is no such absolute right where allegedly obscene material is seized, pursuant to a warrant, to preserve the material as evidence in a criminal prosecution. . . . Even in *United States* v. *Thirty-Seven Photographs*,[4] and the *Revenge at Daybreak* case [58], we did not require that the adversary proceeding must take place prior to *initial* seizure. Rather, it was held that a judicial determination must occur 'promptly so that administrative delay does not in itself become a form of censorship.' . . . In this case, the barrier to a prompt judicial determination of the obscenity issue in an adversary proceeding was not the State, but petitioner's decision to waive pretrial motions and reserve the obscenity issue for trial." Seizing films, Chief Justice Burger continued, "to destroy them or to block their distribution or exhibition is a very different matter from seizing a single copy of a film for the *bona fide* purpose of preserving it as evidence in a criminal proceeding, particularly where, as here, there is no showing or pretrial claim that the seizure of the copy prevented continuing exhibition of the film. If such a seizure is pursuant to a warrant, issued after a determination of probable cause by a neutral magistrate, and, following the seizure, a prompt judicial determination is available at the request of any interested party, the seizure is constitutionally permissible.''

The Court added that ''on a showing to the trial court that other copies of the film are not available to the exhibitor, the court should permit the seized film to be copied so that showing can be continued pending a judicial determination of the obscenity issue in an adversary proceeding. Otherwise, the film must be returned. With such safeguards, we do not perceive that an adversary hearing *prior* to a seizure by lawful warrant would materially increase First Amendment protection. The necessity for a prior judicial determination of probable cause will protect against gross abuses, while the availability of a prompt judicial determination in an adversary proceeding following the seizure assures that difficult marginal cases will be fully considered in light of First Amendment guarantees, with only a minimal interference with public circulation pending litigation. The procedure used by New York in this case,'' the Court concluded, ''provides such First Amendment safeguards. . . .'' The case was remanded to the New York courts for the ''sole purpose of affording [them] an opportunity to reconsider [the] substantive issues'' of obscenity in view of the standards announced in *Miller* v. *California* and the *Magic Mirror* case [102].

Four members of the Court voted to reverse. Justice William O. Douglas, dissenting, ''would reverse the case outright'' as ''the underlying obscenity statute violates the First Amendment. . . .'' Justice William J. Brennan, Jr., joined by Justices Potter Stewart and Thurgood Marshall, also dissented, because the statute, like all such statutes aiming to suppress the dissemination of obscenity among consenting adults, ''was unconstitutionally broad and therefore invalid on its face,'' as explained in Brennan's dissent in *Miller* and the *Magic Mirror* case [102].

1. The general release version of this film opened July 21, 1969 at a running time of 105 minutes. It originally opened at 90 minutes in New York and later screened for the press at 140 minutes. (*American Film Institute Catalog of Motion Pictures: Feature Films 1961–1970*, edited by Richard Krafsur. New York: Bowker, 1976.)
2. People v. Heller, 277 N.E. 2d 651 (1971).
3. Heller v. New York, 413 U.S. 483 (1973).
4. United States v. Thirty-Seven Photographs, 402 U.S. 363 (1971).

[83]
Candy (Candy e il Sul Pazzo Mondo)

Banned in Jackson, Mississippi, 1969.

Italy/U.S., 1968. France, 1970. Dist: Cinerama Releasing Corp., Robert Haggiag–Peter Zoref–Selmur Pictures (ABC), Selig J. Seligman. 119 min.¹ 35mm. Sound. Color. Prod: Robert Haggiag, Dear Films (Italy); Selig J. Seligman, Selmur Pictures (ABC) (U.S.); Peter Zoref, Les Films Corona (France). Dir: Christian Marquand. SW: Buck Henry. Cin: Giuseppe Rotunno. Cast: Ewa Aulin, Charles Aznavour, Marlon Brando, Richard Burton, James Coburn, John Huston, Walter Matthau, Ringo Starr. MPAA: R. Reviews: *Hollywood Reporter*, Dec. 17, 1968, John Mahoney; *Motion Picture Daily*, Dec. 18, 1968, Les Schwartz; *Variety*, Dec. 18, 1968, Murf.; *Cue*, Dec. 28, 1968; *Newsweek*, Dec. 30, 1968, J.M.; *New York Post*, Feb. 18, 1969, Archer Winsten. Articles: *Life*, March 8, 1968, Eileen Lanouette Hughes; *New York Times Magazine*, Feb. 11, 1968, Israel Shenker; *Motion Picture Daily*, March 11, 1968, Charles S. Aronson; *Daily Variety*, Jan. 14, 1969; *Variety*, Jan. 15, 1969; *Motion Picture Daily*, Feb. 26, June 13, 1969.

This film was adapted from the novel *Candy* by Terry Southern and Mason Hoffenberg. Persuaded by a rakish campus-hopping poet that one must give of one's self selflessly, the petulantly endearing young student Candy is molested by the poet and a suburban Mexican gardener. Scandalized, Candy and her sickly father flee town and are rescued by a patriotic pilot who convinces Candy to do her part for her country, with his pistol. While her father, incapacitated by an in-flight head injury, undergoes brain surgery and then disappears, Candy is seduced and molested by the brain surgeon, her lewd uncle, and various other lechers. Finally, she is led by a pseudo-guru through his own artificial bliss till they reach a mystic California temple. There, seduced now by a dirt-caked holy man, Candy recognizes that she has just made love to her father.

Censorship Activity

Three police officers, not in uniform, purchased tickets at the Paramount Theater in Jackson, Mississippi, viewed this film, then arrested the theater manager and projectionist, and seized the print of the film shown. A criminal trial took place and defendants were found guilty of "exhibiting to public view" an obscene picture. They appealed to the county court and also petitioned a federal district court to enjoin enforcement of the law under which they were convicted, order a return of the print seized, and declare their rights to show the film. The parties agreed to await the federal court's ruling before proceeding further in state court. The U.S. District Court for the Southern District of Mississippi found the statute constitutional, the film seizure constitutional, and the film obscene.[2] The decision was, however, vacated by the U.S. Supreme Court.[3]

Legal Importance

The case is remarkable mainly for its illustrating how a court was able to apply the *Memoirs*[4] test of obscenity to a "Hollywood-type" movie rated "R" by the Motion Picture Association of America's classification board and conclude that the film was obscene. The district judge doing this said, "[T]he film is devoid of any literary or artistic merit and presents nothing more than a vivid portrayal of hard-core pornography. The film has no discernible theme or plot and involves a disconnected series of scenes depicting sexual gratification in a shocking and shameful manner." The court found support for its action condemning the film in the *Un Chant D'Amour* case [65].

1. The original release of this film had a running time of 124 minutes. The Paris opening in August 1970 had a running time of 110 minutes. (*American Film Institute Catalog of Motion Pictures: Feature Films 1961–1970*, edited by Richard Krafsur. New York: Bowker, 1976.)
2. Hosey v. City of Jackson, 309 F. Supp. 527 (1970).
3. Hosey v. City of Jackson, 401 U.S. 987 (1971).
4. 'Memoirs' v. Massachusetts, 383 U.S. 413 (1966).

[84]
The Language of Love (Karlekens Sprak)

Banned from entry into the United States, 1969.

Sweden, 1969. U.S., 1971. Dist: Paragon Films. 80 min. 35mm. Sound. Dubbed in English. Color. Prod: Inge Ivarson. Dir/SW: Torgny Wickman. Cin: Max Wilen. Cast: Inge Hegeler, Sten Hegeler, Sture Cullhed, Maj-Briht Bergtrom-Walan. Reviews: *Filmfacts*, v. XIV (1971); *Films and Filming*, v. 17 No. 7 (April 1971), Peter Buckley; *Cue*, June 10, 1971, William Wolf; *New York Times*, July 1, 1979, A. H. Weiler.

The Language of Love is a sex-education film based on the book *The ABZ of Love* by Drs. Inge and Sten Hegeler. The cast members are doctors of sexology and conduct a panel discussion throughout the film. Each topic of discussion is "dramatized and demonstrated by non-professional volunteers, with the additional aid of animation, diagrams, and split-screen techniques."[1]

Censorship Activity

This film was seized in 1969 by the U.S. Customs Service and a proceeding was brought for its forfeiture as obscene pursuant to federal law. Upon a jury trial a federal district court decided the movie was obscene.[2] On appeal, the Second Circuit Court of Appeals reversed that judgment and the film was ordered to be released.[3]

Legal Importance

The federal jury had found the film obscene, but its decision was overruled by the court of appeals, which decided, after seeing the film, that its dominant theme was the "revelation and solution of sexual problems"; that it dealt with sex "in a manner that advocates ideas"; that the First Amendment "protects the expression of ideas regardless of medium or subject"; and that "whatever hard-core pornography is, [this film] considered as a whole is simply not of that genre." This judgment was reached after comparing the film with *I Am Curious—Yellow* [71] and applying the test established in *The Lovers* case [49] for distinguishing an obscene movie from a movie protected by the constitutional guarantees of freedom of expression.

The court of appeals viewed the issue of whether a film is protected by the First Amendment, or obscene contraband, "as a question of law to be decided by the court," in effect making a jury's decision "advisory" only. This is in accord with the views taken by the same federal court of appeals in the *I Am Curious—Yellow* case and by the U.S. Supreme Court in *The Lovers* and *Carnal Knowledge* [105] cases.

The case is interesting also because the government, seeking to condemn the film as obscene, showed the court the film *I Am Curious—Yellow*, which this court had already held not to be obscene, and argued that "the scenes of sexual activity in *Language of Love* are far more numerous and 'shockingly explicit' than those in the former film." The explicitness of the sexual behavior depicted in *Language of Love* was said by the court in this case to be greater "quantitatively and qualitatively than other films of this genre, although at least eight are currently playing or have recently played in New York without government interference, all of which could be said to have maximal explicitness and which enable that segment of the public interested in observing sexual activity in the quiet darkness of a movie theater to do so."

1. *Filmfacts*, v. XIV (1971).
2. United States v. Language of Love, 311 F. Supp. 108 (1970).
3. United States v. Language of Love, 432 F. 2d 705 (1970).

[85]
Odd Triangle

Banned in Nassau County, New York, 1969.

U.S., 1969. Dist: A. L. Shackleton Films. 76 min. 35mm. Sound. B&W. Prod: Rasnel Films. Dir/SW: Joseph W. Sarno. Cast: Barbara Lance, Sidney Laird, Blanche Robins, René Howard.

Allison is bored with her husband and suburban "housewife" life. After observing her neighbor having sex with a gardener and her maid having sex with a boyfriend all in the same afternoon, she is more depressed than ever by her unsuccessful attempts at masturbation. Confiding her troubles to her friend Janet, the two women rent a houseboat and are soon involved with Winnie, a young fishing-party guide. Overcome by her intense feelings, Allison tells her husband she is leaving him. But when she goes to Janet's home, she sees Janet and Winnie in each other's arms, and she runs away.

Censorship Activity

Nassau County police, under the direction of the county district attorney, seized this film and arrested employees of the theater where it was being shown, charging them with a violation of the state obscenity law. The police had search and arrest warrants issued by a judge who had seen the film prior to issuing the warrants. The theater owner sought and obtained an injunction to order the film's return. On appeal, the order to return the film was affirmed.[1]

Legal Importance

It was unnecessary for the court to decide whether the seized film was obscene to determine that the police seizure of the film was unconstitutional and that the film had to be returned to the owner. The controlling rule, established (with respect to book seizures) by two landmark Supreme Court cases,[2] is that in the absence of a prior adversary hearing before a judicial officer to determine the alleged obscenity (or non-obscenity) of a work, any seizure of the work, even one based upon a warrant issued by a judge who has seen the film, is constitutionally deficient, and an abridgment of freedom of expression. In law, such a seizure is considered an unconstitutional "prior restraint." The correctness of the court's decision was subsequently placed in doubt by a decision of the Supreme Court in the 1973 *Blue Movie* case [82], which held that such a seizure was constitutional providing that a copy of the film is or can be made available to the exhibitor "so that a showing [of the film] can be continued pending a judicial determination of the obscenity issue" in a promptly held adversary judicial hearing.

1. Shultz v. Salinas, 416 F. 2d 412 (1969).
2. A Quantity of Books v. Kansas, 378 U.S. 205 (1964); Marcus v. Search Warrants, 367 U.S. 717 (1961).

[86]
Pattern of Evil (Fornicon)

Banned from entry into the United States, 1969.

U.K., 1969. U.S., 1969. Dist: Marvin Films, Jerald Intrator. 72 min. 35mm. Sound. Color. Prod: Chelsea Productions, George Harrison Marks, Al Weiss. Dir: George Harrison Marks. SW: Lawrence Sanders. Cast: Paul Holcombe, Yvonne Paul, Cindy Neal, Rena Bronson, Jutka Goz, Monique Devereaux, Tony Barton, David London, Howard Nelson.

Stripper Dawn Starr performs a dance to suggest Formula-69, a new perfume from Madame LaBanca's cosmetics firm, for whom John Webley handles public relations. A competitor after the formula attempts to kill John, but mistakenly kills his wife. John is a suspect, although lack of evidence causes Scotland Yard to release him. In an effort to find his wife's murderer, John suggests a "truth or consequences" game during a party at Madame LaBanca's home. Greta Marr, the prime suspect, is placed on a medieval torture rack and finally names the killer.

Censorship Activity

The film was refused admittance to the country by the U.S. Customs Bureau on the ground that it was obscene, and proceedings to forfeit the film commenced. Prior to trial, the importer moved to dismiss the proceedings against the film on the grounds that the term *obscene* was unconstitutionally vague, that the proceedings amounted to an unconstitutional prior restraint on freedom of expression, and that the film was not obscene, applying constitutional tests. The motion was denied[1] and the film forfeiture trial was held, but a jury found the film to be not obscene.[2]

Legal Importance

The argument that the customs law providing for the forfeiture of obscene films, and prohibiting their entry into the country, is an unconstitutional prior restraint because it fails to meet the constitutional procedural requirements laid down for film licensing procedures by the U.S. Supreme Court in the *Revenge at Daybreak* case [58] has unsuccessfully been made several times. The Supreme Court, in the 1970 case of *United States* v. *Thirty-Seven Photographs*,[3] construed the customs statute in such a way that its provisions would conform to the constitutional procedural requirements laid down in the *Revenge at Daybreak* case. But in a powerful dissent in that case, Justice Black contended that the Court's four-member plurality (consisting of Justices White, Brennan, and Blackmun and Chief Justice Burger) had engaged in a "rewriting" of this customs statute to a degree constituting "a seizure of legislative power." In his view, the customs law was unconstitutional "on its face" because it specified no time limits within which proceedings must be started to destroy suspect books or pictures, and it did not require a "prompt judicial hearing on obscenity." The plurality in *Thirty-Seven Photographs* had construed the customs law to require judicial proceedings to commence within two weeks following seizure and a final judicial decision to be rendered no longer than 60 days after the commencement of proceedings.

Justice Black also argued that the customs statute was unconstitutionally applied in the *Thirty-Seven Photographs* case to the importation of allegedly obscene photographs concededly for the importer's "private" use, inasmuch as the private possession of concededly obscene films in the privacy of one's home had been found protected by the constitution in the case of *Stanley* v. *Georgia*.[4] Said Justice Black: "The right (recognized in *Stanley*) to read and view any literature and pictures at home is hollow indeed if it does not include a right to carry that material privately in one's luggage when entering the country." And: "Certainly when a man legally purchases such material abroad he should be able to bring it with him through customs to read later in his home."

For other films banned or attempted bannings by U.S. Customs, see the cases of *I Am Curious—Yellow* [71], *The Language of Love* [84], *491* [55], and *Sinderella* [108].

1. United States v. A Motion Picture Entitled *Pattern of Evil*, 304 F. Supp. 197 (1969).
2. *Variety*, Feb. 11, 1970.
3. United States v. Thirty-Seven Photographs, 402 U.S. 363 (1971).
4. Stanley v. Georgia, 394 U.S. 557 (1969).

[87]
Yellow Bird (Curious Yellow Bird)

Banned in Atlanta, Georgia, 1969.

U.S., 1969. Dist: Century Cinema Corp. 62 min. 35mm. Sound. Color. Prod: Century Cinema Corp.

Ellie finds her lesbian lover, Sylvia, in another's arms; her reaction is to go to Skid Row, where she picks up a middle-aged alcoholic named Howard, whom she can sexually dominate. Eventually, Sylvia finds them and the three become a *ménage à trois*. While this is going on, in the same building Lily is being dominated by Jock, who uses her to satisfy the needs of his clients. Lily and Howard meet in the elevator of the building and are united in love.

Censorship Activity

Atlanta, Georgia police seized this film at a theater pursuant to a search warrant issued by the Superior Court of Fulton County. The police intended to exhibit the picture to a grand jury so as to indict all persons responsible for its showing in the county. The film was seized and the search warrant was issued without any prior adversary judicial hearing or any determination whether or not the film was obscene. The theater owner went to court to prevent a possible prosecution against him being secured on the basis of an illegal seizure. A federal court for the northern district of Georgia ordered the film be returned to the owner.[1]

Legal Importance

A prior adversary judicial hearing, "designed to focus searchingly on the question of obscenity, must be held before the State may seize any motion picture film," wrote Judge Albert J. Henderson, Jr., relying on the U.S. Supreme Court's landmark decision in *A Quantity of Books* v. *Kansas*.[2] "The seizure of *The Yellow Bird* was constitutionally deficient because it lacked safeguards to prevent the suppression of non-obscene materials." The judge added: "Let no one infer that this court seeks to impede responsible and vigorous state action designed to check the flow of obscenity in our society. . . . But as the end does not justify the means, here basic constitutional rights may not be trampled under the banner of public morality. If the phrase 'law and order' has any meaning, certainly it requires public enforcement officials to operate within the framework of our Constitution."

1. Central Agency, Inc. v. Brown, 306 F. Supp. 502 (1969).
2. A Quantity of Books v. Kansas, 378 U.S. 205 (1964).

1970–1981

[88]
The Collection

Banned in Los Angeles, California, 1970.

U.S., 1970. Dist: Project One. 35mm. Sound. Color. Prod: Project One. Cast: Max Blue, David Michaels, Ash Grover, Poco Alan.

A homosexual appeases his lust by capturing and enslaving men. The film includes depictions of male homosexual activity, masturbation, flagellation, and sodomy.

Censorship Activity

An exhibitor of this film was convicted in the Los Angeles municipal court of exhibiting this film (and another entitled *Man to Man*) in violation of the California criminal obscenity law. On appeal, the conviction was reversed and the case was remanded for a new trial because of a failure of the prosecution to comply with the "best evidence" rule.[1] On retrial, he was found guilty again and again appealed. The conviction was affirmed by the appellate court,[2] and review by the U.S. Supreme Court was denied.[3]

Legal Importance

When the defendant was first arrested for exhibiting an obscene film, the film itself was not seized. The arresting officers, inside the theater, took pictures of portions of the film and these, rather than the film itself, became evidence at the trial. This was held improper. The film itself was the best evidence of the contents of the film and should have been placed in evidence by the prosecution. Following retrial, the exhibitor unsuccessfully presented an argument that the exhibitors successfully argued in the *Cry Uncle* [106] and *The Exorcist* [110] cases—that since the law under which he had been prosecuted and convicted was patterned after the definition of obscenity presented in the landmark case of *Memoirs* v. *Massachusetts*,[4] and since that definition had been altered in the case of *Miller* v. *California*,[5] the statute here was no longer valid. Justice Brennan's dissent in *Miller* has suggested that virtually all state obscenity laws were impliedly rendered unconstitutional because of the change in the definition made by *Miller*, but this was denied in the majority opinion, written by Chief Justice Burger.

Justices Brennan, Marshall, Stewart, and Douglas dissented from the Supreme Court's refusal to consider this case because as Justice Douglas noted, "any state ban on obscenity is prohibited" and the statute's definition of obscene matter was constitutionally "overbroad" and, therefore, invalid on its face. The position is explained in the *Magic Mirror* case [102].

1. People v. Enskat, 98 Cal. Rptr. 646 (1971).
2. People v. Enskat, 109 Cal. Rptr. 433 (1973).
3. Enskat v. California, 418 U.S. 937 (1974).
4. Memoirs v. Massachusetts, 383 U.S. 413 (1966).
5. Miller v. California, 413 U.S. 15 (1973).

[89]
The Libertine (La Matriarca)

Banned in Fort Smith, Arkansas, 1970.

Italy, 1969. U.S., 1969. Dist: Audubon Films, Inc., Radley Metzger, Euro-International Films (outside U.S.). 90 min. 35mm. Sound. Color. English subtitles. Prod: Clesi Cinematografica, Silvio Clementelli. Dir: Pasquale Festa-Campanile. SW: Nicolo Ferrari, Ottavio Jemma. Cin: Alfio Contini. Cast: Catherine Spaak, Jean-Louis Trintignant, Luigi Proietti. MPAA: X (1969), R (1971 version). Reviews: *Variety*, Jan. 15, 1969, Werb; *New York Times*, May 16, 1969, Howard Thompson; *Film Daily*, May 21, 1969, Mandel Herbstman; *Motion Picture Herald*, May 21, 1969, Barry Glasser; *Independent*, May 26, 1969; *New York*, May 26, 1969, Judith Crist.

After the death of her husband, sexually straitlaced Mimi discovers his private pad of sexual perversion, including among its various devices home movies of some of his adulterous performances. Rather than finding his secret eros morally contemptible, Mimi is outraged at her exclusion from it, sheds her Victorian morals, and sets out to learn what she was missing. Impatient but cold, Mimi seduces virtually everyone she encounters, employing a variety of erotic styles. Nevertheless, she remains unsatisfied until her encounter with a steady, understanding radiologist, DeMarchi. Mimi is attracted to DeMarchi, they have an affair and they fall in love, despite his humiliating disapproval of her bizarre sex life and her aggravating attempts to involve him in it. DeMarchi proposes marriage to Mimi, claiming that he only requires her love, regardless of her sex life. Mimi accepts but insists on being thoroughly satisfied by her husband; together they find a happy erotic middle ground.

Censorship Activity

After three local ministers saw this film, they told a circuit judge what they had seen. The judge directed local police officers to view the film and report back. Since all these people told him that it was obscene, the judge issued a search warrant for the film, which was seized by police while being shown to a paying audience. The theater owner sought a judicial declaration that the search and seizure were unconstitutional, an order to return the film, and an injunction against prosecution for the crime of showing obscenity. A three-judge federal court ordered the film returned to the theater owner, but also directed him to furnish to the state a copy of the movie for use in the pending criminal prosecution; it declined to enjoin prosecution.[1]

Legal Importance

The court held that before a search warrant is issued or a film is seized, an adversary judicial hearing is constitutionally required to determine whether or not the film is obscene. This principle accords with the holdings of later cases, such as *Cindy and Donna* [97] and *Blue Movie* [82], although the U.S. Supreme Court, in the former case, implied that an *adversary* judicial hearing was not required at least where a judicial officer had himself viewed the film prior to authorizing its seizure by police. Here, no such *judicial* "viewing" occurred prior to the film's seizure, and this was sufficient to condemn the process.

1. United Artists Theatre Circuit v. Thompson, 316 F. Supp. 815 (1970).

[90]
The Secret Sex Lives of Romeo and Juliet

Banned in Orlando, Florida, 1970.

U.S., 1969. Dist: Box Office International Film Dist. 96 min. 35mm. Sound. Color. Prod/Dir: A. P. Stootsberry. SW: Jim Schumacher. Cin: Duane

Rayven. Cast: Dicora Carse, Forman Chane, Mickey Jines, Stuart Lancaster.
Review: *New York Times*, Dec. 5, 1979, Howard Thompson.

Loosely based on Shakespeare's *Romeo and Juliet*, this film purports to be
the "true" version of the play as it would have been performed in the Globe
Theater in the mid-1600s. Juliet, promiscuous with men, has a lesbian love
affair with her maid. Romeo, promiscuous with women, sleeps with Juliet's
mother and nurse. Juliet's father arranges a marriage for her and Paris, a
rich homosexual. To avoid marriage, Juliet takes a sleeping potion to feign
death; Romeo finds her and thinks she has died, so he takes the potion too.
Both fathers come upon the sleeping pair, think they have died, and go off
to have a drink together, which allows the lovers to be alone.

Censorship Activity

Orlando police seized a print of this film and arrested the owner and
operator of the theater in which it was being exhibited on the basis of the
film's alleged obscenity, under an Orlando ordinance. The theater owner
and operator brought suit in federal district court, seeking a declaration
that the ordinance was unconstitutional on its face; an order suppressing the
film's seizure and requiring its return; and temporary and permanent injunctions against any further prosecutions in the Orlando Municipal Court.
The district court denied the motion for a temporary restraining order, but
on appeal a three-judge district court held that the seizure and arrests were
unlawful.[1]

Legal Importance

The seizure of the allegedly obscene film and the arrests of the individuals
responsible for exhibiting it were held unconstitutional because of the
absence of a "prior judicially superintended adversary determination of the
obscenity of the moving picture film in question." In effect, this means that
police cannot stop the showing of a film without first going to court. The
court said that this constitutional principle was "settled by the weight of
authority and is an essential safeguard to protect the evanescent guarantee
of freedom of speech." (See the *Revenge at Daybreak* case [58].) For the
court the "real question" posed was whether it was constitutionally permissible for law enforcement officers wishing to obtain evidence for use in a
criminal prosecution to "seize a single print of film . . . without having an
adversary judicial hearing prior to the seizure. . . ." The court observed
that there were a number of ways in which this might be accomplished
without police seizure of a film. For example, the court could direct that a
print be made reasonably available to the prosecution, or a subpoena *duces
tecum*, ordering the appearance of the materials, might be used. The court
declined to grant permanent injunctive relief against future prosecutions of
the owner for exhibiting this motion picture. Instead, the seizure of the film

was suppressed, and it was ordered returned to the theater owner. "In view of our holding . . . ," the court observed, "this prosecution, for practical purposes, is terminated."

1. Carroll v. City of Orlando, 311 F. Supp. 967 (1970).

[91]
Starlet

Banned in Alabama, 1970.

U.S., 1969. Dist: Entertainment Ventures, Inc. 100 min. 35mm. Sound. Color. Prod: Ado Productions, David F. Friedman, William Allen Castleman. Dir: Richard Kanter. SW: David F. Friedman. Cin: Paul Hipp. Cast: Shari Mann, Deirdre Nelson, Joe Gardner, Kathi Cole.

A studio boss spots starlet Carol in a stag film with Doug Davis. He invites Carol and her roommates, Allison, who is bisexual, and Linda, a virgin, to a party, where they meet Maxine, sex star, who is attracted to Allison. Carol has sex with the studio boss to get the lead in his next film, which means that Maxine is left out. Maxine and Allison steal Carol's film, but, in a chase through the lot, Allison is accidentally electrocuted and the film is burned up. Carol becomes a star and, much to everyone's surprise, marries Doug, who is now a contract actor.

Censorship Activity
On July 9, 1969, Alabama state police conducted "raids" on six movie theaters located throughout the state, on the orders of the governor. The police purchased tickets to see *Starlet* and the five other movies being shown at the theaters, viewed the films in their entireties, and, concluding they were obscene, arrested the theater operators and seized the films. The films were introduced as evidence that the exhibitors had violated the Alabama Penal Code. In one case, the exhibitor was also charged with violating ordinances of the city of Birmingham; in another, the operator of a drive-in theater was also charged with contributing to the delinquency of a minor. Defendants requested a three-judge federal court to enjoin the criminal prosecutions and declare unconstitutional police seizures of the films and the laws under which the prosecutions were commenced. The court held unconstitutional all of the seizures and several of the laws invoked to punish the films' exhibitors.[1]

Legal Importance
The federal court ruled that a police seizure of a film based solely on the conclusions of the police that the film is obscene, and incidental to an ar-

rest, violated principles of freedom of expression established by the Supreme Court in the landmark *Revenge at Daybreak* case [58] and others.[2] Those principles require either that an adversary proceeding be held by a judge, prior to any seizure, or that a judge himself view the film and determine whether there is probable cause to consider it obscene before any warrant to seize it is issued, and then only in a situation assuring a prompt final decision after an adversary proceeding. Police officers constitutionally are not qualified to make the judgment required as a condition to seizing a film, and so the film seizures here "fell short of the demanding necessary sensitivity to freedom of expression."

The court also found unconstitutional, as applied to the exhibitor of allegedly obscene motion pictures, an Alabama law punishing the display of "nude pictures of a man, woman, or girl, in any public place, except art galleries," because it was "overbroad," reaching constitutionally protected as well as unprotected materials, and not being limited to the type of materials that the Supreme Court had defined as "outside" constitutional protection in the landmark *Roth* and *Memoirs* cases,[3] as well as in *The Lovers* case [49].

Also ruled as unconstitutional, in its application to a movie's exhibitor, was the Alabama law against "contributing to the delinquency of a minor"; it was held "void for vagueness" because in an area where First Amendment rights were at stake, "precision of regulation must be the touchstone," citing the Supreme Court's decision in the *Viva Maria* case [67], in which a Dallas ordinance prohibiting the exhibition to minors of "harmful" films was declared constitutionally defective because overbroad. The trouble with such a law is that "those who are governed by the law and those who administer it will [not] understand its meaning and application."

1. Entertainment Ventures, Inc. v. Brewer, 306 F. Supp. 802 (1970).
2. For examples: Lee Art Theatre v. Virginia, 392 U.S. 636 (1968); A Quantity of Books v. Kansas, 378 U.S. 205 (1964).
3. Roth v. United States, 354 U.S. 476 (1957); Memoirs v. Massachusetts, 383 U.S. 413 (1966).

[92]
The Vixen

Banned in Ohio and in Duval County, Florida, 1970.

U.S., 1969. Dist: Eve Productions. 71 min. 35mm. Sound. Color. Prod/Dir/Cin: Russ Meyer. SW: Robert Rudelson. Cast: Erika Gavin, Harrison Page, Garth Pilsbury, Michael O'Donnell, Vincence Wallace, Robert Aiken, Jon Evans. MPAA: X. Reviews: *Morning Telegraph*, May 19, 1968; *Variety*, Oct. 30, 1968; *Time*, June 13, 1969.

The owner of a lodge in British Columbia spends too much time away from his wife as a bush pilot and hunting guide to his lodgers. In his absence, his wife seeks sexual encounters, living up to her name, Vixen. She has affairs with "everyone from a Royal Mountie to the wife of a visiting fisherman."[1]

Censorship Activity

A nuisance abatement action was brought to enjoin permanently the distribution and exhibition of *The Vixen* in Ohio because it was obscene. The court of common pleas issued the requested injunction, and this action was upheld by the Supreme Court of Ohio.[2] In an unrelated case arising in Florida, a federal district court enjoined a Duval County, Florida sheriff from seizing a print of *The Vixen* being shown at the Five Points Theater in Jacksonville,[3] without prior notice or adversary hearing to determine the obscenity of the film. Such a seizure was in conflict with the First Amendment's guarantees of free expression, as prescribed by the cases of *Marcus* v. *Search Warrants*[4] and *A Quantity of Books* v. *Kansas*.[5]

Legal Importance

The Ohio Supreme Court's opinion is interesting for its failure legally to distinguish between the "depiction of purported acts of sexual intercourse on the movie screen" and the performance of such acts "in a public place," calling both such activities "conduct, not free speech." The court obscures a difference that is central to free speech theory. Just as speech is protected precisely because it is speech and not conduct, so a film will be protected precisely because it is a filmed depiction of conduct, not the depicted conduct.

Films frequently depict conduct that would be criminal if *actually* performed "in a public place"—for example, a murder; but, whereas the actual act of murder may and should be punished as a crime, common sense as well as the guarantees of free expression preclude the punishment of a film or a play portraying an act of murder. A similar instance of legal obfuscation was engaged in by a majority of the Supreme Court of the United States in 1973, when speaking for the Court in a landmark decision, Chief Justice Burger said: "Conduct or depictions of conduct that the state police power can prohibit on a public street do not become automatically protected by the Constitution merely because the conduct is moved to a bar or a 'live' theater stage. . . ."[6] But, constitutionally, they certainly might be so protected, first, because now they are forms of expression rather than conduct and, second, because they are "consented-to" presentations, not unconsented-to offensive displays.

Another noteworthy aspect of the Ohio Supreme Court's decision in this case involved its application of the "redeeming social value" or "social importance" test for freeing films from suppression as obscene. The court misapplied a "pandering" rule announced in the case of *Ginzburg* v. *United States*[7] by holding that evidence that a film's exhibitor was principally motivated by the prospect of financial gain was equivalent to pandering to prurient interests in sex, and so negatived whatever social value or importance the film might conceivably have. Although half of the movie's footage dealt with "contemporary issues [such] as racism, anti-militarism, communism, and airline hijacking," the court could "pierce the veil of contrived social commentary totally unrelated to the dominant theme of the picture" and find the film obscene. Since *Vixen* showed "sexual intercourse on the movie screen for commercial exploitation," rather than for a genuine scientific, educational, sociological, moral, or artistic purpose, it could validly be condemned.

1. *Time*, June 13, 1969.
2. State *ex rel.* Keating v. A Motion Picture Film Entitled Vixen, 272 N.E. 2d 137 (1971).
3. Mandel v. Carson, 309 F. Supp. 326 (1969).
4. Marcus v. Search Warrants, 367 U.S. 717 (1961).
5. A Quantity of Books v. Kansas, 378 U.S. 205 (1964).
6. Paris Adult Theatre I v. Slaton, 413 U.S. 49 (1973).
7. Ginzburg v. United States, 383 U.S. 463 (1965).

[93]
Where Eagles Dare

Banned in Rutherford County, North Carolina, 1970.

U.S., 1969. Dist: MGM. 158 min. 70mm. Sound. Color. Prod: Jerry Gersawm, Elliot Kastner. Dir: Brian Hutton. SW: Alistair MacLean. Cin: Arthur Ibbetson. Cast: Richard Burton, Clint Eastwood, Mary Ure, Ingrid Pitt. MPAA: M. Reviews: *Variety*, Dec. 11, 1968; *Newsday*, March 13, 1969, Joseph Gelmis; *Christian Science Monitor*, March 14, 1969, Roderick Nordell; *New York* Magazine, March 17, 1969, Judith Crist; *Life*, March 28, 1969, Richard Shickel.

This film is a World War II espionage thriller. An Allied general has been captured by the Germans. He must be rescued from the Bavarian castle where he is being hidden so that he will not divulge the plans for the invasion of Europe by the Allies. In order to rescue him, a British intelligence officer, an American lieutenant, and a woman agent band together and "take over Gestapo headquarters in the Bavarian Alps, rescuing and unmasking a traitor and getting safely home to guarantee our victory while leaving the Alps up to their peaks in blood and corpses."[1] The rescue mission requires parachuting in a blinding snowstorm onto a cliff where the castle is perched. They are discovered and must escape by a daring cable car ride that is the only link between the castle and the town below. The overall tone of the movie is one of violent action with much killing and blowing up of cars and buildings.

Censorship Activity

The sheriff of Rutherford County, North Carolina, undertook a campaign to stop the exhibition within the county of all films not recommended by the Motion Picture Association of America "for general audiences." He threatened to arrest the owner of a theater planning to show *Where Eagles Dare* and to confiscate the film. The plaintiff, the theater operator, discontinued showing adult-rated films and, alleging the ban would put him out of business, sought and secured a court order restraining the sheriff from the described activity. On review, a federal court of appeals affirmed.[2]

Legal Importance

Even assuming that the North Carolina obscenity law that the sheriff purported to enforce was constitutional, it was "clear that the sheriff's conduct cannot be tolerated in a free society." Inasmuch as motion pictures are "speech" within the meaning of the First Amendment, the sheriff's activities amounted to unconstitutional prior restraints on freedom of that speech, analogous to the constitutionally condemned activities of an organization called the "Rhode Island Commission to Encourage Morality in Youth," which had informally coerced, persuaded, and intimidated booksellers into removing from their shelves books the commission had considered objectionable for youth.[3] The sheriff apparently believed he was constitutionally empowered to decide by himself "in any manner he saw fit" what films could not be shown whereas, as the *Revenge at Daybreak* case [58] held, no film could be seized without "a prior judicial adversary proceeding on the issue of obscenity, at which both sides have an opportunity to be heard." The court observed that "it has been noted more than once" that constitutionally protected expression is often separated from obscenity "only by a dim and uncertain line," and that "the separation of legitimate from illegitimate speech calls for . . . more sensitive tools" than the sheriff made use of in his censorship activity.

1. *New York* Magazine, March 17, 1969, Judith Crist.
2. Drive-In Theatres, Inc. v. Huskey, 435 F. 2d 228 (1970).
3. Bantam Books v. Sullivan, 372 U.S. 58 (1963).

[94]
Without a Stitch (Uten En Trad)

Banned from entry into the United States, 1970; banned in California, Tennessee, and Rhode Island, 1970–1972.

Denmark, 1968. U.S., 1969. Dist: VIP Distributors, Inc., Jack H. Harris, Sherpix, Inc., Donald L. Velde Distributors, Tonlyn Productions. 96 min. 35mm. Sound. Color. English subtitles. Prod: A/B Palladium Production, Teuga Nielsen, John Hilbard. Dir: Annelise Meineche. SW: Annelise Meineche, John Hilbard. Cin: Aage Wiltrup. Cast: Anne Grete, Ib Mossin, Niels Borksand, Ki-Jo Feza, Niels Dybeck. MPAA: X. Reviews: *New York Post*, Jan. 10, 1970, Archer Winsten; *New York Times*, Jan. 10, 1970, Roger Greenspun; *Motion Picture Herald*, Jan. 21, 1970, Michael Schau. Articles: *Hollywood Reporter*, Jan. 2, 1970; *Variety*, March 8, 1972; *Box Office*, April 13, 1970.

This film was adapted from the novel *Without a Stitch I*, by Jens Bjorneboe. Fearing herself frigid, Lilian, a high-school girl, seeks the guidance of a handsome, young male gynecologist who is an "orgasm specialist." After the doctor determines that she functions normally, Lilian takes his personal stimuli and response course. To rid Lilian of her inhibiting feeling of guilt, the doctor advises her to "do unto others as you would have others do unto you" and sends her off into the world to open herself to every beckoning experience. Inspired, Lilian hitchhikes her way through Europe, leaving no erotic opportunity unfulfilled. Finally, by now a mature woman, Lilian returns to the handsome young doctor, with a diary for his studies, for one more examination. According to one critic, the young actress who plays Lilian, Anne Grete, "could reasonably pass for Bibi Andersson's kid sister. Her very good looks suggest an active intelligence (her second greatest passion is collecting books—Heine, Strindberg, etc.). Because the face is what we look to, even in erotic movies, Miss Grete carries the film into the slightly deeper, warmer, lovelier intimacies of knowledge that it may have intended."[1]

Censorship Activity

Six private individuals sought an injunction from a California Superior Court to prevent the exhibition of this film and to suppress it as a public nuisance. The court denied the injunction. On appeal, the Court of Appeals affirmed.[2] The film was also determined to be not obscene by a federal court jury after being seized by U.S. Customs; obscene by a Rhode Island Superior Court judge; and obscene by a Memphis, Tennessee court.

Legal Importance

The court held that the provisions of the state "Red Light Abatement Law" did not extend to the exhibition of motion pictures. Thus, even though the film appeared to the court to be "a singularly inartful cinematic effort

[that] depicts sexual activity including, but not limited to, sexual intercourse, lesbianism and sodomy,'' it was shown in a closed theater, and so could not be deemed a public nuisance. Only those persons could view the film who had paid the admission price and entered the theater. Only those members of the community were exposed to the film who voluntarily chose to see it. The "nuisance" could not be said to be one which was "inflicted or imposed on the public.'' The court recognized that the public nuisance statute had been applied to "lewd live stage shows and exhibitions,'' but never "to depictions in closed theaters of those same acts, by still or motion picture, or drawings of any type of exhibits which are limited to closed theaters.'' Furthermore, private citizens could not interfere with the film's exhibition in such a location.

Associate Justice Roy L. Herndon dissented, claiming that "[t]he English language does not provide adjectives sufficient to describe the utter rottenness of this sordid product of subhuman depravity and greed that portrays every known form of sexual perversion.'' Anticipating an approach that would be taken a few years later by Chief Justice Warren Burger of the U.S. Supreme Court in *Paris Adult Theatre I* v. *Slaton*,[3] he maintained that "the nuisance created by hard-core pornography assumes the form of a pollution of the moral environment far more offensive and more damaging in its effects than the nauseous odors produced by the swine . . . or the animals [referred to in other cases].'' Justice Herndon admitted, however, finding no California appellate court decision extending the application of the nuisance act "to authorize an action by a private citizen to abate the exhibition of an obscene motion picture.'' But, he wrote, "I submit that both the literal terms of the act and the public policy which it plainly expresses dictate its application here.'' Since legislature declared houses used for illegal gambling, lewdness, or prostitution to be nuisances in the interests of protecting others than those who chose to frequent such houses, so houses used for the showing of obscene films should be condemned as nuisances, despite their popularity with persons who pay an admission price to enter them.

1. *New York Times*, Jan. 10, 1970.
2. Harmer v. Tonlyn Productions, Inc., 100 Cal. Rptr. 576, 23 Cal. App. 3d 941 (1972).
3. Paris Adult Theatre I v. Slaton, 413 U.S. 49 (1973).

[95]
Woodstock

Banned for persons under 18 in Kenosha, Wisconsin, 1970.

U.S., 1970. Dist: Warner Brothers Pictures. 184 min. 35mm. Sound. Color. Prod: Bob Maurice. Dir/Cin: Michael Wadleigh. Cast: Popular rock musicians. MPAA: R. Reviews: *Village Voice*, March 26, 1970; *Boston After Dark*, April 1, 1970, Deac Rossell; *The Villager*, April 30, 1970, Ellen Cohn; *Punch*, July 1, 1970, Richard Mallett.

This is a documentary film of a three-day music festival that took place in Bethel, New York at the Yasgar Farm in 1969. Over half a million young people turned out for the "Woodstock Music Art Fair" and camped near the sound stage erected on the farm. The festival included performers Joan Baez, Joe Cocker, Country Joe and the Fish, Crosby, Stills, Nash, and Young (who sang the title song "Woodstock," written by Joni Mitchell), Arlo Guthrie, Richie Havens, Jimi Hendrix, Santana, Sha-Na-Na, John Sebastian, Sly and the Family Stone, Ten Years After, and The Who. Amidst the recording of the performances of these artists, the communal life of the audience was interjected, through use of a split-camera technique, thereby showing shots of the performers side by side with the audience's reaction. "The whole uniqueness of the Woodstock festival lay in its communal mood, its liberation of the individual through participation. Skinny-dipping in a pond, childishly sliding in mud, sharing a blanket, a bottle, a joint, Woodstock had that extra dimension of community."[1]

Censorship Activity

Several persons under 18 years of age in the company of two adults who were parents of some of them were denied entrance to a movie theater showing this film because a city of Kenosha ordinance forbade the entrance of minors at theaters showing movies classified by the Motion Picture Association of America as R or X. The adults, on their own and the children's behalf, asked a federal district court to enjoin enforcement of the ordinance because it denied to children their rights of freedom of expression. The court issued the injunction.[2]

Legal Importance

The court ruled that the ordinance amounted to an unconstitutional prior restraint on expression because there was no requirement that the city go to court immediately and prove the movie was of the type banned for minors, and because the standards used by the MPAA to classify films as R or X (and thereby prohibited for minors) were unknown to the city itself, as well as to persons wishing to see the movie. Since the ordinance allowed the prosecution of persons violating its terms, it was likely to deter persons from exercising their First Amendment rights. The case disclosed the unusual situation whereby government officials utilized the views of a private organization to bring about a censorship of expression.

1. *Boston After Dark*, April 1, 1970.
2. Engdahl v. Kenosha, 317 F. Supp. 1133 (1970).

[96]
The Art of Marriage

Banned in Minneapolis, Minnesota, 1971.

U.S., 1970. 62 min. 35mm. Sound. Color. Prod: Nevada Institute for Family Study. Review: *New York Times*, May 10, 1970, Vincent Canby.

In this quasi-instructional film, a bearded host/narrator introduces the audience to a variety of explicitly shown coital positions taken by two "happily married" couples. "The color is good, the camera as mobile as necessary, and the effect as erotic as Algebra One."[1]

Censorship Activity

The owner-manager of a commercial motion picture theater in Minneapolis who showed this film was convicted in municipal court of exhibiting an obscene film, contrary to a Minneapolis ordinance. On appeal, the Supreme Court of Minnesota affirmed.[2]

Legal Importance

The main issue was whether the film had even "a modicum of redeeming social value" for, under the U.S. Supreme Court's decision in the *Fanny Hill* book case,[3] that was said to entitle a work to constitutional protection and preclude it being condemned as obscene. A majority of the state supreme court decided that the film's educational attributes were "mere pretense," that nearly everything the narrator said "could in fact apply to the beasts of the field as well as to human beings," without any reference to "affection, love, respect, marital discipline, or . . . any moral code," and that the film was "utterly without redeeming social value." It was "so-called hard-core pornography." Dissenting Justice Otis found the film "tedious and uninspired . . . quite obviously simulated [and] about as sexually provocative as a documentary on techniques for artificially inseminating cattle." Moreover, in his opinion, the film was one that "might well be of substantial benefit to couples with marriage problems," and since its showing was limited to adults who were "warned" about its character, it was "neither pandered, obtrusive, nor exhibited to juveniles," and so could not properly be condemned as obscene.

The decision of the majority anticipated the decision subsequently reached by the Burger majority of the U.S. Supreme Court in the *Magic Mirror* case [102], while dissenting Justice Otis anticipated the important dissent rendered in the latter case by Justice Brennan.

1. *New York Times*, May 10, 1970, Vincent Canby.
2. State v. Lebewitz, 202 N.W. 648 (1972).
3. Memoirs v. Massachusetts, 383 U.S. 413 (1966).

[97]
Cindy and Donna

Banned in Pulaski County, Kentucky, 1971.

U.S., 1970. Dist: Crown International Pictures. 84 min. 35mm. Sound. Color. MPAA: X. Prod: Robert J. Anderson, Terry Anderson. Dir: Robert J. Anderson. SW: Barry Clark. Cin: J. Barry Herron. Music: Robert O. Ragland. Cast: Debbie Osborne, Nancy Ison, Cheryl Powell, Max Manning, Suzy Allen, Tom Koben.

Fifteen-year-old Cindy is curious about but afraid to discover her own sexual nature. After she sees her half-sister Donna, 17, make love to Cindy's father while high on marijuana, Cindy decides to experiment. With both parents gone one weekend, Donna has sex with three young men, Cindy and her friend Karen get high on marijuana, and Cindy has a sex experience with Karen. When Cindy later tries to have sex with Donna's boyfriend, he throws Donna out of the house and she is hit by a car. Cindy's sexual adventures end.

Censorship Activity

After the sheriff of Pulaski County bought a ticket and viewed the film's public showing, he arrested the theater manager and seized the film because it displayed "nudity" and "intimate love scenes." The manager was convicted of exhibiting obscene material, against the argument that the film was seized illegally and thus evidence of its content (conceded to have been obscene) should have been suppressed. On review by the Court of Appeals of Kentucky, the manager's conviction was upheld.[1] However, the Supreme Court of the United States reversed.[2]

Legal Importance

The behavior of the sheriff in seizing the film solely on the basis of *his own* conclusion that it was obscene violated constitutional standards, inasmuch as there was no opportunity for a magistrate to "focus searchingly on the question of obscenity" before suppression, as required by such cases as *Blue Movie* [82], where a magistrate had viewed the film before warranting its seizure as evidence of the commission of a crime. "Seizing a film," Chief Justice Burger said, speaking for the Supreme Court, "then being exhibited to the general public presents essentially the same restraint on expression as the seizure of all the books in a bookstore." Such a seizure, without a judicial warrant, violated the constitutional prohibition against "unreasonable seizures." Bookstores and commercial theaters are "presumptively under the protection of the First Amendment" and present "a very different situation from that in which contraband is changing hands or where a robbery or assault is being perpetrated." Seizures of weapons, or other evidence or instruments of crime—without a warrant might be justified in the latter situation where it is a "now or never" situation. There, it is "reasonable" to seize "without prior judicial evaluation." The seemingly broad protection afforded films, in this case, from precipitous police seizure does not, it should be noticed, protect films from precipitous judicial action. The case, by implication, holds that a film may be seized without a prior *adversary* hearing—without, that is, an opportunity given to the film's distributor to deny, and defend against, the allegations that the film is obscene, before it is seized—if the film is seen, and believed probably obscene by a judge. However, the *Blue Movie* case [82] did indicate that in such a situation the film may be seized only *as evidence* of the crime of showing obscenity and provided that another copy of the film is available to the exhibitor who wishes to continue showing the film, pending conclusion of "adversary proceedings" to determine whether it is obscene.

1. Roaden v. Kentucky, 473 S.W. 2d 814 (1971).
2. Roaden v. Kentucky, 413 U.S. 496 (1973).

[98]
Computer Game

Banned in Miami, Florida, 1971.

U.S., 1969. Dist: Distribpix. 63 min. 35mm. Sound. Color. Prod: Kirby Films International.

A sexual maniac makes use of a computer dating service to lure women to his home, where he puts them through autoerotic and lesbian activity. The police catch up with him and terminate his and his victims' enjoyment of the practices.

Censorship Activity

After this film and two others[1] were seized by police pursuant to a search warrant, on the ground that they were probably obscene, the owner of the theater at which they were being shown brought suit for a temporary injunction to stop criminal proceedings from taking place. He also asked that the Miami obscenity ordinance be declared unconstitutional and sought return of the prints seized. The Circuit Court of Dade County refused to grant the injunction, thus upholding the police action. The court also entered an order permanently restraining the theater owner from exhibiting anywhere in the state these films or any other movies which were "obscene." On appeal, the District Court of Appeals of Florida affirmed the order, after limiting its scope to the named films and to Dade County.[2]

Legal Importance

The Florida court held in a *per curiam* opinion that the Miami obscenity ordinance was constitutional, not being void for vagueness despite its failure to specify obscenity standards spelled out in the landmark U.S. Supreme Court *Roth* case.[3] "[A]lthough not literally present in the ordinance, [these standards] are to be implied when the ordinance is applied," the court decided. In any event, the court believed the movies to be "hard-core pornography or 'stag movies.' " According to the court, "[T]here are no conceivable community standards which would permit dissemination of this type of motion picture." However, the restraining of other unnamed movies was, in the court's opinion, "not properly included" in the lower court's judgment, as this provision "did not have reference to the films which had been seized or to any specific films and was too broad in scope." Furthermore, it was improperly broad to order a suppression outside of Dade County.

1. The two other films seized, *Fur Piece* and *Married Bachelors*, were also depicted by the court as "hard-core pornography or 'stag movies.' "
2. State of Florida *ex rel.* Little Beaver Theatre, Inc. v. Tobin, 258 So. 2d 30 (1972).
3. United States v. Roth, 354 U.S. 476 (1957).

[99]
It All Comes Out in the End

Banned in Georgia, 1971.

U.S., 1970. Dist: Jo-Jo Distributors. 61–68 min. 16mm. Sound. Color.

Censorship Activity/Legal Importance

See *Magic Mirror* [102], involving the same case.

[100]
The Killing of Sister George

Promotional advertisement banned in Los Angeles, California, 1971.

U.S., 1968. Dist: Cinerama Releasing Corp. 118 min. 35mm. Sound. Color. Prod/Dir: Robert Aldrich. SW: Lucas Heller. Cin: Joseph Biroc. Cast: Beryl Reid, Susannah York, Coral Browne. MPAA: X. Reviews: *Morning Telegraph*, Dec. 17, 1968, Leo Mishkin; *Newark Evening News*, Dec. 17, 1968, Bruce Bahreburg; *Newsweek*, Dec. 23, 1968; *Christian Science Monitor*, Feb. 3, 1969.

The Killing of Sister George is based on the stage play of the same title by Frank Marcus. It reveals the problems of a lesbian love triangle. "Sister George" is a BBC soap opera character who is "killed off" due to low ratings. The aging actress who portrays Sister George is a lesbian living with a childish middle-aged woman named Childie, who works in a factory when not playing with her doll collection. Conflict arises between the two lovers when the hard-nosed BBC female program director, who told George of her canceled part, also steals Childie away. "To make the point perfectly plain the film includes a scene of this program director making love to the blonde girl in the privacy of the latter's bedroom. . . ."[1] As consolation for losing both her job and her lover, George is offered the voice part of a puppet cow in a new animated cartoon series.

Censorship Activity

The film's producer asked a federal district court to stop the *Los Angeles Times* from censoring its proferred advertising copy for the film. The producer claimed that the newspaper's alteration of the drawing of a female figure and the deletion of a reference to deviate sexual conduct abridged the constitutional "right to know." The petition was dismissed and, on appeal, the dismissal was affirmed.[2]

Legal Importance

May a privately owned newspaper constitutionally alter or delete advertising copy because, in its "private" judgment, the copy "is in poor taste or offensive to its readers"? Or does such action violate the would-be advertiser's freedom of expression? Would a court order forbidding such alteration or deletion by the newspaper itself violate the newspaper's freedom of expression? Does the fact that a newspaper has a substantial monopoly, "accounting for 80% of all morning daily circulation," make of that newspaper a "quasi-public" organ whose activities should be deemed tantamount to governmental action? It is a basic principle of constitutional interpretation that only actions by governmental, as distinguished from private, agencies come within the constitutional prohibitions against abridging the freedoms of speech and press. Consequently, the courts usually refuse to characterize as unconstitutional actions by private persons or organizations which, if done by governmental organs, would be held to violate freedom of expression. The result of this case thus accords with the usual approach.

The deficiency of this doctrine is suggested by the situation presented in this case in which the producer of a film, which could not be found obscene because it had social importance (thereby gaining constitutional protection), was prevented from advertising the film (in a non-obscene and lawful manner) in a daily newspaper because the esthetic and moral views presented by the advertisement deviated from those professed by the newspaper's proprietor. There is little doubt that, were the newspaper governmentally owned or regulated, as a "public" organ of communication, the sort of censorship that the *Los Angeles Times* here engaged in would have violated the producer's constitutional rights.

1. *Morning Telegraph*, Dec. 17, 1968, Leo Mishkin.
2. Associates & Aldrich Co. v. Times Mirror Co., 440 F. 2d 133 (1971).

[101]
Lysistrata

Banned in Tucson, Arizona, 1971.

U.S., 1968. Dist: Chancellor Films. 65 min. 35mm. Sound. B&W. Prod: Mod Films, Frank Garto. Dir: Jon Matt. SW: Roly Strong. Cin: Red Del.

Very loosely adapted from Aristophanes' play *Lysistrata*, this film tells of Manhattan model Lysistrata, who hates men after they rape or reject her. She forms a lesbian club, whose members all hate men and vow to frustrate them by making sure they are sexually unsatisfied, at the same time satisfying their own desires with masturbation and cunnilingus. Fred, whose girlfriend Pamela has joined the club, spies on their activities and sees Lysistrata, in a vengeful act of jealousy, stab each of the club members. Fred intends to torture Lysistrata, but before he can do so, she stabs herself to death.

Censorship Activity

After a Tucson, Arizona police lieutenant viewed this film at a drive-in theater, the city attorney brought suit in the Pima County Superior Court for an injunction to restrain further exhibition of the film on the grounds that it was obscene and, being visible from a nearby public highway, that its exhibition was a public nuisance. Although the trial court held that an Arizona statute that expressly authorized the issuance of injunctions against obscene materials was not applicable to motion pictures, the court nevertheless enjoined the theater operator from exhibiting *Lysistrata* or any other film "of the same character" at a drive-in theater in such a manner that the nearby public could view it—as a "public nuisance." Evidence was introduced that the film could be, and was, seen by children under 18 who stood outside the theater and that it could be "potentially harmful" to minors. On appeal, the Court of Appeals of Arizona affirmed the granting of an injunction to prevent the theater from further showing the film.[1]

Legal Importance

The appellate court held that a movie which a child psychiatrist considered "potentially harmful" to minor children who might view it and which could be seen by adults and children from public places outside the theater was a "public nuisance" which could be abated by a court injunction. The court argued that a drive-in theater that exhibited films in such a way that they were visible to the public outside the theater invaded the rights of that public by "imposing its pictures upon persons without their consent." Analogizing the situation to a typical nuisance action in property law, the court reasoned: "If the owner of land can be prohibited from polluting the community with noxious smoke and unpleasant odors, we conceive of no reason why he cannot be prohibited from polluting the neighborhood with visual material harmful to children. We see no reason why a public nuisance which is a menace to the well-being of the children in a community should be protected by the First Amendment. Indeed, speech or conduct which inflicts harm is not protected by the First Amendment."

Although the court's legal analysis of the situation was cogent in the sense that constitutional freedom of expression may not include a right to inflict every sort of sexual image on nonconsenting adults or on children (see, for example, Justice Brennan's dissent in the *Magic Mirror* case [102]), the use of a general public nuisance statute to stop the showing of a film that might be considered potentially harmful to minor children because of its sexually oriented content violates the First Amendment's guarantees of freedom of expression because of vagueness and overbreadth. In 1975, in the *Class of '74* case [114], the U.S. Supreme Court invalidated, as unconstitutionally overbroad on its face, a Jacksonville, Florida ordinance which made it a public nuisance to exhibit films containing nudity when the screen is visible from a public street or place—despite the arguments that such a law was justified in order to protect citizens against unwilling exposure to materials that may be offensive, because of nudity, and that it was a reasonable means of protecting minors from nude displays. "Speech that is neither obscene as to youths nor subject to some other legitimate proscription cannot be suppressed solely to protect the young from ideas or images that a legislative body thinks unsuitable for them." And, "the Constitution does not permit government to decide which types of otherwise protected speech are sufficiently offensive to require protection for the unwilling listener or viewer." The "burden normally falls upon the viewer[s] to avoid further bombardment of [their] sensibilities simply by averting [their] eyes."

The Arizona public nuisance law contained no ascertainable standards and no precise definitions regarding what sorts of films, viewable by persons outside of drive-in theaters, could not be shown by such theaters. Applied to restrain the exhibition of films, it should have been held fatally vague and overbroad, unconstitutional. In 1980, the U.S. Supreme Court found a Texas public nuisance statute unconstitutional, as applied to motion pictures shown indoors at an adults-only theater because it authorized a "prior restraint of indefinite duration on the exhibition of motion pictures without a final judicial determination of obscenity and without any guarantee of prompt (judicial) review of a preliminary finding of probable obscenity," citing the *Revenge at Daybreak* case [58].[2] The Court said, "Nor does the fact that the temporary prior restraint is entered (*ex parte*) by a state trial judge rather than an administrative officer sufficiently distinguish this case from [the *Revenge at Daybreak* case]. That a state trial judge might be thought more likely than an administrative censor to determine accurately that a work is obscene does not change the unconstitutional character of the restraint if erroneously entered."

1. Cactus Corporation v. State *ex rel.* Murphy, 480 F. 2d 375 (1971).
2. Vance v. Universal Amusement Co., 446 U.S. 947 (1980).

[102]
Magic Mirror

Banned in Georgia, 1971.

U.S., 1970. Dist: Stacey Distributors. 61–81 min. 16mm. Sound. Color.

Censorship Activity
The district attorney went to court for an order declaring this and another film, *It All Comes Out in the End* [99], to be obscene and enjoining their exhibitors from showing them. The Superior Court of Fulton County, Georgia viewed the films and found them not to be obscene. Upon appeal, however, the Supreme Court of Georgia reversed that ruling,[1] which decision was affirmed by the U.S. Supreme Court.[2]

Legal Importance
The trial court thought the films degrading to the human body and personality but, since the sexual activity was merely "simulated" and the public had been given notice of the character of the films, which, moreover, were not shown to minors—the court ruled them not to be obscene. On appeal, the exhibitor argued that the recent 1969 U.S. Supreme Court decision in *Stanley* v. *Georgia* required a finding that the films were constitutionally protected expression because there the Court had recognized the constitutional right of an adult to possess and view unidentified, admittedly obscene movies in his home.[3]

The U.S. Supreme Court's decision in this case is a benchmark of the Burger Court's interpretation of the constitutional law of obscenity. In it, and in the case of *Miller* v. *California*[4] decided the same day, the high court denied that "consenting adults" in the United States were constitutionally free, outside the privacy of their homes, to view the movies and read the books of their choice—if these were "obscene."

The possibility of such freedom of expression for adults had been strongly implied by Justice Thurgood Marshall, speaking for a majority of the Supreme Court, in the *Stanley* case: "If the First Amendment means anything," he said, "it means that a state has no business telling a man, sitting alone in his own house, what books he may read or what films he may watch. Our whole constitutional heritage rebels at the thought of giving government the power to control men's minds." Four years later, in his opinion in the present case, Chief Justice Burger denied that *Stanley* meant freedom for adults to see whatever films they wished, and held that a state could prevent the "public" dissemination of obscene materials, including a film, "which, by definition, lacks any serious literary, artistic, political, or scientific value as communication." This, Burger contended, was "distinct from a control of reason and the intellect. . . . [F]or us to say that our constitution incorporates the proposition that conduct involving consenting adults only is always beyond state regulation is a step we are unable to take."

Obscene films could be banned from "commercial premises open to the adult public" in view of the state's "broad power to regulate commerce and protect the public environment." This is not because the conduct depicted by obscene films is considered "wrong" or "sinful" by the state, but because a state is empowered to make the "morally neutral judgment" that the public exhibition or commerce in "obscene" material "has a tendency to injure the community as a whole, to endanger the public safety, or to jeopardize . . . the States' right to maintain a decent society."

One of the earmarks of a decent society, according to Chief Justice Burger, resided in the prerogative of government to prevent "consenting adults" from engaging in "degrading conduct," including conduct brigaded with expression. The laws "against prostitution, suicide, voluntary self-mutilation, brutalizing fist-fights, and duels," although these crimes may only directly involve "consenting adults," were illustrative. For, as Professor Irving Kristol observed: "Bearbaiting and cockfighting are prohibited only in part out of compassion for the suffering animals; the main reason they were abolished was because it was felt that they debased and brutalized the citizens who flocked to witness such spectacles."[5] In refusing to recognize the existence of a constitutional right in American adults to view the movies of their choice, entirely free of government constraint, the

Chief Justice recorded the disinclination of a majority of the Supreme Court to agree with the political philosophy that John Stuart Mill advanced in his classic work *On Liberty*.

Laws preventing and punishing obscene films were said to be akin to "blue-sky" laws that regulate "what sellers of securities may write or publish about their wares." Such laws have their legitimate state purpose "to protect the weak, the uninformed, the unsuspecting and the gullible from the exercise of their volition," from their so-called "free will." Similarly, Chief Justice Burger pointed out, modern societies do not leave the "disposal of garbage and sewage" up to the individual's "free will," but instead "impose regulation to protect both public health and appearance of public places."

The Court recognized that states were free "to follow a *laissez-faire* policy and drop all controls on commercialized obscenity, if that is what they prefer, just as they can ignore consumer protection in the marketplace, but nothing in the Constitution compels them to do so." Thus did the Court hold that citizens are not constitutionally free to see obscene movies if their government is determined that they ought not to see such movies but in the privacy of their homes.

In a dissenting opinion, Justice William O. Douglas recalled having frequently expressed his disagreement with the basic decision that obscenity was not protected by the First Amendment, and with the definitions of obscenity that the Court, principally through Justice William Brennan, had evolved. He also observed that "in a life that has not been short, I have yet to be trapped into seeing or reading something that would offend me." "I never read," he continued, "or see the materials coming to the Court under charges of obscenity, because I have thought the First Amendment made it unconstitutional for me to act as a censor." Although, when a man entered society, controls were necessarily imposed, "our society—unlike most in the world—presupposes that freedom and liberty are in a frame of reference that makes the individual, not government, the keeper of his tastes, beliefs, and ideas; and it is this article of faith that sets us apart from most nations in the world."

Justice William Brennan, joined by Justices Potter Stewart and Thurgood Marshall, also dissented, in a long, discursive opinion in which he admitted that the landmark decision he had written for the Court 16 years earlier in *Roth* v. *United States*—to the effect that obscenity was unprotected by the constitutional guarantees of freedom of speech and press—ought to be abandoned. Brennan now doubted that "there exists a definable class of sexually oriented expression that may be totally suppressed by the federal and state government." Even assuming such a class of expression as "obscenity" exists, he continued, "the concept of 'obscenity' cannot be defined with sufficient specificity and clarity to provide fair notice to persons who create and distribute sexually-oriented materials, to protect substantial erosion of protected speech as a by-product of the attempt to suppress unprotected speech, and to avoid very costly institutional harms.''

The only "legitimate" governmental interests now seen by Justice Brennan as capable of justifying restraints against even the *public* dissemination of obscene materials such as films were to protect "unconsenting adults" and "children" from exposure to erotic communication. "It may well be," he said, "as [Professor Thomas Emerson] has argued, that 'exposure to [erotic material] is for some persons an intense emotional experience.' A communication of that nature, imposed upon a person contrary to his wishes, has all the characteristics of a physical assault. . . . [And it] constitutes an invasion of his privacy. . . . Similarly, if children are 'not possessed of that full capacity for individual choice' which is the presupposition of the First Amendment guarantee . . . then the State may have a substantial interest in precluding the flow of obscene materials even to consenting juveniles.''

According to Justice Brennan, government regulation of obscenity should be limited to those situations where children are involved or where it is necessary to prevent its imposition on unwilling persons of any age. These are the only "legitimate governmental interests for the legal control of obscenity." Only if government activity, with respect to sexually oriented materials, is restricted to those specific areas will "fuller freedom of expression" for films and other expressive materials be guaranteed.

1. Paris Adult Theatre v. Slaton, 185 S.E. 2d 768 (1971).
2. Paris Adult Theatre v. Slaton, 413 U.S. 49 (1973).
3. Stanley v. Georgia, 394 U.S. 557 (1969).
4. Miller v. California, 413 U.S. 15 (1973).
5. Irving Kristol, *On the Democratic Idea in America.* New York: Harper, 1972.

[103]
Pornography in Denmark (Censorship in Denmark; Denmark Report, 1970)

Banned in Essex County, New Jersey, 1971.

Denmark, 1970. U.S., 1970. Dist: Sherpix, Inc. 75 min. 16mm. Sound. Color. Prod/Dir: Alex De Renzy. Cin: Alex De Renzy, Jack Kerpan. MPAA: X. Reviews: *Daily Variety*, April 10, 1970, Rick; *Variety*, April 15, 1970, Har.;

Hollywood Reporter, April 17, 1970, John Mahoney; *New York Times*, June 17, 1970, Vincent Canby. Articles: *Variety*, April 22, 1970, Addison Verrill; *Time*, July 20, 1970; *Motion Picture Daily*, Oct. 5, 1970; *Motion Picture Daily*, March 17, 1971; *Variety*, March 17, 1971.

This documentary illustrates the sort of pornography that became publicly available in Denmark following its legalization there, in 1968. It includes on-the-street interviews of people about to enter Copenhagen's 1969 Pornography Fair; interviews with bookstore and theater managers and with an innocent-looking girl who is a pornographic film star; 16mm. footage of 8mm. theater "porn," showing various forms of heterosexuality and female masturbation with a battery-driven dildo; shots of the making of an 8mm. "porn" film with a model and a sailor having sex with each other; and shots of a sex club show, ending with three women performing cunnilingus on each other all at once, sweating and shrieking, while the smoke and breathing of the audience thickens. One review noted, regarding the Danish couple copulating, "Since the shooting took all day, the actor's ability to perform on cue is a marvel to ponder and the actress' boredom with the whole scene is equally intriguing."[1] "[T]he few remaining barriers to the depiction of the sex act on public screens have been shattered in a manner that makes *I Am Curious—Yellow* seem weasling."[2]

Censorship Activity

After a sheriff's detective and a municipal magistrate viewed this film in three theaters in Essex County where it was showing, warrants were issued and executed for the arrest of the exhibitors and seizure of the films. The managers of the theaters moved to suppress the evidence (the films seized) on the ground that their seizure violated constitutional freedom of expression. The judge denied the motion and, on review, the Superior Court of New Jersey affirmed the denial.[3]

Legal Importance

The case illustrates one solution to the problem presented when law enforcement agents, in the performance of their duties, execute warrants for the seizure of films alleged to be obscene for use as evidence in criminal proceedings. The exhibitors of such films are in risk of forfeiting their constitutional right to exhibit the films—if the films are protected expression and not obscene—if they lack copies that may continue to be shown pending a final judicial determination of the alleged obscenity. One solution is to forbid the police to carry out such seizures, or require the prosecutor to return any films seized, so that the exhibitions may continue, conditioning a return of the films on the exhibitors' being ordered or subpoenaed to supply prints to the government for trials of the criminal charges. Another solution, the one adopted here, is to permit the state to retain the seized films, provided that the exhibitors from whom they were seized have available other prints of the film for continued showing. Only if the state were to seize such other prints would the court order their return and, presumably, restrain any further such interferences with the exhibitors' exercise of their freedom of expression without "prior restraint." The overriding constitutional principle applicable to this sort of case is the one laid down in the *Revenge at Daybreak* case [58], which holds that material alleged to be obscene may not be restrained from dissemination until after an adversary proceeding has taken place, designed to focus searchingly on the issue of the material's obscenity, and providing also for a prompt final judicial determination and expeditious review of any decision adverse to the film's disseminator.

1. *Variety*, April 15, 1970.
2. *Variety*, April 22, 1970.
3. State v. Osborne, 285 A. 2d 43 (1971).

[104]
Sexual Freedom in Denmark (Dansk Sexualitet)

Banned in New York, New York, 1971.

Denmark, 1970. U.S., 1970. Dist: Art Films International. 75 min. 35mm. Sound. Color. Prod/Dir: M. C. Von Hellen. Cin: Finn Thomsen. Cast: Ole Lassen, Karen Biller, Dorrit Frautzen, Elizabeth Bundgaard, Ruth Dymore. Rating: (self-assigned) X. Reviews: *Saturday Review*, May 16, 1970, Hollis Alpert; *Variety*, March 18, 1970; *Hollywood Reporter*, April 1, 1970. Article: *New York Times*, May 10, 1970, Vincent Canby.

An argument for banning all censorship is the message of this semidocumentary of sexual practices. It includes such clips as a man and women nude in the forest, parts of a sex education film on various positions, primitive erotic and contemporary erotic art, a nudist beauty contest, and a cram course in human biology.

Censorship Activity
After having exhibited this film publicly "in midtown Manhattan" for 32 weeks, the defendants were arrested and prosecuted under the New York State Penal Law for having "exhibited to the public" a film "which is obscene in that it depicts acts of sexual intercourse and oral sodomy." At the trial, neither side introduced any evidence other than the film. After viewing it and comparing it with films found not obscene in other cases, the criminal court dismissed the criminal complaint, holding that the film was protected by the First and Fourteenth Amendments.[1]

Legal Importance

The court's opinion holds a certain interest because of its candid admission of the difficulty of reaching sound decisions in obscenity cases. For example: "[T]he term 'pornography' defies definition, and even those judges who agree that a particular film is not legally pornographic cannot agree among themselves why. A case-by-case interpretation hardly results in consistency or stability in principle. . . . The result is hodge-podge. We of the lower courts are constrained to anticipate final action of the majority in a higher court. . . . [W]e flounder in wondering what the Supreme Court will do in each matter. We cross our fingers and hope that our guess is correct."

1. People v. Hilsy, 324 N.Y.S. 2d 164 (1971).

[105]
Carnal Knowledge

Banned in Albany, Georgia, 1972.

U.S., 1971. Dist: AVCO Embassy Pictures. 97 min. 35mm. Sound. Color. Prod: Mike Nichols, Joseph E. Levine. Dir: Mike Nichols. SW: Jules Feiffer. Cin: Guiseppe Rotunno. Cast: Jack Nicholson, Candice Bergen, Art Garfunkel, Ann-Margret, Rita Moreno, Cynthia O'Neal, Carol Kane. MPAA: R. Awards: Ann-Margret nominated for Academy Award (Oscar) for Best Supporting Actress. Reviews: *Daily News*, July 1, 1971, Kathleen Carroll; *Washington Post*, July 2, 1971, Gary Arnold; *Saturday Review*, July 3, 1971, Hollis Alpert; *New York Times*, July 4, 1971, Vincent Canby; *Newsweek*, July 5, 1971, Paul Zimmerman; *Time*, July 5, 1971, Stefan Kanfer. Articles: *Chicago Daily News*, July 24, 25, 1971, Studs Terkel and David Elliot; *New York Times*, Aug. 1, 1971, Stephen Farber; *Washington Post*, July 2, 1974, George F. Will; *Newsweek*, July 8, 1974.

During the postwar 1940s, two college roommates who are best friends discuss the ideal woman. Knowledgeable Jonathan wants only physically perfect girls; nice, bumbling Sandy considers intellect and sensitivity to be of primary importance. Although both are attracted to a lovely student, Susan, whom they spot at a college mixer, Jonathan declares her breasts are too small and leaves her to Sandy. When Sandy confides that Susan, despite her virginity, engaged in bold sexual foreplay, Jonathan pursues her and, pretending an unhappy childhood, seduces her. Next, Sandy, by dint of clumsy advances, seduces Susan too, and both friends continue to date her. When Jonathan insists that Susan choose between them, Susan, being unwilling to hurt Sandy, rejects Jonathan.

Years later, we find Sandy, a well-established New York doctor married to Susan, and Jonathan, running through a dozen women a year in search of the perfect female bedmate. Now Jonathan thinks he has found her in Bobbie, a voluptuous 29-year-old model, with whom he has a dreadful relationship. They break up only after Jonathan rejects Bobbie's request for marriage and a child, and she barely survives an overdose of pills. A decade later, dressed as a member of the "Now Generation," Sandy visits Jonathan at his luxurious bachelor pad with an 18-year-old hippie named Jennifer, who he claims has shown him true love. Jonathan presents slides of the women in his life, revealing that he married and had a child with Bobbie and is now being bled for alimony. When he reduces Jennifer to tears, Sandy takes her home. And Jonathan is visited by his hundred-dollar prostitute, who performs her regular sexual ritual, reassuring him of his virility.

Censorship Activity

Acting pursuant to a search warrant, Albany, Georgia police seized this film and arrested the manager of the theater in which it was being shown on a charge of distributing obscene material. The theater manager was convicted by a jury in the Superior Court of Dogherty County, and the Supreme Court of Georgia affirmed the verdict.[1] The U.S. Supreme Court, however, reversed.[2]

Legal Importance

The Supreme Court overturned the criminal jury's judgment that this film was "obscene" and held that it could not constitutionally be found obscene under the standards announced in the 1973 landmark decision of *Miller* v. *California*.[3] Noting that "[t]here is little to be found in the record about the film . . . other than the film itself," Justice William H. Rehnquist, speaking for the Court, quoted at length from one of the reviews which, together with "a variety of information and critical commentary," the exhibitor had supplied.

The state had argued that "under *Miller* the obscenity *vel non* of the film . . . was a question for the jury," and that its judgment of conviction, after viewing the movie and applying the *Miller* standards, should be affirmed with judicial review of that verdict "virtually precluded." But, in *Miller*, Rehnquist pointed out, the Court had "made it plain [that] no one will be subject to prosecution for the sale or exposure of obscene materials unless these materials depict or describe patently offensive 'hard core' sexual conduct. . . ." For example, he suggested, it would be "wholly at odds with *Miller* to uphold an obscenity conviction based upon a defendant's depiction of a woman with a bare midriff, even though a properly charged jury unanimously agreed on a verdict of guilty."

The Court's viewing of the film had "satisfied" it that *Carnal Knowledge* "could not properly be found under the *Miller* standards to depict sexual conduct in a patently offensive way. . . . While the subject matter of the picture is, in a broader sense, sex, and there are scenes in which sexual conduct including 'ultimate sexual acts' is to be understood to be taking place, the camera does not focus on the bodies of the actors at such times. There is no exhibition whatever of the actors' genitals, lewd or otherwise, during these scenes. There are occasional scenes of nudity, but nudity alone is not enough to make material legally obscene under the *Miller* standards." The showing of the film was "simply not the 'public portrayal of hard core sexual conduct for its own sake, and for the ensuing commercial gain' which we said was punishable in *Miller*." It was, therefore, protected by the free expression guarantee of the First and Fourteenth Amendments.

Justice Brennan, concurring in the Court's reversal of the conviction, repeated his contention, stated in *Miller*, that "the Court's reformulation (of the test for 'obscenity') hardly represented a solution to what Justice Harlan called 'the intractable obscenity problem.' " The Court's new formulation did not extricate it from the "mire of case-by-case determinations of obscenity, [and so] at least in the absence of distribution to juveniles or obtrusive exposure to unconsenting adults, the First and Fourteenth Amendments should prohibit the state and federal governments from attempting wholly to suppress sexually-oriented materials on the basis of their allegedly 'obscene' contents."

The film played in nearly 5,000 theaters in every state and was viewed by almost 20 million people. According to Bob Woodward and Scott Armstrong in *The Brethren*, when the Supreme Court met to decide this case in 1974, all nine justices "were prepared to say" that the film was not obscene and to reverse the conviction. But Justices Douglas, Brennan, Stewart, and Marshall wanted the Court to admit that the necessity for reversing a jury's finding of "obscenity" stemmed directly from Chief Justice Burger's obscenity opinions of the previous year in *Miller* and the *Magic Mirror* case [102]. The Chief Justice, of course, disagreed and wanted only to warn local jurisdictions that there were limits to what a jury could find obscene; under the guidelines he formulated in *Miller*, clearly *Carnal Knowledge* was not obscene. Not wanting to pull back from *Miller*, he assigned the opinion to Justice Rehnquist. According to Woodward and Armstrong, when Justice Rehnquist began work on the opinion, "his job looked simple." But *Miller* presented a problem: The Chief Justice had written that material could be found obscene whether the sexual acts were "acted or simulated," so long as the act itself was "patently offensive." Was not the simulated fellatio of Jonathan in the closing moments of *Carnal Knowledge*, even though not explicit, "patently offensive"? Rehnquist decided he would "carefully re-interpret" Chief Justice Burger's obscenity opinion and declare that "only explicit displays could be ruled obscene by local judges."[4]

1. Jenkins v. State, 199 S.E. 2d 183, 230 Ga. 726 (1973).
2. Jenkins v. Georgia, 418 U.S. 153 (1974).
3. Miller v. California, 413 U.S. 15 (1973).
4. Bob Woodward and Scott Armstrong, *The Brethren* (New York: Simon & Schuster, 1979), 280-281.

[106]
Cry Uncle

Banned in Tennessee, 1972.

U.S., 1971. Dist: Cambist. 87 min. 35mm. Sound. Color. Prod: David Disick. Dir: John G. Avildsen. SW: David Odell. Cin: John G. Avildsen. Cast: Allen Garfield, Madeleine LeRoux, Devin Goldenberg, David Kirk. MPAA: X. Reviews: *Variety*, March 17, 1971, Murf.; *Cue*, July 24, 1971, W.W.; *New York Times*, Aug. 18, 1971, Howard Thompson. Article: *Motion Picture Daily*, March 15, 1972.

This film was adapted from the novel by Michael Brett. A wealthy man, who is being blackmailed by girls who appeared with him in a pornographic film, hires a bumbling and boorish gumshoe to clear him from a murder charge. The detective, who makes love with his hat on, discovers the betrayal of a cool, husky-voiced, gorgeous woman and thereby solves the case.

Censorship Activity

Pursuant to a Tennessee statute, on February 26, 1972, a district attorney requested the Knox County Criminal Court to issue a temporary restraining order to prohibit the further showing of this allegedly obscene film. The same day, the court issued an order to ban showings of the movie—without notice to the exhibitor and without permitting him to be heard in court. Thereafter, the film was found to be obscene, its exhibition was permanently enjoined, and the film itself was ordered to be destroyed. The film's distributor intervened at the appeal stage of the case and in 1973 claimed the statutory definition of obscenity was unconstitutional under the holding of *Miller v. California*.[1] The Supreme Court of Tennessee held the statute unconstitutional and remanded the case to the trial court for a disposition not inconsistent with its opinion.[2]

Legal Importance

The statute found unconstitutional here was, in its definition of obscenity, closely patterned after the definition of obscenity announced by Justice Brennan in the landmark case of *Memoirs* v. *Massachusetts.*[3] There, the definition was framed so as to encompass material that predominantly appealed to prurient interest in sex, was patently offensive, and was devoid of any literary, scientific, or artistic value or other social importance. Since the Supreme Court repudiated this test in the *Miller* case, the Tennessee high court invalidated the state law. The court also declined, as would the state court in 1976 in the case of *The Exorcist* [110], to read into the law the definition recommended by the Supreme Court in *Miller*, saying it could not usurp the prerogatives of the legislature by "supplying essential elements to a statute which have been omitted by that body."

Although neither the exhibitor nor the distributor appears to have raised the issue, it seems clear that the procedure followed by the district attorney and the criminal court in suppressing the film's exhibition without notice or adversary hearing was unconstitutional under the principles of the *Revenge at Daybreak* case [58].

1. Miller v. California, 413 U.S. 15 (1973).
2. Art Theater Guild v. State *ex rel.* Rhodes, 510 S.W. 2d 258 (1974).
3. Memoirs v. Massachusetts, 383 U.S. 413 (1966).

[107]
Deep Throat

Banned in California, Colorado, Florida, Georgia, Illinois, Iowa, Kentucky, Louisiana, Maryland, Massachusetts, Michigan, Mississippi, Missouri, Nebraska, New Hampshire, New Jersey, New York, North Dakota, Ohio, Pennsylvania, South Dakota, Tennessee, and Texas, 1972–1981.

U.S., 1972. Dist: Aquarius. 73 min. 35mm. Sound. Prod: Lou Perry, Vanguard. Dir/SW: Jerry Gerard (pseudonym for Gerard Damiano). Cin: Harry Flecks. Cast: Linda Lovelace, Harry Reems, Dolly Sharp, William Love. MPAA: X. Reviews: *Variety*, June 28, 1972, Verr.; *Film Bulletin*, Sept. 1972; *Saturday Review*, March 1973, Thomas Meehan. Articles: *New York Times*, Dec. 18, 19, 20, 21, 22, 27, 30, 31, 1972, Jan. 3, 4, 1973, Paul L. Montgomery; *Newsweek*, Jan. 15, 1973; *Time*, Jan. 15, 1973; *Variety*, July 11, 1973; *Hollywood Reporter*, Jan. 25, 1974, Will Tushner.

Frustrated by her inability to "hear bells" in orgasm during her many sexual encounters, even with 14 men at once, a young woman consults a promiscuous, accommodating doctor, who diagnoses her problem as having her clitoris in her throat. In search of relief, she tries her mouth out on as many male members as she can, finally settling on one measuring 13 inches, which is said to be four inches more than adequate to make her "hear bells." "Miss Lovelace is at once youthful, passably pretty, and has a lithe and supple body. And while she evidences not the slightest talent for acting, she does not possess what no less authority than the *New York Times* has termed "a virtuoso talent for fellatio."[1] By January 1973, the movie reportedly had played in 73 U.S. cities.[2]

Censorship Activity

This film was involved in litigation in a great number of cities and states because of its alleged obscenity. One such case, which reached the U.S. Supreme Court, arose when the landlord of a theater operator who was exhibiting the movie notified the operator that his lease would be terminated because the county attorney had threatened to "abate the theater as a public nuisance in order to prevent the future showing of allegedly obscene motion pictures." The movie exhibitor went into federal court to have such action by the county attorney declared unconstitutional and be enjoined. The three-judge court assigned the case declared the Texas public nuisance statutes invoked by the county attorney to be invalid prior restraints on the exercise of First Amendment rights as applied to movie theaters.[3] This judgment invalidating the county attorney's asserted power to "abate" a movie theater's operations—its showing *in the future* of unnamed films—was upheld by a federal court of appeals[4] and by the U.S. Supreme Court.[5]

Legal Importance

The constitutional defect of this scheme to close down as a public nuisance a movie theater found to have shown obscene movies in the past resided in its authorizing a court to impose "prior restraints of indefinite duration on the exhibition of motion pictures that have not been finally adjudicated to be obscene." The restraint on movie freedom of expression imposed by this sort of law was even "more onerous and more objectionable" than the threat of criminal punishment "after a film has been exhibited" because the film's non-obscenity would be a defense in any criminal prosecution, but not in a proceeding to punish an exhibitor for "contempt" of court in exhibiting a film ultimately declared to be non-obscene, which, however, had erroneously been found obscene in a nuisance abatement proceeding.

The film was found obscene in a number of state[6] and federal[7] cases. Although produced and released in the United States, a print of the film imported from Canada was seized by U.S. Customs in Boston and, in a subsequent legal proceeding, was ordered forfeited by a Massachusetts federal district court. This suppression was upheld by the first circuit court of appeals[8] notwithstanding the arguments advanced by the importer, and testified to at trial by expert witnesses, that the movie "puts forth an idea of greater liberation with regard to human sexuality and to the expression of it" and would benefit the "many women [who] have an unreasonable fear of the penis." To accept any such argument, the court felt, would be to disregard the reasoning of the U.S. Supreme Court that pornography has no value.

1. *Saturday Review*, March 1973.
2. *Time*, Jan. 15, 1973.
3. Universal Amusement Co. v. Vance, 404 F. Supp. 33 (1975).
4. Universal Amusement Co. v. Vance, 559 F. 2d 1286 (1977).
5. Vance v. Universal Amusement Co., 446 U.S. 947 (1980).
6. People v. Mitchell Brothers, 101 Cal. App. 3d 296 (1980).
7. Colorado v. Tabron, 544 P. 2d 372 (1975). See, for example: United States v. Battista, 646 F. 2d 237 (1981); United States v. Peraino, 7 Media Law Rptr. 1703 (1981); United States v. Marks, 520 F. 2d 913 (1975); United States v. One Reel of Film, 481 F. 2d 206 (1973).
8. United States v. One Reel of Film, 481 F. 2d 206 (1973).

[108]
Sinderella

Banned from entry into the United States, 1972.

U.K., 1972. U.S., 1972. Dist: Sherpix, Inc. 6½ min. 35mm. Sound. Color. Creators: David Hamilton Grant, Ron Inkpen. Review: *Variety*, July 19, 1972.

"Sinderella in this (cartoon) version loses her bra and not her slipper in an animated depiction of intercourse with Prince Charming."[1] While the narrator recites the fairy tale free from vulgarity, the film depicts Sinderella performing sexual acts with Little Red Riding Hood, Puss 'n Boots, Goldilocks, and the Three Bears, as well as Prince Charming.

Censorship Activity

Upon arrival from England at John F. Kennedy International Airport in New York, this short film was offered for entry into the United States by claimant Sherpix, Inc. After viewing it, Customs agents seized the film as obscene and a legal proceeding was instituted to condemn it and prevent its entry into the country. A U.S. district court viewed the film and took evidence proferred by Sherpix from a professor of sociology, a professor of English, and a professor of motion picture history to the effect that the film had redeeming social value and did not offend contemporary community standards, especially because of "its wit, humor, and satire." Nevertheless, the court found the film obscene and ordered it to be forfeited, as provided by the Tariff Act.[2] On appeal, the Court of Appeals for the Second Circuit affirmed the judgment of forfeiture.[3]

Legal Importance

The case is the only known officially reported case to have raised and decided the issue of whether an animated film is obscene. Although the trial court took the view that "humor in material otherwise obscene has social value," and might, on that account, be constitutionally protected from seizure and destruction, the humor of this film was only "purported humor," a "mere gimmick . . . devoid of underlying intellectual or ideological content," which "does not infuse this cartoon with enough social value to retrieve it from the trash can." In thus applying the test for separating obscenity from protected expression, announced by the Supreme Court in the landmark case of *Memoirs* v. *Massachusetts*,[4] the trial court seemed to discount the admonition issued in that case that material must be "utterly without redeeming social value" or "unqualifiedly worthless" before it can be found obscene. While conceding that "exhibitions of genitals or normal or abnormal sexual acts are not obscene if the material advocates ideas or is of some literary or scientific or artistic value," the court held this film obscene. Professor Richard Brown of New York University testified to "novelty in the method of production of the film," it being produced in a style called Feltboard animations. The court decided, however, that such "novelty in production methods was irrelevant to the issues."

On appeal, the U.S. Court of Appeals for the Second Circuit applied the standards announced by the Supreme Court in the landmark case of *Miller* v. *California*,[5] which were decided while the appeal in the present case was pending, and adjudged the film here obscene and unprotected by the constitutional guarantees of freedom of expression. The distributor also argued that because the government had failed to introduce any evidence "other than the film itself," the evidence was insufficient to prove its obscenity. But, as the Supreme Court said in the *Magic Mirror* case [102],[6] decided the same day as *Miller*, there is no error in failing to require "expert" affirmative evidence that materials are obscene "when the materials themselves [are] actually placed in evidence. The films, obviously, are the best evidence of what they represent." The distributor also had argued that the Constitution placed the exhibition of films "to consenting adults" beyond the power of a state to regulate and represented that it would limit exhibition of the film to "consenting adults." The *Magic Mirror* case, however, had rejected that proposition also.

This case appears to represent an example of material principally made

up of the depiction of sexually explicit behavior, artistically and humorous-
ly presented—that is, material that is not "utterly without" artistic or social
importance—being condemned as obscene, under the revised and narrower
tests for distinguishing obscene matter from constitutionally protected
works, announced by the Burger court in 1973[7] and sharply criticized by
Justice Brennan at that time in an extensive dissenting opinion.[8] In this
respect, the case can be compared with the case of *Un Chant d'Amour* [65],
decided under the standards the Supreme Court announced in *Memoirs* v.
Massachusetts.

1. *Variety*, July 19, 1972, p. 5.
2. United States v. One Reel of 35mm Color Motion Picture Film, 369 F.
   Supp. 1082 (1972).
3. United States v. One Reel of 35mm Film Entitled *Sinderella*, 491 F. 2d 956
   (1974).
4. Memoirs v. Massachusetts, 383 U.S. 413 (1966).
5. Miller v. California, 413 U.S. 15 (1973).
6. This *dictum* seems inconsistent with the Court's holding in the landmark
   Revenge at Daybreak case [58] that the censor has the burden to prove that
   material is "obscene."
7. Miller v. California, 413 U.S. 15 (1973).
8. Paris Adult Theatre I v. Slaton, 413 U.S. 49 (1973).

[109]
Behind the Green Door

*Banned in New York, 1973; Texas, 1974–1981; Colorado, 1975; Georgia,
1976; and California, 1979.*

U.S., 1972. Dist: Mitchell Bros. Film. 72 min. 35mm. Sound. Color. Prod:
Jartock, Inc., Art and James Mitchell. Dir: Jim and Art Mitchell. SW: Jim
Mitchell. Cin: Jon Fontana. Cast: Marilyn Chambers, George S. McDonald,
Johnny Keyes, Ben Davidson. Rating: (self-assigned) X. Reviews: *Variety*,
Aug. 16, 1972, Har.; *Film Bulletin*, July 1973. Articles: *Box Office*, June 18,
1973; *New Yorker*, Feb. 11, 1974.

This film, an attempt at "porno art," was adapted from an anonymous
story. A beautiful young woman is kidnapped and sexually molested as the
star attraction of a private club's sex show. Bewildered but not unwilling,
she endures the attention of the masturbating audience and a great variety
of direct sexual use, while the show turns into an orgy. The actress and star
of this sex opus is Marilyn Chambers, the demure Ivory Snow model. In one
scene, the actress is shown having sex with four men at once, while all are on
a sort of trapeze.

Censorship Activity

A Suffolk County, New York jury found the theater operator who showed this film (in his modern 600-seat shopping-center theater) guilty of violating the state's criminal law, which prohibited the exhibition of any film that "appeals to prurient interest in sex, goes substantially beyond the customary limits of candor, and has utterly no redeeming social value."[1] This was the test for distinguishing obscenity from constitutionally protected expression that the U.S. Supreme Court laid down in *The Lovers* case [49]. The film was also the target of a civil action by New York City's corporation counsel and the district attorney of New York County to prevent its exhibition at certain theaters in New York City. The constitutionality of this action was upheld by the state Supreme Court's Appellate Division.[2]

Legal Importance

The prosecutor argued that the film was "unqualifiedly worthless" and therefore obscene, and that if it was not obscene to devote almost an entire film to a sexual orgy of the sort depicted in this film, then "nothing is obscene." The defendant tried unsuccessfully to persuade the judge to have the jury view the film in his "modern non-sleazy theater," which had opened only a few months earlier with *The Sound of Music*. Despite testimony by an impressive array of expert witnesses to the effect that the film had "redeeming social value"—for example, because it was useful in providing viewers with sexual fantasy material, sexual information, and a "vocabulary for dealing with sexual problems they had been reluctant to discuss," and also had "a ritual quality reminiscent of Ravel's *Bolero*"—the film was found obscene and, presumably, without any redeeming social value.

In the civil action brought to enjoin exhibition of the film in New York City theaters, the appellate court found the film was, and was advertised to be, hard-core pornography, involving "multiple and variegated ultimate acts of sexual perversion [which] would have been regarded as obscene by the community standards of Sodom and Gomorrah." The court also held the New York statute that authorized the enjoining of obscene motion pictures was not unconstitutionally overbroad within the meaning of the U.S. Supreme Court's holding in the landmark case of *Miller* v. *California*.[3]

1. This case was officially unreported; the trial is described by Calvin Trillin in "Trying Green Door," *The New Yorker*, Feb. 11, 1974, from which the data in the text were taken.
2. Redlich v. Capri Cinema, 349 N.Y.S. 2d 697 (1973).
3. Miller v. California, 413 U.S. 15 (1973).

[110]
The Exorcist

Banned in Hattiesburg, Mississippi, 1973.

U.S., 1973. Dist: Warner Bros. 121 min. 35mm. Sound. Color. Prod: William Peter Blatty, Noel Marshall. Dir: William Friedkin. SW: William Peter Blatty. Cin: Owen Roizman. Cast: Linda Blair, Ellen Burstyn, Max Von Sydow, Lee J. Cobb. MPAA: R. Reviews: *Variety*, Dec. 26, 1973, Murf.; *New York Times*, Dec. 27, 1973, Vincent Canby; *Box Office*, Jan. 14, 1974. Articles: *Variety*, Jan. 30, 1974; *New York Times*, Feb. 3, 24, 1974; *Newsweek*, Feb. 11, 1974, Kenneth L. Woodward; *Time*, Feb. 11, 1974; *Variety*, May 29, 1974.

This film was adapted from the novel by William Peter Blatty. As aging Jesuit Father Merrin discovers an ancient devil figure in Iraq, 12-year-old Regan, the daughter of a divorced film actress, undergoes a radically destructive personality change. Regan becomes more and more violently malicious. Her mother's fiancé is killed by a fall down a flight of stairs near her house, and a police detective suspects murder. Convinced that Regan is possessed by the devil, her mother consults a young priest, Father Karris, who is troubled by his dying mother and his uncertain faith. He decides that only exorcism by the experienced Father Merrin can save Regan. As the exorcism's violence kills aged Father Merrin, young Father Karris attacks Regan, is himself possessed, and leaps to his own death, leaving Regan apparently free of the devil, recalling nothing of it.

Censorship Activity

Several police officers and a justice of the peace accompanied the district attorney to see this film at the Saenger Theater in Hattiesburg, Mississippi. Thereafter, affidavits were filed, search and arrest warrants issued, the film seized, and the theater manager and projectionist arrested. The charges against them were subsequently dismissed, but the corporate owner of the theater was tried and convicted for publicly exhibiting "an obscene, indecent and immoral motion picture." On appeal, the defendant argued that the statute was constitutionally overbroad, lacked specificity, and failed to comply with the constitutional requirements laid down by the Supreme Court in the landmark case of *Miller* v. *California*;[1] the Supreme Court of Mississippi held the statute constitutionally overbroad, violative of the First Amendment and, as such, unconstitutional.[2]

Legal Importance

The state urged the Supreme Court of Mississippi to "read into" the criminal statute it used to suppress this film the specificity and definiteness required to cure it of its overbreadth, as articulated by the U.S. Supreme

Court in the *Miller* case, but this the court declined to do. To do so with respect to the corporate defendant here would impose an unconstitutional *ex post facto* rule of law on it, for there was no way the defendant could be aware of this more specific meaning at the time it showed the film. Moreover, the court considered such specification to be a legislative, not a judicial, function.

1. Miller v. California, 413 U.S. 15 (1973).
2. ABC Interstate Theatres, Inc. v. State, 325 So. 2d 123 (1976).

[111]
The Last Picture Show

Banned in Phoenix, Arizona, 1973.

U.S., 1971. Dist: Columbia Pictures. 119 min. 35mm. Sound. B&W. Prod: BBS Productions, Inc., Stephen J. Friedman. Dir: Peter Bogdanovich. SW: Larry McMurtry, Peter Bogdanovich. Cin: Robert Surtess. Cast: Timothy Bottoms, Jeff Bridges, Cybill Shepard, Cloris Leachman, Sam Bottoms. MPAA: R. Award: N.Y. Film Critics Award for Best Written Screen Play of 1971. Reviews: *Village Voice*, Feb. 24, 1971, Martina Rubin; *Sunday News*, Sept. 26, 1971, Wanda Hale; *Newsweek*, Oct. 18, 1971, Paul Zimmerman; *New York Times*, Jan. 23, 1972, Stephen Farber. Article: *New York Times Magazine*, April 4, 1982, William K. Stevens.

This film is based on Larry McMurtry's novel of the same title, and captures the slow-paced life of a very small Texas town, Amarene, in the 1950s. Arid and seemingly empty of ambition, the town is trying to adjust to the onset of television, which is bringing about the closing of its only movie house. The story revolves around town characters: the rich girl, trying to escape, and the wife of the athletic coach, seducing the high school hero. The last scene shows the boy going to the movie house for its last showing of *Red River*, before he leaves for Korea.

Censorship Activity

After receiving "several complaints from citizens" concerning this film, which had shown for a week at a Phoenix, Arizona drive-in theater and which apparently could be seen by "neighboring residents and travelers upon the public way," the city attorney wrote the theater manager that "it was [his] opinion" that the film violated both the "explicit terms" and the "spirit as well" of a state criminal obscenity statute. He also requested the manager to "cease exhibiting this film," and stated that its continued showing would result in the manager's prosecution; the manager stopped showing the movie. When the prosecutor, at a meeting one month later, demanded the deletion of a "four-second segment of total frontal nudity of a female swimmer," the producer and distributor brought suit in federal court against the prosecutor, claiming their civil rights were violated and that the criminal statute was unconstitutional on its face and as applied. A three-judge district court declined to resolve the constitutional issues by holding that the film, which it viewed, did not violate the statute, and so could not lawfully be suppressed.[1]

Legal Importance

The prosecutor's "clear and unequivocal threats" were found by the court to have "directly caused the cessation of the exhibition of the Film." This was described as "tantamount to an official suppression" of the producer and distributor, "resulting in injury with no opportunity to obtain a judicial test of the constitutional issues." The prosecutor's threats were not based on a claim that the film was "obscene," but that the challenged four-second segment of "frontal female nudity" violated a statutory prohibition against publicly displaying pictorial depictions of "human genitalia." After studying still pictures of the film frames, the court disagreed that the film violated the statute. "In short," the court said, "the challenged segment of film shows a 'total frontal nudity of a female swimmer' walking forward and climbing the steps, completely straight, legs together, and from knee deep in the pool to the top of the pool's rim, much reminiscent of the early twentieth-century household picture entitled 'September Morn.' We find as an anatomical fact that such a portrayal is not a display of exterior female genitalia." The court declined to accept a "stipulation of fact" tendered by counsel that "the term 'genitalia' in the statute reaches total front male and female nudity," pointing out that "[c]ommon knowledge tells us that is not necessarily so in the case of a female." In the court's view, "the Mount of Venus, revealed by the triangular area of pubic hair, is [not] any component of exterior female genitalia." The court recommended *Dorland's Illustrated Medical Dictionary*, 23rd Edition, "for a view of exterior female genitalia and the names of the components."

1. BBS Productions, Inc. v. Purcell, 360 F. Supp. 801 (1973).

[112]
Last Tango in Paris

Banned in Montgomery, Alabama and Shreveport, Louisiana, 1973.

Italy, 1973. U.S., 1973. Dist: United Artists. 125 min. 35mm. Sound. Color. French with English subtitles. Prod: Alberto Grimaldi. Dir: Bernardo Bertolucci. SW: Bernardo Bertolucci, Franco Arcalli. Cin: Vittorio Storaro. Cast: Marlon Brando, Maria Schneider, Jean-Pierre Léaud, Darling Legitimus. MPAA: X (February 1973); R (April 1974). Festivals: New York Film Festival. Awards: Bernardo Bertolucci nominated for Academy Award (Oscar) for Best Director; Marlon Brando nominated for Academy Award (Oscar) for Best Actor. Reviews: *Playboy*, Feb. 1973; *Time*, Jan. 22, 1973; *Cue*, Feb. 3, 1973, William Wolf; *New York Daily News*, Feb. 6, 1973, Rex Reed.

This film portrays a sexual liaison between an older American expatriate and a young Parisian woman. They meet in an unfurnished apartment by accident and, although total strangers, immediately engage in sexual intercourse. He suggests that they continue to meet in the apartment but that they must remain nameless and not explain anything about their personal histories. He is tormented by the recent suicide of his wife; she is disturbed by the fact that her fiancé is more interested in a television documentary about her than in making love to her. After the American has "worked through his hang-ups," brutalizing her, he realizes she is part of him because she has shared so much of the dark side of his nature. He now exposes a different weakness, a vulnerability, asking her for love. By coming into the open about himself and breaking their pact, he sees a second chance in life; the girl, however, sees a used-up has-been. Familiarity has bred a tragic contempt. In a vain attempt to gain her love at a tango contest, he avidly pursues her back to her mother's apartment, where, out of fright, she shoots him.

Censorship Activity

After the distributor of this film had entered into an agreement with a local movie theater in Montgomery, Alabama for exhibition of this film, the Montgomery chief of police wrote the exhibitor that his showing the film, prior to a judicial declaration that it was not obscene, "might result in [criminal] prosecution" under state law. The distributor went into federal district court to have the statute declared unconstitutional and to restrain its enforcement. The court granted the relief requested.[1]

The manager of a theater showing this film in Shreveport, Louisiana was arrested under a state criminal law and the film was seized by the police on the second day of its showing. When he exhibited another copy of the film on the next day, he was again arrested, and this copy was also seized. The manager and the film's exhibitor thereupon sought and obtained from a federal district court a temporary restraining order prohibiting further arrest of the manager and further seizure of the film. When this order expired, the same plaintiffs filed suit in state district court, seeking the same relief on a temporary and permanent basis—"until there could be a final judicial determination of the obscenity issue in an adversary hearing"—as required by the constitutional principles laid down in both state and federal cases. The Supreme Court of Louisiana issued orders to the district judge requiring him to restrain the chief of police and the state prosecutor from seizing prints of the film and from otherwise interfering with its showing, pending a final determination of the question whether the film was obscene and of the issues raised concerning the constitutionality of the state laws invoked. The district judge, following a trial, found the film obscene and issued an order that enjoined the manager and the distributor from showing it. On review, this judgment was reversed by the state supreme court, which found unconstitutional the state laws invoked to prevent exhibition of the film and prohibited the police and prosecutors of Shreveport from interfering with it.[2]

Legal Importance

The Alabama law provided that prior to the commencement of a criminal prosecution for exhibiting an obscene film, a government official must warn the prospective exhibitor that there is reasonable cause to believe the film violates the obscenity law and advise him of his opportunity to seek a declaratory judgment concerning the validity of the warning. Since, the court found, "few would dare ignore the warning" inasmuch as "people do not lightly disregard public officers' thinly-veiled threats to institute criminal proceedings against them, if they do not come round," the statute was perceived as a system of "prior restraints" on expression. But a system of prior restraints is not "necessarily" invalid. For example, the movie censorship system upheld by the U.S. Supreme Court in the *Don Juan* case [48] was a system of prior restraint. In the *Revenge at Daybreak* case [58], the U.S. Supreme Court invalidated a film censorship system as an unconstitutional prior restraint, but described the requirements for a valid system that would conform to constitutional standards. The constitutional defects in the Alabama system involved the failure to place on the government the burden of proving a questioned film was obscene; the failure to require the government to "go to court" before a determination of "obscenity"; and the failure to provide for "expedited judicial consideration" of the issues. For these reasons, the Alabama law was declared unconstitutional "on its face."

In Shreveport, Louisiana, the statutory scheme that was used to prevent the film being shown was found to be an unconstitutional "prior restraint" because of its failure to meet the constitutional requirements established by both state and federal cases, and notably the requirement for an independent judicial determination, at an adversary proceeding, that the film probably is obscene—prior to any governmental action restraining its exhibition. The Louisiana Supreme Court reiterated the proposition, announced in the landmark U.S. Supreme Court case of *Bantam Books* v. *Sullivan*,[3] that "any system of prior restraints of expression comes to this Court bearing a heavy presumption against its constitutional validity. . . . We have tolerated such a system only where it operated under judicial superintendence and assured an almost immediate judicial determination of the validity of the restraint.''

1. United Artists v. Wright, 368 F. Supp. 1034 (1974).
2. Gulf State Theatres of Louisiana v. Richardson, 287 So. 2d 480 (1974).
3. Bantam Books v. Sullivan, 372 U.S. 58 (1963).

[113]
The Newcomers

Banned in New York, New York, 1973.

U.S., 1972. Dist: Ander Production. 70 min. 16mm. Sound. Color. Prod: Gerry Bronson. Dir/SW: William Logan. Cin: Fox Barton. Cast: Linda Marena, David Strange, Anne Sargent, Alan Randall. MPAA: X. Review: *Variety*, Sept. 6, 1972.

The Newcomers is a story of the sexual discoveries made by six college students when they accept an invitation to the house of a young professor and his wife and explore their sexual boundaries. ''That sensual expedition, which presumably rates them all *A* + in the professor's social hygiene class, is composed of now conventional straight hardcore elements: mixed couplings, a dash of lesbian activity and an orgy.''[1]

Censorship Activity

After judges of the criminal court of New York City personally viewed this movie and four others, including *Behind the Green Door* [109], they issued search warrants commanding seizure of a print of each film, for evidence in criminal prosecutions for violation of New York State's obscenity law that were then initiated against the exhibitors of the films. Respectful of the U.S. Supreme Court's admonition in the *Blue Movie* case [82] that such seizures were valid for evidentiary purposes only and were not constitutional if they prevented exhibition of the films pending a trial to determine whether they were in fact obscene, the judges permitted the films to continue to be shown. To stop this, the corporation counsel of New York City and the New York County district attorney brought civil actions to enjoin temporarily and permanently the exhibitors from showing the films, pursuant to statute. The New York Supreme Court (trial court) denied the requested injunction on the ground that the statute was unconstitutionally overbroad.[2] This judgment was reversed by the appellate division of the same court, which granted a preliminary injunction preventing the movies from being displayed.[3] An appeal from this judgment was dismissed.[4]

Legal Importance

This case illustrates two of three methods by which government may prevent the exhibition of a movie. The method not involved is by administrative censorship boards of the type no longer practiced in New York since the decisions reached by its courts in 1965, invalidating that system, in the *A Stranger Knocks* case [59] and *The Unsatisfied* case [64]. The two methods tried in the present case were (1) by seizure of the film, incident to a criminal arrest, or upon a criminal warrant to search for and seize a film believed to have been used in the commission of the crime of exhibiting an obscene movie; and (2) by civilly enjoining the exhibition of a movie pursuant to a statute specially providing such legal recourse (as here), or as an equitable remedy. If the government proceeds criminally against the movie's exhibitor, it is today well settled that the exhibitor is constitutionally entitled to continue showing the film while the criminal proceeding pends, as was discussed in the *Blue Movie* case. The injunctive action to stop or prevent a movie being shown can serve to restrain its showing immediately upon conclusion of an adversary judicial proceeding designed "to focus searchingly on the question of obscenity." In view of the greater forensic burdens cast upon the government in a criminal proceeding, the civil injunctive action probably is a swifter, surer method of suppressing dissemination of a film.

The case is also of importance for the example provided of a state court curing a state statute of a potentially invalidating defect by reading into its provisions terms that bring the statute into conformity with constitutional requirements. Nothing in the statute stated that it was limited to the suppression of films (or other works) that "taken as a whole, do not have serious literary, artistic, political, or scientific value"—a requirement stated by Justice Brennan in *The Lovers* case [49]—to be necessary lest constitutionally protected works wrongly fall under the ban. The appellate courts held that such a requirement could and would be read into the New York injunctive law, thus saving it from being constitutionally defective. So construed, the statute was held clearly and properly employed to stop the showing of films like the present one and *Behind the Green Door*, which the appellate division viewed as "simple pornography unrelieved by any merit." The "multiple and variegated ultimate acts of sexual perversion" depicted in these films "would have been regarded as 'obscene' by the community standards of Sodom and Gomorrah," the court concluded.

1. *Variety*, Sept. 6, 1972.
2. Redlich v. Capri Cinema, Inc., 347 N.Y.S. 2d 811 (1973).
3. Redlich v. Capri Cinema, Inc., 349 N.Y.S. 2d 697 (1973).
4. Redlich v. Capri Cinema, Inc., 309 N.E. 2d 136 (1974).

[114]
Class of '74

Banned in Jacksonville, Florida, 1974.

U.S., 1972. Dist: General Film Corp. 82 min. 35mm. Sound. Color. Prod: Charles Stroud, Don Gottlieb. Dir: Arthur Marks, Mack Bing. Cast: Pat Woodell, Marki Bey, Sandra Currie, Barbara Caron, Philip Terry, Gary Clarke. MPAA: R. Review: *Box Office*, Feb. 14, 1972.

A young college woman of the early 1970s looks to three aggressively unconventional fellow coed friends for guidance in her search for her own social and sexual identity. Following their lead, she gleefully cavorts with a handsome young photographer, introduced to her by her "free-thinking" friend; a young stud, provided by her yearning black friend; and a jet-set married couple looking for a *ménage à trois*, thanks to another friend of exotic taste. Returning, finally, to campus, she determines to put her well-earned sexual prowess at the disposal of a new freshman coed.

Censorship Activity
The manager of a Jacksonville, Florida drive-in theater was arrested on March 13, 1972 for exhibiting this film in violation of a city ordinance that prohibited, as a "public nuisance," the showing of any movie containing nudity at a drive-in where the screen is visible from "a public street or place." The city attorney agreed not to prosecute the manager until the validity of the statute could be tested in a civil case. The Circuit Court of Duval County upheld the ordinance as a proper exercise of the city's police power, and the District Court of Appeal, First District, affirmed.[1] The Florida Supreme Court declined to hear the case,[2] but the U.S. Supreme Court reversed the judgment of the district court of appeals.[3]

Legal Importance
The Supreme Court held that the Jacksonville ordinance, on its face and as applied in this case, was unconstitutional infringement of First Amendment rights. "The plain, if at times disquieting, truth," Justice Lewis F. Powell, Jr., wrote, "is that in our pluralistic society, constantly proliferating new and ingenious forms of expression, we are inescapably captive audiences for many purposes. Much that we encounter offends our esthetic, if not our political and moral, sensibilities. Nevertheless, the Constitution does not permit government to decide which types of otherwise protected speech are sufficiently offensive to require protection for the unwilling listener or viewer." Justice Powell considered that "the burden normally falls upon the viewer to avoid further bombardment of his sensibilities simply by averting his eyes."

The statute "discriminates among movies solely on the basis of content''; its ''effect is to deter drive-in theaters from showing movies containing any nudity, however innocent or even educational.'' Such a discrimination could not be upheld as ''a means of preventing significant intrusions on privacy.'' Although the statute was defended as ''an exercise of the city's undoubted police power to protect children,'' the restriction was broader than permissible. By sweepingly forbidding ''display of all films containing *any* uncovered buttocks or breasts, irrespective of context or pervasiveness,'' it would ''bar a film containing a picture of a baby's buttocks, the nude body of a war victim, . . . scenes from a culture in which nudity is indigenous [or] of the opening of an art exhibit as well as shots of bathers on a beach. Clearly all nudity cannot be deemed obscene even as to minors.''

Chief Justice Warren E. Burger, joined by Justice William H. Rehnquist, dissented, claiming that the ''screen of a drive-in movie theater is a unique type of eye-catching display that can be highly intrusive and distracting. Public authorities have a legitimate interest in regulating such displays under the police power. . . . The First Amendment interests involved in this case are trivial at best.'' The statute involved, ''although no model of draftsmanship, is narrowly drawn to regulate only certain unique public exhibitions of nudity; it would be absurd to suggest that it operates to suppress expression of *ideas*.''

1. Erznoznik v. City of Jacksonville, 288 So. 2d 260 (1974).
2. Erznoznik v. City of Jacksonville, 294 So. 2d 293 (1974).
3. Erznoznik v. City of Jacksonville, 422 U.S. 205 (1975).

[115]
School Girl

Banned in Memphis, Tennessee, 1974.

U.S., 1971. Dist: Sherpix, Inc. 87 min. 35mm. Sound. Color. Prod: Sherpix, Inc., Art Theater Guild, Inc. Dir: David Reberg. Cast: Debra Allen, Susan George. MPAA: X. Festivals: Amsterdam Adult Film. Awards: Grand Prize, Amsterdam Adult Film Festival 1971–72. Reviews: *Box Office*, May 15, 1972; *Saturday Review*, Sept. 30, 1972, Arthur Knight. Article: *Motion Picture Daily*, Oct. 4, 1972.

For her sociology course, a nubile student investigates the subculture of sex-by-newspaper-ad. In response to sex ads in the *Berkeley Barb*, she has sex with an older man, a father-son pair, a husband and wife, and a man who gets her to respond to his obscene phone calls. Having brought her completed assignment to class, she declares that she enjoyed it all. Although "no one could maintain that *School Girl* is a cinematic triumph," it conveys "an eroticism all too rare in American films," evidently stemming from "our heroine's wide-eyed, half-humorous detachment from the various sexual trips on which she embarks."[1]

Censorship Activity

In this complicated case,[2] an assistant U.S. attorney, with the cooperation of various FBI agents, obtained search warrants and grand jury subpoenas in Memphis, Tennessee, which enabled him to seize and secure some 10 or 12 prints of *School Girl* and the master negative from the film's owner and several exhibitors in possession of prints in Memphis and other parts of the United States; and to institute proceedings that included a criminal indictment, charging the owner and exhibitors with unlawfully using a common carrier to ship an "obscene" film (*School Girl*) in interstate commerce and with a "conspiracy" to distribute this "obscene" film nationally.

The film's owner and its Memphis exhibitor asked a federal district judge to quash the subpoenas (ordering production of the prints) because the "effect of the subpoenas would be to suppress the film"; they also requested an injunction requiring the immediate return of all prints and negatives seized as a result of the search warrants, and restraining the government's agents from any further seizing or suppression of the film.

The trial court made a preliminary determination that the film was obscene and denied the relief requested. On appeal, the issues were remanded to the trial court with instructions to permit copies of the film to be made so that the government could retain the evidence it had obtained in furtherance of *bona fide* investigations and prosecutions for violations of federal laws; but the adverse parties, including the exhibitors, would have prints that could be shown, in the "free exercise of the First Amendment rights of the Constitution," pending final judicial resolution of the issues raised by the government's law enforcement activities.

Legal Importance

The basic issue in this case was how to resolve the conflicting claims and legitimate interests of the government's prosecutorial arm, on the one hand, and the film's owner and exhibitors, on the other. The government should be able to gather evidence (here, a print of the film) needed to prosecute alleged law violations. At the same time, the exhibitors of the film in question have a constitutional right to continue to exhibit the film unless and until it has been shown to be obscene (and therefore not constitutionally protected) through an adversary judicial proceeding designed to focus searchingly on the question of obscenity. The solution seemed to satisfy the legitimate claims and interests of both sides, in accordance with the principles laid down in two landmark cases involving books,[3] as well as in the *Blue Movie* case [82].

1. *Saturday Review*, Sept. 30, 1972.
2. Art Theatre Guild v. Parrish, 503 F. 2d 133 (1974).
3. A Quantity of Books v. Kansas, 378 U.S. 205 (1964); Marcus v. Search Warrants, 376 U.S. 717 (1961).

[116]
Stewardesses

Banned in Louisiana, 1974.

U.S., 1969. Dist: Sherpix, Inc. 93 min. 35mm. Sound. Color. Prod: Louis K. Sher. Dir/SW: Alf Silliman, Jr. Cin: Christopher Bell. Cast: Christina Hart, Paula Erikson, Angelique De Moiline, Michael Barrett, William Basil, Jerry Litivinoff. MPAA: X. Reviews: *Variety*, Feb. 3, 1971, Addison Verrill; *Chicago Sun Times*, Oct. 24, 1971, Joseph Gelmis; *London Observer*, Dec. 16, 1973, George Melly.

Stewardesses takes place during an 18-hour layover of a Boeing 747 in Honolulu. The crew and passengers join together in various sexual encounters. The "stewardesses" include lesbians, "nymphos," and an LSD tripper who imagines "getting it off' with a table lamp in the form of a Greek marble bust. One stewardess meets an advertising executive, hoping to become his new ad campaign model. He, in turn, wants to leave the corporate life he began with a homosexual affair with the boss. The stewardess persuades him to sign her up as a model, but he abuses her sexually. The next morning the memory of the previous night's horrors enrages her; she beats the ad man to death with a small statue and jumps to her death from his apartment window. Later, the crew reconvenes in the airport for the next flight.

Censorship Activity

The exhibition of this film was "permanently" enjoined as a "nuisance" under a Louisiana "Abatement of Nuisances" statute. The exhibitor claimed that the statute was unconstitutional and the film not obscene. After consideration of the issues and remand of the case by the U.S. Supreme Court, the Supreme Court of Louisiana held the statute unconstitutional and reversed the judgment previously rendered that prevented exhibition of the film.[1]

Legal Importance

The Supreme Court of Louisiana held that the statute here was unconstitutional because it authorized a non-judicial government official to obtain court orders to prevent a film being shown upon the simple allegation by the official, "upon information and belief," that it was obscene. Such a procedure fails to conform to the requirements laid down by the U.S. Supreme Court in a line of cases, including the *Revenge at Daybreak* case [58], providing for prior notice and an adversary judicial hearing before a film is banned as obscene. The Louisiana court cited its earlier decision in the *Last Tango in Paris* case [112] as controlling here.

1. State v. Gulf State Theaters of Louisiana, 287 So. 2d 496 (1973).

[117]
The Devil in Miss Jones

Banned in California, Florida, Georgia, Kansas, Massachusetts, Michigan, Missouri, New York, South Dakota, Texas, and Virginia, 1975.

U.S., 1973. Dist: Marvin Films. 74 min. 35mm. Sound. Color. Prod/Dir/SW: Gerard Damiano. Cin: Harry Flecks. Cast: Georgina Spelvin, John Clemens, Harry Reems. MPAA: X. Reviews: *Variety*, Feb. 21, 1973, Verr.; *New York Post*, March 29, 1973, Archer Winsten; *Box Office*, May 7, 1973. Articles: *New York Times*, April 8, 1973, Vincent Canby; *Time*, May 7, 1973, J.C.; *Variety*, Aug. 8, 1973; *Newsweek*, Sept. 17, 1973.

A desperately lonely, repressed, and frustrated virgin kills herself, only to be condemned to eternal damnation for it. Claiming she is guilty of nothing but the single act of suicide, she begs for and is granted a postponement of her fate so that she might well earn it. She eagerly tries and enjoys virtually all forms of sex, insatiably. Finally, her reprieve ended, she is confined forever to a barren room that she shares only with a madman too far gone to be aroused.

Censorship Activity

This film was involved in litigation in numerous cities and states because of its alleged obscenity. The Wayne County, Michigan prosecutor brought civil actions against several theaters as "public nuisances" because they had exhibited "lewd" films, including this one, as well as *Deep Throat* [107] and two others.[1] The nuisance statute was in its terms applicable to "any building, vehicle, boat, aircraft, or place" used for the purpose of "lewdness," prostitution, gambling, etc.

Holding that the terms "lewd" and "obscene" were "synonymous," the court decided that "all four films clearly depicted 'hard-core' sexual conduct in a patently offensive way," and were legally obscene within the threefold definition laid down in the 1973 landmark case of *Miller* v. *California*[2] and applied in such a movie censorship case as *I Am Curious—Yellow* [71]. The Michigan Court of Appeals also found the theaters in which the films had been shown to be "public nuisances," but modified the trial court's order (closing the theaters for one year and perpetually enjoining their future use "for the purpose of lewdness") so that only the particular films found obscene at trial were perpetually enjoined from being shown in the future, as "nuisances."[3] However, the Supreme Court of Michigan reversed, holding that the nuisance statute was not applicable to motion pictures, but only to houses of prostitution.[4]

Legal Importance

The Michigan high court correctly limited the force of the "nuisance" abatement law to any further showings of particular films found obscene after trial. To perpetually enjoin the theaters in question from showing in the future any other "lewd" films would have constituted an unconstitutional "prior restraint" upon the exhibition of unnamed films by the theater owners. As the U.S. Supreme Court ruled in the Texas *Deep Throat* case, the "heavy hand of a public nuisance statute [is] constitutionally deficient in the First Amendment context [because] it authorizes prior restraints of indefinite duration on the exhibition of motion pictures that have not been finally adjudicated to be obscene," contrary to the teaching of such cases as *Revenge at Daybreak* [58].

This case has a certain additional interest in the old-fashioned (circa 1920) way in which the Michigan court "morally" justified its condemnation of the films and the theaters that exhibited them to "consenting adults" under the nuisance statute: The films were said to be "an example of the trash that a few sick, demented minds are spewing out across our country in search of the easy dollar. Films of this type, no doubt, scar the minds of many people, young and old, who, out of a natural curiosity, view them. These films can greatly weaken, if not destroy, the moral and wholesome fiber which the citizens of this country possess in abundance. To permit this moral sabotage to continue would be to ignore the spreading of a deadly plague . . . we are not about to permit this disease to spread."

The appellate court's opinion suggests that the trial court's "padlocking" of the theaters for one year as "public nuisances" was upheld, although it is not entirely clear on this point. If so, this aspect of the nuisance law's sanctions is "punitive"; and a question not explored by the courts in this case is whether it is not an unconstitutional denial of due process of law to "punish" a movie theater owner for showing obscene films without affording him the procedural safeguards constitutionally guaranteed for "criminal" cases, including trial by jury and proof "beyond a reasonable doubt" of each element of the crime alleged, including "scienter" of a culpable mental state.

1. The two other films were *Little Sisters* and *It Happened in Hollywood*.
2. Miller v. California, 413 U.S. 15 (1973).

3. State *ex rel.* Cahalan v. Diversified Theatrical Corp., 229 N.W. 2d 389 (1975).

4. State *ex rel.* Cahalan v. Diversified Theatrical Corp., 240 N.W. 2d 460 (1976).

[118]
Gun Runners (The Gun Runner)

Banned in Huntsville, Alabama, 1975.

U.S., 1969. Dist: Grads Corp. 76 min. 35mm. Sound. Color. Prod: Jabe Films—J. Tananbaum Productions. Dir/SW: Richard Compton. Cin: John Nestor. Cast: Trent Dolan, Victoria Carbe, John Rico, Beach Dickerson. MPAA: X. Review: *Box Office*, Nov. 1, 1971.

A hard-hitting but unlikely hero must endure men's weaknesses as he tries desperately to destroy a gun-running organization that imports weapons from South America for sale to fanatic anti-communists in Texas.

Censorship Activity

Over a period of two weeks, a Huntsville, Alabama police detective visited the Fox Cinema Theater on several occasions, taking numerous photographs and recording the movies being shown, including this one and others entitled *The Making of the Blue Movie, I Am Sandra* [119], *Mary Jane, The Executive Wives*, and *The Mermaids*. With this evidence, the city's chief of police went to court to shut down the theater, claiming that for nearly two years it had "consistently shown" obscene movies and that this violated the state's "public nuisance" law. The Circuit Court ordered that the theater be closed "for all purposes" for one year and "perpetually enjoined" its owner from exhibiting "obscene matter" in the county. On appeal, the Supreme Court of Alabama reversed.[1]

Legal Importance

The Alabama Supreme Court ruled that movies were constitutionally protected expression and that persons cannot be deprived of their rights to free expression in advance of employing them. Although there was "ample evidence" that the films in question were obscene, even if one "is guilty of maintaining an obscenity nuisance, it is not constitutionally permissible to deprive him *prospectively* [italics supplied] of his First Amendment rights. . . . The padlocking of [the theater] for one year constitutes prior restraint at its worst and is patently unconstitutional." The court saw "a dichotomy in the social ills against which obscenity law and public nuisance law are directed." A nuisance action aims to abate a condition which harms a substantial number of people or damages the public safety, health, or morals. It does not attempt to suppress "a particular form of expression." The nuisance law's "imprecise nature" makes it "ill-equipped to cope with the intricacies of First Amendment guarantees," and its failure to conform to the requirements set forth by the U.S. Supreme Court in such cases as the *Revenge at Daybreak* case [58] rendered its application to prospective film showings unconstitutional.

The court did not entirely rule out the possibility of constitutionally applying the state law to ban a *particular* obscene movie from being shown in the future as a "public nuisance," even in an adults-only theater, or to ban movies "not fit for children to see" from "drive-in" movie theaters if visible from public places. Issues relating to the latter situation have been considered by the U.S. Supreme Court in several "drive-in" movie cases, notably in the cases of *Carmen, Baby* [75] and *Class of '74* [114].

1. General Corporation v. State of Alabama *ex rel.* Sweeton, 320 So. 2d 668 (1975).

[119]
I Am Sandra

Banned in Huntsville, Alabama, 1975.

U.S., 1970. Dist: Grads Corporation. 90 min. 35mm. Sound. Color. Prod: Jay Fineberg, Ron Nicholas. Dir: Gary Graver. SW: Robert Aiken, Gary Graver. Cin: Gary Graver. Cast: Monica Gayle, Daryll Largo, Raymond Zona, Jean Clark, James Ritter.

Sandra is a "sexually liberated" woman who recalls the experiences that brought her to San Francisco after her drunken father's death. They include a traveling salesman who makes love to her while wearing one of his sample brassieres, a lesbian who sells cosmetics, a motorcyclist who is brutal, and a psychiatrist who claims that her liberation is "healthy."

Censorship Activity/Legal Importance
See *Gun Runners* [118].

[120]
Naked Came the Stranger

Banned in Oakland County, Michigan, 1975.

U.S., 1975. Dist: Mature Pictures Corp. 89 min. 35mm. Sound. Color. Prod: Catalyst Production; L. Sultana. Dir: Henry Paris (pseudonym for Radley

Metzger). SW: Jake Barnes. Cin: Robert Rochester. Cast: Darby Lloyd Rains, Levi Richards, Mary Stuart, Alan Marlow. MPAA: X. Reviews: *Film Bulletin*, June 1975, Haleff; *Daily Variety*, June 4, 1975, Sege; *Box Office*, June 23, 1975. Articles: *Variety*, Jan. 1, April 30, 1975.

This film was adapted from the novel of the same name, written by 12 journalists of the Long Island newspaper *Newsday* under the name "Penelope Ashe." After catching her husband, her partner in their radio talk show, having sex with one of his production secretaries, a woman ventures into a life of her own erotic affairs. Finally, she has a lesbian fling with the secretary, only to reject her to return to her husband's lovemaking. "[I]t has a playful and good-humored quality, as well as what could even be called a moral climax when the two spouses get together again in a very athletic sex scene at the end."[1] "Director Henry Paris, following up his *The Private Afternoons of Pamela Mann*, again prefers to keep his identity quiet and again is taking bows for what some critics are calling one of the best pornos to date."[2]

Censorship Activity

An Oakland County prosecutor on August 27, 1975 arrested the manager of the theater showing this film and seized the film, pursuant to judicial warrants. Pending his trial for the crime of exhibiting an obscene movie, the manager exhibited it again and was again arrested pursuant to a judicial warrant obtained by the prosecutor, who also seized this second copy of the film. After an adversary judicial hearing, the film was found obscene. However, on the ground that the *Blue Movie* case [82] permitted the prosecutor to seize only one copy of the film for evidentiary purposes, the judge dismissed the second prosecution and ordered the second copy of the film returned to the theater manager. When the prosecutor did not return this copy of the film and stated his intention of seizing a copy of the film each day it was played, the theater manager went to court to prevent this prosecutorial harassment. On the same day, the prosecutor went to court seeking a judicial declaration that the film was a "nuisance" and an order preventing the manager from showing it and removing the theater's fixtures, furniture, and contents.

A circuit court judge issued an *ex parte* (non-adversary) temporary restraining order forbidding the manager from showing the film anywhere in Oakland County, pending a final trial on the obscenity nuisance action. However, this order subsequently was vacated by the court of appeals, acting in response to the manager's "emergency appeal," on the ground that the order was "a forbidden prior restraint on activities presumptively protected by the First Amendment by enjoining the showing of the named motion picture film without first having conducted an adversary proceeding . . . to determine whether said film is 'obscene.' " When this order was vacated, the manager resumed exhibition of the film but was again arrested and, this time, jailed overnight, upon a judicial warrant obtained by the prosecutor. A third copy of the film was seized in that raid. When, nevertheless, exhibition of the film was resumed, the prosecutor obtained a fourth search warrant, raided the theater, seized a fourth copy of the film, and removed the theater's projection equipment. The prosecutor was thereupon ordered by a federal district court, upon the theater manager's application, to refrain from further arrests or seizure and to return the projection equipment.[3]

Legal Importance

In the *Blue Movie* case [82], the U.S. Supreme Court held that law enforcement officers could constitutionally seize a film being exhibited at a theater only if a judicial officer had viewed it and, finding it probably obscene, had ordered its seizure for evidentiary purposes in adversary proceedings to reach a final decision whether the film was obscene in the constitutional sense; and that, pending the outcome of those adversary proceedings, the film's exhibitor could not be prevented from showing another copy, since that would amount to a prior restraint on expression, violating the First Amendment.

In the present case, arguing that it was his duty to enforce the law and that each showing of the questioned film constituted a separate crime, evidence of which would be needed for trial, the prosecutor sought to justify repeated arrests and film seizures and his departure from the principle established in the *Blue Movie* case. The federal court, however, ruled that such prosecutorial behavior was not justified, for the following reasons: first, since the same version of the film was shown on each occasion, the prosecutor had "all the evidence that needs to be seized for any future prosecutions"; second, to prove that the film was shown on repeated occasions, the prosecutor need only introduce testimony from witnesses (e.g., police personnel assigned to view the film) who observed the additional showings. This procedure "would not only be less restrictive of First Amendment freedoms but possibly less expensive to the government than repeated raids upon the theater."

Although the procedure of repeated arrests and seizures might be appropriate law enforcement techniques with respect to crimes such as bank robbery, it was inappropriate, and unconstitutional, when applied to the "dissemination of materials presumptively protected by the First Amendment," for it falls far short of the "necessary sensitivity to freedom of expression" as spelled out by the Supreme Court in the landmark *Revenge at Daybreak* case [58].

1. *Film Bulletin*, June 1975.
2. *Box Office*, June 23, 1975.
3. Llewelyn v. Oakland County Prosecutor's Office, 402 F. Supp. 1379 (1975).

[121]
Caligula

Banned in Atlanta, Georgia, 1981.

U.S., 1980. Dist: Penthouse International, Ltd. 156 min. 35mm. Sound. Color. Prod: Bob Guccione, Franco Rossellini. SW: Gore Vidal.[1] Cin: Tinto Brass. Music: Paul Clemente. Rating: (self-assigned) MA; MPAA: X. Cast: Malcolm McDowell, Peter O'Toole, John Gielgud, Teresa Ann Savoy, Helen Mirren.[2] Reviews: *New York Times*, Feb. 2, 1980, Vincent Canby; *New Republic*, Feb. 23, 1980; *Newsweek*, Feb. 25, 1980; *Los Angeles Times*, April 21, 1980. Articles: *Newsday*, Feb. 10, 1980; *Los Angeles Times*, April 11, 1980.

The film is based on Suetonius's biography of Caligula. It tells the story of the bloody reign of the fourth of the 12 Caesars of the Roman Empire. We follow the mad ruler and his companions through a great variety of explicit sexual activities, as well as assorted decapitations, dismemberments, and disembowelings. These set the scene for the film's climax—the bloody assassination of Caligula himself. "The film is a dizzying display of bodies, genitals, orgies, heterosexual and homosexual activity, masturbation, bodily functions, and sexual content and excesses of all varieties. . . . Violence is as much a part of the film as is promiscuity."[3]

Censorship Activity

By May 15, 1981, according to the federal district court in the Northern District of Georgia that tried this case, the movie had been shown in over one hundred cities in the United States. In Atlanta, the film's distributor asked the court to declare *Caligula* not obscene, but, rather, protected by the First Amendment and to enjoin the Solicitor General of Fulton County from arresting or prosecuting anyone concerned with the film's distribution or exhibition. The court issued the requested declaration but declined to enjoin any criminal prosecution.[4]

Legal Importance

The only issue in the case was whether the movie was obscene in the constitutional sense, applying Georgia law, which incorporated the "three-pronged" legal test for identifying constitutionally unprotected obscenity, set forth by the U.S. Supreme Court in *Miller* v. *California*.[5] An "advisory jury" empanelled by the court viewed the film, listened to expert witnesses, and found the film not obscene. The court, having also viewed the film, agreed with the jury on the grounds that (a) the movie did not appeal to, but instead "inhibit[ed]" sexual stimulation; (b) it was "patently offensive" because the sexual depictions were "an affront to contemporary community standards''; and (c) it had no serious literary or scientific value but did contain serious artistic and political value.

In the court's view, one of the distributor's "most convincing" witnesses was Dr. Robert Sklar, professor and chairman of the department of cinema studies at New York University, and author of many publications on film, history, theory, and criticism. Although he regarded *Caligula* as an artistic failure, with many flaws, Professor Sklar found "serious artistic value" in the ways in which the film communicated ideas of corruptive power, indifference to human life, terror, the relationship of mortality and immortality, and the "apposition of genuine love versus depraved, abusive, and selfish gratification." These "ideas and emotions" were conveyed through the movie's "effective use" of acting, set design, cinematography, music, and the other "elements of the cinematic art."

1. Penthouse v. McAuliffe, 7 Media Law Rep. 1798 (1981): "Whether due to [the producer's] artistic tampering with the movie or due to some other displeasure with the final product, Gore Vidal, Malcolm McDowell, Peter O'Toole, Sir John Gielgud, and others involved in the production have purportedly disassociated themselves from the film."
2. See note 1.
3. Penthouse v. McAuliffe, 7 Media Law Rep. 1798 (1981).
4. Penthouse v. McAuliffe, 7 Media Law Rep. 1798 (1981).
5. Miller v. California, 413 U.S. 15 (1973).

[122]
Emmanuelle

Banned in Covina, California, 1981.

France/Thailand, 1974. U.S., 1974. Dist: Columbia Pictures. 92 min. 35mm. Sound. Color. Prod: Yves Rousset-Rouard, A. Trinacra/Orphee Prod. Dir: Just Jaeckin. SW: Jean-Louis Richard. Cin: Richard Suzuki. Cast: Sylvia Kristel, Alain Cuny, Marika Green, Daniel Sarky, Jeanne Colletin, Christine Boisson. MPAA: X. Reviews: *New York Times*, Dec. 16, 1974, A. H. Weiler; *Time*, Jan. 6, 1975.

Adapted from the novel by Maryat Rollet-Andriane (pseudonym for Emmanuelle Arsan), the film depicts the erotic adventures of the beautiful young wife of a diplomat attached to the French Embassy in Bangkok, Thailand. Bored with the life of a diplomatic community, and in response to her husband's urgings to broaden her horizons, Emmanuelle embarks upon sexual experiments. Starting with a lesbian affair with her older squash partner, Emmanuelle is also raped in an opium den, awarded as a prize in a boxing match, and made a party to a *ménage à trois*. Filmed in Thailand, the movie was banned in France under President Georges Pompidou and subsequently freed by the government of President Valéry Giscard d'Estaing.

Censorship Activity

After notifying the Cinema Theater in Covina, California, which showed this film, that the city was concerned regarding its exhibition of X-rated films, an "interim emergency" ordinance was adopted that prohibited adult films being exhibited while zoning regulations of various "adult" land uses could be studied. (The Cinema Theater regularly offered a repertory program of foreign films, unusual domestic films, classics, and "cult" films.)

When the theater continued to show X-rated films on its calendar, including *Emmanuelle*, town police viewed the films and filed misdemeanor charges with the Los Angeles district attorney's office. Although no criminal proceedings were brought against the theater, the threat discouraged patrons from attending the cinema's shows, rendered its repertory film policy economically unrewarding, and obliged the theater to stop showing X-rated films. Thereafter, the city adopted a comprehensive zoning ordinance prohibiting the location of "adult entertainment business" within 500 feet of a residential area. The Cinema Theater being located within that distance, its operator filed a court action seeking declaration that the ordinance violated the constitutional guarantees of freedom of expression, due process, and equal protection. The trial court denied the operator's request, but an appellate court ruled that although the ordinance was not unconstitutional on its face it could not be construed to prevent the Cinema from showing X-rated films such as *Emmanuelle*, so long as they did not amount to a preponderance of films whose dominant theme was the depiction of specified sexual activities or anatomical areas.[1]

Legal Importance

The appellate court construed the ordinance's prohibitions on "adult" films narrowly so as to save the law from constitutional condemnation as overly broad, such that "men of common intelligence [would] be required to guess at the meaning of the enactment." Recognizing that the U.S. Supreme Court had declared that "where a vague statute abut[s] upon First Amendment freedoms it operates to inhibit the exercise of [those] freedoms" and that the California Supreme Court also had warned that "vague statutory language, resulting in inadequate notice of the reach and limits of the statutory proscription, poses a specially serious problem when the statute concerns speech, for uncertainty concerning its scope may then chill the exercise of protected First Amendment rights," the court construed the Covina ordinance so that it restrained only the showing of "adult" films whose "dominant or predominant character and theme is the depiction of" certain enumerated sexual activities or anatomical areas. Among the activities whose filmed depiction was discouraged by the ordinance were: (a) the fondling of genitals, buttocks, or female breasts; (b) normal or perverted sex acts, actual or simulated; (c) masturbation; and (d) excretory functions in association with any of the foregoing.

The movie exhibitor could not be prevented from *occasionally* showing artistic, serious films rated "X" by the Motion Picture Association of America that contained sexually explicit matter. Construing the ordinance so as not to expose theaters to punishment for following such a policy, it was not necessary to find the ordinance violative of constitutional freedom of expression. The court refused to suppose that the occasional showing of sexually explicit films could be "destructive of the general quality of life in the neighborhood," as contended by the city of Covina. Such a premise would appear as a "misconceived attempt directly to regulate content of expression [by] using the power to zone as a pretext for suppressing expression." The court held that movie theaters located in a restricted zone designed to preserve the quality of a neighborhood from the "blight" of sexually explicit materials could not be prohibited from showing non-obscene sexually oriented films as selective (not as constant or predominant) fare. This holding was consistent with the U.S. Supreme Court's holding in the case of *Young* v. *American Mini Theatres.*[2]

1. Pringle v. City of Covina, 115 Cal. App. 3d 153 (1981).
2. Young v. American Mini Theatres, 427 U.S. 50 (1976).

Epilogue

Controversy over freedom and censorship has punctuated the history of motion pictures. Films have reflected the reality and imagination of society, its changing values, its beauty and violence, hopes and fears, and the confusing paths of social progress. Movies have mirrored virtually all aspects of life and culture, while their censorship has challenged as much what they have portrayed as the way in which it was portrayed.

The sheer diversity of interests and differences of opinion in this country suggest that appeals for censorship will never end. At the same time, advocates of intellectual freedom and freedom of the screen will continue to contend that the "transcedent value of speech," as Justice Brennan happily called it, ought never be subverted. Recently, expressions of concern over excessive freedom have come from some activists in the women's movement, who have urged the banning of pornography because, allegedly, it advocates sexual violence against women and exploits children. Perceiving such expression as "gynocidal propaganda" and a "fascist ideology of female inferiority," these feminists have discounted the fact that, as Justice Brennan stated in *Roth*, the First Amendment protects "unorthodox ideas, controversial ideas, even ideas hateful to the prevailing climate of opinion."

It may even protect the dissemination of films and books that portray children under 16 in sexual acts, or that exhibit their genitals in a "lewd" way. In a recent case challenging the constitutionality of New York's "kiddie-porn" law, as applied to the sale to an undercover policeman of two films "depicting young boys masturbating" (*New York* v. *Ferber*), and which made no claim to having "social value," the Court unanimously upheld the law. The Justices were in sharp disagreement, however, on the issue whether such a law might constitutionally be applied to ban a film or a book containing such depictions—if these had artistic or educational value. Although the Court did not consider such situations likely, one needs only to look at the book *Show Me! A Picture Book of Sex for Children and Parents* or the movies *The Exorcist, Pretty Baby,* and *The Tin Drum*, to realize that such materials may not compose the "tiny fraction" of valuable works that the Court's opinion suggests. Justice Brennan, in any event, flatly stated it to be "inconceivable how a depiction of a child that is itself a serious contribution to the world of art or literature or science" can be excluded from First Amendment protection. The Court's newest member, Justice Sandra Day O'Connor, disagreed: "The Constitution might in fact permit (a state) to ban knowing distribution of works depicting minors engaged in explicit sexual conduct, regardless of the social value of the depictions." Thus, the "social value" test for distinguishing movies and books protected by the Constitution promises to remain pivotal to freedom of expression.

The Chief Justice of the United States believes that censorship is a social good. His approach would subordinate First Amendment values to the values of maintaining a society in which the quality of life is "decent" by his lights. But the values of freedom of expression are as old as the values of decency. One need only recall Plato's *Apology*, in which Socrates described himself as "a sort of gadfly, given to the State by God," whose function it was "all day long and in all places" to fasten on the public, "arousing and persuading and reproaching you." The movies, like all of the press in this country, were meant to have the same gadfly function.

The recent rash of library book bannings and vigilante group book bannings is more than a backlash against a prevailing liberalism. It shows that the censorial impulse retains its vitality, a fact that should alarm those who care about the free flow of ideas. Danger to the open society lurks when any group seeks to impose *its* values on the rest of the populace. At stake is the First Amendment and, ultimately, the mind of America.

When Chief Justice Burger redefined obscenity in *Miller* v. *California*, Justice Douglas voiced a dissent that addressed the dangers posed to libraries. "What we do today is rather ominous as respects librarians," he said. "The net now designed by the Court is so finely meshed that taken literally it could result in raids on libraries. . . . If what is offensive to the most influential person or group in a community can be purged from a library, the library system would be destroyed." The freedom-constraining decisions of the Burger Court placed some librarians under fear of prosecution for lending "obscene" books to adults and children. Perhaps of greater importance is the fact that "influential" persons and groups, members of some of "the most vocal and powerful minorities" in the country (such as the so-called Moral Majority), have found inspiration, if not incitement, to censorship in some of the Court's free speech opinions.

On behalf of the Court's plurality, Justice Brennan recently spoke to curtail such censorship, by extending First Amendment protection to school libraries. In the controversial Island Trees case (*Board of Education* v. *Pico*), he said that "students do not 'shed their rights to freedom of speech or expression at the schoolhouse gate,' and therefore local school boards must discharge their 'important, delicate, and highly discretionary functions' within the limits and constraints of the First Amendment." The decision means that the nation's courts are required to supervise the acts of school boards if they remove books from library shelves because of their ideas. It was not surprising to find the Chief Justice dissenting in this case: he views school libraries as "vehicles for inculcating fundamental values" in the minds of children.

The future will surely bring new kinds of problems. Cable television's "public access" channels that are available to independent programmers are intended to operate on a nondiscriminatory noncensorable basis. At the same time, some subscribers may not care to have opposing viewpoints broadcast, nor politically or sexually exciting ones. The "public access" concept will pose new First Amendment issues. Despite the Supreme Court's unwillingness to free obscenity for adults, obscenity has not gone underground, but into the constitutionally protected privacy of the American home, as recognized in *Stanley* v. *Georgia*. The boom in sexually explicit films, both in videocassette form and on cable television programs, suggests that the public "garbage" of which the Burger Court and neoconservatives despaired, has now settled into homes. Will the Court alter its previous rulings and permit police to invade the privacy of the home?

Obscenity has presented problems of definition as have few other words. Emotion and imagination can, as the history of movie censorship attests, be more influential than reason in lending it content. Inevitably, it means different things to different people. Judges, scholars, religious leaders, and laypersons have tried to define it. They have failed—at least to agree. Grasping it is like "coming to terms with a greased pig," wrote Judge Curtis Bok. Observing its shifting judicial definition, Judge Jerome Frank spoke of its "exquisite vagueness."

What has never been denied about the medium of film is its power, which from the beginning caused reformers to find means to control "the mightiest engine for molding public opinion." Self-regulation was pursued and hailed as the motion picture industry's defense against governmentally imposed censorship. Operating under the watchful eye of competing pressures, the Motion Picture Association of America has increasingly been obliged to defend freedom of the screen. The courts, a handful of resourceful lawyers, and a more open society would not let it be otherwise.

Films, *moving pictures*, entertain, educate, incite, and inspire. Once they were no longer considered mere entertainment or "business pure and simple,'' they came to be appreciated as a form of art and, most recently, as a constitutionally protected form of art. And art, as John Dewey observed, can only be ''responsible to life, to the enriching and freeing of its meaning.''

Substantial gains in freedom of expression were secured by the Supreme Court liberal bloc of Black, Brennan, and Douglas. Today, however, the stark reality of the constitutional situation is that because the Court is so deeply divided, there is no rule of law protecting the freedom to watch or the freedom to read. Nor is there one protecting the disseminators of movies and books. What protects them instead is the rule of men and, ultimately, the favorable votes of five out of nine men, or rather eight men and a woman.

Appendix

Acronyms and Abbreviations

A.	Atlantic Reporter
ACLU	American Civil Liberties Union
AJC	American Jewish Committee
ALA	American Library Association
AAP	Association of American Publishers
App.	Appellate
B&W	black and white
BMP	Bureau of Motion Pictures (of OWI)
Cal.	California Reporter
CARA	Code and Rating Administration (of MPAA)
CIA	Central Intelligence Agency
Cin.	Cinematographer
CPI	Committee on Public Information
CPR	Committee on Public Relations (of MPPDA)
ct.	court
Dir.	Director
EPIC	"End Poverty in California"
F.	Federal Reporter
FBI	Federal Bureau of Investigation
FCC	Federal Communications Commission
F. Supp.	Federal Supplement

G	suggested for general audiences, including children of all ages (CARA rating)
HUAC	House Un-American Activities Committee
IATSE	International Alliance of Theatrical Stage Employees
IFIDA	International Film Importers and Distributors Association of America
MA	Mature Audiences (rating)
MPAA	Motion Picture Association of America
MPPDA	Motion Picture Producers and Distributors Association of America
NAACP	National Association for the Advancement of Colored People
NAMPI	National Association of the Motion Picture Industry
NATO	National Association of Theater Owners
NCOMP	National Catholic Office of Motion Pictures
N.E.	Northeastern Reporter
NIRA	National Industrial Recovery Act
N.W.	Northwestern Reporter
N.Y.S.	New York Supplement
OWI	Office of War Information
P.	Pacific Reporter
PCA	Production Code Administration (of MPPDA/MPAA)
PG	parental guidance suggested, as some material may not be suitable for preteenagers (CARA rating)
Prod.	Producer
R	restricted; persons under 17 not admitted unless accompanied by parent or adult guardian (CARA rating)
Rept.	Reporter
S.E.	Southeastern Reporter
SMA	Suggested for Mature Audiences
So.	Southern Reporter
SW	Screenwriter
S.W.	Southwestern Reporter
X	persons under 17 not admitted (CARA rating)
YMCA	Young Men's Christian Association

Court Case Abbreviations

The following are examples of court case citations with abbreviations explained.

Sample Court Case Citation

	1	2	3	4	5

Jenkins v. Georgia,   418   U.S.   153   (1974).

Explanation of Court Case Citation

1 Name of case
2 Volume
3 Reporter
4 Page in volume
5 Year decision rendered

Typical Examples of Court Case Citations and Abbreviations

418 U.S. 153 (1974)—citation to a case contained in "United States Reports," published by the Government Printing Office.

435 F. 2d 228 (1970)—citation to a case contained in "Federal Reporter—Second Series," published by West Publishing Co., St. Paul, Minnesota.

311 F. Supp. 967 (1970)—citation to a case contained in "Federal Supplement," published by West Publishing Co.

154 N.W. 964 (1915)—citation to a case contained in "Northwestern Reporter," published by West Publishing Co.

14 N.Y.S. 2d 39 (1939)—citation to a case contained in "New York Supplement—Second Series," published by West Publishing Co.

7 S.E. 2d 157 (1940)—citation to a case contained in "Southeastern Reporter—Second Series," published by West Publishing Co.

98 Cal. Rptr. 646 (1971)—citation to a case contained in "California Reporter," published by West Publishing Co.

124 A. 2d 292 (1956)—citation to a case contained in "Atlantic Reporter—Second Series," published by West Publishing Co.

358 S.W. 2d 589 (1962)—citation to a case contained in "Southwestern Reporter—Second Series," published by West Publishing Co.

417 P. 2d 255 (1966)—citation to a case contained in "Pacific Reporter—Second Series," published by West Publishing Co.

230 N.E. 2d 241 (1967)—citation to a case contained in "Northeastern Reporter—Second Series," published by West Publishing Co.

23 Cal. App. 3d 941 (1972)—citation to a case contained in "California Appellate Reports—Third Series," published by West Publishing Co.

258 So. 2d 30 (1972)—citation to a case contained in "Southern Reporter—Second Series," published by West Publishing Co.

Glossary of Legal Terms

amicus curiae   Friend of the court.

bona fide   Good faith.

de novo   From the beginning; over again.

dicta   (plural of *dictum*) Statements in a court opinion not essential to the decision.

duces tecum   Bring with you.

ex parte   Of or from one party or side in a case; appearance made in a court without notice to the adverse party or side.

ex post facto   After the fact or event.

ex rel   (abbreviation of *ex relatione*) On the relation or information of.

holding   The matter or issue or thing decided by the court in a case.

in personam   Against the person; concerning the person.

in rem   Against a thing, as distinguished from a person; concerning the status of a thing.

injunction   A form of action requested of a court that is designed to protect the plaintiff from injury to rights of which the court can take cognizance by prohibiting or commanding the doing of specified acts, including the enforcement of a law or constitutional provision.

ipso facto   By the fact or act itself.

per cur   (abbreviation of *per curiam*)

per curiam   By the court, as a body or whole.

per curiam opinion   An opinion (unsigned) by the court in which the judges are of one view on the issue involved, and there is no need or desirability for extended discussion of the supporting reasons.

per se   By itself; as such.

prima facie   On the face of it; without more.

pro forma   As a matter of form.

vel non   Or not.

writ of certiorari   The process that requires the certification and return of the record and proceedings of an inferior court in order that the record may be corrected in law.

writ of mandamus   The process that institutes a proceeding to require an inferior court, tribunal, or agent to perform an official duty specified.

Selected Bibliography

Aceto, Vincent J., Jane Graves, and Fred Silva, eds. *Film Literature Index: 1973 Annual Cumulation*, New York: R. R. Bowker, 1975; *1974 Annual Cumulation*, New York: R. R. Bowker, 1975; *1975 Annual Cumulation*, New York: R. R. Bowker, 1977.

Ayer, Douglas, Roy E. Bates, and Peter J. Herman. "Self-Censorship in the Movie Industry: An Historical Perspective on Law and Social Change," 1970 *Wisconsin Law Review* 791.

Balio, Tino, ed. *The American Film Industry*. Madison, Wis.: Univ. of Wisconsin Press, 1976.

Bartlett, Donald L. and James B. Steele. *Empire: The Life, Legend, and Madness of Howard Hughes*, New York: Norton, 1979.

Batten, Mary. "An Interview with Ephraim London," *Film Comment*, v. 1, no. 4, 2.

Batty, Linda, comp. *Retrospective Index to Film Periodicals, 1930–1971*. New York: R. R. Bowker, 1975.

Behlman, Rudy, ed. *Memo from David O. Selznick*. New York: Viking, 1972.

Bergman, Andrew. *We're in the Money: Depression America and Its Films*. New York: Harper, 1972.

Berns, Walter. "Pornography v. Democracy: A Case for Censorship," *The Public Interest*, Winter 1971, no. 22.

Bickel, Alexander M. *The Morality of Consent*. New Haven, Conn.: Yale Univ. Press, 1975.

Blanshard, Paul. *American Freedom and Catholic Power*. Boston: Beacon Press, 1958.

Boyer, Paul S. *Purity in Print: The Vice-Society Movement and Book Censorship in America*. New York: Scribner, 1968.

Carmen, Ira H. *Movies, Censorship and the Law*. Ann Arbor: Univ. of Michigan Press, 1966.

"Censorship of Motion Pictures," 49 *Yale Law Journal* 87 (1939).

Ceplair, Larry and Steven Englund. *The Inquisition in Hollywood: Politics in the Film Community, 1930–1960.* Garden City, N.Y.: Anchor, 1980.

Chafee, Zechariah. *Free Speech in the United States.* Cambridge, Mass.: Harvard Univ. Press, 1941.

Chafee, Zechariah, Jr. *Government and the Press: A Report from the Commission on Freedom of the Press.* Chicago: Univ. of Chicago Press, 1947.

Clor, Harry M. *Obscenity and Public Morality.* Chicago: Univ. of Chicago Press, 1969.

Conant, Michael. *Antitrust in the Motion Picture Industry: Economic and Legal Analysis.* Berkeley: Univ. of California Press, 1960.

Corliss, Richard. "The Legion of Decency," *Film Comment*, v. 4, no. 4 (Summer 1968), 24.

Countryman, Vern, ed. *The Douglas Opinions.* New York: Random, 1977 (review by Roger K. Newman, 6 *Hastings Constitutional Law Quarterly* 387 (1978)).

Cripps, Thomas. *Slow Fade to Black: The Negro in American Film, 1900–1942.* New York: Oxford, 1977.

de Grazia, Edward. "Obscenity and the Mail," *Law and Contemporary Problems*, v. 20 (1955).

de Grazia, Edward, comp. *Censorship Landmarks.* New York: R. R. Bowker, 1969.

Dowdy, Andrew. *"Movies Are Better Than Ever": Wide-Screen Memories of the Fifties.* New York: Morrow, 1973.

Emerson, Thomas I. *The System of Freedom of Expression.* New York: Random, 1970.

"Entertainment: Public Pressures and the Law," 71 *Harvard Law Review* 326 (1957).

Ernst, Morris L. and Alexander Lindey. *The Censor Marches On.* New York: Doubleday, 1940.

"Film Censorship: An Administrative Analysis," 49 *Yale Law Journal* 87 (1939).

Fisher, Robert. "Film Censorship and Progressive Reform: The National Board of Censorship of Motion Pictures, 1909–1922," *Journal of Popular Film*, v. 4 (1975), 149.

Friedman, Jane M. "The Motion Picture Rating System of 1968: A Constitutional Analysis of Self-Regulation by the Film Industry," 73 *Columbia Law Review* 185 (1973).

Friedman, Leon, ed. *Obscenity: The Complete Oral Arguments before the Supreme Court in the Major Obscenity Cases.* New York: Chelsea House, 1970.

Geduld, Harry M., ed., *Focus on D. W. Griffith.* Englewood Cliffs, N.J.: Prentice-Hall, 1971.

Goodman, Paul. "Pornography, Art, and Censorship." *Commentary* (March 1961).

Haight, Anne Lyon. *Banned Books*, 4th ed. Revised and enlarged by Chandler B. Grannis. New York: R. R. Bowker, 1978.

Halberstam, David. *The Powers That Be.* New York: Knopf, 1979.

Halsey, William M. *The Survival of American Innocence: Catholicism in an Era of Disillusionment, 1920–1940.* Notre Dame, Ind.: Univ. of Notre Dame Press, 1980.

Haney, Robert W. *Comstockery in America: Patterns of Censorship and Control.* Boston: Beacon, 1960.

Hays, Will H. *Memoirs*. Garden City, N.Y.: Doubleday, 1955.

Hentoff, Nat. *The First Freedom: The Tumultous History of Free Speech in America*. New York: Dell, 1981.

Higham, Charles. *Hollywood at Sunset*. New York: Saturday Review Press, 1972.

Inglis, Ruth A. *Freedom of the Movies*. Chicago: Univ. of Chicago Press, 1947.

Jacobs, Lewis. *The Rise of the American Film*. New York: Teacher's College Press, 1939.

Jacobs, Lewis, ed. *The Compound Cinema: The Film Writings of Harry Alan Potamkin (1900-1933)*. New York: Teacher's College Press, 1977.

Jowett, Garth. *Film: The Democratic Art*. Boston: Little, Brown, 1976.

Kalven, Harry, Jr. "The Metaphysics of the Law of Obscenity," 1960 *Supreme Court Review*, Philip B. Kurland, ed. Chicago: Univ. of Chicago Press, 1960.

Kauffmann, Stanley, ed. *American Film Criticism—From the Beginnings to "Citizen Kane."* New York: Liveright, 1972.

Keats, John. *Howard Hughes*. New York: Random, 1966.

Knight, Arthur. *The Liveliest Art*. New York: New American Library, 1979.

Koppes, Clayton R. and Gregory D. Black. "What to Show the World: The Office of War Information and Hollywood, 1942-1945," *Journal of American History*, v. 64 (1977), 87.

Krafsur, Richard, ed. *The American Film Institute Catalog of Motion Pictures: Feature Films, 1961-1970*. New York: R. R. Bowker, 1976.

Kristol, Irving. *On the Democratic Idea in America*. New York: Harper, 1972.

Kronhauser, Eberhard and Phyllis Kronhauser. *Pornography and the Law*. New York: Ballantine, 1959.

Kurland, Philip B., ed. *Free Speech and Association: The Supreme Court and the First Amendment*. Chicago: Univ. of Chicago Press, 1961.

Leab, Daniel J. *From Sambo to Superspade: The Black Experience in Motion Pictures*. Boston: Houghton Mifflin, 1975.

Limbacher, James L., ed. *Feature Films on 8mm, 16mm, and Videotape*, 6th ed. New York: R. R. Bowker, 1979.

Lockhart, William D. and Robert C. McClure. "Censorship of Obscenity: The Developing Constitutional Standards," 45 *Minnesota Law Review* 5 (1960).

———. "Literature, the Law of Obscenity, and the Constitution," 38 *Minnesota Law Review* 295 (1954).

McCarthy, Kathleen D. "Nickel Vice and Virtue: Movie Censorship in Chicago, 1907-1915," *Journal of Popular Film*, v. 3 (1976), 37.

McClure, Arthur F., ed. *The Movies: An American Idiom*. Rutherford, N.J.: Fairleigh Dickinson Univ. Press, 1971.

MacGregor, Ford H. "Official Censorship Legislation," *Annals of the American Academy of Political and Social Science*, v. 128 (1926).

Magrath, C. Peter. "The Obscenity Cases: Grapes of Roth," 1966 *Supreme Court Review*.

May, Lary. *Screening Out the Past: The Birth of Mass Culture and the Motion Picture Industry*. New York: Oxford, 1980.

Miller, Douglas T. and Marion Nowak. *The Fifties: The Way We Really Were*. Garden City, N.Y.: Doubleday, 1977.

Mock, James R. and Cedric Larson. *Words That Won the War: The Story of the Committee on Public Information, 1917–1919*. Princeton, N.J.: Princeton Univ. Press, 1939.

"Motion Pictures and the First Amendment," 60 *Yale Law Journal* 696 (1951).

Munden, Kenneth W., ed. *The American Film Institute Catalog of Motion Pictures: Feature Films, 1921–1930*. New York: R. R. Bowker, 1971.

Navasky, Victor S. *Naming Names*. New York: Viking, 1980.

O'Connor, John E. and Martin A. Jackson, eds. *American History/American Film: Interpreting the Hollywood Image*. New York: Ungar, 1979.

Paul, James C. N. and Murray L. Schwartz. *Federal Censorship: Obscenity in the Mail*. New York: The Free Press, 1961.

Preminger, Otto. *Preminger—An Autobiography*. Garden City, N.Y.: Doubleday, 1977.

"Private Censorship of Movies," 22 *Stanford Law Review* 618 (1970).

Ramsaye, Terry. *A Million and One Nights*. New York: Simon & Schuster, 1926.

Randall, Richard S. *Censorship of the Movies: The Social and Political Control of a Mass Medium*. Madison, Wis.: Univ. of Wisconsin Press, 1968.

Report of the Commission on Obscenity and Pornography. New York: Bantam, 1970.

Schlesinger, Arthur, Jr. "When the Movies Really Counted," *Show*, April 1963, 77.

Schumach, Murray. *The Face on the Cutting Room Floor*. New York: Morrow, 1964.

Sjöman, Vilgot. *I Was Curious: Diary of the Making of a Film*. New York: Grove Press, 1968.

Sklar, Robert. *Movie-Made America: A Cultural History of American Movies*. New York: Random, 1975.

Steinfels, Peter. *The Neoconservatives: The Men Who Are Changing America's Politics*. New York: Simon & Schuster, 1979.

Talese, Gay. *Thy Neighbor's Wife*. New York: Dell, 1981.

Truitt, Evelyn Mack, comp. *Who Was Who on Screen*, 2nd ed. New York: R. R. Bowker, 1977.

Vizzard, Jack. *See No Evil: Life Inside a Hollywood Censor*. New York: Simon & Schuster, 1970.

Walker, Alexander. *Sex in the Movies*. Baltimore, Md.: Penguin, 1968.

Weber, Francis J. "John J. Cantwell and the Legion of Decency," *American Ecclesiastical Review*, v. 151 (1964), 237.

Westin, Alan F. *The Miracle Case: The Supreme Court and the Movies*. Inter-University Case Program No. 64. University, Ala.: Univ. of Alabama Press, 1961.

Winer, Ehihu. "See Nothing but Evil: Recollections of a Hollywood Censor," *International Writers Guild Journal*, July 1970, 24.

Woodward, Robert and Scott Armstrong. *The Brethren*. New York: Simon & Schuster, 1979.

Tables of Cases

Cases by Case Name

Note: These tables provide citations for the major film-related court cases discussed in this book. Italic numbers refer to text pages, not film account numbers.

ABC Interstate Theatres, Inc. v. State, 325 So. 2d 123 (1976). *The Exorcist, 110, 361–362*

American Committee on Maternal Welfare v. Mangan, 14 N.Y.S. 2d 39, (1939); affirmed 283 N.Y. 551 (1940). *The Birth of a Baby, 218–220*

American Museum of Natural History v. Keenan, 89 A. 2d 98 (1952). *Latuko, 234–235*

Art Theatre Guild v. Parrish, 503 F. 2d 133 (1974). *School Girl, 369–371*

Art Theatre Guild v. State ex rel. Rhodes, 510 S.W. 2d 258 (1974). *Cry Uncle, 327, 354–355*

Associates & Aldrich Co. v. Times Mirror Co., 440 F. 2d 133 (1971). *The Killing of Sister George, 341–343*

BBS Productions, Inc. v. Purcell, 360 F. Supp. 801 (1973). *The Last Picture Show, 362–366*

Bainbridge v. City of Minneapolis, 154 N.W. 964 (1915). *The Birth of a Nation, 180–183*

Block v. City of Chicago, 87 N.E. 1011 (1909). *The James Boys in Missouri; Night Riders, 177–180*

Brattle Films v. Commissioner of Public Safety, 127 N.E. 2d 891 (1955). *Miss Julie, 236–238*

Brooks v. City of Birmingham, 32 F. 2d 274 (1929). *The Road to Ruin, 208–209*

Distinguished Films v. Stoddard, 68 N.Y.S. 2d 737 (1947). *Amok,*
227–228

Drive-In Theatres, Inc. v. Huskey, 435 F. 2d 228 (1970). *Where Eagles*
Dare, 333–334

Duggan v. Guild Theatre, 258 A. 2d 858 (1969). *Therese and Isabelle,*
311–312

Dunn v. Maryland State Board of Censors, 213 A. 2d 751 (1965). *Lorna,*
276–277

Eisenstadt v. Baird, 405 U.S. 438 (1972). *17, 188*

Embassy Pictures Corporation v. Hudson, 226 F. Supp. 421 (1964); 242
F. Supp. 975 (1965). *Women of the World, 271–272*

Engdahl v. Kenosha, 317 F. Supp. 1133 (1970). *Woodstock, 336–337*

Entertainment Ventures, Inc. v. Brewer, 306 F. Supp. 802 (1970). *Starlet,*
330–331

Erznoznik v. City of Jacksonville, 280 So. 2d 260 (1974); reversed 422
U.S. 205 (1975). *Class of '74, 368–369*

Eureka Productions v. Byrne, 300 N.Y.S. 218 (1937). *Ecstasy, 210–211*

Eureka Productions v. Lehman, 17 F. Supp. 259 (1936). *Ecstasy,*
210–211

Excelsior Pictures Corp. v. Regents of the University of the State of New
York, 156 N.Y.S. 2d 800 (1956); affirmed 144 N.E. 2d 31 (1957). *The*
Garden of Eden, 247–248

Fanfare Films, Inc. v. Motion Picture Censor Board, 197 A. 2d 839
(1964). *Have Figure Will Travel, 275–276*

Federal Communications Commission v. Pacifica Foundation, 438 U.S.
726 (1978). *268–269*

Fox Film Corporation v. Chicago, 247 F. 231 (1917). *The Spy, 194–195*

Foy Productions v. Graves, 299 N.Y.S. (1937); affirmed 3 N.Y.S. 2d 573
(1938); affirmed 15 N.E. 2d 435 (1938). *Tomorrow's Children, 215–217*

Gelling v. State of Texas, 247 S.W. 2d 95 (1952); reversed 343 U.S. 960
(1952). *Pinky, 238–240*

General Corporation v. State of Alabama ex rel. Sweeton, 320 So. 2d
668 (1975). *Gun Runners; I Am Sandra, 374–375*

Goldstein v. United States, 258 F. 908 (1919). *The Spirit of '76, 193–194*

Goldwyn Distributing Corp., In re 108 A. 816 (1919). *The Brand,*
197–198

Gulf State Theatres of Louisiana v. Richardson, 287 So. 2d 480 (1974).
Last Tango in Paris, 363–366

Hallmark Productions v. Pennsylvania Board of Censors, 121 A. 2d 584
(1956). *Wild Weed, 250–252*

Cases by Film Title

Index